THE ETERNAL CHRIST

God With Us

WILLEM J. OUWENEEL

AN EVANGELICAL INTRODUCTION TO
REFORMATIONAL THEOLOGY
VOLUME II/2

PART II: GOD:
THE PERSONAL SOURCE BEHIND THEOLOGY

An Evangelical Introduction to Reformational Theology

Part I: Scripture: The Revealed Source For Theology
    I/1 *The Eternal Word*: God Speaking To Us
    I/2 *The Eternal Torah*: Living Under God

Part II: God: The Personal Source Behind Theology
    II/1 *The Eternal God*: God Revealing Himself To Us
    II/2 *The Eternal Christ*: God With Us
    II/3 *The Eternal Spirit*: God Living In Us

Part III: Redemption: The Christ-Centered Heart of Theology
    III/1 *The Eternal Purpose*: Living In Christ
    III/2 *Eternal Righteousness*: Living Before God
    III/3 *Eternal Salvation*: Christ Dying For Us
    III/4 *Eternal Life*: Christ Living In Us

Part IV: Consummation: The Lived Shape of Theology
    IV/1a *The Eternal People*: God in Relation To Israel: Israel in the Tanakh and the New Testament
    IV/1b *The Eternal People*: God in Relation To Israel: Post-New Testament Israel
    IV/2 *The Eternal Covenant*: Living With God
    IV/3 *The Eternal Kingdom*: Living Under Christ

Part V: Method: The Comprehensive Foundation of Theology
    V/1 *Eternal Truth*: The Prolegomena of Theology

THE ETERNAL CHRIST

God With Us

WILLEM J. OUWENEEL

The Eternal Christ: God With Us

This English edition is a publication of the Reformational Publishing Project (www.reformationalpublishingproject.com) and Paideia Press (P.O. Box 500, Jordan Station, Ontario, Canada L0R 1S0). Copyright © 2022 by Paideia Press. All rights reserved. Except for brief quotations in critical publications or reviews, no part of this book may be reproduced in any manner without prior written permission from Paideia Press at the address above.

Unless otherwise indicated, Scripture quotations are from the ESV® Bible (The Holy Bible, English Standard Version®). Copyright © 2001 by Crossway, a publishing ministry of Good News Publishers. Used by permission. All rights reserved.

Scripture quotations or references marked as NKJV are taken from the New King James Version®. Copyright © 1982 by Thomas Nelson, Inc. Used by permission. All rights reserved.

Scripture quotations or references marked as NIV are taken from the Holy Bible, New International Version®, NIV®. Copyright © 1973, 1978, 1984, 2011 by Biblica, Inc.™ Used by permission of Zondervan. All rights reserved worldwide. www.zondervan.com. The "NIV" and "New International Version" are trademarks registered in the United States Patent and Trademark Office by Biblica, Inc.™

ISBN 978-0-88815-323-4

Printed in the United States of America

Bethlehem Ephrathah, you are small among the clans of
Judah;
    One will come from you to be ruler over Israel for Me.
His origin is from antiquity,
    from **eternity**.

Micah 5:2 (HCSB)

In the beginning was the Word,
    and the Word was with God,
    and the Word was God.
He was **in the beginning** with God. . . .
And the Word became flesh
    and dwelt among us,
    and we have seen his glory,
glory as of the only Son from the Father,
    full of grace and truth. . . .

John 1:1–2, 14

[F]rom their [= Israel's] race, according to the flesh,
    is the Christ,
who is God over all,
    blessed **forever**. Amen.

Romans 9:5

[W]e are in him who is true, in his Son Jesus Christ.
    He is the true God and **eternal** life.

1 John 5:20

Table of Contents

Table of Contents (Expanded)		
Series Preface		i
Author's Preface		v
Abbreviations		vii
Chapter 1	Preliminary Orientation in Christology	1
Chapter 2	Development of Christology	53
Chapter 3	Twentieth Century Christology	101
Chapter 4	Messianic Hopes in the Tanakh	145
Chapter 5	Christ in the Historical Sources	215
Chapter 6	The Pre-Incarnate Christ	271
Chapter 7	The Deity of Christ	323
Chapter 8	The Humanity of Christ	373
Chapter 9	The Virgin Birth of Christ	423
Chapter 10	The Sinlessness of Christ	449
Chapter 11	The Life of Jesus	489
Chapter 12	The Passion Story	541
Chapter 13	Jesus' Resurrection and Ascension	571
Bibliography		615
Scripture Index		663
Subject Index		695

Table of Contents Expanded

Series Preface		i
Author's Preface Author's Preface		v
Abbreviations		vii
1 Preliminary Orientation in Christology		1
1.1 Worship Versus Reflection		1
1.1.1 Worship		1
1.1.2 The Gospel's Heart		3
1.2 Theological Reflection		5
1.2.1 The Existential Depth Dimension		5
1.2.2 The Praying, Praising Theologian		7
1.3 The Person and Work of Christ		9
1.3.1 Inseparable Matters		9
1.3.2 Yet Distinguishable		11
1.4 Intramural Christian Debate		13
1.4.1 No Acquiescence		13
1.4.2 Modern Debate		15
1.4.3 Pale Pictures		17
1.5 Gnostic Christology		19
1.5.1 Alternative Christianity		19
1.5.2 Paganism		21
1.5.3 The Key: the Old Testament		23
1.6 Islamic Christology		24
1.6.1 The Significance of Jesus		24
1.6.2 Who Was Jesus' Successor?		26

1.7	Jewish Christology	27
	1.7.1 Messianic Jews	27
	1.7.2 Messianic Christology	29
	1.7.3 Sympathizing Jews	32
	1.7.4 The Jewish Jesus	34
1.8	Christology in Modern Times	36
	1.8.1 Proof Texts	36
	1.8.2 "Repeating" Scripture	37
	1.8.3 Scripture as a Unity	39
	1.8.4 Revelational Paradigm	41
1.9	The New Testament Portraits of Jesus	43
	1.9.1 The Synoptics, Especially Mark	43
	1.9.2 The Letters of Paul	46
	1.9.3 Other New Testament Writers	48
	1.9.4 Final Remarks	51
2 Development of Christology		**53**
2.1	Introduction	53
	2.1.1 Two Natures	53
	2.1.2 A Man of Contrasts	55
2.2	The Two Natures: Biblical Testimony	56
	2.2.1 The Divine and the Human	56
	2.2.2 One Person, Perfect Humanity	59
2.3	Development of the Doctrine of the Two Natures	60
	2.3.1 First Solution: Apollinaris of Laodice	61
	2.3.2 Second Solution: Theodore of Mopsuestia	62
	2.3.3 Third Solution: Nestorius of	

	Constantinople	63
	2.3.4 Additional Comment (1)	64
	2.3.5 Additional Comment (2)	65
2.4	The Chalcedon Formula	66
	2.4.1 The Two Natures	66
	2.4.2 Critical Questions	68
2.5	Developments After Chalcedon	70
	2.5.1 Monophysitism and Dualism	70
	2.5.2 Anhypostasis and Enhypostasis	71
	2.5.3 Summary	74
2.6	Chalcedon and the Reformation	75
	2.6.1 Some Confessional Documents	75
	2.6.2 The Extra-Calvinisticum	78
	2.6.3 Did God Die on the Cross?	81
	2.6.4 Anti-Docetism and Dichotomy	82
2.7	The Enlightenment	84
	2.7.1 Reason and Rationalism	84
	2.7.2 From Above, from Below	86
	2.7.3 The Old Jesus Quests	87
2.8	The First Quest	88
	2.8.1 History and Kerygma	88
	2.8.2 Various Approaches	90
	2.8.3 A Third Approach	92
2.9	The End of the First Quest	93
	2.9.1 Philosophical Backgrounds	93
	2.9.2 History and Faith	95
	2.9.3 Again: Above and Below	97
3	Twentieth-Century Christology	101

3.1	Non-Questers	101
	3.1.1 Karl Barth	101
	3.1.2 Rudolf Bultmann	103
3.2	The Second Quest	106
	3.2.1 Introduction	106
	3.2.2 Evaluation	107
3.3	The Third Quest	108
	3.3.1 The Position of Conservative Christianity	108
	3.3.2 What Way?	111
3.4	New Interests	113
	3.4.1 The Jesus Seminar	113
	3.4.2 Old Things in a New Garment	114
	3.4.3 New Elements	116
3.5	Misunderstandings in the Earlier Quests	118
	3.5.1 First Misunderstanding	118
	3.5.2 Second Misunderstanding	120
3.6	Christology among Dutch Theologians	121
	3.6.1 Hendrikus Berkhof	121
	3.6.2 Jakob van Bruggen	124
	3.6.3 Abraham van de Beek	127
3.7	Is Chalcedon Obsolete?	130
	3.7.1 A Better Formula?	130
	3.7.2 Duality and Dualism	132
3.8	Jesus' Self-Awareness	134
	3.8.1 A Messianic "Secret"?	134
	3.8.2 Deceit?	137
3.9	Jesus' Jewishness	139

		3.9.1 Denial in the First and Second Quests	139
		3.9.2 Jesus: Meaning and Goal	141
4	Messianic Hopes in the Tanakh		145
	4.1	The Messiological Significance of the Tanakh	146
		4.1.1 The Tanakh and the New Testament	146
		4.1.2 The Gospels and Paul about the Tanakh	148
	4.2	Balance	149
		4.2.1 Interpretation and Application	149
		4.2.2 The *Entire* Torah Speaks of the Messiah	151
		4.2.3 Recognizable Messianic Predictions	153
	4.3	From Adam to Judah	154
		4.3.1 Adam	154
		4.3.2 Shem and Eber	156
		4.3.3 Abraham and Isaac	157
		4.3.4 Jacob	158
		4.3.5 Judah	160
	4.4	The Shoot of Jesse	163
		4.4.1 Bethlehem	163
		4.4.2 Jesse	165
	4.5	David	166
		4.5.1 "My Servant David"	166
		4.5.2 The Son of David	167
		4.5.3 David and Amos	168
	4.6	Sons of David	170

	4.6.1 Ahaz	170
	4.6.2 Jeconiah	172
4.7	Son of God	174
	4.7.1 Psalm 2	174
	4.7.2 Isaiah 9:6–7	176
4.8	The Son of Man in Daniel 7	178
	4.8.1 *Ben-Adam*	178
	4.8.2 Daniel 7:13	179
	4.8.3 A Messianic Figure	181
4.9	The Son of Man in the Psalms	182
	4.9.1 Psalm 8 and Hebrews 2	182
	4.9.2 The Messianic Thrust	184
	4.9.3 Psalm 80	186
4.10	The Messianic Prophet	187
	4.10.1 Moses' Announced Prophet	187
	4.10.2 More than Moses	189
4.11	The Messianic Priest	191
	4.11.1 Psalm 110:4	191
	4.11.2 Zechariah 6:12–13	192
4.12	The Messianic King	194
	4.12.1 Introduction	194
	4.12.2 Psalms	195
	4.12.3 Zechariah	196
4.13	Other Messianic Psalms	198
	4.13.1 Psalm 16	198
	4.13.2 Psalm 22	200
	4.13.3 Psalm 40	201
	4.13.4 Psalm 69	202

	4.13.5	Psalm 118	203
4.14	The Servant of YHWH	204
	4.14.1	The Four Poems	204
	4.14.2	Various Layers	206
	4.14.3	Servant-Messiah	208
4.15	Two More Messianic Passages	210
	4.15.1	Daniel 9	210
	4.15.2	Hosea 11	212
5	Christ in the Historical Sources	215
5.1	No Fear of Historical Studies	215
	5.1.1	Biblical Criticism	215
	5.1.2	Various Approaches	216
5.2	What Is Authentic?	218
	5.2.1	No "Harmonies"	218
	5.2.2	Peter's Confession	219
	5.2.3	Theological Compositions	221
	5.2.4	Unity in Diversity	223
5.3	The Four Gospels	225
	5.3.1	The Synoptics	225
	5.3.2	Oral Tradition	226
	5.3.2	John's Gospel and the Spirit	227
5.4	New Testament Testimony	229
	5.4.1	Jesus' Life in the Gospels	229
	5.4.2	Jesus' Teaching in the Gospels	230
	5.4.3	The Remainder of the New Testament	232
5.5	Again: Theological Compositions	236
	5.5.1	Paintings, Not Photographs	236

	5.5.2 Neither Journalism Nor Fantasy	237
5.6	"Contradictory" Passages	239
	5.6.1 Who Said What?	239
	5.6.2 Other Examples	241
5.7	"Contradictory" Events	242
	5.7.1 Discrepancies	242
	5.7.2 Three Approaches	244
5.8	Biases	245
	5.8.1 Our Own Biases	245
	5.8.2 Liberal Biases	247
5.9	Nine Passages and Comments	249
	5.9.1 The First Five Passages	249
	5.9.2 Comments	252
	5.9.3 Trust	253
	5.9.4 The Last Four Passages	254
5.10	Jesus' Historicity: Early Christian Testimony	257
	5.10.1 The New Testament Writers	257
	5.10.2 The Apostolic Fathers	258
5.11	Jesus' Historicity: Pagan Testimony	260
	5.11.1 Roman Writers	260
	5.11.2 Other Authors	263
5.12	Jesus' Historicity: Jewish Testimony	265
	5.12.1 Flavius Josephus	265
	5.12.2 The Talmud	267
	5.12.3 Other Sources	268
6 The Pre-Incarnate Christ	271
6.1	Seven Positions	271

	6.1.1	Description	271
	6.1.2	Corresponding Christologies	274
	6.1.3	Corresponding Titles	275
6.2	Old Testament Evidence		277
	6.2.1	Eternal Existence	277
	6.2.2	Divinity	279
	6.2.3	YHWH and Messiah	281
6.3	The Angel of YHWH		285
	6.3.1	*Mal'akh Habb'rit*	285
	6.3.2	*Mal'akh YHWH*	287
6.4	The Divine "Man"		289
	6.4.1	Three Impressive Examples	289
	6.4.2	The Messenger	290
	6.4.3	Messiah and YHWH	292
6.5	The Angel and the Logos		294
	6.5.1	Image, Radiance, Imprint, Form	294
	6.5.2	Sonship	295
6.6	Christ's Pre-Existence in John 1		297
	6.6.1	The Logos	297
	6.6.2	*Theos* and *Ho Theos*	299
6.7	New Testament Hints		301
	6.7.1	Other Passages in John	301
	6.7.2	*Egō Eimi*	303
	6.7.3	The Epistles	305
6.8	Deviant Views		307
	6.8.1	The Liberal View	307
	6.8.2	Was Jesus As a Man Pre-Existent?	309
	6.8.3	Evaluation	311

	6.9	Typological Christology	312
		6.9.1 The Significance of Typology	312
		6.9.2 Personal Types	315
		6.9.3 Types in Genesis and the Feminine Bible Books	318
		6.9.4 Non-Personal Old Testament Types	319
7	The Deity of Christ		323
	7.1	Jesus Is God	323
		7.1.1 John's Writings	323
		7.1.2 Paul's Writings	326
	7.2	Jesus' Claims to Deity	328
		7.2.1 Equality with God	328
		7.2.2 Four Other Claims to Deity	331
		7.2.3 Three Other Claims to Deity	335
	7.3	Jesus' Divine Attributes	337
		7.3.1 The God–Christ Connection	337
		7.3.2 List of Attributes	338
		7.3.3 Implications	341
	7.4	The Eternal Father and the Eternal Son	342
		7.4.1 Fatherhood and Sonship	342
		7.4.2 Eternal Sonship	344
	7.5	God Manifested	345
		7.5.1 Son and Sons of God	345
		7.5.2 Co-Equality	347
		7.5.3 God's Self-Revelation	349
	7.6	The Eternal Father-Son Relationship	350
		7.6.1 John 1:14–18	350
		7.6.2 Only Begotten and Firstborn	352

		7.6.3 Colossians 1 and Proverbs 8	354
	7.7	Eternal Generation	357
		7.7.1 Main Arguments	357
		7.7.2 More Arguments	358
		7.7.3 Collateral Arguments	360
		7.7.4 Evaluation	362
	7.8	The Father and the Son	365
		7.8.1 Subordinationism	365
		7.8.2 Synergy	367
		7.8.3 The Three Together	370
8	The Humanity of Christ		373
	8.1	Human Properties	373
		8.1.1 Youth and Relatives	373
		8.1.2 Humanness	376
		8.1.3 The "Ordinary" Jesus	377
		8.1.4 Human Soul/Spirit	379
	8.2	Human Knowledge	381
		8.2.1 Perfect Knowledge	381
		8.2.2 Limited Knowledge?	383
		8.2.3 Complication	384
	8.3	Jewish Characteristics	386
		8.3.1 The Importance of the Matter	386
		8.3.2 More Jewish Characteristics	389
		8.3.3 Jesus the Faithful Jew	391
	8.4	Confidence in God	393
		8.4.1 The Praying Jesus	393
		8.4.2 The Trusting Messiah	395
		8.4.3 Nine Mountains of Prayer and	

		Worship	396
		8.4.4 Humiliation, Yet Greatness	398
	8.5	Jesus' Personality	400
		8.5.1 Grief and Joy	400
		8.5.2 Rage and Tenderness	403
		8.5.3 Other Features	405
		8.5.4 Divine Suffering?	407
	8.6	The Exceptional Incarnation	409
		8.6.1 A Truly Human Body	409
		8.6.2 Jesus Still Human Today	411
		8.6.3 Mythological Aspects?	414
	8.7	Self-Emptying	415
		8.7.1 Becoming Man, Even Slave	415
		8.7.2 What Is *Kenōsis*?	417
		8.7.3 The Kenotic Theory	420
9	The Virgin Birth of Christ		423
	9.1	Jesus Begotten of a Virgin	424
		9.1.1 The Miracle of the Virgin Birth	424
		9.1.2 The Holy Spirit: Begetting or Giving Birth?	425
		9.1.3 Virginal Begetting or Virgin Birth?	427
		9.1.4 The Virgin Birth in the Quran	429
	9.2	Biblical Testimony	430
		9.2.1 The Testimony of Matthew and Luke	430
		9.2.2 Other Biblical Testimony	433
	9.3	Objections	435
		9.3.1. Mythology	435
		9.3.2 An Ovum of Mary?	437

	9.3.3	Other Objections	440
9.4	Theological Significance		443
	9.4.1	Link with the Incarnation	443
	9.4.2	Link to Jesus' Sinlessness	445
	9.4.3	Significance of the Biblical Testimony	447
10 The Sinlessness of Christ			449
10.1	Jesus' Guiltlessness		449
	10.1.1	Is It Human to Sin?	449
	10.1.2	Jesus' Moral Excellence	451
	10.1.3	Deeper Testimony	453
	10.1.4	A Sinless Nature	454
10.2	The Temptation of Jesus		455
	10.2.1	To Sin and to Be Able (Not) to Sin	455
	10.2.2	Temptation and Weakness	457
	10.2.3	Physical and Moral	460
10.3	The "Likeness of Sinful Flesh"		461
	10.3.1	The Meaning of Romans 8:3	461
	10.3.2	Objections	463
10.4	Could Jesus Err?		465
	10.4.1	Smaller Examples	465
	10.4.2	More Substantial Examples	466
10.5	Was Jesus' Baptism Needed?		468
	10.5.1	The Anticipation of the Cross	468
	10.5.2	Sin and Righteousness	469
	10.5.3	Did Jesus Reject the Qualification "Good"?	472
10.6	The Holy and Righteous One		474

10.6.1	Jesus Is "Risky"	474
10.6.2	A Place of Rest	475
10.6.3	The Mount of Transfiguration	477
10.7	Stumbling Over Jesus	478
10.7.1	"Sweet" Jesus	478
10.7.2	Dubious Actions	480
10.7.3	The Irritating Jesus	481
10.8	Jesus and Women	484
10.8.1	Lust: the Gravest Sin	484
10.8.2	Sinlessness and Women	485
10.8.3	Touch Without Lust	487
11	The Life of Jesus	489
11.1	Circumstances of Jesus' Birth	489
11.1.1	Nazareth	489
11.1.2	Time of Birth	492
11.1.3	The Census	494
11.2	The Birth of Jesus	495
11.2.1	Stable or Cave	495
11.2.2	The "Kings" (?)	497
11.2.3	The Star and the Shelter	499
11.3	Jesus' Youth	500
11.3.1	High or Low Status?	500
11.3.2	Visit to Jerusalem	502
11.4	Historical Context	504
11.4.1	Pompei and Antipater	504
11.4.2	Herod and Archelaus	505
11.4.3	The Forerunner	507
11.5	Jesus' Ministry	510

11.5.1 Dating	510
11.5.2 Spiritual Background	512
11.5.3 Pharisees and Sadducees	514
11.5.4 Other Movements	515
11.6 The Beginning of Jesus' Ministry	517
11.6.1 The First Disciples	517
11.6.2 The First Passover	519
11.7 First Journey through Galilee	520
11.7.1 Healings and Deliverances	520
11.7.2 The Twelve Disciples	522
11.7.3 The Sermon on the Mount	525
11.8 Second Journey through Galilee	526
11.8.1 Preaching and Expounding	526
11.8.2 New Tokens of Power	528
11.9 Third Journey through Galilee	529
11.9.1 New Preaching	529
11.9.2 Feeding the Crowd	530
11.9.3 Walking on the Lake	531
11.10 Jesus' Final Activities	532
11.10.1 Various Places	532
11.10.2 The Transfiguration	534
11.10.3 The Feast of Booths	536
11.10.4 To Perea and Back	538
12 The Passion Story	541
12.1 The Passion Week	541
12.1.1 Palm Sunday and Monday	541
12.1.2 Tuesday and Wednesday	543
12.1.3 Thursday	546

12.2 The Last Night	548
12.2.1 Gethsemane	548
12.2.2 Deliberations	550
12.3 The Jewish Trial	551
12.3.1 The Accusing Witnesses	551
12.3.2 Another Illegal Act	553
12.4 The Roman Trial	555
12.4.1 No Immediate Ratification	555
12.4.2 Trying to Save Jesus	557
12.5 The Crucifixion of Jesus	558
12.5.1 The Act of Crucifying	558
12.5.2 The Bystanders	561
12.6 The Death of Jesus	563
12.6.1 Last Sayings	563
12.6.2 The Events Surrounding Jesus' Death	565
12.7 Jesus' Burial	566
12.7.1 The Rich Man's Tomb	566
12.7.2 Descending into the Netherworld?	567
13 Jesus' Resurrection and Ascension	571
13.1 The Resurrection of Jesus	571
13.1.1 Introduction	571
13.1.2 The Discovery of the Empty Tomb	572
13.2 The First Appearances	574
13.2.1 The Women and Peter	574
13.2.2 The Emmaus Disciples	576
13.2.3 The Twelve and Many Others	578
13.3 Later Appearances	579

	13.3.1 In Galilee	579
	13.3.2 Once More in Jerusalem	580
13.4	The Significance of Jesus' Resurrection	582
	13.4.1 A Historical Turning Point	582
	13.4.2 Scientific Argumentation	585
	13.4.3 Alternative Hypotheses	588
13.5	Three Facts	591
	13.5.1 The Empty Tomb	591
	13.5.2 The Changed Disciples	591
	13.5.3 The Appearances	592
13.6	Why No Public Appearance?	594
	13.6.1 Three Reasons	594
	13.6.2 Two More Reasons	596
13.7	The Theological Significance of Jesus' Resurrection	598
	13.7.1 Natural and Spiritual	598
	13.7.2 Seven Truths	600
13.8	Jesus' Ascension	601
	13.8.1 The Reports	601
	13.8.2 The Testimonies	603
	13.8.3 Jesus' Glorification	606
13.9	Jesus' "Anakenōsis"	609
	13.9.1 A Man Clothed in Divine Glory	609
	13.9.2 Shared With, and Beheld By, Believers	611
Bibliography		615
Scripture Index		663
Subject Index		695

Series Preface

BY MEANS OF THIS PREFACE, the editor and publisher of this series wish to help the reader both understand and process the content of these volumes.

The capacities and erudition of Dr. Willem J. Ouweneel need no demonstration or defense from us. His voluminous work and prodigious writing stand as a testimony to his love for the Lord Jesus Christ, God's Word, and God's people.

But these volumes present ideas that will surprise some, anger others, and possibly confuse still others. Both the editor and publisher disagree with some of Dr. Ouweneel's assertions and conclusions, but this is not the place for offering our counter-arguments. That requires an altogether different venue. Nevertheless, discerning readers will legitimately wonder why this editor and publisher invested effort and resources in putting these volumes into print.

At least three reasons justify that investment. Each of them is very sensitive.

The first reason is: *self-examination*. Some of our readers may conclude that, in presenting his exegetical, doctrinal, and historical case, Dr. Ouweneel is "coloring outside the lines" of what they have come to believe. He challenges deeply and firmly held convictions and beliefs, like those associated with Israel, with the law of God, with election and reprobation, with infant baptism, with covenant theology, and with justification. At each point, his challenges call us readers to self-examination, regarding our love for Scripture, for the God of Scripture, and for the Truth revealed and incarnated personally in Jesus Christ. One of Ouweneel's challenges is for us believers in Jesus Christ who are Reformed and Presbyterian church members to recognize that there are millions, even billions, of Jesus-believers who disagree with us *and are nevertheless genuine Christians*. And they ought to be acknowledged as such.

The second reason is: *repentance*. Coming, as they do, from one who lives and teaches outside the orbit of many of our readers, Dr. Ouweneel's observations about the state of our (numerous) churches and of our (interminable) doctrinal squabbles ought to embarrass us Reformed and Presbyterian church members. Our incessant polemicizing, our cantankerous stridency, and our offenses against the unity of Christ's church seriously compromise the gospel's witness to the watching world. Brothers and sisters, we must repent of these, for the sake of the gospel, for the sake of the church's witness, and for the sake of our children.

The third reason is: *ecumenicity*. This reason may indeed strike you as strange, but one of the salutary outcomes of reading Dr. Ouweneel's arguments can be this: *not* that you surrender your commitments and convictions that are being challenged, but instead that you come to *respect* and *love* those Jesus-believers who don't share them with you. These Christians are those whose spiritual pilgrimage and gospel-guided history have not brought them to the same place on the road, but who nonetheless are walking the same road as we.

You may well be asking: How, then, is this different from advocating doctrinal relativism? If these distinctive features of Reformed confession and theology are biblical, then why is Dr. Ouweneel being given a microphone for proclaiming

Series Preface

his criticisms and rejections of these distinctive emphases of Reformed teaching? The short answer is this: So that from this brother in Christ, this close cousin in the faith, this fellow pilgrim-soldier, we may learn how to lock arms with other Jesus-believers as we face unbelief in our day, even if we can't hold hands. So that we may learn what it means to be Jesus-believers *first*, Reformed or Presbyterian confessors *second*, and only then, *thirdly, theological advocates*.

So we leave you with this challenge: Why do you believe what you believe? What is your biblical warrant? Dr. Ouweneel presents fairly the various positions prevalent within Christianity. The reader will learn why others believe what they believe, and why they don't emphasize certain teachings in the same way that we do.

These books, then, are *not* for the faint of faith. But they *are* for those wanting to grow up and mature into the unity of faith in our Lord Jesus Christ (John 17: 20-23; Eph. 4:13).

Nelson D. Kloosterman, editor
John Hultink, publisher

Author's Preface

THIS IS VOLUME II/2 in a systematic-theological series on the "unseen, eternal" things of God (cf. 2 Cor. 4:18). The first two volumes, I/1 and I/2, deal with bibliology, and more specifically with the Torah. Then follows the first volume of a new part that contains volumes II/1–II/3, dealing with the Deity: the first with theology proper (the doctrine of God), the second (present) volume with Christology, and volume II/3 with pneumatology. The present volume deals with comparative-religious and historical aspects of Christology, with the Messianic message in the Old Testament, with the pre-incarnate Christ, with the deity of Christ, with the humanity of Christ, with his virgin birth, with his sinlessness, and with the life, death, resurrection, and ascension of Christ.

This volume is a re-working and expansion of parts of my *Evangelisch-Dogmatische Reeks* ("Evangelical Dogmatic Series," published by Medema, in Vaassen, and later, Heerenveen, Netherlands, consisting of twelve volumes in total). The part used here comes from chapters 1 and 3–12 from the Dutch volume 2 (*De Christus van God*). Each volume title in the Dutch series ends with the words *van God* ("of God"). For the English series I have chosen the key term "Eternal" in each title.

Bible quotations in this book are usually from the English

THE ETERNAL CHRIST: GOD WITH US

Standard Version.

I thank Dr. Nelson D. Kloosterman again very warmly for his expert editorial work on the manuscript of this book. And I am again deeply thankful to my publisher, John Hultink, for his constant encouragement in this entire project.

Willem J. Ouweneel
Fall 2019

Abbreviations

Bible Versions

AMP	Amplified Bible
AMPC	Amplified Bible, Classic Edition
ASV	American Standard Version
CEB	Common English Bible
CEV	Contemporary English Version
CJB	Complete Jewish Bible
DLNT	Disciples' Literal New Testament
ERV	Easy-to-Read Version
ESV	English Standard Version
GNT	Good News Translation
GW	God's Word Translation
HSV	Herziene Statenvertaling
ICB	International Children's Bible
ISV	International Standard Version
KJV	King James Version
LEB	Lexham English Bible
NASB	New American Standard Bible
NET	New English Translation
NIV	New International Version
NKJV	New King James Version

NLV	New Life Version
RSV	Revised Standard Version
TLB	Living Bible
WEB	World English Bible

Other Sources

AB	Anchor Bible Commentary
BT	Kelly, W., ed. 1856–1920. *Bible Treasury: A Monthly Review of Prophetic and Practical Subjects.* Available at https://bibletruthpublishers.com/bible-treasury/lpvl22465.
CD	Barth, K. 2009. *Church Dogmatics. Study Edition.* Translated by G. W. Bromiley et al. Vols. I/1–IV/1. New York, NY: T&T Clark. (Editor's Note: The original fourteen volumes have been published in the *Study Edition* as thirty-one volumes. For citation purposes, the original volume enumeration is followed by the number of the equivalent new volume: e.g., III/3=18. The sections [§] are identical in both editions. The final number[s] refer[s] to the page[s] in the new *Study Edition*. Sample citation convention: CD III/3=18, §51.2:130.)
CNT	Commentaar op het Nieuwe Testament
COT	Commentaar op het Oude Testament
CW	Darby, J. N. n.d.-a. *The Collected Writings of J. N. Darby.* Available at https://bibletruthpublishers.com/john-nelson-darby-jnd/collected-writings-of-j-n-darby/luc13-14921

Abbreviations

DD	Kuyper, A. n.d. *Dictaten Dogmatiek.* 5 vols. Kampen: J.H. Kok.
DJG	Green, J. B., S. McKnight, and I. H. Marshall, eds. 1992. *Dictionary of Jesus and the Gospels.* Downers Grove, IL: InterVarsity.
DNTT	Brown, C., ed. 1992. *The New International Dictionary of New Testament Theology.* 4 vols. Grand Rapids, MI: Zondervan.
DOTT	Van Gemeren, W. A., ed. 1997. *The New International Dictionary of Old Testament Theology and Exegesis.* 4 vols. Grand Rapid, MI: Zondervan.
EBC	Expositor's Bible Commentary
EDR	Ouweneel, W. J. 2007–2013. *Evangelische Dogmatische Reeks.* 12 vols. Vaassen/Heerenveen: Medema.
EGT	Nicoll, W. R., ed. 1979. *The Expositor's Greek Testament.* Grand Rapids, MI: Eerdmans.
KDC	Keil, C. F. and F. Delitzsch. 1976–1977. *Commentary on the Old Testament.* 10 vols. Grand Rapids, MI: Eerdmans.
KV	Korte Verklaring der Heilige Schrift
NICNT	New International Commentary on the New Testament
NICOT	The New International Commentary on the Old Testament
NIGTC	New International Greek Text Commentary
RC	Dennison, J. T., Jr., ed. 2008–2014. *Reformed Confessions of the 16th and 17th Centuries in English Translation.* 4 vols.

	Grand Rapids, MI: Reformation Heritage Books.
RD	Bavinck, H. 2002–2008. *Reformed Dogmatics*. Edited by J. Bolt. Translated by J. Vriend. 4 vols. Grand Rapids, MI: Baker Academic.
RGG	Galling, K. ed. 1986. *Die Religion in Geschichte und Gegenwart*. 6 vols. Tübingen: Mohr (Siebeck).
RT	Ouweneel, W. J. Forthcoming. *An Evangelical Introduction to Reformational Theology*. Edited by N. D. Kloosterman. 13 vols. Jordan Station, ON: Paideia Press.
SBB	Cohen, A., ed. 1982–1985. *The Soncino Books of the Bible*. 14 vols. London: Soncino.
SBK	Strack, H. L. and P. Billerbeck. 1922–1928. *Kommentar zum Neuen Testament aus Talmud und Midrasch*. 4 vols. München: C. H. Beck.
ST	Chafer, L. S. 1983. *Systematic Theology*. 15th ed. 8 vols. Dallas, TX: Dallas Seminary Press.
TDNT	Kittel, G. et al., eds. 1964–1976. *Theological Dictionary of the New Testament*. Translated by G. W. Bromiley. 10 vols. Grand Rapids, MI: Wm. B. Eerdmans.
TNTC	Tyndale New Testament Commentary

Chapter 1
Preliminary Orientation in Christology

What do you think about the Christ?
Whose son is he?
                                    Matt. 22:42

1.1 Worship Versus Reflection
1.1.1 Worship

JUST AS DOGMATICS constitutes the heart of theology, Christology constitutes the heart of dogmatics.[1] The subject of the person and the work of Jesus Christ belongs to the core of Christianity. Throughout the ages, the questions of the people around him keep resounding: "Who is this?" (Matt. 21:10; Mark 4:41; Luke 5:21; 7:49; 8:25; 9:9; cf. John 5:12; 9:36; 12:34), or directly addressed at Jesus, "Who are you?" (John 8:25). We also hear the echoes of the questions that Jesus himself once asked, "[W]ho do you say that I am?" (Matt. 16:15), and, "What do you think about the Christ? Whose son is he?" (22:42).

Here we must stress, however, that in the New Testament

---

1. Cf. the subtitle in Van de Beek (2002a): "Christology as the Heart of Theology," and the opening line in Bloesch (1997, 15), in which the same terms are used.

these are not systematic-theological questions. If Peter replies to the penultimate question mentioned, "You are the Christ, the Son of the living God," Jesus responds with this: "Blessed are you, Simon Bar-Jonah! For flesh and blood has not revealed this to you, but my Father who is in heaven. And I tell you, you are Peter [Gk. *petros*], and on this rock [Gk. *petra*] I will build my church, and the gates of Hades shall not prevail against it" (Matt. 16:16–18). Peter did not just supply a correct answer to an academic question, but his reply had at least a twofold character. First, it illustrated that it is possible to truly know Christ only through divine revelation (objective aspect), and with the enlightened eyes of the heart (Eph. 1:18; cf. 1 Cor. 2:14–15) (subjective aspect). Second, Peter's reply had the character of a confession, even worship. Therefore, Jesus said, as it were, that from such "material" as this "rock," Peter, he would build his church.

Conversely, the overt confession of Christ himself that he was the Son of God led the high priest Caiaphas to tear his garments (Mark 14:61–64). Between these two options, worship and dismay, there is, unfortunately, much room for disinterest, but no room for neutrality, no matter how much many people have sought this space. Ultimately, one is either a worshipper or an opponent; it is either adoration or aversion. "Whoever is not with me is against me," said Jesus himself (Matt. 12:30; Luke 11:23; cf. Mark 9:40; Luke 9:50).

The church of Christ consists primarily not of orthodox people, but of confessors and worshippers. In this respect, it is remarkable that the Greek word *doxa* means "opinion, presentation"; being "orthodox" (Gk. *orthos* = right) means having the "right opinion of a matter." However, within the New Testament we observe an interesting shift. Via the meaning "(favorable) opinion that others have of someone," the Greek noun *doxa* came to mean "glory"; the corresponding Greek verb *doxazō* actually means "to opine," but in the New Testament it means "to boast, to praise" (cf. the word "doxology"). Being "orthodox" concerning God thus receives a much wider meaning than many realize: it means having the right opinion of him, *and thus praising him, glorifying him.*

1.1.2 The Gospel's Heart

Such acts of worship as that of Peter toward Christ belong to the heart of the gospel. Therefore, Jesus says of the woman who, as an act of worship, anointed his head: "[W]herever this gospel is proclaimed in the whole world, what she has done will also be told in memory of her" (Matt. 26:13).[2] Christ is primarily to be worshiped in the church, less to be reasoned about. Therefore, the New Testament rarely argues about Jesus but instead glorifies him, as Thomas did: "My Lord and my God!" (John 20:28). The apostle Paul did the same: ". . . the Christ, who is God over all, blessed forever. Amen" (Rom. 9:5), and Peter: ". . . our Lord and Savior Jesus Christ. To him be the glory both now and to the day of eternity. Amen" (2 Pet. 3:18), and John: "Jesus Christ . . . [t]o him who loves us and has freed us from our sins by his blood and made us a kingdom, priests to his God and Father, to him be glory and dominion forever and ever. Amen" (Rev. 1:5-6).[3]

Philip Melanchthon sensed this clearly: "We do better to worship the mysteries of the Deity than to research them."[4] In this respect, it is remarkable that John Calvin described his *Institutes* not as a summary of theology (Lat. *summa theologiae*) but as a summary of piety (Lat. *summa pietatis*),[5] where "piety" refers to "that reverence joined with love of God which the knowledge of his benefits induces."[6] Donald Bloesch ar-

---

2. This promise pertains not so much to the person of Mary of Bethany. Where this word of Jesus is quoted (see also Mark 14:9) her name is not mentioned, and where her name *is* mentioned (John 12:1–8) this statement of Jesus is lacking. It is her *act* that matters, not her *name*. (Actually, the commentaries give very different interpretations of Matt. 26:13 and Mark 14:9.)
3. Cf. Schweizer (1971a, 1–76): the belief that Christ is God is primarily a matter not of theory but of doxology, of personal commitment, of a Christian lifestyle.
4. Quoted in Ford and Higton (2002, 209).
5. Calvin (1960), subtitle of the 1536 edition.
6. Ibid., 1.2.1.

gued that Jesus Christ is accessible, not (primarily) to the historian's investigations, nor to the theologian's speculations, but to the supplications of the humble and the penitent.

Anyone who confesses and worships Christ in this way apparently *knows* him.[7] People do not "know" Christ through Christology; the latter offers them at most some (defective and constantly changing) *information* about him. However, truly knowing Christ involves a *relationship*.[8] This is what the apostle Paul means: "Indeed, I count everything as loss because of the *surpassing worth of knowing Christ Jesus* my Lord. For his sake I have suffered the loss of all things and count them as rubbish, in order that I may gain Christ . . . *that I may know him* and the power of his resurrection, and may share his sufferings, becoming like him in his death, that by any means possible I may attain the resurrection from the dead" (Phil. 3:8-11; cf. 2 Cor. 5:16-17; Eph. 3:19; 4:13). This is what the apostle Peter means: "[G]row in the grace and *knowledge* of our Lord and Savior Jesus Christ" (2 Pet. 3:18). And this is what Jesus himself means: "[T]his is eternal life, that they know you, the only true God, and Jesus Christ whom you have sent" (John 17:3).

This knowing Jesus leads not only to engaging in praise but also to being shaken, to humbling oneself. For instance, this is what happened to Thomas and to Saul of Tarsus when they met the risen Lord. As A. van de Beek put it, "Being a Christian means that no ideology is ever comfortable. Any confessing of the Lord causes dislocation. We are therefore Christians in fear and trembling" (cf. Phil. 2:12-13).[9] Knowing Christ is a comprehensive event, one that claims the entire person. This knowledge makes one dance and sing, but it also

---

7. See McGrath (2001).
8. About *this* knowing Christ, see Macquarrie (1998, chapter 5). There are people "who have somehow or other come to know Christ, who have perhaps even made a scholarly study of him, but have not encountered Jesus himself in his utter uniqueness and otherness," said Ratzinger (2007, 292).
9. Van de Beek (2002a, 133).

renders one small.

1.2 Theological Reflection
1.2.1 The Existential Depth Dimension

Not only is Jesus Christ confessed and worshiped, but the theological reflection on his person and work is indispensable, if only to counter every doctrine that dishonors him. The apostle John told an ordinary woman and her children:[10]

> Everyone who goes on ahead and does not abide in the teaching of Christ,[11] does not have God. Whoever abides in the teaching has both the Father and the Son. If anyone comes to you and does not bring this teaching, do not receive him into your house or give him any greeting, for whoever greets him takes part in his wicked works (2 John 1:9–11).

What is involved here is the specific heresy of Docetism (see further in §2.6); but the general message is that each individual believer must advocate the true teaching concerning Christ.

Such a commitment is impossible without reflecting on what exactly this true doctrine concerning Christ involves. For the woman mentioned, and her children, this teaching was not one about natures and substances, but about the "unsearchable riches of Christ" (Eph. 3:8). This involves not an arid, abstract treatise about him, but an existential orientation toward him, more or less in the sense of the urgent question that the imprisoned Dietrich Bonhoeffer asked a friend: "Who is Jesus for us today?"[12] Bonhoeffer would not have denied that the "doctrine of Christ" contains many timeless elements; but for him as well as for the woman addressed in 2 John, the primary issue was what Jesus means here and now for me.

At the same time it is true that, even if the "doctrine of

---

10. Ordinary, that is, if the terms "woman" and "children" are meant literally; some have understood these as figurative references to a local church; see, e.g., Marshall (1978a, 10, 60–61; Lalleman (2005, 36–38).
11. This refers not to what Christ taught, but to the doctrine (KJV) *concerning* Christ.
12. Bonhoeffer (1967, 139).

Christ" is viewed as an existential, personal matter, it evokes questions. Take, for instance, the question mentioned: "What do you think about the Christ? Whose son is he?" (Matt. 22:42). Whose son is Jesus Christ? The son of Joseph, the carpenter of Nazareth? The son of David? In what sense? Does this mean that he is the Messiah of Israel? And in particular: is he the Son of God? And what does this mean? That from eternity he is the Son of the Father? Or is he Son of God only because he was begotten by the Holy Spirit? Or only because he was adopted as Son by God at his baptism? Or is he the Son of God in the same way every believer—or even every human being (cf. Luke 3:23, 38)—is a son or daughter of God?[13]

These questions are of crucial importance. They were this already for the apostles. We say that the Letter to the Romans is especially about justification by faith—but Paul is primarily concerned with God's "Son, who was descended from David according to the flesh and was declared to be the Son of God in power according to the Spirit of holiness by his resurrection from the dead, Jesus Christ our Lord" (Rom. 1:3-4). We say that 1 Corinthians is about the order in the church—but Paul is primarily concerned with "Christ the power of God and the wisdom of God. . . . Christ Jesus, who became to us wisdom from God, righteousness and sanctification and redemption, so that, as it is written, 'Let the one who boasts, boast in the Lord'" (1 Cor. 1:24, 30-31). We say that 2 Corinthians is especially about the defense of Paul's ministry, but Paul is not primarily concerned with himself but with

> the light of the gospel of the glory of Christ, who is the image of God. For what we proclaim is not ourselves, but Jesus Christ as

---

13. Brown (1994a, 4) distinguishes between the *degree* of divinity (e.g., in Job 1 and 2 angels are called sons of God, too) and the *way* of being Son of God (e.g., from eternity, from Jesus' incarnation, from his baptism [adoption]). He also speaks of a two-step Christology (114), but one could just as legitimately speak of a four- or five-step Christology: Jesus is Son of God from eternity (John 17:5, 24), *and* from his incarnation (Luke 1:35), *and* from his baptism (3:22), *and* from his resurrection (Rom. 1:4).

Lord, with ourselves as your servants for Jesus' sake. For God, who said, 'Let light shine out of darkness,' has shone in our hearts to give the light of the knowledge of the glory of God in the face of Jesus Christ (2 Cor. 4:4-6).

Thus it is with many New Testament letters. In Galatians, Paul is primarily concerned with the "faith in the Son of God, who loved me and gave himself for me" (Gal. 2:20). Ephesians is about "the Beloved" (Eph. 1:16), and about the "unsearchable riches of Christ" (Eph. 3:8). Philippians is about "Christ Jesus, who, though he was in the form of God, did not count equality with God a thing to be grasped, but emptied himself, by taking the form of a servant, being born in the likeness of men" (Phil. 2:5-7). Colossians is about the Father's "beloved Son . . . the image of the invisible God, the firstborn of all creation. For by [rather, in] him all things were created, in heaven and on earth" (Col. 1:12-16).

1.2.2 The Praying, Praising Theologian

Even the most expert theologian must always be, and remain, a worshipper of Christ. Karl Barth claimed that dogmatics is not possible without the attitude of prayer, and to show this, he quoted Aurelius Augustine, Anselm of Canterbury, and Thomas Aquinas.[14] Helmut Thielicke wrote: "The man who studies theology, and especially he who studies dogmatics, might watch carefully whether he increasingly does not think in the third rather than in the second person."[15] That is, beware of thinking more in terms of "he" (God/Christ) than of "you," more speaking *about* God or Christ than *to* him. As Emil Brunner wrote: "[T]his process of turning to the 'third person', and the impersonality which this engenders, means that the personal element, the 'heart' — so long as the theological process of reflection goes one — is practically ruled out."[16] Theological knowledge stems from the prayer of faith, and

---

14. Barth (*CD* I/1=1, §1:23–24).
15. Thielicke (1962, 33).
16. Brunner (1950, 74).

Bible passages must be read and understood in a dialogical openness from the human being to God, and in applying oneself to prayer.[17] Prayer and praise ought to be the highest interest of dogmatics.[18]

Wolfgang Trillhaas called Christianity the world's "most thoroughly reflected upon" religion, which for him implied a loss of "faith immediacy":[19] true faith always contains something of the naiveté of the childlike confidence in God the Father, whereas the scope and essential necessity of a critical (and thus not naïve) dogmatics are less than the church's preaching, less than her hymns and prayers, even less than faith itself. Thus, G. C. Berkouwer wrote about

> the auxiliary function of dogmatics. It does not intend to reach up into a gnosis higher than the simple faith of the church; there is no gnosis which would enable one to elevate himself above the "communio sanctorum" composed of those of whom the Savior said: "I thank thee, O Father, Lord of heaven and earth, that thou didst hide these things from the wise and understanding, and didst reveal them unto babes" (Matt. 11:25).[20]

And Joseph Ratzinger wrote:

> The saints are the true interpreters of Holy Scripture. The meaning of a given passage of the Bible becomes most intelligible in those human beings who have been totally transfixed by it and have lived it out. Interpretation of Scripture can never be a purely academic affair, and it cannot be relegated to the purely historical.[21]

---

17. Ott (1972, 36).
18. Schlink (1983, 33–35, 64–65).
19. Trillhaas (1972, 7, cf. 10).
20. Berkouwer (1954, 352).
21. Ratzinger (2007, 78); he was referring to Francis of Assisi, who wished to bring the people to "listen anew to the word—without evading the seriousness of God's call by means of learned controversies" (79). Cf. 393: "Not the biblical scholars, those who are professionally dealing with God, recognize him; they remain stuck in the thicket of their detailed knowledge. The simple look at the whole, at God's own reality revealing itself, is, through

Within no domain of dogmatics, aside from the doctrine of God (see the previous volume), are all these remarks more applicable than Christology. The "mystery of Christ" (cf. Eph. 3:4; Col. 1:27; 2:2; 4:3) is not contemplated by the theologian as such, who reasons about the mystery, but by the ordinary believer to whom the mystery has been *granted*. The word "ordinary" does not mean less gifted, or childish, or naïve, but the quality of being like children with their plain, down-to-earth faith (Matt. 18:3); it is the "simplicity that is in [ESV: sincere and pure devotion to] Christ" (2 Cor. 11:3 KJV). This gift involves the "revealing" (Gr. *apokalupsis*) about which Jesus speaks in Matthew 16:17. On the most profound level, Jesus' own word remains applicable: "[N]o one knows the Son except the Father" (Matt. 11:27). However, faith *grasps* what reason cannot *fathom*: "Everyone who *believes* that Jesus is the Christ has been born of God" (1 John 5:1).

1.3 The Person and Work of Christ
1.3.1 Inseparable Matters

Within systematic theology, Christology constitutes such a vast topic, but I am using the term in its *limited* meaning, namely, as referring only to the *person* of Christ. And here, too, the subject is limited since the topic of the Trinity has been discussed thoroughly in the previous volume. The *work* of Christ will be discussed in subsequent volumes. Naturally, there are many overlaps with respect to the topics of the person of Christ and the work of Christ.[22] Therefore, in this volume, too, there will be several direct or indirect references to the redemptive work of Christ. It is difficult to speak of the coming of God's Son into this world without referring to its aim: "I have not come to call the righteous but sinners

---

all their knowledge, distorted for them—this is because they believe that things cannot be that simple for him who knows so much of the complexity of the problems" (cf. Isa. 29:14b; 1 Cor. 1:18–19, 26–29; 3:18).

22. Berkouwer (1965, 19). McGrath (2007, 292) argued that the distinction between the person and the work of Christ is increasingly viewed as useless, except for purposes of organizing and presenting the relevant material.

to repentance" (Luke 5:32; cf. 9:56; 19:10); "I did not come to judge the world but to save the world" (John 12:47); "the Son of Man came not to be served but to serve, and to give his life as a ransom for many" (Matt. 20:28; Mark 10:45).

In the New Testament, we find various examples of Christological passages that, in one breath, speak of the person *and* the work of Christ, such as:

> [A]ll things were created through him and for him. And he is before all things, and in him all things hold together. And he is the head of the body, the church. He is the beginning, the firstborn from the dead, that in everything he might be preeminent. For in him all the fullness of God was pleased to dwell, and through him to reconcile to himself all things (Col. 1:16–20).

Similarly, we read about ". . . our great God and Savior Jesus Christ, who gave himself for us to redeem us from all lawlessness and to purify for himself a people for his own possession who are zealous for good works" (Tit. 2:13–14). Finally, the apostle Peter wrote "[t]o those who have obtained a faith of equal standing with ours by the righteousness of our God and Savior Jesus Christ" (2 Pet. 1:1).

We find this coupling also throughout church history. Church father Athanasius claimed that Christ had to be both divine and human in order to save us: divine, to be able to save us, human, to identify himself with us. His view of the two natures of Christ was not purely ontological, but also of a soteriological nature.[23] We encounter the same thought in the Heidelberg Catechism, Lord's Day 6:

> *16. Why must [the mediator] be a true and righteous human?*
> Because the justice of God requires (Rom. 5:15) that the same human nature which has sinned should make satisfaction for sin; but one who is himself a sinner cannot satisfy for others (Isa. 53:3–5).

---

23. Kärkkäinen (2003, 11).

17. Why must [the mediator] also be true God?
That by the power of His Godhead He might bear in His manhood the burden of God's wrath (Isa. 53:8; Acts 2:24), and so obtain for us (John 3:16; Acts 20:28) and restore to us righteousness and life (1 John 1:2).[24]

The identity of the person of Christ comes to light in his work, while, conversely, his work was possible only because of the person he was. For some critics, the two therefore cannot be separated; according to them, one who nevertheless tries to do so, turns the confession of the person of Christ into an abstraction.[25] As a starting-point, people like to refer to a statement by Philip Melanchthon: "To acknowledge Christ is to acknowledge his benefits, not, as is sometimes taught, to behold his natures or the modes of his Incarnation."[26] In other words, it is not simply Christ's "being" that matters, but his "being for us," what he has done for us. This is more or less like the meaning of the name YHWH: not simply "I am" (in any philosophical sense), but "I am *there*," namely, for you.[27]

1.3.2 Yet Distinguishable

People who place one-sided emphasis on Melanchthon's comment overlook that, at other places where Melanchthon wished to defend the doctrine of the Trinity or the two natures of Christ, he clearly did acknowledge the importance of these matters. He was simply seeking, as should we, to warn against a Christology that is exclusively ontological, and not also soteriological. What does it mean that Christ is truly *God* if it is not realized that precisely because of this, he could accomplish the work of redemption (cf. Ps. 49:7–9)? And what does it mean that Christ is truly *Man* if it is not realized that precisely because of this, he could become the Mediator be-

---

24. Dennison (*RC* 2:774).
25. See Berkouwer (1954, chapter 6); McGrath (2007, 292–94).
26. *Loci communes*, 1521, quoted in Berkouwer (1954, 102); Bonhoeffer (1966, 30–31).
27. Cf. the translation by Martin Buber: *Ich bin da*, "I am there" (Exod. 3:14).

tween God and humanity (cf. 1 Tim. 2:5)? All speaking of the *person* of Christ receives its deepest meaning and significance from the *work* of Christ. However, this does not mean that the reflection upon the person of Christ as such would be meaningless or superfluous. Apparently, questions such as "Who do you say that I am?" (Matt. 16:15), and "What do you think about the Christ? Whose son is he?" (22:42), are also meaningful even though they are not immediately linked with soteriology.

In practice, it may be true that people come to know Christ experientially first through his work. Thus, the man at Bethesda who had been ill for thirty-eight years was healed by Jesus before he came to know the Lord: "They asked him, 'Who is the man who said to you, "Take up your bed and walk"?' Now the man who had been healed did not know who it was" (John 5:12-13). The man who was born blind was first healed by Jesus before he came up with the question: "And who is he [i.e., the Son of Man], sir, that I may believe in him?" (9:36). However, the experiential route is not identical to the theological route. Whereas a person comes to Jesus' person through Jesus' work, the theologian moves from Christ's person to his work. Berkouwer mentioned the example of Emil Brunner, who tried to follow the opposite route but, in Berkouwer's view, hardly succeeded in this.[28]

Immanuel Kant claimed that, in general, we can know things immediately only insofar as we can observe their effects. In agreement with this, Albrecht Ritschl claimed that we must not separate Christology and soteriology because the only way to obtain knowledge about something is to observe its effects upon us.[29] However, Bonhoeffer preferred to follow Luther: the work does not explain the person, but the person explains the work.[30] Otto Weber pleaded for *both* approaches:

---

28. Berkouwer (1954, 106).
29. Kärkkäinen (2003, 12).
30. Bonhoeffer (1966, 30–31).

each explains the other.³¹

It is certainly true that, if we were to limit ourselves to Jesus' person, his work would be of no avail to us. However, conversely, there is a danger of trying to construe a Christology purely on the basis of soteriological considerations, which would thus no longer have any basis in the history of the person of Jesus.³² Therefore, Christology is entirely correct in moving from the person Christ to his work. Scripture contains plenty examples of this. In Hebrews 1:1-3, Christ is first the Son, the heir of all things, the One through whom God creates and sustains all things, before he is the One who carried out the "purification for sins." A similar sequence is found in John 1: first, Christ is the Logos with God, then the incarnated Logos, then the Lamb of God (vv. 1-3, 14, 29, 35). We mention yet a third author: Paul (Col. 1), who does begin with redemption (vv. 13-14), but then comes to Jesus as the Son of the Father's love, the One through whom all things have been created, and are sustained (vv. 15-17), and then, through the resurrection (v. 18), arrives again at reconciliation (vv. 19-22).

1.4 Intramural Christian Debate

1.4.1 No Acquiescence

Regardless of which Christology ordinary believers adopt, the theologians at least cannot simply and blindly repeat the orthodox³³ viewpoint (the Nicene Creed, the formula of Chalcedon, etc., all of which we will discuss extensively). No, the discussion with Christian movements that reject Nicaea and

---

31. Weber (1983, 2:12).
32. McGrath (2007, 293), with reference to Wolfhart Pannenberg, who signals this danger.
33. The term "orthodox" (apart from reference to Eastern Orthodox Churches and orthodox Jews) in this book means nothing other than standing in the tradition of the Councils of Nicaea (325), Constantinople (381), and Chalcedon (451). The term "liberal" refers to the theology that rejects the statements of these Ecumenical Councils. Of course, there are many intermediate positions, such as: acceptance of Nicaea and Constantinople but doubt with respect to the Chalcedonian formula.

Chalcedon cannot and should not be avoided, even though we have our own critical questions about these and related credal conclusions, such as: Can we accept a formula such as "God of God, Light of Light" (Nicene Creed) or Christ's "rational soul" (Athanasian Creed)? At the same time, we see that some liberal experiments have already run aground, and that some liberals are showing new, though reluctant interest in the more traditional viewpoints. As C. Graafland put it, the church

> was not able, and not allowed, to simply repeat what Chalcedon had stated. It was called upon to confess anew. This involved the task of interpretation, and this interpretation is directed to the concrete questions and views that appear at certain moments. In that latter sense, it is true that the confessing tradition has continued after Chalcedon, also with respect to the confession of Christ.[34]

Each generation and every audience have their own challenges and needs. Against unbelieving Jews, Saul/Paul endeavored to prove from the Scriptures that Jesus is the Messiah and the Son of God, who had to suffer and to rise from the dead (Acts 9:20, 22; 17:3; 18:5, 28). He could do so because, for his Jewish listeners, the authority of the Scripture was beyond discussion. Against non-Jews, however, Paul had to choose a different starting point: linking to the pagans' own experiences, but without telling them what they wished to hear, he proclaimed the message of the risen Lord (Acts 17:22-31). And against Judaizing and pseudo-Christian heretics, other approaches had to be chosen (e.g., 1 Cor. 15; Gal. 3-6; Col. 2-3; 1 Tim. 4:1-5; 2 Tim. 4:1-4; see also 2 Pet. 3; 1 John 2 and 4; 2 John 1; Jude 1).

Today the systematic theologian, starting from the Scriptures, has the task of linking to the experiences of modern people and, without making concessions, bringing them the message of the risen Lord. This is not simple, as Paul explained to

---

34. Graafland (1982, 52; see more extensively, 100–104).

Timothy (2 Tim. 2:8–10). Today's challengers are easily identifiable. First, there is still the intramural Christian discussion between the orthodox and the heretics, or, to express the matter in a more prudent and contemporaneous way, between conservatives and liberals (and the many views in between) (for this, see §1.4). Secondly, at the fringes of Christianity we encounter Gnostic Christology (see §1.5). Then there are discussions, thirdly, with Islamic views of Christ (see §1.6) and, fourthly, with Jewish Christology (see §1.7).

1.4.2 Modern Debate

Especially since the Enlightenment and the rise of investigation into the life of Jesus (Ger. *Leben Jesu Forschung*), the theological debate around the person of Jesus has been enormous, including the modern Jesus Seminar with its post-Christian Jesus (§3.4.1). Throughout history, every conceivable viewpoint has been defended. As a consequence, today there seems to be a Christology for every taste and preference. Of course, there is still one for extremely liberal theologians,[35] but also one for adherents to federalism (covenant theology),[36] one for Latin Americans,[37] one for feminist theologians,[38] and last but not least—especially since the Nag Hammadi findings—one for the Gnostic theologians (see §1.5).[39]

J. P. Meier observed that, as in the first century, so today: no one Jesus suits everybody.[40] The cause of this is that all theology is paradigmatically determined; as Graafland put it: it is striking "that what is presented as the outcome of scholarly biblical research fits amazingly well the already established (faith) position of the researcher."[41] Concerning the study of

---

35. Some examples are Kuitert (1999) and Funk (1999).
36. See Horton (2005).
37. Sobrino (1978).
38. See, e.g., Schüssler Fiorenza (1994), and the comments by Witherington (1997, 163–185).
39. See, e.g., Slavenburg (1992).
40. Meier (1991, 3).
41. Graafland (1982, 28).

the Gospels, H. Kuitert had to admit that scholarship produces little more than contradictory hypotheses, sometimes even circular arguments.[42] F. H. Klooster wrote about the liberal New Testament scholars and the Christologists that their claim of being objective and without prejudice was itself a myth.[43]

According to Meier, generally speaking, Roman Catholics worship a Catholic Chalcedonian Jesus, Protestants warm to a Protestant Jesus, while Jews seek to recover the Jewish Jesus. Whether we call it a prejudice, a *Tendenz*, a worldview or a belief, every person writing about the historical Jesus does so from a certain ideological viewpoint; no critic is exempt from this.[44] Another Roman Catholic New Testament scholar, K. Berger, called certain "fundamental 'results of liberal exegesis' an example of ideological wishful thinking."[45]

All the more astonishing, then, that C. den Heyer claimed with respect to the traditional approach of the New Testament: "In this case, there can be no question of an unprejudiced exegesis of the texts"[46] — as if any unprejudiced exegesis *exists* at all; Den Heyer's own Christological publication is part of the evidence indicating that this is not the case.[47] I prefer the conclusion of Van de Beek:

> Ever since New Testament scholarship began to make a distinc-

---

42. Kuitert (1999, 33).
43. Klooster (1977, 26).
44. Meier (1991, 5).
45. Berger (2004, 532–33).
46. Den Heyer (2003, 11).
47. A remarkable example of Den Heyer's own prejudicial style is the following (2003, 130): "One of the consequences of the investigation into the origins of the Gospels in the nineteenth century was the discovery of the Q source . . . a surprising discovery. . . . Now we know [!] that this Q-source is of inestimable significance for the knowledge of early Christianity." Of course, the truth is that a Q-source was never "discovered" but only "postulated"— something that, from the viewpoint of scholarly precision, constitutes an enormous difference. The most we can "know" is that the Q-*hypothesis* is significant, *not* that this source that exists only in scholarly imagination is significant; cf. Meier (1991, 44, with references); Stein (1996, 38–40).

tion between what is historical and theological, we have found that same divide among theologians as well. Which way the decision goes largely depends on the theological position (or the worldview underlying that theology). The theological argumentation usually decides the historical outcome of the debate.[48]

1.4.3 Pale Pictures

Paul Barnett rightly argued that any Jesus reconstructed from the Gospels—apocalyptic prophet, devoted *chasid*, social reformer, cynic with esoteric knowledge[49]—never attains Sonship, Messiahship, or Lordship in the missionary preaching reflected in the New Testament epistles.[50] He also observed that little attention is paid to the divine dimension in Jesus, a very conspicuous element in the faith of the early church. As a consequence, these reconstructions of Jesus closely resemble the "pale Galilean"[51] of nineteenth-century liberal Protestantism, against which Albert Schweitzer reacted so strongly.[52]

In the liberation theology of Gustavo Gutiérrez, Leonardo Boff, and others,[53] Jesus is not only the Savior of sinners but also the Liberator of the oppressed. In itself, from a Christian viewpoint, stressing social justice, combating poverty, and pleading for human rights may be beneficial. But a Christology in which Jesus cares for the poor merely because they are poor misses the point.[54] Liberation theology interprets Je-

---

48. Van de Beek (2002a, 150).
49. Regarding Jesus as an adherent of cynicism (a Socratic Hellenist movement), see especially Burton Lee Mack, John Dominic Crossan, and F. Gerald Downing; see Borg (1994a, 15–18, 28–32); Witherington (1997, 58–92); Knight (2004, 51–54).
50. Van de Beek (2002a, 52–57).
51. The phrase comes from the "Hymn to Proserpine," a poem by A. G. Swinburne published in 1866.
52. Van de Beek (2002a, 133–35).
53. Gutiérrez (1988); Boff (1984); see also M. Bonino (1974); De Ru (1974); Küster (1999, especially §4).
54. See Van de Beek (2002a, 236–50), who calls it the "deficit of the traditional liberation theologians" that being "lost" refers only to the absence of "mate-

sus' mission in terms of liberation and introducing justice — if necessary with the use of force (in spite of Matt. 26:51-52). However, the justice that Jesus preaches is not first a political justice, and certainly not one of a (semi-)Marxist type, but the righteousness of the kingdom of God (Matt. 6:33), and this is a state that possesses not a leftist government but the rule of Christ.

This theology often appeals especially to what Luke said about the poor (e.g., 4:18; 6:20; 7:22; 14:13, 21; 18:22; 19:8), without acknowledging that Luke does not envision a liberation of the poor and afflicted as such. In his Gospel, the poor are saved not because they are poor but because they repent and receive forgiveness of sins (1:77; 3:3; 5:20; 7:47; 24:47). We have already seen this in Jesus' own mission statement: "I have not come to call the righteous but sinners to repentance" (Luke 5:32). Only when this is understood will we understand the story of the rich man and poor Lazarus (16:19-31): Lazarus was accepted not because he is poor and afflicted but — as his name indicates[55] — he knows God as his helper. And the rich man landed in Hades not because he was rich but because he does not care about God and his commandments (cf. 2 Tim. 4:3, "lovers of pleasure rather than lovers of God"). Our conclusion might not follow from the exegesis of this single story, but it does follow from the context of the entire Gospel of Luke (cf. the wicked judge in Luke 18:4, "I neither fear God nor respect man").

As Meier observed, only through distorted exegesis and bizarre reasoning can Jesus be transformed into a this-worldly political revolutionary. The historical Jesus overthrew not just some ideologies but *all* ideologies, including liberation theology. Indeed, the significance of the historical Jesus for theology is that in the end he escapes all our modern theological programs; he renders all of them dubious by refusing to

---

rial dignity or autonomy."
55. Heb. *El'azar*, "God helps." Whether or not this story is a parable, we must notice that only in this story of Jesus is the name of a person used.

Preliminary Orientation in Christology

fit into the boxes that we create for him.[56] Importantly, this is true about both orthodox and liberal boxes. Jesus does not allow himself to become anyone's theological servant, whether the liberation theologian or the fundamentalist theologian, or any theologian in between.

1.5 Gnostic Christology
1.5.1 Alternative Christianity

Another example of a modern Christology is that of neo-Gnosticism. In a certain sense, Gnosticism is the very opposite of liberal theology. Liberal theology holds that Jesus is truly Man but not God, while Gnosticism teaches that Jesus is truly God but averse to physical matter, including what is genuinely human. In antiquity, Gnosticism arose within Christianity especially through the extremely popular Marcion of Sinope. Today, especially the discovery of the Nag Hammadi writings (1945) gave neo-Gnosticism a tremendous boost. On the basis of these writings, many opine that these Gnostic writings present the authentic picture of the person and the teaching of Jesus, in contrast with the New Testament. They contain the so-called "Gospels" of Thomas, of Philip, of Mary [Magdalene], of the Truth, the Apocryphon of John, the Sophia of Jesus Christ, the Dialogue of the Savior, and many other works.[57] One of the subjects in them is the prominent position of Mary Magdalene, especially with respect to Peter.[58]

Concerning the Nag Hammadi writings a flood of literature has appeared, especially regarding the significance of

---

56. Meier (1991, 199).
57. For a helpful online introduction, see http://www.gnosis.org/naghamm/nhl.html; cf. Pagels (1992). Funk (1999, 110–117) enumerates twenty-two Gospels, partly hypothetical (e.g., Q), partly small fragments found in Oxyrhynchus, partly Gospels found in Nag Hammadi, partly proto-Gospels (those by James and Thomas). Much more extensive is Meier (1991, 114–166, 439–40). For a discussion of the thirteen most important ones, see Theissen and Merz (1998, 17–59); cf. also Van Bruggen (1998, 45–52); Stein (1996, 35) enumerates twenty-three Gospels.
58. See extensively Ouweneel (1998).

these works for Gnosticism,[59] sometimes with rather wild speculations.[60] On the basis of these writings, modern Gnostics accuse the church of having ensured the triumph of the Petrine line, in at least two ways. First, the church supposedly and intentionally left the Gnostic writings out of the New Testament and destroyed them. Secondly, the church is accused of having degraded Mary Magdalene to a converted prostitute. This was caused by pope Gregory the Great, who made a composite from three New Testament women: Mary Magdalene, Mary of Bethany, and the sinful woman of Luke 7.[61] The Gnostics claim that this fit into the strategy of the official church. They speak of *two* apostolic successions, one beginning with Peter—this is the line of the official church—and one beginning with Mary Magdalene. The early church called her the "apostle [feminine] of the apostles" (Lat. *apostola apostolorum*) because she was the risen Lord's messenger to the apostles (John 20:17), and also called her the archetypal bride of Jesus, the heavenly Bridegroom. Thus, Mary Magdalene is supposed to have been the actual successor of Jesus, not Peter. The Gnostics claim that this is supported by the Gnostic Gospels, which view Mary as the actual leader of the Christian church.

Basically, according to modern Gnostics, we are dealing with two different kinds of Christianity, and therefore with two Christs and two Christologies. In the Petrine line, what matters is true doctrine, pure confession, orthodoxy, the rigid structure and hierarchy of the church. However, in the Mag-

---

59. See Quispel (1972); Hoeller (1989, 2002); Walker (1990); Ehrman (1996, 2003a, 2003b); Markschies (2000); King (2003).
60. See Baigent et al. (1983, 1991); Picknett and Prince (1998).
61. Mary of Bethany was the woman who anointed Jesus' feet, but afterward does not appear again in Jesus' passion story, whereas Mary Magdalene does. Were the two identical? Both the "sinner"—who almost certainly was an adulterous woman or a prostitute—and Mary of Bethany wet the feet of Jesus, and wiped them with their hair. Thus, the two were identified as well. Conclusion: the assumed prostitute of Luke 7 is Mary Magdalene (she is mentioned immediately after this in 8:2).

dalene line, what matters is the personal, mystical relationship with Christ, the validity of personal visions and revelations, merging into and uniting with God, the discovery of the divine that, at creation *and* re-creation, God himself lived in humans, and continues to do so.

1.5.2 Paganism

Through the novel, *The Da Vinci Code*, by Dan Brown,[62] the Magdalene view mentioned has been popularized, partly because Jesus is presented as the lover or husband of Mary Magdalene, and father of a daughter from whom the Merovingian kings (the fathers of modern Europe[63]) would have descended. Apart from such literary speculation — which actually had been propagated already long before Dan Brown[64] — the Gnostics have many other arguments undergirding their claim that the true Christology is presented not by the biblical Gospels but by the Gnostic Gospels. In fact, this issue is more of a bibliological issue than a Christological issue. Which Gospels are genuinely canonical?[65]

The only Christological aspect that I wish to emphasize here is this: New Testament Christology joins with, and builds upon, the Old Testament Messianic prophecies, whereas Gnostic Christology breaks with the Old Testament, and presents a thoroughly Hellenized picture of Christ, a composite of Persian, Syrian, and Greek elements. To be sure, it contains Jewish elements, but few Old Testament elements. Judaism developed its own mysticism and Gnosticism, and thereby distanced itself from its Old Testament roots, not only according to current Christian theology but also according to many rabbis.[66] Thus, Gnosticism has mainly extra-bib-

---

62. Brown (2004).
63. Through a foremother, *the* "father of Europe," Charlemagne, was a descendent of them.
64. See Burstein (2004) regarding Dan Brown's novel, with references to many contemporary Gnostic publications.
65. See *RT* I/1, as well as, e.g., Green (1992); McDowell (2006).
66. Especially a Sophiology that clearly went over the edge plays a great role in

lical roots. The Jesus of the New Testament is a Jesus who is thoroughly and pervasively connected to the Old Testament (see next section). But the Jesus of the Gnostics may originally have been a Jew, but then a Jew who, to a large extent, tore himself away from his roots to become the founder of a completely new world religion.

This new Gnostic religion has more similarities to the great pagan thought movements than to Jewish religion. Its teachings are typically pagan, and thus unbiblical, such as:

(a) the material world as such is evil;

(b) humanity fell from a purely spiritual state to the material (and thus evil) state;

(c) through the transfer of *gnosis* (esoteric knowledge), redemption consists of self-elevation from the material state; only a small number of elite "spiritual" people are saved;[67]

(d) the Redeemer is a mythical figure, a syncretized composite drawn from many movements ([neo-]Platonism, Hermetism, Zoroastrianism, the teaching of Simon Magus, etc.);

(e) Christ—the Christ adapted to Gnostic thought—is merely one of the many Redeemers, who at times are sent into this world; this spiritual Christ lived in the Man Jesus of Nazareth, which is taught also by Rosicrucians and other esoteric thinkers.

In the New Testament, Jesus is the One who brings *redemption*; in Gnosticism, he is the One who brings *gnosis*, "knowledge, understanding." In the Bible what matters is *faith*, an intimate surrender to God's promises. This faith began already with Adam and Noah, and continued with the patriarchs, with Moses and the great prophets. In Gnosticism, however, what matters is the *understanding* that brings true liberation, *insight* into one's own being, into God, into the need for en-

---

Gnosticism (see Ouweneel [*EDR* 1:§3.4]).

67. This kind of "spiritual" people (pre- or proto-Gnostics) belonged to Paul's opponents in Corinth (see especially 1 Cor. 2, 6–7, 15) and Colossae (see especially Col. 1–2).

lightenment, for self-redemption. In the Bible, in both the Old and New Testaments, people cannot redeem themselves; instead, they intimately surrender to God, who in both the Old and in the New Testament redeems people on the basis of a substitute sacrifice.

1.5.3 The Key: the Old Testament

Since the time of Marcion, Gnostics have made a virtual separation between the God of the Old Testament and the God of Gnosticism. In their view, Old Testament YHWH, God the Creator, is especially the God of avenging justice. In contrast to this, Gnosticism teaches the Father of Jesus Christ, that is, God as Redeemer, the God who redeems through *gnosis*. This supposedly is the God of love and mercy, in contrast to the Old Testament God. The New Testament God is ostensibly elevated far above the Old Testament God. In this way, Gnostics abandon the Old Testament.

In contrast to this approach, Jesus did the very opposite: he connected completely to the Old Testament. He did so with ease because the God of the Old Testament is definitely also the God of love. When God reveals himself to Moses on Mount Sinai, he calls himself "[t]he LORD, the LORD, a God merciful and gracious, slow to anger, and abounding in steadfast love and faithfulness, keeping steadfast love for thousands, forgiving iniquity and transgression and sin" (Exod. 34:6-7; cf. Neh. 9:17; Ps. 86:15; 103:8; 145:8; Joel 2:13; Jonah 4:2). Indeed, the text continues by saying that God "will by no means clear the guilty," but the picture of the loving God prevails. Conversely, the God of the New Testament is definitely also the God of avenging justice (e.g., Rom. 2:3-10; 14:10; 2 Cor. 5:10; Heb. 10:31; 12:29; Jude 1:4, 6-7, 15; Rev. 4-20). In this respect, there is not a single essential contrast between the Old and New Testaments—the contrast exists between the Bible and Gnosticism.

It is enlightening to understand the Apostles' Creed as a testimony of the early church against Gnosticism. The statement "who was conceived by the Holy Spirit, born of the Virgin Mary" is primarily a testimony not about Jesus' deity but about his humanity. He was so genuinely human as to have been begotten of a woman, even though at the same time he was such a special human (namely, divine) that this woman was a virgin, and he had been begotten by the Holy Spirit (Luke 1:35). He is the One who "suffered under Pontius Pilate," that is, one can localize and identify him in world history. He "was crucified, died, and was buried"—his death not some mystical death in a historical vacuum. Nor did he directly ascend from the cross to heaven, as some Gnostics asserted; his body was truly buried in a grave, with a stone in front of it. These things were so tangible that the resurrection that followed on the third day, and his ascension and second coming, are equally concrete and tangible: the genuinely dead body of Jesus really came to life again.[68]

1.6 Islamic Christology
1.6.1 The Significance of Jesus

A third example of a Christology that conflicts with the New Testament, yet is highly significant today, is Islamic Christology. As long as the topic is the doctrine of God, there are surprising similarities between the Christian and Muslim portraits of God, more similarities than many fundamentalists on both sides seem prepared to accept.[69] In the discussions about whether the God of the Koran and the God of the Bible are identical, people should be more aware of this fact. Such discussions are often pointless because the answers are both affirmative (the word *Allah* goes back to the same general Semitic appellative for the [chief] Deity; Muhammad derived his knowledge of God especially from Jews and Christians) and negative (the picture of God in the Koran is so distorted that it shows little resemblance to the God of the Bible).

---

68. Van de Beek (2002a, 171–72) seemed to create too much distance between what he called the "immanent" (from Jesus' conception to his funeral) and the "transcendent" (from Jesus' resurrection to his second coming).
69. Ibid., 269–70.

However, as soon as Christology becomes the topic for discussion, pervasive differences become apparent. In the dialogue with Islam, the person of Jesus (*Isa*) plays a great role. It is remarkable that, in some respects, Islam has maintained a picture of Jesus that is more conservative than that of liberal Christian theology. However, the significance of Jesus in Islam must not be exaggerated. Olaf Schumann has observed that Christology has not produced its own article of faith in Islam; it is hardly anything more than an aspect of prophetology.[70] A. van de Beek wrote that for many Muslims the role of Jesus is similar to that of Jeremiah for many Christians — and that role is not very conspicuous.[71]

The Koran calls Jesus the Messiah (*al-masikh*),[72] but this is more a vague title than an indication of a special relationship to Israel as the latter's anointed King. The Koran also acknowledges that Jesus — often called the "son of Mary" — was supernaturally begotten within the pure Mary (*Maryam*),[73] though this is viewed on the same level as the creation of Adam.[74] With respect to Jesus, the Koran refers to the "Word [*kalima*] of God" and the "Spirit [*rukh*] of God,"[75] and calls him "prophet [*nabi*] of God,"[76] and even sinless.[77] He healed the sick as no other prophet did, raised the dead, and created life from inanimate matter.[78] Further, it is said, "Christ Jesus, the son of Mary, is only the messenger [*rasul*] of God,"[79] namely,

---

70. Schumann (1988, 15).
71. Van de Beek (2002a, 294).
72. Eleven times in the Medinensic Surah's, including 3:45; 4:157,171; 5:72.
73. Surah 3:42-47; 19:16-36; cf. 21:91; 66:12; see further §9.1.1.
74. Surah 3:59, "Indeed, the example of Jesus to Allah is like that of Adam. He created Him from dust; then He said to him, 'Be,' and he was."
75. Surah 4:171; 5:110; 21:91; 66:12.
76. E.g., Surah 19:30.
77. In later Islamic tradition; actually, for Islam, Jesus shares this characteristic with the other great prophets.
78. Surah 3:49; 5:110-115; some of the miracles mentioned were adopted from the apocryphal Gospels, e.g., the Gospel of Thomas and the Arabic Infancy Gospel.
79. Ibid.

in the sense that he brought to people the "gospel" (*indjil*, a word derived from Gk. *evangelion*). In Islam, Jesus is great, but no greater than other messengers[80] of God; he is subordinate to Muhammad. However, it *is* said about Jesus alone, not even of Muhammad, that he is a "sign for the people."[81] Apparently, this means that God miraculously revealed through him his powerful acts to the world in order to lead people to repentance and faith.

1.6.2 Who Was Jesus' Successor?

Muslims acknowledge Jesus especially as an ascetic prophet. According to a famous *hadith* (saying of Muhammad, outside the Koran), Jesus supposedly said,

> My seasoning is hunger, my undergarment is the fear of Allah, my upper garment is wool, my fire in winter is the sun's radiation, my lamp is the moon, my mount is my feet, and my food and fruit are what the earth produces. At night I have nothing, and in the morning I have nothing. Yet, no one on earth is richer than I am (cf. Matt. 8:20; 2 Cor. 8:9).[82]

Another *hadith* says of Jesus that he "was an ascetic in the world, longing for the next world, and eager for the worship of Allah. He was a pilgrim on earth until the Jews sought him, and wished to kill him. Then Allah elevated him to heaven; and Allah knows what is best."[83]

Islam claims that, especially in John's Gospel, Jesus himself pointed to his great successor, Muhammad, namely, in the passages that speak of the Paraclete (14:16, 26; 15:26; 16:7). The Greek term *Paraklētos* is interpreted as *Periklutos*, "blessed one," in Arabic *Ahmad*, one of the names of Muhammad. It is remarkable to see how Islam uses these passages because

---

80. The Koran mentions a total of nine messengers: Noah, Lot, Ishmael, Moses, Su'aib, Hud, Salih, Jesus, and Muhammad, and five prophets with whom God entered a covenant: Noah, Abraham, Moses, Jesus, and Muhammad.
81. Surah 19:21; cf. 21:91.
82. Quoted in Ng Kam Weng; see Chung (2005, 181).
83. Ibid., 182.

the context makes it perfectly clear that Jesus referred to the Holy Spirit—and Muhammad never claimed to be the Holy Spirit. What he reportedly did say about himself is this: "I am the closest relative of Jesus, son of Mary, in this world and the next. The prophets are brothers, sons of one father through fellow-women. Their mothers differ, but their religion is one. There has been no prophet in between the two of us."[84]

I will not dwell on what Islam has said about the message of Jesus, nor about his death and resurrection, because Islamic theology is strongly divided over these matters. Those who emphasize the (supposed) similarities between Islam and Christianity refer to these and similar matters. However, it is more important to stress that Islam cannot accept Jesus as the Son of God. On the contrary, Islam strongly emphasizes that Allah has no son, and *cannot* have a son, nor could he ever assume a body of flesh and blood. This means that Islam has no room at all for the deity of Christ. Some Muslims speak with more reverence about Jesus than do some so-called Christians, but despite this, they have no room for the most important aspects of the person of Jesus.[85] The lesser the importance of the deity of Christ in the thinking of modernist Christians, therefore, the easier it will be for them to engage in ecumenical dialogue with Muslims.

1.7   Jewish Christology
1.7.1   Messianic Jews

Until the middle of the twentieth century, there was hardly any question of a Jewish Christology,[86] that is, of orthodox Jewish views of Jesus. This has changed completely. In 1982, the orthodox Jewish New Testament scholar Pinchas Lapide

---

84. According to Abu Huraira, reported by Imam al-Bukhari and Sahih Muslim (ninth century); quoted in Ford and Higton (2002, 152–53).
85. Parrinder (1977); Räisänen (1980); Kuitse (1992); Bouman (1994); Schirrmacher (1994, 206–28); Knight (2004, 226–29).
86. Or more correctly: Jesuology (because orthodox Jews do not acknowledge Jesus as Messiah/Christ)—to be distinguished from a general Messiology (doctrine concerning the Messiah).

said that, in the state of Israel alone, between 1952 and 1982, 187 Hebrews books about Jesus had appeared—more than in all nineteen preceding centuries combined.[87] If one added the studies about Jesus written by Jewish scholars in Europe and America since 1950, they numbered more than three hundred.[88] All these Jewish portraits of Jesus share a growing appreciation of the life and death of the Man of Nazareth, an empathy that often can hardly be distinguished from sympathy, an awareness of a spiritual affinity that calls for a belated "homecoming" of Jewish thinkers, according to Lapide.[89] Moreover, after the revived interest in the historical Jesus, new interest arose in the Jewish Jesus.[90]

Since the time of Lapide's observation, a global Messianic-Jewish movement has appeared consisting of an estimated 250,000 to 300,000 persons, and several hundred congregations, whereas merely seventy-five years ago only a handful existed. In Israel, present estimates claim about ten thousand Messianic Jews. Especially after the conquest of old Jerusalem in 1967, hundreds of Jews came to believe in Jesus as the Messiah, and a number of Messianic congregations arose in Israel. Since the fall of communism in the former Soviet Union (1989), thousands of Jews have come to faith in Jesus. Among Jews who emigrated from the former Soviet Union to

---

87. Works that have come to us from Israel in Western languages include those of Ben-Chorin (2001) and Flusser (2007).
88. In addition to Shalom Ben-Chorin and David Flusser, well-known twentieth-century Jewish writers about Jesus (see extensively, Van der Linden [2001]) include Claude G. Montefiore (1910, 1930); Leo Baeck (1938); Sholem Asch (1939); Martin Buber (1961); Joseph Klausner (1964); Avraham Aharon Kabak (1972); Geza Vermes (1973, 1983, 1993, 2002); Gaalya Cornfeld (1982); Pinchas Lapide (1983; 1988; and Luz, 1985); Margareta Susman (1987); Yehezkel Kaufmann (1988); Ellis Rivkin (1984); Jacquot Grunewald (2000); Jacob Neusner (2000); and Franz Rosenzweig (1971).
89. Rahner and Lapide (1987, 104–105).
90. E.g., Vermes (1973, 1983, 1993); Sanders (1984); Charlesworth (1991); Meier (1991/4); Witherington (1994; see also 1997, 197–232); Dunn (2003; 2005).

Preliminary Orientation in Christology

Israel, hundreds have found Jesus the Messiah in this land.[91] Most Messianic Jews accept the orthodox doctrine concerning Christ—or Yeshuah, as they prefer to call him—but in addition to this, they emphasize more strongly his Jewishness and his Jewish way of life. In other words, their Christology is far more Jewish and might instead be called a Yeshuology (cf. §8.3).

Usually, a meaningful distinction is made between Hebrew Christians and Messianic Jews. The former are Christians of Jewish descent belonging to established churches (Roman Catholic, Protestant, Evangelical), who thus have largely or entirely surrendered their Jewish identity. Their Christology is formally the same as that of Christian tradition, that is, Nicene and Chalcedonian. The latter group are believers in Yeshuah who have retained their Jewish identity. Some of them limit themselves to the institutions of the Torah (Shabbat, biblical festivals, circumcision, food laws), while others also accept the rabbinic tradition (yarmulke, separation of the meat and the milk kitchen, etc.). There are all kinds of intermediate groups between Hebrew Christians and Messianic Jews (e.g., Calvinists keeping the Shabbat). As far as Christology is concerned, we find among Yeshuah believers an entire array of attitudes to the Christological tradition.

1.7.2 Messianic Christology

Messianic theologian David Stern took a strong stand against those Messianic Jews who oppose traditional Christology.[92] He acknowledged that the *term* "trinity" does not appear in the Bible, but the *substance* does appear,[93] clearly expressed in the New Testament and hinted at in the Tanakh (Old Testament). Stern also wished to acknowledge, in addition to absolute equality among the divine persons, also a hierarchy among them—a dangerous expression, bordering on subor-

---

91. See Ouweneel (2001a, 13 et passim).
92. Stern (1997, 68–69).
93. Cf. Stern (1992, 86, 476).

dinationism.[94] I believe this is acceptable only if Stern intended to say that as a *Man* Yeshuah was less than God the Father: "[T]he Father is greater than I" (John 14:28). For the rest, Stern is correct that, a Jew who confesses to be Messianic but who does not acknowledge the deity of Jesus and the equality of Father, Son, and Holy Spirit, at best does not know what they are talking about, and at worst is not a Christian.

Another Messianic theologian in Israel, Dan Juster, also defended the biblical doctrine of Yeshua's deity.[95] He emphasized more than Stern did that the Tanakh reveals a certain multiplicity in God's being, clear from the plural Hebrew term *Elohim* ("God") and the "Us" in Genesis 1:26 and 3:22. Thus, both the Shekhinah (i.e., the Holy Spirit[96]) and the Angel of YHWH are identified with God, but also distinguished from him (see §6.3). Juster also dealt with indications in the Tanakh that the Messiah is more than merely human (Ps. 110:1; Isa. 9:6–7; Micah 5:2; see §4.7). In the New Testament, the distinct deity of Yeshuah and of the Holy Spirit come to light much more clearly, according to Juster.

Dan Juster argued that the Jews thought functionally, in terms of different manifestations of God, and never felt the need of thinking numerically, in terms of oneness and threeness. Also, the Hebrew *Sh'ma Yisrael* ("Hear, Israel," Deut. 6:4) is not a statement about the simplicity of God's being but about the one God over against the many gods of paganism. Juster believed it was the Hellenistic Christians who drew ontological conclusions from the Bible's functional language. Here, Juster came dangerously close to Sabellian modalism,[97] the more so because he called Yeshuah "one person or one aspect of that plural manifestation of God."[98] Juster made a fascinating reference to the *Zohar*, the well-known main work

---

94. See Ouweneel (*RT* II/1:§10.3.3).
95. Juster (1995, 181–90).
96. Cf. Ouweneel (*EDR* 1:§3.4.2).
97. See Ouweneel (*RT* II/1:§10.2.3).
98. Juster (1995, 187).

Preliminary Orientation in Christology

of the Kabbalah, in which the Ancient of Days (Dan. 7:13, 22) is manifested with three heads "that are united into one . . . described as being three. . . . But how can three names be one? . . . [This] can be known only through revelation of the Holy Spirit."[99]

Another Messianic theologian who has dealt with the subject is Michael Schiffman.[100] He described the resistance among some Jews against the supposedly Hellenistic term "Trinity," and claimed (erroneously[101]) that the doctrine of the Trinity was articulated first at the Council of Nicaea (AD 325), where no bishops of Jewish descent had been invited, where the anti-Semitic emperor Constantine presided. Yet, Schiffman accepted Trinitarianism, and clearly—in my view correctly—distinguished it from tritheism and modalism.[102] Like Stern, he affirmed that Jews who believe in Yeshuah as the Messiah but not as true God, and do not believe in his incarnation and virgin birth, are not truly Messianic.[103] He also explained the mistake of Jews who believe that the doctrine of the Trinity conflicts with Jewish monotheism.

Schiffman did have trouble with the Greek philosophical mold in which the doctrine of the Trinity has been cast. He emphasized, more than a non-Jewish theologian would do, that the Greek *form* of the doctrine of the Trinity constituted a stumbling block for Jews.[104] However, he also acknowledged that earlier attempts to reformulate this doctrine were nothing but semantic variations, which were only worse than the Hellenistic format of the doctrine. Schiffman fell into the snare of biblicism by attempting to formulate the doctrine exclusively in the form of Bible quotations, apparently without realizing

---

99. Ibid., 188; see more extensively, the Messianic rabbi Tzvi Nassi (1990).
100. Schiffman (1996, 93–104).
101. The doctrine of the Trinity was implicitly affirmed no earlier than by the Council of Constantinople (381), which confessed the full deity of the Holy Spirit.
102. See Ouweneel (*RT* II/1:§§10.2.2 and 10.2.3).
103. Schiffman (1996, 98).
104. Ibid., 102.

that the development of this doctrine by the church fathers was a bitter necessity to mitigate all kinds of heresies.[105]

In his commentary on Romans, the strictly rabbinic Messianic Jewish theologian Joseph Shulam was not very clear about the divinity of Yeshuah. He did not clearly distinguish between the *ideal* pre-existence of the Messiah in Midrashic literature and the *ontic* pre-existence of Yeshuah.[106] He also asserted that the apostle Paul nowhere referred to Yeshuah as "God"[107] (in spite of, in particular, Rom. 9:5 and Tit. 2:13), and expressed himself vaguely, or in an explicitly subordinationist way, concerning the relationship between Yeshuah and God.[108] He did acknowledge, however, the Messiah's divine attributes: sonship, divine name, redeemer, righteousness, and so on.[109] Shulam's approach seems characteristic of those Messianic Jews who most resent Christian Trinitarian terminology, and who for this very reason risk falling into various snares that the church fathers purposely sought to expose and avoid.

1.7.3 Sympathizing Jews

In addition to the remarkable phenomenon of Messianic Jewry, there are also orthodox Jewish leaders who do not acknowledge Jesus as Messiah—if they did so, they would have become unacceptable to other orthodox Jews—but come very close. As Jewish scholar Pinchas Lapide observed,

> . . . the Church prays daily for the parousia of Christ, the synagogue for the arrival of the Messiah. Because there can only be one single and universal bringer of salvation according to Christian soteriology as well as in Jewish teaching about the

---
105. See Ouweneel (*RT* II/1:chapter 10).
106. Shulam (1998, 31).
107. Ibid., 340n11.
108. See ibid., as to whether Yeshuah is identified as God himself or partakes in his divinity; the strictness with which the description "God" is limited to no other person, including the Messiah, is reflected in the use of Isa. 9:6 in 1QH 3.9–10, one of the Dead Sea scrolls, according to Shulam.
109. Ibid.

Messiah, so the fervent expectation must be for our common redeemer.[110]

Jewish philosopher Martin Buber wrote: "From my infancy, I found in Jesus my big brother. The fact that Christianity viewed, and views, him as God and Savior always seemed to me a fact of the highest importance, which I, for my and for his sake, must try to understand."[111] The Yiddish writer Sholem Asch once said, "Jesus Christ is for me the eminent personality of all times, entire history, both as Son of God and as Son of Man."[112] Rabbi Kaufman Kohler wrote: "Jesus, the humblest of all people, the most despised of the despised Jewish nation, mounted the world throne to become the great King of the entire earth."[113]

Both Israeli scholars Joseph Klausner and Yehezkel Kaufmann were prepared to acknowledge Jesus as "a [!] Jewish apocalyptic messiah, who through his life and his teaching comes to stand outside Jewish society."[114] At the same time, Klausner could not accept Jesus as *the* Messiah; this was because—here, Klausner used an age-old[115] Jewish argument—the kingdom of heaven had not arrived with Jesus.[116]

In his conversation with Roman Catholic theologian Karl Rahner, Pinchas Lapide said this:

> If Paul is right ... and the coming redeemer turns out to be Jesus, then all of Israel will surely welcome him as the anointed of the Lord. "Until he comes" (1 Cor. 11:26), we both live in hope that must remain open as long as God does not give us

---

110. Rahner and Lapide (1987, 79).
111. Buber (1961, 12).
112. Quoted in Siegel (1976, 148).
113. Kohler (1894).
114. Van der Linden (2000, 86).
115. This argument was used in debates between Jewish rabbis and Christian theologians during the Middle Ages; see Ouweneel (2000, 286) for references.
116. Van der Linden (2000, 82); Jacob Neusner (2000) used this argument as well; see Ratzinger (2007, 149).

certainty. Just as hard to dispute would be the possibility that God could surprise us both as he has already done so often, "for my thoughts are not your thoughts, neither are your ways my ways, says the Lord" (Is. 55:8).[117]

And later he observed:

> In his book *The Church in the Power of the Spirit* [Jürgen Moltmann] writes: "Through his crucifixion, Jesus became savior of the Gentiles. In his Parousia [Return], however, he will prove himself also to be Israel's Messiah." That seems to me [says Lapide] to be a strong formula for reconciliation—until God gives us the fullness of certainty. For if on the day of the Lord it should be revealed that the Christian hope was legitimated, then that should be fair for all religious people [including Jews!]. God knows what he is doing and Jews loyal to the Bible trust his will blindly and without question. In the meantime, though, "until he comes" (1 Cor. 11:26), we all live in hope, we travel as pilgrims toward the same Messiah and we build hopefully on one and the same gracious love of God, without which our earthly existence would be meaningless.[118]

1.7.4 The Jewish Jesus

Jewish thinkers, whether Messianic (i.e., confessing *Jesus* as Messiah) or not, have strongly emphasized the *Jewish* Jesus. Orthodox Jews can accept this *Jewish* Jesus, stripped of what they see as Christian additions. Israeli author Shalom Ben-Chorin has beautifully formulated this in terms of the relationship between Jews and Christians: "The belief *of* Jesus unites us, the belief *in* Jesus separates us."[119] The faith of Jesus is a thoroughly Jewish faith, rooted in the Old Testament; on this, Jews and Christians can agree. But faith *in* Jesus as the Messiah of Israel and the Son of God separates Jews and

---

117. Rahner and Lapide (1987, 81).
118. Ibid., 110.
119. Ben-Chorin (2001, cover).

Christians.[120]

The Jewishness of Jesus has a remarkable consequence. Against the scholarly movement that was skeptical about the life of Jesus, and against liberal theology, claiming inability to access the Jesus of history but only the Christ of faith, the orthodox Jewish scholar David Flusser wrote his book about Jesus, which begins by telling us that "[T]he main purpose of this book is to show that it is possible to write the story of Jesus' life."[121] His sentiment was echoed by Lapide who, in conversation with Karl Rahner, emphasized that the Jewishness of Jesus was theologically important:

> ... if you deem the Jewishness of the person of Jesus unimportant or theologically irrelevant, then fundamentally you commit the error of "deincarnation" — the reduction of a living human figure to an abstract, bodiless idea.[122]

He is suggesting that kerygmatic thinkers are afraid of a Jesus who is (all too) *Jewish*. To me, this seems exaggerated. But it *is* true that Flusser, Lapide, and like-minded thinkers seek to stress the Jewishness of Jesus, whereas the mass of liberal *and* orthodox theologians share a similar disinterest in this Jewish Jesus.

For Flusser, the Jesus of history is definitely accessible: "The early Christian accounts about Jesus are not as untrustworthy as people today often think. The first three Gospels not only present a reasonably faithful picture of Jesus as a Jew

---

120. In Lapide and Luz (1985, 27–61), Lapide endeavors, unlike Kaufmann (1988), to show that Jesus never announced himself as Messiah toward his people. His conversational partner, Swiss theologian Ulrich Luz, replied to this (129): "Not only did Jesus not declare himself to his people as the Messiah; more than likely he did not even consider himself to be the Messiah." In contrast with this, the *Jew* David Flusser (2007, 200–201) assumed that Jesus certainly viewed himself as the Messiah (no wonder: "Are you the Christ [= Messiah], the Son of the Blessed?" And Jesus said, "I am," Mark 14:61–62). On this subject, see Vlaardingerbroek (1989, chapter 2).
121. Flusser (2007, 18).
122. Rahner and Lapide (1987, 54).

of his own time, ..."[123] Especially Jewish expositors have sought our attention for this Jewish Jesus, in whom both liberal and orthodox theologians seem to have so little interest. In our times, a Christology with no place for this Jewish Jesus is no longer conceivable (§8.3).

1.8 Christology in Modern Times
1.8.1 Proof Texts

Since the rise of Enlightenment theology, and in particular since the rise of the scholarly research into the historical Jesus, deriving the details of Jesus' person and life from proof texts has become problematic. This is due to the dominant conviction that all four Gospels are theologically biased (see §§5.3 and 5.4), and cannot be understood as biographies, and certainly not as objective biographies (in the sense of historical science or journalism). Is it possible to really discover anything objective about Jesus' person and life behind the doctrinal biases of the evangelists (and possibly of the faith communities to which they belonged)?

In general, many theologians understandably abhor appealing to proof texts, for two reasons (for the second one, see §1.8.3). First, behind such an appeal we often find a rather positivistic intellectual attitude, as if a theological theory can be proven by means of such proof texts. People collect such passages, which if correctly interpreted automatically yield the correct dogmatic model. People fail to realize that their interpretation is always affected by dogmatic biases.[124] In the great majority of cases, the dogmatician "knows" already—for instance, on the basis of tradition (creeds, church dogmas)—what the proof texts broadly tell him. Thus, an ap-

---

123. Flusser (2007, 20).
124. Brown (1994a, 25–30) mentioned the remarkable example of two extremes. On the one hand, there are (liberal) theologians who limit Jesus' divinity to their "he must" ("if Jesus is Man, he must . . .") or "he cannot" ("Jesus cannot do this or that, for that is impossible"). On the other hand, there are (fundamentalist) theologians who limit Jesus' humanity to *their* "he must" or "he cannot" ("if Jesus is God, he cannot . . .").

peal to proof texts will be meaningful only if the interpreter is fully aware of his own dogmatic prejudices, and dares to call them into question.

The clearest examples of such a positivist approach to the Bible appeared in previous eras. Charles Hodge viewed the goal of systematic theology to involve systematizing the facts of the Bible, and determining the principles or general truths that lie enclosed in these facts.[125] For William H. Griffith Thomas, theology must investigate all the facts of revelation, estimate their value, and arrange them into a doctrinal whole.[126]

Viewing the Bible's facts as neutral biblical data is characteristic of the positivist attitude mentioned. It overlooks the fact that facts are never unbiased, but always facts-for-people, facts that *become* facts only on the basis of the paradigmatic viewpoint from which one looks at them. For instance, the Chicago Statement on Biblical Hermeneutics (art. XXI) denies that "genuine scientific facts" could ever be in conflict with the true meaning of any biblical passage.[127] To them this is self-evident, since all supposed scientific facts that (really or seemingly!) conflict with the Bible are necessarily "non-genuine scientific facts." Such circular reasoning is self-incriminating.[128] Add to this the naiveté in the assumption that the true meaning of any biblical passage can be ascertained *a priori* to possessing an interpretive paradigm.

1.8.2 "Repeating" Scripture

We encounter a similar naiveté among dogmaticians who claim to be simply repeating (cf. Dutch *naspreken*, Ger. *nachsprechen*) what Scripture is saying. Emil Brunner claimed that all dogmatics is a repeating of the divine Word,[129] and Jochem Douma claimed that both church and dogmatics repeat Scripture

---

125. Hodge (1872, 18).
126. Griffith Thomas (1930, xxi).
127. Radmacher and Preus (1984, 886).
128. See more extensively, Ouweneel (*RT* I/1:chapter 9).
129. Brunner (1950, 84).

in the form of dogma.[130] Willie van der Merwe used the word "repeat" (Dutch *naspreek*) with regard to theology three times on one page.[131] In each of these cases, no one acknowledged the difference between Scripture's non-theological language and speech, and the theoretical nature of theological parlance. Only in Herman Bavinck, who belonged to the Reformed tradition of the late nineteenth- and early twentieth-centuries, did I encounter some critical awareness of this distinction. In reference to earlier theologians, he wrote: "Dogmatics is . . . a fallible human attempt, in one's own independent way, to think and say after God what he in many and various ways spoke of old by the prophets and in these last days has spoken to us by the Son [cf. Heb. 1:1]."[132] But later he added (as a second thought): "Scripture is not designed so that we should parrot it but that as free children of God we should think his thoughts after him. But then all so-called presuppositionlessness and objectivity are impossible."[133]

Bavinck wrote this at the end of the nineteenth century, but in the twentieth century Norman Geisler believed that, in opposition to the (supposed) humanistic roots of errantism (the doctrine that the Bible is not inerrant with respect to matters of science), one could simply appeal to the factual evidence of the Bible. If a philosophical foundation existed for his hermeneutic, he believed it was a version of theism, a supernaturalistic and metaphysical realism taught or presupposed by the Bible[134] — if we may presume that the Bible either teaches or is interested in any "-isms."[135]

Such an uncritical attitude by a scholar is rather futile. An ordinary believer must have the courage to simply say at a certain moment: "It is written . . .," as Jesus did to the devil

---

130. Douma (1974, 18).
131. Van der Merwe (1991, 66).
132. Bavinck (*RD* 1:55).
133. Ibid., 83.
134. Geisler (1979, 333–34); see more extensively, Geisler (1981).
135. See Ouweneel (*RT* I/1:§9.7.2).

(Matt. 4:4, 7, 10). However, in theological discussions, a direct appeal to Scripture is usually ineffective, since opponents already familiar with the passages involved interpret them differently. It is written, to be sure, but does the theologian *understand* what they are reading (cf. Acts 8:30)? Does their appeal to the facts of Scripture contain all sorts of hidden premises—biases that might not be as faithful to the Bible as they imagine? To what extent are their way of reading and theologizing determined by traditions that they have not critically examined? If only it were true that theologians simply repeat Scripture! If that were true, why do they so often reach contradictory conclusions? Of necessity, between the activities of reading Scripture and declaring its truths lies the activity of theological reflection—and in this reflection, we are not only fallible, but our horizon is limited, and we are children of our age more than we realize.[136]

1.8.3 Scripture As a Unity

The second argument against appealing to proof texts (see §1.8.1) is very different in nature. It holds that such an appeal is possible only if one accepts the unity of the Bible. And even then, we must be careful in applying passages from the synoptic Gospels to interpret Johannine or Pauline passages, and the reverse. If people believe, for instance, that the synoptic, Johannine, and Pauline portraits of Jesus are in conflict—as has been often asserted—their appeal to proof texts is even less persuasive. Such passages, as people claim, at most disclose how the Synoptics, or John, or Paul, or Peter viewed Jesus, that is, their portraits of Jesus or Christologies—not how modern theologians ought to view Jesus.

One perspective encountered in the New Testament might be that Jesus was identified with God, or was filled with God, either from his resurrection (whether historical or not), or from his baptism, or from his conception. Other perspectives might be that Jesus had a unique, divine relationship with

---

136. On this, see extensively, Ouweneel (*EDR* 1:§13.4).

God, or that he was adopted by God as his Son, or that God revealed himself to him in a special way.[137]

Of course, such approaches to the New Testament are based partially upon exegesis. But they are fundamentally governed—just like the traditional approach, of course[138]—by a certain theological paradigm. This is true for the exegesis as such. The main difference between the approaches just mentioned and the traditional approach is the attitude—pro or con—toward supernaturalism: belief in things that cannot be explained in terms of normal scientific categories. Questions involving incarnation and resurrection, for example, are determined by whether the investigator deems it possible *a priori* that a pre-existent, transcendent being is made flesh (cf. John 1:14), or that a human corpse becomes alive again (cf. Luke 24:39-43). This choice involves primarily not one's theology, but one's worldview, and is fundamentally a choice of *faith*. Therefore, A. van de Beek said of the resurrection: "It is hard to believe that someone was raised from the dead. It is incredulous not to modern folk alone [cf. Acts 17:32]. However, events are not about what can possibly happen but what has actually happened."[139]

Enough difficult theological questions remain, such as: How must we construe an incarnation or bodily resurrection? How strong is the testimony about these events? How can the various traditions be harmonized? What are the theological as well as the scientific implications of the virgin conception of Jesus, related to the incarnation, and a bodily resurrection? What is the theological *necessity* of these events, or why do people *need* to believe in them?

All of these are valuable questions. However, the basic question has already been answered: Does the theologian's worldview have any room *a priori* for such events? Whether

---
137. See, e.g., the extensive discussion by Pannenberg (1977, 53–187).
138. See Ouweneel (1995, chapter 5); cf. Ouweneel (*EDR* 12:chapters 6 and 9); Ouweneel (*RT* V/1).
139. Van de Beek (2002a, 1176–77).

the answer is affirmative or negative, the theologian will exhibit the tendency of steering his investigation of Scripture into the direction of his biases; no informed scientist today believes in neutral, objective, unbiased scholarship. This does not imply that theological work has become useless; to the contrary, despite their inherent biases, advocates of various paradigms continue to face the exciting task of showing what approach is intellectually most defensible.

1.8.4 Revelational Paradigm

The paradigm I am defending claims that in the New Testament, we are dealing primarily not with theology produced by the church (Ger. *Gemeindetheologie*, pious speculations about Jesus by the early church),[140] but with divine revelation. This does not necessarily exclude a certain element of such theology. However, what is important are not the ideas of the early Christians about Jesus—even though this reflection was of some significance—but the thoughts of God about Jesus, as these are revealed through apostolic forms. We are dealing primarily not with *acquired* truths but with *revealed* truths; not with wishful representations that the early church supposedly projected upon Jesus, but with its *faith* in divine revelation. Our access to this message follows a path that is neither psychological[141] or anthropological, but revelational.[142] Psychological and anthropological aspects are not unimportant, but they are subordinate to divine revelation.

While acknowledging the obvious differences in approach between John, Peter, Paul, and the Synoptics, we begin by affirming the essential revelational unity of the New Testament, in terms of its central scope. Within this paradigm, one can show that the alleged contradictions between the portraits

---

140. The expression goes back to German theologian Johann Gottfried Herder, who spoke of the church's "creative power" in elaborating the portrait of Jesus.
141. "Jesus is beyond our psychologies," said Romano Guardini, quoted in Ratzinger (2007, 50–51).
142. Cf. Berkouwer (1954, 129–70; on projection: 161, 178).

of Jesus of Paul, John and the Synoptics are easily explained, and are only imaginary.

Some may consider this to be a dogmatic starting point. In reply, my hope rests in the persuasive power of this book as the best foundation for this starting point. I will not avoid the debate; already in this first chapter, I have entered into the discussion. Now, in the first part of the twenty-first century, this task appears easier than it would have been fifty or one hundred years ago. At that point, modernism was flourishing, with its naturalism and scientism, and its strong faith in universal reason, to which Christology also had submit. This situation allowed little room for a more traditional Christological approach. The Jesus of history portrayed by this modernism—insofar as something meaningful could be said about him at all—was far removed from the Christ in whom the average Christian believed. Today, this distance has been reduced considerably.

My paradigm offers a Christological approach that builds on the foundation of the Council of Chalcedon (AD 451). I am convinced that this Christology cannot be adopted directly from the Bible naïvely or positivistically, but it does greater justice to the biblical material than many modernist approaches. Today, in our post-modern time, now that modernism has experienced a stalemate on many fronts, including within theology, it is easier to make this claim. In a post-modern intellectual climate, where naturalism is not more plausible *a priori* than supernaturalism, a new, often cautious interest arises in many viewpoints that modernism had dismissed with such a cavalier attitude.

I am *not* seeking a revival of pre-modernism, such as, for example, early Protestant theology. Because of its acquiescence to scholasticism, this theology was pervasively rationalistic, so that when Enlightenment theology arose, it did not need to alter its (rationalist) methodology at all. Any revival of pre-modernism would be merely a form of reactionism.

Instead, every theologian, including the most conservative, must engage with modernism without seeking to avoid its challenges.[143] We need, now as always, a *contemporary* Christology, one that has engaged the history of modernism and meets the requirements and questions of contemporary people.

1.9 The New Testament Portraits of Jesus
1.9.1 The Synoptics, Especially Mark

We will now look more closely at the various portraits of Jesus in the New Testament. First, it can be established that the Synoptic Gospels, despite their varied doctrinal orientations, agree remarkably well with each other in historical and biographical respects.[144] It matters little whether people explain this similarity either from the assumption that both Matthew and Luke used Mark, or from the assumption that all three are rooted in shared sources — including Q (the *Quelle* that supposedly contained *logia* [sayings] of Jesus), about which people can only speculate, since it has never been discovered.[145] The important point is that Matthew and Luke (and Mark) started from these same supposed (oral and written) sources because, no matter how different their doctrinal aims were, they apparently could do nothing else than start from the well-known historical facts of the life of Jesus. Luke (1:1-4) claims to have "carefully investigated" the matter (v. 3 NIV), apparently among the "eyewitnesses and ministers of

---

143. Marshall (1977, 136) mentions the negative example of New Testament scholar Donald Guthrie, who knew the methods of modern historical research but did not engage them in his book. As a result, readers were left confused by the historical questions and received no help with their problems. Moreover, the legitimate insights supplied by historical methods are lacking. The modern reader needs more help than Guthrie supplied, and might erroneously conclude that no historical problems exist, according to Marshall.
144. In §13.1, I deal with some alleged contradictions between Matthew, Mark, and Luke.
145. G. N. Stanton (*DJG* 644–50); cf. R. H. Stein (*DJG* 784–92: "Synoptic Problem").

the word" (v. 2). If someone like him would have been completely uninterested in facts but only in a doctrinal portrait of Jesus, why would he have consulted sources? To this we must add that, for the Gospel writers, the divine origin and nature of Jesus were matters of certainty.

Many assume on good grounds that Mark was the first and John the last written Gospel (see §5.3). Though John's Gospel is filled with allusions to Jesus' deity, we supposedly find few if any of them in Mark. Yet, this seems to me incorrect. Let us consider a few examples of this, even though Enlightenment theology considers the clearest allusions to Christ's deity to be later insertions, or theological elements produced by the church—which claims must be proven first if one wishes to avoid the fallacy of begging the question.[146]

A first argument commonly adduced is that in Mark, Jesus is referred to as the "Son *of Man*." Our first response is that in John's Gospel, which emphasizes so strongly that Jesus is the Son of God, the term "Son of Man" is mentioned almost as frequently (twelve times *versus* fourteen times in Mark). Second, in Mark as well, Jesus is often referred to as the "Son of God" (1:1 [variant reading]; 3:11; 5:7; 15:39), or as "my beloved Son" (1:11; 9:7), or simply as "the Son" (13:32). This does not permit us, however, to interpret these expressions as referring always to the eternal Son (see further in chapter 7). For instance, in 14:61–62 the title "Son of the Blessed" is linked with Jesus' Messiahship (cf. 1:11; 9:7; 15:39; for this Messiahship, see also 2:19; 8:29; 10:47-48; 11:10; 15:32), and this need mean no more than the phrase "You are my Son" in Psalm 2:7 (cf. Luke 1:35; see §4.7.1).

Yet, in Mark the title "Son of God" means more than simply a Messianic honorary title, as is clear from, among other things, the testimony of the demons (3:11; 5:7). They call him the "Holy One of God," and are afraid that he will destroy them; so apparently they assume that he has the power to do

---

146. R. A. Guelich (*DJG* 518–22).

this (1:24). Jesus does not call himself only the Messiah, as is evident in his discussion with the religious leaders, where he states, on the basis of Psalm 110:1, that the Messiah is not only David's son but also David's Lord (Mark 12:35-37).

Quite remarkable is the parable of the tenants, in which Jesus compares the prophets with "servants" (12:2-5) but elevates himself far beyond the latter by comparing himself with the "beloved son" of the vineyard's owner (v. 6). The authenticity of this passage has been doubted because of its allegorical features. However, similar features are present in the parable of the sower (4:13-20). This is no compelling reason to question the parable's genuineness.[147] C. F. D. Moule wrote that because Jesus' story so obviously addresses the irresponsible religious leaders of his time, it presents a truly contemporary, unchanged piece of teaching by Jesus.[148] In this story he not only presents himself as the beloved Son of his Father, but also predicts his own death. This story also agrees with the twofold testimony from heaven that he is the "beloved Son" of God (1:11; 9:7).

I will discuss below (§7.1) how various acts of Jesus point to his divine character, even though they do not constitute real *proofs*. People fall down before him and worship him in a way that is only fitting for God (Mark 1:40; 5:6, 22, 33; 7:25; 10:17; cf. Acts 10:26; 14:13-15; Rev. 19:10; 22:8-9). He cleanses lepers (Mark 1:40-42), which only God can do (2 Kings 5:7). Nature submits to him (Mark 4:39 [cf. the question of v. 41!]; 6:48, 51). He forgives sins (2:5,7), as only God can do, though emphasizing that he has received this authority as Son of *Man* (v. 10). Such an indirect reference to his divinity in which his humanity is simultaneously emphasized is found in 13:32 as well, where his ignorance is a typically human feature while at the same time he refers to himself with the typically divine name "the Son" (§§2.2.1, 5.9.1, and 8.2.3). Conversely, in verse 26 he calls himself the "Son of *Man*," but in verse 27 speaks of

---

147. See Lane (1974, 416–17); Wessell (1984, 731).
148. Moule (1965, 94).

"*his* angels" in a way that is fitting for God alone (cf. "angels *of God*" in Matt. 22:30; Luke 12:8-9; 15:10; John 1:52).

In light of the rest of the New Testament, if we accept the unity of Scripture, we can say that, although Mark strongly emphasizes Jesus' humanity (see also 3:20; 4:38; 6:31; 14:33-34),[149] he does so against the backdrop of Jesus' deity. Matthew contains some passages absent in Mark, which point to Jesus' deity (or to his divinity, if we wish to distinguish between the two expressions). This is true especially for the following passages: "[N]o one knows the Son except the Father, and no one knows the Father except the Son and anyone to whom the Son chooses to reveal him" (11:27; cf. Luke 10:22). "You are the Christ, the Son of the living God" (16:16; cf. 26:63); and ". . . baptizing them in the name of the Father and of the Son and of the Holy Spirit" (28:19). In Luke we notice the following passage: "The Holy Spirit will come upon you, and the power of the Most High will overshadow you; therefore the child to be born will be called holy—the Son of God" (1:35). The testimony of the Synoptics regarding Jesus' deity cannot be denied.

1.9.2 The Letters of Paul

According to the critics, Mark's Gospel shows deep interest in Jesus' course of life but little interest in his divine character, whereas with the apostle Paul the reverse is true. The quest for the historical Jesus, in particular the assertion that many New Testament statements about Jesus are not historically reliable but products of the church's theology, presents as one of its theses that Paul's interest in Jesus is highly soteriological but hardly biographical. Paul is supposedly concerned only with the suffering, death, and resurrection of Christ. Without a doubt, these events are central for him, since without

---

149. This might be related to Mark's doctrinal aim: in a time when Jesus' deity was overemphasized at the expense of his humanity (Docetism), Mark wished to emphasize Jesus' true humanity, especially his sufferings, according to Martin (1972, 161).

the work of atonement it would make little sense to speak of the person of Jesus. However, this does not mean that Paul has little interest in Jesus' person and historical life. On the contrary, for him *who* the person is who accomplished the work of redemption is very important. There are plenty of examples. We will see that Paul clearly emphasizes the deity of Christ (chapter 7), but he also pays attention to the facts of Jesus' human life (see extensively, §5.4.3).

In Paul's epistles, the title "Lord" (Gk. *kurios*) for Jesus Christ played a significant role; many times he used expressions like "the Lord Jesus Christ," and "Christ Jesus our Lord" (some significant examples: Rom. 10:9; 14:8; 1 Cor. 1:2; 2:9; 8:6; 10:21; 12:3; 2 Cor. 4:5; Phil. 2:11). It can hardly be maintained that these passages in such early epistles are merely examples of theology produced by the church. This title is encountered in the Gospel of Mark as well; the way of the "Lord" had been prepared by John the Baptist (1:3), and after his ascension, the "Lord" blessed his followers (16:19-20). Jesus declared himself to be the "Lord" of the sabbath (2:28), and referred to himself as the "Lord" (11:3). The fact that elsewhere in Mark the term "Lord" clearly referred to God in heaven (5:19; 11:10; 12:11, 30, 36; 13:20) is problematic only for those who believe that Mark did not know about Jesus' divinity.

Wilhelm Bousset believed that *kurios* worship had originated in the Hellenistic context of the church in Antioch.[150] In response, Gerhard Sevenster argued that the Palestinian Christian church knew the title *kurios*, namely, in the Aramaic expression *Maranatha* that was common there.[151] This probably means *marana tha*, "our Lord, come" (cf. 1 Cor. 16:22 and the petition "come, Lord Jesus" in Rev. 22:20). In 1 Corinthians 8:5, Jesus is the one true Lord among the many who are worshiped as divine "lords." The significance of the early use of this title is that in the Septuagint, the Greek term *kurios* is used for YHWH, so Jesus is being equated with God (see §7.1.2

---

150. Bousset (1970).
151. Sevenster (*RGG* 1:1748).

for a discussion of Old Testament *kurios* passages that are applied to Jesus in the New Testament). At the same time, Jesus was explicitly called *kurios* as the Man glorified at God's right hand (Mark 16:19–20; Acts 2:36; 10:36–37).

Thus, there is no basis for construing essential differences between Paul and the Gospel writers. At most, the writings of Paul lacked certain well-known notions found in the Gospels, such as Jesus being the "Son of Man" (unless Paul was the author of Hebrews; see 2:6). However, his quoting Psalm 8:6b ("you have put all things under his feet," 1 Cor. 15:27; Eph. 1:22) suggests that Paul was definitely familiar with the interpretation that Jesus is the Son of Man of Psalm 8 (§4.9.1).[152] The Jesus of Paul's epistles is essentially the same person as the Jesus of the Synoptic Gospels.

In the pastoral epistles (1 and 2 Tim., Titus) we notice in particular the term "Savior" (Gk. *sōtēr*), which was used both for God and for Jesus Christ. Perhaps, the term was being used polemically here as a testimony against the imperial cult — the Roman emperor was considered to be *theos* ("god"), *kurios* ("lord"), and *sōtēr* ("savior") — but we think this usage continues the soteriological parlance found in the rest of the New Testament. There is here no divergent Christology.

1.9.3 Other New Testament Writers

I see no essential difference between the Jesus of the Synoptics and the Jesus of John's Gospel. There are different accents, though: John is far more doctrinal, and much less historical and biographical than Matthew, Mark, and Luke. If the tradition is correct that John was written as the last of the four Gospels,[153] then one could presume that John was assuming the biographical data in the Synoptics to have been well-known

---

152. Cf. also his parallel between the first man and the second Man in Rom. 5:15–19 and 1 Cor. 15:45, 47.
153. Cf. Clement of Alexandria: "Last of all, John, seeing that the bodily [or external] facts had been expounded in the [other] gospels, composed at the urging of his followers and with the inspiration of the Spirit a spiritual gospel"; quoted in Guthrie (1970, 273).

among his readers (see §5.3.2). Still more important than this is that everything we know from the Synoptics and that John omits, and everything mentioned by John and omitted in the Synoptics, can be easily explained from the doctrinal messages of John and the others. Later in this book, especially in chapters 7 and 8, we will investigate this so-called theology of John more closely. At present, it is sufficient to note that John explicitly affirms Jesus' deity, as the following remarkable examples show: "In the beginning was the Word, and the Word was with God, and the Word was God" (1:1). Jesus was "calling God his own Father, making himself equal with God" (5:18). "[B]efore Abraham was, I AM" (8:58; cf. Exod. 3:14). "I and the Father are one" (10:30). "The Jews answered him, 'It is not for a good work that we are going to stone you but for blasphemy, because you, being a man, make yourself God'" (10:33).

A study of the Book of Acts yields a Christology that does not differ essentially from that of the Synoptics, which is to be expected, of course, given the shared authorship of Luke and Acts. Attempts to discern especially in Acts 2:36 and 13:32–33 adoptionistic[154] features fail simply because there is no inherent need for this. On the contrary, Luke identified Jesus as Son of God before Jesus' baptism (1:32, 35; 2:49). Moreover, he showed that Jesus' sonship is based not on adoption but on descent (3:23–38).[155] God did not *make* Jesus his Son at the latter's baptism but declared him to *be* his Son.

---

154. One of the best known advocates of classical adoptionism was Paul of Samosata, who viewed Jesus as a Man who was inhabited by the eternal Logos (see §3.1.1). Adoptionists begin with the Man Jesus, who was later animated by the Holy Spirit (at his conception, his birth, or his baptism) or by the eternal Logos, whereas official church doctrine begins with the eternal Logos, who then became flesh in the person of Jesus (see also §§2.1–2.3). The sequence is not that Jesus was deified, but that the divine Word was made flesh; see Hengel (1995, 368, 374).

155. Actually, in this way Jesus would be a son like *all* people, as descendants of Adam, are "sons (daughters) of God"; but Luke 1:35 indicates the uniqueness of Jesus' sonship.

The Book of Revelation contains its own specific Christology, which, however, nowhere conflicts with other New Testament Christologies. We notice especially the unique title "Lamb" (Gk. *arnion*):[156] Jesus is both the Lamb who died in weakness (cf. 2 Cor. 13:4) and atones sins with his blood, and the Lamb who will come, judge, and triumph. Here again, we are dealing with representations that, in spite of the particular terminology, correspond entirely to other parts of the New Testament.

Consider also 1 and 2 John, in which the incarnation of Christ takes a central position. Here again, there is a specific theological orientation without contradicting other theological orientations in the New Testament. One of the most powerful statements about the deity of Jesus (contrary to suggestions to identify the antecedent of the pronoun "this" [Gk. *houtos*] the phrase "him who is true," that is, God[157]) is 1 John 5:20, ". . . we are in him who is true, in his Son Jesus Christ. He is the true God and eternal life."

With respect to Hebrews, the epistle clearly employs its own specific terminology and theology, which are unique in the New Testament, especially concerning Jesus' priesthood. But does this theology conflict with any other New Testament Christologies? I do not think so. For instance, elsewhere we also find allusions to Jesus' high priestly intercession (Rom. 8:34; 1 John 2:1; Rev. 1:13; cf. 8:2) and to Jesus' involvement in the work of creation and sustenance (cf. Heb. 1:2b with John 1:3 and Col. 1:16–17). Central in Hebrews are well-known names and titles such as "Son" (1:1, 5, 8), "Lord" (1:10; 2:3), and "Christ" (3:6, 14).

---

156. Unique indeed, for in John 1:29 and 36, Acts 8:32, and 1 Pet. 1:19, the Greek word for "lamb" is *amnos*!
157. Lalleman (2005, 217) mentions J. R. W. Stott, S. S. Smalley, and D. Rensberger, who understand the end of v. 20 to refer to God the Father; he mentions C. H. Dodd and G. Strecker, who believe it refers to the Father *and* the Son. Lalleman himself, and other authors whom I have consulted, understand it to refer to the Son.

Preliminary Orientation in Christology

1.9.4 Final Remarks

G. Sevenster warned against presuming a *development* of Christology within the New Testament as such.[158] Especially the apostle Paul gives us the impression that everything he writes about the person and the work of Christ was well-known in the apostolic church, and needed no further explanation. In 1 Corinthians 15:3, he explicitly declares ("what I also received") that he is relying on the Jesus tradition of the first believers. What he preached belonged for years to the universal confession of these Christians. Philippians 2:6-11 is also of interest because, according to many expositors, Paul is quoting here an early Christian hymn or creed (on this, see §8.7).

Sevenster also pointed out that Paul fulminates against all kinds of errors and heresies that threatened the early Christians, but never against teachings of the other apostles, or doctrines defended elsewhere in the New Testament. Paul also shows that from the beginning Christians prayed—not only to God but—to Christ (Rom. 10:12-13; 1 Cor. 1:2; 16:22 [Gk. *Marana tha!* "Our Lord, come!"]; 2 Cor. 12:8; cf. Acts 7:59; 8:22; 9:13-14; Rev. 22:20). This means that these Christians ascribed to Christ divine properties. All the essential qualities that the quest for the historical Jesus often claims to have been invented subsequently by the church, dismissing them as the theological product of the church, such as Christ's being *kurios* and Son, his pre-existence, his vicarious, atoning suffering, seem instead to have been part of the earliest confession of the Christian church. Every attempt to play off a Jewish Christology against a Hellenistic Christology, or a Jerusalem Christology against an Antioch Christology, is defeated.

In summary, when we begin with the unity of the New Testament, we indeed may appeal to proof texts, as long as (a) we remain aware of the paradigm within which we are interpreting these proof texts, and (b) take into account—not the

---

158. Sevenster (1986, *RGG* 1:1760-61).

contradictions but — the distinct doctrinal orientations within the various parts of the New Testament. We understand individual passages from our perspective on the entire New Testament, just as the latter perspective results from our understanding of individual passages (the hermeneutical circle[159]). In other words, there is a bidirectional path from exegesis to dogmatics, and from dogmatics to exegesis.

---

159. See Ouweneel (*RT* I/1:§1.7).

Chapter 2
Development of Christology

[Christ desires that]
we all attain to the unity of the faith
and of the knowledge of the Son of God,
to mature manhood,
to the measure of the stature of the fullness of Christ.

Ephesians 4:13

2.1 Introduction
2.1.1 Two Natures

IN ITS REFLECTION on Christ as true God and true Man, while opposing a multitude of heretical ideas, theologians had to consider the relationship between Jesus' deity and humanity. Accepting that Jesus is both God and Man is good, but for the thoughtful believer this is insufficient; such a believer wants some idea of how one and the same person can be fully God and fully Man. What is the coherence, within the one Jesus, between his divine and his human nature? Notice the terms used here: a "person" is a rational being, a responsible subject of his actions; "nature" is the totality of all essential properties of a thing, that which makes it what it is.[1] The *person* of the Logos (the Word)—who is God, that is, who possessed and possesses the divine *nature*—"became flesh" (John 1:14), that is, partook of human *nature* as well. But what does this mean? How are continuity and discontinuity related here?

Let me give some examples. If water turns into ice, it is no longer water, but it is still H_2O. If a caterpillar turns into a butterfly, it is no longer a caterpillar, but it remains the same biological species, and on the cellular level there is continuity. What happened with the Logos? When it became flesh, did it remain the Word? Yes, says Revelation 19:13. What does it mean that, from then on, the Logos was and is both Word and flesh? How can we understand that the *person* of the Logos, who had the *divine* nature, now also has a *human* nature—and this in one and the same person?

By way of introduction to this problem, let me provide four quotations from the early church, the first from Clement of Alexandria: at the incarnation, the flesh was not "changed into the nature of the Godhead, and the unspeakable nature of the Word of God was not transformed into the nature of the flesh."[2] The phrase "the Word became flesh" (John 1:14) does not mean that the Word was *transformed into* flesh, but that the Logos shared in flesh and blood (Heb. 2:14). Compare the second quotation, from the Athanasian Creed (Art. 35): Christ is "One; not by conversion of the Godhead into flesh: but by taking [assumption] of the Manhood into God" (Lat. *Unus autem, non conversione divinitatis in carnem: sed assumptione humanitatis in Deum*).[3] Third, Augustine wrote: "Christ added to himself that which he was not [viz., his humanity]; he did not lose what he was [viz., his deity]."[4] God became

---
1. Berkhof (1981, 321). It is remarkable that Melito of Sardis and Tertullian did not speak of "nature" but of "substances" in the one person of Christ (cf. Ouweneel [*RT* I/2]); Tertullian saw a parallel here with the two "substances" in humans: soul and body; see Pannenberg (1994, 2:382–83).
2. Quoted in Bromiley (1978, 134).
3. Schaff (1919, 99).
4. Quoted in Berkouwer (1954, 94).

Man without ceasing to be God.

2.1.2 A Man of Contrasts

The fourth and longest quotation, rendered (and abridged) freely here (with Bible passages added), comes from one of the famous "Theological Orations" by Gregory of Nazianzus, one of the three Cappadocian church fathers, who speaks here about the two natures of Christ.[5] The Man Jesus was wrapped into swaddling clothes (Luke 2:7), but took away the tomb clothes through his resurrection (24:12; John 20:5-7).

He had no form or majesty in the eyes of the Jews (Isa. 53:2), but to David he was the most handsome of all humans (Ps. 45:2).

He was baptized as a Man (Matt. 3:15-16), but he forgave sins as God (9:2).

He was tempted as a Man, but he triumphed as God (4:1-10); yes, he asks us to be of good courage, for he has overcome the world (John 16:33).

He was hungry (Matt. 4:2), but he fed thousands (14:19-21); yes, he is the bread that gives life and that is from heaven (John 6:33-51).

He was thirsty (19:28), yet he cried out: "If anyone thirsts, let him come to me and drink" (7:37); yes, he promised that rivers would flow from those who believe (v. 38).

He was tired (4:6), but he is the rest of those who labor and are heavy laden (Matt. 11:28).

He was sleepy (8:24), yet he walked lightly over the sea (14:25).

He paid tax, but this comes from a fish (7:37); yet, he is the King over those who demanded it.

He was called a Samaritan and demonic (John 8:48); yet, he saved him who went down from Jerusalem and fell into the hands of robbers (Luke 10:30).

He prayed, but also answered prayers.

---
5. Quoted in Ford and Higton (2002, 93–94).

He wept (19:41; John 11:35), but also stopped tears (20:15-16).

He asked where Lazarus had been laid (11:34), for he was a Man; but he raised Lazarus (vv. 43-44), for he was God.

He was sold, and very cheaply, for only thirty pieces of silver (Matt. 26:15); yet, he ransomed the world, and this at a high cost, his own blood (20:28; 26:28).

Like a sheep he was led to the slaughter (Isa. 53:7); yet, he was the Shepherd of Israel, and now also of the entire world (John 10:11, 14, 16).

2.2 The Two Natures: Biblical Testimony
2.2.1 The Divine and the Human

In the one person of Jesus, the divine and the human natures are necessarily as different as God and humanity are. How must we ensure that these two natures nonetheless are not separate in such a way that Christ in fact would be *two persons*? The *Man* Christ Jesus is the bridge between God and humanity (cf. 1 Tim. 2:5) — but this can be understood only if we first grasp (insofar as this is possible) the nature of the bridge between the divine and the human within the one person of Jesus. We assume this *a priori* to be a challenging issue; Danish philosopher Søren Kierkegaard therefore called this the "absolute paradox."[6] This is because the divine is infinite, the human is finite; the divine is immortal, the human is mortal; the divine is omniscient and omnipotent, the human is limited in knowledge and power; the divine is omnipresent and time transcending, the human is bound to space and time. How then can it be said that one person is both these things at the same time? The church was confronted with these questions at an early stage because people asked these questions in such a way that the church had to answer *them*.

Let us begin with the biblical testimony, which, to be sure, does not speak of the "person" and the "natures" of Christ,

---

6. Kierkegaard (1936, 29).

but it does emphasize the absolute unity of the divine and the human in him. Thus, Jesus says, "[C]oncerning that day or that hour [of the second coming], no one knows, not even the angels in heaven, nor the Son, but only the Father" (Mark 13:32). This passage clearly warns against any false separation within his personality by joining a typically divine title, "Son," with a typically human trait: "not knowing" (see also §§1.9.1, 6.3.2, and 9.1.3). Theologians speak here of the communication of properties (Lat. *communicatio idiomatum*): properties characteristic of one of the two natures are ascribed to the entire person, sometimes even with the emphasis upon the other nature.[7]

The Bible seems always to guard the absolute unity of Jesus' person, and even when sometimes his divine side comes more into the foreground, and at other times his human side, he is never only God or only Man. Compare Hebrews 5:8, "Although he was a son, he learned obedience [as a Man]." That is, although he is God, he exhibits human traits; and, conversely, we may add that, although he is a Man, he exhibits divine traits.

When a human trait such as ignorance or obedience was being emphasized, Jesus was sometimes referred to with a divine title, and the reverse.[8] As to the *former* (divine title, human trait), take John 5:19 ("the Son can do nothing of his own accord, but only what he sees the Father doing"), 1 Corinthians 15:28 ("then the Son himself will also be subjected to him who put all things in subjection under him"), and Colossians 1:13 ("the kingdom of his beloved Son"). In all these

---

7. Gregory of Nazianzus and John of Damascus spoke of a mutual interpenetration (Gk. *perichorēsis*; Lat. *circumincessio*) of the divine and the human in Christ, which involves a (risky!) transfer of the divine attributes to the human nature, so that the latter is deified; see Pannenberg (1994, 2:407); see further in §2.3.
8. The Reformer Ulrich Zwingli spoke here of "exchange" (Gk. *alloeosis*), viz., when one nature is mentioned and the other one is intended (zh.ref.ch/content/e3/e1939/e10912/e10999/index_ger.html); cf. Berkouwer (1954, 276).

cases, just as in Mark 13:32, the divine title of "the Son" was linked with a human limitation (not-being-able, subjection) or activity (kingship). In 1 Corinthians 2:8, he was called the "Lord of glory," which is a typical Old Testament reference to the deity ("the glory of YHWH," mentioned from Exod. 16:7 to Hab. 2:14). Yet, this title was applied here to the crucified One, who died on the cross as a Man. It is as Man that he is the son of David, and thus the King in the Messianic kingdom—whereas Paul does speak of the "kingdom of the Son of [the Father's] love" (Col. 1:13 NKJV).

As to the *latter* phenomenon (human title, divine trait): when a divine attribute such as omnipresence or omnipotence was being emphasized, Jesus was sometimes referred to with a human title, such as in the variant reading in John 3:13 ("the Son of Man who is in heaven," NKJV); further in 5:27 (the Son executes judgment "because he is the Son of Man"). In John 6:62, he speaks of "the Son of Man ascending to where he was before." Notice two things: he was not just passively "taken up" (as, e.g., in 1 Tim. 3:16) but was actively "*going* up" (CEB), in his own divine majesty;[9] and he was ascending to where *he* had been earlier, though he had not been there earlier as Son of Man but only as Son of God.

It is typically divine to forgive sins, but Jesus said that "the *Son of Man* has authority on earth to forgive sins" (Matt. 9:6). It is typically divine that he had the power (or authority) to "lay down my life that I may take it up again" (John 10:17-18)—but as a dependent Man he added, "This charge I have received from my Father [and who could do this except the Son?]" (v. 18b). We read the same in John 12:49-50: no one other than the Son of the Father could proclaim eternal life to people (see especially 1 John 1:1-3), whereas, as a dependent Man on earth, he spoke of a commandment.

---

9. There is also a difference between "he was raised" (as a Man by God) and "he has risen" (through his own divine power)—but the meanings of the Gk. verbs *egeirō*, "to raise," and *anistēmi*, "to rise," do overlap.

2.2.2 One Person, Perfect Humanity

Nowhere in the New Testament do we find any separation between what, especially since the Council of Chalcedon (451), is called the two natures of Christ. The one nature nowhere stands in opposition to the other nature, as if there could be any contradiction between the two. Nor are we allowed to say that, on one occasion, it was the divine nature of Christ that spoke or acted, and, on another occasion, the human nature. Always the *one person* was speaking or acting. No doubt sometimes the divine nature and sometimes the human nature of Christ comes to the fore, but without the one being severed from the other. Since his incarnation, Jesus never spoke or acted *only* as God, and never *only* as Man. This is precisely what we mean in saying that he is not two persons but one person.

Here is an important example: God is the only One who is immortal (cf. 1 Tim. 6:16); he *cannot* die, whereas humans can. Therefore, when Jesus died on the cross, we say that the *Man* Jesus died — but also in his death he did not cease being God. We do not mix the natures such that we say that *God* died on the cross (theopaschitism; see §8.5.4) — but we do not separate the natures such that we would claim that in his dying Jesus was no longer God. The divine was clothed in the garment of the human, and is always present in this garment, even though veiled. Jesus' divine glory is concealed behind the veil of his humanity, but from time to time that glory clearly shines through the veil for those who can see (John 1:14). His omnipotence, his omniscience, and his omnipresence remain intact, but have become incarnated in the limited power, knowledge, and space of a human being. His divine infinity remains fully infinite but is veiled in the garment of finiteness.

"He that is able to receive it, let him receive it," Jesus said in a different context (cf. Matt. 19:12 KJV). That is, these things are "hard to understand" (cf. 2 Pet. 3:16). It would therefore be arrogant to imagine that all this can be precisely mapped out theologically. First, it is impossible to form a rational concept of what surpasses all conceptualization.[10] Second, we know what is human only as we know it in ourselves and in our fellow humans—and this is a *fallen* humanity. The humanity that the Logos took upon himself is not this (fallen) humanity, for he was indeed perfect Man, but without sin (Heb. 4:15; 1 Pet. 2:22; 1 John 3:5). It was only on the cross that he "who knew no sin" was "made to be sin" for our sake (2 Cor. 5:21). The Logos took upon himself the humanity God had originally intended for us—in the image and after the likeness of God—and which we, since the Fall, no longer know; or more correctly, humanity as we *will* know it, in the new creation (see §10.1.1). The question is not whether Jesus was perfectly human, but whether *we* are. He was *as human* as we are—he was *more human* than we are, if we mean human in its truest sense. Spiritually speaking, his was the humanity that believers will possess when they are glorified (cf. Phil. 3:20-21), according to Millard Erickson.[11] In order to understand Jesus' humanity, then, we must not start from our own (natural) humanity, but the reverse: in order to understand believers' *new* humanity we must start from Jesus' humanity.

2.3 Development of the Doctrine of Two Natures[12]

It was one thing to have to defend Christ's perfect deity (and therefore his ontic equality with the Father) over against, in particular, the Arians, and his true humanity over against, in particular, the Docetists and the Gnostics. It was another thing to take a stand against those who accepted both the deity and the humanity of Christ, but viewed the relationship between the two in a deviant way. In this discussion, the terms *person* and *nature* were used in a way that, at different times, almost every possible combination of these two terms has been de-

---

10. For the precise meaning of what is being said here, see, e.g., Ouweneel (*RT* I/1:§§1.1.1, 3.9, and *RT* I/2:§1.9).
11. Erickson (1985, 753).
12. Here is a small selection from the literature: Berkouwer (1954); Grillmeier (1975); Loofs (1975); Moule (1977); Pannenberg (*RGG* 1:1762–77); Hengel (1995).

fended: Christ is one person, but then also one nature (such that his humanity was thought to have merged into his divinity, or this one nature was viewed as divine-human); or, if two natures, then also actually two persons: a divine person and a human person in one body. As we will see, the Council of Chalcedon (451) produced the intermediate—and, according to all orthodox Christians, correct—solution: one person, two natures. Or, if the term "correct" is too strong (too definitive), this approximation was at least the best conceivable.

One starting point for the debate was the question flowing from John 1:14 (the *Logos* [Word] became *sarx* [flesh]): How could *Logos* and *sarx* be united? In this debate, Greek anthropological aspects played a clear role: did the Logos *absorb* the supposed "rational soul" (the *anima rationalis* in the sense of Aristotle[13]) that belongs to humanity (dynamic view), or did the Logos *replace* this soul (static view), or did this soul in the neo-Platonic sense play a mediatory role in the union of the transcendent Word with the immanent flesh?

2.3.1 First Solution: Apollinaris of Laodicea

Apollinaris of Laodicea construed the connection between Logos and flesh in such a way that Jesus' humanity was literally limited to his flesh, that is, without a human soul/spirit. In this case, he has only one nature, that of the Logos. This view was the origin of one of the many forms of monophysitism, the view that Christ had only one nature. Apollinaris argued

---

13. Cf. the Athanasian Creed (Art. 32): "[Christ is] perfect God: and perfect Man, of a reasonable soul and human flesh subsisting" (Lat. *Perfectus Deus: perfectus homo, ex anima rationali et humana carne subsistens*) (Schaff [1919, 98]). Also the Confession of Chalcedon, the Westminster Larger Catechism (A. 37), and the Second Helvetic Confession (chapter 11) speak of Christ's "rational (or reasonable) soul." In the latter (highly appreciated Reformed) confessional document we read in chapter 7 that a human being "consists of two, and those divers substances in one person; of a soul immortal ... and a body mortal, ..." (Dennison [*RC* 2:820]). Louis Berkhof spoke of the "essential elements of human nature, that is, a material body and a rational soul" (1981, 318) and of "two substance" humans: "matter and spirit" (ibid., 325).

that one could not speak of the *personality* of Christ as Man. Christ was truly human; but in him, the Logos took the place that in ordinary people is occupied by the human soul/spirit. We speak here of a Logos–*flesh* Christology in contrast with a Logos–*Man* Christology, the latter doctrine holding that Christ was so fully human that he had a human will, human thoughts, and human feelings.

The Synod of Alexandria (362) insisted that the Logos had also assumed a human soul/spirit because otherwise the human body would be able to partake in salvation, but the human soul/spirit would not. After this Synod, Apollinaris accepted the decision, and from then on maintained only that Jesus did not possess a human mind (Gk. *nous*), but that the Logos in him took the place of the *nous*. Gregory of Nazianzus could not accept this, because in this way the human *nous* would not be able to share in salvation. He and that other Cappadocian father, Gregory of Nyssa, spoke of *two* complete natures in Christ, the divine and the human.

Arguing from the thesis that only a human could become a substitute for a human (1 Tim. 2:5), the church insisted that only what Christ had assumed in the incarnation could be redeemed. I cannot see any counter-argument against this: why would Christ have to assume human flesh in order to redeem *our* flesh, if, at the same time, he did not assume a human soul/spirit, or human mind, in order to redeem *our* soul/spirit or mind?

2.3.2 Second Solution: Theodore of Mopsuestia

Alexandria and Antioch, both within the Roman Empire in the fifth century AD, were home to Christian communities from an early date. Both had produced important Christian thinkers: Antioch identified with the apostle Paul, of course; but Alexandria, with a thinker such as Athanasius, could certainly claim to be Antioch's equal. The entire Christological discussion of those days consisted of a conflict between the Alexandrian school (especially Cyril) and the Antiochian school (especially Theodore, Nestorius).[14]

Theodore of Mopsuestia, belonged to the latter school and emphasized that the Logos had become not only flesh but fully human. The emphasis on the human soul was so important to him because he viewed sin as having proceeded from the soul. Because of the independence that he ascribed to Jesus as Man, some people accused him of separating Christ's deity and humanity. In response, he was the first to articulate the formula "two natures, one person," which later became so well-known via the Council of Chalcedon (451).

Whereas Gregory of Nazianzus and Gregory of Nyssa did not express the unity of the divine and the human nature in Christ in a single term, Theodore chose the concept of person (Gk. *prosopon*) to express this unity. A good example of a New Testament passage where the Greek term *prosōpon* means "person" is 2 Corinthians 1:11 ("many persons," NKJV). (A good example of a New Testament passage where the Greek term *physis* means "nature" is 2 Pet. 1:4, "the divine nature.")

2.3.3 Third Solution: Nestorius of Constantinople

From the same Antiochian school as Theodore of Mopsuestia was Nestorius of Constantinople, who distinguished the two natures such that he wished to call Mary "mother of God" only insofar as she gave birth to the Man who was the bearer and temple of the Deity. He feared that such parlance — "mother of God" — would lead to a form of monophysitism because the human nature of Christ was in danger of merging into his divine nature. At the instigation of Cyril of Alexandria — a representative of the Alexandrian school — Nestorius was excommunicated by the Council of Ephesus (431), and Mary was officially hailed as the "mother of God" (Gk. *theotokos*).[15] Among Roman Catholics and Lutherans, this title is still officially accepted, but Calvin and the Reformed rejected it.

---

14. See Pannenberg (1994, 2:300); McGrath (2007, 286–90); Van de Beek (2002a, 72–77).
15. On this, see Ouweneel (1998, §§1.4.3 and 6.3.1).

The views of Nestorius continue to be held today. This is because many Protestants in particular will, perhaps without knowing Nestorius, sympathize with his standpoint, and ask: Can God have a mother? Does not the term *theotokos* come dangerously close to monophysitism, perhaps also to Apollinarianism, or even Arianism, which views Christ as a created being?

Actually, such questions can also be reversed: Is not Mary the mother of the one person of Jesus, who is not only human but also divine? This question is related to a question like: Can God die? If one answers affirmatively, the counter-question is: But how then can God be called the only immortal One (1 Tim. 6:16)? If one answers negatively, the counter-question is: But is it not the one Jesus, who is both human and divine, who died on the cross?

Nestorianism would be really objectionable if Nestorius claimed to discern in Christ two *persons*, which he did not do, though his successors came dangerously close to doing so.[16]

2.3.4 Additional Comment (1)

From those early days, the battle continued along the narrow dividing-line between Nestorianism, emphasizing the twoness, and monophysitism, emphasizing the unity. It is difficult to avoid sympathizing occasionally with either side (with Nestorianism when their opponents seemed to overemphasize the unity, or with monophysitism when their opponents overemphasized the twoness). Two comments can clarify these issues a bit more.

First, the term "monophysitism" is actually a collective term for rather divergent views. A monophysite teaches that Christ had only one nature. But what is meant by this—a divine nature? A human nature? Or a merged God-Man nature? In a sense, all liberal theologians who deny the deity of Christ are monophysite, for they acknowledge only the humanity of Christ. Conversely, all Docetists who deny the humanity of

---

16. See Van de Beek (2002a, 18–26).

Christ are monophysite, for they acknowledge only the deity of Christ. Apollinaris was a monophysite, for he denied the human soul/spirit of Christ and asserted that the Logos occupied the place of this soul/spirit in Christ. But someone who does accept the notion of a human soul/spirit in Christ but believes that Christ's humanity has merged into his deity, or that he had one single God-Man nature, or that his divine nature had merged into his human nature (a form of kenoticism; §8.7), is also monophysite.

At Chalcedon (451), all monophysites were more or less lumped together, and were admonished with the exhortation, "Two natures!" In this, there certainly might have been some unfairness because it is not clear *a priori* why someone teaching that the one person of Christ possessed one God-Man nature would be a heretic. The same would be equally true for the person who maintained the distinction (not separation!) between the divine and human properties of Christ, and would have supported their view by pointing to the danger of a certain dualism in the Chalcedonian formula (see §2.4). If the term "nature" refers to the totality of all essential properties of a matter—that which makes it what it is—one may wonder how something or someone can have *two* natures (characters that exclude each other). This is not inherently impossible—we also describe the believer as having an old nature and a new nature—but asking the question is not *a priori* heretical.

2.3.5 Additional Comment (2)

Our second comment is that, when studying the history of church and theology, it is not always easy to determine whether a certain view was condemned for theological reasons or rejected mainly for political reasons.[17] For example, an important representative of monophysitism, Eutyches, was excommunicated with the consent of pope Leo I, but the "robber synod" of Ephesus (449)—so called because the one party

---

17. Regarding the Nestorians, see Loofs (1975); see also Van de Beek (2002a, 93–95).

tried to convince the other party with the help of clubs—tried to rehabilitate him. Its leader, Dioscurus, was removed from office by the Council of Chalcedon. The more that one feels affinity for the Ecumenical Councils for reasons of church history and theological tradition (this is true for Roman Catholics, but also for Lutherans, Calvinists, and Anglicans), the greater one's inclination to cover the strong political aspects of these Councils with the mantle of love. The less one feels this bond, as is often the case in the Evangelical tradition, the more one feels irritated by the political power games that were played, and the more one would wish to distance oneself from them. Unfortunately, this is not an option because the *matter at issue* at the Councils is far too important.

Even Nicea (325), the mother of all Councils, leaves a bit of a bad taste. It rightly combated Arianism, but it also allowed the (probably non-Christian) emperor Constantine to acquire primacy within the church (caesaropapism). Moreover, it gave the green light to the first widespread persecutions of Jews by Christians. When the persecution of Christians ended, the suppression of the Jews began, because they refused to submit to the demands of the Christian church.[18] How could the same church fathers who introduced caesaropapism and Jewish persecution have been led by the Holy Spirit in their Trinitarian and Christological debates? To ask this question is not necessarily to condemn the conclusions of (especially) Nicea and Chalcedon, but rather it is to be all the more amazed by the grace of God, which, despite the works of the human flesh, preserved the Trinitarian and Christological truth so well.

2.4 The Chalcedon Formula
2.4.1 The Two Natures

The Council of Chalcedon (451) sought the middle road between Nestorianism and Eutychianism—and according to both the Eastern and the Western churches, and according to

---
18. See Ouweneel (2003, 127–28, 135).

both Roman Catholics and traditional Protestants, found it.[19] The solution was presented in this formula: "One Christ consisting of two natures," one person working in two natures according to the character of each nature. The two are united in and through one person (or hypostasis).

According to Chalcedon, these two natures exhibit the following characteristics. First, *contra* Eutyches and the monophysites: "acknowledged in two natures":

(a) "Unconfusedly" (Gk. *asynchytōs*): the two natures are clearly distinct, so that what can be said of the divine nature is not true for the human nature, and vice versa. For instance, one cannot say that, when Jesus died on the cross, God died (*contra* Luther; cf. §2.6.2).

(b) "Unchangeably" (Gk. *atreptōs*): by assuming flesh, the divine nature did not change, for instance, by becoming human (or a bit more human); and the human nature of Jesus is just as human as that of other people; the Logos did not alter it; nor did the human nature merge into the divine nature.

Second, *contra* Nestorius and the Nestorians:

(c) "Indivisibly" (Gk. *achōristōs*): Christ is not a split being, divided into a divine half and a human half, but, as Chalcedon put it: he is "the Self-same Son and Only-begotten God, Word [*Logos*], Lord, Jesus Christ."[20]

(d) "Inseparably" (Gk. *adiairetōs*): there is nothing that is true of the one nature such that the other nature would not share it; that is, since his incarnation, the Logos never speaks or acts as only God or as only Man, for this would inevitably lead to the notion that Jesus is in fact two persons. Even at the moment when Jesus died he did not cease to be God. We

---

19. Sellers called the Council of Chalcedon the place where three roads (Alexandrian, Antiochian, and Western) merged (1961, 203). Grillmeier said of Chalcedon that, in its Formula, all important centers of church life and all important theological trends—Rome, Alexandria, Constantinople, and Antioch—contributed to the formulation of a common expression of faith (1975, 544).
20. https://en.wikipedia.org/wiki/Chalcedonian_Definition.

THE ETERNAL CHRIST: GOD WITH US

hesitate to say that *God* died, yet we cannot deny that the *Man* who died was God.

2.4.2 Critical Questions

The Chalcedonian formula, to which many interpretations and clarifications have been added subsequently, has become part and parcel of orthodox (Roman Catholic and Protestant) belief, as it received form in the Creed named after Athanasius (c. AD 296–373), but which originated around AD 500. However, this does not mean that the debate ended after Chalcedon, because the Chalcedonian solution answered the prevailing questions only in a relative sense. The issue of the *relationship* between the two natures in Christ still remained essentially unresolved. How can we speak of two natures without splitting Jesus into two persons? And how can we maintain the one person (with one personality center, one consciousness, one mind, one will, one feeling) without mingling the two natures, or make the one merge into the other?

The most influential theologian of the nineteenth century, Friedrich Schleiermacher, summarized these questions as follows:

> [H]ow can the unity of life coexist with the duality of natures, unless the one gives way to the other, . . . or unless they melt into each other, both systems of ways of action and laws really becoming one in the one life?—if indeed we are speaking of a person, *i.e.* of an Ego which is the same in all the consecutive moments of its existence.[21]

Who would venture a definitive answer to such questions, especially when *each* possible answer has been condemned as a heresy in some way or other? Where Jesus' humanity was overemphasized, adoptionism regained the upper hand; where his deity was overemphasized, monophysitism reap-

---

21. Schleiermacher (1928, 393); he spoke of two possible heresies: either Jesus is humanized to such an extent that he can no longer be Redeemer; or he is deified to such an extent that he is irrelevant for the human condition, and therefore cannot be Redeemer; cf. Macquarrie (1998, 18–19, 27).

peared; and where the twoness in his person was exaggerated, some variety of Nestorianism reappeared.

The function of the Chalcedonian formula is therefore negative: it tells us what the one person and the two natures are *not*. It is no coincidence that each of the four terms mentioned — unconfused, unchanged, indivisible, inseparable — has a negative prefix.[22] Chalcedon did not wish to enclose the mystery of Christ's person in a formula; that was impossible. Rather, it wished to indicate with its formula especially what the mystery is *not*.[23] Willem Aalders saw the four negative terms as four signals placed where the breach in the dike is most threatening.[24] Klaas Runia wrote: "Through these *negativa* the fathers of the Council pointed out four boundaries so to say, and said: somewhere between these boundaries lies the mystery."[25] Cornelis van der Kooi described this moving within the boundaries pointedly as "hopscotching within the lines."[26]

Here, the question may be asked whether A. van de Beek was right in calling Chalcedon a Western council in the sense that, contrary to the Eastern Orthodox churches, the emphasis is clearly especially on the two natures: "The formula of Chalcedon is rarely referred to as the *unio personalis* but almost always as the 'two-nature doctrine.' This 'two' is much more important than the 'one.'"[27] There may be some truth in this. Perhaps this was because, after Chalcedon, the danger of monophysitism did seem to be greater than that of Nestorianism.

---

22. Adolf von Harnack found this a difficulty; he spoke of negative, bare provision; but, said Berkouwer (1954, 68), "These complaints evince a misunderstanding of the fifth century conflict."
23. This is called an *apophatic* speaking of God; saying (in particular) who and what God is *not*, in order not to violate the mystery of God; another term is "negative theology."
24. Aalders (1933, 150).
25. Runia (1992, 10).
26. Van der Kooi (1999, title).
27. Van de Beek (2002a, 78; see 77–83).

2.5 Developments After Chalcedon
2.5.1 Monophysitism and Dualism

After the fourth century the danger of monophysitism (especially Eutychianism) turned out to be the most pressing. Here, the one person of Christ is linked so closely with the divine nature that his human nature is essentially impersonal. Jesus' Ego is exclusively the divine Ego, and not the human Ego as well. It can be hardly denied that the doctrine of *anhypostasis*, the view that there is no (*an*) distinct human hypostasis in Jesus, is inclined to the latter view. The ultimate consequence is that this view becomes a form of monophysitism.

The same danger existed in monotheletism, the belief that Jesus possessed only one (divine-human) will. This doctrine was rejected by the Council of Constantinople (680).[28] But what about this view today? Those committed to monophysitism will rejoice; those sympathetic to Nestorianism will fear that, here again, the humanity of Jesus is in danger of being absorbed by his divinity.

Behind such debates we repeatedly encounter the complex issue of the (im)personal character of Jesus' human nature — an ancient theological battle.[29] Please note that neither side denies that Jesus is an integral human person; neither side has any sympathy for Docetism. This debate must also be distinguished from the one about Apollinarianism, which involved whether Jesus had a human soul/spirit; Apollinaris claimed that the Logos had assumed the place of this human soul/spirit. However, in the debate about the personal or impersonal character of Jesus' human nature we encounter a new aspect of the ancient conflict between Eutychian monophysitism and Nestorian dualism. The one (monophysite)

---

28. See Ford and Higton (2002, 127–28). Cf. the will of God the Son in John 17:24, and the will of the Man Jesus, distinct from the will of the Father, in Luke 22:42.
29. Berkouwer (1954) devotes an entire chapter (chapter 12) to this one question.

party[30] claims that the Logos had joined with the impersonal human nature (the doctrine of *anhypostasis* just mentioned). The other (dualistic) party[31] postulates the human nature's own personality; in this case, the Logos joined with a human person (*enhypostasis*).

Here again, the differences are razor-thin. In the debate between Valentijn Hepp and Dirk Vollenhoven, who represented the former and the latter view respectively,[32] Hepp claimed that Vollenhoven's viewpoint was semi-Nestorian, whereas Vollenhoven, if he were consistent, had to call the Reformed confession, as represented by Hepp, monophysite. However, Berkouwer argued that the two were employing different concepts of "person." Vollenhoven did not wish to say that in Christ there are actually *two* persons, a divine person and a human one; nor did Hepp wish to deny that Jesus Christ was a human person.

2.5.2 Anhypostasis and Enhypostasis

The church never formally taught that, according to his human nature, Christ was impersonal, but it did teach that the Logos did not unite with an independent human being (cf. §2.6.4).[33] Louis Berkhof summarized this well (and I am summarizing *him*).[34] On the one hand, the human person of Christ does, as such, not constitute a person. The "Logos person" did not assume a human person—so that we would have two persons in Christ—but a human nature. On the other hand, we must not call the human nature of Christ impersonal; it

---

30. E.g., Thomas Aquinas and John Calvin; also Bavinck (*RD* 3:307); Barth (*CD* I/2=3, §15.2, "Very God and Very Man"); Aalders (1933, 159); Hepp (1937); Pannenberg (1977; 1994).
31. E.g., Vollenhoven (1933, 189; cf. 132–33, 140–41); Korff (1940, 194); Althaus (1952, 225).
32. Described by Berkouwer (1954, 313–19).
33. The latter has indeed been asserted by, e.g., Schoonenberg (1969): he put the Man Jesus first, and saw the divine person (the Logos) assumed in this (a kind of reversed *anhypostasis*: the human person of Jesus has assumed the impersonal divine nature); cf. Graafland (1982, 55, 86).
34. Berkhof (1981, 322; see 322–29).

is impersonal only insofar as this nature does not have any independent existence. It has its personal existence and individuality in the person of the Logos. Since Leontius of Byzantium, this viewpoint is referred to as *enhypostasis* (which is closely related with *anhypostasis*): the human nature of Christ enjoys a personal existence, but exclusively *in* the Word who became flesh.[35]

This entire debate turns on the question: How human is Christ? Though Chalcedon wished to do full justice to Jesus' humanity, that humanity remained underemphasized in subsequent centuries. Therefore, after the Reformation, among some Anabaptists, the Socinians, the Unitarians, and especially during the Enlightenment, an understandable reaction arose, due to the traditional one-sided emphasis upon Jesus' deity. This reaction, however, was not a return to Chalcedon, but an extreme overreaction, leading to the denigration of Jesus' deity. These newer Christologies will be discussed more extensively in §§2.7–2.9; but it may be useful at this point to investigate how these newer approaches play off Jesus' humanity against his deity.

It cannot be denied that the Chalcedonian formulation—"Christ in one person and two natures: divine and human"—at a minimum presents the *danger* of dualism, which can lead quite easily to distinguishing two personalities in Jesus. This danger can be avoided if "natures" are not understood as "substances" (as some called them originally), but as "characters," or even "sides." It is similar to the old nature and new nature in the regenerated person; here, too, we are not dealing with a split personality with two substances but with the *character* of the old self, and the *character* of the new self, both of which can be manifested in the reborn person. Similarly, in the one person of Jesus we see both the divine and the human *characters* or *sides* manifested.[36] At times, the

---

35. So, too, Schilder (1950, 3:37–49); Van Genderen and Velema (2008, 461–62); cf. the criticism by Macquarrie (1998, 43–60).
36. Pannenberg (1977) spoke of "two complementary total aspects of Jesus'

human side becomes so manifest that he stands *as a Man* over against God (e.g., Matt. 27:46; Luke 18:19; John 13:31) — which must be carefully distinguished from his standing as Son over against the Father (e.g., John 17). At other times, the divine side becomes so manifest that he can say: "I and the Father are one" (John 10:30).

Given the threat of a Chalcedonian dualism, Wolfhart Pannenberg rightly said,

> The issue in the question of the deity of Jesus Christ is the deity of the man Jesus. We are not dealing, then, with the divine nature considered in isolation. We must discover the contours of the divine sonship of Jesus in his human reality, which as eternal sonship precedes his historical existence.[37]

In addition, Pannenberg claimed that the divine and the human in Jesus Christ are not two "natures" that are ontologically on the same level and, apart from their connection in the person of the God-Man, are separate from each other.[38] I can follow Pannenberg here but, in my view, he went too far in asserting that "[h]uman nature as such is ordained for the incarnation of the eternal Son in it."[39] Here again, we encounter the danger of monophysitism, when he said, "The person of Jesus Christ is identical with the eternal Son. But this does not mean that the human reality of Jesus lacks personality. Precisely in his human history Jesus has his personal identity solely in being the Son of his heavenly Father."[40] But in this case, Jesus is, or has, no *human* personality. Thus, has Jesus' humanity merged into his deity — or has his deity merged into

---

existence."
37. Pannenberg (1994, 2:325).
38. Ibid., 2:385; cf. the critical comment by Bloesch (1997, 68–69), who thought Pannenberg's view was influenced too strongly by the Enlightenment and by Hegel.
39. Pannenberg, (1994, 2:385–86); cf. a similar generalization by O'Meara (1974, 76): the incarnation is God's attempt to become flesh and blood in each of us.
40. Pannenberg (1994, 2:389).

his humanity?

2.5.3 Summary

With regard to the divine and the human in the person of Jesus, the views range along a continuum in degree of emphasis on Jesus' humanity.

1. *Docetism:* Jesus only seemed to be human; he was the divine Logos in a temporary human-like appearance.

2. *Apollinarianism:* Jesus had only a human body, not a human soul/spirit; the divine Logos was the person (hypostasis) dwelling in Jesus' human body.

3. *The anhypostasis doctrine (Cyril of Alexandria):* Jesus had a human body as well as a human soul/spirit, and also two natures (divine and human); these two natures have been united in one person (hypostasis), and this person was the divine Logos. (The human soul/spirit here is nothing more than an animating or life-giving principle.)

4. *The doctrine of Chalcedon:* identical to the previous one with this difference: the one person of Christ essentially one with the Father, but just as much essentially one with humankind. The one hypostasis is here divine-human.

5. *The enhypostasis doctrine (Leontinus of Byzantium):* identical to the previous one with this difference: also as a Man, Jesus was a person, but this personality (hypostasis) had merged into that of the divine Logos.

Many modern authors—I've already mentioned Macquarrie and Pannenberg[41]—were unsatisfied with the last-mentioned solution because it still underrates Jesus' humanity. This is because one could say of the one hypostasis—which is both divine and human—that it is actually neither really divine nor really human, but a "third something" (Lat. *tertium quid*), as Leontius emphasized.[42] Here, the dilemma resurfaces: those who emphasize the distinction between the divine

---

41. See also the discussion by Jenson (2001).
42. According to Hall (1968, 87–88, 104) and Bloesch (1997, 56), Calvin, too, tended into this direction: "a level halfway God and us."

and the human seem unable to avoid a dualism. But those who emphasize the unity of the two, or the merging of one into the other, seem ultimately to lose *both*.⁴³

Yet, the Chalcedonian formulation seems more acceptable—more prudent, leaving more room for the mystery—than, for instance, Macquarrie's solution, who reversed the matter; he claimed that Jesus' hypostasis was the human hypostasis transformed through a continual submersion in the divine Spirit.⁴⁴ This sounds too much like a certain form of adoptionism, a doctrine he criticizes in the same chapter. Wiser were the words he added to the quotation just given, namely, that our theology has its limitations, and that one could continue forever refining and arguing about the subtle concepts used in Christological debates.

I conclude with a well-known illustration, used by several church fathers (Origen, John of Damascus). A mass of iron is placed in the fire; it continually receives the fire's heat so that it is completely permeated by that heat and transmits the light and the heat it receives from the source. The iron receives the fire's color, yet does not stop being iron; it is not intermingled with some other substance, for fire is another mode of being; yet, the iron has become more than it was.⁴⁵ The illustration is not entirely accurate, for it might incorrectly suggest that Christ's human nature was transformed.⁴⁶ As with the traces of the Trinity (Lat. *vestigia trinitatis*),⁴⁷ so here as well: perhaps these traces have value only for those who already believe in the Trinity or the doctrine of Christ's two natures, respectively.

2.6 Chalcedon and the Reformation
2.6.1 Some Confessional Documents

We cannot set out the entire post-Chalcedonian history of the

---

43. Macquarrie (1998, 56–59).
44. Ibid., 79.
45. Ibid., 80; Bloesch (1997, 57).
46. See Mackintosh (1914, 222).
47. See Ouweneel (*RT* II/1:§10.6.2).

two-natures doctrine here. But one part cannot be overlooked, namely, the Chalcedonian elements in Reformational creeds. Let us look first at the Heidelberg Catechism, which contains various hints of Chalcedon.[48] In Answer 15 it is said that we need a Mediator "who is a true (1 Cor. 15:21-22, 25-26) and righteous man (Jer. 33:16; Isa. 53:11; 2 Cor. 5:21; Heb. 7:15-16), and yet more powerful than all creatures, that is, one who is also true God (Isa. 7:14; Heb. 7:26),"[49] who is Jesus Christ (Answer 18). For the term "true," the Catechism refers to 1 Corinthians 15:21, where the Man (Christ) through whom resurrection has come is "Man" just like the man (Adam) through whom death came. In Answer 17 it is stated that Jesus bore "in His manhood the burden of God's wrath," and in Answer 35: "[T]he eternal Son of God, who is (John 1:1; Rom. 1:3-4) and continues true and eternal God (Rom. 9:5), took upon Himself the very nature of man, of the flesh and blood of the virgin Mary (Gal. 4:4; John 1:14), by the operation of the Holy Ghost (Matt. 1:18-20; Luke 1:35); . . . ."[50] The latter is not without problems: Jesus was born of Mary's womb, but this does not necessarily mean that her "flesh and blood" contributed anything to the body of Jesus. Specifically, did Jesus grow from one of Mary's ova? We will return to this question in §9.3.

The Belgic Confession enters more extensively into the matter of Jesus' two natures. It says in Article 19:

> We believe that by this conception the person of the Son is inseparably united and connected with the human nature; so that there are not two Sons of God, nor two persons, but two natures united in one single person; yet each nature retains its own distinct properties. As, then, the divine nature has always remained uncreated, without beginning of days or end of life [Heb. 7:3], filling heaven and earth [Eph 1:23; 4:10], so also has the human nature not lost its properties but remained a creature, having beginning of days, being a finite nature, and re-

---

48. See Ouweneel (2016); cf. Berkouwer (1954, chapter 4).
49. Dennison (*RC* 2:773).
50. Ibid., 2:778.

taining all the properties of a real body [1 Tim. 2:5]. And though He has by His resurrection given immortality to the same, nevertheless He has not changed the reality of His human nature [Matt. 26:11; Luke 24:39; John 20:25; Acts 1:3,11; 3:21; Heb. 2:9]; forasmuch as our salvation and resurrection also depend on the reality of His body [1 Cor. 15:21; Phil. 3:21].

But these two natures are so closely united in one person that they were not separated even by His death. Therefore, that which He, when dying, commended into the hands of His Father, was a real human spirit, departing from His body [Matt. 27:5]. But in the meantime the divine nature always remained united with the human, even when He lay in the grave [Rom. 1:4]; and the Godhead did not cease to be in Him, any more than it did when He was an infant, though it did not so clearly manifest itself for a while. Wherefore we confess that He is **very God** and **very man**: very God by His power to conquer death; and very man that He might die for us according to the infirmity of His flesh.[51]

Here again, one might wonder whether the Confession does not say too much: his "human spirit, departing from His body" might entail Greek dualism. For the rest, we may be satisfied with the formulations of the Confession.

The Westminster Larger Catechism says in Answer 36:

The only Mediator of the covenant of grace is the Lord Jesus Christ (1 Tim. 2:5), who, being the eternal Son of God, of one substance and equal with the Father (John 1:1, 14; 10:30; Phil. 2:6), in the fulness of time became man, and so was and continues to be God and man, in two entire distinct natures, and one person, forever (Luke 1:35; Rom. 9:5; Col. 2:9; Heb. 7:24–25).[52]

It follows with Answer 40:

It was requisite that the Mediator, who was to reconcile God and man, should himself be both God and man, and this in one

---

51. Ibid., 2:435; emphasis added.
52. Ibid., 4:305

person, that the proper works of each nature might be accepted of God for us (Matt. 1:21, 23; 3:17; Heb. 9:14), and relied on by us as the works of the whole person [of Christ].[53]

2.6.2 The Extra-Calvinisticum

In the Heidelberg Catechism, in answer to Question 47, "But is not Christ with us even unto the end of the world (Matt. 28:20), as he promised us?" we read: "Christ is true man and true God. According to His human nature He is not now on earth (Matt. 26:11; John 16:28; 17:11), but according to His Godhead, majesty, grace, and Spirit, He is at no time absent from us (John 14:17-18; 16:13; Eph. 4:8)." With a glance toward the Lutherans, this is followed by Question 48: "*But are not, in this way, the two natures in Christ separated from one another, if the manhood is not wherever the Godhead is?*" To which the answer is: "Not at all, for since the Godhead is incomprehensible and everywhere present (Acts 7:49; Jer. 23:24), it must follow that it is indeed beyond the bounds of the manhood which it has assumed, but is yet nonetheless in the same also, and remains personally united to it (Col. 2:9; John 3:13; John 11:15; Matt. 28:6)."[54]

We are amazed to find this fascinating polemic in what was intended as a Bible course for young believers! It has been referred to as the "extra-calvinisticum," although it is indeed anti-Lutheran but not specifically Calvinistic.[55] This Catechism answer seeks to avoid the Lutheran notion that Christ's divinity is enclosed within his human nature, with a consequence that Christ is omnipresent also according to his human nature.[56] Luther was employing the ancient idea of the "communication of properties" (Lat. *communicatio idio-*

---

53. Ibid., 4:306.
54. Ibid., 2:780.
55. See Berkouwer (1954, 76, 81, 88); Beker and Hasselaar (1981, 58–66); Bonhoeffer (1966, 95–97); Pietro M. Vermigli (1561), quoted in Ford and Higton (2002, 233–34); Kärkkäinen (2003, 80–82).
56. See extensively, Bavinck (*RD* 3:308–16); Emmen (1935, 40–43); Berkouwer (1954, 282–300); Graafland (1982, 66–69).

matum), that is, the transfer of the properties of one nature to the other,[57] in this case, the transfer of divine omnipresence to Christ's human nature. In opposition to this, the Heidelberg Catechism states that Christ's divine nature is not enclosed within his human nature, as if his divine nature could be only where his human nature is, too. According to his divine nature, Christ is omnipresent—now on earth as well—but according to his human nature, he is no longer on earth.

In other words, Lutherans teach that "the finite [viz., the Man Jesus] is capable of bearing (or carrying) the infinite" (Lat. *finitum capax infinitii*). Calvinists teach that "the finite is incapable of bearing (or carrying) the infinite" (Lat. *finitum non capax infinitii*). Lutheranism, said Donald Bloesch, runs the risk of monophysitism and Docetism, whereas Calvinism runs the risk of Nestorianism.[58] No other possibilities exist; as *always* in this matter, theologians risk falling off the path toward either the left or the right.

The Belgic Confession has the same view as the Heidelberg Catechism. The phrase, "so also has [Christ's] human nature not lost its properties but remained a creature" (Art. 19), opposes every attempt to deify Christ's human nature and to humanize his divine nature. The Confession implicitly opposes monophysitism as well; both the divine nature and the human nature remained what they were. Here again, the Lutheran notion of enclosing the divine within the human nature is being opposed.

This tension between Christ's divine omnipresence and his human limitation to space and time does not result from theological speculation. The tension is present in the Bible; consider: on the one hand, "[Y]ou will not always have me [with you]" (Matt. 26:11; John 12:8), and on the other hand: "I am with you always, to the end of the age" (Matt. 28:20; cf. John 14:18). On the one hand, Jesus ascends to heaven and leaves behind his disciples (John 14:1–3); on the other hand,

---

57. See note 6 above.
58. Bloesch (1997, 62).

he promises in the same chapter: "If anyone loves me, he will keep my word, and my Father will love him, and we will come to him and make our home with him" (v. 23).

This debate had significant implications for the Lord's Supper.[59] According to Zwingli and Calvin, Christ cannot, as a Man, be personally present in the signs of bread and wine (as a *Man*, for his body and blood are involved). This is because, as a Man, Christ is always at one location at any given time, and since his ascension, this place is the right hand of God. However, according to Luther, Jesus' deity permeates his humanity such that his humanity, too, can be everywhere, so that he can be *bodily* present in the Lord's Supper. For Luther, it was important that, wherever Christ is present, he is always present as one person, without a separation of the divine and the human natures (as occurs in asserting that the latter is in heaven, and the former on earth). Here again, one might argue that Zwingli and Calvin tended more toward Nestorianism, and Luther more toward monophysitism.

Both parties pay too little attention to the pneumatological aspect.[60] Jesus Christ is present among believers as the Spirit of Jesus (Acts 16:7), or of Jesus Christ (Phil 1:19), or of Christ (Rom. 8:9; 1 Pet. 1:11), or of God's Son (Gal. 4:6). This is not the divine nature of Christ, nor his human spirit. Rather, it is what is called the third person of the Godhead. When he says, "I will not leave you as orphans; I will come to you" (John 14:18), this is *not* the "I come again" of verse 3 but what precedes immediately in the text: "I will ask the Father, and he will give you another Helper [Gk. *Paraklētos*, Advocate, Counselor], *to be with you forever*, even the Spirit of truth, whom the world cannot receive, because it neither sees him nor knows him. You know him, for *he dwells with you and will be in you*" (vv. 16-17). Jesus' presence in the Lord's Supper pertains neither to his divine, nor to his human nature, but to the Spirit of Christ — as the third person who is distinct from the second

---

59. Bavinck (*RD* 4:468–90).
60. This despite the words "and Spirit" in Heidelberg Catechism Answer 47.

person of the Godhead, yet who is closely linked with, and represents, him.

2.6.3 Did God Die on the Cross?

Luther's view of the *communicatio idiomatum* led to another unacceptable conclusion: if Jesus is God and Jesus were crucified, then God was crucified.[61] Luther's well-known expression "the crucified God" returns, for instance, in the title of a publication by Jürgen Moltmann.[62] This idea is just as extreme as its very opposite: the classical theological, though pagan, notion that God cannot suffer, a notion going back, for instance, to the Stoic idea of the divine apathy or inability to suffer (Gk. *apatheia*).[63] The Bible speaks differently: "[T]he LORD regretted that he had made man on the earth, and it *grieved* him to his heart" (Gen. 6:6). "How often they rebelled against him in the wilderness and *grieved* him in the desert" (Ps. 78:40). "In all their suffering, *He suffered*" (Isa. 63:9 CSB).

Such passages state that God sometimes suffers, so we may assume that the Father certainly suffered with the Son when he was on the cross (cf. John 16:32b). However, the New Testament never claims that it was *God* who died on the cross. He who was God was born of Mary as a male human being without ceasing to be God (see §2.3.3); similarly, he who was God died as a Man on the cross without ceasing to be God. But such a statement does not entitle us to say that *God* was born of Mary, or *God* died on the cross. Here again, we encounter the tension that will always characterize the doctrine of Christ's two natures.

The dividing line between Lutherans and Calvinists with regard to the *communicatio idiomatum* is razor-thin, and each side can easily slide off the path. The Lutheran view carried to its logical conclusion approaches monophysitic Eutychianism

---

61. McGrath (2007, 289–90); Graafland (1982, 69).
62. Moltmann (1993); so too Zephyrinus and Athanasius, according to Van de Beek (2002a, on Moltmann: 50–51; on the extra-calvinisticum: 52–57).
63. Regarding Luther's Christology, see Lienhard (1980).

(the human and divine nature merge), and perhaps Docetism (disregard for Jesus' human nature's own character). Conversely, the Calvinist view carried to its logical conclusion approaches dualistic Nestorianism (the human and the divine nature are separated). Similar razor-sharp distinctions occur with tritheism and modalism, leading us to wonder who can find the exact middle path without slipping either to one side or the other? We can only confess here that the two natures of Christ must always be sharply distinguished — not separated — and their absolute unity in the one person of Jesus Christ must be maintained, without any merging.

2.6.4 Anti-Docetism and Dichotomy

The Belgic Confession describes Christ as "that true, eternal, and almighty God whom we invoke, worship, and serve" (Art. 10). In Article 18, it says that Christ

> did not only assume human nature as to the body, but also a true human soul, that He might be a real man. For since the soul was lost as well as the body, it was necessary that He should take both upon Him, to save both.
>
> Therefore, we confess (in opposition to the heresy of the Anabaptists, who deny that Christ assumed human flesh of His mother) [that Christ was fully human]....[64]

This confession is supported by many Bible passages (Isa. 11:1; Jer. 33:15; Matt. 1:23; Luke 1:42; Acts 2:30; Rom. 1:3; 9:5; Gal. 4:4; Heb. 2:14, 16–17; 4:15; 7:14). This confession joins with the Lutherans in opposing not only the Anabaptists, but also Docetism and certain forms of Gnosticism, all of which taught that the womb of Mary did not contribute anything to Christ's humanity, and was merely the channel through which he entered this world (see more extensively §9.3).[65]

We notice here also the thesis that Christ's "two natures are so closely united in one person that they are not separated

---

64. Dennison (*RC* 2:434).
65. Cf. Erickson (1985, 771–75).

even by His death" (Art. 19). Because Christ is one person, the divine and human natures can never be separated, not even in physical death. Here again, we encounter the basically unfathomable mystery of the person of Christ: on the one hand, we maintain that God is immortal (cf. 1 Tim. 6:16), and therefore it seems to be difficult to say that God the Son died. On the other hand, in death, Jesus could lay aside his bodily mode of being but not his divine nature; otherwise, the unity of his divine-human being would have been disrupted. It was the *Man* Jesus who died—for humans can die, God cannot—but this Man was, also in death, uninterruptedly the Son of God. Moreover, this is true both for Jesus in the tomb—not only "the body of Jesus," but *Jesus* was laid in the grave (John 19:40, 42)—and for Jesus in Hades (Acts 2:27, 31), or Paradise (Luke 23:43). Jesus' *human* body went to the grave, and his *human* soul/spirit to the hereafter, whereas at the same time his humanity was, and remained, inseparably connected with his deity.

In fact, it would be better to say that *he* was in the grave for three days, as well as that for three days *he* lived the afterlife, while this "he" was continually the one God-Man Jesus Christ. Here we encounter the boundary of what we can still claim and account for. In itself, it is correct to state that the idea of a separation between body and soul at death looks too much like a Greek dichotomy.[66] This is true, not only for the Belgic Confession but also for the Heidelberg Catechism, which claims in Answer 57 that, in the resurrection, the body will be "reunited" with the soul. In Answer 52, the Westminster Larger Catechism says the same about the resurrection of Christ: his body was "united to his soul." The same is said in Answers 86 and 87 about the resurrection of the dead.[67]

---

66. See Ouweneel (1986a, chapter 5).
67. Cf. Calvin (*Comm. Philippians* ad loc.), who at Phil. 1:23 ("to be dissolved," DRA) noted that, according to Paul here, death is a separation of soul and body: "Paul overtly witnesses that we will be with Christ when our soul will be separated from our body."

However, it is wise to remember that the creeds and confessions are not primarily theological statements, but church documents, which cannot be judged according to the same criteria as academic publications. They speak the language of faith (although such language is permeated with references to past theological debates), not the language of scholarship.

2.7 The Enlightenment
2.7.1 Reason and Rationalism

Roughly speaking, the period of modernism was from 1789 (fall of the French *Bastille*) until 1989 (fall of the Berlin Wall); however, just as there was a long prelude to modernist tendencies before 1789, there was a long prelude to postmodernist tendencies before 1989.[68] The lengthy transition from the premodern era, which included the Reformation, to the modern era began with British empiricism in the seventeenth century. Historians often mark the beginning of the Enlightenment with British empiricism (John Locke, George Berkeley, David Hume).

We see a similar lengthy prelude within Christology. Not long after the Reformation, there was a turning point with regard to what had been regarded since the Council of Chalcedon as orthodox Christology. We see this among some Anabaptists, and then among the Socinians and the Unitarians, and massively in the time of the German and French Enlightenment (eighteenth century). Whereas, after Chalcedon, Roman Catholics and Protestants placed imbalanced emphasis on Jesus' deity, resistance against this went to the other extreme during the time of Enlightenment. Not much of Jesus' deity remained. Enlightenment rationalism had no room for the notion of a God who revealed himself in his Son. For the modern mind, Jesus was nothing but a great wisdom teacher,[69] a great ethical example, a Man superior to other human

---

68. See Ouweneel (2000b, §13.2).
69. On the basis of some renderings of Joel 2:23 (GW), some prefer the title "Teacher of Righteousness."

beings, differing from them in terms of degree, not essence.

At least two things can be said in defense of the Enlightenment. First, the slogan of the Enlightenment, as formulated by Immanuel Kant, was "Have the courage to use your own mind!" (Ger. *Habe Mut, dich deines eigenen Verstandes zu bedienen*).[70] That is, do not blindly accept what earlier generations, or certain institutions such as the church or the government, have told you, but scrutinize *everything*, and retain only what you can truly accept for yourself. For a more conservative Christian this would mean: Do not accept something because Nicaea or Chalcedon, or Luther or Calvin, have claimed it, but because you have established for yourself that this or that agrees most with the Bible. Of course, do not despise tradition; rather, let yourself be inspired by it. Basically, this was the attitude of Luther as he stood before the Diet of Worms: Even if all popes and councils would have said one thing, and I find that the Bible says another thing, then I believe the Bible. Therefore, confessional doctrine is fundamentally non-academic because a number of church beliefs are *a priori* undebatable.[71]

Second, the similarity between Enlightenment theology and early Protestant scholasticism is much greater than people are often prepared to acknowledge. This is because the rationalistic method, which endeavored to grasp all God's mysteries with the tool of reason, did not essentially change. One need only consult the *Synopsis purioris theologiae* ("Summary of a Purer Theology," 1625) by Joannes Polyander, Antonius Walaeus, Antonius Thysius, and Andreas Rivetus, in order to see rationalistic orthodoxy.[72] To put it a bit starkly, pre-Enlightenment rationalism paused before certain mysteries, such as the virgin birth, the miracles and the resurrection of Christ, and notions such as revelation and inspiration. En-

---

70. Kant (2013, 2).
71. See more extensively, Ouweneel (1995, §3.3).
72. Polyander et al. (1625); we encounter the same spirit in Abraham Kuyper's *Dictaten Dogmatiek*.

lightenment rationalism was more consistent: it did not accept that, by the authority of the church, these mysteries had an exceptional position, and began scrutinizing them as well, with the consequence that little remained of these mysteries.[73] The problem here was not the Enlightenment; the problem was rationalism.

2.7.2 From Above, from Below

Indeed, pre-Enlightenment Christology was a Christology "from above," moving from the eternal Logos to the Man Jesus.[74] In the Enlightenment, this approach gave way to a Christology "from below," one that was developed from what could be established with reasonable certainty concerning the historical Jesus.[75] One could put it this way: a Christology "from above" moves from belief concerning the eternal Logos to the science concerning the historical Jesus, whereas a Christology "from below" moves from the science concerning the historical Jesus to belief concerning the eternal Logos. To be sure, this is rather simplistic because there is no "neutral" science concerning the historical Jesus, one that precedes belief. Thus, Enlightenment theology cannot be severed from the deism and anti-supernaturalism of that time.

It is important to state that the distinction between a Christology "from above" and one "from below" does not necessarily coincide with the distinction between a conservative and a liberal theology. Some liberal theologians wish to begin with the church's convictions concerning Jesus, and some conservative theologians wish, for educational or apologetic reasons, to begin with the historical Jesus.

Donald Bloesch pleaded for a synthesis between the two approaches; he argued that we should not begin with an ab-

---

73. See the useful remarks about Enlightenment theology by Kärkkäinen (2003, 85–89).
74. See, e.g., Anselm of Canterbury's *Cur Deus Homo?*, "Why Did God Become Man?"
75. Althaus (1932, 85); Berkouwer (1954, 107); Weber (1983, 2:16–30); Bloesch (1997, 17); Macquarrie (1998, 19–20); Kärkkäinen (2003, 12–13).

stract concept of deity (as occurs in many Christologies "from above"), nor with the historical Jesus (as happens in Christologies "from below"), but with the living God incarnated in the Man Jesus.[76] He warned that a Christology "from above" can easily lead to Docetism, modalism, monophysitism, or Apollinarianism, and a Christology "from below" can easily lead to adoptionism, Arianism, Nestorianism, or subordinationism.[77] The best approach would be to reject the entire distinction between "from above" and "from below": we know only the Man Jesus who is the incarnated Logos, which is the same as saying that we know the Logos as incarnated in the Man Jesus.

2.7.3 The Old Jesus Quests

Scholarly research into the historical life of Jesus, which began in the Enlightenment, is also called "the quest for the historical Jesus." To distinguish it from the twentieth-century quests (see the next chapter), this is referred to as the *Old* or the *First Quest*. We could distinguish seven *stages* in the quest for the historical Jesus.[78]

Eighteenth and nineteenth centuries:
Stage 1:   preparatory stage (H. S. Reimarus, G. E. Lessing, F. Schleiermacher)

Nineteenth century:
Stage 2:   the first designs (D. F. Strauss, E. Renan)
Stage 3:   the Old or First Quest (W. Bousset, E. Troeltsch, A. Harnack; §2.8)

Twentieth century:
Stage 4:   refutation of the Old Quest (M. Kähler, A. Schweitzer; §2.9)
Stage 5:   the *no questers* (K. Barth, R. Bultmann; §3.1)

---

76. Bloesch (1997, 57).
77. Ibid., 70–71.
78. See Theissen and Merz (1998, 1–15) for a related introduction.

Stage 6: the New or Second Quest (E. Käsemann, G. Bornkamm, E. Fuchs, J. Jeremias; §3.2)

Stage 7: the Third Quest (§3.3)

First, the *preparatory* stage presented the critical groundwork for the "Jesus Quest." This involved the work of Enlightenment theologians Hermann S. Reimarus and Gotthold E. Lessing, and first beginnings by Karl F. Bahrdt, Johann Jakob Hess, and especially Friedrich Schleiermacher.

The *second* stage involved the first *designs* of the historical Jesus; here, we must mention especially the German Hegelian David F. Strauss,[79] and the French liberal Ernest Renan.[80] After the historical approach advocated by H. S. Reimarus, Strauss was the first to elaborate the *mythical* approach: in his view, the Jesus tradition, especially in John's Gospel, is thoroughly mythical. He believed this pertained to all the supernatural features in the Gospels. Within five years, Strauss' work was followed by about sixty responses, among which that of the converted Jew August Neander may be mentioned with honor.[81] In the British world, the converted Jew Alfred Edersheim was a worthy counterpart to Strauss, Renan, and their consorts;[82] in addition to this, the work of J. B. Lightfoot (1889), F. J. A. Hort, and B. F. Westcott may be mentioned.

2.8 The First Quest
2.8.1 History and Kerygma

The third stage involved the optimistic *Old* or *First Quest* for the historical Jesus; the main protagonists were F. C. Baur and H. J. Holtzmann. Their aim was a historical-critical reconstruction of Jesus' life on the basis of the oldest sources (the so-called two-source theory: Mark and Q; see §5.3). They hoped thereby to liberate the "true" Christian faith from the

---

79. Strauss (1972).
80. Renan (1863); the theologians mentioned here are mostly German, and their influence far surpassed that of others in this field; see Kopmels (2005).
81. Neander (1847).
82. Edersheim (1979).

"claws" of the dogmas, and in this way to revitalize faith.

The summit, but also the terminus of this classical "Life of Jesus" theology, was reached by Adolf von Harnack,[83] near the turn of the century. The pre-existence and the virgin birth of Christ, along with every form of his divinity, were sacrificed on the altar of anti-supernaturalism. If the eighteenth-century portrait of Jesus embodied the Enlightenment's rationalistic ideal, the nineteenth-century portrait embodied the religious personality ideal of Romanticism.[84] As Carl Braaten put it, the nineteenth-century biographers of Jesus were like plastic surgeons remodeling the face of their patient according to their own image.[85] Martin Hengel warned more broadly: "We all have the tendency of interpreting and adapting him in ways that fit us, to form him theologically 'according to our own image,' and in this point we are not far from the psychologizing 'Life of Jesus' research of the latter part of the nineteenth century."[86]

I. Howard Marshall acutely depicted what happens when the historian or the theologian excludes the supernatural or miraculous *a priori* from his research.[87] Take, for instance, the fact that miracles played an essential role in Jesus' ministry. The modern historian will respond that miracles fall outside his scholarly field of inquiry; at best, he can state that many of Jesus' followers believed that he performed miracles. Thus, the modern historian will feel compelled to write a history of Jesus without anything about the supernatural (which is like writing a book on astronomy without anything about stars). The historical Jesus of the modern historian or theologian can *a priori* be nothing else than an ordinary human being.[88]

In this way, the well-known chasm developed between the

---

83. Harnack (1957).
84. Cf. McGrath (2007, 312).
85. Braaten (1966, 55).
86. Hengel (1995, 67).
87. Marshall (1977, chapter 3: "Faith and the Supernatural").
88. Ibid., 59.

"historical Jesus" (the Jesus of history), who is a special person, yet a human being like us, and the "kerygmatic Christ" (the Christ of faith), whom we know from the preaching (Gk. *kerygma*) of the early church, a miracle worker, who, according to his followers, experienced a supernatural conception as well as a supernatural resurrection. In itself, the *distinction* between the "historical Jesus" and the "kerygmatic Christ" is not wrong if it means that the great majority of Christians have believed in Christ without much knowledge of the historical context in which Jesus of Nazareth lived.[89] However, if this distinction were to become a chasm because of the anti-supernaturalist prejudice, a form of Docetism would arise because the Christ of faith is severed from the real Man Jesus, as Donald Bloesch argued.[90] In opposition to this, Bloesch insisted that we do not believe in the "historical Jesus" or in the "kerygmatic Christ," but in the historical God-Man Jesus.

Those who do wish to make the distinction mentioned must first answer the question whether, on the basis of the Enlightenment biases, a bridge is still possible between the "historical Jesus" and the "kerygmatic Christ." Actually, this is impossible, for the former is thoroughly natural, the latter thoroughly supernatural. Second, the supernatural is interwoven with the life of Jesus to such an extent that we must ask: After subtracting the miraculous, how much of the "historical Jesus" remains? Little more than the fact that he really existed, said Rudolf Bultmann — and how can one even be sure of *that*? When one peels layer after layer from an onion, aiming to reach the core, at a given moment one is left empty-handed.

2.8.2 Various Approaches

Various liberal theological ways of arguing away Jesus' deity include the method of crediting this notion to the early church, one that is supposedly foreign to the New Testament.

---

89. Cf. Meier (1991, 197–98).
90. Bloesch (1997, 71–72).

The first is the *euhemeristic* view, such as the one defended by W. Bousset and E. Troeltsch.[91] By euhemerism we understand the view that ascribes the origin of the gods to the deification of historic heroes. Ostensibly, Jesus had been such a historic hero, who, after his death, had been put on a pedestal by his followers. First, the simple carpenter had been elevated to the status of Messiah, and finally to that of God.[92] During the time of the Enlightenment, Reimarus asserted that all of Christology went back to deceit perpetrated by the apostles. They knew who Jesus really was, and were supposedly responsible for his deification.

If this were so, how could the apostle Paul, whose writings belong to the earliest ones of the New Testament, so ardently oppose all pagan deifications, and present Jesus as the true God and Lord (Rom. 9:5; 1 Cor. 8:5)? The apostles refused to participate in such euhemeristic games, so to speak; they fiercely opposed them. They believed that the Man Jesus had not become God, but that in him God had become Man. The euhemeristic view would lead one to expect that the *Man* Jesus would appear in the earliest New Testament writings, and the *deified* Jesus in the later ones. In reality, the earliest writings assume the deity of Jesus, whereas the writings that aim at presenting to us the historical Jesus, namely, the Gospels, arose in a much later period.[93] Several authors have emphasized that the reason why the very early church believed in Jesus as the Son of God can be explained only by assuming that Jesus himself presented himself as such.[94]

This fact is important also with regard to the second approach, the *Hellenizing* view: Jesus' elevation to a divine status arose from a Hellenization of the Jewish rabbi from Nazareth. One version of this view saw this elevation as based upon confusing the Greek philosophical Logos (Heraclitus) with the New Testament Logos. This

---

91. Bousset (1906; 1970); Troeltsch (1971; 1911).
92. Elsewhere, I have pointed out that something similar possibly occurred with the biblical Nimrod; he is supposedly identical to the Babylonian god Marduk; see Ouweneel (1998, 221; 2003, 60–62).
93. Berkhof (1986, 277).
94. Meyer (1979, 252); Witherington (1990, 1–2); Bockmuehl (1994); Dunn (2003; 2005); Barnett (1998, 96).

view claims that the Trinitarian and Christological dogmas are not only clothed in Hellenistic dress (Gk. *ousía, prosōpon, hypostasis, phusis*), but also permeated with Hellenistic content. An important example of this criticism was Adolf von Harnack; he wished to free Christology from every form of Hellenism, but at the same time also from all supernaturalism. His book is still a standard work for every liberal Christology. According to him, the notion of Jesus as the Son of God is a Hellenistic idea, one that is foreign to Judaism, which entered early Christianity from outside.

This is a strange standpoint for at least three reasons. First, for several centuries, Judaism had been thoroughly Hellenized, so that there was no need for any "penetration" from the outside world. Secondly, the notion of the "Son of God" entered not from Hellenism but from the Old Testament (Ps. 2:7). Thirdly, given the strongly Jewish-Christian character of the New Testament infancy narratives, it is highly unlikely that their "inventors" would have made use of stories about gods that lay entirely beyond their horizon.[95]

Finally, it is good to realize how an approach like Harnack's is linked to Romanticism, to pre-existentialists such as Søren Kierkegaard and Friedrich Nietzsche, and a philosophy of religion scholar, Max Müller. In other words, while Harnack attributed early Christology to extra-biblical influences, his own Christology was largely determined by this very kind of influence. A. van de Beek summarized:

> The popular notion that Jesus of Nazareth as a regular human being was gradually hell[e]nized into God in a process of a few centuries with Chalcedon as capstone, is sheer nonsense. The earliest writers in the church . . . not only teach the incarnation of God, but are all fully aware of the paradox involved.[96]

2.8.3 A Third Approach

I interrupt my historical treatise here for a moment in order to identify a third approach, the *functionalistic* approach. It

---
95. Berger (2004, 53).
96. Van de Beek (2002a, 98).

arose more recently, long after the First Quest had ended. This approach claimed that New Testament Christology must be viewed in a functional way, as part of redemptive history, rather than in an ontological way.

One advocate of this approach was Oscar Cullmann.[97] He considered the Chalcedonian formula to be outdated because of its ontological character, since it makes claims about the being or essence of Christ's person. The New Testament, however, along with modern humanity, are supposedly more interested in functional questions, like: What is the meaning of this thing or that person? What is important is no longer the essence of humanity but humanity's purpose on this earth. Similarly, with regard to Christ, what is important is not who he is in himself, but who he is for us.[98] Postmodern people ostensibly view notions like incarnation, virgin birth, and bodily resurrection as no longer relevant. What is important is no longer whether Chalcedon is correct (as premoderns claimed) or incorrect (as moderns asserted), but the meaning and use of the Chalcedonian formula (as postmoderns ask).

There is certainly some truth in this approach. It was always good to assess whether one is asking the right or relevant questions. Yet, theologians cannot help asking, even today, whether Jesus was God—not only in the sense of what this might mean practically for us today, but also in the essential sense: What exactly are we claiming if we suggest that Jesus is God?

2.9 The End of the First Quest
2.9.1 Philosophical Backgrounds

Nineteenth-century liberal Christology did not retain anything of the biblical Jesus, and thus was not left with any Christianity either. Therefore, this "dead end," or "blind alley," as Martin Kähler called it, was ardently combated by

---

97. Cullmann (1963).
98. Cf. Dietrich Bonhoeffer's question (see §1.2.1): "Who is Jesus for us today?" (1967, 139).

theologians like Kähler himself and Albert Schweitzer.[99] However, the latter two rejected the Chalcedonian Christology as well. Schweitzer blamed the nineteenth-century theologians for having tried to fashion Jesus into a modern (i.e., nineteenth-century) person after their own image and likeness. Their aim had been noble: they wished to put a solid scholarly historical foundation under faith—but this attempt had simply failed. Schweitzer's historiography of the investigation into the life of Jesus describes this failure. Euhemerism and Hellenism were ultimately unable to offer a scholarly explanation for the faith of the earliest church. This was because the oldest Christological tradition in the New Testament (the letters by Paul,[100] which are based upon yet older layers of tradition, e.g., 1 Cor. 15:1-7 and Phil. 2:6-9) appeals in a straightforward way to the historical Jesus. Schweitzer sought to understand Jesus from the latter's eschatological view, which according to Schweitzer was the view of an idealist, devoid of any historical sense of reality.[101]

Colin Brown interestingly observed that whereas Harnack's historical Jesus was a reflection of the liberal Protestant scholar, Schweitzer's Jesus had an element of the heroic "Superman" of Nietzsche, a philosopher that was admired by Schweitzer.[102] Brown spoke here of a "Christ mysticism." While Kähler and Schweitzer accused their predecessors of philosophical biases (going back to Thomas Hobbes, David Hume, Immanuel Kant, and others), they were little aware

---

99. Kähler (1964); Schweitzer (1956); other theologians from this period, such as Wilhelm Wrede and K. L. Schmidt, will be mentioned later in this book.
100. Barnett (1998, 86; see further 86–96) pleaded for Jesus' deity based on the evidence in Paul's letters because these can be dated with certainty close to the time of Jesus, written by someone who had been part of New Testament history almost from the beginning, first as persecutor and later as apostle. Elsewhere (88–89) he claimed that, in each reconstruction of the pre-Easter Jesus, there must be obvious similarity between him and the person in whom the churches believed immediately after Easter, and for whom they were persecuted by Saul of Tarsus and other Jews.
101. Regarding contemporary theologian Wilhelm Wrede, see §3.8.1.
102. Brown (*DJG* 332).

Development of Christology

of their own. They were well described by the famous metaphor of George Tyrrell, who compared the behavior of the modernists, especially Harnack, with that of a man peering to see what is at the bottom of a deep well, seeing nothing but his own image in the water.[103] "[Y]ou thought that I was one like yourself," says Psalm 50:21 appropriately. John P. Meier said that all these continually changing and often contradictory portraits of the historical Jesus, no matter how useful in the academy, cannot be the object of Christian faith for the worldwide church.[104] And Joseph Ratzinger wrote that those who read several of these reconstructions side by side soon discover that they are more like photographs of the authors and their ideals than the polishing of an icon that had become obscure.[105]

2.9.2 History and Faith

Martin Kähler also made the sharp distinction between the Jesus of history (with whom the investigation into the Life of Jesus had been exclusively occupied, as Kähler reproached it) and the biblical Christ of faith, who is the One who really matters. The Gospels are no biographies of the historical Jesus, but faith testimonies concerning the Christ who is the object of Christian faith, the original document (Ger. *Urkunde*) upon which the preaching, the *kerygma*, is based. This insight signaled some progress in the "life of Jesus" movement. At the same time, however, Kähler severed the historical Jesus from the Christological dogma with the argument that this dogma does not follow from the personal observation of Jesus' contemporaries, but from theological conceptualizations of later generations. Thus, empirical observation (the experience of Jesus) was played off against reason (reflection upon Jesus).

The basis for this consisted of the distinction between the

---

103. Tyrrell (1963, 44).
104. Meier (1991, 198).
105. Ratzinger (2007, xii).

objective ordinary history of the "historical Jesus" (Ger. *Historie*) and the subjective higher history of the kerygmatic Christ (Ger. *Geschichte*), like a lower level history and an upper level history. In the Anglo-Saxon world, this corresponds with the distinction between the *historical* Jesus, that is, the Jesus of objective history, and the *historic* Jesus, that is, the Jesus of faith experience; the latter Jesus is the object of Christian faith.[106] This distinction goes back to the philosophers of German idealism, Johann G. Fichte and Georg W. F. Hegel, who assigned to Jesus a place within idealistic philosophy.

Herman Ridderbos sought to harvest the positive elements in Kähler's thinking, while bringing together the historical Jesus and the Christ of faith. For him, this is the central question: "In the Gospels are we dealing with the figure of Jesus Christ as he existed for the church's faith, and on that basis was antedated in the life of Jesus of Nazareth, or is this same figure at the same time the Christ of history, that is, the One who at one time indeed preached, performed miracles, suffered, died, rose from the dead?"[107] Ridderbos decidedly chose the latter, and Carl Braaten did the same: a kerygma without a truly historical Jesus is a verbal vacuum, and a Jesus without the apostolic kerygma is a meaningless "surd."[108] Eduard Schweizer similarly claimed that Mark's Gospel really *was* a book of history, since Mark knew that the essential elements of the Good News being preached would be found nowhere else than in the report of the events during the years of Jesus' ministry.[109]

Where people did not know how to deal very well with the historical Jesus, but believed to find the solution in the kerygmatic Christ, they began to speak so tirelessly about the "Word of God" (Karl Barth), or the "kerygma" (Rudolf Bult-

---

106. This distinction was advocated later by Karl Barth, but effectively combated by Pannenberg (1977) and others.
107. Ridderbos (1946, 33).
108. Braaten (1966, 62).
109. Schweizer (1971b, 24).

mann), or "personal encounter" (Emil Brunner), or "I-thou relationships" (Friedrich Gogarten), that historical interests were snowed under in an avalanche of theological rhetoric, as Carl Braaten put it.[110]

The ultimately unfortunate separation between the Jesus of history and the Christ of the *kerygma* found its all-time low in the theology of Rudolf Bultmann (§3.1.2), at which point a new notion arose: that of the *Easter Chasm* (Ger. *Ostergraben*). According to this thinking, the Easter event (no matter how understood) constituted a deep cleft between the historical Jesus who died on the cross, and the ideal Christ figure, who rose from the dead and constitutes the object of Christian faith.

2.9.3 Again: Above and Below

Kerygmatic theology followed Kähler in distinguishing the preached Christ from the historical Jesus; according to Bultmann, modern people were interested not in the historical (events around) Jesus (*contra*, e.g., 1 Cor. 15:3-19) but only in the Christ of faith.[111] In spite of this, or rather for this very reason, this theology viewed itself as a Christology "from above": the kerygmatic Christ can be known only through an existential (read: irrational) leap of faith, elevated beyond all conclusions of rational theoretical theology. Conversely, a Christology "from below," which begins with the historical Jesus, does not have to be liberal. An example is Wolfhart Pannenberg,[112] who acknowledged Jesus' divinity.[113]

Millard Erickson sought a way between the kerygmatic Christology "from above" and a Christology "from below," based upon a supposedly objective rationalism.[114] I prefer a middle path found in the correct philosophical view of the

---

110. Braaten (1996, 25).
111. Bultmann (1958).
112. Pannenberg (1977; 1994); cf. Runia (1992, 29–30).
113. Regarding Christologies "from above" and "below," see Kärkkäinen (2003, 12–15).
114. Erickson (1985, 673–75).

relationship between faith and reason in *all* science. This relationship is based upon the anthropological relationship between believing and thinking as immanent functions of the transcendent heart. It follows from this insight that theology, like all science, is simultaneously existentially determined and capable of being fully rational.[115] I am pleading for a Christology that is both "from above" and "from below," the former *via* the Logos who became flesh (cf. John's Gospel), and the latter *via* the Man Jesus of Nazareth, who is divine (cf. the Synoptics).

Kerygmatic theologians adduce an argument from 2 Corinthians 5:16, "From now on, therefore, we regard no one according to the flesh. Even though we once regarded Christ according to the flesh, we regard him thus no longer." John H. Bernard paraphrased Paul's words as follows:

> [T]hough there was a time in my life when I, like my Judaising opponents now, laid great stress on the local and hereditary, and, so to speak, fleshly "notes" of the Messiah who was to come.... I know better now.... In personal religion the merely *historical* must yield precedence to the *mystical* [read: experiential] element; it is of great interest and of real value to learn all that can be known about the Birth, Life, Death and Resurrection of Jesus of Nazareth, but it is the *present* Life of Christ, "in whom" we may be found if we will, that is of religious importance.[116]

What John Bernard, in the wake of especially F. C. Baur and A. P. Stanley, is saying is this: the historical Jesus is interesting but religiously irrelevant; what matters is the "present" Christ (note here the shift from "Jesus" to "Christ"). The apostle Paul supposedly developed this insight during a so-called "second" conversion. Murray J. Harris wrote in a

---

115. See extensively Ouweneel (1995, especially §§2.3, 2.4, 3.3.5, and 4.4; *RT* I/2).
116. Bernard (1979, 70–71).

very different, and in my view, more biblical, way.[117] He did set off a historical Jesus against a present Christ, but this referred to a Christ carnally viewed against a Christ spiritually viewed. Paul is rejecting not a knowledge of, or interest in, Christ-after-the flesh (viz., the historical Jesus), but a carnal view of Christ, whereas he himself had a Spiritual view and a cross-oriented attitude.

The viewpoint of Baur, Stanley, Bernard, and others cannot be harmonized with the testimony of Paul's letters. The apostle was definitely interested in the facts of Jesus' earthly life, from his birth (Gal. 4:4) until his death and resurrection (see also 2 Cor. 5:18–21) (see §5.4.3). Paul saw no antithesis between the objective facts concerning the historical Jesus and a subjective surrender to the glorified Christ.

New approaches advocated in the twentieth century, both from "non-questers" and from "new questers," demand our attention now. To these approaches we now turn.

---

117. Harris (1976, 355); see also Hughes (1962, 199–200).

Chapter 3
Twentieth-Century Christology

> *Then he said to Thomas,*
>   *"Put your finger here, and see my hands; and put out your hand, and place it in my side.*
>   *Do not disbelieve, but believe."*
> *Thomas answered him,*
>   *"My Lord and my God!"*
>
> John 20:27–28

3.1 Non-Questers
3.1.1 Karl Barth

AFTER THE MASSACRE resulting from the initial "Life of Jesus" Quests, and after their equally liberal opponents, what remained was at best a form of adoptionism: Christ is Son of God,

(a) because the Logos dwells in the Man Jesus; various versions of this view can be found among the early Christian Ebionites (who accepted Jesus as Israel's Messiah but not as divine) and with Paul of Samosata;[1] or

---
1. See chapter 1, note 155 above.

(b) because, at his baptism, Jesus had been adopted by God as his Son;[2] or

(c) because in him the divine reality is present in a special way ("dynamic incarnation"[3]); or

(d) even weaker, because he had a unique awareness of God.

A very different path was chosen by Karl Barth, whose thought dominated theology through the middle of the twentieth century, characterized as thoroughly Christocentric, if not Christomonistic. People have spoken of the "old questers" (§§2.8 and 2.9), whereas the so-called neo-orthodox theologians (Karl Barth, Emil Brunner, Rudolf Bultmann, Friedrich Gogarten, Eduard Thurneysen, Paul Tillich) stood between the "old questers" and the "new questers"; therefore, they were referred to as "no questers."[4] In Karl Barth's theology, the notion of revelation again occupied a primary position, which led to a sharp conflict with his teacher, Adolf von Harnack. Their abrasive correspondence has been analyzed by Martin Rumscheidt.[5]

Barth wished to theologize in a contemporary way, though entirely in line with Chalcedonian thought; in this respect, he differed sharply with the First Questers. He did, however, slide unmistakably toward Apollinarianism, the doctrine that Jesus did not have a human soul/spirit (his human nature was non-personal, although it did possess individuality), but that the Logos filled the place of this human soul/spirit. In

---

2. Ratzinger (2007, 23–24): "A broad current of liberal scholarship has interpreted Jesus' Baptism as a vocational experience. . . . It was then, we are told, that he became aware of his special relationship to God and his religious mission. . . . But none of this can be found in the texts. However much scholarly erudition goes into the presentation of this reading, it has to be seen as more akin to a 'Jesus novel' than as an actual interpretation of the texts."
3. Erickson (1985, 733–34).
4. Spykman (1992, 383, 386, 391).
5. Rumscheidt (1972).

other words, the Son was the spirit of Jesus' human body.[6] In this respect, Barth was certainly *not* orthodox, although Klaas Runia claimed he was.[7] Nor was Barth orthodox in the way he viewed typically human traits of Jesus such as obedience and humility as characteristics of *God*, namely, for the Son with respect to the Father. Not only is this subordinationism[8] objectionable, but the tension between the divine and the human within Jesus is thereby shifted to the being of God himself.

The most important reason why Barth exerted such a great influence on Christology was his Christomonism, which permeated his theology. Here, we may admire Barth for his opposition against liberal theology as he presented a Christology "from above" concerning the transcendent God revealing himself in Christ to people, and concerning the Logos who, on behalf of God, assumed human nature in order to redeem humanity. Orthodoxy is a relative notion. But despite criticism of Barth from those holding to traditional Christology, in comparison with all nineteenth-century liberalism, to describe him as "neo-orthodox" was certainly appropriate.

3.1.2 Rudolf Bultmann

Although the voice of the Barthians continued to be heard long after World War II, soon after the War the *central* position of Karl Barth in dogmatics, and especially in Christology, came to be occupied by Rudolf Bultmann[9] and his program of demythologizing the New Testament. The return to orthodox Christology, which we observe with Barth, was reversed. According to Bultmann, the New Testament offers no history of Jesus and early Christianity, but only theology produced

---

6. Barth (*CD* I/2 = 3, §15.3). At the end of the nineteenth century, a division occurred in England within the Brethren Movement (Plymouth Brethren) on this same question (among other things), which led to the rise of the Exclusive Brethren, who adhere to a form of Apollinarianism.
7. Runia (1992, 14–15).
8. See Ouweneel (*RT* II/1:§10.3.3).
9. See especially Bultmann (1984; as well as 1958; 1963); see the analysis by Berkouwer (1954, 1952, 36–42; 1965, 45–50).

by the church, in which the facts of Jesus' life have been intermingled with mythical elements, adopted especially from Hellenism.[10] In the wake of Martin Heidegger's existentialism, Bultmann was no longer interested in who or what Jesus means *in himself* (historically, ontologically) but in what he (existentially) means *for the believer*, for one's faith. The thoroughly mythical garment in which Jesus in the New Testament is clothed is unacceptable for modern humans. Therefore, they will accept the New Testament message only if and when the New Testament has been radically demythologized.

Bultmann expressed this in the following famous words:

> We cannot use electrical lights and radios and, in the event of illness, avail ourselves of modern medical and clinical means and at the same time believe in the spirit and wonder world of the New Testament. And if we suppose that we can do so ourselves, we must be clear that we can represent this as the attitude of the Christian faith only by making the Christian proclamation unintelligible and impossible for our contemporaries.[11]

These are fascinating words, especially for us who, more than three-quarters of a century later, have experienced the transition from the modern to the postmodern spiritual climate, in which the "the spirit and wonder world" is entirely acceptable again—though usually not in the way of the New Testament.

Bultmann did not wish to conduct his demythologizing program in the manner of nineteenth-century liberal theology, which, so to speak, removed one layer after another from the historical Jesus until nothing of him remained. No, said, Bultmann, we must reinterpret (Ger. *umdeuten*) the New Testament by seeking the existential message hidden behind the New Testament's mythical statements. All statements about the pre-existence, virgin birth, vicarious sacrifice, bodily resurrection and ascension of Christ are supposedly purely mythological; that is, these things never really occurred. Nev-

---

10. Regarding myth, see J. D. G. Dunn (*DJG* 566–69).
11. Bultmann (1984, 4–5).

ertheless, they are true—if only we are prepared to understand them existentially. Behind this entire mythical façade lies the salvation of God, which radiates through Jesus, according to Bultmann. However, this salvation involved no redemptive *fact* like those confessed, for instance, in the Apostles' Creed or the Nicene Creed. That is, Christ brought me salvation, but without rendering a vicarious atoning sacrifice, without having risen bodily, and without being glorified in heaven as the risen One.

Bultmann asserted that modern Christian faith is thoroughly disinterested in such redemptive facts. He wrote, "The Easter event as the resurrection of Christ is not a historical event.... Christian faith, however, is not interested in the historical question;...."[12] In other words, Christ's resurrection is part of the *kerygma* only.[13] Against this, one might argue that, for the apostle Paul, the resurrection definitely *was* a real, historical event (1 Cor. 15:17, 19). In answer to many letters that Bultmann received concerning this matter, he replied, "They refer to Bible passages without considering that the latter are since long familiar to me, and without trusting that I already have professionally pondered over their meaning."[14] He went on to call these correspondents, who said that they were praying for his conversion, people "misled by blind guides of the blind."

Berkouwer rightly spoke of

> the theological presumption of this undertaking [of Bultmann]. The conflict over the church's dogma of the two natures ends here with a declaration that what the church regards as Christ's essence is myth. What in the dogma of the church are regarded as God's acts in history are devaluated by Bultmann to the status of a religious fancy. Theology can sink no farther. ... The biblical Jesus Christ, whom the kerygma-theologians wished to

---

12. Ibid., 39–40.
13. See Braaten and Harrisville (1964, 42).
14. Bultmann (1984; 1952, 1:8).

find, is bidden adieu at the suggestion that now the mythical world-view has become untenable.[15]

And Joseph Ratzinger concluded from Bultmann's errors: with Bultmann, "we see how little protection the highly scientific approach can offer against fundamental mistakes."[16]

3.2 The Second Quest
3.2.1 Introduction

During the last two centuries, Christology underwent a remarkable swing. If nineteenth-century liberalism provided a swing to the left, Karl Barth offered a swing to the right (even though, according to many, not far enough), and Bultmann provided a large swing to the left (with this difference from earlier liberalism: Bultmann retained the kerygmatic Christ).[17] All of this prepared for a new swing to the right, though not a reactionary swing: what was sought was a Christology that differed from both classical orthodoxy and Karl Barth.

We can easily guess what this new development would look like: a renewed interest in the historical Jesus. After the failure of the First Quest and the attempts of the Non-Questers, a Second Quest began. This new approach rejected Bultmann's thesis that we can know very little about the historical Jesus.[18] In October 1953, interestingly enough at a reunion of Bultmann's own pupils, one of them, Ernst Käsemann, gave a lecture in which he called Bultmann's stand-

---

15. Berkouwer (1954, 41–42).
16. Ratzinger (2007, 220; cf. 323, where, in a different context, the author speaks of "a certain kind of logic that meticulously classifies the different aspects of a title. While that might be appropriate for rigorous professorial thinking, it does not suit the complexity of living reality, in which a multilayered whole clamors for expression").
17. Cf. Klooster (1977, 63), who argued that the unsolved theological problem of one generation becomes the starting point for the next.
18. Meier (1991, 196) saw here a similarity between Bultmannians and "diehard fundamentalists": both groups view the quest for the historical Jesus as irrelevant, or even as harmful for Christian faith; the Bultmannian claims that the historical Jesus cannot be found, whereas the fundamentalist views the historical Jesus as identical with the Jesus of the four Gospels.

point a form of Docetism since for Bultmann the real Man Jesus was not relevant.[19] To be sure, Käsemann and his colleagues did not want to ignore the results of historical-critical New Testament research,[20] but they sought to delineate the historical Jesus.[21] According to them, the Gospels disclose both the historical Jesus and the kerygmatic Christ, the latter based upon the acts and preaching of the former. Thus, Käsemann claimed that, for both, the coming of God's kingdom was of foremost importance.

In this way we see, after the First Quest for the historical Jesus in the nineteenth century, since about 1954 the rise of the New Quest[22] or Second Quest for the historical Jesus. Well-known theologians in this field, in addition to Ernst Käsemann, were Joachim Jeremias, Ernst Fuchs, and Günther Bornkamm.[23]

3.2.2 Evaluation

One of the fascinating aspects of this New Quest was that, just as with Barth, room was created for the notion of revelation (especially with Fuchs) and for the historicity of the resurrection. Although the resurrection lies outside the reach of historical investigation, Bornkamm argued that what formed the foundation for belief in the resurrection was not a myth, but Jesus' appearances and the testimony of eyewitnesses. Jeremias emphasized that there is a historical basis for Christian belief, which can be scientifically determined.

There were more positive points. Traditional Christians argue that theologians should be demonstrating not the authenticity but the inauthenticity of statements of Jesus; but Jeremias felt compelled to emphasize this anew. The start-

---

19. Käsemann (1954); see further, e.g., Ebeling (1961).
20. Cf. Ouweneel (*RT* I/1:chapter 12).
21. Regarding the most recent development, see Evans (1992); Chilton and Evans (1994); Borg (1994a); Witherington (1997); Barnett (1998); Theissen and Merz (1998); and Knight (2004).
22. Notice the title of Robinson (1959): *A New Quest of the Historical Jesus*.
23. Bornkamm (1960); Fuchs (1964); Jeremias (1971).

ing point is accepting that the Gospels are what they claim to be, namely, a presentation—no matter how subjective—of what Jesus has really said and done, until scientific analysis demonstrates the opposite, or at least makes the opposite plausible.[24] C. H. Dodd added an interesting argument: Jesus' doctrine is simply too brilliant to have been invented by the early church. A genius was needed for this, and the New Testament describes just such a genius; why would we not take the New Testament seriously on this point?[25] The view that Jesus' doctrine came from Jesus himself yields far fewer problems than the view that attributes it to the early church.

Colin Brown compared the "Old," the "Non-," and the "New" Questers as follows (cf. §2.7): Harnack's Jesus looked like a liberal Protestant, Schweitzer's Jesus resembled Nietzsche's Superman, and the Jesus of the New Quest looked like an existentialist philosopher, whose presence in history was hardly discernible behind the kerygma.[26] He is encountered in a kind of existential vacuum, from which the historical circumstances of the first century have been largely removed. Thus, the New Quest ended scarcely two decades after it began. Its decline coincided with the end of the Bultmann era, and the disappearance of existentialist philosophy, according to Brown. With this, the Third Quest began.

3.3 The Third Quest
3.3.1 The Position of Conservative Christianity

In the 1970s and 1980s, great interest arose with regard to the Jewish roots (see §1.7) and other backgrounds of Jesus and his teaching. This movement produced so many new results that it gradually became known as the Third Quest, assuming this can be viewed as a consolidated movement. The Dutch edition of a book by Marcus Borg speaks in the subtitle of a "renais-

---

24. Marshall (1977, 200).
25. Dodd (1952, 109–10; 1971, 49).
26. C. Brown (*DJG* 337).

sance" of Jesus research.[27] The orthodox Jewish scholar David Flusser wrote a book about Jesus in which he attacked the modern disconnection between Jesus' view of his task within the divine plan and the church's kerygma.[28] Another Jew, Géza Vermes, reproached Christian New Testament scholars for paying too little attention to the Jewish backdrop of Jesus' ministry. In his view, the numerous similarities between Jesus and contemporary enthusiastic Jewish prophets and miracle workers strengthened the reliability of the Gospels.

Before discussing this further, we need to provide a provisional assessment of the significance of those Quests and their results. In chapter 2, I argued that no theologian can escape the challenges that the Questers placed before them. The theologian who believes in the inspiration of Scripture and in the supernatural (virgin birth, miracles, bodily resurrection) cannot evade the questions raised by the historical sciences — and these questions can be answered only with arguments derived from these very same historical sciences. Only in this way can justice be done to the claims of opponents, and only in this way could they ever be persuaded.

Let us establish one thing at the outset: neither the historical Jesus described by the historical sciences, nor the kerygmatic Christ resulting from an ecclesiastical Christological development, is the object of Christian faith.[29] Christians believe in a living person, Jesus Christ, God manifested in the flesh, descended to earth as a Man, shortly before the beginning of the present era, who died for the sins of the believers, arose, and was glorified, and now lives with the Father. Christian faith is directed first toward this person, the incarnate, crucified, and risen Lord, and only secondarily toward church teachings and statements concerning him. The Christian believer is interested first and foremost, not in the right Christology, but in *Jesus Christ*.

---

27. Borg (1994b).
28. Flusser (2007, 175).
29. See extensively, Meier (1991, 198).

However, many believers rightly do not wish to stop at this point. Anselm of Canterbury spoke of faith that seeks a deeper insight (Lat. *fides quaerens intellectum*) into both the person and the life and work of Christ. Theology reflects on, among many other things, Jesus' historical context and his functioning in this context (the historical Jesus), as well as on the ecclesiastical Christological development involving his person (the kerygmatic Christ). Such theology is always culturally conditioned; if it were to withdraw to an island, this would signal the end of theology as an academic discipline. Therefore, when during the Enlightenment the historical-critical approach arose in Western culture, theology could not avoid the historical approach either, without necessarily adopting the Enlightenment's anti-supernaturalist biases.

The uses of research into the historical Jesus, the flesh and blood Jesus who lived in a specific historical context—"who suffered under Pontius Pilate"—are manifold.[30] First, such research may keep us from every form of Docetism, which elevates the kerygmatic Christ to an ahistorical, timeless, mythical, existential level. Such Docetism occurs not only in liberal theology. Orthodox theology also faces the (basically Docetic) danger of emphasizing Christ's divinity one-sidedly and excessively, at the expense of his humanity. As an example, I mention the grumblings in certain Reformational circles, especially where supersessionism is very strong, against the emphasis on "Jesus the Jew" in the Third Quest (§3.3).[31] It is precisely the Jewish (and thus historical) Jesus, the non-conformist Jesus, who criticized all the proud traditionalism and religious hypocrisy found in the Judaism of his day. It is this very Jesus who can keep us from settling for a *bourgeois* Christianity, which refuses to be admonished concerning its own traditionalism and its own outward religiosity.

---

30. Cf. ibid., 199.
31. A striking example is Jewish Calvinist and preacher Baruch Maoz (2003), who sharply opposed anything that he calls a Judaizing of Christianity; cf. Ouweneel (2001a).

3.3.2 What Way?

Orthodox Christians have nothing to fear from investigating the historical Jesus; on the contrary, they can learn much from such research. The only thing they must avoid is the strong anti-supernaturalism of theologians still working in the spirit of the Enlightenment. But although this resurfaces repeatedly, as in Bultmann's demythologizing program, greater awareness exists today than during the Enlightenment in two respects. First, there is the awareness that all science, including all theology, is paradigmatically determined. Second, there is the insight that (antisuper-)naturalism is not *a priori* better (more scientific) than supernaturalism.[32]

Thus, today, the Easter event no longer constitutes a cleft between the Jesus of history and the Christ of faith. On the contrary, Jesus' bodily resurrection is at the center of theological interest—though in many cases it remains obscure how people wished to understand this resurrection. Wolfhart Pannenberg in particular strongly pleaded for the bodily resurrection of Christ, and made clear that this event can be made plausible within the well-known historical categories, and must not be burdened with biases about what is and is not thought to be scientifically possible.[33] Pannenberg made the resurrection the cornerstone of his entire theology.

At the same time, in this way the ancient Christological questions concerning the *person* of Christ came to the fore again. If we do have (some) access to the historical Jesus, then who *was* he? True God, true Man? One person, two natures? Chalcedon is on the agenda again. What must we do with it? Should we expand on Chalcedon, as advocated by Karl Barth, and later by Wolfhart Pannenberg[34] and Jürgen Moltmann,[35]

---
32. Of course, the reverse is true as well: one may believe in supernatural miracles, but this does not entail accepting *every* claim that such a miracle has occurred (Meyer [1991, 209]).
33. Pannenberg (1977; 1994). I find it strange that Van de Beek (2002a, 260–64) takes such a negative attitude to this view.
34. Ibid.
35. See especially Moltmann (1993), who, in *The Crucified God*, approaches

as well as by Roman Catholics like Karl Rahner[36] and Walter Kasper?[37] Or can we no longer use Chalcedon, and instead move in a different direction, as many Roman Catholic[38] and Protestant theologians[39] have done? Or can we unashamedly retain Chalcedon as an enduring expression of the faith once delivered to the saints (Jude 1:3), as Donald Bloesch put it?[40] He was quoting Dietrich Bonhoeffer, who wrote: "The Chalcedonian Definition is an objective, but vivid statement, which breaks through all forms of thinking."

We observe that the vigorous Christological battle that erupted after the Enlightenment did not lead any of the great churches of the Reformation (Lutheran, Reformed, Anglican) to annul any of the ancient creeds, or to renounce the Trinitarian and Christological dogmas. Instead, traditional theologians were supported by the creeds of their own churches, whereas liberal theologians resisted the confessional foundation of their own churches. But the battle nowhere resulted in the removal of this foundation.

---

theopaschitism (see §8.5.4).

36. Rahner and Thüsing (1980); see Rahner (1961, 149): "The clearest formulations, the most sanctified formulas, the classic summaries of the church's age-old work in prayer, reflection and wrestling with regard to God's mysteries: these all derive their life from the fact that they are not end but beginning, not aim but means, truths that open the way to the always greater Truth." He also said (1971, 34) that "today, the classic formulas of Christology . . . in a slow process that is just beginning, are gradually—not suppressed or replaced to be sure but certainly—completed by other formulations, which for us today are perhaps easier to understand, and which more clearly exclude certain mistakes, for which we today are rightly sensitive, than the classic formulas did on their own."
37. Kasper (1976).
38. Runia (1992, 38–53) mentions Piet Schoonenberg, Edward Schillebeeckx, and Hans Küng.
39. Runia (1992, 54–68) mentions Ellen Flesseman-van Leer (see 1985), Hendrikus Berkhof, and Simon Schoon (see 1991).
40. Bloesch (1997, 69–70).

3.4 New Interests
3.4.1 The Jesus Seminar

The New Testament scholars engaged in the Third Quest are interested not primarily in the classical redemptive facts but in Jesus' *self-understanding*. What did he believe and preach about himself? This is because there must be some continuity between Jesus' self-understanding and the way the early church understood him. To be sure, theologians still believe that there is an important difference between the two: Jesus preached the kingdom of God, and the early church preached Jesus, as some like to say. The *preacher* Jesus became the *preached* Jesus. The believing Jesus became an object of believing. Yet, the continuity turned out to be much stronger and more important than people had assumed.

In the Anglo-Saxon world, the liberals took up the gauntlet especially in the Jesus Seminar, founded in 1985 by Robert W. Funk. This is a large group of New Testament scholars searching for the historical Jesus, in particular, for the things he supposedly *really* said,[41] *really* did,[42] and *really* taught.[43] The aim is to liberate Jesus from the dogmatic prisons in which he is confined: this pale, bloodless, iconic Jesus compares poorly with the raw reality of the true Jesus.[44] This real Jesus was supposedly a philosophical teacher of Greek wisdom; the Jesus Seminar accuses the Synoptic writers of having invented the myth of the Jewish Jesus.

In addition to Funk, other important representatives of the Jesus Seminar are John Dominic Crossan[45] and Marcus Borg.[46] All of them began with what British scholar James D. G. Dunn rightly called a questionable starting point: it is sim-

---

41. Funk and Hoover (1993).
42. Funk (1998).
43. Funk (1999; see also 1996; 1998; 2002). For a critical analysis, see Witherington (1997, 42–57, 272–76).
44. Funk (1996, 300).
45. Crossan (1991, 1995a, 1995b).
46. Borg (1987; 1994a; 1994b; 1998); see also the debate between Borg and Wright (1999); regarding Borg, see Witherington (1997, 93–108).

ply erroneous to believe that the real Jesus must necessarily be disconnected from faith, in contrast with the Jesus of the Gospels—this in spite of the fact that it is only through the faith of the first disciples that we can obtain any knowledge of Jesus.[47] Therefore, the scientific findings of the Jesus Seminar have been fiercely opposed by Evangelical authors.[48] In previous decades, brave defenders of the Evangelical approach to the New Testament have included scholars Charles F. D. Moule, Graham N. Stanton, and I. Howard Marshall.[49] Quite fascinating is the sympathetic-critical way Marcus Borg and N. T. Wright have subjected one another's Christology to a comparative analysis.[50]

The Christologies of New Testament scholars and systematic theologians from the nineties, such as Raymond Brown, John Macquarrie, Martin Hengel, I. Howard Marshall, Nils Alstrup Dahl (2001), Markus Bockmuehl, Robert Stein, Hans Schwarz, Klaus Berger, John Cochrane O'Neill, N. T. Wright, J. van Bruggen, A. van de Beek, Ben Witherington III, Darrell L. Bock, and Sung Wook Chung,[51] differ widely from each other. Many of them, however, exhibit a new trend: no longer emphasizing the differences among the Gospels, but their agreement.

3.4.2 Old Things in a New Garment

Several of the New Testament scholars just mentioned are unafraid to defend Trinitarianism and the two-natures doc-

---

47. Dunn (2005, 22).
48. Wilkins and Moreland (1995); Johnson (1996); Wright (1996a); Witherington (1997); Wright in Borg and Wright (1999); Dunn (2003; 2005).
49. Moule (1977); Marshall (1977; 1978a; 1978b; 1990a; 1990b); Stanton (1989; 1995).
50. Borg and Wright (1999).
51. Marshall (1990a; 1990b); Macquarrie (1990; 2003); Dunn (1990a; 1990b; 2003; 2005); Dahl (1991); Bockmuehl (1994); Brown (1994a); Farmer (1994); Hengel (1995); O'Neill (1995); Stein (1996); Van Bruggen (1998; 1999); Wright (1996a; 1996b; 2003); Bloesch (1997); Witherington (1997); Van de Beek (2002a); Schwarz (1998); Bock (2002); Berger (2004); Chung (2005); cf. also De Jonge (1990; 1997).

trine. On the contrary, the insight has gained ground that first-century Christology was far more unified, and connected far more closely with the New Testament, than people had thought for a long time. John O'Neill wrote that the dogmas concerning the Trinity and the incarnation were not a late development in Christian thought, ideas that some had claimed were surreptitiously introduced into the church. The core of Christology, which survived more than nineteen centuries, could have been set forth within fifteen years after the death and resurrection of Christ.[52] Raymond Brown defended the general claim that a moderate, conservative Christology can garner the broadest agreement among scholars.[53]

The same can be said today. Of course, we neither can nor wish to return to pre-Enlightenment views in a reactionary and ahistorical way. We have no other option than to move forward. At the same time, we find in these postmodern times that the Enlightenment paradigm, with its emphasis on universal reason and its related anti-supernaturalism, is clearly obsolete. Church attendance may be less than in earlier centuries, but religion is far from gone.[54] To be sure, in most cases today's religion is not the old, familiar, orthodox Christian faith, but there is room again even for this. Let's draw the lessons from the past. One lesson might be that, if the liberal Enlightenment approach had triumphed, this would have led ultimately to the darkening of Christianity, and thus to its end. In other words, if it continues to adhere to what it believed thousands of years ago, Christianity will survive, not only in non-Western countries (Africa, China, South America) but also in Europe and North America. But it will have to do this in a self-critical way, understanding the challenges of our times.[55]

In his comprehensive study, New Testament scholar Klaus

---

52. Macquarrie (1990, 44–47); Dahl (1991, 167); Hengel (1995, 389).
53. Brown (1994a, 102).
54. See, e.g., Van de Donk et al. (2006).
55. Cf. Van de Beek (2006, 253).

Berger came to the following conclusions with respect to the reliability of the Gospels.[56]

(1) In light of the Dead Sea Scrolls, many facts in the Gospels must be designated as historically sure, and thus as true—many more than people would have thought possible in the first half of the twentieth century.

(2) Whereas people formerly viewed everything attested by the New Testament alone, and not by sources outside of it, as untrue, many today assume the New Testament stories are historically true until the opposite has been demonstrated.

(3) When Gospel writers report the same things in different ways this by itself is no reason to doubt the historical correctness of the things described.

(4) The Gospels' time of origin is closer to Jesus' earthly life than was formerly believed.

(5) The (what Berger calls) "mystical" stories (visions, appearances of angels, etc.) do not necessarily plead against the historicity of the Gospels.

3.4.3 New Elements

Such a plea for the basic historicity of the Gospels received support from an unexpected and unsuspected corner, namely, from orthodox Jewish circles. The well-known rabbi David Flusser (see §1.7.4) is one of the scholars who in recent decades have led us back to the historical Jesus. He clearly stated that the Jesus sketched in the Synoptic Gospels is the historical Jesus, and not some "kerygmatic Christ."[57] Even a Jewish thinker like Flusser was of the opinion that we are allowed to return to our earlier view, namely, that the portrait of Jesus in the Gospels is theologically tinted and incomplete, but it is definitely historically reliable.

At the same time, we should acknowledge not only that the ancient message must continue to be preached, but also

---

56. Berger (2004, 41–52).
57. Flusser (2007, 21–22).

that entirely new Christian accents are coming to the fore. These should be given room. We may not change the essence of the message, but that does not mean that the message as we have known it thus far has contained the *entire* Christian truth. Let me give some examples of new accents.

(1) The Jewishness of Christ and of his message, in which there were elements that were often neglected until now, such as Jesus' attitude toward the Mosaic Torah.

(2) The relationship between Jesus and the great renewals in the pneumatological domain.[58]

(3) The biblical significance of the kingdom of God, not only in its spiritual meaning but also in connection with the spiritual as well as physical restoration of Israel (this matter will be discussed in later volumes).

(4) The testimony about Jesus in the Bible as compared with the testimony about him in the Koran (see §1.6), which is important for our dialogue with Muslims.

(5) In addition, there is interest in Jesus' possible significance for the liberation movement, the environmental movement, the feminist movement, and neo-Gnosticism (see §1.5). To be honest, in these domains we expect fewer great and lasting results. Yet, these and other matters may be viewed as mines to be tested to see whether they produce any mineral ore, and if so, what kind and how much.

The interests of recent Christology have been so varied that we can hardly speak of a coherent Third Quest. Craig A. Evans rightly stated that the so-called Third Quest for the historical Jesus is characterized by a diversity of portraits: Jesus the rabbi, Jesus the sage, Jesus the prophet, Jesus the philosopher (perhaps of the Cynical school), Jesus the saint, and Jesus the Messiah.[59]

Richard A. Burridge and Graham Gould distinguished two lines in modern research: the first is the Jesus Seminar,

---

58. See *EDR* 1, especially chapters 1 and 2, and the next volume in this series.
59. In Bockmuehl (2001, 11).

which presents Jesus as the Greek wisdom teacher; the second presents Jesus as the Jewish rabbi.[60] In addition to these, Veli-Matti Kärkkäinen[61] pointed to a third approach, the more traditional conservative one, as presented, for instance, by Charles F. D. Moule.[62]

James Dunn preferred to restrict the name "Third Quest" to the search for Jesus *the Jew*.[63] In a broader sense, we can assign to the Third Quest especially the new interest in the Jewish roots of Jesus and his doctrine (see §§1.7, 3.5, 13.1, and 13.2). The study of the Dead Sea Scrolls, which put to an end the idea of a rigid, uniform Judaism, has been tremendously significant for this Quest. The study of the apocryphal and pseudepigraphic Jewish literature has put on display the multifaceted Judaism of the time. We now know Second Temple Judaism as a multicolored and multilayered religion, with which Jesus and the "sect of the Nazarenes" (Acts 24:5) were quite at home. What we call Christianity began as a Jewish sect.

At the same time, we must beware of this Judaizing of Jesus. Sometimes, the emphasis on the Jewishness of Jesus' person and teaching was so strong that the work of redemption that he came to accomplish shifted into the background.[64] What Jesus was and said were thought to be more important than what he came to do here on earth. In such presentations, he is the Jewish rabbi or wisdom teacher rather than the promised Redeemer.

3.5 Misunderstandings in the Earlier Quests
3.5.1 First Misunderstanding

To me, some of the most fascinating contributions during the Third Quest have been those of the New Testament scholar James D. G. Dunn. I refer especially to his great work *Christol-*

---

60. Burridge and Gould (2004, 17, 32–34).
61. Kärkkäinen (2003, 106).
62. Moule (1977).
63. Dunn (2005, 62); cf. Duvekot (1998).
64. Cf. Van de Beek (2002b, 264).

ogy in the Making, volume 1: *Jesus Remembered*, of which the essence can be found in a concise collection of lectures, entitled *A New Perspective on Jesus: What the Quest for the Historical Jesus Missed*.[65] This subtitle is remarkable: Dunn wished to identify elements that previous quests for the historical Jesus had overlooked. Here is my summary of Dunn's findings.

His first point was that the "Easter Gulf" (see §2.9.2 above), imagined to exist between the pre-Easter Jesus of history and the post-Easter Christ of faith, is an illusion because the disciples' faith in Jesus did not originate after Easter.[66] Christianity could arise through the lasting impression that Jesus made upon his followers from the beginning. This was an impression that shaped the Jesus-tradition from the beginning, so that long before Easter reliable stories about him were being disseminated. The claim is incorrect that Jesus' statements began to circulate for the first time after Easter, when they supposedly were shaped to a lesser or greater extent by the church's theology. On the contrary, they originated a considerable time before Easter with the disciples, indeed, with Jesus himself.[67] As an example, Dunn mentioned the ongoing discussion concerning the so-called "Q-material" (the material

---

65. Dunn (2003; 2005).
66. Dunn (2005, chapter 1: "The First Faith"). For instance John P. Meier (1991, 167–95), who has extensively investigated the criteria to determine what came from Jesus and what did not, began with the (unproven and improbable) assertion criticized by Dunn that the Gospels are permeated with the Easter faith of the early church (167). Raymond Brown (1994a) and Martin Hengel (1995) emphasized, like Dunn, that the post-Easter origin of Christology is inconceivable if its essential elements had not been accepted by the disciples before Easter; cf. Ratzinger (2007, 303): "Where is post-Easter faith supposed to have come from if Jesus laid no foundation for it before Easter? Scholarship overplays its hand with such reconstructions."
67. Dunn discussed (2005, chapter 2: "Behind the Gospels") the enormous significance, as well as the reliability, along with the proper character of the oral tradition that went from Jesus to the first written sources, a fact that, because of their literary mindset, the Questers have largely neglected; the nature of the Synoptic Gospel tradition might have been largely determined during the oral period, and before it was written down in Mark and Q (58; cf. the Appendix).

that supposedly belonged to the hypothetical Q-document), which seems strongly Galilean in nature, and which lacked a story of Jesus' suffering. The most obvious explanation of this, according to Dunn, is *not* that the Q-material originated *after* Easter within some "Q-community," but that it originated in Galilee, and received its ultimate shape before Jesus' death.[68]

3.5.2 Second Misunderstanding

A second misunderstanding that Dunn encountered in the Quests for the historical Jesus is that this figure must necessarily *differ* from the Jesus of faith, of the kerygma. According to Dunn, the historical Jesus is not a kind of objective scientific Jesus that, as a kind of "thing-in-itself" (Kant's *Ding an sich*), can be identified *behind* the Jesus of the Gospels and *behind* the Jesus of the Christian faith. A kind of genuine Jesus cannot be isolated from the traditions about him, which from the outset were *faith* traditions. We possess no other Jesus than the Jesus of faith; only a positivistic scientific view of science can claim that *therefore* we cannot know Jesus as he really was.

The only historical Jesus we know is the Jesus who, from the beginning, made the overwhelming impression upon people that constituted the beginning of the Jesus-tradition. The notion of a fifth Gospel propagated by Martin Kähler, and long after him, the Jesus Seminar—the supposedly sci-

---

68. Ratzinger (2007, xxii) pointed out that, about twenty years after Jesus' death, we find in the Christ hymn of Phil. 2:6–11 a fully developed Christology, and wondered how this is possible. The notion of theology produced by the church does not help here at all: "How could these unknown groups be so creative? How were they so persuasive and how did they manage to prevail? Isn't it more logical, even historically speaking, to assume that the greatness came at the beginning, and that the figure of Jesus really did explode all existing categories and could only be understood in the light of the mystery of God?" (xxii–xxiii). Ratzinger's convincing conclusion: "The anonymous community is credited with an astonishing level of theological genius—who were the great figures responsible for inventing all this? No, the greatness, the dramatic newness, comes directly from Jesus; within the faith and life of the community it is further developed, but not created. In fact, the 'community' would not even have emerged and survived at all unless some extraordinary reality had preceded it" (324).

entifically sound Gospel of theologians and historians—is an illusion. Or to put it another way: it is the gospel of another kind of "believer": modern rationalists, scientists, or anti-supernaturalists. There *is* no Jesus of history distinct, or even radically different, from the Christ of faith. The only Christ we know is the "Christ of faith," regardless of what "faith glasses" we are wearing.

As James Dunn put it, the more that the Synoptic portrait of Jesus is reconstructed, the more it must express the agendas of the individual Questers.[69] That is to say, the greater the distance between the reconstructed portrait of Jesus and the portrait of Jesus in the Gospels, the more evidence we find that various Questers applied their own ideas and ideologies to their portrait.

3.6 Christology among Dutch Theologians

My number of examples is few. I will omit discussion of the Roman Catholic Edward Schillebeeckx,[70] who also began with the distinction between the historical Jesus and the kerygmatic Christ, and for whom the central element in his portrait of Jesus was Jesus' unique Abba experience. My examples are three Protestant authors from the closing decades of the twentieth century.

3.6.1 Hendrikus Berkhof

Many theologians have abandoned the ancient Chalcedonian formula, among them Hendrikus Berkhof, who rejected what he called the "static notions of 'nature'." Concerning the "duality of the structure of the being of Jesus' person" he said that the New Testament "does not speak of the two structures as being found statically on top of each other but *as historically following each other*."[71] Remarkably, in order to support this

---

69. Ibid., 34.
70. In particular, Schillebeeckx (1979).
71. Berkhof (1986, 292; italics added). This is an example of what Erickson (1985, 679) called the replacement of a metaphysical Christology by a historical Christology.

claim he referred to some irrelevant passages (Acts 2:22-36; Rom. 1:3-4; Phil. 2:8-11; 1 Tim. 3:16; Heb. 5:7-9). This is quite amazing, for apparently Berkhof did not see, or wish to acknowledge, the fundamental difference between Jesus' deity *from eternity* and Jesus' glorification *as Man, after* he had accomplished his work. This is all the more amazing because in particular Philippians 2:5-7 ("being in the form of God," KJV) and 1 Timothy 3:16 ("He was manifested in the flesh") are *based* upon Jesus' deity (God became Man).

This confusion continues when he writes:

> The NT shows us a history in which the man Jesus, because of his total obedience even to death, may share in the life and rule of God. In this history Jesus transcends the boundaries of what we understand by the "human." However, he does not lay aside the "human"; but on the way of a progressive obedience and glorification he exhibits more and more new and to us unknown dimensions of the divinely intended humanity.[72]

Apparently, Berkhof's view involved the deification of the Man Jesus, not the incarnation of the divine Logos in Jesus.

At the same time, Berkhof warned that he who wishes to express this deification in words, "comes understandably and dangerously [!] close to dualistic-sounding formulations like 'God-man,' and 'two natures.'"[73] Here, indeed, Chalcedon is being pushed entirely to the background, and nothing seems to be left of the divine nature of Christ. Yet, matters are not so simple, for Berkhof had also said:

> There are thus not two subjects in Jesus, but his human "I" is, out of free will, fully and exhaustively permeated by the "I" of God; and in virtue of this permeation he becomes the perfect instrument of the Father. This completed covenant relationship signifies a new *union of God and man*, far beyond our experience

---

72. Ibid.
73. Ibid.

and imagination.⁷⁴

However, what this "permeating" means *in concreto* is evident from the following: "after much inner turmoil and struggle, [Jesus] ends by fully participating in the life of the Father and in his work in the world." God "permeates [the human person of Jesus] entirely with his Spirit, that is, with himself."⁷⁵ In this respect, Jesus apparently differs from each believer only in terms of degree. What is entirely proper to Jesus is, in Berkhof's view, not expressed by Jesus' deity, but in names like Lord, Savior, and Firstborn. Indeed, as I said, there is here no room for an incarnation of God, of God becoming Man; the Word that became flesh is nothing but God's creative speaking, which received form in the Man Jesus.⁷⁶

Berkhof no longer had room for classical Trinitarianism, Christ's pre-existence, and the virgin birth. Yet, his theology could not simply be classified as liberal theology, at least not nineteenth-century liberal theology. He did maintain a divine mystery of Christ, which no historical research could grasp, and which such research could not argue away. But this divine mystery never pertained to Jesus' own divinity.⁷⁷ For Berkhof, human thought ruled supreme over the New Testament, many of whose statements were simply laid aside, and from which only what suited Berkhof's Christology was considered valid. Of course, to a certain extent *every* Christology is the construct of its theologian or theological school. But the difference between a construct resulting from one's (largely naturalistic) biases, and one drawn from an unabridged Bible, is quite significant.⁷⁸

In Berkhof's thought, the relationship between theology

---

74. Berkhof (1986, 291 [emphasis added]).
75. Ibid.
76. Ibid., 294.
77. Runia (1992, 61–62); Berkouwer (1954, 327–31) warns against speaking of a "mystery of Christ," which only involves covering up a certain heresy.
78. See the critical evaluation by Beker and Hassclaar (1981, 241–49).

and culture played a great role.⁷⁹ Theology should not sever itself from the culture within which it is constructed, but neither may it merge with that culture.⁸⁰ Within Christology as well, Berkhof placed heavy emphasis on the significance of Christ for the entire culture, as was already evident from his book *Christ the Meaning of History*.⁸¹ The salvation realized in Christ is not salvation for the soul alone, but for the world, for our culture. Hence his interest in ecumenism; for years, he was the chairman of the Dutch Council of Churches, and he also held several positions within the World Council of Churches. By strongly emphasizing the *earlier* redemptive-historical significance of Israel, Berkhof also demonstrated his great interest in Jesus the *Jew*. "Jesus was a Jew, and that is no coincidence," he once wrote in a newspaper article.⁸² At the same time, the power of this remark is reduced by Berkhof's failure to acknowledge any contemporary or future redemptive-historical role for Israel.

3.6.2 Jakob van Bruggen

The third series of the well-known New Testament commentary (Dutch *Commentaar op het Nieuwe Testament*, edited by Jakob van Bruggen) contains two perspectival volumes authored by the editor, now in English: *Christ on Earth: The Gospel Narratives as History* and *Jesus the Son of God: The Gospel Narratives as Message*.⁸³

It makes quite a difference whether a Christological work is written by a New Testament scholar like Van Bruggen, or a systematic theologian like Berkhof, or Wentsel,⁸⁴ or Van de Beek. From the latter group, we may expect extensive expositions concerning the development and the present status of the doctrine of the Trinity and the doctrine of two-natures.

---

79. See the summary by Van de Beek (2006, 157–62).
80. Berkhof (1990, chapter 1).
81. Berkhof (1966).
82. Quoted in Van de Beek (2006, 162).
83. Van Bruggen (1998) and Van Bruggen (1999).
84. Wentsel (1981, chapters 9–10).

In Berkouwer's treatise on Christology, he deals exclusively with these matters;[85] he does not deal at all with literary and historical criticism of the four Gospels, nor with the life and teaching of Jesus, which are the very matters that Van Bruggen does discuss.

In the face of many liberal Christologies produced for Christians, Van Bruggen's Christology is a refreshing exception. He takes seriously the literary and historical dimensions of the Gospels. Nonetheless, I observe a deficit in Van Bruggen's work, for one may wonder whether, in describing the life of Jesus,[86] he engaged inadequately with the critical literature on this subject. For instance, little is written about the Quests for the historical Jesus and the relationship of the latter to the kerygmatic Christ. His volume *Christ on Earth* is in fact a kind of commentary on a harmony of the Gospels. As one volume in a New Testament commentary series, this may be understandable; but as an introduction to the commentaries on the various Gospels, we would expect a much more extensive treatment of the many questions with which New Testament scholarship has been occupied in the last century, as well as questions in the field of systematic theology.[87]

Van Bruggen's volume, *Jesus the Son of God*, deals with, among other things, the *person* of Jesus according to the four Gospels, makes up somewhat for the omission. But his Christological core chapters (4 and 5) contain only fifty-eight pages,[88] whereas Van Bruggen devotes no fewer than sixty pages to discussing the Jews from the first century, in particular the Pharisees.[89] I perceive a clear imbalance here.

Van Bruggen devoted only eight pages to Jesus' teaching in §3.2, apart from references distributed throughout the oth-

---

85. Berkouwer (1954).
86. Van Bruggen (1998, especially chapter 4).
87. To a large extent, this criticism is also true for comparable works like those by Dwight Pentecost (1981) and Darrell Bock (2002).
88. Van Bruggen (1999, 93–150).
89. Ibid., 13–35, 236–72.

er chapters, especially chapter 7. In this very short treatise on Jesus' teaching, Jesus' preaching of the kingdom of God rightly takes a central position. But unfortunately, Van Bruggen concluded:

> Thus the fact that the concept of "the kingdom of God" is not central in the later development of the teaching of the church is consonant with the flow of history. The early church and the Reformation clearly understood the striking way in which Jesus dealt with the concept of the kingdom of God when they placed at the center the satisfaction by means of Jesus' atoning death and the salvation through God's only Son. Today the gospel of the kingdom of God consists in bestowing the power of faith in Christ. This faith preserves us and lets us inherit the future. . . .[90]

Let us notice what happens here. Jesus' emphasis upon eschatology merges entirely into Van Bruggen's soteriology. This may be in line with Augustine, but not with the New Testament, as I hope to show in later volumes in this series. Consider for now this one point: the book of Acts mentions the kingdom of God eight times, and most letters in the New Testament refer to it. After Jesus' resurrection, the kingdom of God was the core of his message (Acts 1:3), and Paul's message was not only "repentance toward God and faith in our Lord Jesus Christ" (20:21) and "the gospel of the grace of God" (v. 24), but also going about "proclaiming the kingdom" (v. 25). He was taken captive in Thessalonica, not for preaching Jesus the Redeemer but Jesus the King (17:7). Van Bruggen might have concluded instead that the message of the kingdom of God became lost in the ancient church and in the Reformation.

In summary, we can say that these two volumes by Van Bruggen are of great value for the study of the Gospels, but their contribution to modern Christology is limited. Even though Van Bruggen is a New Testament scholar and not a

---

90. Ibid., 83.

systematic theologian, we may regret that he missed opportunities here. As quoted from Howard Marshall in chapter 1 (note 144) with regard to Donald Guthrie: the reader, confused by the historical questions, did not receive any help with his problems from Guthrie, and the insights that could be given through the application of historical methods were lacking.

3.6.3 Abraham van de Beek

In the Christology of systematic theologian Abraham van de Beek[91] we encounter all the essentials of early Christian Christology: Christ as the eternal Son of the Father, the incarnation of the Logos, the virgin birth, and the bodily resurrection. The things one might still wish to criticize are more marginal—fascinating for connoisseurs, but no longer touching upon the core of his view. As A. A. van Houwelingen et al. write:

> The approach of Van de Beek is high. He begins with Jesus as the church fathers taught him and as was decided at the Ecumenic Councils: Jesus, truly Son of God, according to his nature and his personality. Everything depends on this, for it is only in this way that we will get to know something about God himself. However, that high Christological approach ends low: with humanity in its misery and grief. The approach with regard to God is not that of humans ascending to God, for imitation, but of God himself who most fundamentally as Man carries the world.[92]

As an academic systematic theologian—and thus more than a traditionalist—Van de Beek enjoys writing occasionally in a somewhat provocative way. For instance, he writes about Zephyrinus, who said: "I know but one God, Christ Jesus, and apart from him no other who was born and suffered," to which Van de Beek responded: "That did not sit well with many. Yet I am of the opinion that we can not make

---

91. Van de Beek (1980; 2002a; see also 2002b); cf. Kuitert, Van de Beek et al. (1999).
92. Kuitert, Van de Beek, et al. (1999, 9).

do with less in Christian theology."[93] However, ultimately Zephyrinus was a monophysite and a theopaschite, and such thinkers are not our primary sources for constructing Christian theology.

Here is another provocative statement: "Can someone be truly human without this pain [of one's own consciousness of sin]? In short: is not sin so quintessentially a part of being human that someone without sin is not really human? In brief, does sin not belong so essentially to the human being that he who does not sin cannot be truly human? Apollinaris of Laodicea . . . helped me the most with this conundrum"[94] — though later he distanced himself somewhat from Apollinaris.[95] The way he defended the *anhypostasis*, and claimed that the Chalcedonian formula tilted toward two natures, Van de Beek showed that on the monophysitism–Nestorianism continuum, he leaned toward the former side. But this is not all that alarming, since any theologian who wants to oppose him will risk tilting toward the opposite side.

We should note further that Van de Beek resisted a statement such as this one: "Christ suffered as a human being and healed as God. As a human being Christ wept, and as God Christ was raised from the dead."[96] I agree with Van de Beek's resistance, although perhaps not quite for the same reason. I find it essential to emphasize that Christ healed and raised the dead also *as Man* — in the power of the Holy Spirit — because it was only in this way that he could become an example for all believers after him (cf. Matt. 10:1, 8; Mark 16:17-18; Luke 10:9; John 14:12).[97]

Van de Beek exposed in a refreshing way how the Jesus of history has been played off against the Christ of faith, and he placed this phenomenon within the wider framework of

---

93. Van de Beek (2002a, 14–15).
94. Ibid., 41–42.
95. Ibid., 108–109.
96. Ibid., 84.
97. See extensively *EDR* 1.

spiritualizing:

> Whenever we have problems with the Great Flood we declare it to be a theological flood; we make Jonah a theological Jonah, and the fish a theological fish. Likewise, the virgin Mary becomes a theological virgin and the resurrection a theological resurrection. Before long everything has become theological and no longer historical. This used to be called "spiritualizing" the matter. I am not saying that everything in the Bible must be read in a literal and historical manner. However, we can not simply dismiss the historical problem. For the story of God has to do with concrete people and their history.[98]

I am less happy with the third part of Van de Beek's book ("Jesus in Every Culture"), specifically with his provocative way of writing about pagan ancestral veneration.[99] We find many problematic phrases, calling Jesus the "first ancestor," and ancestors "indirect mediators" between God and humanity, but we find few Bible references. This is not the strongest part of the book. The same is true for what he says about evangelicals,[100] who, like Christian existentialists, do not sever meaning from facts, but consider facts themselves to be meaning.[101] In my opinion, only thoughtless Christians do this. I recognize, however, that many Evangelicals defend the self-evident nature of redemptive facts, display a frequent lack of wonder, and lack sensitivity for the paradoxical, for the "impossibility" of Christ. So I do understand why he writes: "As for my own stance, I would like to incorporate a much greater uncertainty at every turn in theological thinking. We are searching for the right words and our faith is tested. For we believe that God acts in [human] history yet we do not know how."[102] Though this may be a bit exaggerated, theology is and remains a form of groping and stammering.

---

98. Van de Beek (2002a, 152).
99. Ibid., 213–226.
100. Ibid., 256–59.
101. Ibid., 256–57.
102. Ibid., 259.

In his book, *De kring rond de Messias*, Van de Beek made interesting Christological comments as well. Consider this single example, where he refers to the rise of liberal theology:

> It is only when the balance tips and Christians begin to think that they should improve the world through their good works, beginning with themselves, and thus forget that with Christ they have died to the world [Gal. 6:14], the tide of orthodoxy turns. This tipping of the balance is almost always linked with a change of Christology, in which it is denied that in Christ God himself became flesh.[103]

3.7 Is Chalcedon Obsolete?
3.7.1 A Better Formula?

Three important theological questions emerge from the very concise summary of the most recent developments provided above.

(1) To what extent is the formula of Chalcedon—"one person, two natures"—still useful today? With regard to the terminology used, can we speak of "natures" without ending up in Greek metaphysics? Does such talk of two natures hide a dangerous dualism? With regard to the Christological reality denoted by the terminology, can we still speak of the divinity, or deity of Jesus today?

(2) What constituted Jesus' self-awareness, that is, what did he believe concerning himself (e.g., that he was the Messiah of Israel, the Son of God, the God of Man)? Is there indeed a contrast between Jesus the preacher and Jesus the One preached, between Jesus the believer and Jesus the One believed?

(3) What is the significance of the facts that Jesus was a Jew, understood himself to be such, and presented himself as such? What does it mean for his relationships with fellow Jews, and for the similarities and differences between his teaching and that of contemporary Judaism? Were the First

---
103. Van de Beek (2002b, 242–43).

and Second Quests right in emphasizing the differences, or the Third Quest in emphasizing the similarities?

Regarding the first question, it is undoubtedly true that the Chalcedonian formula uses terms (Gk. *prosōpon*, Lat. *persona*; Gk. *physis*, Lat. *natura*) that are suspect because, though they do occur in the New Testament, theology has filled them with Hellenist content (see §§2.3.2 and 2.8.2 above). We would rather limit ourselves to the actual intention of Chalcedon, and state that the one Man Jesus Christ was and is not only a perfect Man but also perfect God. This is the way it has been handed down to us in this related formula: *vere deus, vere homo*, "truly God, truly Man." But can we indeed limit ourselves to this? Is this sufficient to fend off all heresy, ranging from monophysitism to Nestorianism?

It reminds us of the complaint of Augustine, and later the Reformers: concerning the mystery of the Trinity, one would prefer to say nothing more than that there is only one God, *and* that the Father is God, the Son is God, and the Holy Spirit is God, *and* that Father, Son, and Spirit are not identical.[104] However—they added—heretics force us to say more. But, in doing this, we are speaking about a mystery where every extra word leads us further away as well. This is the tension we face. Heretics say more than they can account for, but to answer them we are forced to say more than we might be able to account for. Thus, Chalcedon felt compelled to say more than *vere deus, vere homo*, in order to confront Apollinaris, Nestorius, Eutyches, and many more. In the end, though we may not be sure that "one person, two natures" is the best way of speaking, and though we meet various objections against this formulation, *the point is that we have no better formulation in hand*—if we wish to proclaim, together with Chalcedon, that Jesus was a true Man, with a human body, a human soul, and a human spirit, and at the same time truly God, the eternal Logos who became flesh (John 1:14), the eternal Son of God—

---

104. See Ouweneel (*RT* II/1:§9.2.1).

co-equal with the Father—manifested in human flesh (cf. 1 Tim. 3:16).

3.7.2 Duality and Dualism

Berkouwer rightly remarked that, on the one hand, every attempt to improve Chalcedon came into conflict with

> what the church intended, namely, to confess that Christ was truly man, and not to offer a scientific formulation of the mystery of the Incarnation. It is surely no sign of traditionalism to take more pleasure in the Christological conflict of the first few centuries than in nineteenth-century efforts to make the unity of Jesus Christ humanly conceivable.[105]

On the other hand, it also goes too far to assert, for instance with A. G. Honig, that the doctrine of Chalcedon had been formulated already "to its full extent": "On this point, the doctrinal development has progressed as far as was possible." Honig added, "I do not hesitate to state that the doctrine of the Person of the Mediator, as it was established by the church, is not open for further development."[106] This is strong language! Perhaps we ourselves will not surpass Chalcedon either, although we do postulate, with strong qualifications, one divine-human nature in Christ (cf. §2.3). However, asserting *a priori* that the Chalcedonian doctrine "is not open for further development" suggests that one can envision all Christological thinking until Christ's return.

There is no doubt that the formula of Chalcedon contains a certain duality (God and Man in one person), but a *duality* is not automatically a *dualism*. That would happen only if the divine and the human were positioned antithetically, over against each other, such that we would speak of two persons. True enough, many New Testament passages show a tension between the divine and the human in Jesus, as we will see in the next chapters. But this tension exists already *within the*

---

105. Berkouwer (1954, 71).
106. Honig (1910, 74).

New Testament, and not within the solution offered by Chalcedon. To be sure, the New Testament does not speak of two natures in Jesus. But this silence does not invalidate such a description, as long as we understand it correctly, not in a dualistic or substantialistic way. This way of speaking is the fruit of centuries-long theological reflection, similar to the terms Trinity, substitution, and satisfaction (the latter two referring to the redemptive work of Christ). These terms do not occur in the Bible either, but this does not mean they are wrong.

It cannot be denied that there is a complementary duality, which comes to light in many New Testament passages. Recall the examples of §2.2 above. It is the tension in Mark 13:32 between "the Son" (an obviously divine description) *and* his "not knowing," or in 1 Corinthians 2:8 between "the Lord of glory" *and* his death on the cross, or in Matthew 9:6 between the "Son of Man" (the human *par excellence*) *and* his divine authority to forgive sins, and in John 5:27 between "the Son" (notice the name) who exerts judgment in divine majesty *and* can do so "because he is the Son of Man." If Chalcedon is guilty of espousing a dualism, or a duality, then so too is the New Testament. We find this twoness in the New Testament; it was not invented by the church fathers.

For reasons mentioned earlier (in §2.5.3 above), I am very reluctant to try to clarify this twoness with the help of anthropological parallels. This occurs in the Athanasian Creed: "For as the reasonable soul and flesh is one man: so God and Man is one Christ" (Art. 37). This comparison is heavily freighted with the Greek-substantialistic dualism consisting of the rational soul (Lat. *anima rationalis*) and the material body (see §2.3). Nonetheless, this dualism is encountered in both Luther and Calvin, whereas Abraham Kuyper and Gerrit Berkouwer rightly distanced themselves from it.[107] As a popular analogy used in a sermon, some might find it acceptable, as long as the pastor speaks of soul and body in a philosophically and

---

107. See Berkouwer (1954, 296–97).

theologically responsible way, and rejects the Greek dualism. However, the analogy is theologically worthless; it can lead only to confusion.

3.8 Jesus' Self-Awareness
3.8.1 A Messianic "Secret"?

What did Jesus believe concerning himself? Did he know, or believe, that he was the Messiah of Israel, and/or the Son of God, and/or the Son of Man? Here again, everything depends on the theologian's biases, since it is rather easy simply to declare all statements in which Jesus sees himself as the Messiah, the Son of God, or the Son of Man, to be non-authentic.[108]

An example of this was the ingenious hypothesis of Wilhelm Wrede of more than a century ago.[109] In his work, *The Messianic Secret*, Wrede asserted that it was the early church who began to believe that Jesus was the Messiah of Israel, and was then confronted with the question why this fact did not come to light more clearly during Jesus' life. According to Wrede, the church's reply was that, at his baptism, Jesus had indeed been declared to be the Messiah, and therefore was aware of his Messiahship, but kept this from outsiders as a secret, so that during his life this hardly became known. Especially in Mark, we see how Jesus knew of his Messiahship, but entrusted this secret to his followers alone (1:44; 3:12; 5:43; 7:36; 8:30; 9:9). In opposition to this, Wrede asserted that Jesus *never* presented himself as the Messiah, but this idea was a product of church produced theology, and this idea was subsequently inserted into the life of Jesus in Mark's Gospel.

Wrede the pioneer was followed by form criticism[110] and

---

108. See extensively, Brown (1994a, 73–80) and Hengel (1995, chapter 1) on Jesus' claim of Messiahship; also Brown (1994a, 80–100) on Jesus' claim that he was the Son of God and the Son of Man.
109. Wrede (1971); see R. A. Guelich (*DJG* 521–22).
110. See especially Schmidt (1969); Dibelius (1919); Bultmann (1963); this school has been summarized by Rohde (1968). The aim of form criticism was to trace the literary genres of Jesus' stories and statements, and to relate them to their sociological context (Ger. *Sitz im Leben*).

redaction criticism[111] in reading Mark and the other Gospels in this new way. According to this view, the Gospels are not a source of historical data about Jesus, but a source for the sociological contexts in which the various literary genres originated, and for the editors who collected and shaped the texts. There is a grain of truth in this, as New Testament scholars since Wrede have realized more clearly that in addition to being historiography, Mark is also a work of theology; since the middle of the twentieth century, this insight has been generally accepted.

This is acceptable if this work of historiography is left intact. Therefore, William L. Lane has identified the mistaken presupposition that a literary work could be a primary source for the historical source from which it originated (as form criticism claims), and only a secondary source for the historical matters about which it supplies information. Historical questions are properly asked about the content of early church proclamations, whereas the existence of the four Gospels bears witness to the church's interest in the earthly life of Jesus.[112] In short, a Gospel may claim to tell us the story of Jesus, but form critics claim that this Gospel is instead telling us the story of the source from which it arose. This is like saying that a certain book about the American Revolution hardly tells us anything about this Revolution as such, but instead about the circles from which the book arose.

Wrede's hypothesis was attractive because of its originality, not because of its plausibility. It is pure speculation to say that the early church would have *invented* the idea that Jesus was the Messiah instead of assuming that Jesus himself already knew and testified to this. Of course, expositors must offer a plausible explanation for why Jesus often did not want his miracles to be generally known. However, Wrede's expla-

---

111. The term goes back to Marxsen (1969); its aim was to trace in the biblical texts the possible work of editors, who collected and edited the texts according to their own theological interests.
112. Lane (1974, 7).

nation is certainly not the only possible one, or even the most likely one. For instance, with an unmistakable reference to himself, Jesus asked: "How can the scribes say that the Christ is the son of David?" (Mark 12:35). Why are there so many explicitly Messianic miracles of Jesus in Mark that occurred either in public or more in private without him forbidding the person healed or set free to tell about the miracle (1:21-28, 39; 2:1-12; 3:1-6)? In Mark 15:19-20 we read that Jesus encouraged the man who had been set free of demons: "'Go home to your friends and tell them how much the Lord has done for you, and how he has had mercy on you.' And he went away and began to proclaim in the Decapolis how much Jesus had done for him, and everyone marveled."

In some cases where Jesus silenced the person who was healed or set free, the issue involved not that he was the Messiah but rather that he was the Son of God (3:11-12; 9:7-9). Therefore, Joachim Bieneck preferred to speak of a "Son Secret" rather than of a "Messianic Secret."[113]

In my view, a plausible explanation of the supposed Messianic secret is that Jesus did not wish to draw attention to the signs and miracles as such, but rather to the One who had sent him, as well as to Moses and the prophets who had testified about him.[114] This is because the point of the coming of God's kingdom is not just the Messiah himself, but the salvation that he, on behalf of God, brings to this world. The point was not that he would not have known about his Sonship and Messiahship, but that, to him, that was not where the emphasis should be placed. In other words, we can agree with Johan Verkuyl that ". . . in no way did Jesus make any concessions to the nationalistic Messiah expectation. . . . Therefore he says repeatedly that people should tell no one that he is the Messiah; that is to say, in a rather concealed manner he says yes to the Messiahship, but on his own conditions and those of

---

113. Bieneck (1951, 46–48).
114. Cf. Van de Beek (2002a, 140).

him whom he called Abba, Father."[115] And Raymond Brown wrote that Jesus did not intend to do things that many would associate with the Messiah, such as establishing an earthly kingdom, conquering foreign rulers, and functioning as an earthly ruler himself.[116]

3.8.2 Deceit?

Some say that Jesus never viewed himself as the Messiah,[117] or as the Son of God, or Son of Man, and that these identities were invented by the early church or by the Gospel writers. If this were correct, then the conclusion of Reimarus is inescapable, that the Gospel writers *deceived*. Their Gospels appeared so early after the facts they described that there can be no question of good faith. No matter how pious their intentions, no matter how popular their religious imagination, these do not alter our conclusion. It does not matter how differently than us the early Christians' mind may have functioned, or how great the cultural differences between us. The fact is that, if Jesus never viewed himself as the Messiah or as the Son of God, and those who accompanied him for several years asserted shortly after his departure that he did, they committed something that, in every culture and in every age, is called deceit.

Since Reimarus, theologians have attempted to cover this up in all possible ways, but the fact remains: according to many modern theologians, the Gospels give us not just a colored, theologized portrait of Jesus, but a *false*, if not *deceptive* portrait of him.

It is an inherent contradiction to claim that Jesus could be the Son of God — as Christians believe — without Jesus himself having known this. The Gospels tell us the opposite: already

---

115. Verkuyl (1992, 217).
116. Brown (1994a, 79).
117. Den Heyer (2003, 125) asserted that even though Paul often called Jesus "Christ," he never said that Jesus was *the* Christ (i.e., Messiah). However, in Greek Paul often wrote "*the* Christ" (Gk. *ho Christos*), which most translations render simply as "Christ" (Eph. is a good example).

at twelve years old, Jesus knew about his (heavenly) Father (Luke 2:49). And the thirty-year-old Jesus heard the voice from heaven saying: "You are my beloved Son; with you I am well pleased" (3:22; cf. Matt. 17:5). The Gospels may be theological compositions (see §§5.2.3 and 5.5 and vol. I/1 of this series), but they definitely intended to give us facts ("the things that have been accomplished among us . . . an orderly account," Luke 1:1, 3). They tell us that there was a Man on earth who was addressed even by the devil and the demons as Son of God (Matt. 4:3, 6; 8:29; Mark 3:11; 5:7; Luke 4:3, 9, 41; 8:28), a Man who addressed God as Father (Matt. 11:25 par.; Mark 14:36 par.; John 11:41; 17:1), who referred to himself as the Son of the Father (Matt. 11:27 [cf. 21:37]; Mark 13:32; Luke 10:22; many times in John), who by his followers was recognized as Son of God (Matt. 14:33; 16:16; cf. 27:54; Mark 15:39), and who openly and freely acknowledged before his judges that he was the Son of God (Matt. 26:63-64; cf. 27:43; Mark 14:61-62; Luke 22:70).

In all these statements, there may be traces of the Gospel writers' own theological interpretation of the facts. However, if their descriptions had no kernel of truth, if Jesus did *not* know himself or present himself as the unique Son of God (no matter how far the theological reach of this title may extend with the Synoptic writers), then the Gospel writers are pulling our legs. In that case, they have at most some church historical significance. They may be of some interest for those who wish to search for the *pious portraits* of Jesus that the early church developed, but not for those who wish to know who Jesus *really was*. In that case, the Gospels present to us church *projection*, not divine *revelation*. Then Paul also is deceiving us, or he himself had been deceived, for his portrait of Jesus does not differ essentially from that of the Gospel writers.

Jesus presented himself not only as the Messiah and as the Son of God, but also as the Son of Man. The significance of this goes beyond his being a special Man, or beyond his being human, though some twentieth century scholars wished to interpret the title in this way. The texts clearly show that Jesus was openly alluding to the Son of Man in Daniel 7:13, who is coming on the clouds of heaven. Jesus used this title very often, in speaking both to his own people and to outsiders and opponents, and he sometimes explicitly referred to Daniel 7:13, especially in the expression "coming on the clouds of heaven" (Matt. 24:30; 26:64; Mark 14:62). We will return to this matter in §4.8.

3.9 Jesus' Jewishness
3.9.1 Denial in the First and Second Quests

One of the most remarkable misunderstandings on the part of the earlier Questers was that Jesus' uniquenesses consisted in the things in which he *differed* from his surroundings. Thus, John P. Meier presented as a second criterion to determine what came from Jesus and what did not, the *criterion of discontinuity* (or, *dissimilarity*): considered as authentic were words or acts of Jesus that could not be derived either from Judaism in Jesus' time, or from the early church after him.[118] This means that, from the beginning, the Questers were searching for a non-Jewish Jesus. James Dunn spoke here of "traditional Christian antisemitism," and ascribed it to the supersessionism that had arisen in the second century. Supercessionists taught that the church superseded Israel, replacing it as a spiritual Israel, and standing antithetically over against Judaism.[119] In our own day, this means that people begin their study of Jesus with the serious error that, in his Jewishness, Jesus was different from the other Jews and became the founder of a new religion: Christianity.[120]

This error significantly affected the search for authentic statements of Jesus. Norman Perrin asserted that a statement could be considered authentic if it could be shown that it differed from characteristic accents in ancient Judaism and in the early church.[121] To-

---

118. Meier (1991, 171); he did realize, though, the shortcomings of this criterion: 172–74. Thus also Perrin (1967, 39–43).
119. See extensively, the criticism of Dunn (2005, chapter 3: "The Characteristic Jesus").
120. See extensively, *RT* IV/1a-b on Israel.
121. Perrin (1967, 39); cf. the similar view of Schillebeeckx (1979, 91–95).

day, many New Testament scholars seem to think this way: a saying of Jesus is authentic if it betrays no influence of contemporary Judaism or the Christian post-Easter faith. Not only is this *a priori* a mistaken starting point, but it also led to multiple contradictory and conflicting portraits of the historical Jesus.

Dunn pointed to Jewish scholar Susannah Heschel, who criticized the earlier Questers sharply. She pointed out that Judaism, in its Jewishness, represented a number of qualities associated with everything Christian theologians wished to reject: false religiosity, immorality, legalism, hypocrisy, carnality, seductiveness, dishonesty, and so on.[122] Heschel claimed that liberal theologians painted a picture of first-century Judaism that was as negative as possible in order to elevate Jesus as a unique religious figure, who was sharply opposed to his Jewish surroundings.[123] For instance, she quoted Ernest Renan, who had written that there was nothing essentially Jewish about Jesus, and that after his visit to Jerusalem, Jesus no longer functioned as a Jewish reformer, but as the destroyer of Judaism. Renan said that Jesus was no longer a Jew.[124] And Albrecht Ritschl asserted that Jesus' rejection of Judaism and its Torah sharply demarcated his own teachings from those of the Jews.[125] The truth is, of course, that Jesus never rejected Judaism and the Torah (cf. Matt. 5:17)—he rejected only false religiosity, legalism, hypocrisy, and dishonesty, in whatever form it appeared. (He would be doing the same today if he encountered these things in Christianity.)

According to Dunn, later kerygmatic Christology did not do any better: it was radically opposed to anything Jewish about Jesus. The Second Quest called the Judaism of Jesus' days "late Judaism" (Ger. *Spätjudentum*); this is a remarkable misidentification, since this same Judaism has continued to flourish until the present day. According to critics, this late Judaism was the last Judaism, which prepared the way for the supposedly new religion that Jesus brought. Dunn expressed his dismay that, even after the Holocaust, some

---

122. Heschel (1998, 75 and passim).
123. Ibid., 9, 21.
124. Ibid., 156–57.
125. Ibid., 123.

Christian theologians continued to assert that Jesus had put an end to Judaism.[126] The neo-liberal quest of John Dominic Crossan and Burton Mack, who did acknowledge Jesus' Jewishness, preferred to emphasize the *similarities* between Jesus and Hellenism, and the *differences* between him and his Jewish environment.

3.9.2 Jesus: Meaning and Goal

The Third Quest should not fall into the other extreme, which is the risk faced by Géza Vermes and Ed Sanders.[127] For them, Jesus is *only* a Jew—though a special Jew—and the tensions between him and Pharisaism are minimized, which makes it difficult to understand why the Jewish leaders rejected him and had him executed. Basically, the core question is not at all how Jewish or non-Jewish Jesus was; the point is not what was different about Jesus, but what was characteristic of him. This is what impressed his followers most, whether it was Jewish or less Jewish. Part of this characteristic picture are indubitable facts such as the starting point of Jesus' mission in his encounter with John the Baptist, his main activities in Galilee within the framework of the Judaism of those days, his main message, namely, the kingdom of God, his use of the title "Son of Man," as a description both of his ministry then and of the future kingdom; and so on.

More in general, the statement by K. Schilder is applicable here:

> ... [I]n his works [Jesus] is never understood in isolation from, but definitely also not on the basis of, the time which he spent among the people here on earth. He is indeed known by way of, but not on the basis of, his days, for he dominates, directs, and governs all ages. . . . Neither does the knowledge of Judaism

---

126. Dunn (2005, 61); he referred to Wolfhart Pannenberg and Leonhard Goppelt. A favorable exception was Martin Hengel (1995, 72): "[Jesus'] person and work charge us with the task of a 'whole' *biblical theology*, which in particular is fully conscious of its Jewish heritage, a biblical theology that does not erase the lines between the Old and the New but defines them correctly."
127. For criticism of them, see Witherington (1997, 108–12, and 118–32).

explain him, although (provided that this knowledge produces good results) it will sharpen every exegete's pencil.[128]

Jesus can never be entirely explained from his Jewishness or from the Judaism of his days, just as he cannot be explained from the Hellenism of his day, or from the social or political situation of his day. Jesus is not explained from history or culture, or any -ism, but each history, every culture, and each -ism is ultimately explained from *him*. This is because he is the starting point, foundation, and goal of all history and all culture, as well as the meaning and aim, *or* the refutation, of every -ism. Judaism does not explain Jesus, but Jesus exposes the deepest meaning, root, and goal of Judaism.

Let me close this chapter with two interesting quotations. The first one comes again from K. Schilder:

> We must remember that Jesus has declared himself to be the Christ.[129] This self-declaration (in accordance with, and with reference to, the Scriptures) is accepted on authority by the one and rejected by the other. And this rejection often camouflages itself with the cloak of ignorance. At that point, the complaint runs as follows: He is such a riddle; please allow me to pray the prayer of the ignorant, in order that someday I may know how to determine what qualities can be attributed to this Jesus.
> Some will then themselves construct some Jesus-image or oth-

---

128. Schilder (2016, 32–33).
129. J. Douma has a footnote at this point (ibid., 26n34; expanded by the translators):
"The Dutch clause contains a play on words. It actually says 'as *the* [*de*] and as *the* [*den*] Christ.' The first 'the' (*de* in Dutch) is in the nominative (subject) case and the second (*den* in Dutch) is in the accusative (direct object) case. [The difference cannot be expressed in modern English. Indeed, it is lost in modern Dutch as well.] What Schilder intends to convey with the play on words is this: Jesus, in his capacity and with his authority as Christ (as *de/the* Christ, in the nominative case), explained who he was, namely, the Christ (as *den/the* Christ, in the accusative case). This duality is repeated. Christ's self-declaration is in accordance with the Scriptures (I am *de/the* Christ) and takes place with reference to the Scriptures (they describe *den/the* Christ)."

er. Not the One sent by God, Jesus himself, but a humanly conceived notion of Jesus is then likewise made into a sphinx by those who have not acknowledged him as the Christ. That is not what he is, for his self-declaration is clear enough. But he becomes a sphinx to those who discard what he declares himself to be. Then for those people a riddle is propounded in him, and this riddle is not solved as long as Jesus is acknowledged only as "Jesus.". . . People were able to see the "historical Jesus" with their eyes, but, in order really to know and acknowledge him, faith was needed. The fact that the man Jesus was God's Christ (Messiah), that he was called the son of Joseph, though without having been begotten by him, and so much more than this, remained a matter of faith. . . .[130]

The second quotation comes from Klaus Berger, and is given here as a synopsis of our summary of the history of Christology:

> Many people talk about Jesus but nobody weeps for him. People analyze his words, make him the object of Christology, of their creed. That is quite all right. But the key is the lamentation. This was the case with Mary Magdalene [John 20:11, 13, 15], and also with Peter [Matt. 26:75]. Peter laments after a desperate detour, Mary directly, spontaneously. Jesus was the center of their lives.[131]

What I understand Berger to be saying here is that argumentation belongs to theology, and that is all right. Lamentation belongs to faith. Reasoning about Jesus creates distance; lamenting about him arises from a relationship. Those Christians are poor who only reason about Jesus, but have never wept about the dead Lord, and have no relationship with the living Lord.

---

130. Ibid., 26–27.
131. Berger (2004, 244–45).

Chapter 4
Messianic Hopes in the Tanakh

For to us a child is born,
   to us a son is given;
and the government shall be upon his shoulder,
   and his name shall be called
      Wonderful Counselor,
      Mighty God,
      Everlasting Father,
      Prince of Peace.
Of the increase of his government and of peace
   there will be no end,
on the throne of David and over his kingdom,
   to establish it and to uphold it
with justice and with righteousness
   from this time forth and forevermore.
                      Isaiah 9:6–7

4.1 The Messiological Significance of the Tanakh
4.1.1 The Tanakh and the New Testament

THE TANAKH (WHICH Christians call the Old Testament) is permeated with the expectation of the Messiah,[1] that is, the anointed king from the tribe of Judah, and, as with time became clear, from the house of David. The Messiah is the eschatological king who will receive world dominion, and who will establish peace and righteousness, not only for Israel but for the entire world. If we pass over for a moment Genesis 3:15 (see §4.3.1), we find his first announcement in the blessing of Jacob: "The scepter shall not depart from Judah, nor the ruler's staff from between his feet, until Shiloh comes, and to him [shall be] the obedience of the peoples" (Gen. 49:10 NASB; see §4.3.5).

In the first century of our era, the Messianic expectation among the Jews was universal.[2] Even a Samaritan woman could say, "I know that Messiah is coming. . . . When he comes, he will tell us all things" (John 4:25). The Jewish fisherman Andrew told his brother Simon, "We have found the Messiah," referring apparently to the One they were awaiting (1:42).

According to Christians, the appearance of Jesus in this world was the (partial) fulfillment of this Tanakh Messianic hope, and according to Jews, it was not. This does not change the existence of this Messianic hope as such, and it deserves our full attention. This matter presupposes another question, namely, the relationship between the Tanakh and the New Testament. In the twentieth century, there was much debate on this matter. Not a few theologians underestimated the significance of the Tanakh in comparison with the New Testa-

---

1. Heb. *mashiach*, "anointed," from *m-sh-ch*, "to anoint"; cf. Gk. *christos*, from *chriō*, "to anoint"; see extensively, Schirrmacher (2001); Raymond (2003). In New Testament citations from the Tanakh, I take the liberty of using "Messiah" instead of "Christ."
2. Regarding the Messianic hope (including that of the pagan nations), from the second century before until the second century after the beginning of our era, see Oegema (1991).

ment, or at least they devalued the Messiological exegesis of the Tanakh.[3] For instance, W. E. Vischer strongly defended this exegesis,[4] whereas E. Hirsch viewed the Tanakh only as the proclamation of a legalistic religion, which had supposedly been annulled by Jesus.[5]

In addition to these are others who wish to do justice to the Tanakh, but wish to interpret it by itself, and not through the glasses of the New Testament. For example, the New Testament appeals extensively to the Tanakh to make clear that Jesus is the fulfillment of the Messianic predictions. But this does not mean that in all these quotations the actual grammatical-historical exegesis of the Tanakh passages is presupposed. For instance, in some cases we are dealing with Messianic applications of Tanakh sayings that refer to the Davidic king in general (see Ps. 2:7 and 2 Sam. 7:14 in Heb. 1:5). In other cases, the relationship is even weaker; they involve midrashic (i.e., typological) applications of the Tanakh that could never have come up in straightforward grammatical-historical exegesis (see Hos. 11:1 in Matt. 2:15, and Jer. 31:15 in Matt. 2:18).[6]

However, it is equally true that the exegesis of the Tanakh must never consciously exclude the New Testament's testimony. For instance, it cannot be insignificant to expositors that a Jewish man in Acts 2:25-31 gives a Messianic interpretation of Psalm 16:8-11. Another Jewish man does the same in Hebrews 2:6-9 with respect to Psalm 2:5-7, a third Jewish man gave in John 12:41 a Christological interpretation of Isaiah 6, and a fourth Jewish man in Acts 8:32-35 interpreted Isaiah 53 Messiologically.

---

3. See Berkouwer (1954, chapter 7).
4. Vischer (1935/42).
5. Hirsch (1936); I have tried to refute this underlying error, in Ouweneel (2001a); see also *RT* II/1.
6. The rabbis speak here of a *pesher* interpretation, in which the expositor taps into a deeper layer of the text than the one to which the usual (grammatical-historical) exegesis refers (*pesher* overlaps here with midrash); see also §§4.10.2, 4.10.2, 4.13.1, and 4.13.5.

4.1.2 The Gospels and Paul about the Tanakh

The enormous emphasis of especially the Gospels on the overall Messianic significance of the Tanakh is unmistakable.[7] Jesus himself said, "the Scriptures [i.e., the Tanakh] . . . bear witness about me" (John 5:39), and, "Moses . . . wrote of me" (v. 45). Philip said, "We have found him of whom Moses in the Law and also the prophets wrote, Jesus of Nazareth, the son of Joseph" (John 1:45). And to the Emmaus disciples Jesus said, "'O foolish ones, and slow of heart to believe all that the prophets have spoken! Was it not necessary that the Messiah should suffer these things and [thus] enter into his glory?' And beginning with Moses and all the Prophets, he interpreted to them in all the Scriptures the things concerning himself" (Luke 24:25-27). And somewhat later:

> "These are my words that I spoke to you while I was still with you, that everything written about me in the Law of Moses and the Prophets and the Psalms[8] must be fulfilled." Then he opened their minds to understand the Scriptures, and said to them, "Thus it is written, that the Messiah should suffer and on the third day rise from the dead, and that repentance for the forgiveness of sins should be proclaimed in his name to all nations, beginning from Jerusalem" (vv. 44-47).

So too the apostle Peter wrote: the "Spirit of the Messiah" within the Tanakh prophets "predicted the sufferings of Christ and the subsequent glories" (1 Pet. 1:11).

The apostle Paul also made a direct connection between the Tanakh predictions and the life and sufferings of Jesus: ". . . the utterances of the prophets, which are read every Sabbath, [his enemies] fulfilled them by condemning him. . . . And when they had carried out all that was written of him, they took him down from the tree and laid him in a tomb"

---

7. See C. A. Evans (*DJG* 579-90).
8. This formulation agrees with the Jewish tripartition of the Tanakh: T-N-Kh = *Torah*, *Nevi'im* (= prophets) and *K'tuvim* (= [other] writings, of which the Psalms are the first and largest book).

(Acts 13:27, 29). Thus, Paul could testify that, during his entire ministry, he had been "saying nothing but what the prophets and Moses said would come to pass: that the Messiah must suffer and that, by being the first to rise from the dead, he would proclaim light both to our people and to the Gentiles" (Acts 26:22-23). And when the Ethiopian eunuch asked whether the prophet in Isaiah 53 was speaking about himself or about somebody else, "Philip opened his mouth, and beginning with this Scripture he told him the good news about Jesus" (Acts 8:34-35).

Nowhere does the New Testament speak of the Tanakh in a critical way; on the contrary: "Scripture [i.e., the Tanakh] cannot be broken" (John 10:35). Nowhere is there any suggestion of a conflict between the New Testament and the Tanakh.[9] With regard to the Tanakh, the New Testament has at least a threefold function: it is the fulfillment, *and* the continuation, *and* the interpretation of the Tanakh. Berkouwer said of this Christian (read: Messianic) character of the Tanakh: "One can boil down the church's credo regarding the Scriptures into the statement that it is no anachronism to say that the Old Testament is Christian."[10] In other words, the Christological (or Messiological) interpretation is not being read into the Tanakh; rather, the Tanakh is explicitly Messianic, concerning both the person and the redemptive work of the Messiah.

4.2 Balance
4.2.1 Interpretation and Application

It is important to follow a balanced approach here.[11] On the one hand, the *entire* Tanakh is fundamentally Messianic, from the promise in Genesis 3:15 (the woman's descendent

---

9. Some have suggested such a conflict in the six "antitheses" of Matt. 5:21–22, 27–28, 31–32, 33–34, 38–39, 43–44 ("You have heard ... but I say to you"); however, Jesus was not thereby correcting the Torah itself but only certain rabbinic interpretations of it; see Vermes (1993, 37); Ouweneel (2001, 124–25).
10. Berkouwer (1954, 117).
11. Cf. Heyns (1988, 232).

will bruise the head of the serpent, i.e., the devil and Satan; cf. Rev. 12:9; 20:2) to the rise of the "sun of righteousness" in Malachi 4:2, no doubt a reference to the Messiah (cf. Matt. 17:2; Acts 26:13; Rev. 1:16). The scope of the Tanakh is thoroughly Messiological. I maintain this over against the historical-critical exegesis of the Scripture, which has rejected the Messianic interpretation of, for instance, Genesis 3:15, Psalm 22, and the songs of the Servant of YHWH in Isaiah 42–53,[12] and has thoroughly psychologized the Messianic hope itself.[13]

On the other hand, the propriety of grammatical-historical exegesis must never be despised. It has priority over the typological (or allegorical,[14] or midrashic) interpretation of any Tanakh passage. In rabbinic terms, the *peshat* (grammatical-historical exegesis) always comes before, and must not be contradicted by, *remez* (allegorical exegesis), *derash* (midrashic exegesis), and *sod* (mystical-esoteric exegesis).[15] In a somewhat simplified description, we would say that *interpretation* must always be distinguished from, and always precede, *application*. Indeed, the New Testament's use of the Tanakh often has more to do with application (though, to be sure, Spirit-inspired application!) than only with interpretation.

Losing one's balance here is easy, whereby one theologian places more emphasis on a strictly grammatical-historical exegesis (a typically Western imbalance), and another more on a typological, allegorical, or midrashic approach (more in line with certain rabbinic schools). Personally, any approach that detracts from the pervasively Messianic character of the Tanakh (at least if properly understood) is suspect. This includes any approach that affects the way the New Testament deals with the Tanakh. In summary, grammatical-historical exegesis must always precede any form of typological exegesis, without minimizing the propriety of typological exegesis,

---

12. See, e.g., Von Rad (1935).
13. Regarding this, see Berkouwer (1954, 142–51).
14. Regarding the difference between typology and allegory, see §6.9.
15. Regarding the typology in the Psalms, see Thompson (1996, 51–59).

as the New Testament itself extensively demonstrates. However, this exegesis must never go beyond the New Testament midrashic exegesis of the Tanakh, and never be done at the expense of the literal sense (Lat. *sensus literalis*), that is, of the grammatical-historical exegesis of the Tanakh.

In brief, we look for a balance between the grammatical-historical exegesis and the midrashic or typological exegesis. Only in this way can we do justice to the Messiological scope of the Tanakh. However, many Tanakh passages that according to the New Testament midrashic exegesis are Messiological are not so according to their *sensus literalis*, and this must be fully maintained. On the other hand, consider Berkouwer's wise word: "No one may say that a given part of the Old Testament is without bearing on Jesus Christ, even though certain parts do not belong to what are generally called Messianic prophecies."[16]

4.2.2 The *Entire* Torah Speaks of the Messiah

To put it more strongly, *everything* in the Tanakh has to do with the Messiah: the patriarchs in Genesis, the priests, and the sacrifices in Exodus to Deuteronomy,[17] the judges in the book of Judges, the kings in 1 Samuel to 2 Chronicles and in the Psalms. Even the wisdom in Proverbs is none other than the Messiah (Prov. 8; cf. 1 Cor. 1:24; Col. 2:3),[18] and in my view he is also the "man" in Ecclesiastes 7:28 ("One man among a thousand I found, but a woman among all these I have not found") and 9:15 ("there was found in [the city] a poor, wise man, and he by his wisdom delivered the city. Yet no one remembered that poor man"). Typologically, he is Isaac and Joseph in the book of Genesis, Joshua in the book of Joshua, Boaz in the book of Ruth, Elijah/Elisha in the book of Kings, Mordecai in the book of Esther,[19] Job in the book of Job,[20] the

---

16. Berkouwer (1954, 128).
17. Ouweneel (n.d.-a).
18. Ouweneel (1998, 50–51).
19. Ouweneel (n.d.-b).
20. Ouweneel (2000a).

bridegroom in the Song of Solomon,[21] Jonah in the book of Jonah (cf. Matt. 12:40),[22] and so on.

With regard to Jesus' statement concerning all that was written *about* him in the Law of Moses (Luke 24:44), K. Schilder rightly argued that it is futile to "nose around" in the Mosaic literature trying to "dig up" some "tiny speck" that might "lend" itself to a Messianic interpretation.[23] On the contrary, Christ is the all-pervasive subject or topic or theme of the *entire* Torah (Pentateuch), as well as of the rest of the Tanakh. Schilder developed this in his unique way:

> [Thus, in Luke 24:27, 44 and John 5:39, Christ] would *not* have been thinking particularly of some detail A, or type B, or event C, or text D, or priestly garment E, or tabernacle furnishing F, or festival day G, or festival menu H, *but* of the *pattern*: Moses was a *mediator*; what is mediatorship? Moses wished to *die* for others, but he was not allowed or able to do this [Exod. 32:32-33]; what is mediatorship-without-exhaustive-sacrifice? Moses gave laws, laws, laws, but how can he [in Deut. 30:11-14] in looking back on his entire course as lawgiver and mediator posit as the preeminent commandment-with-threat: Now don't bring to me your final supreme effort, but acknowledge that the bread-from-heaven lay, as cut bread, for a long time on your table, within your reach, indeed, in your mouth, indeed, already in your heart (cf. Rom. 10:6-8)? And then: Moses wrote the history of the *toledot*,[24] of the decisive births and twists in history. All those *toledot* are *my* toledot, Christ wants to say. And Moses wrote about Melchizedek [cf. Heb. 7:1-10], and about Isaac, in whom the promised seed [i.e., Christ; Gal. 3:16] would be called, would be begotten. I am *the* begotten One! It is about *me* that Moses wrote, also in those historical portions.[25]

---

21. Ouweneel (1973).
22. Ouweneel (1989).
23. Schilder (1949, 2:309).
24. Heb. *toledot* means births, origins, history (Gen. 2:4; 6:9; 10:1; 11:10, 27; 25:12, 19; 36:1, 9).
25. Ibid., 2:310-11.

Messianic Hopes in the Tanakh

The *entire* Tanakh speaks of the Messiah, not just certain Messianic prophecies—even though also Schilder did not avoid selecting some elements from the Torah in order to illustrate this Messiological character.

4.2.3 Recognizable Messianic Predictions

We will do well here to distinguish between Messianic predictions that are recognizable as such only in the light of the New Testament, and Messianic predictions that were recognized as such by the rabbis.[26] A clear example are the Psalms. Some of these (Pss. 2, 45, 72, 132) have been accepted by the rabbis as Messianic, at least indirectly or secondarily. But other Psalms were not accepted by them as such; we recognize them as Messianic only because the New Testament treats them as such; take, for instance, Psalms 8 (see Heb. 2:5-9), 16 (see Acts 2:31; 13:35), 22 (see Matt. 27:39, 43, 46; John 19:24; Heb. 2:12), 40 (see Heb.10:5-10), and 69 (see John 2:17; Rom. 15:3).

Because of this distinction, we want to listen to the orthodox Jewish testimony concerning the Tanakh, but with a few restrictions. First, for us the New Testament is the divinely inspired key to the Tanakh, and cannot be surpassed by any rabbinic comments. Second, Jewish interpretation has certainly suffered under constant opposition to the Christological interpretations in the New Testament regarding the Tanakh. For instance, where early Jewish expositors had no difficulty recognizing the Messiah in Isaiah 53, later rabbis rejected this interpretation because it came too close to the New Testament interpretation of it (cf. Matt. 8:17; Luke 22:37; Acts 8:32-33; 1 Pet. 2:22, 24) (see further in §4.14).

There is an obvious tension here. On the one hand, for centuries Jews have accused Christians of reading their beliefs into the Tanakh.[27] On the other hand, Christians followed the

---

26. A Jewish tally identified 75 Messianic prophecies in the Torah, 243 in the Nevi'im, and 138 in the Ketuvim, according to Edelkoort (1951, 507).
27. For instance, Schoeps (1932, 25).

apostle Paul in speaking of a veil covering Jewish hearts when they read the Tanakh (2 Cor. 3:14), so that they do not understand it as they should.[28] We could put it this way: Jews read the Tanakh through the glasses of the Talmud, and Christians read it through the glasses of the New Testament.

We may add, though, that both groups receive help today beyond what they enjoyed earlier. Jews receive help from liberal Christian theologians who reject many Christological interpretations of Tanakh passages. The Soncino Books of the Bible series contains many rather triumphant references to such liberal expositors, who inadvertently come to the aid of Jewish scholars by denying the application of many passages to Jesus. But conversely, there are also orthodox Jewish theologians who have come much closer to the Christian approach. One well-known example is Pinchas Lapide, who considered it to be a "non-excludable possibility" that the Messiah expected in the Tanakh would have the traits of Jesus of Nazareth.

Lapide also said that Christians and Jews "await one and the same resolution as fulfillment of the promises; . . . ."[29] We can state without any reservation that conservative, non-supersessionist Christians and orthodox Jews are looking forward to that one great and glorious event: the appearance of the Messiah of Israel on the clouds of heaven (Dan. 7:13), who will sit on the throne of David to rule over Israel (Isa. 9:7), and from there over all the earth (Ps. 72:8; Isa. 49:6).

4.3   From Adam to Judah
4.3.1   Adam

The New Testament opened with calling Jesus "son of David, son of Abraham" (Matt. 1:1), and ultimately "son of Adam" (Luke 3:23–38). The messages concerning the Davidic descent of the Messiah (according to his human nature) gradually reached a single focus during the writing of the Tanakh. They

---

28. Berkouwer (1954, 116).
29. In Rahner and Lapide (1987, 80; cf. also 101).

began with Adam.

In Genesis 3:15, we find a promise that has been referred to as the *Proto Evangelium*: "I will put enmity between you [i.e., the serpent] and the woman, and between your offspring and her offspring; he [i.e., the woman's offspring] shall bruise your head, and you shall bruise his heel." Conservative Christian expositors invariably find a Messianic prophecy here: the Messiah is the woman's offspring, and thus also Adam's offspring (Luke 3:23–38), and the serpent is Satan (cf. Rev. 12:9; 20:2, "that ancient serpent, who is called the devil and Satan, the deceiver of the whole world"). No doubt the references in the book of Revelation have strongly supported this exegesis.

Jewish expositors have never identified a Messianic prophecy here. Modernist Christian expositors see no Messianic prediction here, either; liberals believe that traditional exegesis has read far too much into the text. This is not entirely without basis: Francis A. Schaeffer and Josh McDowell thought they saw a reference to Jesus' virgin birth in the text.[30]

In the primary sense (*peshat*, see §4.2.1), the text obviously refers to two real progenies: the literal world of serpents and the human world (cf. Isa. 65:25). In the secondary sense (*remez* or *derash*), the text refers to two races: that of Satan (in addition to Rev., see also John 8:44, "You are of your father the devil") and that of the (reborn) woman, that is, the race of death and the race of life, respectively (cf. Gen. 3:20, Eve = life). Cain and Abel constituted the first fulfillment of Genesis 3:15 because they were the first representatives of these two spiritual races. Cain, as an instrument of Satan, was the first to "bruise the heel" of the woman's offspring, by inflicting a crippling but not definitively destructive blow. This is how it always went in history, from the murder of Abel (cf. Matt. 23:35; Luke 11:51; Heb. 12:24) to the murder of Jesus (cf. Acts 3:15; 5:30; 7:52). Conversely, one day Satan's "head" will be "bruised," and this means ultimate destruction. Messiah's

---

30. McDowell (1972, 116); Schaeffer (1982, 73–74).

followers will also be involved in this—"The God of peace will soon crush Satan under your feet" (Rom. 16:20)—but the ultimate conqueror of Satan will be the Messiah (Heb. 2:14; 1 John 3:8; cf. Rev. 20:1, 10).

The prediction of Genesis 3:15 could be called an indirect Messianic prophecy: the time when the Messiah was "pierced" (Zech. 12:10)—"they have pierced my hands and feet" (Ps. 22:16); "he was pierced for our transgressions; he was crushed for our iniquities" (Isa. 53:5)—was the same as the time when, figuratively speaking, Messiah's "heel" was "bruised." But it turned out to be also the time when he "bruised" the serpent's "head."

In Genesis, the Messianic line runs from Adam through Seth, Enosh (Gen. 4:25-26), Noah (6-9), Shem, Eber (10:21), Terah, and the patriarchs (11:27). They were all representatives of the woman's offspring in the spiritual sense.

4.3.2 Shem and Eber

The insider knows, in the light of the Tanakh historical narrative, that in Noah's predictions concerning his sons, the line of Shem will become the Messianic line, or the line of divine blessing: "May God enlarge Japheth, and let him dwell in the tents of Shem" (Gen. 9:27). For Japheth the divine blessing can be realized only in and through the "tents of Shem." In subsequent parts of the Tanakh, it becomes evident that the divine blessing, which also extends to the Japhethites, is realized through Shem's descendent, the Messiah. But the attentive Torah reader recognized this in principle back in Genesis 9:27.

In Genesis 10:21, the line is narrowed still further: Shem is the ancestor of Eber, and Eber is, according to Genesis 11:10-27, the forefather of Abr(ah)am, who is nicknamed "the Hebrew" (ᶜibri, Gen. 14:13). This expression can mean either a descendent of Eber (ᶜeber), or the one who has crossed the Euphrates (from ᶜ-b-r, "to cross, to pass").

4.3.3 Abraham and Isaac

YHWH said about Abraham under oath: "In your seed all the nations of the earth shall be blessed" (Gen. 22:18 NKJV). In Galatians 3:16, the apostle Paul argues in a midrashic way to draw from this the conclusion that the text is speaking ultimately of *the* seed of Abraham, that is, the Messiah. In opposition to B. Loonstra,[31] I claim that this argument of Paul is not just a "Jewish method of Scripture exegesis" and the "Jewish redemptive pattern of his days," but a responsible exposition of Genesis 22:18. Abraham's seed, his offspring, is the people of Israel. But, as we will see repeatedly, the Messiah is the true Israel; the true Israel of God is concentrated in his person. Therefore, *the* seed of Abraham is ultimately the Messiah.

Interestingly, Paul suggests that, if the Galatian believers had listened carefully to the Torah (see Gal. 4:21), they could have deduced what Paul deduced here from Genesis. That is, as far as we can assess, Paul did not follow some existing Jewish interpretation, nor did he invent some explanation; he was convinced that his exegesis followed from the text itself.[32] In the same self-evident way he drew far-reaching conclusions from the story of Sarah and Hagar, in Galatians 4:21–31, and from the stories of Israel's travels through the wilderness, in 1 Corinthians 10:1–12.

The "seed" of Abraham involves three things. First, it refers to the people of Israel because it is Abraham's "seed" that will inherit the promised land (cf. Gen. 17:9; 21:12; 26:3, 24; 28:4, 13). Second, it refers to the Messiah, who is the true Israel. And third—we should not forget this—it is Abraham's physical son Isaac. After Abraham, the first new phase in the Messianic line is Isaac: "In Isaac your seed shall be called" (Gen. 21:12 NKJV), and to Isaac it is said, "[I]n your seed all the nations shall be blessed" (26:4 NKJV).

Isaac is not only the Messiah's forefather but also a model.

---

31. Loonstra (1994, 50–51).
32. See more extensively, Ouweneel (1997a, 203–206, 287–89).

Abraham had many sons (cf. Gen. 25:2), yet he had only *one* son: the one beloved (22:2). Similarly, Isaac had millions of descendants, yet he had only *one* descendant: the one beloved son, the Messiah. If the Messiah is both "son of Abraham" and "son of David" (Matt. 1:1), we may think here of Solomon as well. Like Abraham, David had many sons, yet there was only one son who was in particular loved by the Lord. YHWH gave him the name Jedidiah, which means "beloved of YH" (2 Sam. 12:24–25). Isaac, the son of his father's love, and Solomon, the son of God's love, remind us of the great son of both Isaac and Solomon: the One who is called "the son of his [the Father's] love" (Col. 1:13 ASV).

The writer of the letter to the Hebrews (Jesus-believing Jews), who is so strong in his midrashic approach to the Tanakh, implicitly presents Isaac as a figure of the Messiah:

> By faith Abraham, when he was tested, offered up Isaac, and he who had received the promises was in the act of offering up his only son, of whom it was said, "Through Isaac shall your offspring be named" [Gen. 21:12]. He considered that God was able even to raise him from the dead, from which, figuratively speaking, he did receive him back (Heb. 11:17–19).

The son of his father's love had to be sacrificed, and in a figurative way, the son did indeed pass through death, and was given back to his father through resurrection.

4.3.4 Jacob

The name "Israel" was given first to a person, who is normally called Jacob, but is sometimes called by his name Israel (Gen. 32:28; 35:10, 21–22; 37:3, 13; 42:5; 43:6, 8, 11; 45:21, 28; 46:1–2, 5, 8, 29–30; 47:27, 29, 31). Thus, the primary person who could be called the true Israel — so literally that he was the first to carry the name "Israel" — was Jacob. In this sense, Jacob, too, prefigured (foreshadowed) the Messiah, in spite of the vicissitudes of his life which were due mainly to his own mistakes. In Isaiah, the servant of YHWH is primarily "Israel, my servant,

Jacob" (Gen. 41:8; 44:1, 21; 45:4; 49:3). But sometimes this s/Servant is distinguished from Israel: "And now the LORD says, he who formed me from the womb to be his servant, to bring Jacob back to him; and that Israel might be gathered to him. . . . 'It is too light a thing that you should be my servant to raise up the tribes of Jacob and to bring back the preserved of Israel'" (Isa. 49:5-6). The *servant* is Jacob/Israel — the *Servant* is the true (self of) Jacob/Israel, who brings the latter back to the Lord. Jacob is a type of the Messiah — and he is the one who will be brought back by the Messiah.

Of the two sons of Isaac, Jacob became the bearer of the Messianic promise. As the apostle Paul says,

> [W]hen Rebekah had conceived children by one man, our forefather Isaac, though they were not yet born and had done nothing either good or bad — in order that God's purpose of election might continue, not because of works but because of him who calls — she was told, "The older will serve the younger" [Gen. 25:23]. As it is written, "Jacob I loved, but Esau I hated" [Mal. 1:2] (Rom. 9:10-13).

God told Jacob: "[I]n you and in your seed [Israel *and* the true Self of Israel: the Messiah] all the families of the earth shall be blessed" (Gen. 28:14 NKJV).

The remarkable prophecy by the false prophet Balaam (from whom we know only God-inspired prophecies) fits in with this:

> [A] star shall come out of Jacob,
>   and a scepter shall rise out of Israel;
> it shall crush the forehead of Moab
>   and break down all the sons of Sheth.
> Edom shall be dispossessed;
>   Seir also, his enemies, shall be dispossessed.
>   Israel is doing valiantly.
> And one from Jacob shall exercise dominion
>   and destroy the survivors of cities! (Num. 24:17-19).

The "star" turned out to be a ruler (cf. Isa. 14:12; Ezek. 32:7; Rev. 22:16), underscored by the parallel word "scepter." This ruler would triumph over all the neighboring people around Israel, including Balaam's own sponsor: Moab.

One might argue that these words were fulfilled in David's victories over Moab and Edom (2 Sam. 8:2, 13-14; 1 Kings 11:15-16), but this was at best a preliminary fulfillment, because both Moab and Edom regained their power. Therefore, the prophecy will be definitively fulfilled only in the Messiah.[33] The Targums of Onkelos and of Jonathan understood the text to be Messianic. Great Jewish expositors — Rashbam (Rabbi Shemuel ben Meir, grandson of Rashi) and Nachmanides — also saw the Messiah in Numbers 24.[34] It is all the more remarkable that Martin Luther did not wish to view the passage as Messianic because he deemed Balaam to be unworthy of such a lofty subject.[35] Church fathers like Justin Martyr and Athanasius had no difficulty with the Messianic interpretation, nor did many after Luther.

4.3.5 Judah

The Messianic line narrowed down still further. Among the twelve sons of Jacob, Joseph is the clearest *type* of the Messiah in his person (Gen. 49:22-26, ". . . him who was set apart from his brothers," v. 26) and in his life (from glory to his downfall — sold by his own brothers — and then back to still higher glory). It is remarkable that, after Reuben's fall, the right of the firstborn was not given to Judah, but to Joseph (1 Chron. 5:1). Joseph became what is said of Jesus as well: "the firstborn among many brothers" (Rom. 8:29).

Yet, it is Judah who is the bearer of the Messianic promise: "[I]t is evident that our Lord was descended from Judah" (Heb. 7:14; cf. Matt. 1:3; Rev. 5:5). Of great significance is Ja-

---

33. Allen (1990, 909–911); Ashley (1993, 502–503, and references).
34. Cohen (1983, 926); see also jerTaanith 68.4; Debarim Rabba chapter 1; Pesiqta Sotarta 58.1; 1QM:VII.
35. Quoted in Bornkamm (1969, 240n72).

cob's prophecy concerning his son Judah, and thus concerning the tribe of Judah: "The scepter shall not depart from Judah, nor the ruler's staff from between his feet, until tribute [or, Shiloh] comes to him; and to him shall be the obedience of the peoples" (Gen. 49:10). The first difficulty is the Hebrew word *shiloh*. Is it a name (as many traditional translators conclude), or an ordinary word that must be translated? Some render as follows: "he whose right it is to come" (CSB), or "he whose right it is comes" (HCSB), or "he to whom it belongs shall come" (NIV). Others, "until tribute comes to him" (ESV). If Shiloh is a location (see, e.g., 1 Sam. 1:3, 9, 24), it is possible to render it as "until he comes to Shiloh" (EXB alternate reading). Each of these renderings has been defended by expositors.³⁶

The usual rendering is difficult, first, because a feminine subject ("Shiloh") is connected here with a masculine verbal form ("comes"), and second, because in the Tanakh Shiloh is exclusively the name of a location, not in Judah but in Ephraim. Nonetheless, many Jewish and Christian expositors have understood the name Shiloh here as referring to the Messiah. Some have connected the root here to *shalom*, "peace," so that the meaning could be something like *sar-shalom*, "prince of peace," in Isaiah 9:6.

The rendering in the Septuagint is clearly Messianic: ". . . until the things come that are kept in store for him." One could think here of (his title to) the Davidic scepter and the "ruler's staff," these two expressions being more or less synonymous. It is significant that the Dead Sea scrolls also view the passage as Messianic by speaking explicitly of "the Messiah of righteousness, the branch of David."³⁷ Those from the tribe of Judah who would wield the scepter would do so in expectation of him to whom kingship would truly belong.³⁸ And this would not only be a royal rule over the *tribes* of Is-

---

36. See the extensive discussion by Sailhamer (1990, 279–80) and Hamilton (1995, 659–62, including the references).
37. 4QPBless, quoted in Hamilton (1995, 660).
38. Sailhamer (1990, 276).

rael, but also over the *nations* of the world (cf. Ps. 2:8; 72:8-11; Isa. 49:5-6; Dan. 7:13-14; Rev. 5:5, 9). No Davidic king ever possessed *this* kingship, though Solomon approached it most closely (1 Kings 4:21, 24; cf. the heading of Ps. 72).

When this Messianic king appears, the time of abundance will arrive that is described so poetically in Genesis 49:11-12 (CJB): "Tying his donkey to the vine, his donkey's colt to the choice grapevine, he washes his clothes in wine, his robes in the blood of grapes. His eyes will be darker than wine, his teeth whiter than milk."

Genesis 49 does not appear to allow the possibility that there would ever be a time that this (royal) scepter would no longer be available to Judah; the royal tribe would keep it until he would come whose right it is, or to whom it belongs. We think here of another Messianic reference: "A ruin, ruin, ruin I will make it [i.e., Judah/Jerusalem]. This also shall not be, until *he comes, the one to whom judgment belongs* [lit., *whose right* (Heb. *mishpat*) *it is*], and I will give it to him" (Ezek. 21:27; in some Bibles v. 32).[39]

Even after the fall of the Davidic royal house, Israel retained a certain measure of independence—under the Persians (cf. Ezra 1:5, 8), later under the Greeks, and later again under the Romans. Therefore, we can understand what happened when, in the year AD 7, the Romans took from Judea its last exercise of sovereignty, namely, the right of the sword (Lat. *ius gladii*, the right to implement the death penalty; cf. John 18:31). We read that pious Jews sprinkled ashes on their heads, covered themselves with sackcloth, and shouted: "Woe over us, for the scepter has departed from Judah, and the Messiah has not come!"[40] They did not know about a certain boy, perhaps ten or twelve years old, who at that very moment was living in the inconspicuous town of Nazareth. Of this boy, the angel Gabriel had said, "[T]he Lord God will

---

39. Fisch (1978, 141).
40. Assuming the story is authentic, though it has not been verified to have originated earlier than the thirteenth century.

give to him the throne of his father David" (Luke 1:32). That same year, or shortly after, this same boy was sitting in the temple during Pesach among the rabbis, and he told his astonished parents that he had to be occupied with his Father's business (Luke 2:49 NKJV). The *ius gladii* had been taken away, but Shiloh's work had just begun.

4.4 The Shoot of Jesse
4.4.1 Bethlehem

Several times, Jesse, or Isai, the father of David (Ruth 4:17), is called Jesse the Bethlehemite (1 Sam. 16:1, 18; 17:58), and once "an Ephrathite of Bethlehem in Judah, named Jesse" (17:12). At a much later time, when it was generally known that the Messiah would come from the house of David, Micah explicitly referred to "Bethlehem Ephrathah" (Bethlehem of the Ephrathites, to distinguish it from other Bethlehems), the dwelling place of Jesse, the "city of David,"[41] and thus the city of the Messiah:

> [Y]ou, O Bethlehem Ephrathah, who are too little to be among the clans of Judah, from you shall come forth for me one who is to be ruler in Israel, whose coming forth is from of old, from ancient days. Therefore he shall give them up until the time when she who is in labor has given birth; then the rest of his brothers shall return to the people of Israel (Micah 5:2–3; some Bibles: 5:1–2).[42]

Interestingly, the Jewish scholars in Herod's time did not hesitate for a moment to interpret this passage as Messianic (Matt. 2:4-6; cf. John 7:42). We may assume that this was common in those days. However, in the time of the early church, in reaction to the Christian interpretation of the passage, some Jewish expositors tried to rob it of its Messianic meaning, for

---

41. Bethlehem must share the title "city of David" (Luke 2:4, 11) with Jerusalem (2 Sam. 5:7, 9; 6:10, 12, 16).
42. For more extensive analysis of this passage, see Ouweneel in Knevel and Paul (1995, 168–83).

instance, by applying it to Zerubbabel.[43]

In spite of its low reputation, Bethlehem Ephrathah was chosen to become the birthplace, not only of David but also of his greatest son, *the* ruler of Israel. The great majority of the Davidic kings were born in Jerusalem, with two exceptions: David himself, as well as the Messiah, who were both born in Bethlehem. There are more parallels: both are shepherds (1 Sam. 16:11; Micah 5:4; cf. vv. 5–6, 8; Ezek. 34:23; 37:24), and both have been chosen by God "for himself" (cf. the remarkable "for me" in Micah 5:2 and in 1 Sam. 16:1; cf. 13:14 and Acts 13:22).

The city is the "woman" who will give birth to the Messiah; at least, this is a possible explanation of verse 3, because the "she" in this verse must be a figure mentioned a little earlier in the text.[44] Many others, however, think of Israel as a whole, one argument being that the "daughter of troops" in Micah 5:1 (some Bibles: 4:14) might be Israel as well; but this might also be Zion (Jerusalem; cf. v. 13). Indeed, Rashi (acronym of Rabbi Shlomo Yitzchaqi, d. 1105) and Malbim (acronym of Meir Leibush ben Yechiel Michel, d. 1879) find here a reference to Zion (cf. Isa. 66:8).[45] The underlying question is whether verse 3 is speaking of Messiah's birth, or rather of Zion "giving birth" in the end time (cf. 4:9–10), during which the believing remnant of Israel is born (cf. Isa. 49:21; 54:1; 66:8).

The fulfillment of the prophecy refers to the end time, when "the rest of his brothers shall return to the people of Israel," and the Messiah will shepherd his people (v. 4) and will have triumphed over all his enemies (vv. 5–9).

In §6.2.1 we will return to the remarkable words at the end of verse 2: "whose coming forth is from of old, from ancient days" (cf. NKJV: "Whose goings forth [are] from of old, from everlasting"; DRA: "his going forth is from the beginning, from

---

43. Keil (KDC 10:480–81).
44. McComiskey (1985, 428); the suggestion by Allen (1976, 345) that the "she" must be linked with Isaiah 7:14 is far-fetched and unnecessary.
45. Goldman in Cohen (1980, 175).

the days of eternity").

4.4.2 Jesse

In Romans 15:12, Paul quotes Isaiah 11:10, where the Messiah is called the "root of Jesse." The full verses 1 and 10 say this: "There shall come forth a shoot from the stump of Jesse, and a branch from his roots shall bear fruit.... In that day the root of Jesse, who shall stand as a signal for the peoples—of him shall the nations inquire, and his resting place shall be glorious." The army of Assyria, resembling a forest (Isa. 10:33-34), will be reduced to stumps, whereas from the "stump of Jesse" a shoot, a branch will come forth. It says Jesse, not David. In opposition to the pride of Assyria, the emphasis lies not on some royal figure but on the common Judean farmer, Jesse—although the point of the passage of course is David and his offspring (cf. Isa. 9:6-7; 16:5).[46]

The traditional rendering "root [Heb. *choter*] of Jesse" is fundamentally mistaken. If A is the root of B, B comes forth from A; but what the text says is that A (the shoot) comes forth from B (Jesse). We have the same problem in Revelation 5:5 and 22:16: the Messiah is not the "root" (Gk. *rhiza*) of David (as if David sprouted from *him*) but the "shoot" (descendant) of David.

Jewish tradition did not hesitate to say that Isaiah 11 referred to the Messiah, as we find in the Targum, the Talmud, and Rashi.[47] Above the interpretation of Isaiah 11, Rabbi Israel W. Slotki placed the words "The Messianic Age."[48] The New Testament alluded to the passage several times (e.g., Matt. 2:23; Acts 13:22-23; Rom. 15:12; Eph. 1:17; Rev. 5:5; 19:11, 15, 21; 22:16; see also Isa. 11:4c ["with the breath of his lips he shall kill the wicked"], which we find repeated in 2 Thess. 2:8).

By the time the Messiah would be born, the house of Da-

---

46. Grogan (1986, 87); Oswalt (1986, 278–79).
47. Sanhedrin 93b.
48. Slotki (1983, 56).

vid would have become a "stump" (cf. 6:13; 53:2); it still existed, but for six centuries it had not produced a king. In the imagery of Isaiah, the Messiah is a "shoot," a "branch" (cf. Isa. 4:2; 6:13), a metaphor that we will meet again later.

Just as in Genesis 49, the prophecy extends to all nations: "In that day the shoot of Jesse . . . —of him shall the nations inquire" (Isa. 11:10). In Isaiah, the expression "in that day" consistently refers to the Messianic age: *then* the Messiah "shall stand as a signal" (or, banner, ensign), which will exert attractive power on all the nations (cf. Isa. 2:1–4; 49:6; 60:1–3; see also John 12:32).

4.5 David
4.5.1 "My Servant David"

In some Tanakh passages of David, such as Psalm 2, the question is whether they were speaking of David himself or of the great son of David, the Messiah,[49] or of both (see §4.7.1). Of course, there is a profound connection between these two interpretations because, in the Tanakh, David was one of the great types (prefigurations, foreshadowings) of the Messiah. This extended to the point that the Messiah was sometimes called "David" himself. But there can be no doubt who was meant in Hosea 3:4–5: "[T]he children of Israel shall dwell many days without king or prince, without sacrifice or pillar, without ephod or household gods. Afterward the children of Israel shall return and seek the LORD their God, and David their king, and they shall come in fear to the LORD and to his goodness in the latter days." These final words, "in the latter days," are characteristic of (the beginning of) the Messianic age.[50] The Targum identified "David their king" here as the Messiah. "Seeking" the Messiah can hardly refer to the first coming of the Messiah in the person of Jesus Christ; it will be fulfilled only in the Messianic kingdom (Isa. 12:1–6; 66:23; Jer.

---

49. See D. R. Bauer (*DJG* 766–69).
50. Lehrman in Cohen (1980, 13).

33:11; Ezek. 20:40).[51]

The same name "David" is found in Ezekiel: "I will set up over them one shepherd, my servant David, and he shall feed them: he shall feed them and be their shepherd. And I, the LORD, will be their God, and my servant David shall be prince among them" (34:23-24). Later, Ezekiel says,

> My servant David shall be king over them, and they shall all have one shepherd. They shall walk in my rules and be careful to obey my statutes. They shall dwell in the land that I gave to my servant Jacob, where your fathers lived. They and their children and their children's children shall dwell there forever, and David my servant shall be their prince forever (37:24-25).

There can be no reasonable doubt that here "David" is a name for the Messiah.[52]

4.5.2 The Son of David

At other places, the text spoke of the seed (descendant) or son of David, where the reference was to the Messiah. We find this is the background of the prophecy of Nathan, given to David (2 Sam. 7:12-16). Hebrews 1:5 applied verse 14 to the Messiah. Rabbi Solomon Goldman wrote on this passage that its promise concerning an everlasting kingship of the house of David strongly influenced the development of Messianic hope in Israel.[53] And A. S. van der Woude wrote: "Even though this prophecy, viewed by itself, is originally not a Messianic promise, the Messianic expectation did sprout from it under certain conditions."[54]

Indeed, there is a Messianic perspective in these verses, which unfolds only in the subsequent divine revelation. Therefore, A. H. Edelkoort certainly went too far in saying that, in 2 Samuel 7, David was "allowed to hear that the Mes-

---

51. See Wood (1985, 183).
52. Mulder in Knevel and Paul (1995, 127–29, 136–38).
53. Goldman (1983, 229).
54. Van der Woude (1973, 5–6).

siah would come forth from his family."⁵⁵ Yet, the *root* of the Messianic hope in Israel can certainly be sought here (cf. Ps. 89:19-29).⁵⁶ For the first time in history, it is made clear that the great Messianic king would sprout from the house of David, and nowhere else.

There has been some debate about whether David's "seed" and "son" in verse 12 referred to Solomon alone, or to each Davidic king.⁵⁷ In either case, the warning is understandable, though not applicable to the Messiah: "When he commits iniquity, I will discipline him with the rod of men, with the stripes of the sons of men" (v. 14). However, verse 16, with its promise of a continual Davidic house and kingship and a throne that is everlasting, does find its ultimate fulfillment in the Messiah. If the passage refers primarily to Solomon, the physical son of David, he is a type (prefiguration, foreshadowing) of the Messiah (cf. Matt. 12:42).

4.5.3 David and Amos

David himself had some awareness of the coming Messiah, as we see in Psalm 110:1 ("The LORD says to *my Lord*: 'Sit at my right hand, until I make your enemies your footstool'") (see the interpretation given by Jesus in Matthew 22:42-45; see further §4.12.2). In 2 Samuel 23:3-5, God was speaking either in general terms of how a good ruler should behave (as we find in many translations), or in more specific terms of the coming Messiah:

> The Rock of Israel said to me: "One shall come who rules righteously, who rules in the fear of God. He shall be as the light of the morning; a cloudless sunrise when the tender grass springs forth upon the earth; as sunshine after rain." And it is my fam-

---

55. Edelkoort (1941, 162).
56. Brown (1994, 130, 156–60); he saw a second phase in the Messianic hope in, e.g., Isa. 7:14; 9:6–7; 11:1–5; Micah 5:2; Jer. 23:5; 30:9; Ezek. 17:23; 34:23–24; 37:24–25, and a third, post-exilic phase in, e.g., Zech. 9:9–10, the Psalms of Solomon, the Dead Sea scrolls, and 1 Enoch.
57. In addition to Goslinga (1962, 139–40), see Peels in Knevel and Paul (1995, 45).

ily He has chosen! Yes, God has made an everlasting covenant with me; his agreement is eternal, final, sealed (TLB).

In my view, it is difficult to picture someone other than the Messiah in words such as: "he dawns on them like the morning light, like the sun shining forth on a cloudless morning" (v. 4 ESV), at least in the ultimate sense of these words. They remind us of Malachi 4:2 (some Bibles: 3:20), where many expositors see the expression "the sun of righteousness" as a reference to the Messiah.

In Amos 9:11-12 we read: "'In that day I will raise up the booth of David that is fallen and repair its breaches, and raise up its ruins and rebuild it as in the days of old, that they may possess the remnant of Edom and all the nations who are called by my name,' declares the LORD who does this." These words were quoted by Jesus' brother James (Acts 15:16-17). He did so mainly in the Septuagint version, with the implication that, in the end time, David's "booth" or "tent" will be restored in the great son of David, and that this will have tremendous consequences for Israel and the nations. It is sufficient to note here that the perspective in Amos 9:11-15 was clearly Messianic,[58] and this was also the way James understood it in Acts 15.[59]

The notion of a "booth" or "tent" may suggest that, at the time of fulfillment, David's house or dynasty will have shrunk to nothing. Yet, in Isaiah 16:5 as well, we find this expression "tent," without any notion of little esteem: ". . . a throne will be established in steadfast love, and on it will sit in faithfulness in the tent of David one who judges and seeks justice and is swift to do righteousness."

---

58. So also Lehrman in Cohen (1980, 123).
59. The strange differences between the Masoretic text and the Septuagint, and between the Septuagint and Acts 15, need not occupy us here; see, e.g., Bruce (1988, 293–94); Mudde in Knevel and Paul (1995, 157–66).

4.6 Sons of David
4.6.1 Ahaz

In Isaiah 7, the Messianic line involved king Ahaz: from him the Messiah would come forth. This is not so astonishing: apart from Joahaz and Zedekiah, *all* Davidic kings were forefathers of the Messiah (Matt. 1:6–11). In this respect, it is remarkable that the prophet Isaiah in 7:13 does not give the promise to king Ahaz, but more generally to the "house of David," as if the wicked Ahaz had personally forfeited all promises.

Most conspicuous is verse 14, "Behold, the virgin shall conceive and bear a son, and shall call his name Immanuel." Not only conspicuous, but confusing; it is said that there are at least eight different interpretations of the verse.[60] It would lead us too far afield to discuss all eight here. I believe that Matthew 1:18–23, where the verse was applied to Jesus, offers not only a figurative or associative exegesis but a genuine grammatical-historical exegesis. My two core arguments are these:

(1) The text may certainly refer to a "virgin" (see below).

(2) Whether Isaiah 7:14 speaks directly of the Messiah or of a son who would be born in the immediate future but would be a type (prefiguration) of the Messiah, this Messianic dimension is present *in the text itself*, and was not read into it by Matthew.

As for (1): indeed, the Hebrew text does not use the common word for "virgin," *b'tulah*, but the word *almah*, which means "girl" or "young woman." However, in the seven places where *almah* (singular) occurs in the Tanakh, it always refers to a girl that is unmarried and chaste. Genesis 24 calls Rebekah both a *b'tulah* (v. 16) and an *almah* (v. 43). Although *almah* is linked less directly with virginity as such than *b'tulah*, in common Hebrew parlance it certainly did refer to an un-

---

60. In Knevel and Paul (1995, 78–85); see also Berkouwer (1965, 112–16); Grogan (1986, 62–66); Oswalt (1986, 206–13).

married, chaste young woman, that is, a "virgin."[61] Therefore, it is perfectly understandable that the Septuagint renders *almah* in Isaiah 7:14 with a word that unequivocally means "virgin," namely, *parthenos*. From the Septuagint, *parthenos* was adopted in Matthew 1:23. It is said of Luther that he once promised one hundred florins to anyone who could prove to him that *almah* ever referred to a married woman.

If the text had a primary fulfillment in a child that was soon to be born, then the young woman intended by these words—whether a princess at Ahaz' court,[62] or the future wife of Isaiah (Isa. 8:3)—was still a virgin at the moment of the prophecy. If the text does not have any preliminary fulfillment but was directly fulfilled in the Messiah (see further point [2]), the text indicates that, during her pregnancy, the *almah* would still be a virgin.

As for (2): whether the text has one or two fulfillments—opinions may legitimately differ on this point—the text itself contains a depth-dimension that surpasses its short-term fulfillment. First, the "sign" in 7:11–14 is a *miraculous* sign, which goes far beyond the fact that a young married woman would get pregnant and give birth to a child. Second, the sign is not given directly to Ahaz, but to the "house of David" (v. 13), which strongly seems to favor a long-term fulfillment. And especially third, Immanuel is not just any child: the land of Israel is *his* land (8:8). Of what prince could such a thing be said (except of Hezekiah, but his birth was very ordinary; moreover, he had probably been born at the time of Isaiah 7). The land belongs to the LORD (Lev. 25:23; Hos. 9:3); indeed, Immanuel is "God with us."

We must consider here that these passages belonged to one extended prophecy, which extended from Isaiah 7:1 to 9:7. This means that 7:14 and 8:8 culminated in 9:5–6: the Child born, the Son given, is the Messiah from the house of David, who will one day rule in justice and righteousness,

---

61. Bloesch (1997, 94).
62. Loonstra (1994, 49).

on the throne of David (§4.7.2). Even if Isaiah 7:14 had a contemporary fulfillment, Matthew quoted the verse correctly by viewing it as having been basically and ultimately fulfilled in the Messiah. The same is true for the Messianic prophecy of Isaiah 16:4-5, which connected directly to 9:6-7:[63] "When the oppressor is no more, and destruction has ceased, and he who tramples underfoot has vanished from the land, then a throne will be established in steadfast love, and on it will sit in faithfulness in the tent of David one who judges and seeks justice and is swift to do righteousness."

4.6.2 Jeconiah

The prophecies in Jeremiah concerning the "Branch" (23:5; 33:15; Heb. *tzemach*) were given after a remarkable divine statement concerning Jeconiah, or, as he is called elsewhere, Jehoiachin (e.g., 2 Kings 24:6) or Coniah (e.g., Jer. 22:24). The statement is this: "Write this man down as childless, a man who shall not succeed in his days, for none of his offspring shall succeed in sitting on the throne of David and ruling again in Judah" (Jer. 22:30). This verse is remarkable because the names of Jeconiah as well as his son Shealtiel and the latter's son Zerubbabel appear in Matthew 1:12 in the legal ancestry of Jesus (legal because it is the line of Joseph, legal father of Jesus and heir to the throne of David). In the genealogy of Luke 3:23-38, the names of Zerubbabel and Shealtiel appear as well, but not that of Jeconiah; in verse 27 Shealtiel is called a son of Neri. Perhaps we should take Jeremiah 22:30 to mean that Jeconiah had no sons of his own, but that Shealtiel was appointed as his legitimate heir.[64] Other ingenious solutions have been proposed, such as levirate marriages. The solutions are relativized by the great diversity of the manuscript varieties in the Tanakh genealogies (Masoretic text and Septuagint).

---

63. Oswalt (1986, 343).
64. See Godet (1879, ad loc.); Plummer (1922, ad loc.). In Talmud tract Sanhedrin 37b, it is supposed that Jeconiah received forgiveness (cf. 2 Kings 25:27–30), and therefore yet received his son Shealtiel.

If indeed Jeconiah himself had seven biological sons, including Shealtiel (1 Chron. 3:17-18), Jeremiah 22:30 might only be telling us that none of the seven sons of Jeconiah would occupy the Davidic throne.[65] It is all the more remarkable that, a few verses later, the Messiah from the house of David is announced: "Behold, the days are coming, . . . when I will raise up for David a righteous Branch, and he shall reign as king and deal wisely, and shall execute justice and righteousness in the land. In his days Judah will be saved, and Israel will dwell securely. And this is the name by which he will be called: 'The LORD is our righteousness'" (Jer. 23:5-6; cf. 33:14-16). The name of the Messiah, "The LORD our righteousness" (YHWH *Tzidkēnu*), is an obvious allusion to the name of the last pre-exilic Davidic king, Zedekiah (Heb. *Tzidqiyyahu*, "YHWH, my righteousness"), who could be called a kind of anti-messiah (cf. the concept of the *antichristos*, "anti-messiah," in 1 John 2:18, 22; 4:2; 2 John 1:7).

The notion of the "Branch" reminds us of Isaiah 11:1, although the Hebrew term there is different (§4.4.2). After the exile, we find it again in Zechariah: "[B]ehold, I will bring my servant the Branch [*tzemach*] . . . and I will remove the iniquity of this land in a single day. In that day, . . . every one of you will invite his neighbor to come under his vine and under his fig tree" (Zech. 3:8-10; cf. 1 Kings 2:25; Micah 4:4). "Behold, the man whose name is the Branch: for he shall branch out from his place, and he shall build the temple of the LORD . . . and shall bear royal honor, and shall sit and rule on his throne. And there [or, he] shall be a priest on his throne, and the counsel of peace shall be between them both" (Zech. 6:12-13). The Branch metaphor does not mean that the Messiah — for he is being referred to, as the Targum of Jonathan tells us already — is a Branch from the tree of David, but he "branches out from his place," possibly a reference to his humble and unclear origin.

---

65. According to Irenaeus, *Adversus Haereses* 3.21.9.

Just as in Jeremiah 23 and 33, the eschatological terminology can refer only to the Messianic kingdom; the temple here can be nothing other than the temple described in Ezekiel 40-44 (cf. Isa. 2:2-4; Hag. 2:7-10). The priesthood of the Branch in Zechariah 6 will be discussed further in §4.11.2.

4.7 Son of God
4.7.1 Psalm 2

When we speak now of the Messiah as "Son of God," we have in view the Tanakh, without considering for now the New Testament view of the "Son of God" (see chapter 7).[66] First and foremost, Israel among the nations is referred to as God's "firstborn son" (Exod. 4:22-23; cf. Hos. 11:1, "out of Egypt I called my son"; cf. the plural "sons" in Deut. 14:1). Next, it is the Davidic king who in particular is described as God's "son" (2 Sam. 7:14; Ps. 2:7; 89:26-27): "Israel's privileged status as God's firstborn son is personified in the kings; he embodies the dignity of Israel in person."[67] This is meant by saying that the Messiah is the true Israel.

In various New Testament passages, the Tanakh was quoted to support the notion of Jesus' divine sonship. In Acts 13:33, the apostle Paul applied Psalm 2:7 ("You are my Son; today I have begotten you") to Jesus, and the same occurred in Hebrews 5:5. In Hebrews 1:5, Psalm 2:7 and 2 Samuel 7:14 ("I will be to him a father, and he shall be to me a son") are applied to him. Remarkably enough, one passage was not quoted: "For to us a child is born, to us a son is given" (Isa. 9:6).

As for Psalm 2, in Acts 4:25-26 (quoting Ps. 2:1-2), and in Revelation 2:27 and 19:14 (quoting Ps. 2:9), a Messianic interpretation of Psalm 2 was implied. It is also assumed that God's words to the Messiah—"You are my beloved Son" (Mark 1:11; Luke 3:22)—were alluding to Psalm 2:7. However, this does not mean that the Psalm is primarily a Messian-

---

66. Cf. Wentsel (1981, 278-86).
67. Ratzinger (2007, 336).

Messianic Hopes in the Tanakh

ic psalm.⁶⁸ Many interpreters, like John Calvin, thought first of an ordinary Davidic king, who prefigured *the* great son of David.⁶⁹ Yet, we can understand why F. Delitzsch called the Psalm prophetic and Messianic.⁷⁰ The full reality of the Psalm extends far beyond whatever Davidic king, including Solomon, especially because of the world rule of the anointed king (vv. 8-9; cf. Rev. 19:19-21; 20:7-9).

Jewish expositors have wrestled with the same problem: is the Psalm primarily or secondarily Messianic? Rashi wrote: "Our Rabbis expound [the psalm] as relating to king Messiah; but according to its plain meaning it is proper to interpret it in connection with David, in the light of the statement: *And when the Philistines heard that David was anointed king over Israel, all the Philistines went up to seek David* (2 Sam. v. 17)."⁷¹ Not a son of David, but David himself would thus be the "begotten" (i.e., set, installed; v. 6) son of verse 7. However, in the Dead Sea scrolls Psalm 2 seems to be viewed as primarily Messianic.⁷²

The statement "you are my son" (in Psalm 2:7) is thought to refer to David, whereas in 2 Samuel 7:14 and Psalm 89:26 a similar expression is applied to Solomon, the son of David—but in their ultimate significance, these passages are Messianic as well. In its primary meaning, this sonship does not necessarily tell us anything about the king's descent. Nor must we think here of a deification of the Davidic king, like certain heathen nations viewed their kings as gods. The point involves an adoption in the sense of an official relationship between God and his anointed one established on the day of the latter's enthronement. No doubt the expression also involves favor and familiarity, but as such it does not point to

---

68. Cf. Van Estrik in Knevel and Paul (1995, 53, 55–56).
69. Ridderbos (1955, 19); Van Gemeren (1991, 65).
70. Delitzsch (KDC 5:89–91).
71. Quoted in Cohen (1985, 3).
72. Quotations in Longenecker (1981, 426), which also refers to 2 Sam. 7:14; here again some have thought primarily of a Messianic meaning, e.g., Schneider (1953, ad loc.).

an ontic relationship between God and his anointed one.[73] It is only in its Messianic *application* that it can be related to the divine birth of the Messiah (cf. Isa. 9:6; Micah 5:2 and Luke 1:35).

However, in Acts 13:32-33, the verb "begotten," quoted from Psalm 2:7, did not signify a "begetting" in the womb but an installing in the Messianic office, perhaps in connection with Christ's resurrection from the dead (cf. Rom. 1:4).[74] Therefore, some translations render verse 33 as follows: "Today I have begotten (or fathered) you" (NKJV), but others: "Today I have become your father" (NIV).

4.7.2 Isaiah 9:6-7

Of quite a different nature is Isaiah 9:6-7:

> For to us a child is born, to us a son is given; and the government shall be upon his shoulder, and his name shall be called Wonderful Counselor, Mighty God, Everlasting Father,[75] Prince of Peace. Of the increase of his government and of peace there will be no end, on the throne of David and over his kingdom, to establish it and to uphold it with justice and with righteousness from this time forth and forevermore. The zeal of the LORD of hosts will do this."

The first point of interest is that this passage is even more explicitly Messianic than Isaiah 7:14 or Psalm 2:7, yet is never quoted in the New Testament. (Another, almost as clearly Messianic, passage is Psalm 72, which is not quoted in the New Testament either.)

The second point of interest is that Isaiah emphasized the *childhood* of the redeemer, just as in 7:14 in comparison with 8:1-4, 18. The Talmud and medieval Jewish expositors such

---

73. Thus also Goslinga (1962, 143–44) on 2 Sam. 7:14.
74. This is related to how one understands the verb "to beget" in v. 33 *and* v. 34; cf. Knowling (1979, 295–96); Longenecker (1981, 428); Bruce (1988, 259–60).
75. It is remarkable that the "son" is described as "Everlasting Father," i.e., someone who, as the God-king, is the father of his people.

as Rashi and Abraham Ibn Ezra tried to combat the Christological exegesis of the passage by asserting that the text is referring only to the birth of crown prince Hezekiah. However, this does not agree with the chronology of Hezekiah's life. American theologian Joseph A. Alexander [76] argued that the four verbs of verse 6 must refer to the same moment in time, and this moment must be either before Hezekiah's birth or after his enthronement. Neither can be historically correct: the prophecy of Isaiah 7:1–9:7 dates from the time of the Syro-Ephraimite war (734–732 BC); at that time, Hezekiah had already been born (c. 741 BC), but he was not yet co-regent (c. 729 BC), nor was he king (c. 716 BC).

Moreover, the text implies that this is not an ordinary man; among his names are "Mighty God" and "Everlasting Father," and he receives an eternal rule.[77] Therefore, the Targum says emphatically that this refers to the "anointed one, in whose days there will be peace for us." However, this does not necessarily mean that the Targum is thinking of *the* Messiah in the eschatological sense. Rabbi Samson H. Levey assumed that the word "Messiah" (anointed one) in the Targum refers only to Hezekiah.[78]

According to one rabbinic tradition, God originally wished to make Hezekiah the Messiah, but he changed his mind after Hezekiah had failed to sing a hymn for him after his miraculous healing.[79] (We would rather point to a more serious failure by Hezekiah: see Isa. 39.) The greatest Messianic kings in the Tanakh are no doubt David, Solomon, Hezekiah, and Josiah—and they all failed miserably. There is only One who will never fail, and that is the One to whom these persons point.

Rabbi Slotki hid behind "modern non-Jewish exegetes" (read: liberal Christian theologians) who understood the text

---

76. Alexander (1980, 203); others have thought of different crown princes; see Buitink-Heijblom in Knevel and Paul (1995, 88–90).
77. Oswalt (1986, 245).
78. Quoted by Buitink-Heijblom in Knevel and Paul (1995, 88).
79. Sanhedrin 94a.

to be referring to a "contemporary person," namely Hezekiah; they quoted rabbi Isaac Abarbanel, who put the names into a separate sentence: "Wonderful in counsel is God the Mighty, the Everlasting Father, the Ruler of Peace."[80] In this way, not only is the link with the context severed, but it also ignores that, according to verse 7, the born child himself is the Peace-Bringer.[81] This cannot refer to Hezekiah, however, because he waged war, and was attacked by others.

Regarding the parallel phrases "to us a child is born" and "to us a son is given," the former refers to the human origin of the Messiah; he is the child that was born of the virgin (7:14). In the light of the New Testament, the latter phrase, concerning the *given* Son, seems to fit better with his divine nature, indicated also by the names "Mighty God, Everlasting Father".[82] I will return to these names later (§6.2.2); our present focus is the name "Son." The claim that the two names "Child" and "Son" refer to the humanity and deity of the Savior[83] is not exegesis but an interpretation in retrospect, inspired by the New Testament. The "given Son," who is a divine Son, supplies us with the answer to the question who is the Father of the Son born of the virgin (7:14). According to his divine nature, he is the Son of the Father; according to his human nature, he is the child of the virgin.

4.8   The Son of Man in Daniel 7
4.8.1   *Ben-Adam*

In the New Testament, Jesus referred to himself many times as the "Son of Man" — thirty times in Matthew alone. In the entire New Testament, no person ever mentioned this title except Jesus himself, and outside the Gospels, three others: Stephen (Acts 7:56), the writer of Hebrews 2:6, and the apostle

---

80. Slotki (1983, 44).
81. Rashi and Kimchi solve this by translating: "And the Wonderful One, the Counselor, the Mighty God, the Everlasting Father calls his [= Hezekiah's] name Prince of Peace."
82. See extensively, Davis (2004).
83. Bultema (1981, 123).

John (Rev. 1:13 and 14:14).[84]

The remarkable fact that Jesus so often called himself the Son of Man can be understood only from the Tanakh (the same is true of most other key notions in the New Testament). The Hebrew expression *ben-adam*, literally "son of a (or, the) man (human)," primarily means "human being," member of the human race.[85] Because the Hebrew *adam* does not have a plural form, the notion of "humans" is often rendered as *b'nē-(ha)adam*, "humans, people" (lit., "sons of a/the human," members of the human race).

The singular *ben-adam* in the simple meaning of "human being" occurs more than ninety times in Ezekiel; it is the Lord addressing the prophet in this way (2:1, 3, 6, 8). It is here "a depicting of weakness and mortality, powerlessness and dependence, humility and submission"[86] (cf. Job 25:6; Isa. 51:12, and especially in contrast with God's greatness: Num. 23:19; Job 35:7-8; Ps. 146:3). At the same time, the association of *ben-adam* ("Son of Man") with the Messiah is so strong that some understood this title in Ezekiel to be a foreshadowing of the Messiah.[87]

4.8.2 Daniel 7:13

Occasionally, Hebrew uses *ben-enosh* ("son of a mortal") for "son of man," as in Psalm 144:3. The Aramaic text of Daniel 7:13 reflects this by using the expression *bar-enash*, "son of man." In Daniel 2:38 and 5:21, the Aramaic *b'nē-anasha* means "children of man" (humans, people). Within the context of Daniel 7, too, the primary meaning of *ben-enosh* is simply "human being"; here the term does not yet have the specific meaning that it acquired later. In Daniel 7:13, there is someone "*like* a son of man" appearing—simply someone who looked

---
84. This fact that hardly anyone other than Jesus uses this title for Jesus has led to vigorous debates; see Ratzinger (2007, 321–35).
85. See the extensive study by Michel (1992); cf. Wentsel (1981, 270–78); Sevenster (1986, 1749–52); I. H. Marshall (*DJG* 775–81).
86. Noordtzij (1932, 57); cf. Alexander (1986, 761).
87. Grant and Bloore (1931, 24).

THE ETERNAL CHRIST: GOD WITH US

like a human being (cf. Ezek. 1:26, "a likeness with a human appearance"; Rev. 1:13 GNT: "like a human being").[88]

There are at least two major differences with what we find earlier in Daniel 7: the four beasts.

(1) The beasts *come up* out of the sea (Dan. 7:2), presumably a picture of the restless nations (cf. Isa. 17:12; Rev. 17:15), whereas the Son of Man *comes down* from heaven. The beasts are products of human history, whereas the Son of Man is a divine intervention from above.

(2) The beasts are *like* a lion, a bear, a leopard, respectively (Dan. 7:4-6) — the fourth beast was different (vv. 7, 23-24) — whereas the person coming down is "*like* a son of man" ("like a human being," GNT); he is not a beast but a human, someone of the species of Man (*Homo sapiens*).

We sense immediately that this is not just a common man; and this is our experience wherever this title is used in the Bible.

> In the Son of Man, man is revealed as he truly ought to be... . The enigmatic term "Son of Man" presents us in concentrated form with all that is most original and distinctive about the figure of Jesus, his mission, and his being. He comes from God and he is God. But that is precisely what makes him — having assumed human nature — the bringer of true humanity.... He comes from God and hence establishes the true form of man's being.[89]

In Daniel 7, he is the Human of humans, just like the fourth beast is a kind of "Beast of the beasts" ("terrifying and dreadful and exceedingly strong. It had great iron teeth; it devoured and broke in pieces and stamped what was left with its feet. It was different from all the beasts that were before it," v. 7).

This *bar-enash*, this Man *par excellence*, comes on the clouds

---

88. *Contra* Van Genderen and Velema (2008, 442), who saw in the title "Son of Man" as occurring in Dan. 7:13 a title of royal rank.
89. Ratzinger (2007, 325, 333–34); we should become such a human too (1 Cor. 15:48–49; Eph. 4:24; Col. 3:9–11).

of heaven, and receives from God (the "Ancient of days," v. 9) "dominion and glory and a kingdom, that all peoples, nations, and languages should serve him; his dominion is an everlasting dominion, which shall not pass away, and his kingdom one that shall not be destroyed" (v. 14). Note the contrast with the fourth beast, which strives for world dominion: "[I]t shall devour the whole earth, and trample it down, and break it to pieces" (v. 23).

4.8.3 A Messianic Figure

It is no wonder that ancient Jewish expositors have referred verses 13-14 to the Messiah, even though a modern exegete like Rabbi Israel Slotki, in the light of verse 27, wishes to think of the reborn nation of Israel.[90] The rabbis did feel a tension, though, with Zechariah 9:9: will the Messiah come on the clouds of heaven, or riding on a donkey? In the Talmud, one of them says, "If they [i.e., Israel] are meritorious, [he will come] with the clouds of heaven; if not, lowly and riding upon an ass."[91] This is not the place to enter into the difficulties of such a view: *both* prophecies are unconditional, and *both* must have their fulfillment, but (as the New Testament shows) at different times.

In the Septuagint, more strongly than in the Targum and in Theodotion's Greek translation, it comes to expression more clearly that the "Son of Man" receives nothing less than God's authority as judge. Some suggest that this implies the notion of a pre-existent Messiah.[92] This is supported by the fact that, in verse 13, the Septuagint renders Hebrew *im* ("with") with Greek *epi* ("upon"), whereas appearing *on* clouds normally is said of God alone (cf. Ps. 68:33-34; 97:2; 104:3; Lam. 3:44; and especially Isa. 19:1).

In Jewish apocalyptic writings, the "Son of Man" became

---

90. Slotki (1985, 60, 63).
91. Sanhedrin 98a.
92. Hengel (1995, 183-84 and references).

an important Messianic figure.[93] In the parables of 1 Enoch, he is the object of the hope of a pious community. He is the chosen One, the righteous One, the representative of God's righteousness and wisdom, One who had existed before the foundation of the world, One who enters into the Messianic conflict with the spiritual powers, and comes out of this as the Overcomer (46:3 etc.; 48:2 etc.; 62:7). The text clearly reflects Daniel 7, but also the psalms and the prophets, Isaiah in particular. We must be careful with 1 Enoch, though, because it is not clear whether there are Christian influences in the book (it originated between AD 40 and 70, the parables possibly even later).[94] We can conclude, however, that 1 Enoch understands the Son of Man in Daniel 7 to be a Messianic figure, without the expression "Son of Man" having become a Messianic *title*.

In 2 Esdras (= 4 Ezra) 13 as well, the expression "Son of Man" is a reference to a Messianic figure, although quite different from 1 Enoch. Especially the fantastic imagery is remarkable here. At any rate, the apocalyptic literature is important in the transition to the New Testament period, when the title "Son of Man" plays a great role within the Jewish community. Here, Jesus applies this title unhesitatingly to himself, with all the Messianic connotations involved in this (see further in chapter 8).

Rabbi Akiva seemed to clearly identify the Son of Man in Daniel 7:13 with the Davidic Messiah; the rabbinic tradition, including the Talmud, has many similar suggestions.[95]

4.9 The Son of Man in the Psalms
4.9.1 Psalm 8 and Hebrews 2

In Hebrews 2:6–8, the writer quotes Psalm 8:4–6 and applies it to Jesus. The text of the Psalm says,

> [W]hat is man [Heb. *enosh*] that you are mindful of him, and

---

93. Michel (1992, 614–17); Zwiep (2003, 17–31); Knight (2004, 117–20).
94. Brown (1994a, 93).
95. Hagigah 14a; Sanhedrin 38b (see SBK 1:238; 4:871, 1104–1105); see Hengel (1995, 194–95).

the son of man [*ben-adam*] that you care for him? Yet you have made him a little lower than the heavenly beings [or gods, or God, Heb. *elohim*] and crowned him with glory and honor. You have given him dominion over the works of your hands; you have put all things under his feet.

It is quite remarkable to see how the writer of Hebrews applies this Psalm; here we have an excellent example of a Tanakh passage where the grammatical-historical exegesis would hardly arrive at a Messianic interpretation.[96] As far as I know, Jewish exegesis has never proposed a Messianic understanding of this Psalm. On the contrary, the primary meaning of the Psalm is evident: God has established man as lord over the earth, and endowed with powers that make him only little less than God himself.[97]

All the more striking, then, that the writer of Hebrews 2 finds in the Psalm a Messianic thrust. The "Son of Man" is now the One "who for a little while was made lower than the angels, namely Jesus, crowned with glory and honor because of the suffering of death, so that by the grace of God he might taste death for everyone" (v.9). It is quite possible that the writer was well aware of the primary — or literal historical — meaning of Psalm 8, but in addition recognized the eschatological significance of the Psalm.

Interestingly, the notion of a Messianic significance of the Psalm is not exclusive to the writer of Hebrews. When Jesus quoted the saying from Psalm 8:2 — "Out of the mouth of infants and nursing babies you have prepared praise" (Matt. 21:16) — was this based upon merely an aural association? Or was he not actually claiming for himself the honor that is brought to God because he, Jesus, is the Messianic God-Man? At least he assigned to the Psalm a Messianic orientation. The apostle Paul did exactly the same by quoting twice the words of verse 6b ("you have put all things under his feet"), both

---

96. See more extensively, Ouweneel (1982, 1:32–37).
97. See Cohen (1985, 18–19).

times applying them to the Messiah (1 Cor. 15:27; Eph. 1:22). Thus, we are not dealing with an idiosyncrasy of the writer of Hebrews, for Jesus and especially Paul testified indirectly to the Messianic thrust of Psalm 8.

4.9.2 The Messianic Thrust

What arguments could we adduce for arguing that this Messianic significance must be present in the Psalm, and was not read back into it in order to salvage certain New Testament quotations of it? First, we notice the idealizing way the Psalm speaks about "man" (the human race). How can Psalm 8 offer us such an optimistic picture of man as ruler over the creation? Does David not know about the Fall and its consequences? Compare this with Psalm 144:3-4: "O LORD, what is man [Heb. *adam*] that you regard him, or the son of man [Heb. *ben-enosh*] that you think of him? Man is like a breath; his days are like a passing shadow." Is not the portrait of Psalm 144 far more realistic? Here, David wonders how God can take care of such tiny and unworthy beings as humans.

However, in Psalm 8:4-6, David asks almost the same question, but now considering the *greatness* of humanity; only the Hebrew terms *enosh* and *adam* are reversed. Psalm 144 represents the overall teaching of the Tanakh: what is tiny humanity, such that God is at all interested in it? In my view, Psalm 8 is the striking *exception*: what is man that God has elevated him to such a height that man is allowed to rule over all God's works, yea, all created things have been put under his feet? It may be true that the Psalm is primarily describing the greatness of the *first* Adam, though with a remarkable optimism and idealism that overlooks the human Fall (Gen. 3). However, secondarily, the Psalm is speaking of the *last* Adam (cf. 1 Cor. 15:45). It does so in a language that, to make the parallelism between the first and the last Adam quite clear, obviously draws on Genesis 1. Psalm 8 echoed what the first Adam had possessed originally but forfeited through the Fall, while it also anticipated what the last Adam will possess during the Messianic kingdom (cf., e.g., Isa. 11:1–10; 65:21–25).

If we are willing to entertain this understanding of Psalm 8, we can begin to understand how verse 5 was understood by the author of Hebrews 2: "[Y]ou have made him a little lower than the *elohim*, and crowned him with glory and honor." Let us remember first that translating *elohim* as "angels" originated not with the author of Hebrews but with the Septuagint. Why the Septuagint did this seems clear: the thought that humanity would be just a little lower than YHWH seems almost blasphemous. Others have preferred the rendering "gods";[98] in the Bible the "gods" are created angelic powers (cf. Col. 1:16).[99] At any rate, the translation "angels" or "gods" (ESV: "heavenly beings") is not only acceptable but also preferable to the rendering "God."

The "Son of Man" has been "made a little lower than the heavenly beings." What a wonderful example of a double entendre! With reference to the first Adam, these words refer to his *greatness*: in the creation order he is only a little lower than the "gods" (angelic powers). But with reference to the last Adam, these same words refer to his *humiliation* in his incarnation, and in his sufferings and death, when he was placed even below the angels.

In summary, I agree with W. Van Gemeren, who argued that this Psalm is not Messianic in the narrow sense of the term, yet it is applicable in a Messianic way in the sense that Jesus is perfect Man, and has realized God's expectation of humanity in perfect obedience and holiness.[100] At the same time, I emphasize that the Psalm goes further than this: it refers to the Messiah not only in the moral sense but especially in the eschatological sense, that is, as the ultimate human ruler of the world (the Messianic kingdom).

---

98. Ridderbos (1955, 74–75).
99. See Ouweneel (2003, especially chapter 2; Eng. translation forthcoming).
100. Van Gemeren (1991, 110).

4.9.3 Psalm 80

There is one other passage that demands our attention when it comes to the expression "son of man." This is Psalm 80:17, "[L]et your hand be on the man of your right hand [Heb. *ish yeminehka*], the son of man (Heb. *ben-adam*) whom you have made strong for yourself," especially together with verse 15: "... the stock that your right hand planted, and for the son [*ben*; others: branch] whom you made strong for yourself." In light of the preceding verse, verse 15 clearly refers to Israel, which came under judgment because of its infidelity. Over against this, the faithful ones now place their hope in the son of David, referred to as "the man of your right hand" (cf. Ps. 110:1) and the "Son of Man," who ultimately is *the* son of David, the Messiah.[101] The Targum, along with many older Christian expositors, thought here of the Messiah.

J. Ridderbos could not accept such a transition from the collective interpretation (in v. 15) to an individual one (in v.17).[102] However, on the basis of many Tanakh passages—most of them discussed in this chapter—we find that the collective interpretation (Israel) and the individual one (the Messiah) often merge, because the Messiah is the true (faithful) Israel.[103]

Charles Spurgeon wrote about Psalm 18:17:

> There is no doubt here an outlook to the Messiah, for whom believing Jews had learned to look as the Saviour in time of trouble. . . . It is by the man Christ Jesus that fallen Israel is yet to rise, and indeed through him, who deigns to call himself the Son of Man, the world is to be delivered from the dominion of Satan and the curse of sin.[104]

And Joseph Ratzinger wrote: "Psalm 80:18 closely associates the 'Son of man' with the vine [v. 14]. Conversely: Although

---

101. See ibid., 527–28 and the references there.
102. Ridderbos (1958, 315).
103. Ouweneel (2000a, chapter 2).
104. Spurgeon (2008, ad loc.); also cf. Alexander Pirie, quoted by him (197–98).

the Son has now himself become the vine [John 15:1], this is precisely his method for remaining one with his own, with all the scattered children of God whom he has come to gather (cf. Jn 11:52)."[105] The vine taken out of Egypt (Ps. 80:8, 14) corresponds with the son called out of Egypt (Hos. 11:1). The primary referent of both is Israel, but their secondary referent is the Messiah, the Vine and Son *par excellence* (cf. Matt. 2:15; John 15:1).

4.10 The Messianic Prophet
4.10.1 Moses' Announced Prophet

It is customary in theology, most prominently since Calvin and in the Reformed tradition, to describe the ministry of the Messiah in terms of his threefold office (Lat. *munus triplex*). These three offices have in common that all three of them are based upon *anointing*: the office of *prophet* (cf. 1 Kings 19:16; Isa. 61:1-3; see also the parallelism in Ps. 105:15), the office of *priest* (cf. Exod. 29:7; 30:30; Lev. 8:12; Num. 3:3), and the office of *king* (cf. 1 Sam. 16:13; 2 Sam. 2:4; 5:3). In this volume, we are devoting limited attention to the matter because a treatment of the three offices can be given more extensively only in connection with the *work* of the Messiah (see the forthcoming soteriological volumes).

The first and most important reference to the Messiah as prophet is found in these words of Moses:

> The LORD your God will raise up for you a prophet like me from among you, from your brothers—it is to him you shall listen—just as you desired of the LORD your God at Horeb on the day of the assembly, when you said, "Let me not hear again the voice of the LORD my God or see this great fire any more, lest I die." And the LORD said to me, "They are right in what they have spoken. I will raise up for them a prophet like you from among their brothers. And I will put my words in his mouth, and he shall speak to them all that I command him" (Deut. 18:15-18).

---

105. Ratzinger (2007, 260).

From the New Testament it is clear that the Jews in Jesus' day understood this passage eschatologically.[106] They expected a special prophet, as shown by their question to John the Baptist: "Are you the Prophet?" (John 1:21, 25); at the same time, this passage shows that, to these people, it was not self-evident that the Messiah and the Prophet would be identical because they distinguished between the two: "They asked him, 'Then why are you baptizing, if you are neither the Christ, nor Elijah, nor the Prophet?'" (v. 25).

When Philip told Nathanael, "We have found him of whom Moses in the Law and also the prophets wrote, Jesus of Nazareth, the son of Joseph" (v. 46), he was likely thinking of Deuteronomy 18 (cf. John 5:46). In John 6:14, the Jewish people said of Jesus, "This is indeed the Prophet who is to come into the world!" In Acts 3:22-23, the apostle Peter applies our text unequivocally to Jesus, and not to the prophets in general, as Rashi does in Deuteronomy 18 and Edelkoort in Acts 3.[107]

These examples do not necessarily imply that Deuteronomy 18:15-18 is primarily Messianic.[108] Moses primarily announced only a successor (Joshua? Samuel? see 1 Sam. 3:20; Acts 13:20), followed by an entire series of prophets, who usually did not prophesy simultaneously, but one after the other. The singular "prophet" is no problem here; in Deuteronomy 17:14-20, Moses also speaks of "the king" (singular), whereas there have been many kings in Israel. However, in addition to this primary meaning there has been some expectation of one very special prophet, as is clear from the Gospels. Thus, Rabbi Levi ben Gershom (or Gersonides, d. 1344) in his *Sefer Milhamot Adonai* ("Book of the Wars of the Lord," finished 1329) expressed the belief that Moses' words referred to the Messiah.

---

106. Cf. Also 1QS IX, 9–10; 4QTest. and see Hengel (1995, 39).
107. Cohen (1983, 1085); Edelkoort (1941, 76–78).
108. Craigie (1976, 262); Paul in Knevel and Paul (1995, 33–36).

4.10.2 More than Moses

Perhaps this expectation was inspired more by Deuteronomy 34:10-12, where we read:

> [T]here has not arisen a prophet since in Israel like Moses, whom the Lord knew face to face, none like him for all the signs and the wonders that the Lord sent him to do in the land of Egypt, to Pharaoh and to all his servants and to all his land, and for all the mighty power and all the great deeds of terror that Moses did in the sight of all Israel.

As Israel declined, the longing for a "second Moses" was deepened. What the faithful wanted was a prophet of his stature (cf. Num. 12:6-8), who would perform equally great or even greater miracles against the people's enemies and would usher in definitive redemption.[109]

What Israel needs most is a prophet like Moses, "whom the Lord knew face to face." As the Lord said himself, "With him I speak mouth to mouth, clearly, and not in riddles, and he beholds the form of the Lord" (Num. 12:8). This is the Prophet with a capital P:

> He shows us the face of God, and in so doing he shows us the path that we have to take. . . . And the characteristic of this "prophet" will be that he converses with God face-to-face, as a friend does with a friend [Exod. 33:11]. His distinguishing note will be his immediate relation with God, which enables him to communicate God's will and word firsthand and unadulterated. And that is the saving intervention which Israel — indeed, the whole of humanity — is waiting for.[110]

Recall that Moses was allowed to see only God's "back" (Exod. 33:20-23); therefore, the "new Moses" (cf. Heb. 3:1-6) was expected to receive what was not granted to the first Moses:

---

109. Craigie (1976, 406–407).
110. Ratzinger (2007, 4–5; see 1–8).

> . . . a real, immediate vision of the face of God, and thus the ability to speak entirely from seeing, not just from looking at God's back. . . . [Jesus] lives before the face of God, not just as friend, but as Son; he lives in the most intimate unity with the Father. . . . Jesus' teaching . . . originates from immediate contact with the Father, from "face-to-face" dialogue–from the vision of the one who rests close to the Father's heart [John 1:18].[111]

From John 1:25 and 7:40–41 ("When they heard these words, some of the people said, 'This really is the Prophet.' Others said, 'This is the Messiah'") we learn that in New Testament times a distinction was made between the prophet and the Messiah; possibly the former was viewed as the forerunner of the latter.

Isaiah 61:1–3 is not necessarily primarily Messianic, either:

> The Spirit of the Lord GOD is upon me, because the LORD has anointed me to bring good news to the poor; he has sent me to bind up the brokenhearted, to proclaim liberty to the captives, and the opening of the prison to those who are bound; to proclaim the year of the LORD's favor, ...

This speaker is first of all the prophetic writer, who secondarily, in his very quality of prophet, may be understood as a type of the Messiah. In the synagogue of Nazareth, Jesus applied the prophecy to himself (Luke 4:17–21), which again is an example of a *pesher* interpretation.[112] The latter is highly important, but does not prove that the prophecy is primarily Messianic; it can be taken to refer to the prophets in general.[113] It is equally clear, though, that it is only in the Messiah that the prophecy finds its ultimate fulfillment.[114] And it is important that this very prophecy makes the notion of the Messiah accessible to believers from the Gentiles: the Man with the oil bringing the happy message of healing, redemption, deliver-

---

111. Ibid., 5–7.
112. See note 6.
113. Calvin (*Comm. Isaiah* ad loc.).
114. Young (1972, 458–59).

ance.[115]

4.11 The Messianic Priest
4.11.1 Psalm 110:4

We read in Psalm 110:4, "The LORD has sworn and will not change his mind, 'You are a priest forever after the order of Melchizedek.'" These words are quoted several times in Hebrews (5:6, 10; 6:20; 7:11, 17).[116] This could be one of the Tanakh passages of which the Jews were thinking, when they said, "We have heard from the Law [Torah, here in the sense of Tanakh] that the Christ remains forever" (John 12:34). Other possible Tanakh passages are Isaiah 9:7 and Daniel 7:14 (see also Luke 1:32–33).

Rabbi Abraham Cohen distanced himself not only from the Christological exegesis of this Psalm,[117] but also from the view that the protagonist was Simon the Maccabee, who combined the monarchy with the office of high priest.[118] Cohen referred to Rashi, who thought of Abraham (Gen. 14), and to Ibn Ezra, Bible scholar Alexander F. Kirkpatrick, and chief rabbi Hermann Adler, who, like Cohen, thought of David (see also §4.12.2). David was a priest, not in the Levitical sense, but "after the order" (i.e., the ideal model, example) of Melchizedek, who was both king and priest (Gen. 14:18). Harold H. Rowley saw a connection between king David and the Zadokian priesthood.[119]

Seeing David as the referent here is highly suggestive because to some extent all *three* offices mentioned were combined in him.

(1) Especially in 2 Samuel 23:1-7 (apart from many prophetic psalms) he is clearly a *prophet*: "The oracle of David, the son of Jesse, the oracle of the man who was raised on high,

---

115. Cf. Grün (2002, 134–36).
116. See more extensively, Ouweneel (1982, 1:68, 84–85, 91–94).
117. See Berkouwer (1954, 178) on the (non-)Messianic character of Ps. 110.
118. Cohen (1985, 371).
119. Rowley (1950).

the anointed of the God of Jacob, the sweet psalmist of Israel: 'The Spirit of the LORD speaks by me; his word is on my tongue,'" and so on.

(2) In passages such as 2 Samuel 6:13-18 and 1 Chronicles 21:28, David acted like a *priest*: he offered sacrifices, was clothed like a priest (v. 14), and laid a priestly blessing upon the people (v. 18). (Solomon, too, offered sacrifices and blessed the people [1 Kings 8:14, 55, 62-64], while even the Levitical high priest stood under him [2:27, 35].)

(3) And of course, David was *king*, as we will consider below.

As we saw in other cases as well, Psalm 110 is not primarily Messianic but generally applicable, in this case, to the Davidic kings.[120] But here again, we must say that the Psalm is understood in its full depth only if the Messianic thrust is recognized, as is worked out in the New Testament. Interestingly, Jesus himself pointed to the remarkable fact that David in verse 1 addresses the protagonist as "my Lord" (Matt. 22:43-45 par.). How can David address either himself or one of his own descendants as "my Lord," unless this very special "son of David" is the Messiah himself?

4.11.2 Zechariah 6:12-13

Zechariah 6:12-13 also suggests a remarkable connection between kingship and priesthood:

> Behold, the man whose name is the Branch: for he shall branch out from his place, and he shall build the temple of the LORD. It is he who shall build the temple of the LORD and shall bear royal honor, and shall sit and rule on his throne. And there [or, he] shall be a priest on his throne, and the counsel of peace shall be between them both.

Notice here the two different renderings in verse 13, which can both be defended: either "[besides the king] there shall be a priest on his throne," or "he [i.e., the king] shall [also] be a

---

120. Cf. Paul (1987); Van Gemeren (1991, 696–700); Hengel (1995, chapter 3).

priest on his throne."

The Dead Sea scrolls expect two Messianic figures: a high priest of the house of Phinehas (cf. Num. 25:10-13; hence the "sons of Zadok" in Ezek. 40:46; 43:19; 44:15; 48:11) and a king from the house of David. Also Rabbi Eli Cashdan read the text in this way, and assumed that the Branch was Zerubbabel (though with Messianic overtones; Zech. 4:6-10), and the intended priest was Joshua (3:1-9; 6:11).[121]

The difficulty with this interpretation is, first, that in chapter 3:8 the Branch is presented as future, whereas Zerubbabel was already present, and, second, that the latter has never received any royal dignity, and never has occupied a royal throne. More remarkably, in 6:11 it is not Zerubbabel but Joshua who receives a crown, although he himself never received the office of king-priest.[122] This is one of the arguments for translating verse 13 not as "there will be a priest," but as "he will be priest."[123] Thus, the ending of verse 13, "the counsel of peace shall be between them both," means nothing else than that, within the Messiah, there will be perfect harmony between the two offices. Zerubbabel and Joshua,[124] the two "messiahs" ("anointed ones," 4:14), constitute together a type prefiguring the one Messiah, the crowned King-Priest on the throne.[125]

Joseph Ratzinger pointed to another, deeper hint of Jesus' priesthood.[126] In addition to Melchizedek, the great prototype of all biblical priesthood, the high priest Aaron is called in Psalm 106:16 "the holy one of the LORD." Something similar

---

121. In Cohen (1980, 293); Edelkoort (1941 and 1945) connected with this point various speculations about whether Haggai and Zechariah might have erroneously viewed Zerubbabel as the Messiah.
122. The suggestion by Edelkoort (1945, 81; cf. 83) and others that in v. 11 we must read "Zerubbabel" does not find any support in the manuscripts.
123. Ridderbos (1935, 105); Baldwin (1972, 137); Barker (1985, 640).
124. In Ezra and Nehemiah he is called "Jeshua," which in the Septuagint is rendered as *Iēsous*, "Jesus" (cf. Heb. 4:8 *Iēsous* = Joshua).
125. Unger (1962, 609–610); Barker (1985, 638–41).
126. Ratzinger (2007, 302–303).

was also written on his turban, on a golden plate: "Holy to the LORD," that is, "Consecrated to the LORD" (Exod. 28:36; 39:30). In Hebrew, the word for "consecrating" to the priesthood is from the same root *q-d-sh*, "holy" (28:3, 41; 29:1, 21, 33, 44; Lev. 8:12, 30). Given these facts, it is remarkable that Peter says of Jesus: "[W]e have believed, and have come to know, that you are the Holy One of God" (John 6:69; cf. Mark 1:24; Luke 4:34). He says this immediately after Jesus' exposition that he would give his "flesh" for the life of the world (v. 51), which is a priestly (sacrificial) act (cf. Heb. 2:17, Jesus was "a merciful and faithful high priest in the service of God, to make propitiation for the sins of the people").

4.12 The Messianic King
4.12.1 Introduction

As we saw, the title "Messiah," the Anointed One, is related to all three Messianic offices: prophet, priest, and king. Nevertheless, the title is linked in particular with Messiah's kingship; especially in the Psalms, the "anointed one" is always the king (2:2; 18:50; 20:6; 28:8; 84:9; 89:38, 51; 132:10, 17), often with obvious Messianic traits.

In the New Testament, "the Christ" (Gk. *ho christos*, "the anointed one") is originally simply the Greek rendering of "the Messiah"; but gradually this title developed into a name. In the combination "Jesus Christ," "Christ" is hardly recognizable as a title. Especially where "Christ" occurs as a subject, without the article and without the addition "Jesus" (Rom. 5:6, 8; 6:4, 9), it has become a full name. As Joseph Ratzinger expressed it: "What began as an interpretation ended up as a name [Christ], and therein lies a deeper message: He is completely one with his office; his task and his person are totally inseparable from each other. It was thus right for his task to become a part of his name."[127]

I may add to this that, at the same time, the name always reminds us of the link with Israel: he is the Messiah of *Israel*.

---
127. Ibid., 319.

"Christ [Messiah!] became a servant to the circumcised [i.e., Israel] to show God's truthfulness, in order to confirm the promises given to the patriarchs" (Rom. 15:8) — promises that are irrevocable (cf. 11:29).

4.12.2 Psalms

We have seen examples of the Messianic royal office, such as Genesis 49:10 and Daniel 7:13-14, and all the passages that link the Messiah with (the house of) David. In this section, some other royal psalms must be dealt with. I reserve Psalm 45 for §6.2.2.

Psalm 72 offers the ideal picture of the Davidic king, with a strong emphasis on righteousness and peace, as is common in Messianic prophecies.[128] Rabbinic tradition, too, discerns in the Psalm a Messianic thrust; see Targum and Talmud.[129] Rashi interpreted the Psalm as David's prayer for his son Solomon; compare the first words: the Hebrew *lish'lomoh*, which can mean "of Solomon" (ESV, NIV) but also "for Solomon" (NKJV). Connected with this is the question what translational form is chosen: the declarative ("He *will* judge Your people with righteousness, and Your poor with justice," v. 2 NKJV), or the hortative ("May he judge your people with righteousness, and your poor with justice," ESV). Obviously, the declarative fits the Messianic thrust better.

Having considered Psalm 110:4 (§4.11.1) we must now look at verse 1. There is no verse in the Tanakh to which the New Testament alludes more often: "The LORD says to my Lord: 'Sit at my right hand, until I make your enemies your footstool'" (see Matt. 22:44 par.; 1 Cor. 15:25; Heb. 1:13; 10:12-13). This is no wonder: no Tanakh passage seems to speak more clearly of the ascension and heavenly glorification of the Messiah than this one (cf. Acts 2:34-35). Jesus did *not* link the sitting at God's right hand with, for instance, the temple on earth, where the ark of the covenant is placed, which some-

---

128. Van Gemeren (1991, 469).
129. Cohen (1985, 227).

times is also called the throne of God (1 Sam. 4:4; 2 Sam. 6:2; 2 Kings 19:15; 1 Chron. 13:6; Ps. 80:1; 99:1; Isa. 37:16). No, he linked it with heaven by adding immediately that he would come down from there on the clouds of heaven (Matt. 26:64 par.). All the relevant New Testament passages speaking of the Messiah's sitting at God's right hand *in heaven* (e.g., Acts 7:55–56; Rom. 8:34; Eph. 1:20; Col. 3:1; Heb. 1:3; 1 Pet. 3:22) go back to Psalm 110:1.

Yet, as we saw, the Psalm does not necessarily have a primary Messianic meaning. For instance, Psalm 110:1 can be linked with 1 Chronicles 29:23, where Solomon is sitting on the "throne of YHWH" (cf. 28:5, "the throne of the kingdom of YHWH over Israel"). Psalm 110:1 does not explain where the protagonist sits down at God's right hand, and a simple earthly meaning is most natural. Verse 1b finds a direct application to David in 1 Kings 5:3, where Solomon says, "You know that David my father could not build a house for the name of the LORD his God because of the warfare with which his enemies surrounded him, *until the LORD put them under the soles of his feet.*" Secondarily, however, it cannot be denied that the Psalm finds its highest and most complete fulfillment in the Messianic King-Priest, just as do Psalms 2, 45, 72, and 132.

4.12.3 Zechariah

The final part of Zechariah contains some remarkable Messianic references; I limit myself here to two passages (see also §6.2.3). The first says,

> Rejoice greatly, O daughter of Zion! Shout aloud, O daughter of Jerusalem! Behold, your king is coming to you; righteous and having salvation is he, humble and mounted on a donkey, on a colt, the foal of a donkey. I will cut off the chariot from Ephraim and the war horse from Jerusalem; and the battle bow shall be cut off, and he shall speak peace to the nations; his rule shall be from sea to sea, and from the River to the ends of the earth (9:9–10).

Three things are mentioned of the Messiah: (1) he is righteous, (2) he is *nosha*, literally "saved" *or* "bringing salvation" (NRSV: "victorious"), and (3) he is humble.

Rabbi Ibn Ezra saw here a reference to Judas the Maccabee, others to Nehemiah, but Rashi believed that the passage "can only refer to King Messiah of whom it is said, 'And his dominion shall be from sea to sea,' since we do not find any ruler with such wide dominion during the days of the Second Temple."[130] Also Rabbi Cashdan recognized in verse 10a the "first effect of the Messianic age: the destruction of all implements of war."[131]

Matthew 21:4-5 and John 12:14-15 referred the passage to Jesus, specifically to his entry into Jerusalem, riding on a young donkey. Of course, this entry could only be a preliminary fulfillment; ultimately, the passage refers to the Messianic kingdom of peace (v. 10). In those days we expect an entry that will be more in line with Psalm 24:7, "Lift up your heads, O gates [of Jerusalem]! And be lifted up, O ancient doors, that the King of glory may come in."

Zechariah 12:10 is the second important Messianic passage: "I will pour on the house of David and on the inhabitants of Jerusalem the Spirit of grace and supplication; then they will look on Me whom they pierced. Yes, they will mourn for Him as one mourns for [his] only [son], and grieve for Him as one grieves for a firstborn" (NKJV). The middle part is quite remarkable; one could read here: ". . . they will look on *me* because they pierced him." Many Jewish expositors believe in this case that "they" are the nations, and that "him" refers to Israel. But Rashi refers the passage to the so-called "Messiah son of Joseph," who is supposed to die in battle.[132] Again, Cashdan hides behind liberal Christian expositors, who do not wish to assume any Christological meaning in the text but

---

130. Quoted in Cohen (1980, 305).
131. Ibid., 306.
132. In reference to Soekkah 52a, Kimchi, and Ibn Ezra; cf. De Wilde (1929, 247).

think it refers to some unknown martyr.[133]

The apostle John said of Jesus on the cross: "And again another Scripture says, 'They will look on him whom they have pierced'" (John 19:37). Elsewhere John said, "Behold, he is coming with the clouds, and every eye will see him, even those who pierced him, and all tribes of the earth will wail on account of him" (Rev. 1:7). Evidently, the piercing was in the past; but of course, the complete fulfillment of Zechariah's prophecy lies in the end times: the mourning will be at the return of the Messiah, followed by the Messianic kingdom as described in the remainder of the book of Zechariah.

4.13 Other Messianic Psalms
4.13.1 Psalm 16

Psalm 16 is one of the many Psalms of which certain parts are related to the Messiah in the New Testament. The apostle Peter in Acts 2:24–32, and the apostle Paul in 13:35–37, adduced Psalm 16:10 as evidence for the resurrection of the Messiah. The verse says, "For you will not abandon my soul to Sheol, or let your holy one see corruption [or, see the pit]." To us, this may seem a rather weak piece of evidence; but in Acts 2 Peter gives a *pesher* interpretation. At first sight, the text simply seems to say that David was confident that God would *keep* him from death, and not that God would *raise* him from death. However, the verse also allows for a different interpretation. The expression "you will not abandon my soul to Sheol" *can* mean: you will make sure that I will never get there; but also: After I have arrived in Sheol, you will not abandon me to it (or, leave me there), that is, you will raise me from death. The second line is perhaps even clearer: "you will not . . . let your holy one see corruption." This *can* mean: You will make sure that I do not die (and thus will see corruption), but also: You will make sure that, when I will be in Sheol, I will not see corruption.

The Septuagint seems to go more into the direction of this

---
133. In Cohen (1980, 321–22).

second interpretation than the Masoretic text does: "You will not abandon my soul to [in the sense of: leave my soul in] the Sheol." This means: my soul will have to spend some time in Sheol, but not forever. We must consider here that the Septuagint, as a Jewish translation, reflects to some extent the Jewish *understanding* of the text, prevalent a few centuries before the birth of Christ. Peter and Paul cite something close to the text of the Septuagint.

Thus, there is a deeper significance in this Psalm, which Peter and Paul have in view.[134] Their argument is: nobody can claim that *David* was rescued from the tomb, and therefore the text must be referring prophetically to another person. This was someone who was prefigured by David, but was himself greater than David: the son of David, the Messiah. As far as we can assess, the apostles were connecting here with the current Jewish exegesis, that is, an older exegesis, which could not yet have been (anti-)Christologically biased.

Rabbinic tradition sees in this verse a reference to the immortality of the righteous.[135] The text is also used in the liturgy in this sense. Some rabbis saw here a hint of the Messiah. That is to say, there is a midrash of the Psalms in which a line in Psalm 16:9 is as follows: "[M]y glory[136] rejoices in the Lord, the Messiah, who will come forth from me [i.e., David]." This midrash was written down at a much later time than the book of Acts; after the arrival of Christianity some rabbis apparently associated Psalm 16 with the Messiah.

There is yet another interesting connection between the apostolic and the rabbinic interpretation. According to tradition, it was Rabbi Hillel who formulated some rules for the midrash. The second of these was that of "word analogy" (*g'zērah shawah*). This rule means that, if in two Bible passages the same (key) words occur, the interpretation of the one passage is also true for the other one. The apostle Peter was

---

134. Cf. Ridderbos (1955, 131–32); Van Gemeren (1991, 159).
135. Cohen (1985, 39).
136. Heb. *kebodi*, i.e. here, "my heart"; cf. Ps. 30:13; 57:9.

apparently following this rule. He first quoted Psalm 16:8–11, and then Psalm 110:1. In both Psalms, we find the expression "at my right hand," so that these two passages can be linked together. This implies that, if Psalm 110 is Messianic, so is Psalm 16. We find a similar argument with the apostle Paul in Acts 13. He first quotes Isaiah 55:3, and then Psalm 16:10. In both passages, we find the Hebrew term *chesed* (Gk. *hosios*, rendered as "mercies" and "merciful/godly/faithful," respectively). Because the two passages share this term, a connection can be made between them, so that both can be applied to the resurrection of Christ.

4.13.2 Psalm 22

As for Psalm 22, Rabbi Abraham Cohen, who wished to give an *orthodox* interpretation, hid behind *liberal* Christian expositors in order to avoid the Christological application of the Psalm.[137] He preferred the interpretation according to which an unknown protagonist is expressing his feelings here as a member of the suffering nation of Israel (cf. Rabbi David Kimchi, who thought in particular of the time of Esther).

At the present time, we no longer have difficulty admitting that the Psalm is not primarily Messianic;[138] thus, John Calvin suggested that the Psalm presents David as suffering under Saul (although there are many objections against this interpretation[139]). Only secondarily, it can be accepted that, in his descriptions, David is reaching beyond himself, so that the Psalm receives a Messianic significance.[140] This explains why we find many Messianic allusions to this Psalm in the New Testament, not only with respect to verse 2 ("My God, my God, why have you forsaken me?" Matt. 27:46; Mark 15:34), but also many other verses, such as verses 8–9 (see Matt. 27:39, 43), verse 14 (see 1 Pet. 5:8), the end of verse 17 (see John 19:18;

---

137. Cohen (1985, 61); cf. Mudde in Knevel and Paul (1995, 60–61).
138. *Contra* many church fathers; see Mudde in ibid., 59–60, 67–68.
139. Ridderbos (1955, 185–86).
140. Ibid., 182–86; Van Gemeren (1991, 199).

20:25, 27), verse 19 (see John 19:24), verse 23 (see John 20:17; Heb. 2:12), verse 25 (Heb. 5:7), and verse 28 (Rev. 15:4).

At the most profound level, we may wonder whether any holy man or woman was forsaken by God. The idea even conflicts with other statements in the Psalms, such as 9:10 ("you, O LORD, have not forsaken those who seek you"), 37:25 ("I have not seen the righteous forsaken"), and 94:14 ("the LORD will not forsake his people"). David may have *felt* forsaken in Psalm 22:2, but only Jesus was *really, truly* forsaken, on the cross, when the chastisement of God was upon him because of the sins of his people (Isa. 53:4-5).

4.13.3 Psalm 40

Psalm 40 seems to have originated while David was fleeing from King Saul. Here again, the Psalm can at best be understood as indirectly Messianic. (One may wonder how many *direct* Messianic psalms there are—probably none.) Rabbi Abraham Cohen identifies no possible Messianic overtones, while others are remarkably brief on this aspect.[141]

Nevertheless, in Hebrews 10:5-7, the writer quoted Psalm 40:6-8 and applied it Messianically: "In sacrifice and offering you have not delighted, but you have given me an open ear. Burnt offering and sin offering you have not required. Then I said, 'Behold, I have come; in the scroll of the book it is written of me: I delight to do your will, O my God; your law is within my heart.'" In my view, this quotation cannot be dismissed as simply a thoughtless interpretation of Psalm 40, irrelevant for the further understanding of the Psalm.[142]

First of all, there is the striking way in which the Septuagint renders the words "you have given me an open ear" (better: "ears you have prepared me," GNV), namely, "a body you have prepared for me." Whereas the Hebrew text spoke of the preparation of only the ears (which presupposes an entire body), the Septuagint took the liberty of extending this

---

141. Noordtzij (1934, 129); Ridderbos (1955, 354); Van Gemeren (1991, 321).
142. See more extensively, Ouweneel (1982, 2:28–31).

phrase to the entire body. These words received their proper sense only in the incarnation of the Logos.

Second, the quotation of Psalm 40:6–8 in Hebrews 10 was one of the clearest proofs that in the Tanakh, animal sacrifices could provide no real satisfaction to God in view of sin, and that a Redeemer was needed who could and would present himself as the true sacrifice:

> For if the blood of goats and bulls, and the sprinkling of defiled persons with the ashes of a heifer, sanctify for the purification of the flesh, how much more will the blood of the Messiah, who through the eternal Spirit offered himself without blemish to God, purify our conscience from dead works to serve the living God (Heb. 9:13–14; cf. 10:4, 11).

Third, I prefer to relate the line "in the scroll of the book it is written of me" to the book of God's eternal counsel,[143] as in 1 Peter 1:19–20, which spoke of the "lamb without blemish or spot . . . foreknown before the foundation of the world." The author of Hebrews based so many important conclusions on Psalm 40:6–8 that, if we accept the unity of the Bible, we cannot possibly conclude we are dealing here with a thoughtless allusion. Therefore, I appreciate commentaries that, in addition to explaining the primary interpretation, endeavor to trace these Messianic lines through the remainder of the psalm.[144]

4.13.4 Psalm 69

Psalm 69 describes an episode from the life of the persecuted David, but the New Testament quotations of this psalm reveal a Messianic thrust: verse 4b is quoted in John 15:25, verse 9a in John 2:17, verse 9b in Romans 15:3, verses 22–23 in Romans 11:9–10, and verse 25 in Acts 1:20. And last but not least, John 19:28 ("I thirst") alluded to Psalm 69:21. In this way, Psalm

---

143. See ibid., 30.
144. See, e.g., Grant (1897a, 165–69); Gaebelein (1965, 175–81); Spurgeon (2008, ad loc.).

69 displays Messianic features, which sheds light on a line like verse 4 (end, ASV): "That which I took not away I have to restore" — a reference to the doctrine of sacrificial substitution (the innocent one paying for the trespasser).

However, large parts of the psalm do not refer to the Messiah at all but rather to believing Israel (e.g., v. 5, "the wrongs I have done"; cf. v. 19). Thus, in Psalm 69 we see primarily the suffering David, and subsequently the suffering (but not innocent) faithful in Israel, with whom the Spirit of Christ apparently identified himself.

Something similar — a reference to Israel, especially the righteous among them, which then in the New Testament was applied to the Messiah[145] — is seen at various places in the Psalms. Let me mention only Psalm 34:20 (cf. Exod. 12:46; Num. 9:12), applied to Jesus in John 19:36. Similarly for Psalm 22:1, see Matthew 27:46 and Mark 15:34. For Psalm 41:9, see John 13:18. For Psalm 109:25, see Matthew 27:39 and Mark 15:29. Sometimes the subject was specifically David (see, e.g., Ps. 89:27 in Rev. 1:5).

In the prophetic books, Isaiah was sometimes a type of the Messiah (see 8:17 in Heb. 2:13; cf. 61:1–2 in Luke 4:18–19), or Eliakim was such (see Isa. 22:20-22 in Rev. 3:7), and further the prophet Zechariah (see Zech. 11:4-7 in Luke 15:1-7; John 10:11, 14; Zech. 11:9-14 in Matt. 27:9–10; cf. Zech. 13:7 in Matt. 26:31).

4.13.5 Psalm 118

As for Psalm 118, it is instructive that, in New Testament times, Israel's spiritual leaders clearly understood and accepted the Messianic significance of the Psalm. The New Testament seems to be giving a *pesher* interpretation of the psalm. Verses 22–23 say, "The stone that the builders rejected has become the cornerstone. This is the LORD's doing; it is marvelous in our eyes." For this passage, see Matthew 21:42 par.;

---

145. The reverse occurs as well: the clearly Messianic prophecy in Isa. 50:8–9 is generalized in Rom. 8:33–34, and then applied to all believers.

Acts 4:11; 1 Peter 2:7.

Verses 25-26 say, "Save us, we pray,[146] O LORD! O LORD, we pray, give us success! Blessed is he who comes in the name of the LORD! We bless you from the house of the LORD." For this passage, see Matthew 21:9 par.; 23:39 par.

Unfortunately, the Messianic significance of the Psalm became lost in later Jewish tradition, due to a negative reaction to Christianity. This occurred in many cases where the rabbis became aware of the Christological use that Christian theologians made of certain Tanakh passages. For instance, Rabbi Abraham Cohen applied verse 22 to Israel,[147] as he did in so many cases where the text speaks of the suffering *tzaddiq* (see §4.14).

4.14 The Servant of YHWH
4.14.1 The Four Poems

In Isaiah we find four poems on the suffering servant of YHWH, namely, in 42:1-7; 49:1-7 (or -9a), 50:4-11, and 52:13-53:12.[148] The interpretation of these four "servant songs" has a complicated history. The traditional Jewish interpretation sees in the servant of YHWH either the suffering people of Israel, or the prophet himself, or another biblical figure such as Moses, Uzziah, Hezekiah, Josiah, Zerubbabel, Jehoiachin, Cyrus, Jeremiah, or Ezekiel, or reads in some verses the people, and in other verses a certain person. However, there were definitely also Jewish traditions and expositors who saw the Messiah in certain passages on the servant of YHWH.[149] Thus, the Targum of Jonathan reads in Isaiah 52:13a "my servant the Messiah" (even though it applies the next verses to Israel). Rabbis Ibn Ezra, Rashi, Abarbanel, and others, who themselves had giv-

---

146. "Save us please": Heb. *anna hoshi'ah*; from *hoshi'ah anna* the word "Hosanna" was derived (Matt. 21:9, 15 par.).
147. Cohen (1985, 392).
148. See more extensively, Ouweneel (2000a, chapter 2 for many more references); see also Ouweneel in Knevel and Paul (1995, 94–112); see also R. T. France (*DJG* 744–47).
149. So Ridderbos (1934, 33).

en up the Messianic interpretation, recognized that the latter is the oldest Jewish interpretation.[150] Not only the Midrash Tanchuma and Yalkut Shimeoni, but the two Rabbis Eliyahu de Vidas and Moses Alshech saw Isaiah 53 as referring to the Messiah. Also the Zohar, the famous medieval kabbalistic work, connected Isaiah 53 explicitly with the Messiah. A prayer by Rabbi Eleazar HaQalir is read in the synagogues on Yom Kippur, in which Isaiah 53 is related directly to the sufferings of the Messiah.[151]

With the rise of Christianity, the Messianic interpretation of Isaiah 53 was relegated more and more to the background in Judaism. However, the Jewish men (and the proselyte Luke) who wrote the New Testament had been raised in Judaism and related Isaiah 53 directly to the Messiah. John the Baptist seemed to allude to Isaiah 53:4 and 7 (John 1:29: "Behold, the lamb of God"). In response to the Ethiopian eunuch, the evangelist Philip immediately applied Isaiah 53 to the Messiah (Acts 8:30–35).

In Matthew 20:28 par. ("give his life as a ransom for many"), Jesus himself seemed to allude to Isaiah 53:10 ("his death was a sacrifice to bring forgiveness," GNT). In Luke 22:37, he referred to Isaiah 53:12 ("was numbered with the transgressors"), and in Luke 18:31 and 24:16 — entering into glory through sufferings — probably to Isaiah 53 in general (cf. also Matt. 8:16–17; 12:15–21; Mark 9:12b; 14:24; John 12:37–38). The apostolic writers followed the same interpretation. Thus, the message of Isaiah 52–53 was interpreted in John 12:38 and in Romans 10:16 and 15:21 as the message of the Messiah. And some verses in Isaiah 53 were directly related to him: verse 4 in Matthew 8:17, verses 5 and 9 in 1 Peter 2:22–25, verses 7–8 in Acts 8:32–33, and verse 12 in Luke 22:37 (cf. also Rom. 4:25; 1 Cor. 15:3; 2 Cor. 5:21; Heb. 9:28; 1 Peter 1:11, 19; 3:18; 1 John

---

150. Alexander (1980, 129, 285, and references).
151. Santala (1992, 164–172); see also Wolff (1984) on the interpretation of Isa. 53 in Second Temple Judaism.

2:1-2; 3:5).[152]

In general, Jews see Israel in Isaiah 53, and Christians see Jesus in it. However, the reverse occurs as well. On the one hand, we saw that the earlier rabbis definitely saw the Messiah in Isaiah 53. On the other hand, especially in recent times Christian expositors have seen in the prophecies concerning the servant of YHWH primarily, or exclusively, Israel. They are prepared to admit that Isaiah can be *applied* to Jesus, since this is what is done in the New Testament. Yet they are of the opinion that the primary referent of the prophecy is Israel. Several authors have properly summarized the multifaceted and complicated problem of these prophecies.[153]

4.14.2 Various Layers

It is unsurprising that the interpretation of the prophecies concerning the suffering servant of God apparently is so complicated. In studying Isaiah 40-53 we soon find that the expression "my servant," or "his servant," or "servant of YHWH," refers sometimes to Israel (41:8-9; 43:10; 44:1-2, 21, 26; 45:4; 48:20; cf. also the plural "servants" in 54:17). And if one sees in certain passages that Isaiah is referring to the Messiah, and the prophet seems then to be speaking of *two* servants, one can still be confused by the striking similarities between the servant Israel and the servant Messiah within the four songs.

However, in addition to the similarities there are also noticeable differences between the two. Thus, in Isaiah 42:19-22 Israel was the blind and imprisoned servant, whereas earlier, in verses 6-7, the servant was the one who opened the eyes of the blind and brought out the prisoners from the dungeon (cf. 49:8-9; 61:1-2). Similarly, in Isaiah 44:21-22 God blotted

---

152. See extensively Wolff (1984, 71–143) regarding references to Isa. 53 in early Christian literature. See also the quotation of Isa. 42:1–4 in Matt. 12:18–21, and of 49:6 in Luke 2:32; Acts 13:47; 26:23. The only passage where Isa. 53 is not applied to Jesus is Acts 13:47; here, Paul and Barnabas apply the notion of the servant to themselves.
153. Ridderbos (1934, 33–36); Rowley (1952, 49–53, 61–88); North (1956, 192–219); Wolff (1984).

out the sins of the unfaithful servant (Israel), but in 53:5-12 the servant blotted out the sins of Israel[154] through his atoning sufferings.

This is the general line: in the passages mentioned, Israel, God's servant, was comforted and was promised redemption (from Babylon); but the true servant, the Messiah, the true Israel (49:3), was the One *through whom* redemption is brought about. Generally speaking, it is clear to which of the two servants Isaiah was referring; at various places, the two are contrasted with each other. Thus, the servant is given as a covenant for the people of Israel (42:6; 49:8); he is called to bring back Israel to God (49:5-6; cf. 42:3); he is the One despised by Israel (49:7; cf. 50:6; 53:2-4); he has a message for Israel (50:10); and he was stricken for the transgression of "my people," says the Lord (53:8). In all these cases, the servant is sharply distinguished from the people of Israel.

However, what is distinguished must not be separated. Especially in the first two songs, we cannot exclude the possibility that the prophet is also thinking of Israel, or at least of the faithful remnant of Israel. We need only think of Isaiah 49:3, where the prophet explicitly used the name "Israel" for the servant of YHWH. In summary, one can distinguish the following layers in the prophecies concerning the servant of YHWH.

(1) Apart from the four songs mentioned, the servant is always the people of Israel.

(2) In the earlier of these four songs, it is possible that Israel, or the remnant of Israel — the true Israel — is also in view: the true people of God. However, the very first prophecy (42:1-7) has a very personal character (see especially vv. 2-4), and here the servant stands over against the entire nation, including the faithful remnant.

---

154. *Not* the sins of the nations, as some expositors have it, because God was speaking of "*my* people" (53:8); it is not Israel vicariously suffering for the nations—a thought unknown in the Tanakh—but the Messiah vicariously suffering for God's people.

(3) Especially in the later songs, the prophet has one individual in mind, one who is rejected by the people, and atoningly suffers for them. According to many (older) Jewish sources as well as the New Testament, this person is the Messiah.

4.14.3 Servant-Messiah

Isaiah 52:13 ties in directly with verses 11–12, where the remnant of Israel is described leaving Babylon at the end of the exile (cf. 48:20) and returning to Zion. In addition, Isaiah 52–53 possesses a deeper dimension, since its ultimate fulfillment will occur in the kingdom of the Messiah (cf. 52:7-10, 15; 53:12). However, this Messianic kingdom cannot be established without the many sins of the people, which had led to the exile, having been blotted out. The people must also recognize that their sins cannot be taken away by anyone other than the Messiah, the One whom they themselves, remarkably enough, had rejected. This insight is expressed in the fourth servant song. It is YHWH, the same One who in 52:12 brings his people back to the promised land, who in verse 13 draws their attention to the Messiah.

The Messiah is the One who, although he was rejected by Israel, is nonetheless *God's* servant (cf. 42:1; 49:3). As such, he is sharply contrasted with Israel itself, the unfaithful servant of YHWH. In 41:8-9; 43:10; 44:1-2; 45:4; 48:20, Israel, God's servant, is comforted, and its deliverance is prophesied. However, this redemption is not possible without a sin offering for all the sins committed. Therefore, 52:13–53:12 shows the One *through whom* the redemption is possible: the Messiah is both God's sin offering for the people, and the Redeemer, the One who delivers from Babylon and from all the other powers that have oppressed Israel, *and* the One who redeems Israel from itself, from its sins and trespasses. The Messiah is both the divine *ground* for God's forgiveness and redemption, as well as the *instrument* through whom the deliverance is brought about.

In Isaiah 53 the servant of the Lord must be a single person; this person is primarily the Messiah, and secondarily the true Israel. Apparently, the servant is a man; the literal translation of verse 3 is: "He was despised and ceasing [or, taking an end] [among the] *men* [Heb. *ishim*], a *man* [Heb. *ish*] of sorrows." Subsequently, this man is put to death. Verse 5 says that he was "pierced," and verse 10, that it was God's will to "crush" him. Verse 7 compares him with a "lamb led to the slaughter"; verse 8 describes him as "cut off out of the land of the living." Verse 9 even puts it in still stronger terms: "[T]hey made his grave with the wicked and with a rich man in his death." In verse 10 he dies the death of a guilt offering, and verse 12 says most clearly: "[H]e poured out his soul to death."

It is my conclusion that the four prophecies concerning the servant of YHWH, especially the last one, give us a clear picture of the Messiah, the One who is described in the New Testament as the Redeemer who, on the cross of Golgotha, bore the sins and sicknesses of his people, as well as of all those who would believe in him. At the same time, the many passages mentioned in which the servant of YHWH is obviously Israel indicate that, in the description of God's servant, the true Israel is also the referent. Both the Messiah and (the true) Israel are "chosen," "called from the womb," "upheld," led by God's "Spirit," are in the "shadow of his hand," and he "glorifies himself" in them (on the one hand, see Isa. 41:8-10; 43:10; 44:1-3, 23; 45:4; 46:3; 51:16, on the other hand 42:1 and 49:1-5).

Viewed in this way, there is only one servant in Isaiah: the Messiah is the true Israel, or rather the true Remnant of Israel, faithful Israel. However, at the same time there is a profound internal tension for, on the one hand, the servant is the One who takes away the sins of the people (53:8-12), and on the other hand, the servant is the one whose sins are taken away (44:21-22). Throughout the centuries, the servant (Israel) has been the "scapegoat" (cf. Lev. 16:10, 20-22) of all nations. And at the same time, the servant (Messiah) has been the "scapegoat" for the faithful from all nations as well as from Israel itself. Thus, in the broadest sense, the "we" in 53:1–6 basically includes each faithful person in each age, of any and every nation. The true faithful one is he/she who finds his/her eternal salvation in Israel's Messiah, *and* grieves over what has been inflicted upon Israel throughout the ages. Salvation is from the Messiah, but this is the same as saying that salvation is from the Jews (John 4:22). The Messiah cannot be severed from Israel, and *vice versa*. Israel is God's firstborn son (Exod. 4:22), and the Messiah is God's firstborn Son (Rom. 8:29; Col. 1:15; Heb. 1:6), and yet, God can have only one firstborn son.

4.15 Two More Messianic Passages
4.15.1 Daniel 9

Of great interest is that, in the entire Tanakh, only one passage contains the word *mashiach* with a truly Messianic meaning, and this is Daniel 9:24–27:

> Seventy weeks [lit., sevens] are decreed about your people and your holy city, to finish the transgression, to put an end to sin, and to atone for iniquity, to bring in everlasting righteousness, to seal both vision and prophet, and to anoint a most holy place. Know therefore and understand that from the going out of the word to restore and build Jerusalem to the coming of Messiah, the prince, there shall be seven weeks and sixty-two weeks: it shall be built again with squares and moat, but in a troubled time. And after the sixty-two weeks, the Messiah shall be cut off and shall have nothing. And the people of the prince who is to come shall destroy the city and the sanctuary. Its end shall come with a flood, and to the end there shall be war. Desolations are decreed. And he shall make a strong covenant with many for one week, and for half of the week he shall put an end to sacrifice and offering. And on the wing of abominations shall come one who makes desolate, until the decreed end is poured out on the desolator (ESV, with a few adaptations from NKJV).

Messianic Hopes in the Tanakh

The Hebrew text is very complicated, and at various points alternative translations are conceivable; this is not the place to examine all the details.[155] I agree here with commentators who interpret the text in a Messianic sense.[156] Briefly stated, I understand the "weeks" (literally "sevens") to be sevens of years. They must be counted from the moment that the order was given to rebuild the city; in 457 BC, Ezra received from the Persian king Artaxerxes I Longimanus the order to rebuild the temple (Ezra 7:12–26), and Ezra rightly concluded that this also entailed the restoration of the walls (9:9); no safe restoration of the temple was possible without the restoration of the city's fortifications. From the time of this royal command, it was seven "sevens" (49 years) for the restoration of city and temple. Seven plus sixty-two "sevens" (483 years) were to occur before the Messiah came. Verse 24 makes clear that the seventy "sevens" terminate when Israel's unrighteousness is atoned; this will be fully realized at the beginning of the Messianic kingdom. On the basis of both internal and external exegetical arguments, I believe, with many other expositors, that there is a great gap between the sixty-ninth and the seventieth "seven."[157] If we begin in the year 457 BC, then the sixty-nine "sevens" (483 years) bring us just about to the beginning of Jesus' ministry in Israel.

The text says that, after the sixty-nine "sevens" the Messiah is "cut off." This is followed by the mysterious Hebrew words *l'ēn lo*, which is literally: "and not for (or, to, against) him." These words have been interpreted in various ways: (a) "he shall have nothing" (i.e., he dies poor and bereft), (b) "it will not be for himself" (i.e., he dies for others), (c) "there is nothing against him" (i.e., he dies innocently), (d) "there is no

---

155. Regarding this, see Ouweneel (1997b, §1.7; *EDR* 10:§6.5).
156. See, e.g., Anderson (1990; n.d.); Kelly (1902, ad loc.); Gaebelein (1911, ad loc.); Lang (1942, ad loc.); Hoehner (1977, 117); McDowell (1979, 15–22); Maier (1982, ad loc.); Archer (1982, 289–92); Fijnvandraat (1990, ad loc.).
157. An internal argument is that v. 26 mentions events that apparently occur after the sixty-ninth but before the seventieth "seven"; an external argument is that v. 26 has been entirely fulfilled, but v. 27 not at all.

one for him" (i.e., no one defends him or helps him). Each of these interpretations is applicable to Jesus. Interpretations (b) and (c) present him as the innocent substitute. This suggests a connection with verse 24, which becomes apparent only in the light of the New Testament: the One who atones for unrighteousness is the One who dies innocently for others.

4.15.2 Hosea 11

Finally, we close this chapter with a consideration of Hosea 11:1, "When Israel was a child, I loved him, and out of Egypt I called my son." This verse must be mentioned because in Matthew 2:15 it was applied to the Messiah. Matthew's theological basis for this lies in the profound unity between Israel and its Messiah. We have seen several times that the Messiah is the true Israel. This also implies that, in his life, the entire history of Israel repeats itself in miniature, in such a way that, in contrast with Israel, he magnificently remains upright. Thus, Jesus calls himself the true vine (John 15:1), and there can hardly be any doubt that with this identification he is placing himself over against Israel, which is often compared to a vine (Ps. 80:8–15; Isa. 5:1–7; Jer. 2:21; Ezek. 15; 19:10; Hos. 10:1). Whereas, in all these passages, Israel is pictured as an unfaithful and guilty, "false vine," Jesus presents himself as the "true vine."

Since Israel is viewed in Psalm 80 as a "vine" "dug up [or, uprooted] from Egypt" (v. 8 HCSB), and is also called "son" (v. 15), there seems to be a parallel here with Hosea 11:1. We have seen (§4.9.3) that the text in Psalm 80:15 and 17 seems to move smoothly from Israel to the Messiah. Verse 15 might still refer to Israel—Israel is the firstborn "son" of God (Exod. 4:22)—but although verse 17 is indisputably speaking of the same figure as verse 15, this figure assumes in verse 17 unmistakably Messianic features. In the light of the New Testament, terms such as "man of your right hand" and "son of man" obtain their full significance in the Messiah. If this line of thought is correct, both the New Testament and the Tanakh writer himself merge the figures of Israel and the Messiah.

Chapter 5
Christ in the Historical Sources

[The Messiah] shall have dominion also from sea to sea,
  And from the River to the ends of the earth.

Psalm 72:8 (NKJV)

5.1 No Fear of Historical Studies
5.1.1 Biblical Criticism

For our knowledge of the person, life, and teaching of Christ, we depend almost exclusively on the four canonical Gospels; we will see that, on this point, other sources yield only a meagre result (§§5.10–5.12). This does not mean, however, that the four Gospels provide easy access to the historical Jesus; we have examined this in chapters 2 and 3. In these two chapters, we were occupied with the development of Christology, especially since the Enlightenment: the three Quests for the historical Jesus.

We may wonder what results these Quests have actually produced. We saw how scholars such as Martin Kähler and Albert Schweitzer dominated the field with nineteenth-century Christology (§2.9). Yet, one positive result of this Christology was the insight that the Gospels, too, may be submitted to historical research, and that Christians have nothing to fear from such examination. Today, many orthodox Christians respond negatively to phrases like "biblical criticism" or "historical criticism," as if they entail "criticizing the Bible." That is historical nonsense. "Biblical criticism" means "critical (i.e., scholarly) Bible research," whether of the text (lower criticism, or textual criticism), which aims at establishing the Bible text as accurately as possible, or of the nature and origin of the text's contents (higher criticism).[1] Such "criticism" can be liberal, fundamentalist, orthodox, and everything in between.

For instance, every serious reader of the New Testament encounters questions like: In what sense and to what extent do the Gospels depend on each other for their content? How can their differences and similarities be explained? Dismissing such a question by ascribing these differences and similarities to a form of mechanical inspiration occurs nowadays only among a small fundamentalist minority.[2] Moreover, the supposed contradictions between the Gospels can hardly be explained through an appeal to inspiration; it would make God a liar because apparently he says one thing here and something else there. No, historical and literary questions must be answered not by an appeal to the supernatural, but only by means of historical and literary scholarly arguments. To be sure, we must always be aware of the (often profound) paradigmatic or worldview differences between two opponents, such as the contrast between naturalism and supernaturalism. But the actual discussion must occur on the level of the historical and literary sciences.

5.1.2 Various Approaches

I. Howard Marshall pointed to the remarkable example of the

---

1. See Ouweneel (1978b, chapters 7 and 8; *RT* I/1, chapter 11).
2. Unfortunately, Darby went rather far in this direction (*CW* 6:359–64 ["Inspiration of the Scriptures"]).

thoroughly orthodox English theologian J. B. Lightfoot,³ who followed the very approach just described.⁴ Lightfoot rightly wrote that renouncing reason is not evidence of faith, but the acknowledgement of despair.⁵ In other words, the fundamentalists' appeal to the supernatural (in this case, inspiration) is not *answering* but *avoiding* the questions asked, perhaps out of fear of confrontation. Lightfoot fully believed in the inspiration of Scripture, but he wished to answer historical questions with historical answers. Only in this way, he argued, we can do justice to opponents, and perhaps even win them over. This is what the apostle Paul did as well: to the Corinthians who did not accept the (bodily) resurrection, he did not say: You simply have to *believe* it, but he employed *arguments* for the resurrection (1 Cor. 15).

Conversely, we should not expect too much of reason. M. Hengel warned that New Testament exegesis is open to danger not only from an uncritical, sterile fundamentalistic apologetic, but also from a no less sterile "critical ignorance," which — Hengel believed — has little in common with sound *historical* critical methods.⁶ He wrote: "The old 'orthodox' rationalism, which betrays an ahistorical and fundamentalist longing for security, and modern forms of rationalism, which try to domesticate Jesus according to selfish interests and ideologies, are ultimately, in their roots, not very different from each other."⁷ And elsewhere: "Orthodox-fundamentalist biblicism finds its counterpart in critical biblicism. Both are naïve, and run the danger of violating the historical reality — one through its ahistorical biblical literalism, and the other by selecting and interpreting according to its worldview and theological interests."⁸

---

3. Lightfoot (1889).
4. Marshall (1977, 112).
5. Lightfoot (1865); quoted by Cassels (1874), in the beginning of his book, which book was being combated by Lightfoot (1889).
6. Hengel (1995, 57–60).
7. Ibid., x.
8. Ibid., 71.

R. Brown helpfully distinguished between (a) an "uncritical conservative" approach, which sees no difference between Jesus' own Christology and that of his followers, (b) an "uncritical liberal" approach, which unnecessarily creates between the two a deep cleft, (c) a "critical liberal" approach, which accepts limited continuity between the two, or believes that this cannot be demonstrated (Bultmann), and (d) a "critical conservative" approach, which sees much continuity between Jesus' own Christology and that of his followers, but also leaves room for a certain amount of theology produced by the church and doctrinal supplementing by the apostolic writers.[9]

5.2 What Is Authentic?
5.2.1 No "Harmonies"

Many scholars, including conservative theologians, have rightly stated that the Gospels are not journalistic reports, not biographies in any sense, not objective historiography. Each event, each statement of Jesus in the Gospels, stands in a thoroughly theological context; in other words, the Gospels are more theology than historiography.[10] Therefore, it will not be easy to find today a theologian who would write a harmony of the Gospels, as Tatian did in the second century; later, John Calvin did the same, and wrote a commentary on the harmony that he constructed. I found a note, written in 1864 (probably by Bible scholar William Kelly), with which I fully agree. It rejects all harmonies of the Gospels because the Gospels contain a mixture of reports, and each was written with a distinct divine aim. The facts have been collected by the Holy Spirit with a clear goal, such that each Gospel presents both Christ and the ways of God in a different light. Blending them

---

9. Brown (1994a, 6–15).
10. Here I am using the term "theological" in the broader sense of "religious doctrinal," in order to adapt to common parlance. Actually, I prefer to use the term "theology" not in the sense of "religious doctrine," but rather in the sense of the *theoretical scientific* reflection on this doctrine; see extensively, Ouweneel (1995; 2015), and *RT* V/1.

together destroys this goal and darkens insight into the Gospels.[11]

Indeed, in our time, we understand so much better that a certain event described in all the Synoptic Gospels, or in all four Gospels, is narrated within a different theological perspective in each Gospel, depending on the scope and theological direction of each Gospel.[12] Therefore, today we feel much less inclined to harmonize the parallel passages in the Gospels in order to salvage their historicity.

5.2.2 Peter's Confession

Let us choose for our discussion a well-known example with several important Christological implications. As Peter's reply to Jesus' question: "[W]ho do you say that I am?," the presumably earliest Gospel gives only these words: "You are the Christ [i.e., the Messiah]" (Mark 8:28–29). In Luke 9:20, the reply is this: "The Christ of God," but in Matthew 16:16 it is: "You are the Christ, the Son of the living God," followed by this important comment by Jesus: "Blessed are you, Simon Bar-Jonah! For flesh and blood has not revealed this to you, but my Father who is in heaven" (v. 17).

Why this difference between, on the one hand, Mark and Luke, and on the other hand, Matthew? It seems easy to suggest that, for reasons unknown to us, Mark and Luke omitted the words "the Son of the living God," as well as Jesus' comment. In this way, the historicity of each account is salvaged.[13] But is the opposite also a possibility? Could it be that the additional words in Peter's confession are a theological elaboration by Matthew himself — perhaps in full accord with Peter's actual views, as they came to light on various occasions? I am not sure *whether* this is the case; perhaps Peter did literally say the full sentence (even though I do not understand why

---

11. *The Bible Treasury*, V (1864), 46.
12. See extensively, Van Bruggen (1998, chapter 2: "Four Gospels—One History?"
13. This is how many apparent discrepancies in the Gospels are smoothed over in Archer (1982).

Mark and Luke left out the fuller reply). But it does not *need* to be this way. I have no difficulty assuming that we have here an element of church produced theology, as long as my comment is understood in the sense of theological elaboration of historical facts *and not some pious projection in place of historical facts*. What Matthew 16 may have added to Peter's confession is not an invention by the Gospel writer himself, or by the circle to which he belonged, but is entirely in line with the total revelation in the New Testament.

Now this example illustrates how the theologian's frame of thought comes to light. We are not amazed when, for instance, theologians Rudolf Bultmann[14] and Harry Kuitert[15] declare the words "the Son of the living God" together with verses 17-19 to be non-authentic. This conclusion is easily drawn; the words simply do not fit the ideas these theologians have about Jesus. The conclusion of some fundamentalists is just as easily drawn: they look not for an explanation for the differences but simply ascribe them to divine inspiration. We ask such people: But *why* did Matthew, Mark, and Luke tell things in a different way? And we ask Bultmann and Kuitert: But *why* could the words ascribed to Jesus not be authentic?

B. F. Meyer argued that the words mentioned could definitely be genuine words of Jesus:[16] they explain more easily the origin of the other forms—not only in Mark and Luke, but also Peter's description of "the Holy One of God" (John 6:69)—than the shorter text of Mark 8:29 does. Oscar Cullmann, too, pleaded for the authenticity of the words,[17] even though he believed that they originally belonged in a different setting, namely, that of Jesus' sufferings (see, e.g., Luke 22:31-38). Others have made similar suggestions. Thus, the words can definitely be authentic, either in the sense that Peter literally spoke them on this occasion, or that he said sim-

---

14. Bultmann (1952, 1:45).
15. Kuitert (1999, 62–63).
16. Meyer (1979, 189–91); cf. Tasker (1961, 160–61); Carson (1984, 365–66).
17. Cullmann (1953, 158–70).

ilar words on this or another occasion. Actually, at this point we need not read into the phrase "Son of God" anything more than a purely Messianic honorary title (cf. Ps. 2:7; Matt. 14:33; Luke 1:35; John 1:50).

5.2.3 Theological Compositions

A very different example of what is accepted as authentic or non-authentic involves Jesus' self-designation "Son of Man."[18] Some critics accept only two of Jesus' statements in Luke as authentic, namely, 12:8 ("everyone who acknowledges me before men, the Son of Man also will acknowledge before the angels of God") and 17:24 ("as the lightning flashes and lights up the sky from one side to the other, so will the Son of Man be in his day"). The reason is that Jesus supposedly distinguishes himself from the Son of Man here. However, how can verse 25 continue as follows: "But first he must suffer many things and be rejected by this generation"? And how can the parallel of Luke 12:8 be as follows in Matthew 10:32: "So everyone who acknowledges me before men, *I* also will acknowledge before my Father who is in heaven"?

Of course, we can imagine how the critics would answer such questions, but we must determine which hypothesis best fits all the facts. In Luke 12 and 17, the context makes it plausible that Jesus was referring to no one other than himself when using the title "Son of Man." But plausibility is subjective. Ultimately, one's paradigm of thought—say, one's basic *beliefs*—determines the outcome of this discussion. This is true for both liberal and conservative theologians.

Yet, conservatives and liberals have come to agree that the Gospels are theological *compositions*, in which the various Gospel writers have taken the liberty of arranging distinct events and Jesus' sayings, or ordering them differently, according to their theological design (see more extensively §5.5). The problem, again, is not that we have a Gospel writer's theology or the theology produced by the church, but rather the

---

18. See Ratzinger (2007, 328–30).

claim that *for this reason* certain of Jesus' sayings and narrated events cannot be authentic, did not really happen, but are the fruit of pious imagination. The moment we accept this claim, the flood of options overwhelms the discussion, because almost every critic has their own selection of Jesus' sayings and narrated events that are authentic or non-authentic. This result is unsurprising given the absence of objective scientific criteria and of extra-biblical sources to which one could appeal. Ultimately only the theologian's pre-theological paradigm determines what is *allowed* to be authentic, and what is not. This path leads us into one grand roundabout of circular reasoning: what is authentic in the Gospel determines our Christology—but our Christology in turn determines what in the Gospels is considered authentic.[19]

In my view, the only argument that has a measure of apparent objectivity—though it turns out to be false—is the claim that the earliest New Testament writings are closest to the historical Jesus, whereas the writings whose origin is later exhibit more signs of theology produced by the church, and thus signs of a "higher" Christology, one that increasingly elevates Jesus. Such a claim advocates a doctrinal development within the New Testament. However, as we have seen, the situation is the very opposite. According to some, Galatians was written early (after Paul's first missionary journey[20])—yet in this epistle we encounter a very "high" Christology: God revealed his Son in Paul (1:16); God sent his Son, "born of woman, born under the law, to redeem those who were under the law, so that we might receive adoption as sons" (4:4–5).

1 and 2 Thessalonians were written during Paul's second missionary journey, in AD 50/51, about twenty years after Jesus' death and resurrection; notice how Paul can write here: "[M]ay our God and Father himself, and our Lord Jesus, direct our way to you" (1 Thess. 3:11). Notice how the singular

---

19. Regarding this, see Brown (1994a, 24).
20. But see Ouweneel (1997a, 13–17), where the date of the third missionary journey is preferred.

verb (Gk. *kateuthunai*) places here "our God and Father" and "our Lord Jesus" on one level, and joins them as one. Similarly, the singular is used in 2 Thessalonians 2:16-17: "[M]ay our Lord Jesus Christ himself, and God our Father . . . comfort [Gk. *parakalesai*] your hearts and establish [Gk. *stērixai*] them in every good work and word." According to many, the Gospels were written later than these epistles; Mark was written perhaps between AD 60 and 70. But it is these very Gospels that bring us closest to the historical Jesus — while at the same time displaying the same "high" Christology (regarding Mark, see §1.9.1).

5.2.4 Unity in Diversity

In chapters 3 and 4 we asked whether there is indeed a contrast between Jesus the Preacher and Jesus the preached One, between Jesus the believer and Jesus the object of faith. Some theologians may think so, but that is not the picture that the Gospels or the epistles present. First, central in Jesus' preaching was the coming of the kingdom of God.[21] But this is central also in Acts (1:3; 8:12; 14:22; 19:8; 20:25; 28:23, 31), the epistles (Rom. 14:17; 1 Cor. 4:20; 6:9-10; 15:24, 50; Gal. 5:21; Eph. 5:5; Col. 1:13; 4:11; 1 Thess. 2:12; 2 Thess. 1:5; 2 Tim. 4:1, 18; Heb. 12:28; James 2:5; 2 Pet. 1:11), and Revelation (1:6, 9; 5:10; 11:15; 12:10). In fact, there are many more similarities between Jesus' teaching and that of the epistles.

Second, in the Gospels Jesus certainly did present himself as an object of faith: "Come to me, all who labor and are heavy laden, and I will give you rest" (Matt. 11:28). "Follow me, and I will make you become fishers of men" (Mark 1:17 par.). "If anyone comes to me and does not hate his own father and mother and wife and children and brothers and sisters, yes, and even his own life, he cannot be my disciple. Whoever does not bear his own cross and come after me cannot be my disciple" (Luke 14:26-27 par.). "[W]hoever comes to me shall not hunger, and whoever believes in me shall never thirst . .

---

21. See the volume in the present series entitled *The Eternal Kingdom*.

. whoever comes to me I will never cast out" (John 6:35, 37; cf. 3:15-16; 5:40). "Whoever believes in me, as the Scripture has said, 'Out of his heart will flow rivers of living water'" (7:38). "Whoever believes in me, though he die, yet shall he live, and everyone who lives and believes in me shall never die" (11:25-26; cf. 12:44, 46; 14:12). "Let not your hearts be troubled. Believe in God; believe also in me. . . . I am the way, and the truth, and the life. No one comes to the Father except through me" (14:1, 6).

Taking into account the special character of each of the Gospels, we proceed in this study from the conviction that they are unified and coherent, as Scripture itself testifies.[22] This does not mean that we close our eyes to the many problems that have been posited (properly or not) by New Testament scholarship and Christology. On the contrary, we take them seriously. But we do so in recognition of our own paradigm, which accepts supernaturalism and the notions of revelation and inspiration, and thus the unity of the New Testament, and Scripture in its totality: "Scripture cannot be broken" (John 10:35).

This posture does not result from a rigid binding to Nicaea and Chalcedon, for the truly Protestant attitude is to accept the beliefs of such Councils only *because* and *insofar as* they agree with the Bible. Thus, Herman Bavinck could write:

> Theology, if it truly wants to be scriptural and Christian, cannot do better for now than to maintain the two-natures doctrine. In the process it may thoroughly convince itself of the inadequate character of its language, specifically also in its doctrine of Christ. But all other attempts undertaken up until now to formulate Christological dogma and to bring it home to us fail to do justice to the riches of Scripture and the honor of Christ.[23]

---

22. See extensively, *EDR* 1:chapter 13, and *RT* I/1. We must "read the Bible, and especially the Gospels, as an overall unity expressing an intrinsically coherent message, notwithstanding their multiple historical layers" (Ratzinger [2007, 191]).
23. Bavinck (*RD* 3:304).

In short, we accept the formula of Chalcedon, not because it is perfect but because until now we have nothing better.

Please note Bavinck's expression "for now." In principle, it always remains possible that someday a more adequate formula will be produced. Therefore, each generation of theologians is challenged to show that the tradition is really rooted in the Scripture—taking into account all the hermeneutical presuppositions playing a role in this—and to consider how the tradition can be improved, that is, how the doctrine concerning the person of the God-Man Christ can be formulated in a way closer to Scripture. This remains a struggle, and the discussion is not advanced when people take refuge in "mystery." Theologians must respect mysteries, but they also have the duty to explicate them as clearly as possible (see chapters 6-9 below).

5.3 The Four Gospels
5.3.1 The Synoptics

In subsequent chapters we will examine the pre-existence of Christ, the divine and the human aspects of Christ, and the life of Christ. In preparation, we must ask whether such an examination is possible. We have four canonical Gospels, and this implies at least four different "Jesus portraits," four Christological "designs."[24] Consider this bold parallel: just as in the case of the triune God, we can speak of the one God but also of the three distinct divine hypostases, the present subject is somewhat similar. We can attempt to trace the main line in the life of Jesus and the core elements of his teaching. But if we were to limit ourselves to this, we would do injustice to the various "Jesus portraits" of the four Gospels.

Thus, let us look first at the four canonical sources for the life and the teaching of Jesus: the three Synoptic Gospels and the Gospel of John. The most important views of their origin

---

24. Cf. S. C. Barton in Bockmuehl (2001, chapter 11): "Many gospels, one Jesus?" He spoke of "four portraits, not one" (175). Burridge and Gould (2004, 53) also spoke of "four portraits of Jesus."

are the following.[25]

(1) The two-source hypothesis: Mark originated with the help of oral and possibly written traditions between AD 60 and 70. Matthew and Luke originated between 70 and 100 (or even 80 and 90?) independently of each other, with the use of Mark and Q,[26] and special traditions that are characteristic of Matthew and Luke, respectively. Today this is the most widely accepted view.[27]

(2) The Griesbach hypothesis, still defended, for instance, by Farmer, Mann, and Peabody et al.:[28] Matthew originated first, then Luke using Matthew, and finally Mark as a summary of both Matthew and Luke.

(3) The single-source hypothesis (without Q): Mark originated first, but the existence of Q is considered dubious.[29]

5.3.2 Oral Tradition

In addition to these hypotheses, the theory of *oral tradition* is not obsolete.[30] Here, Luke 1:1–2 is significant: "Inasmuch as many have undertaken to compile a narrative of the things that have been accomplished among us, just as those who from the beginning were eyewitnesses and ministers of the word have delivered them to us, ..." Possibly, these "ministers of the word" (Gk. *hupēretai tou logou*) had an official function in handing down Jesus' words and deeds (cf. Acts 1:1–2, ". . . all that Jesus began to do and teach, until the day when he was taken up").[31]

---

25. See Meier (1991, 43–44) and Brown (1997, chapter 6), with references.
26. Q comes from Ger. *Quelle* ("Source"), the hypothetical document from which Matthew and Luke supposedly adopted the passages that they have in common.
27. See, e.g., Head (1997).
28. Farmer (1964); Mann (1986); Peabody et al. (2002).
29. E.g., Goulder (1974).
30. Dunn (2003; 2005) directed our attention to the oral tradition; Brown (1994a, 108) argued that part of the Gospel material was formed long before the first Gospel, Mark, was written (presumably in the sixties of the first century).
31. Guthrie (1970, 227–28); Bruce (1979, 459).

According to this theory, the Synoptic Gospels go back not to written sources but to oral tradition, partly that of the writers themselves. According to Papias (a second-century Christian author),[32] Matthew personally wrote down the statements by Jesus in Aramaic, while Mark was the secretary and interpreter of the apostle Peter. Irenaeus called Luke's Gospel a representation of Paul's preaching, and ascribed John's Gospel to the "disciple loved by Jesus" (John 13:23; 19:26; 20:2; 21:7, 20).[33] Of course, we are not sure whether Papias and Irenaeus were right, but they do provide the earliest testimony about the authorship of the Gospels: the latter were written by eye- and earwitnesses.

This does not explain every aspect, of course; for instance, it does not explain why the very John who was present at the events in the house of Jairus, on the Mount of Transfiguration, and in Gethsemane, did not describe them, or why Mark and Luke who presumably were not present at Jesus' ascension did describe it, whereas Matthew and John, who *were* present, did not. This illustrates that the Gospel writers were not *only* witnesses but also composers: their Gospels are theologically designed compositions (§5.2.3). In addition, one may wonder why—if Matthew was the writer of the Gospel named after him—he would have depended so strongly on Mark's Gospel, whereas from personal experience he knew Jesus' life and sayings much better than Mark.

Nonetheless, there may be some support for hypotheses (1) and (2) above, since Matthew and Mark must have known each other in Jerusalem (cf. Acts 1:13; 12:12), and Luke and Mark were companions at a later stage (Col. 4:10, 14; 2 Tim. 4:11).

5.3.2 John's Gospel and the Spirit

Regarding the origin of John's Gospel there are two main views: the older view is that John knew and used the Synop-

---

32. Eusebius, *Historia Ecclesiae* III.39.
33. Ibid., V.8.ii–iv.

tic Gospels; the newer view is that John's Gospel represents an entirely distinct Jesus-tradition. According to the majority view, we have three main sources for our knowledge of Jesus: Mark, Q, and John, in addition to other material found in Matthew, Luke, and the rest of the New Testament. However, opinions differ strongly.

Ultimately, we believe that the unity and coherence of the four Gospels are guaranteed through the work of the Holy Spirit. This claim does not dismiss the problems of origin, but rather indicates the underlying paradigm from which to view the problems. No matter how different the Gospels' origins may be, the Holy Spirit is the ultimate guarantor of their unity. It is not correct to call such an appeal to the Holy Spirit an unscientific statement. New Testament scholar J. P. Meier rightly argued that no science, including New Testament scholarship, is neutral and objective;[34] it always starts from a certain ideological paradigm, which does — or does not — allow for supernaturalism, and thus for the inspiring and conserving work of the Holy Spirit.[35]

On the other hand, Meier argued, many authors deal with the matter by mistakenly viewing all passages in the Gospels as historically equally accurate. That is, our appeal to the Holy Spirit should not annul our critical scholarly approach to the Gospels. For instance, serious New Testament scholarship must seek to account for the remarkable (often verbal) similarities between the Synoptic Gospels as well as for the many points of dissonance, both within the Gospels and between them (see §§5.6 and 5.7). But we do this with the acceptance of the Bible's self-testimony that "All Scripture is breathed out by God" (2 Tim. 3:16) — and that the Gospels are "Scripture" (1 Tim. 5:18). Jesus promises that "the Helper, the Holy Spirit, whom the Father will send in my name, he will teach you all things and bring to your remembrance all that I have said to you" (John 14:26). Thus, we trust that we find a reliable re-

---

34. Meier (1991).
35. Guthrie (1970, 231–33).

port of this in the Gospels (cf. John 15:26; 16:13-14). The full tradition concerning "all that Jesus began to do and to teach" (Acts 1:1) was much more extensive than what was ultimately recorded in the Gospels (cf. John 20:30-31; 21:25); the Holy Spirit led the writers in their selection, without diminishing their personal responsibility and investigations (Luke 1:1-4).

5.4 New Testament Testimony
5.4.1 Jesus' Life in the Gospels

Irenaeus called the Gospel writers the "four pillars of the world,"[36] corresponding to the four corners of the world (Job 9:6; 26:11; Ps. 75:3; cf. Jer. 49:36; Ezek. 7:2; Rev. 7:1; 20:8). They are four, and there must be four, so to speak, just as there are four winds (1 Chron. 9:24; Ezek. 37:9; Dan. 8:8; 11:4; Zech. 2:6; 6:5), four bloody sacrifices (Lev. 1-7) — each referring to a different Gospel — four tabernacle colors (Exod. 25:4; 35:6), and four celestial beings (Ezek. 1:5-10; 10:14, 21; Rev. 4:6-8).

I am convinced that these four portraits of Jesus supplement one another, that they are not contradictory, and that the *four* portraits are needed to do justice to the diversity of Jesus. This is what the Holy Spirit intended, as was emphasized, for instance, by Abraham Kuyper: "When in the four Gospels Jesus, on the same occasion, is made to say words that are different in form of expression, it is impossible that He should have used these four forms at once. The Holy Spirit, however, merely intends to make an impression upon the Church which wholly corresponds to what Jesus said."[37] Herman Bavinck said something similar:

> No life of Jesus can be written from the four Gospels, nor can a history of Israel be construed from the OT. That was not what

---

36. *Adversus Haereses* III.11.8: "Just as there are four parts of the world in which we live, and four universal winds, and just as the church is dispersed over all the earth, and the gospel is the pillar and foundation of the church, and the breath of life, it is natural that it has four pillars ... the Word ... gave us the gospel in a fourfold form, but kept together by one Spirit."
37. Kuyper (2008, 383).

the Holy Spirit had in mind. Inspiration was evidently not a matter of drawing up material with notarial precision. . . . Scripture does not satisfy the demand for exact knowledge in the way we demand it in mathematics, astronomy, chemistry, etc. This is a standard that may not be applied to it.[38]

However, if no "Life of Jesus" can be reconstructed from the Gospels, we must let the four portraits remain side by side. We may try to sketch the main contours of Jesus' life and sufferings, as I will do in chapters 11 and 12. And we may also try to sketch the main contours of Jesus' teachings, as I will do in forthcoming volumes in this series. However, this should not go too far; when it comes to the details, both in Jesus' life and in his teaching, there are four inspired designs of Jesus' life, and it should remain this way. By means of a harmony of the Gospels in the sense of Tatian or Calvin, we may try to make the main line of Jesus' life transparent; however, such a harmony will never yield a coherent theological Jesus picture (see §5.2).

5.4.2 Jesus' Teaching in the Gospels

With the teaching of Jesus—as some might say, with Jesus' theology—it is even more complicated than with Jesus' life. This is because we are dealing first not with the theology of Jesus but with the theologies of the four Gospel writers. These are definitely not the same. Each of them creates a portrait of Jesus that is historical, to be sure, but especially theological. From each of these four theologies of the Gospel writers we must determine what each considered the theology (or, more simply, the message) of Jesus to be. Through the theological spectacle of the four Gospel writers, we look at the theology (message) of Jesus, but the result is four theologies (messages) of Jesus. This is no problem; it is probably the way the Holy Spirit wanted it to be—not in order to make things more complicated but to make them more transparent. We never directly hear Jesus' teaching; if this had been the Spirit's intention,

---

38. Bavinck (*RD* 1:444).

Jesus would have written down his teaching himself. Rather, we hear four different voices of those who *reflected* upon that teaching and that life of Jesus.

Stated most concisely, the four messages of Jesus might perhaps be formulated as follows.

(1) Matthew: "The kingdom of heaven is descending to earth, already now, and soon in glory and majesty; if you wish to receive a part in it, become my follower now, and go, with me, through suffering to glory, on the basis of the sin-offering that I brought to God, also for you."

(2) Mark: "The kingdom of God is being manifested on this earth, inevitably in direct conflict with the kingdom of Satan. But I have defeated Satan on the cross, and I invite you to come with me to fight what remains of the demonic powers, until the victory will be ushered in."

(3) Luke: "The grace and mercy of God have entered into this world in my person, for even the greatest sinner. I became on the cross the true sacrifice to God, in order that all sinners, Jew or Gentile, may come to me, truly repent, and receive forgiveness of your sins and eternal salvation."

(4) John: "I am the eternal Son of the Father, who has become truly Man, to reveal the love of God, in order that lost men and women, through my work on the cross, may believe in me, come to the light, and receive eternal life, that is, true and eternal communion with the Father."

Four messages—and yet one message: "Believe in me, the Sovereign, the Satan Fighter, the Savior, the Son!"

As (Roman Catholic) J. P. Meier put it, every Synoptic writer has arranged the rosary beads (i.e., the sections) on the rosary (i.e., the Gospel's structure) in a way that suited his theological view.[39] In a harmony of the Gospels, the differences, along with the (supposed) contradictions, among the Gospels are erased. However, it is these very differences, these mutual tensions, that make the four Gospels so fascinating. Since God

---

39. Meier (1991, 42).

gave the Synoptic Gospels as three, not one, obviously the differences among them are what will lead us to their meaning; often the worst difficulties for unbelief will yield the fullest meaning for any believing examination.[40]

These differences form the marrow of each of the four Gospels, their specialty; they each constitute a theological tract.[41] Without these differences and these tensions, we could just as well have had one Gospel. They are not a threat to orthodox faith—so that they would have to be erased—but a challenge to sketch the four portraits of Jesus being presented to us in the Gospels.

Even the descriptions of the crucifixion given by each of the four are fascinating in their differences. I find the rendering by German monk Anselm Grün, who isolates the cross for a moment from its merely soteriological meaning, remarkably beautiful (though occasionally somewhat dubious).[42] The cross has a different meaning for each Gospel writer. To Matthew, it symbolized Jesus' non-violence. Jesus is the merciful prophet who is not seeking power, [but] lets himself be taken prisoner without any violence, and be killed. To Mark, the cross was a victory of Jesus over the powers of darkness. With Luke, the cross expressed the troublesome situations that we, too, must endure on our way to God's glory. John's interpretation of the cross probably went the deepest: on the cross Jesus displayed his love to us to the utmost (John 13:1; 15:9). He inaugurated us into the mystery of the love of God, who gave us his Son in order that we would find life in him.

5.4.3 The Remainder of the New Testament

Imagine someone who knows nothing of Christianity but discovers only a portion of the Bible, namely, only Acts and the New Testament letters (including Revelation, which actually is a letter to the seven churches of Asia; Rev. 1:11, 19). In this

---

40. Grant (1897b, 22); see extensively, Ouweneel (1980).
41. Kuitert (1999, 59).
42. Grün (2002, 172).

portion, they would read very much about a person referred to as Jesus, or Christ, or the Lord Jesus Christ. Imagine trying to construct from that portion of the Bible a biography of this Jesus, and a description of his teaching. How far would they get?

The result would be rather meagre. The writers of Acts, the epistles, and Revelation focus intently on the sufferings, death, and resurrection of Christ, and especially on the significance and effects of these events, and tell us little about the life of Christ. The reason for this was not that they knew little about it, but that they assumed these to be rather well-known among the early Christians. Here is a list of the sparse biographical data from Acts and the letters.[43]

(1) ". . . Christ Jesus, who, though he was in the form of God, did not count equality with God a thing to be grasped, but emptied himself, by taking the form of a servant, being born in the likeness of men" (Phil. 2:5-7); "He was manifested in the flesh, vindicated by the Spirit, seen by angels" (1 Tim. 3:16).

(2) Jesus was "born of woman, born under the law [of Moses]" (Gal. 4:4), and therefore circumcised (cf. Rom. 15:8; Col. 2:11).

(3) Already at this birth he was threatened by evil powers (Rev. 12:1-5; cf. Matt. 2:16-18).

(4) Jesus originated from Israel (Rom. 9:5), more narrowly: from the tribe of Judah (Heb. 7:14; Rev. 5:5; cf. Matt. 1:2-16).

(5) Jesus belonged to the royal family of David (Acts 2:30; 15:16; Rom. 1:3; 2 Tim. 2:8; Rev. 5:5; 22:16; cf. Matt. 22:42).

(6) Jesus came into the world to save sinners and to grant them forgiveness (Acts 10:43; 13:38-39; 1 Tim. 1:15; cf. Luke 19:10).

(7) Jesus led a humble life (Phil. 2:7-8) under poor conditions (2 Cor. 8:9; cf. Matt. 8:20).

---

43. Cf. Van Bruggen (2005, 178–85).

(8) Jesus was a meek and gentle person (2 Cor. 10:1).

(9) After John's baptism of Jesus, Jesus began his ministry in Galilea (Acts 10:37; 13:23-25).

(10) Jesus had brothers (Acts 1:14; 1 Cor. 9:5; Gal. 1:19; cf. Mark 6:3).

(11) Jesus was sent primarily to the people of Israel (Rom. 15:8; cf. Matt. 15:24).

(12) During his ministry, Jesus had twelve disciples who accompanied him, and were his eye- and earwitnesses, and afterward were called apostles (Acts 2:21-22, 26; 1 Cor. 15:5; Rev. 21:14).

(13) Jesus performed many signs and wonders of healing and deliverance while living on earth (Acts 2:22; 10:35).

(14) Jesus appeared on the Mount of Transfiguration (2 Pet. 1:17-18; cf. Matt. 17:1-5).

(15) Jesus instituted what we call the Lord's Supper, and was delivered to the enemy (1 Cor. 11:23-26; cf. especially Luke 22:19-20).

(16) Jesus experienced agony amid his supplications (Heb. 5:7-8; cf. Mark 14:32-42).

(17) Jesus' testimony before, and condemnation by, Pontius Pilate, who released a murderer in his stead (Acts 3:13-14; 13:27-28; 1 Tim. 6:13; cf. John 18:36-37).

(18) Jesus was mocked by his enemies (Rom. 15:3; Heb. 12:3): "When he was reviled, he did not revile in return; when he suffered, he did not threaten, but continued entrusting himself to him who judges justly" (1 Pet. 2:23).

(19) "And being found in human form, he humbled himself by becoming obedient to the point of death, even death on a cross" (Phil. 2:8).

(20) Jesus was crucified (Rom. 6:6; 1 Cor. 1:17-18, 23; 2:2; 2 Cor. 13:4; Gal. 2:20; 3:1; 5:11; 6:12, 14; Eph. 2:16; Phil. 2:8; 3:18; Col. 1:20; 2:14-15; Heb. 6:6; 12:2; Rev. 11:8) by the "rulers of this age" (1 Cor. 2:8), "outside the gate [of Jerusalem]" (Heb.

13:12; cf. Rev. 11:1-2, 8).

(21) Jesus was killed by his own people (Acts 2:23, 36; 3:15; 4:10; 5:30; 7:52; 10:40; 1 Thess. 2:15), at the time of the Passover (cf. 1 Cor. 5:7).

(22) At the same time it must be said that *God* delivered him up (Acts 2:23; 20:28; Rom. 8:32; cf. John 3:16), and that he delivered *himself* to death (Gal. 1:4; 2:20; Eph. 5:2; 1 Tim. 2:6; Titus 2:12; cf. Matt. 20:28; 26:28).

(23) The water and blood flowed from Jesus' side (as some explain 1 John 5:6; cf. John 19:34).

(24) Jesus' burial (Acts 13:29; Rom. 6:4; 1 Cor. 15:4; Eph. 4:9; Col. 2:12).

(25) Jesus' resurrection on the third day and his appearances, of which those to Cephas (i.e., Simon Peter) and to the twelve apostles are mentioned in the Gospels as well (1 Cor. 15:3-7 and many other passages; cf. Matt. 28:16-17; Mark 16:14; Luke 24:34, 36; John 20:19); in addition to these, Paul mentions Jesus' appearances to the "more than five hundred brothers at one time," to James, and to Paul himself (1 Cor. 15:6-8; see Acts 1:1-8; 9:1-9; 13:31).

(26) Jesus' ascension (Acts 1:9; 2:33-34; Eph. 4:8-10; Phil. 2:9; 1 Tim. 3:16; Rev. 12:5).

(27) Jesus' glorification at God's right hand (Acts 2:35-36; 5:31; 7:55-56; Rom. 8:34; Eph. 1:20; Col. 3:1; Heb. 1:3; 8:1; 10:12; 12:2; 1 Pet. 3:22).

In addition to all this, the apostle Paul gives us the following quotations from or allusions to Jesus' teaching:

(28) "In all things I [i.e., Paul] have shown you that by working hard in this way we must help the weak and remember the words of the Lord Jesus, how he himself said, 'It is more blessed to give than to receive'" (Acts 20:35).

(29) In his discussion of marriage and divorce (1 Cor. 7:10-11), Paul refers to what the Lord Jesus had personally said about these things (Matt. 5:32; Mark 10:11-12; Luke 16:18).

(30) In 1 Corinthians 9:14 Paul refers implicitly to what the Lord had said, "The laborer deserves his food (or, wages)" (Matt. 10:10; Luke 10:7).

There are many more allusions to statements and teachings of Jesus,[44] but our fictional Bible reader who possesses only Acts and the epistles could not know of this. This is why I mentioned only those examples in which the New Testament writers themselves appeal to sayings by Jesus.

5.5 Again: Theological Compositions
5.5.1 Paintings, Not Photographs

Without dispute, the Gospels are theological compositions. As Johan Verkuyl put it, "The Gospels are compositions whose goal is to move people to faith in Jesus, and to move them to take their place in the church of all ages."[45]

In terms of the well-known image, the Gospels do not offer us four different photographs of Jesus, but rather four paintings, or if one wishes (to underscore their unity), a *tetraptychon* (a four-part painting). They involve four coherent portraits, which — because we are dealing with four excellent painters — tell us very much about Jesus, more than would be possible with a photograph. The portraits tell us much about the painters as well. As J. Dwight Pentecost put it, each Gospel writer selects and arranges from the same extant material, according to his individual emphasis and interpretation, what he wishes his portrait to convey.[46]

We should read the Gospels like we would a biography, knowing that the authors were enthralled with this person, and wished to sketch the significance of his life.[47] They did this not by presenting facts in the most detailed way possible but by painting a careful impression of his person. In this way,

---

44. E.g., with Paul: Rom. 12:14 (cf. Matt. 5:44); 1 Cor. 7:10; 1 Tim. 5:18b, accepting the traditional view that the pastoral letters were written by Paul; see, e.g., Earle (1978, 341–43) (cf. Matt. 10:10).
45. Verkuyl (1992, 192).
46. Pentecost (1981, 24).
47. Van de Beek (2002a, 134).

a Gospel is like a work of art. It offers more than just the material — it also presents the impression that the person made upon the artist. And in a footnote, Van de Beek adds, what is involved is a person who is described in the manner of art; the significance of the person is rendered in a concentrated form, in a "recognition of the essence."[48] Abraham Kuyper spoke of "impressionism": biblical historiography "does not supply us with a notarial record of actions, but reproduces what has been caught in one's consciousness, and does not do so with the sharpness of lines characteristic of architecture, but with the impressionistic certainty of life."[49]

By way of illustration, consider the chronology of the events and sayings of Jesus. In Matthew, a number of sayings by Jesus have been gathered together into one "Sermon on the Mount" (Matt. 5-7), whereas in Luke we find these words distributed among chapters 6, 11, 12, 13, 14, and 16. In Matthew, we find a number of miracle stories gathered together (Matt. 8-9), which we find in Mark distributed throughout chapters 1, 4, 5, 2, and 5 (in this order), and in Luke throughout chapters 5, 7, 4, 9, 8, 5, and 8. The woes Jesus spoke against the scribes and the Pharisees, plus the lament over Jerusalem, are found in Luke in 11:37-54 and 13:31-35, respectively, but in Matthew 23:1-39. In Matthew 4:1-10, the order of the three temptations is different than in Luke 4:1-12, so that in each case a different climax is reached. In Matthew 26:20-29 and Mark 14:17-25, we get the impression that Judas left before the institution of the Lord's Supper, but in Luke 22:14-23 he left afterward. In Matthew 27:50-51 and Mark 15:37-38, the veil was rent after the death of Jesus, in Luke 23:45-46 it is the reverse.

5.5.2 Neither Journalism Nor Fantasy

Our interest at the moment is not to explain all these differences (presuming that were possible); they serve only to il-

---

48. In reference to Macquarrie (1981, 30).
49. Quoted in Harinck (2001, 113).

lustrate that the Gospels are compositions, in which the various parts as well as the overall design of each Gospel have a theological purpose. For example, in Matthew's genealogy, three names are omitted to arrive at 3 x 14 generations (Matt. 1:17), and after Solomon it follows a royal pedigree (vv. 6-12), whereas Luke 3:27-31 follows an unknown (non-royal, i.e., humble) pedigree. Another example: Matthew 27:46 and Mark 15:34 mention one (viz., the same) saying of Jesus on the cross, whereas Luke 23:34, 43, and 46 mention three others, and John 19:26-28 and 30 three more sayings of Jesus on the cross.

It is essential to understand what conclusion may *not* be drawn from these differences, namely, that because the Gospels are theological compositions, much of what they tell us is presumably rooted in the Gospel writer's imagination.[50] It is of vital importance that the portrait of Jesus *resembles* him, otherwise it is useless. Like the three others, Luke may have had a clearly theological goal, yet he definitely intended to carefully examine the testimonies of the "eyewitnesses and ministers of the word," and "to write an orderly account for you, most excellent Theophilus, that you may have certainty concerning the things you have been taught" (1:2-4).

Luke's Gospel is not a journalistic report, nor a scholarly biography of Jesus. But neither is it a pious fantasy; Luke was concerned with nothing less than "the things that have been accomplished among us" (v. 1), and "all that Jesus began to do and teach, until the day when he was taken up," as he writes at the beginning of Acts (1:1-2), the sequel to his Gospel. Luke's description of the facts was colored by his theological goal—but they remained facts. He writes with the same practical sobriety with which his missionary partner Paul refers readers to the five hundred brothers who had seen Jesus (1 Cor. 15:6). The resurrection is not a mysterious thing for esoteric people only—if you have difficulty believing it you

---

50. Thus, e.g., Den Heyer (2003, 21-24).

may ask those brothers who were still living. Pursue the *facts*, not ethereal and hazy stories.

No theologian needs to demonstrate that certain sayings ascribed to Jesus are authentic; the way the Gospels present themselves to us forces any theologian who wishes to do so to demonstrate that certain sayings ascribed to Jesus *are not* or *cannot be* authentic. In this evaluation, no anti-supernaturalist biases should play a role, but only historical and literary arguments. Various past judgments of inauthenticity were based upon dubious grounds.[51]

No one would deny that Luke's goal is theological, but this is very different from saying that history has been adapted to theology. It is more correct to say that Luke brings out the theological meaning of the history of Jesus.[52]

5.6 "Contradictory" Passages
5.6.1 Who Said What?

Alleged contradictions between the Gospels *cannot* be used as an argument against the authenticity of the described events, just as the great differences between three (imaginary) portraits of a person by, for instance, Caravaggio, Rembrandt, or Nicolas Poussin do not mean that these portraits could not reflect that person. Similarly, these supposed contradictions *are* interesting. For instance, Matthew 27:37 tells us that above the cross was written: "This is Jesus, the King of the Jews"; Mark 15:26 in short, "The King of the Jews"; Luke 23:38, "This is the King of the Jews"; and John 19:19, "Jesus of Nazareth, the King of the Jews." These four inscriptions cannot all be exactly correct. We can no longer establish what was *literally* written above the cross: at least "King of the Jews," but also "This is" and "of Nazareth"? Yet, we are convinced *that* there was an inscription above the cross saying something about the Jewish King Jesus. Each Gospel writer with his different theological perspective communicated this inscription in his

---
51. Berger (2004, passim).
52. Guthrie (1970, 94).

THE ETERNAL CHRIST: GOD WITH US

own way; but none invented the fact of the inscription.[53]

The same is true about the words that the centurion spoke at the cross. In Matthew 27:54 we read, "Truly this was the Son [or, a son] of God"; in Mark 15:39, "Truly this man was the Son [or, a son] of God"; in Luke 23:47, "Certainly this was a righteous Man!" (NKJV). Some assure us that, of course, the centurion said both;[54] but this is not the point. The really interesting question is not whether we can make it fit historically, but rather how the descriptions "S/son of God" in Matthew and Mark, and "righteous" in Luke, fit into their respective theological compositions.

The same is true about the words that the Father spoke on the Mount of Transfiguration (Matt. 17:5; Mark 9:7; Luke 9:35). Only in Matthew do we find the words "with whom I am well pleased"; they are omitted in Mark and Luke. Only in Luke do we find "my Son, my Chosen One"; in Matthew and Mark it is "my beloved Son." The Father can have made only one statement, and perhaps none of the Gospel writers has handed down the literal words; however, in essence the words used do describe what the Father said and intended. All of this implies, though, that where we do not have the possibility of comparison, we can hardly claim that a certain person said this or that *literally* in this or that way.

In the examples mentioned (the inscription at the cross, the words of the centurion, the Father's saying on the mountain) we could simply merge all the variations. The inscription would then say, "This is Jesus of Nazareth, the King of the Jews." The centurion would then have said, "Truly this man was the Son of God; he was a righteous Man!" And the Father would have said: "This is my beloved Son, the Chosen One, with whom I am well pleased; listen to him." However, first, this gives the impression of being forced. Second, we must still conclude that not a single Gospel handed down the true text correctly, so that the question "Are the Gospels his-

---
53. Cf. Archer (1982, 345–46).
54. Ibid., 346–47.

torically accurate?" has still not been properly answered.

5.6.2 Other Examples

In Mark 10:17-18, Jesus answered the question by the rich young man as follows: "Why do you call me good? No one is good except God alone." But in Matthew 19:16-17 the answer is this: "Why do you ask me about what is good? There is only one who is good." Here we are dealing with not simply different wordings but with quite a different meaning: Mark suggests that Jesus does not accept *himself* to be good, but Matthew circumvents this problem (see further §5.9.1, point [1]).[55]

Consider the words of Jesus at the institution of the Lord's Supper, which come to us in four rather different versions (Matt. 26:26-29; Mark 14:22-25; Luke 22:19-20; 1 Cor. 11:23-26). When distributing the bread Jesus says, "Take, eat; this is my body" (Matt.), or "Take; this is my body" (Mark), or "This is my body, which is given for you. Do this in remembrance of me" (Luke; cf. 1 Cor.). When offering the cup he says, "Drink of it, all of you, for this is my blood of the covenant, which is poured out for many for the forgiveness of sins. I tell you I will not drink again of this fruit of the vine until that day when I drink it new with you in my Father's kingdom" (Matthew; cf. Mark). Or "This cup that is poured out for you is the new covenant in my blood" (Luke; at an *earlier* cup Jesus had already said, "Take this, and divide it among yourselves. For I tell you that from now on I will not drink of the fruit of the vine until the kingdom of God comes." Or "This cup is the new covenant in my blood. Do this, as often as you drink it, in remembrance of me" (1 Cor.).

The writers are clearly speaking of one and the same event, and Jesus could have made only one correct statement. One of the writers has possibly handed down the correct wording, but it is more likely that none of them gives the *exact* wording, but each of them is communicating the essence. If we have at

---

55. Strangely, Archer (1982, 329–32), who deals extensively with this story, does not offer an explanation for this remarkable difference.

most an agreement in essence, do we have any reason to suppose that other words of Jesus have been preserved with any more diligent pursuit of word-for-word literalness?[56]

Many other examples could be given. Consider the two versions of the Beatitudes (Matt. 5:3-12; Luke 6:20-23). In Luke, Jesus says, "Blessed are you who are poor," and, "Blessed are you who are hungry now," but in Matthew, "Blessed are the poor *in spirit*," and, "Blessed are those who hunger and thirst *for righteousness*" — quite different approaches.[57] One might claim, of course, that Jesus gave different versions of the Beatitudes on different occasions, but this does not impress us as a very plausible explanation of the different approaches.

Similarly, there is a number of differences in the Lord's Prayer (Matt. 6:9-13; Luke 11:2-4), which is all the more remarkable because Christians have taken this to be a model prayer for liturgical and personal use. Why, then, do the Gospel writers give us two versions of it?

In all these examples, we are not dealing with the precision of a journalistic report, nor of a scholarly historical report. Rather, we encounter narrative paintings and portraits in which the theological impulse is more important than *verbatim* literalness.

5.7 "Contradictory" Events
5.7.1 Discrepancies

We find differences, to say nothing of apparent contradictions, among the Synoptic Gospels not only in the sayings of Jesus but also in the events involving his person. For instance, in Matthew 20:20-21 the mother of James and John asks Jesus: "Say that these two sons of mine are to sit, one at your right hand and one at your left, in your kingdom." But in Mark 10:35-37 these two men themselves ask this question. Here

---
56. Meier (1991, 43).
57. It is fascinating to see, though, how Ratzinger (2007, 76–77) brings the two together.

again, some propose a simple solution, namely, that both the mother and the sons have probably asked this question.⁵⁸ But let us not overlook the immensely interesting (theological) question about why Matthew has the mother ask the question, and Mark the two sons. It is like asking why, according to Matthew 8:5-9, the centurion of the paralyzed servant comes personally to Jesus and speaks with him, whereas in Luke 7:2-8 the centurion sends Jewish elders, and afterward friends to Jesus.⁵⁹ Those seeking journalistic literalness here will have to conclude that the two stories cannot be reconciled.

And why does Matthew 8:28 speak of two possessed men, whereas Mark 5:2 and Luke 8:27 each speak of only one? Why does Matthew 20:30 talk about two blind men, whereas Mark 10:46 and Luke 18:35 each talk about only one (viz., Bartimaeus)? To me, it is a subterfuge to claim that in both cases there were two men but that Mark and Luke concentrate upon one.⁶⁰ One could just as easily imagine that Matthew doubled the number, possibly because of the Old Testament principle of Matthew 18:16 (cf. Deut. 17:6; 19:15), ". . . that every charge may be established by the evidence of two or three witnesses." It is conceivable that Matthew wished to indicate that Jesus healed more possessed and blind people than these two, but that there was no room to describe these healings.⁶¹

Speaking of numbers: why does the rooster reported to have crowed twice in Mark (14:30, 68, and 72), exactly as Jesus had announced, and in Matthew (26:34 and 75) and Luke (23:34 and 60) only once, exactly as Jesus had announced in these Gospels? Why does Mark, the shortest Gospel, supply many more details in other stories than do Matthew and

---

58. Archer (1982, 332).
59. Cf. ibid., 321–22.
60. So too ibid., 325; see also how Van Bruggen (1998, 85–91) deals with this kind of apparent discrepancy. The claim of Meier is quite harsh, namely, that "[a]ll tensions and contradictions in the four narratives are harmonized by hilarious mental acrobatics" (1991, 197).
61. Marshall (1977, 158).

Luke? Here again, the key is grasping the theological intention that gave rise to these differences, and not smoothing out those differences.

5.7.2 Three Approaches

The following provides another clear example. In Matthew 21:41 it is the spiritual leaders who reply to Jesus' question: "He will put those wretches to a miserable death and let out the vineyard to other tenants who will give him the fruits in their seasons." But in Like 20:16 it is Jesus himself replying to his own question ("He will come and destroy those tenants and give the vineyard to others"; cf. Mark 12:9), to which the leaders respond with indignation, "Surely not!" Thus, in Luke they reject what, according to Matthew, they themselves had asserted. Perhaps it is significant that Gleason Archer does not mention this remarkable discrepancy, which can hardly be reconciled.

People who boast of taking the Bible literally would do well to consider such examples. If it were a matter of rational, scholarly, historical literalness, at least one of the two writers simply gave a false version. But if the Gospels are theological compositions, things are quite different. Here again, the truly fascinating feature is the theological significance of this difference. Roughly speaking, three views are conceivable.

(1) In the liberal view, the Gospel writers have simply passed on mutually contradictory, and thus unreliable traditions.

(2) In the fundamentalist view, the literal accuracy is so important that all discrepancies must be ironed out at all costs.

(3) The intermediate view accepts the *essential* agreement of the Gospels, and tries to explain many of the differences on the basis of the theological purposes of the writers.

View (2) runs the danger of an artificial historical reconstruction, while views (1) and (3) run the danger of dismissing biblical historiography. If (1) is too facile, and if (2) is too forced, then (3) will be able to plausibly explain the discrepancies from the writers' theological purposes.

The reports of Jesus' resurrection also contain many discrepancies. To mention just a few: in Matthew 28:1 and 8, the two Marys go to the tomb, who also come back with joy, and meet Jesus on the road. In Mark 16:1 and 8 there are three women, who flee from the tomb in fear; an encounter with Jesus is not mentioned. Luke 24:1 and 10 mentions the two Marys as well as "the other women," but no encounter with Jesus. John 20:1–2 and 11–18 mentions only Mary Magdalene, who returns immediately from the empty tomb to report to the disciples, then returns to the tomb, and meets Jesus there all alone. Matthew 28:2 and 5 speaks of one angel *near* the tomb (sitting on the stone that he had rolled back), Mark 16:5 of a "young man" *in* the tomb, and Luke 24:4 of "two men," presumably in the tomb.

I. Howard Marshall rightly concluded that we cannot take one Gospel, or all the Gospels together, and assert that the story they contain is the story of the historical Jesus, telling everything exactly the way it happened. The assumption that the "biblical Jesus," or "the Jesus of the Gospels," is the same as "the historical Jesus," or "Jesus as he really was" is basically misleading because "the biblical Jesus" is an abstraction. Even though we believe in the inspiration of the Bible, we must inquire about the historical facts that lie behind the Gospels. We cannot assume that everything happened precisely the way it is described for the reason that the same events are described differently in the various Gospels, according to Marshall.[62]

5.8 Biases

5.8.1 Our Own Biases

As we saw, underlying paradigmatic biases play an essential role in reading the Gospels. This is true with respect to not only the *form* in which the Gospels have been handed down

---

62. Marshall (1977, 23–24).

to us, but also their theological *content*. As we now enter a little more deeply into the underlying presuppositions, we will focus on dogmatic questions. For instance, I believe that all four Gospels clearly teach the pre-existence and the full deity of Christ (see chapters 6 and 8). So why do so many theologians take aim at these important doctrines?

The main objections against the doctrine of the pre-existence and the full deity of Christ are based upon the biases of Enlightenment thinking, especially anti-supernaturalism, which I have mentioned several times. Throughout his work, G. C. Berkouwer entered repeatedly into the objections of Enlightenment theology with regard to the deity of Christ.[63]

On the basis of my own paradigmatic biases, I suggest we do the following three things.

(1) Especially if we call ourselves Christians, we take the biblical testimony seriously, that is, we do not judge it by means of criteria foreign to Scripture itself.

(2) We begin our investigation from the presupposition of the unity of the Bible because that is the comprehensive testimony of the Holy Spirit.

(3) We reject anti-supernaturalism on philosophical grounds, that is, we believe that there are no philosophical reasons to view anti-supernaturalism as more scientific than supernaturalism.

As we do these things, we can reach no other conclusion than that the biblical evidence for the eternal pre-existence and the full deity of Christ is abundant and overwhelming.

However, this conclusion must not make us lazy. The theologian must endeavor repeatedly to enter into the arguments of their opponent. It is no use combating them from one's own paradigm, which in such a case would function as an ivory tower. Rather, one should combat the opponent from the inner contradictions of their own arguments.[64]

---

63. E.g., Berkouwer (1954, 18–56, 153–61, 176–78, 184–92).
64. Cf. Stein (1996, 17–24) on the supernaturalism-anti-supernaturalism debate

5.8.2 Liberal Biases

On the basis of Enlightenment biases, generally only two attitudes toward traditional Christology are conceivable. Either theologians try to interpret it away, so that nothing remains of it. Or it is accepted, but theologians declare themselves not bound to it. With both attitudes, the biblical data are not taken seriously, but the second attitude openly admits doing so.

A remarkable example of the first attitude is given by P. W. Schmiedel. I use this New Testament scholar as a case study. He pointed to five passages in the Gospels that, according to B. B. Warfield,[65] conflict with the reverence for Jesus permeating the Gospels, and therefore could not have been invented by the writers of the Gospels but must have been included on the basis of the tradition fixed earlier; therefore they are preserved in only one or two of them, whereas the other Gospels, if they mention these doubtful statements, modify them to suit their own reverent standpoint.[66]

Such an argument begins from what must first be proven. It is rather subjective to determine what is and is not in harmony with the tenor of the Gospels, since this tenor can be determined only on the basis of distinct passages. The five passages to be dealt with in §5.9 can definitely be in full harmony with the reverence for Jesus permeating the Gospels, if they are interpreted in a way that preserves this harmony.

I claim in advance that the five passages, and the four I will add to them (§5.10), can be easily explained from the biblical testimony that Jesus is not only truly God but also truly Man, who, as the humble and obedient Man, always pays due homage to God. Without separating the two natures (see chapter 2), we must ask whether, in a given passage, Jesus is being viewed especially from his divine side, or especially from his human side. If this question is not raised, one could easily derive from certain New Testament passages a sub-

---

in Christology.
65. Warfield (1929, 189–90).
66. Schmiedel (1901).

ordinationism (Jesus' subordination to God) that seems to conflict with his deity[67] (cf. Matt. 27:46; John 17:3; 1 Cor. 8:6; 12:4-6; Eph. 1:17; 4:4-6; and 1 Tim. 2:5, where Jesus is clearly distinguished from God[68]).

Sometimes the critics construe a contradiction between these passages and those emphasizing the equality of the Father and the Son. One example is John 10:30 ("I and the Father are one") and 14:28 ("the Father is greater than I"). It is a mistake to posit such a contradiction, since the text can easily be interpreted in a way that eliminates any supposed contradiction. But the critics prefer that element in the supposed contradiction that best fits their anti-supernaturalist bias. So they accept the phrase "the Father is greater than I" at the expense of the phrase "I and the Father are one," because the subordinate Man Jesus fits their paradigm better than the divine Jesus.

Such an approach is of little help to the critics. Even on their standpoint there is no logical necessity why the fact that the Father being greater than the Son would exclude the consubstantiality of the Father and the Son (their being-of-one-and-the-same-being, *homoousios*). If we accept that, with respect to the divine being, the Father and the Son are co-equal, but as the humble Man the Son in his self-emptying has taken a lower place than the Father, there need be no contradiction.[69] The critics' view would be stronger if it proceeded from the unity and harmony of the text.

---

67. Cf. Berkouwer (1954, 163).
68. Cf. Brown (1994a, 174–76).
69. Cf. the Athanasian Creed: Jesus Christ is "[e]qual to the Father, as touching his Godhead: and inferior to the Father as touching his Manhood" (Lat. *Aequalis Patri secundum divinitatem: minor Patre secundum humanitatem*) (Schaff [1919, 98]). Berkouwer (1954, 187–88): "It is the Son of Man in his humiliation who now proceeds by way of suffering to the Father who will glorify him. . . . [T]he mystery of the incarnation is denied as well as the act of *submission* to the Father implied in it. . . ."

5.9 Nine Passages and Comments
5.9.1 The First Five Passages

(1) In *Mark 10:18* (cf. *Luke 18:19*) Jesus says "Why do you call me good? No one is good except God alone." According to Schmiedel, the harmonized version is that of Matthew 19:17, "Why do you ask me about what is good? There is only one who is good." In §10.5.3 I will deal extensively with this passage; at this point, I am claiming only that, even on the standpoint of the critics, it does not necessarily follow from Mark and Luke that Jesus denied his deity. We could just as well conclude that Jesus intended to say: If you call me good, then realize that no one is good except God alone, so that either I am God, or you should not call me good at all. At the very least we could say that Jesus also suggests the former ("if I am good, I am God"), because he sovereignly commands the rich young man to follow him (v. 22).

In passing, I note that there are other ways to explain the version of Matthew 19:17, ways that do not necessarily support Schmiedel's view.[70]

(2) In *Matthew 12:31-32* (cf. *Mark 3:28-30*; *Luke 12:10*) we read: "Therefore I tell you, every sin and blasphemy will be forgiven people, but the blasphemy against the Spirit will not be forgiven. And whoever speaks a word against the Son of Man will be forgiven, but whoever speaks against the Holy Spirit will not be forgiven, either in this age or in the age to come."

Some expositors claim that these verses suggest that the Holy Spirit is more than Jesus, because the former can be blasphemed, and the latter cannot. They overlook that, within the context of Matthew 12, it is the operation of the Holy Spirit *within Jesus* that could be blasphemed. What ordinary person would ever venture to say that the Holy Spirit who worked through him could be blasphemed? In no ordinary human be-

---
70. Berkouwer (1954, 242–44); Grosheide (1954, 294–95); Carson (1984, 421–23); Brown (1994a, 174).

ing does the Spirit work in such an evident way that the presence of the Spirit in such a person could not be denied. This is, very powerfully, a presence not mingled with the workings of the person's own mind and their own flesh. In Christ, the Holy Spirit as the true source of their wondrous acts could not be overlooked.

If a person were not to recognize the true deity of the Son of Man, this sin, if confessed, could be forgiven. But equating the Holy Spirit, who was undeniably working in Jesus, with Satan was unforgivable. Even on the critics' own standpoint, it must be acknowledged that the verse simply does not make any statement about the deity of Jesus. The logical error committed here is that Bible passages underscoring Jesus' humanity, or assigning certain perfections to God alone, are taken to be denials of Jesus' true deity.[71]

(3) *Mark 3:21* says, "[W]hen his family heard it, they went out to seize him, for they were saying, 'He is out of his mind.'" The only significance of this verse for liberal expositors seems to be that modifications in verse 21 in the original manuscripts are taken to suggest that in certain parts of the early church it was deemed inconceivable that some people would consider Jesus to be mad.[72] But what does the verse really suggest? It shows only that some people, whether relatives or others, thought Jesus was mad. How can the fact that some people thought Jesus was out of his mind be an indication that he could not be God? On the contrary, a person with such tremendous claims as Jesus is precisely this: either mad (or at best a misled erring spirit), or a conscious liar, or God.

Josh McDowell rightly argued that Jesus' claims of divinity were right or wrong.[73] If right, he was God. If wrong, there are again two options. Either he himself did not know that his claims were untrue, in which case he was sincerely misled.

---

71. See further *EDR* 1:150–52.
72. Lane (1974, 138); some textual witnesses read, ". . . when the scribes around him and the others heard this."
73. McDowell (1972, 107–12).

Or he did know that his claims were untrue, in which case he was a liar. Moreover, in the latter case he was a hypocrite because he taught others to be honest. He was a demon because he taught others to trust him for their eternal salvation, and he was a fool because his false claims took him to the cross. This third alternative is the most unlikely. Therefore, the people around Jesus were right: if he was not God—an option they did not consider—he had to be mad.

(4) *Mark 13:32* says, "[C]oncerning that day or that hour, no one knows, not even the angels in heaven, nor the Son, but only the Father." The argument goes like this: if God the Father does know certain things in the future, but the "Son"—whatever this title may convey—does not, then he cannot be God as the Father *is* God. Here again, Jesus apparently speaks as a humble, obedient human being, not in his quality of God the Son. Moreover, what is "not knowing"? In 1 Corinthians 2:2 the apostle Paul had "decided" to know certain things, and "decided" not to know certain other things—whereas, of course, he knew all these things very well.

But there is something else here: this Gospel passage warns us against any false separation within Jesus' personality, namely, by describing Jesus here in his humanity but using the divine name "Son" for him (see earlier in §1.9.1, 2.2.1, and 9.1.3).

(5) In *Mark 15:34*, (cf. *Matt. 27:46*) Jesus says, "My God, my God, why have you forsaken me?" The liberal argument is obvious: How can someone who feels, or knows, himself to be forsaken by God himself be God, if there is only one God? Here again, the traditional (and in my view, correct) answer is based on the hypostatic union of the divine and the human natures in the one person of Christ (see chapter 8). Christ was so perfectly God that no one other than he was able to endure so perfectly the sufferings of the cross, and in this way bring about redemption. And at the same time, he was so perfectly Man that, *in this quality*, the God of Scripture was *his* God (cf.

John 20:17; Rev. 3:12).[74] Tertullian explained it this way: it was not the divine nature of Christ that suffered on the cross and was forsaken by God, but the human nature.[75]

5.9.2 Comments

The danger of Nestorianism is always present, where part of Jesus was God, and part of him was not (see §§2.5.1 and 2.6.3). But the opposite danger of monophysitism is equally present, like the Lutheran view of the "crucified God" and of "God forsaken by God" on the cross.[76] The tension between such extremes is the tension within the mystery of Christ's own person: God and Man in one. Everything depends on our starting point: if we accept the doctrine of the two natures in one person — true God, true Man (Lat. *vere Deus, vere homo*) — we will believingly accept that the *Man* who was forsaken by God was himself God. At the same time, we will continue to say that a *Man* was forsaken, not *God* was forsaken by God.

If we reject the two-natures doctrine, we will use the saying on the cross about being forsaken as evidence for our point of view that someone forsaken by God cannot be God. Conversely, some have observed that Karl Barth emphasized Jesus' deity so strongly and his humanity so minimally that Matthew 27:46 *almost* seems to narrate a battle being fought within God himself. Barth seems not to have avoided some form of theopaschitism (the doctrine that it was God who suffered and died on the cross).[77]

In contrast to this, the statement of the Heidelberg Catechism (Answer 37) is wiser: ". . . [Christ] bore, in [his human!] body and [his human!] soul, the wrath of God against the sin of the whole human race (1 Peter 2:24; Isa. 53:12); . . . ." A separation of natures will inevitably yield (dualistic) Nestorian-

---

74. In the passages mentioned, Jesus says "my God" seven times in all.
75. *Adversus Praxean* 29–30. Actually, at other places he says just as easily that *God* suffered on earth (*De carne Christi* 3); it just depended on the person to—or about—whom he was writing, emphasizing the one or the other.
76. Gollwitzer (1973, 258).
77. Runia (1992, 16).

ism ("Jesus was forsaken by God according to his human, not his divine nature"), whereas a mixture of natures will yield (monophysite) Eutychianism ("God was forsaken by God").

This discussion is very similar to that about Mary as *theotokos* ("she who gave birth to God," mother of God), as the Council of Ephesus (431) officially named her.[78] Saying that Jesus was Mary's son according to his human nature, but not according to his divine nature, tends toward Nestorianism; we cannot separate the two natures. Saying that Mary gave birth to God (as such) tends toward Eutychianism; a human being cannot cause God to exist in any form. Protestantism defends the conclusion of the Council of Ephesus in resisting Nestorianism, but hesitates to adopt the term *theotokos*. This is first because of the development of Mariology—some might say Mariolatry—within Roman Catholicism, but second, also because of the danger of monophysitism within the term itself.

5.9.3 Trust

In light of these considerations, it is remarkable that in Hebrews 2:13 the true humanity of Christ is illustrated not by an ontological argument about the two natures of Christ but by an existential argument, namely, a quotation from Isaiah 8:17 (LXX): "I will put my trust in him," that is, in God. Jesus did not assume a human form ("share in flesh and blood," Heb. 2:14) in some Docetic sense, but really was "made like his brothers in every respect" (2:17), "yet without sin" (4:15).

Jesus was so perfectly human that he who was God could as a Man express his trust in and dependence on God (see more extensively, §8.4). Even his enemies said of him, "He trusts in the LORD; let him deliver him; let him rescue him, for he delights in him!" (Ps. 22:8; cf. Matt. 27:43). Precisely because of this very trust in God, his being forsaken by God was so grievous. He who, as a human being, had enjoyed more perfect fellowship with God than any other human being, ex-

---

78. Berkouwer (1954, 290–93).

perienced this forsakenness all the more painfully, more than any other human being. And yet, even in his being forsaken by God, Jesus never ceased being God.

The same is true of the death of Christ. We believe that God cannot die, whereas it is also true that what died was not a *part* of Christ, but the *person* of Christ.[79] To be sure, it is the *Man* Christ Jesus who is mediator between God and humanity (1 Tim. 2:5), but he could be so only "by the power of His Godhead" (Heidelberg Catechism, Answer 17). K. Schilder rightly said, "[W]e can safely say that neither in the past nor in the present only a single work of the Mediator has been performed 'in' or 'according' to one single straightforward nature [Dutch *'in' of 'naar' één enkele bloote natuur*]; the natures *are not 'straightforward,'* [Dutch *zijn niet 'bloot'*], since this magnificent Person-of-Mediator, as has been said, is constituted synthetically out of two natures, ..."[80]

In summary we can say that on the basis of the doctrine of the hypostatic unity of the divine and human natures in the one person of Christ, no aspect of his perfect humanity can be used as an argument against his deity (nor is the reverse possible). This is true also in those cases where he is viewed, according to his human nature, as distinct from God, his Father in heaven.

5.9.4 The Last Four Passages

To the five Bible passages mentioned above, Schmiedel added four that he referred to as "the ground pillars for a truly scientific life of Jesus" (which, of course, should be read as follows: "a truly scientific *view of* the life of Jesus"). Here, the term "science" is used in its limited critical naturalistic (i.e., anti-supernaturalistic) meaning, as has become common among many scholars since the Enlightenment.

(1) *Matthew 12:39–40* (cf. Mark 8:12): "An evil and adulterous generation seeks for a sign, but no sign will be given

---
79. See Berkouwer (1954, 294).
80. Schilder (1949, 2:211).

to it except the sign of the prophet Jonah. For just as Jonah was three days and three nights in the belly of the great fish, so will the Son of Man be three days and three nights in the heart of the earth." It seems that the passages that fit the anti-supernaturalist worldview are often considered the most original in the Gospels. Thus, according to liberal theologians, the statement that Jesus refused to do a sign must necessarily be original. This is because miracles are viewed as impossible by anti-supernaturalists, so that stories about supposed miracles by Jesus must be inventions of the early church. However, even the Enlightenment theologian cannot deny that, according to the Gospel writer, Jesus' refusal to do a sign in a certain situation was based not on inability but on unwillingness. When it was clear that no miracle would meet with the proper response from the viewers, Jesus refused to do them, and referred his listeners to the main signs of his suffering, death, and resurrection[81] (cf. 1 Cor. 1:18–25).[82] The fact that Jesus refused to perform a miracle for stubborn unbelievers is evidence that, under different circumstances, he apparently did perform miracles. This point is closely related to the following one.

(2) *Mark 6:5–6* (cf. Matt. 13:58): "[Jesus] could do no mighty work there, except that he laid his hands on a few sick people and healed them. And he marveled because of their unbelief." Compare this with the previous point, and again consider the context. Is the fact that, at a certain moment, Jesus could do no miracles in Nazareth evidence that he was unable to do *any* miracles? If this statement is viewed as authentic, does it not clearly suggest that this was an exceptional situation, and that under other circumstances Jesus did perform miracles? The exceptional character of the situation is evident from the

---

81. Of course, according to the critics, Jesus' implicit reference to his resurrection on the third day *cannot* be authentic.
82. Regarding the authenticity of this statement, see Carson (1984, 295–96). Cf. Martin (1972, 174): by definition, faith can never be based on proofs or signs because this would annul its character; rather it is Jesus' *cross* in which faith sees the demonstration of God's power and wisdom.

following verses: he who "could do no mighty work" in Nazareth immediately sent out his twelve disciples and *gave them authority* over the unclean spirits, and "they cast out many demons and anointed with oil many who were sick and healed them" (vv. 7, 12–13). Any liberal expositor who wishes to give a consistent exegesis of the passage will have to wonder what the word "could" in verse 5 means: does it mean not being able to do miracles at all, *or* encountering hindrances of any kind to effectuating his power, without the implication that he had no miraculous power at all? In my view, the context clearly points to the latter, and not the former interpretation.

(3) *Mark 8:14–21* (the "leaven of the Pharisees and of Herod") refers not to bread but to the teachings of these people (cf. Matt. 16:12; Luke 12:1). Critics may insist that verse 15 ("Watch out; beware of the leaven of the Pharisees and the leaven of Herod") is an isolated saying of Jesus, which has been artificially inserted because of the association between leaven and bread.[83] However, not only does this conflict with Mark's usual way of treating Jesus' sayings, but eliminating verse 15 would break the argument in verses 14–21. Moreover, there definitely is a connection with what precedes (cf. the previous point): Jesus had just admonished the Pharisees, whose "teaching" demanded manipulative signs instead of trusting the rich abundance that had just been displayed in the feeding of the four thousand. And now the disciples in verses 16–17 came very close to the same kind of unbelief by not understanding the lessons presented by such signs.[84]

(4) *Matthew 11:5* (cf. Luke 7:22): "[T]he blind receive their sight and the lame walk, lepers are cleansed and the deaf hear, and the dead are raised up, and the poor have good news preached to them." The critics suggest that the signs of the Messiah are miraculous in the figurative sense. In my view, there is no doubt that the miracles of Jesus often, if not always, had a sign character, that is, they signified something, and

---

83. Lane (1974, 280 note).
84. Carson (1984, 362–63).

had a figurative meaning;[85] see especially the extensive explanation in John 6 about the "bread of life" after, and because of, the miraculous feeding of the five thousand. However, it would be a logical error to conclude that miracles that have a figurative meaning could for that reason have occurred only figuratively. John 6 does not make sense unless it is viewed against the backdrop of people's misunderstanding about Jesus' literal multiplication of the loaves. To use a parallel: baptismal water, the wine of the Lord's Supper, and anointing oil have figurative meanings, yet are real water, real wine, and real oil. The miracles of Jesus have a figurative meaning, yet have really occurred.

In my view, the conclusion must be that Enlightenment theology can maintain its distinction between reliable and unreliable traditions in the Gospels mainly on the basis of its anti-supernaturalist prejudice.

5.10 Jesus' Historicity: Early Christian Testimony
5.10.1 The New Testament Writers

In a chapter about the sources from which we learn about the historical Jesus we must also speak of extra-biblical sources.

Today there are still authors who deny that Jesus ever existed, but they form a small minority. Even the most liberal theologians rarely called into question Jesus' existence. However, some argue that Jesus was a mythical and not a historical figure.[86] Others deny that the early Christians believed that Jesus had lived as a human being on earth.[87] Francesco Carotta asserted that the story of Jesus was nothing but a dis-

---

85. Berger (2004, 423): "No one combats the symbolic aspects of the miracle stories. Feeding stands for receiving the Word of God, healing of the blind signifies opening of the eyes of the heart for the reality of Jesus, raising the sick, stands for the beginning of new everlasting life. However, this second, sign-like level always presupposed the first level, the real sign."
86. E.g., Wells (1996; 1998; 2004).
87. Freke and Gandy (1999); other deniers include Doherty (1999) and Price (2000).

tortion of the story of Julius Caesar.[88]

Some writers may play with the invention of a "Christ myth," but they do so not on the basis of historical evidence. For an unbiased historian the historicity of Christ is just as axiomatic as the historicity of Julius Caesar. It is not historians who propagate the "Christ myth" theories, but theologians.[89] Pagan and Jewish authors referred to Jesus, matter-of-factly or with horror; but one thing they never did: cast doubt on his historicity. At the outset of our investigation, we encounter the historical person of Jesus Christ, living and preaching in what we call the Holy Land.

The New Testament itself is our first and foremost source of evidence. The first letters of Paul were written around AD 50, twenty years or fewer after the death and resurrection of Christ. The first Gospel was likely Mark, written ten to twenty years later. This means that many eye- and ear-witnesses of Jesus must still have been alive. These writings could never have enjoyed such enormous and widespread credibility if the events they narrated had never occurred, or had occurred in a very different way. Around the year 55, the apostle Paul wrote that at a given moment the risen Lord "appeared to more than five hundred brothers at one time, most of whom are still alive, though some have fallen asleep" (1 Cor. 15:6). In other words, Paul was dealing with facts that could be verified with the survivors who had been there. In other words, the existence of the Gospels cannot be explained without positing the existence of Jesus.[90]

5.10.2 The Apostolic Fathers

In addition to the New Testament, we have the writings of the Apostolic Fathers, in particular Ignatius and Polycarp, who were pupils of the apostles, and wrote extensively about Je-

---

88. Carotta (2005); on this, see Ouweneel (2002).
89. Bruce (1972, 83).
90. Marshall (1977, 237).

sus. Consider these examples from Ignatius:[91] "There is one Physician [Jesus Christ] who is possessed both of flesh and spirit; both made and not made; God existing in flesh; true life in death; both of Mary and of God."[92] "[O]ur God, Jesus Christ, was, according to the appointment of God, conceived in the womb by Mary, of the seed of David, but by the Holy Ghost."[93] And this:

> [O]ur Lord . . . was truly of the seed of David according to the flesh, and the Son of God according to the will and power of God; . . . He was truly born of a virgin, was baptized by John, in order that all righteousness might be fulfilled by Him; and was truly, under Pontius Pilate and Herod the tetrarch, nailed [to the cross] for us in His flesh. Of this fruit we are by His divinely-blessed passion, that He might set up a standard for all ages, through His resurrection, to all His holy and faithful [followers], whether among Jews or Gentiles, in the one body of His Church.[94]

We must also mention here the *First Apology* by Justin Martyr (c. AD 150), addressed to Emperor Antoninus Pius, and referring to the report that Pontius Pilate must have written concerning the lawsuit against Jesus, and that must have been available in the imperial archives. Justin wrote: "And after He was crucified they cast lots upon His vesture, and they that crucified Him parted it among them. And that these things did happen, you can ascertain from the Acts of Pontius Pilate."[95] And again:

> And that it was predicted that our Christ should heal all diseases and raise the dead, hear what was said. There are these words: "At His coming the lame shall leap as an hart, and the

---

91. See http://www.earlychristianwritings.com/ignatius.html (trans. Roberts-Donaldson).
92. His letter to the Ephesians 7:2.
93. Ibid., 18:2 (cf. 20:2).
94. His letter to the Smyrnaeans 1:1–2.
95. *First Apologia* 35.

tongue of the stammerer shall be clear speaking [Isa. 35:6]: the blind shall see, and the lepers shall be cleansed; and the dead shall rise, and walk about [Matt. 11:5]." And that He did those things, you can learn from the Acts of Pontius Pilate.[96]

Mentioning the existence of these "Acts of Pilate" (Lat. *Acta Pilati*), with its references to the person, life, and work of Christ, is quite special. Notice that Justin is using the same method the apostle Paul used: Paul tried to convince his opponent by referring him to objective external evidence, viz., the five hundred brothers (most of them still alive), whereas Justin appealed to the written *Acta Pilati*.

In the Greek *Acts of Peter and Paul* and as an appendix to the medieval Latin *Gospel of Nicodemus*, there is an interesting passage assigned to Pontius Pilate, in which he describes Jesus, his work, and his trial. The authenticity of the passage is dubious.[97]

5.11 Jesus' Historicity: Pagan Testimony
5.11.1 Roman Writers

In addition to the sources just mentioned, we find in the extra-biblical history of the first two centuries only a few references to Jesus, but this is quite understandable. In the large Roman Empire there was a wide diversity of religions. Usually these religionists scarcely interested the Roman elite, as long as they did not conflict with the state. Some ancient Roman testimonies are worth mentioning, although some scholars have designated them as later (Christian) additions to the writings concerned.[98]

Pliny the Younger, governor of Bithynia and Pontus, wrote

---

96. *First Apologia* 48. Regarding the "quest of the historical Pilate," see Barnett (1998, 79–84).
97. http://www.earlychristianwritings.com/text/reportpilate.html.
98. These testimonies have been summarized and dealt with many times; some more recent examples: Meier (1991, 89–92); C. A. Evans (*DJG* 365–66); Stein (1996, 25–31); Barnett (1998, 24–28); Theissen and Merz (1998, 76–85); Van Bruggen (1998, 24–29); cf. also Wilken (1984) and Van Voorst (2000).

Christ in the Historical Sources

a famous letter (nr. X.96) to the emperor Trajan about his measures against the Christians (c. AD 106). He wrote among other things:

> Those who denied that they were or had been Christians, when they invoked the gods in words dictated by me, offered prayer with incense and wine to your image, which I had ordered to be brought for this purpose together with statues of the gods, and moreover cursed Christ — none of which those who are really Christians, it is said, can be forced to do — these I thought should be discharged.[99]

He described their practices as follows:

> They ... were accustomed to meet on a fixed day before dawn and sing responsively a hymn to Christ as to a god [Lat. *Christo quasi deo*], and to bind themselves by oath, not to some crime, but not to commit fraud, theft, or adultery, not falsify their trust, nor to refuse to return a trust when called upon to do so. When this was over, it was their custom to depart and to assemble again to partake of food — but ordinary and innocent food.[100]

Scholars generally agree that this passage of Pliny is authentic.

The Roman historiographer Tacitus (c. AD 112) wrote about the false accusations by the emperor Nero against the Christians (*Annales* XV.44), and continued:

> Christ, from whom the name [Christians] had its origin, suffered the extreme [death] penalty during the reign of Tiberius [cf. Luke 3:1] at the hands of one of our procurators, Pontius Pilatus [Lat. *Christus Tibero imperitante per procuratorem Pontium Pilatum supplicio adfectus erat*], and a most mischievous superstition, thus checked for the moment, again broke out not only in Judaea, the first source of the evil, but even in Rome, where all things hideous and shameful from every part of the world find

---

99. http://faculty.georgetown.edu/jod/texts/pliny.html.
100. Ibid.

their center and become popular.[101]

Unfortunately, much of the work of Tacitus was lost, including a writing about the years 29–32, when the trial of Jesus took place. Most scholars believe that the passage just quoted is authentic: the style is altogether Tacitean, the passage occurs in each extant manuscript of the *Annales*, and the tone is so hostile that it is difficult to imagine that Christians would have invented the passage and would have inserted it.

The Roman historiographer Suetonius, court official under Emperor Hadrian, wrote around AD 120 (*Life of Claudius* XXV.4): "Since the Jews constantly made disturbances at the instigation of Chrestus [Lat. *impulsore Chresto*], he [i.e., Emperor Claudius] expelled them from Rome" (cf. Acts 18:2).[102] There are very good reasons to assume that by "Chrestus" Suetonius meant Christus (Christ). In the New Testament as well, we find the spelling "Chrestos" in some manuscripts.[103] Suetonius also knew the spelling "Christos," for elsewhere he says (in *Nero* XVI), "Punishment was inflicted [by Emperor Nero] on the Christians, a class of men given to a new and mischievous superstition."[104] Interestingly, the same Suetonius wrote (*Vespasian* IV): "There had spread over all the Orient an old and established belief, that it was fated at that time for men coming from Judaea to rule the world."[105] The testimony of Suetonius implies that, between AD 40 and 50, Jesus-believing Jews were communicating their faith in Roman synagogues.

---

101. https://en.wikipedia.org/wiki/Tacitus_on_Christ.
102. https://en.wikisource.org/wiki/The_Lives_of_the_Twelve_Caesars/Claudius#25.
103. E.g., we find in a variant reading of Acts 11:26 *chrēstianous* instead of *christianous*.
104. https://en.wikipedia.org/wiki/Suetonius_on_Christians#The_Nero_reference.
105. http://www.preteristarchive.com/Rome/articles/0110_suetonius_vespasian.html.

5.11.2 Other Authors

Lucian of Samosata, a Syrian satirist, probably wrote shortly after AD 165 a satirical letter in Greek, *Peri tēs Peregrinou Teleutēs* ("On the Passing of Peregrinus"),[106] about a Cynic philosopher who temporarily joined Christians. Lucian tells us (§11) about the man "whom they still worship, the man who was crucified in Palestine because he introduced this new cult into the world." In §13 he writes: "[T]heir first lawgiver [i.e., Christ] persuaded them that they are all brothers of one another after they have transgressed once, for all by denying the Greek gods and by worshipping that crucified sophist [i.e., heretical teacher] himself and living under his laws." Thus, Lucian also knew about the Man who had been crucified in Palestine and was worshiped by Christians.

There are also some interesting testimonies from the Middle East itself. Thus, the Christian traveler and historian Sextus Julius Africanus, in his *History of the World*, referred to much older writings, now lost, by the Samarian historiographer Thallus (c. AD 52). Julius discussed the three hours of darkness that occurred at Jesus' crucifixion (Luke 23:44) and wrote: "In the third book of his history, Thallus calls this darkness an eclipse of the sun—wrongly in my opinion"—wrongly, of course, because an eclipse of the sun cannot take place at the time of the full moon, and it was during the full moon of Passover that Jesus was crucified.[107] The fascinating element in this quotation is that, already around the year 52 (twenty-two years after Jesus' death) pagan authors were assuming as real both the historical Jesus and the miraculous events during his life.

There is a letter by a Syrian, Mara Bar-Serapion, sometime after AD 73, but probably before AD 165, written to his son. In this letter, he compared the murdering of Socrates, of Pythagoras, and (apparently) of Christ:

---

106. http://www.earlychristianwritings.com/text/peregrinus.html.
107. http://christianthinktank.com/jrthal.html.

What advantage did the Jews gain from executing their wise king? It was just after [viz., AD 70] that their kingdom was abolished. God justly avenged these three wise men: the Athenians died of hunger; the Samians were overwhelmed by the sea and the Jews, desolate and driven from their own kingdom, live in complete dispersion. But Socrates is not dead, because of Plato; neither is Pythagoras, because of the statue of Juno; nor is the wise king, because of the "new law" [i.e., teaching] he laid down.[108]

This is taken to mean that Jesus lived on after his death (Mara did not know of the resurrection) because his new teaching lived on among his followers.

In addition to these written sources, it is worth mentioning findings of archeology,[109] like the quadrant found in Herculaneum:

```
R O T A S
O P E R A
T E N E T
A R E P O
S A T O R
```

Michael Green suggested a Christian interpretation of these letters because they can be transformed into two words placed in the form of a cross: A PATER NOSTER O. *Pater noster* are the first words (in Latin) of the Lord's Prayer; the additional letters A and O might refer to the alpha and omega (Rev. 1:8; 21:6; 22:13).[110] If this interpretation were correct, it would be a very early testimony of the penetration of Christianity into this Roman city. The Coptic *Prayer of the Virgin in Bartos* tells how Christ was crucified with five nails, which were named Sator, Arepo, Tenet, Opera, and Rotas. This reading of the words subsequently entered the Ethiopic tradition, where

---

108. https://en.wikipedia.org/wiki/Mara_bar_Serapion_on_Jesus
109. Green (1992, 118–21).
110. Ibid., 118–20.

they became known as the names of the wounds of Christ.[111]

Green also referred to the family tomb discovered in Jerusalem in 1945.[112] Two of the ossuaries (bone chests) found were dated between the first century BC and c. AD 50 and contained the name "Jesus" in Greek. On one of them four large crosses had been drawn. If the finding is authentic, and the interpretation correct—many men were called Jesus (Joshua) in those days—it would be one of the earliest references to Jesus outside the New Testament. We also remember the more recent debate surrounding the James ossuary, containing the inscription "James, son of Joseph, brother of Jesus."[113]

5.12 Jesus' Historicity: Jewish Testimony[114]
5.12.1 Flavius Josephus

Among the ancient extra-biblical testimonies, probably the most famous are two passages written by the great Jewish historiographer Flavius Josephus, although there has been much debate about their authenticity.[115] The shorter passage, dealing with the high priest Annas (Luke 3:2; John 18:13, 24; Acts 4:6), says this (*Jewish Antiquities* XX.9.1 §200): "[H]e assembled the Sanhedrin of judges, and brought before them the brother of Jesus, who was called Christ, whose name was James, and some others; and when he had formed an accusation against them as breakers of the law, he delivered them to be stoned."[116] This passage is almost unanimously considered to be authentic because it exhibits no evidence of being a later Christian insertion: the significance of James is not emphasized, he is called the brother of Jesus, not of the Lord (cf. 1 Cor. 9:5; Gal. 1:19), and Jesus is the One "called Christ." The

---
111. See https://en.wikipedia.org/wiki/Sator_Square for references.
112. Green (1992, 121).
113. https://en.wikipedia.org/wiki/James_Ossuary.
114. In addition to other authors mentioned below, see Meier (1991, 94–111); Bockmuehl (1994, 11–14); Stein (1996, 31–34); and Van Bruggen (1998, 29–41).
115. Meier (1991, 56–88); C. A. Evans (*DJG* 364–65).
116. https://en.wikipedia.org/wiki/Josephus_on_Jesus.

Christian historiographer Eusebius quoted this passage.[117]

The longer passage, the famous *Testimonium Flavianum*, reads as follows (*Jewish Antiquities* XVIII.3.3 §63–64):

> About this time there lived Jesus, a wise man, *if indeed one ought to call him a man*. For he was one who performed surprising deeds and was a teacher of such people as accept the truth gladly. He won over many Jews and many of the Greeks. *He was the Christ*. And when, upon the accusation of the principal men among us, Pilate had condemned him to a cross, those who had first come to love him did not cease. He appeared to them spending a third day restored to life, *for the prophets of God had foretold these things and a thousand other marvels about him*. And the tribe of the Christians, so called after him, has still to this day not disappeared.[118]

Many scholars believe that the passage contains some insertions from a later time; I have put them in italics. Perhaps the passage is authentic, but in the course of time was embellished by Christians. At any rate there exists a more sober version of it in a tenth-century Arabic manuscript of bishop Agapius of Hierapolis. The latter made this interesting general remark: "We have found in many books of the philosophers [read: scholars] that they refer to the day of the crucifixion of Christ." Agapius moreover gave a list plus quotations from these ancient works, some of which are no longer extant. His version of Josephus' words is this:

> At this time there was a wise man who was called Jesus. And his conduct was good, and he was known to be virtuous. And many people from among the Jews and the other nations became his disciples. Pilate condemned him to be crucified and to die. And those who had become his disciples did not abandon his discipleship. They reported that he had appeared to them three days after his crucifixion and that he was alive; according-

---

117. *Historia Ecclesiastica* II.23.22.
118. *Jewish Antiquities* XVIII.3.3 (§§63–64); italics added.

ly, he was perhaps the Messiah concerning whom the prophets have recounted wonders. . . .[119]

It is not unlikely that we have here (an approximation of) the original text as Josephus had written it. If this is correct, as many assume, then the passage offers us an interesting testimony concerning Jesus and his ministry, from a time shortly after the last apostle had passed away.

5.12.2 The Talmud

In the Talmud we find various allusions to Jesus, but these are rather obscure, and therefore the opinions about them differ widely.[120] Some believe that the Talmud, including the Mishnah, contains no statement going back to Jesus' time, and no authentic, direct reference to Jesus; all such references are supposedly later, medieval interpolations.[121] If there are Jesus passages, these are supposedly directed more against the Christ preached by Christians than against the historical Jesus.

For various reasons, it is difficult to evaluate possible Jesus passages in the Talmud and Tosefta (additions to the Mishnah).[122] First, in 1554 the Vatican ordered that all passages that could be thought to refer to Jesus be removed from the Talmud. Since that time, we have censored and uncensored versions of the Talmud. In uncensored versions, the name *Yeshu* occurs, sometimes with the addition *haNotzri*, that is, "Jesus the Nazarene." Jewish expositors do not emphasize this, because these passages speak negatively about Jesus, and in the past offered an excuse for antisemitism. Actually, some deny any relationship between Yeshu haNotzri and Jesus of Nazareth.

In the uncensored tract Abodah Zarah,[123] we are told how Rabbi

---

119. Flusser (2007, 157) argued that this form of the Testimonium Flavianum is essentially that of Josephus; cf. extensively, Theissen and Merz (1998, 64–74).
120. C. A. Evans (*DJG* 366–67); Theissen and Merz (1998, 74–76).
121. Lauterbach (1951); Maier (1978, 263–75).
122. See the studies by Klausner (1964); Herford (1975); and Zindler (2003).
123. Abodah Zarah 27b; cf. jerTalmoed: Abodah Zarah 2:2 IV.I.

THE ETERNAL CHRIST: GOD WITH US

Eleazar ben Dama was bitten by a snake. A certain Jacob of Kefar-Sekaniah (i.e., Suchnin in Galilee) wished to heal him; this Jacob may have been James the son of Alphaeus (Mark 3:18) or James the younger (Mark 15:40).[124] In one Talmud manuscript this James is called one of the disciples of Jesus the Nazarene.[125] Later we are told that Rabbi Ishmael, ben Dama's uncle, did not permit him to heal the rabbi. During the dispute between the two rabbis, ben Dama died. Rabbi Ishmael explained that the "teaching of *Minim* [heretics, including Christians]" is attractive, and that one who has dealings with them "may be drawn after them."[126] Elsewhere, the same Jacob/James, appealing to Deuteronomy 23:19 as well as the teaching that he had received from Jesus, asks ben Dama in a critical tone whether it is permitted to hire a harlot to build a toilet for the high priest.[127]

In the tract Sanhedrin 43a, we read in the uncensored Talmud:

> On the eve of Passover Yeshu [one manuscript adds: the Nazarene] was hanged. For forty days before the execution took place, a herald went forth and cried, "He is going forth to be stoned because he has practiced sorcery and enticed Israel to apostasy. Anyone who can say anything in his favor, let him come forward and plead on his behalf." But since nothing was brought forward in his favor he was hanged on the eve of the Passover [one manuscript adds: and the eve of Shabbath].[128]

5.12.3 Other Sources

It is also reported that Yeshu had five disciples, whose names exhibit some resemblance with those of Jesus' disciples: Mati (= Matthew), Nakai (= Luke?), Nezer (= Nazarene = Christians?), Boni (= Nicodemus?), and Todah (= Thaddaeus).[129]

---

124. *The Soncino Talmud, Nezikin* Vol. IV, Abodah Zarah 17a (85n3).
125. Ibid., 85n2.
126. Ibid., 137.
127. Ibid., 16b–17a (85); cf. Tosefta Hullin 2.24; cf. Jeremias (1957).
128. *The Soncino Talmud, Nezikin,* vol 3, Sanhedrin 43a (281).
129. Thus *The Jewish Encyclopedia* 7, 171; the article also refers to the Jewish writing *Toledoth Yeshuah haNotzri,* which mentions the following disciples:

The name Yeshu appears at other places, without any parallel with the New Testament Jesus, yet (in some uncensored manuscripts) with the addition *haNotzri*. In the time when the Babylonian Talmud came about, *Yeshu haNotzri* had become the common Hebrew designation for "Jesus the Nazarene."

What must we think of the addition "ben Pandera (or Pandira)"?[130] Some have thought of a Latin name Pantera, others of an allusion to the traitor Pandaros in Homerus' *Ilias*. Thus, *qol Pandar* in Genesis Rabbah 50 means "voice of Pandar," referring to false promises of a traitor. In this case, "ben Pandera" would be a generic name, just like "son of Belial." Others see in Pandera (= Panthera) a variant of the Greek *parthenos*, "virgin." Those who called Jesus "ben Pandera" had become confused: the original intention of the expression was Jesus, the son of the virgin.

Joseph Klausner was sure that "ben Pandera" referred to Jesus; he defended the authenticity of some Talmud passages mentioned in the previous section, and their reference to "Jesus of Nazareth." He thought that the variants "Yeshu ben Pantere" or "Yeshu ben Pandera" instead of "Yeshu of Nazareth" were due to the fact that, from an early time, the name Pantere or Pantera became current among the Jews as the name of Jesus' supposed father.

The name "ben Pandera" is important, for instance, because the pagan writer Celsus, in combating Christianity (AD 178), claimed that he had heard from a Jew that Mary's husband had divorced her because of her adultery with a Roman soldier named Pantheras, who supposedly became the father of Jesus. In later Jewish writings, Yeshu ben Pandera became a common designation for Jesus. In his refutation of Celsus, Origen claimed that Pantheras was the patronym of Joseph,

---

Simeon (= Peter), Mattia (= Matthew), Elikum (= Luke), Mordechai (= Mark), Todah (= Thaddaeus), and Johannos (= John), that is, the four Gospel writers plus Peter and Thaddaeus.

130. In the Talmud: Shabbath 104b (*The Soncino Talmud*, *Mo'ed*, 1:504 plus note 2; also see *Nezikin*, vol. 3, Sanhedrin, 456n5).

since the latter's father, Jacob (Matt. 1:16), was nicknamed Panther.

Appealing to the Talmud to find evidence for the historical existence of Jesus is a double-edged sword. On the one hand, we could find in the vague references a corroboration of Jesus' existence. On the other hand, we could just as easily conclude that the stories about Jesus go back to vague, mutually contradictory legends, and thus cast doubt on the historical existence of Jesus. Thus, the Egyptologist Gerald Massey asserted that ben Pandera had really lived sometime in the second century, and that the (distorted) stories about Jesus were based upon him; tradition had simply located them in the wrong century.[131] Apart from this, there is still the genuine possibility that most, if not all, of the references to Yeshu have nothing to do with Jesus of Nazareth.

---

131. Massey (1886).

Chapter 6
The Pre-Incarnate Christ

No one has ever seen God;
the only One, who is God,
who is at the Father's side,
he has made him known.

John 1:1–2, 14, 18

6.1 Seven Positions
6.1.1 Description

BY WAY OF introduction to this and the following chapters, we must first recognize the three states of Christ: the pre-incarnate (transcendent) Christ, the humbled (historical-immanent) Christ, and the glorified (supra-historical-transcendent) Christ. As for the latter two, some speak of the doctrine of the twofold state (Lat. *status duplex*) of Christ in his humanity: his state of humiliation and his state of exaltation;[1] in the broader sense, we can speak of his threefold state: Christ's pre-incarnate state, his state of humiliation, and his state of exaltation.

The doctrine of the *status duplex* is based especially on Phi-

---

1. See, e.g., Bavinck (*RD* 3:406–10); Berkouwer (1965, chapter 3); Heyns (1988, 253–69); Van Genderen and Velema (2008, 468–72).

THE ETERNAL CHRIST: GOD WITH US

lippians 2:

> ... Christ Jesus, who, though he was in the form of God, did not count equality with God a thing to be grasped, but emptied himself, by taking the form of a servant, being born in the likeness of men. And being found in human form, he *humbled* himself by becoming obedient to the point of death, even death on a cross. Therefore God has highly *exalted* him and bestowed on him the name that is above every name, so that at the name of Jesus every knee should bow, in heaven and on earth and under the earth, and every tongue confess that Jesus Christ is Lord, to the glory of God the Father (vv. 5-11).

The same fundamental idea appears frequently in the New Testament: "Was it not necessary that the Christ should suffer these things and[2] enter into his glory?" (Luke 24:26). "In saying, 'He ascended,' what does it mean but that he had also descended into the lower regions, the earth? He who descended is the one who also ascended far above all the heavens, that he might fill all things" (Eph. 4:9-10; see also John 12:23-24; Acts 2:22-36; 1 Tim. 3:16; Heb. 1:1-4; 1 Pet. 1:20-21). Since Friedrich Schleiermacher, much criticism has been leveled at this doctrine, related to one's view of the self-emptying (Gk. *kenōsis*) of Jesus (on this, see §8.7), but also to one's view of the full ontic reality not only of Christ's state of humiliation but also of his pre-incarnate state and his state of exaltation.[3]

Within the three states of Christ, we may further distinguish seven positions of Christ according to location and time: one in the first, three in the second, and three in the third state.[4] Each of the seven positions of Christ can be further defined by an adjective, a time reference, and a location. They are the following.

---

2. The idiomatic sense is: "and thus."
3. Berkouwer (1965, 36–37).
4. Chafer (1983, 3:12–17).

A. The Pre-incarnate State

1. The *pre-incarnate* Christ (in heaven, from all eternity until the incarnation).

B. The State of Humiliation

2. The *incarnate* (i.e., *humiliated*) Christ (on earth, from his incarnation until his death, i.e., at least 34 years).

3. The *dead* Christ (from his death until his resurrection, perhaps about forty hours, in the tomb as well as in the hereafter[5]).

4. The *risen* Christ (on earth, from his resurrection until his ascension, i.e., forty days [Acts 1:3][6]).

C. The State of Glorification

5. The *exalted* Christ (in heaven, at the right hand of God, from his ascension until his second coming, i.e., an undefined time period, today almost two thousand years).

6. The *returned* Christ (in heaven, but also appearing on the throne of David on earth, from his second coming until the end of the Messianic kingdom, i.e., one thousand years[7]).

7. The *eternally ruling* Christ (in the new heaven and on the new earth, after surrendering the kingdom to the Father, and then for all eternity; "God all in all" [1 Cor. 15:28], meaning the *Triune* God[8]).

In this chapter we will deal with position 1; in chapters 7–10, we will discuss the two natures that Christ has since the

---

5. On the phrase "he descended into hell" (Lat. *descendit in inferos*) from the Apostles' Creed, see §12.7.2.
6. Or more correctly, Christ was in the "hereafter" (but not yet ascended to heaven), and from there he frequently appeared on earth.
7. If we may understand the "thousand years" in Rev. 20:1–6 literally; see Ouweneel (1988, 58–60; 1990, 209).
8. It is inconceivable that here the term "God" means "the Father," excluding the Son from the eternal reign, given the fact that (a) before his incarnation the Son held all things together (Col. 1:17; cf. Heb. 1:3), and (b) even God's servants "will reign forever and ever" (Rev. 22:4).

incarnation, as well as his sinlessness; in chapter 11, we will deal with position 2; in chapter 12, we will consider the end of position 2, along with positions 3-5. I have dealt with the positions 6 and 7 elsewhere.[9]

6.1.2 Corresponding Christologies

One could distinguish Christologies according to four of the positions of Christ described in the previous section. I mention them here with a name and a description according to the traditional Christian feasts.[10]

1. The *Christmas* Christology of the early church and of the Roman Catholic Church ties in especially with the *incarnation* of Christ. In this tradition, Christmas was always emphasized more than Easter (of course, without disavowing Good Friday and Easter). Roman Catholic church buildings are never so full as on Christmas Eve. The emphasis on the incarnated Word led to, among other things, the concept of Mary as "mother of God," and the veneration for the Madonna with Child as a symbol of early Christian and Roman Catholic piety.

(b) The *Good Friday* Christology of Protestantism, particularly in the Lutheran tradition with its theology of the cross (Lat. *theologia crucis*), without disavowing Christmas and Easter. In both Lutheranism and Calvinism (as well as Evangelicalism), Jesus is viewed first and foremost as the Redeemer, the One who died on the cross for our sins. Practices of piety reflect this: remembering Christ's sufferings in the Lord's Supper, and imitation of the suffering Christ.

(c) The *Easter and Ascension* Christology of Eastern Orthodoxy: not only is Easter far more important than Christmas, but the Orthodox focus is not so much on the crucifix but on Christ Pantokrator, the triumphing Christ rising from the tomb or at God's right hand (consider how differently Christ is depicted in the average Roman Catholic and an Eastern Or-

---

9. *EDR* 10:chapters 12–14.
10. Kärkkäinen (2003, 15–16; see also 82–83).

thodox church). In Orthodox soteriology, what is central are not the experiences of guilt, atonement, and forgiveness, but achieving the glory of Christ. Here, the magnificent liturgy of the church on earth is only an icon (image, foreshadowing) of the heavenly liturgy.

(d) The *Pentecost* Christology of the Pentecostal and Charismatic movement does not disavow Christmas, Good Friday, and Easter, of course, but emphasizes that all these feasts remind us only of what Christ did *for* us, whereas at Pentecost—the culmination of the liturgical year—we are reminded of what Christ does *in* us, on the basis of what is remembered in the previous feasts. The emphasis is more on the exalted Lord than on the suffering Lord. But we could also say that the emphasis is more on the earthly life of the Jesus who worked miracles, who offered healing and deliverance, who was announced as baptizing in the Holy Spirit, and who grants prophecies and glossolalia to his people. All of this involves a Christology: if Pentecostals and Charismatics have their theology in order, the emphasis still rests more on Christ than on the Holy Spirit, as it should: the Spirit glorifies Christ, not the other way around (John 16:4). But the emphasis is particularly on Christ as the Savior, the Baptizer in the Spirit, the Sanctifier, the Healer, and the returning King, as the fivefold (or full) gospel of the Pentecostal movement described him.[11]

6.1.3 Corresponding Titles

Jesus has various titles, which can be arranged according to his various positions, as Oscar Cullmann emphasized.[12] Here is my own concise summary. The titles that I mention are usually not *limited* to the "position" indicated, but are particularly characteristic of it. I mention them here with some typical Bible passages).

1. The *pre-incarnate* Christ
    * the (eternal) Word (the Logos) (John 1:1–14)

---
11. See Thomas (2010).
12. Cullmann (1963).

THE ETERNAL CHRIST: GOD WITH US

  * the (eternal) Son of God (John 17:1-5)
  * in short: God (John 1:1, 18; Rom. 9:5; Titus 2:13; 1 John 5:20)
  * the Wisdom of God (Prov. 8:22-31; 1 Cor. 1:24).

2. The *incarnate* Christ
   * Son of Man (Matt. 8:20; 9:6; 12:40; 17:22-23)
   * Son of David (Matt. 9:27; 12:23; 15:22; 20:30-31)
   * King (Matt. 2:2; 21:5; 27:12, 29, 37, 42)
   * Messiah (the Christ) (Matt. 2:4; 11:2; 16:16; 26:63-64; John 1:42; 4:25)
   * Prophet (Matt. 13:57; 21:11; Luke 7:16; 13:33; John 4:19; 6:14; 7:40)
   * Servant (Matt. 12:18; 20:26-28; Acts 3:13, 26; 4:27, 30)
   * Shepherd (Matt. 18:12-14; 26:31; John 10:2, 11, 14; 1 Pet. 2:25)
   * Bridegroom (Matt. 9:15; John 3:29)
   * Rabbi (Mark 9:5; 11:21; John 1:39, 50; 3:2, 26; 4:31; 6:25; 9:2; 11:8)
   * Master/Teacher (Matt. 8:19; 12:38; 19:16; 22:16, 24, 36; 26:18).

3. The *dying* Christ
   * the Lion of Judah (Rev. 5:5)
   * the Lamb (John 1:29, 36; 1 Cor. 5:7; 1 Pet. 1:19; Rev. 5:6, 8, 12-13 etc.)
   * High Priest (Heb. 2:17; 3:1; 9:11)
   * Savior/Redeemer (Luke 2:11; John 4:42; Acts 5:31; 13:23).

4. and 5. The *risen* and *exalted* Christ
   * Lord (Acts 2:36; Rom. 10:9; 1 Cor. 12:3; 1 Pet. 3:15)
   * High Priest (Heb. 3:1; 4:14-15; 5:5, 10; 6:20; 7:26; 8:1)
   * Advocate (1 John 2:1)
   * the last Adam (1 Cor. 15:45).

6. and 7. The *returned* and *eternally ruling* Christ
   * King (Matt. 25:34, 40; Rev. 19:16)

* Messiah (the Christ) (Rev. 11:15; 20:4, 6)
* Bridegroom (Matt. 25:1–12; cf. Rev. 19:7; 21:2, 9; 22:17)
* Son of Man (Matt. 13:41; 16:27; 19:28; 24:27, 30, 37, 39; 25:31; 26:64)
* Son of David (Matt. 21:9, 15)
* Shepherd (Heb. 13:20; 1 Pet. 5:4).

6.2 Old Testament Evidence
6.2.1 Eternal Existence

Is there anything the Old Testament can tell us about the pre-existence of Christ, that is, his having existed before his incarnation? The prophecy in Micah 5:2 (NKJV) says, "But you, Bethlehem Ephrathah, [though] you are little among the thousands [or, clans] of Judah, [yet] out of you shall come forth to Me The One to be Ruler in Israel, Whose goings forth [are] from of old, from everlasting."[13] Rabbi Solomon Goldman presumed that the final words of the verse gave rise to the later Jewish view that the Messiah existed in the mind of God since time immemorial, as part of the Creator's plan at the beginning of the universe. In the Talmud, the name of the Messiah is one of the seven things that were created before the foundation of the world.[14] Please note that this involves the *name* of the Messiah, not the Messiah himself; Judaism does not acknowledge the pre-existence of the Messiah.

Some Christian expositors believe that the second "going forth" (Heb. *motzaot*, from *y-tz-'*, "to go forth") of the Messiah is explained by the first mention of this verb in the verse: *yētzē*, "he shall come (or, go) forth." This would mean that the coming son of David will be ruler on the basis of the very

---

13. See more extensively, Ouweneel in Knevel and Paul (1995, 174–75, with references).
14. In Cohen (1980, 175); cf. SBK 2:334–35; the other six things are: the Torah, the throne of glory, the sanctuary, the (names of the) patriarchs, the (idea of) Israel, and repentance; occasionally two more are added: the garden of Eden (Paradise) and Gehenna (hell), and occasionally a tenth: the (idea of the) Holy Land (see, e.g., http://jewishencyclopedia.com/articles/12339-preexistence).

ancient rights of the Davidic dynasty of Bethlehem.[15] I believe rather that the second expression goes further than the first one: he will go forth from Bethlehem, *yea*, his goings forth are *even* from of old, from everlasting, or "from the days of eternity" (NASB). The latter expression is doubtful, though. The ESV and others have "from ancient days," or "from days long ago." However, there is wide difference between "long ago" and "from eternity."

Now we cannot deny that in no Bible passage does the phrase "from of old" (Heb. *miqqedem*) refer to *eternity* past; it always refers to a *historical* past (Ps. 74:12; 77:5, 11; 143:5; Isa. 45:21; 46:10; Hab. 1:12). Sometimes this is even explicitly the ancient time of David (Neh. 12:46). In Micah 7:20, the Hebrew phrase *mimē qedem* means "the days of old," which again unmistakably refers to the historical past. Nowhere in the Old Testament does the phrase *mimē ʿolam*, "from the days of eternity (or of long ago)," refer to eternity past, but always to the historical past. In Amos 9:11 this is again the ancient time of David.

Yet, it is equally true that the Hebrew word *qedem* definitely *can* mean "eternity," as in the expression "the eternal God" (Deut. 33:27, Heb. *Elohey qedem*). And the Hebrew word *ʿolam can* mean "eternity," too, especially when applied to God (Gen. 21:33, Heb. *El ʿolam*; Ps. 90:2; 93:2; Isa. 26:4; 40:28, Heb. *Elohey ʿolam*; Jer. 10:10). In Proverbs 8:23-31 both expressions refer to the eternity preceding creation. Thus, it is certainly not inappropriate to read "days of eternity" in Micah 5:2,[16] since the Old Testament does acknowledge the divine character of the Messiah (see next section). The double "going forth" in Micah 5:2 thus becomes a meaningful parallel: on the one hand, the Messiah within earthly time goes forth from Bethlehem as David's son; on the other hand, he also has an eternal

---

15. See, e.g., Deden (1953, ad loc.); Allen (1976, 343); cf. Bleeker (1934, 171–72).
16. See, e.g., Ridderbos (1930, 95); Bentzen (1952); McComiskey (1985, 427); and many older expositors, such as Keil (KDC 10, ad loc.).

"going forth," or origin. And if one prefers expressions such as "ancient" or "of old," we may say that the Messiah dates from ancient times, *long before creation existed.*

This must not necessarily be taken as a reference to the eternal generation of the Son from the Father, as older expositors wished to understand it. That notion of the eternal generation of the Son is a theological idea that goes far beyond the scope of the present passage, which only deals with the question from where and when the Messiah comes (see §7.6).

Lastly, it is possible to explain the plural Hebrew word *motzaot* ("goings forth") such that before his birth in Bethlehem, the Messiah had "gone forth" several times earlier, in the sense of "appeared," that is, within human history.[17] According to this view, it is possible to think here of Messiah's Old Testament appearances, especially—but not exclusively—as the Angel of YHWH (see §6.3).

6.2.2 Divinity

One of the most remarkable differences between the Jewish and Christian views of the Messiah is that in the former view, the Messiah is not, and in the later view is, a divine figure. This is why the former view must seek to avoid applying the Messianic names in Isaiah 7:14 and 9:6 to the Messiah himself, but apply them only to God (see §§4.6.1 and 4.7.2). The traditional Christian view understands these names to indicate the Messiah's divine character.

Among Israel's pagan neighboring nations it was very common to deify the king, and to adorn him with divine names. In Israel this was not the case at all; at most, the Davidic king was viewed as a "son" of God through adoption (2 Sam. 7:14; Ps. 2:7), but this did not give the king any divine status. In this respect, the Messiah is the great exception; the passages just mentioned imply therefore especially that the Davidic

---

17. Cf. Keil (KDC 10, ad loc.). The plural "goings forth" can also simply be the expression of a heightened sentimental emphasis, according to Wolff (1982, ad loc.).

kings were types of the Messiah. A name like Immanuel (Isa. 7:14; 8:8; cf. 8:10) is comparable to other Hebrew names that included the word *el*, like Eleazar, Eliakim, Michael, and Daniel, but these names indicate what God means to the person involved. The name Immanuel, however, indicates that in the child born of the virgin *God himself* would be with his people (Matt. 1:23). Compare Isaiah 8:10, "Take counsel together, but it will come to nothing; speak a word, but it will not stand, for God is with us [Heb. *ki immanu el*]," namely—and this is vital for understanding Isaiah 7–8—in the person of the Messiah.

Similarly, the names in Isaiah 9:6 do not tell us that the God of the Messiah is a Wonderful Counselor, a Mighty God, and an Everlasting Father, but rather that the Messiah *himself* is such.[18] The Counselor is wonderful because his counsel surpasses human counsel (cf. Isa. 11:2). "Mighty God" is also a name for God himself (in Isa. 10:21; cf. Deut. 10:17; Jer. 32:18). "Everlasting Father" means that Messiah's fatherhood over his people lasts forever. "Prince of Peace" is not a divine name; yet, it constitutes a culmination because it is none other than the Wonderful Counselor, the Mighty God, and the Everlasting Father who brings peace to his people, and rules in peace over them, "from this time forth and forevermore" (see Isa. 9:7).

Very special is Psalm 45:6-7, "Your throne, O God, is forever and ever. / The scepter of your kingdom is a scepter of uprightness; / you have loved righteousness and hated wickedness. / Therefore God, your God, has anointed you / with the oil of gladness beyond your companions." Apart from the question whether this psalm is directly or indirectly Messianic,[19] the divinity of the protagonist is expressed here so explicitly that Rabbi Abraham Cohen said of verse 6a, "The Hebrew is difficult.... *Thy throne, O God*, appears to be the obvious translation but does not suit the context."[20] He should

---

18. See more extensively, Oswalt (1986, 246–48).
19. See Ridderbos (1958, 31–34).
20. Cohen (1985, 141).

have said that this translation does not suit his *prejudices*. Cohen came with the distorted solution: "thy throne given by God," or possibly, "thy throne is divinely ordained." Yet, the Septuagint gives the same translation: "Your throne, O God" (Gk. *ho thronos sou ho theos*). Apparently, the Messianic interpretation of Psalm 45 does have ancient Jewish approval.[21] In Hebrews 1:8, the author appeals to this psalm in order to cast light on the Messiah's divinity.[22]

It has been argued that the Hebrew term *elohim* can refer to the judges of Israel, as in Exodus 21:6; 22:8–9, 28, and Psalm 82:2 and 6, and thus can refer to human beings; therefore, the term in Psalm 45:6 does not necessarily prove the divinity of the Messiah. However, I have argued elsewhere that *nowhere* in the Old Testament does *elohim* refer to humans; in Exodus it refers to the place where God dwells (before whom justice is practiced), and in Psalm 82 it refers to angelic powers (cf. Ps. 8:5 with Heb. 2:7).[23] The only exception seems to be Psalm 45, where, according to most translations, the *human* Messiah *is* being addressed as *elohim*. Indeed, the Messiah *is* the exception because he is God and Man in one person. He is not just "a god," but "God"—no less YHWH than the Father and the Holy Spirit. For the apostle John it was evident that when Isaiah beheld the glory of YHWH (Isa. 6), he beheld Christ (John 12:36–41).

6.2.3 YHWH and Messiah

Can it be made plausible from the Old Testament, too, that the Triune God is Father, Son, and Holy Spirit, and that thus the Messiah is YHWH just as the Father and the Son are YHWH (see §§6.5)? Since the rabbis never reached this thought—they would radically reject it—we can say that this is possible only in the light that the New Testament sheds on the Old Testament.

---

21. Van Uchelen (1977, ad loc.).
22. See Brown (1994a, 185–87; cf. 193).
23. Ouweneel (2003, 32).

(a) In *Psalm 102*, an afflicted person addresses their lament to YHWH, and it is not hard to see in this figure also the suffering Messiah. However, in Hebrews 1:10-12, verses 24b-27 are applied to Jesus; he who is YHWH in Psalm 102 is the Messiah in Hebrews 1. Perhaps there is no other place in the Bible where Christ's humanity is so contrasted with his deity as here. The afflicted one says in verse 12a, "But you, O LORD, are enthroned forever"; but according to Hebrews 1, verse 27 says about the *Messiah*: "[Y]ou are the same, and your years have no end." We see the contrast especially in the great denouement of verse 24: in verses 23-24a, it is the Messiah (in the Messianic application of the psalm) as a Man, begging God, who has broken his (Messiah's) strength and has shortened his days: "O my God, . . . take me not away in the midst of my days," that is, halfway the normal age of a human being (cf. 90:10). But then, in verse 24b, God replies to the Messiah, as is suggested by Hebrews 1:10-12, and assures him that he, the cast down and perished Messiah, is the same as the eternal God—"you whose years endure throughout all generations . . . your years have no end"—the Creator of heaven and earth (v. 25), and that the One whose days were shortened here on earth is the same as YHWH who lives forever, even after the present creation will have passed away (v. 26).[24]

We must conclude that in applying Psalm 102:24b-27 to the Messiah, the author of Hebrews is either the worst expositor one could imagine (confusing God and the Messiah, confusing the one addressing and the One addressed)—or he expresses one of the deepest truths of the Bible: the Messiah is God and Man in one person.

(b) In the light of the latter, we perceive in the Old Testament various connections between the coming Messiah and the coming YHWH, and between the kingship of the Messiah and that of YHWH (see also §4.12). In Daniel 7:13 the Son of Man is coming with the clouds of heaven, but the moment we

---

24. Ouweneel (1982, 28).

count upon hearing more about this, it is the Ancient of Days who is coming (v. 22). Thus, in Revelation 1:13-14 we find in the description of the Son of Man features of the Ancient of Days (cf. Dan. 7:9-10), as well as features of the mysterious Man in Daniel 10:5, who I believe to be the pre-incarnate Christ. In §6.5 we will encounter many more Old Testament passages in which we hear about YHWH, but which in the New Testament are applied to the Messiah.

(c) In Isaiah 31:4b-5 it is YHWH who "will come down to fight on Mount Zion and on its hill. Like birds hovering, so the LORD of hosts will protect Jerusalem; he will protect and deliver it; he will spare and rescue it" (cf. 30:27, 30) — but five verses later we hear of a Messianic figure: "Behold, a king will reign in righteousness. . . ." (32:1). Of course, the first referent of 31:4b-5 is the time of Hezekiah; but the very connection with the eschatological Messianic message of Isaiah 32 gives a Messianic bearing to 31:4b-5 as well. That is, in the light of the New Testament we may say that the LORD who descends in Isaiah 31 is basically the same as the King reigning in Isaiah 32.

(d) Isaiah 40:3-5 refers to John the Baptist (see Matt. 3:3; Mark 1:2-3; John 1:23), who prepares "the way of the LORD . . . a highway for our God. . . . And the glory of the LORD shall be revealed." The Messiah's herald prepared the way for him, and in the Messiah the glory of YHWH is manifested. Verse 10 says of the coming Messiah, "Behold your God! Behold, the Lord GOD comes with might, and his arm rules for him; behold, his reward is with him, and his recompense before him" — and the latter phrase is applied to Christ in Revelation 22:12.[25] This verse indicates that YHWH is coming, not as he came at his first coming, in utter weakness, but with a mighty arm to establish a rule that will rectify all evil on earth, will heal its wounds, and will bring peace forever.[26]

(e) In Isaiah 59:19-20 the prophet says, "So they shall fear

---
25. Young (1972, 39–40).
26. Jennings (1966, 468).

the name of the LORD from the west, and his glory from the rising of the sun; for he will come like a rushing stream,[27] which the wind of the LORD drives. And a Redeemer will come to Zion, to those in Jacob who turn from transgression." According to 59:15b, this Redeemer is YHWH himself; but in verse 20 YHWH speaks of him in the third person, whereas Romans 11:26 applies this verse to Christ.[28]

(f) Isaiah 60:1 says, "Arise, shine, for your light has come, and the glory of the LORD has risen upon you" — but in 42:6 and 49:6 it is the Messiah who is the "light of the nations" (cf. Luke 2:32; Acts 13:47; see also 26:23).

(g) In Zechariah 9:9, the King is the humble rider on the donkey; but in 14:9 and 16 the King is none less than YHWH himself. In 11:13 the reward for the good shepherd is called the "price" that "they" set on YHWH, but in Matthew 27:9-10 this very price is set upon the Messiah. In Zechariah 12:4-9 it is YHWH who sets Jerusalem free, but in verse 10 YHWH says, ". . . then they will look on *Me* whom they pierced" (NKJV), a word that in John 19:37 is referred to Jesus. In Zechariah 13:7 God says about the Messiah that he is God's "shepherd . . . the man who stands next to me" (cf. Matt. 26:31), but in Zechariah 14:5, where one expects to hear about the coming of the Messiah on the Mount of Olives (see the connection between the Messiah and the Mount of Olives in Acts 1:11), the name of the coming One is "YHWH my God."

From all this, it does not follow that the Old Testament teaches that according to his divine nature, the Messiah is YHWH (just like the Father and the Spirit); it is only in the light of the New Testament that we begin to recognize the connections that are implicitly present in the Old Testament. Thus, we understand the deeper, eschatological significance of Psalm 96:13, ". . . the LORD . . . comes to judge the earth. He will judge the world in righteousness, and the peoples in

---

27. An interesting phrase, which has been rendered and interpreted in various ways.
28. Bultema (1981, 580–82).

his faithfulness" (cf. 98:9), and of verse 10: "The LORD reigns! Yes, the world is established; it shall never be moved; he will judge the peoples with equity" (cf. 95:3; 97:1; 98:6; 99:1-5). When the floodlight of the New Testaments shines on many such passages, we see the figure of the Messiah radiating in him who is called YHWH.

6.3 The Angel of YHWH
6.3.1 *Mal'akh Habb'rit*

One of the remarkable figures of the Old Testament, one that Christians have traditionally identified as the pre-incarnate Christ, is the "Angel of the LORD" (Heb. *mal'akh* YHWH). No matter how this figure is viewed, at first sight it seems rather daring to identify it as the Messiah. An important argument for doing so, however, is the way the New Testament deals with Malachi 3:1, "Behold, I send my messenger,[29] and he will prepare the way before me. And the Lord whom you seek will suddenly come to his temple; and the messenger [or, angel] of the covenant in whom you delight, behold, he is coming, says the LORD of hosts." In my view, this passage speaks of three figures: (1) YHWH ("LORD") who is speaking here; (2) the *adon* ("Lord") who is being announced by YHWH and is identical[30] to the *mal'akh habb'rit* (the "Messenger/Angel of the covenant," the Angel who is the keeper as well as guarantor of the covenant), and (3) the "messenger" who prepares the way, not of the *adon* or of the Angel of the covenant, as one might expect, but of YHWH. This remarkable point is unproblematic if we assume that YHWH is identical to the *adon*, that is, with the Angel of the covenant. In this case, the passage is referring not to four figures, nor to three figures, but to two figures: the

---

29. Heb. *mal'akhi*, which can also mean "my angel" (DRA), and is identical with the name of the prophet Malachi; *mal'akh* is either an earthly "messenger," or a celestial "messenger," that is, "angel" (from Gk. *angelos*, which also means both messenger and angel), as in the expression "Angel of the covenant" in the same verse.
30. Cf. "the Lord . . . , even the messenger" ([N]KJV) . . . ;"the Lord . . . , yes, the messenger" (CJB) . . . ; cf. Verhoef (1987, 289).

messenger who prepares the way, and he for whom the way is prepared.

Jewish tradition has identified the "messenger" in various ways:[31] the angel of death (thus Rashi, Kimchi), the (suffering) Messiah ben (= son of) Joseph, who is thought to precede the (triumphing) Messiah ben David (the *adon*) (thus Ibn Ezra), or the resurrected prophet Elijah (cf. Mal. 4:5).[32] In the New Testament, the question arose whether John the Baptist was perhaps this Elijah. He himself denied it (John 1:21, 25), whereas Jesus confirmed it (Matt. 17:12-13 par.), or made the answer conditional: John would be Elijah only if Israel accepted that in Jesus himself the kingdom of God had arrived (Matt. 11:14; cf. Luke 1:17; 17:21). The tension between these three different answers is due to the fact that both Jesus and John were rejected by the majority of the Jewish people; in John 1:21 and 25 Israel's rejection of the Messiah is already presupposed (see v. 11).

As for the identification of *adon* and *mal'akh habb'rit*, we interpret the "and" that separates the two expressions as explicative, as do many Bible translations. However, it should be mentioned that, in Jewish tradition, Rashi interpreted the *adon* as the God of justice, and the *mal'akh habb'rit* as a common angel. David Kimchi saw in the *adon* King Messiah, and in the *mal'akh habb'rit* the prophet Elijah.[33]

The first part of Malachi 3:1 is quoted in Matthew 11:10, Mark 1:2,[34] and Luke 7:27 (cf. 1:76), and applied to John the Baptist by Jesus himself. Here the "messenger" is the herald, who apparently prepares the way for YHWH because it says "*my* messenger," who prepares the way "*for* me . . . says the LORD of hosts." But at the same time, the text makes clear

---

31. Ibid., 287.
32. Cashdan in Cohen (1980, 349).
33. Ibid.
34. Mark 1:2 is a composite of three passages: Exod. 23:20 (LXX), Mal. 3:1, and Isa. 40:3, which evoke the image of the forerunner Elijah (cf. Mal. 4:5), and which in their totality are ascribed to their main source: Isaiah; see more extensively, Lane (1974, 45–47).

that the "messenger" prepares the way of the *adon*, that is, the *mal'akh habb'rit*. If John the Baptist is the herald, Jesus is, according to the implication of his own words, both YHWH (cf. §7.3) and the Angel of the covenant.[35] One day, God's glory will return to his temple (cf. Ezek. 43:4; Hag. 2:8), but in the Man Jesus Christ the Shekhinah came to his temple two thousand years ago (from Luke 2:42-43). Therefore, Malachi 3:1 gives us every reason to identify the Angel of YHWH as the pre-incarnate Christ.[36]

6.3.2 *Mal'akh* YHWH

The way YHWH and the Angel are connected in Malachi 3:1 is obviously the same as the way this happens elsewhere in the Old Testament.[37] Usually the expression used is *mal'akh* YHWH, the Angel of the LORD, sometimes *mal'akh (ha)Elohim*, the Angel of God. Please note that the expression *mal'akh* YHWH does not necessarily refer to this unique "Angel of the LORD"; it can also refer to any angel of the LORD (so, e.g., in 1 Kings 19:5, 9; 2 Kings 1:3, 15; 19:35 [= Isa. 37:36; cf. 2 Chron. 32:21]; 1 Chron. 21:12-30; cf. "his angel" in Gen. 24:7, 40; Dan. 6:23). It is the same in the New Testament (Matt. 1:20, 24; 2:13, 19; 28:2; Luke 1:11; 2:9; John 5:4; Acts 5:19; 8:26; 12:7, 23). However, in many other cases the text clearly refers to *the* "Angel of the LORD."

Thus, we can distinguish three categories. In the first category, *mal'akh* (Gk. *angelos*) refers to a human messenger (e.g., Mal. 3:1a; also 2:7, where *mal'akh* YHWH refers to the priest; see further 1 Sam. 29:9; 2 Sam. 14:17, 20; 19:27; Luke 9:52; Gal. 4:14). In the second and the third categories, the *mal'akh* is a heavenly messenger (e.g., Mal. 3:1b). The latter two categories can be divided as follows. In the second, the *mal'akh* YHWH (or *mal'akh ha-Elohim*, "angel of God") is distinct from YHWH, whereas in the third category he is more or less clearly iden-

---

35. Van Veen-Vrolijk in Knevel and Paul (1995, 205–207).
36. Vos (1948, 72–76); Payne (1962, 167–70); Von Rad (*TDNT* 1:77); Kidner (1967, 33–34); Chafer (1983, 327–31); and the commentaries ad loc.
37. Verhoef (1987, 289).

tified with YHWH. Examples of the second category are Exodus 14:19 (but cf. 13:21, YHWH, i.e., his angel, went before the people); 23:20 (not just an angel, for he can forgive sins, and God's "name is in him"; v. 21; see also 32:34; 33:2); Judg. 5:23; Ps. 35:5-6; Zech. 1:11-12; 12:8).

For our purpose, the third category is more interesting because it supplies us with an indirect argument for the deity of the pre-incarnate Christ. Thus, the Angel of YHWH in Genesis 16:11 speaks about YHWH in the third person, but in verse 10 he speaks in the first person as if he is YHWH himself. Verse 13 says explicitly that it is YHWH who has spoken. In Genesis 21:17 it is God who hears the voice of Ishmael, but it is the Angel of God who answers. In Genesis 22:11-12 the Angel of YHWH speaks in the first person *as* YHWH, but in verses 15-18 *on behalf of* YHWH. In Genesis 31:11-13 the Angel of YHWH says, "I am the God of Bethel. . . ." In Genesis 48:15-16 Jacob identifies God more or less with "the angel who has redeemed me from all evil" (see below, Isa. 63:9); the verb "bless" in verse 16 refers to both God and the angel, but it is singular.[38]

In Exodus 3:2 it is the Angel of YHWH who appears in the burning bush, but in verse 4 it is God who speaks from the bush (cf. Deut. 33:16). Stephen says that it was an angel who appeared to Moses in the burning bush, but the voice that Moses heard was the voice of the Lord (Acts 7:30-31, 35). He also said that the person who spoke with Moses on Mount Sinai was an "angel" (v. 38; cf. v. 53; Gal. 3:19; Heb. 2:2).

In Numbers 22:31 YHWH is distinguished from the Angel of YHWH, but in verses 32-35 the Angel speaks in the first person *as* YHWH. In Judges 2:1-5 it is the Angel of YHWH who appears, but he speaks *as* YHWH. In Judges 13:12-13 and 16 the Angel of YHWH (or "the man of God") is distinguished from, but in verse 22 identified with God. Also verse 18: the name of the Angel is "wonderful"; in Isaiah 9:6 this is (part of) one of Messiah's names, and in 28:29 one of the attributes of YHWH. In

---

38. See extensively, Venema (1850, 210–11).

Psalm 34:7 the Angel of YHWH is identical with YHWH, for the text speaks of "those who fear him," which is parallel with "fearing" YHWH in verses 9 and 11 (see also 35:5-6). In Isaiah 63:9 the "Angel of his presence [lit., face]," that is, the Angel who represents YHWH, is parallel with YHWH in verses 7-15. In Daniel 3:28 it is God's angel who delivers Daniel's three friends, but in verse 25 he resembles a *bar-elahin*, Aramaic for "son of the gods," or if we extend the deeper meaning beyond the understanding of Nebuchadnezzar, this refers to "Son of God" (cf. Isa. 43:2). In Zechariah 3:1-4 the Angel of YHWH is identified with YHWH, but in verses 6-10 distinguished from YHWH; in 12:8 he is evidently identified with God.

In summary, the Angel of YHWH resembles the Logos in John 1: he is *with* God (goes out from him, represents him, expresses him), and he is *God*; see further in §6.6.

6.4 The Divine "Man"
6.4.1 Three Impressive Examples

In this context, something must be said about Old Testament theophanies in which God is not referred to with the word "angel" but with the word "man." In Genesis 18 three "men" come to visit Abraham (v. 2), two of whom turn out to be angels (19:1, 15), while the third one turns out to be YHWH (vv. 1, 13, 17-33). It definitely goes too far to view these three "men" as a reference to the Trinity.[39] It is far more probable that the three are angels,[40] one of whom seems to be the uncreated Angel of YHWH (thus Calvin). Or all three were created angels, in and through whom YHWH revealed himself in a special way.[41]

In Joshua 5:13-15, a "man" appears to Joshua who presents himself as "the commander of the army of YHWH." At the same time, he seems to be YHWH himself, for he calls the

---

39. Eastern Orthodoxy sees in the famous icon of Andrei Rublev, depicting the three "men" of Gen. 18, a reference to the Trinity.
40. Rabbinic tradition thinks of Michael, Raphael, and Gabriel; Gispen (1979, 150).
41. So, e.g., Augustine (*De Civitate Dei* XVI.29), but see Gen. 18:17, 22: "YHWH"; cf. Bavinck (*RD* 2:264, 463-68).

ground where Joshua is standing "holy" (cf. Exod. 3:5, where the ground is holy because God himself appears to Moses), while seeming to be the same as YHWH who speaks in 6:2. In a similar way, the "man" who showed to Ezekiel the new temple (40:3-5) speaks in 43:6-7 in the first person as YHWH.

The most remarkable is the "man" in the vision of Daniel 10:5-9, because five of his features return in the description of Christ in Revelation 1:13-16: the golden belt, the eyes like flaming torches, the legs (feet) gleaming like burnished bronze, the voice like the sound of a multitude, and the face like the appearance of lightning, or the sun.[42] We encounter the same "man" in Daniel 12:6-7; his description closely resembles that of the "other mighty angel" in Revelation 10:1-7, who is probably Christ (see below). When all these details are taken together, it seems appropriate to assume that in Daniel 10:5-9 we are dealing with an appearance of the Angel of YHWH, that is, the pre-incarnate Christ. An important objection against this view is that this "man" needs the help of Michael (v. 13). However, it is doubtful whether the angel in verses 10-15 is the same as the "man" in verses 5-9.[43]

6.4.2 The Messenger

In passages where the Angel of YHWH speaks in the first person as YHWH, Jewish expositors understand that the Angel is speaking *on behalf of* YHWH.[44] As for Exodus 3, Nachmanides believed that Moses first saw the Angel of YHWH but upon looking more closely, he caught a glimpse of the Shekinah itself.[45] It may be true that in some passages, an ordinary angel is referred to who, speaking in the first person, is passing on a message from YHWH. Often, prophets do the same thing; but in such cases they add the phrase, "Thus says the LORD," which

---

42. In addition to these, notice the similarities between the Ancient of Days (Dan. 7:14) and the Son of Man (Rev. 1:14).
43. See extensively, Kelly (1902, 195–97); Gaebelein (1911, 154–56); and Fijn-vandraat (1990, 189–210).
44. E.g., Cohen (1983, 181).
45. Ibid., 328.

the Angel never does. Enough evidence exists that points to a figure for whom Jewish thinking has no place, a figure who is both representative of YHWH and YHWH himself.

This is the *mal'akh* YHWH in the most emphatic meaning of the expression. To consider this simply another name for God fails to explain why this figure is called a *mal'akh* ("messenger"). Nor does it explain why this figure is often sharply *distinguished* from YHWH. In such cases (e.g., Gen. 16:11; 21:17; Judg. 13:16; Zech. 1:12–14; 3:7), the Angel is a "messenger" in the truest sense of the word, that is, someone who passes on a message from, and about, God; a sent one, clearly distinct from his Sender, a representative, clearly distinct from the Represented One.

Usually, the church fathers had no difficulty discerning in this figure the pre-incarnate Christ (see §6.5). However, Augustine believed that the glory of God cannot be beheld immediately, and therefore the Old Testament theophanies were always mediated by created angels. This view was adopted by the scholastic and Roman Catholic theologians. Luther and Calvin spoke at times of a created angel, at other times of an uncreated angel, but later Protestant expositors usually thought of the Logos, that is, the pre-incarnate Christ. Bavinck pointed out that perhaps the difference between the two views is not as large as it may seem: either the Angel of YHWH is the Logos, or he is a created angel in whom the Logos manifests himself in a special, unique way.[46] Earlier he had noted that "[t]his *Malak* YHWH is not an independent symbol nor a created angel but a true personal revelation and appearance of God, distinct from him . . . and still one with him in name. . . ."[47]

Robin Wakely claimed that, as seen clearly in Exodus 3:4 and 6, the expression "Angel of the LORD" is almost certainly a reverent synonym for God's presence instead of a reference

---

46. Bavinck (*RD* 2:262–63).
47. Ibid., 1:329.

to a celestial being subordinate to God.⁴⁸ More daring is the view that the Angel of YHWH is the pre-incarnate second person of the Trinity.⁴⁹ One argument for this identification is the ministry of intercession that the Angel of YHWH has according to Zechariah 1:12 and 3:1-5 (cf. Rom. 8:34; Heb. 7:25; 1 John 2:1).⁵⁰

Thus, in light of the New Testament, we may discern in the figure of the Angel of YHWH one of the most remarkable implicit references to the pre-incarnate Christ. In John 1:1-2, the Logos is a representative and a manifestation of God, and is himself God, while in verse 14 this Logos is shown to be Christ (see §6.6). Similarly, the *mal'akh* YHWH is this person in the Old Testament. The light that this discovery sheds on the deity of Christ is brighter than we saw in the earlier part of this chapter. The Bible assigns to the Messiah not just divinity (Gk. *theotēs*, but deity (Gk. *theotēs*). He is called the Son of YHWH — this name entails that of the Father — but the name YHWH applies to him just as much as to the Father and to the Holy Spirit. This is the enormous significance of the key verse in John 12:41, "Isaiah said these things [in Isa. 6] because he saw his [i.e., Jesus'] glory and spoke of him" — and the One whose glory he saw was YHWH (vv. 3 and 5).

6.4.3 Messiah and YHWH

In the light of what we have considered so far, it is unsurprising that New Testament writers apply to Jesus a number of Old Testament passages that explicitly refer to YHWH. This is true in particular about passages in the Psalms: YHWH is the Shepherd of his people (23:1; 80:2;⁵¹ Jesus: John 10:11, 14; Heb.

---

48. Wakely (1996, 685).
49. Chafer (1983, 327); also Niehaus (1996, 1249).
50. Bowling (1980, 465); on the basis of Acts 8:26 and 29, J. B. Taylor (1962, 38) identifies the Angel of YHWH as the Holy Spirit—in my view incorrectly, because it is questionable, first, whether the angel (without the article: *an* angel) in v. 26 is the Angel of YHWH, and second, whether the angel of v. 26 is identical with the Spirit in v. 29.
51. Consider also those passages that speak of a "flock" or "sheep": Ps. 74:1;

13:20; 1 Pet. 2:25; 5:4; cf. also Luke 15:5). YHWH ascended on high (Ps. 68:18; Jesus: Eph. 4:8). YHWH comes to judge the earth in righteousness and faithfulness (Ps. 96:13; Jesus: Rev. 19:11). YHWH has created all things, always remains the same, and will never cease existing (Ps. 102:24-27; Jesus: Heb. 1:10-12; cf. 13:8). YHWH redeems his people from all their iniquities (Ps. 130:8; Jesus: Matt. 1:21; Titus 2:4).

In Isaiah, YHWH manifests himself to the prophet (6:1-3), but what the latter saw was the glory of Jesus (John 12:41; as well as the Holy Spirit: Acts 28:5). YHWH is a stone of offense and a rock of stumbling (Isa. 8:14; 28:16), and so is Jesus (Rom. 9:33; 1 Pet. 2:6-8). For YHWH the way is prepared (40:3), as it is also for Jesus (Matt. 3:3 par.). YHWH comes with reward and recompense (40:10b; 62:11b), and so does Jesus (Rev. 22:12). YHWH gives his glory to no other (42:8; 45:23), but he does give it to Jesus (Phil. 2:9-11). YHWH is the first and the last (44:6b; 48:12b), and so is Jesus (Rev. 1:17; 2:8; 22:13). To YHWH every knee will bow, every tongue will swear allegiance to him (45:23), and so too with Jesus (Phil. 2:10-11; cf. Rom. 14:11). YHWH comes as Redeemer to Zion (59:20), and so does Jesus (Rom. 11:26). YHWH will come in fire, and by fire will enter into judgment (66:15-16), and so does Jesus (2 Thess. 1:7-8).

See also Jeremiah 9:24 (Jesus: 1 Cor. 1:31; 2 Cor. 10:17); 11:20; 17:10; 20:12 (see Rev. 2:23); 23:5-6 (see 1 Cor. 1:30); Daniel 7:9 (see Rev. 1:14); Joel 2:32 (see Rom. 10:12-13); Zechariah 12:10 (see John 19:34, 37; Rev. 1:7); 11:13 (see Matt. 27:9-10); Malachi 3:1 (see Matt. 11:10 par.).

The name YHWH applies to the Messiah, but at the same time he is distinguished from YHWH. In this light it is remarkable that sometimes the Old Testament seems to distinguish different figures within the being of God. In Genesis 19:24, the LORD who rains sulfur and fire on Sodom and Gomorrah is distinguished from the LORD from whose heavenly presence this rain descends on the earth: the LORD rained from the LORD

77:21; 78:52; 79:13; 95:7; 100:3; also Isa. 40:11; Jer. 31:10; Ezek. 34:11-23; Micah 5:3.

in heaven. Similarly, in Hosea 1:7, God saves the house of Judah "by the LORD, their God" (Heb. *b'YHWH elohēhem*). YHWH acts on behalf of YHWH. Is it saying too much if, in the light of the New Testament, we read here that the second person in the Godhead acts on behalf of the first person?

In Psalm 45:6–7 the Messiah is called "God" (see §6.2.2), but at the same time he is distinguished from the God who anointed him. In Psalm 110:1, the Messiah is the "Lord" (Heb. *adon*) who is seated by YHWH at his right hand until YHWH will make the "Lord's" enemies the latter's footstool—an expression usually reserved for YHWH himself (1 Chron. 28:2; Isa. 66:1; Matt. 5:35). This psalm implies a duality in the person of the Messiah: as a Man he is David's son, and as God, he is David's Lord. The consequence of this remarkable fact was that the rabbis temporarily abandoned the Messianic interpretation of the psalm in hostility toward Christianity.[52]

6.5 The Angel and the Logos
6.5.1 Image, Radiance, Imprint, Form

As we saw, the early church fathers had no difficulty recognizing the Angel of YHWH as the pre-incarnate Christ. No matter how paradoxical it may sound, this representative of God *par excellence*, sent by him and performing miracles in his name, can represent him in a perfect way because he *is* YHWH. This is the way the New Testament presents him: he is perfectly God and at the same time he perfectly represents or manifests God. In the words of the apostle John: the Logos, who was with God, was at the same time God (John 1:1–2).[53] The Logos is the One who reveals God as the latter's representative

---

52. Berkouwer (1954, 177–78); cf. SBK 4:453–55. Cf. the interesting hypothesis of Medema (1990, 42–66) regarding the question why the Sanhedrin judged Jesus' application of Ps. 110 to himself as blasphemy (Matt. 26:63–66); this was because of the combination with Dan. 7: from that moment, the temple in Jerusalem would no longer be the dwelling-place of the Shekhinah; rather, the latter would find itself, embodied in Jesus, at the right hand of the Majesty in heaven. To deny to the temple the presence of God was the worst conceivable blasphemy against the holy place.
53. D. H. Johnson (*DJG* 481–84, s.v. "Logos"); Brown (1994a, 187–88).

or manifestation, and can do so perfectly because he is God. He is "the image of the invisible God," who can be this because he is God, God the Son, the One in whom, through whom, and for whom all things were created (Col. 1:15–16). He is the "radiance" of God's glory in an absolute way, like the sun's essence is present in its rays. He is also the "exact imprint" of God's being, just like a stamp's essence is present in its imprint (Heb. 1:3). Philippians 2:6 expresses this as follows: Jesus was "in the form [Gk. *morphē*] of God," possessing the "form" or "appearance" or "image of sovereign divine majesty."[54]

All this helps us understand how the Angel of YHWH can be both identified with YHWH and distinguished from YHWH. Christ did not become the Logos first at his incarnation, but he was the Logos from eternity, God's representative and revealer. Wherever God manifests himself in the past, present, and future, he does so in and through the Logos, the Son. Again, I point here to John 12:41: when Isaiah saw the Lord (*Adonai* and YHWH) sitting on his heavenly throne (Isa. 6:1, 5), he saw "his," that is, Christ's, glory. In other words, from Isaiah 6 we learn that YHWH was manifested to Isaiah in and through the pre-incarnate Christ. The glory of YHWH that Isaiah saw was the glory of Christ; the glory of the Father was revealed in that of the Son. Already then Jesus' word was true: "Whoever has seen me has seen the Father" (John 14:9). In the pre-incarnate Christ, the glory of YHWH was being revealed, and this was possible because he fully participated in the divine being as the Logos who was with God *and* who was God.

6.5.2 Sonship

In John 1:18, the Logos of verses 1–2 and 14 is seen to be the only (unique, only begotten) Son of the Father. To what extent is the relationship of the Angel of YHWH to YHWH connected to the relationship of the Son to the Father? As we saw, in Psalm 2:7 the Messiah is called the Son begotten by God, which is applied in Acts 13:33, Hebrews 1:5, and Hebrews 5:5 to Jesus. Isaiah 9:6 tells us that a

---

54. Behm (1967, 751).

child is born, and a son is given. Since sonship is linked here with begetting and birth, it does not seem to extend beyond Luke 1:35, where Jesus' Sonship is explicitly linked with his birth and human descent. This is not necessarily *eternal* Sonship, as we find that revealed in many other New Testament passages (see §7.4). The truth of the eternal Father and the eternal Son was not yet revealed in the Old Testament. On the contrary, in Isaiah 9:6 the Messiah-Son is called "Everlasting Father"—in the sense of Creator (cf. 64:8), or the One who cares for his people as a father for his children (cf. 22:21)—as well as "Mighty God." Thus, the verse does emphasize that he is eternal and divine. The *born* Child is the *given* Son, and as such an eternal, divine person. This comes very close to the New Testament revelation.[55]

Some expositors point here to Proverbs 30:4, "What is his name, and what is his son's name?" This is taken as evidence for some Old Testament awareness that God has a Son. The capitalization in the NKJV suggests that this verse is speaking of God's Son, as older Reformed expositors have claimed with some certitude.[56] But others doubted that this verse is really speaking about God and his Son,[57] believing that the answer to the four "Who?" questions in this verse is not "God" but "no one." It is impossible for any human being to have the knowledge of verse 3 because, in order to acquire this knowledge, one must be able to ascend to heaven and descend again, and so on, and no one is able to do so. Others believe that the questions do refer to God.[58] In the Jewish tradition, Rashi accepted the former interpretation, but there is a Midrash that believes God is intended, his son being the people of Israel (cf. Exod. 4:22).[59] In light of the New Testament, this Son is the Messiah, who is the true Israel.

Finally, I would mention the remarkable figure of the

---

55. Cf. Oswalt (1986, 244–48).
56. See, e.g., the marginal note in the Dutch States Translation of the Bible (1637).
57. Gispen (1954, 314–16).
58. E.g., Ironside (1907, 436–39); Ross (1991, 1119–20).
59. Ross (1991, 1119).

"other angel" in Revelation 8:3; 10:1 and 18:1. In 7:2; 14:6-9 and 15-18 the expression refers to an ordinary angel (see, e.g., "we" and "our God" in 7:3).[60] But in 8:3 we see him act in a quality that reminds us of the Angel of YHWH in the Old Testament. The idea that these passages refer to Christ is suggested by the fact that he gives power to the prayers of the saints by mixing them with frankincense from the (heavenly) golden altar, and only the high priest is able and allowed to do that.

In my view, the clearest reference to Christ's angelic form is Revelation 10:1-3, where the mighty Angel comes down "from heaven, wrapped in a cloud, with a rainbow over his head, and his face was like the sun, and his legs like pillars of fire.... And he set his right foot on the sea, and his left foot on the land, and called out with a loud voice, like a lion roaring" (cf. 1:15-16; 5:5). So too we read in Rev. 18:1: "After this I saw another angel coming down from heaven, having great authority, and the earth was made bright with his glory" (21:23).

6.6 Christ's Pre-Existence in John 1
6.6.1 The Logos

Wolfhart Pannenberg wrote:

> The idea of a preexistence of the Son of God, who manifested himself historically in Jesus' relation to the Father, is inescapable not only if we assert the fellowship of Jesus with the eternal God but also if we maintain the link between the eternal identity of the Father God whom Jesus proclaimed and the relation to Jesus as his Son.[61]

With such impossible sentences (translated from an even more impossible German), Pannenberg defends a very important matter: the pre-existence of the Son, which necessarily results from the relationship between the eternal Father and the eternal Son.

Much of the biblical evidence dealt with in this chapter has

---

60. See Ouweneel (1988, 253n5; 1990, 3–4n3, 28–31n3, 112–13n12, 172n2, where also some counterarguments are dealt with).
61. Pannenberg (1994; 2:370).

been discussed by Berkouwer.⁶² He defended it over against the liberal exegesis, which either argues away the idea of the pre-existence (e.g., by idealizing it in a Platonic way; see below), or accepts the undeniable presence of the idea in the Bible, but views it as a mythical insertion (Bultmann). Those who attempt to ascribe the doctrine of the Trinity to early Jewish or early pagan doctrines⁶³ can do so only by not (sufficiently) recognizing that this doctrine is profoundly rooted in the Bible itself.

Among the Gospel writers, the apostle John is by far the most outspoken with regard to the pre-existence of Christ.⁶⁴ His prologue (1:1-18) begins as follows: "In the beginning was the Word, and the Word was with God, and the Word was God. He was in the beginning with God. All things were made through him" (vv. 1-3a). The Greek term *logos* ("word") not only means "a saying" (like Gk. *rhēma*), but also implies the inner thought that is being expressed.⁶⁵ This Logos was "in [the] beginning" (Gk. *en archē*, without the article: the beginning is undetermined). Whether we think here of the beginning of creation, as in Genesis 1:1, or of a beginning preceding creation (cf. 1 John 1:1), the Word *was* already there. That is to say, it had existed before all other things (Col. 1:17), from eternity. There never was a time or eternity when the Word did not exist. Any form of Arianism is unacceptable, which teaches that the Word was created at a certain point, even if that point be sometime before Genesis 1.

No matter how complicated the notion of the Logos may be,⁶⁶ it implies that God is the self-revealing God, and this

---

62. Berkouwer (1954, 161–67, 179–85).
63. E.g., Kretschmar (1956).
64. See extensively Morris (1971, 72–79, and references).
65. Cf. the Dutch noun *rede,* which means "reason (ratio)" but also "speech"; cf. the Ger. verb *reden,* "to speak."
66. Some have argued that the Alexandrian church fathers are of little use here because they interpreted the Johannine Logos idea in a (neo-)Platonic way, and derived from it a doctrine of the Son of God that no longer had any connection with the historical Jesus of the Gospels, whereas John derived his

God, through the Logos, creates (v. 3) and gives life (v. 4). This Logos is not some attribute or an activity of God, for this Word has become flesh (v. 14), and in this way came to us in the person of Jesus Christ; the Word is identical with the only begotten (or, unique) Son who is in the bosom of the Father (v. 18 NKJV). Or, in the Nestle-Aland text: ". . . the only begotten God [or, the Only Begotten One, God] who is in the bosom of the Father" (ESV; see §7.6.1). Comparable expressions are "image" (Gk. *eikōn*) of God (Col. 1:15), "radiance" (Gk. *apaugasma*) of God's glory and "exact imprint" (Gk. *charaktēr*) of his being (Heb. 1:3). In various ways, all these terms entail that the glory or the being of God was and is perfectly represented, reflected, and expressed in the person of Jesus Christ, the Son of God. 2 Corinthians 4:4–6 speaks of "the light of the gospel of the glory of Christ, who is the image of God . . . the light of the knowledge of the glory of God in the face of Jesus Christ."

6.6.2 *Theos* and *Ho Theos*

"The Word was God," literally, "was turned toward God" (Gk. *pros* plus accusative), that is, not only existing next to him but accompanying him, in personal fellowship with him (cf. Gk. *kolpos* ["lap, bosom"] of the Father in John 1:18). At the same time, the Logos himself was God (cf. v. 18 CSB, NIV, "the only and one Son, who himself is God"). This does not just mean he was divine. If John had wished to say this, he could easily have used the Greek adjective *theios*; in such a sentence it is even more common to use an adjective than a noun. But John does use the Greek noun *theos*. He omits the article, which does not make the predicate indefinite or qualitative (which would in effect amount to the adjective "divine"[67]) if it precedes the verb. This would be the case only if the context conclusively demands this, which is not the case here.[68]

Logos doctrine from Jesus' very life and works (cf. 1 John 1:1–2). Clement of Alexandria claimed that the Logos spoke as a moral Pedagogue not only through Moses, but also through the ancient philosophers.

67. Cf. the New World Translation of the Jehovah's Witnesses: "the Word was a god."
68. Colwell, quoted in Morris (1971, 77).

John could not have used here the article (Gk. *ho*), for this would annul the distinction contained in the phrase "the Word was with God"; at that point, the article would have identified the Son with the Father, which is the error of Sabellianism or modalism.[69] That is, the Son is not *ho theos* ("the Deity"), for the Father and the Spirit are *theos*, too. Only together they are *ho theos*.

In the footnotes in the Recovery Version Bible translation, going back to the teachings of (the highly appreciated) Chinese Bible expositor Witness Lee, the strange view is defended that the Logos is the *Triune* God, and in John 1:14 it is the *Triune* God who becomes flesh. This would lead one to conclude from verse 1 that the Triune God was with the Triune God—which is absurd—and that the Father and the Holy Spirit became flesh, too, which is equally absurd. All these errors flow from not understanding the phrase "the Logos was God," as though it meant "the Logos is the Triune God," which it does *not* mean. In Trinitarian language, we should instead paraphrase John 1:1 as follows: "In the beginning was the Son, who was the expression of the Triune God; as 'expression' he is distinguished from the Triune God as such, but he *can* be the perfect expression of the Triune God because he himself, as the Son, is just as divine as the Father and the Holy Spirit."

The distinction between *theos* and *ho theos* should be made only in a context that requires it. In John 20:28, Thomas addresses Jesus as *ho theos mou*, but this is probably just a vocative. In Romans 9:5 ("the Christ, who is God over all"), the article is lacking, but *theos* is here predicative. In Titus 2:13 ("our great God and Savior Jesus Christ"), *tou theou* clearly refers to Jesus (perhaps also in 2 Pet. 1:1, but less clearly[70]),

---

69. Cf. *RT* II/1 in this series, §§10.2.3 and 10.7.
70. In Titus 2:13, the Gk. reads *tou megalou theou kai sōtēros hēmōn Iēsou Christou*, but in 2 Pet. 1:1, Gk. *hēmōn* follows directly upon *theou*, so that it is possible to translate that phrase as "of our God and of [the] Savior Jesus Christ."

and has the article. This may be a reference to the full Deity of the Trinity in the sense that Jesus is not only *theos* but also the human expression or representative of *ho theos*. The same is true even more clearly in 1 John 5:20 (". . . him who is true, in his Son Jesus Christ. He is the true God [Gk. *ho alēthinos*]").

6.7 New Testament Hints
6.7.1 Other Passages in John

There are more references to Christ's pre-existence in John's Gospel. Although John the Baptist was half a year older than the Man Jesus (Luke 1:36), he says in John 1:15 and 30: "[H]e was before me," which can point only to the pre-incarnate Christ. Many passages speak of Christ as the One who "descended (or, came down) from heaven" (John 3:13; seven times in 6:33-58). Notice how in John 6:42 the Jews were struck by the implications of this statement ("How can he say, 'I came down from heaven'?"). Jesus also speaks of "ascending to *where he was before*" (6:62). He says, "I know him [i.e., the Father], for I come from him, and he sent me" (7:29); "I am from above . . . I am not of this world" (8:23); "I speak of what I have seen with my Father" (v. 38); "I came from the Father and have come into the world" (16:28). He knew "that he had come from God and was going back to God" (13:3). In all these passages, he is the One who, through the incarnation, had come from a world where he, before this incarnation, had existed from eternity.

Christ has "come in the flesh" (1 John 4:2; cf. 2 John 1:7). This important statement not only contradicts Docetism but also implies Christ's pre-existence. It cannot be said of any ordinary human being that he or she has *come* in the flesh, that is, has entered into the condition of flesh and blood, simply because his or her existence from the very beginning *was* flesh. Even without the reference to his "flesh," his coming into this world may point to his pre-existence: ". . . the light has come into the world" (3:19). "I know where I came from and where I am going" (8:14). "I came from God and I am here. I came not of my own accord, but he sent me" (v. 42).[71] "For judgment I came into this world" (9:39). "I have come into the world as light" (12:46). "I came from the Father and have come into the world" (16:28). "For this purpose I was born and for this purpose I have come into the world — to bear witness to the truth" (18:37).

Other evidence helps us to understand that Jesus' "coming into the world" is special because he was pre-existent. No one has "come into the world" in *this* sense except Jesus.[72] Hence the small but important verbal distinction in Hebrews 2:14, "Since therefore the children share (Gk. *kekoinōnēken*) in flesh and blood, he himself likewise partook (Gk. *meteschen*) of the same things."[73] The expression "he who was manifested in the flesh" (1 Tim. 3:16 ASV) may be understood as pointing to a person who had already existed before he publicly entered into the existence of flesh and blood.[74]

In John 17:5 and 25, the Son speaks of the glory that he possessed with the Father before the world existed, and of the

---

71. This phrase *could* be said of any prophet: he comes from God, he is sent by God; therefore, in the case of Jesus the emphasis lies on the words "come *into the world*" (John 1:9; 3:17, 19; 10:36; 12:46; 16:28; 17:18; 18:37). But even in this case, the evidence must be supported by other evidence because *each* human being is "born *into the world*" (16:21), and when the people spoke of the Prophet who was to "come into the world" (6:14; cf. 11:27), it is highly unlikely that they were thinking of his pre-existence.
72. Therefore, we *could* translate it this way: "This was the true light that gives light to every person coming into the world" (John 1:9), as De Graaff wished (1987, 134), although the context makes this rather unlikely. Nor would such a translation prove the pre-existence of the human soul (in some Platonic sense), as De Graaff suggested.
73. Both the Greek verbs (*koinōneō* and *metechō*) and their forms (perfect and aorist, respectively) are different: humans *have* (by nature, from their conception) part in something in which the pre-incarnate Christ *took* part in at the fullness of time.
74. This is clearly the case in the reading of the Received Text (which has the Gk. noun *theos* instead of the relative pronoun *hos*; see KJV): "God was manifest in the flesh," because this *could* mean that God manifested himself in the flesh of the Man Jesus, without the latter needing to be pre-existent; cf. Kelly (1884, 185–86; 1895a, 331).

love with which the Father had loved him before the foundation of the world. In John's Gospel, and in the New Testament generally, these are some of the clearest references to his pre-existence. I may add here that the same John expresses the past and future eternity of Christ in Revelation 1:17; 2:8; 22:13 in the formula: "I am the first and the last" (cf. "I am the alpha and the omega" in 1:8; 21:6; 22:13). The formula is quoted from Isaiah 41:4, 44:6, and 48:12, where it is used with regard to God. This usage shows that the phrase about Jesus being "the beginning and the end" (22:13; cf. 3:14, "the beginning of God's creation") does not mean that he *has* a beginning in some Arian sense, but that he *was* and *is* the beginning (Gk. *archē*, "origin") of the old creation as well as the new creation. Similarly, he does not *have* an "end" but he *is* the "end" (*telos*, "goal, fulfillment, consummation") of creation (cf. Rom. 10:4, the *telos* of the law).

6.7.2 *Egō Eimi*

In John 8:58 Jesus speaks the astonishing words, ". . . before Abraham was, I AM [Gk. *egō eimi*]." Abraham belonged to the world of "becoming" (rising and falling), Jesus to the world of "being" (eternally being the same).[75] He does not say, "I was," which would have been remarkable enough, but he alludes to the name YHWH, the great "I AM" (Heb. *ehyeh*; cf. Exod. 3:14 Septuagint: *egō eimi ho ōn*, "I am the being [or, existing] One"). This is what Moses was commanded to tell the Israelites (v. 14b): "I AM has sent me to you." As a follow-up to this, Jesus now says, "Before Abraham became, I already was as the I AM."

The Greek expression *egō eimi* is the Septuagint rendering of Hebrew *ani hu*, "I am he [i.e., I am the same]," which God says of himself (e.g., Deut. 32:39; Isa. 41:4; 43:10, 13, 25 [LXX]; 46:4; 48:12; 51:12). Thus, John 8:59 is a reference not only to Jesus' pre-existence but also to his deity. There are several such "I am" statements by Jesus: "[U]nless you believe that I am he

---

75. Ratzinger (2007, 350).

you will die in your sins" (v. 24); "then you will know that I am he" (v. 28); "when it does take place you may believe that I am he" (13:19). The latter two passages are peculiar: through my very elevation on the cross you will get to know me as the "I am."[76] In John 18:5-8, saying "I am he" is sufficient to make his opponents fall to the ground.

The "I am" passages in John remind us of the seven comparisons he reports Jesus making: "I am the bread of life" (6:35, Gk. *egō eimi ho artos tēs zōēs*), "I am the light of the world" (8:12), "I am the door of the sheep" (10:7), "I am the good shepherd" (10:11), "I am the resurrection and the life" (11:25), "I am the way, and the truth, and the life" (14:6), and "I am the true vine" (15:1).

One special "I AM" (Gk. *egō eimi*) saying appears not only in John's Gospel, but also in the Synoptic Gospels; it appears literally in Matthew 14:27 (par.): "Take heart; I AM. Do not be afraid." That we are justified in seeing this as more than a simple "It is I, Jesus, and not a phantom," is evident from his walking on the water and his victory over wind and water, which implicitly point to his divinity. The disciples obviously understood this; hence their confession: "Truly you are the Son of God!" (v. 33).[77] We think here of the translation by Jewish scholars who rendered the Hebrew *ehyeh* as "I am there" (Ger. *Ich bin da*), namely, for you, yesterday, today, and tomorrow. This is in fact what is said in Hebrews 13:8, "Jesus Christ is yesterday and today and forever the I AM," that is, the "I am there" *for you*.

The Synoptic passages show that Matthew, Mark, and Luke presuppose Christ's pre-existence as well.[78] This might also be the case in the ēlthon ("I have come") passages (Matt. 5:17; 9:13; 10:34-35; 20:28; Luke 12:49; also compare Mark

---

76. Cf. ibid., 349.
77. Brown (1994a, 137n202); Ratzinger (2007, 352).
78. *Contra*, e.g., Bousset (1970, 48); Heering (1950, 148); cf. Berkouwer (1954, 166–67).

1:24.[79] But this argument is not decisive because Jesus speaks in a similar way of John the Baptist (Matt. 11:18–19; 17:12).

6.7.3 The Epistles

The apostle Paul refers to the pre-incarnate Christ in 2 Corinthians 8:9, where he describes him as the One who, through he was rich (apparently before his incarnation), for the sake of his people he became poor. Paul points to this even more clearly in Philippians 2:5–7, "... Christ Jesus, who, though he was in the form of God, did not count equality with God a thing to be grasped, but emptied himself, by taking the form of a servant, being born in the likeness of men." The matter of the self-emptying (Gk. *kenōsis*) of Jesus will be dealt with in §8.7. My point here is that he existed before the *kenōsis*, namely, in the "form" (*morphē*) of God, that is, everything that characterized the being of God also belonged to him; the form of God was his mode of existence.

Such a claim is not contradicted by a Pauline passage like this: "[W]hen the fullness of time had come, God sent forth his Son, born of woman" (Gal. 4:4). This notion of "born," literally "become" (Gk. *genomenon*), and thus the entire idea of a "becoming" of Jesus in time, does not conflict with the idea of an eternal pre-existence, as long as we distinguish the divine and human natures of Christ. To put it more strongly, this very verse, Galatians 4:4, offers us an argument for the pre-existence of Christ: apparently, God sent him who, before the "fullness of time," was his Son. He who, as God the Son, had existed from eternity, as a Man, born of woman, had a beginning in time. This is similar in John 1:1–2 and 14: the Word that *was* from eternity *became* flesh; so too in Philippians 2:6–7: he who *was* in the form of God *became* like men. Remaining what he was, he became what he was not. What he was from eternity—the Logos, the Son—he remained in his incarnation; what he was not, is what he became "in the fullness of time"—flesh, Man.

---

79. Sevenster (*RGG* 1:1753; see more extensively, 1948).

THE ETERNAL CHRIST: GOD WITH US

One of the most far-reaching descriptions, briefly touched upon before, is found in Hebrews 1:2-3, "... in these last days [God] has spoken to us by his Son, whom he appointed the heir of all things, through whom also he created the world. He is the radiance of the glory of God and the exact imprint of his nature, and he upholds the universe by the word of his power." To be precise, the author does not say "in" or "by" or "through the Son" (Gk. *en tōi huiōi* or *dia tou huiou*, cf. Col. 1:16a and c), as if God spoke in/by/through someone who himself was not necessarily God, just as God had spoken "by/through the prophets" (Gk. *en tois prophētais*, v. 1). Rather, God spoke "in [the person of the] Son" (Gk. *en huiōi*, without the article, Darby [brackets original]; cf. AMP: "in [the person of One who is by His character and nature] His Son [namely Jesus]"). That is, the Son who spoke *is* God; one could almost translate: "as [i.e., in the quality of] Son." God speaks—but the One whom we hear speaking is the second person of the Trinity: God the Son.[80]

Notice further that he is called the "heir of all things" even before it is said that God through him had created the worlds. Both phenomena point to his pre-existence. Thus, the Greek present participles in verse 3 suggest timelessness: both in eternity and on earth, Christ was, and is, and will forever be the radiance of God's glory and the exact imprint of his being.[81]

Later in Hebrews we read: "[W]hen Christ came into the world, he said, 'Sacrifices and offerings you have not desired, but a body have you prepared for me....' Then I said, 'Behold, I have come to do your will, O God, as it is written of me in the scroll of the book'" (10:5, 7). This "coming into the world" suggests the pre-existence of the Son of God. What

---

80. Ouweneel (1982, 1:23–24).
81. It is astonishing with what ease Berkhof (1986, 293) rejects passages like Phil. 2:6, Col. 1:15–17, and Heb. 1:1–3 as evidence for the personal pre-existence of Christ, the Son of God; his liberal bias is clearly overruling the clear sense of Scripture.

was written about him in the scroll (the heavenly book of God's counsel, or the books of the earthly prophets) pertained not to a person whose existence was future, but to a person who existed before anything was written about him. The person is just as eternal as everything that is written about him in God's book.

6.8 Deviant Views
6.8.1 The Liberal View

The phrase "pre-incarnate Christ" refers to Christ before his incarnation. Can we speak of Christ in this way? Can we use the names "Jesus" or "Christ"[82] before the incarnation of the eternal Son? Yes, just as we can say in a retrospective way that "President Reagan was born in 1911," although he became president in 1981. Thus, 2 Timothy 1:9 can speak of "grace, which [God] gave us in Christ Jesus before the ages began," that is, in the pre-incarnate Christ, even though the *Man* Jesus Christ did not exist in eternity past. This raises an important theological problem: what can we say about the relationship between Jesus' pre-existence and Jesus' humanity?

Some argue that we can have the humanity of Jesus without his pre-existence, or we can have his pre-existence without his humanity, but there is absolutely no way we can have both.[83] The former combination is the modern liberal view, the latter combination is the traditional Christian view: Christ existed in eternity past, but before his incarnation he was not yet a human being. Thus, a middle view is excluded, namely, Jesus' supposed humanity from eternity (see the next section). What remains is this: either from eternity past Jesus was the Son and the Logos, but only since his incarnation is he the Man Jesus (the traditional view), or only the Man Jesus exists since his conception; there is no eternal Son or Logos, unless perhaps in an ideal way, in the counsel of God (the liberal

---

82. I distinguish here between "Christ" as a name and "*the* Christ," i.e., the Messiah, as a reference to an office.
83. Knox (1967, 106).

view).

Since the Enlightenment, the liberal view has become self-evident for many theologians. The starting point is here the fundamental rejection of the deity of Christ. In this view, a true Man cannot at the same time be true God. You cannot have both. What is acknowledged about Jesus as possibly being divine is viewed at best along adoptionist lines: Jesus was declared to be divine, or rather, was adopted as Son of God, through either his conception or birth (cf. Luke 1:35), or through his baptism (cf. 3:22), or through his resurrection (regardless of how the latter is viewed) (cf. Rom. 1:4). Liberal theology felt obliged to re-interpret the traditional view concerning Jesus' pre-existence in various ways. In the school of Albrecht Ritschl, the notion of an ontic pre-existence was replaced by an ideal pre-existence of Christ in the counsel of God, comparable to the notion of the ideal pre-existence of the Messiah in Jewish tradition. In this sense, however, this pre-existence differs only in degree from that of any other human being.

Other schools, such as that of Rudolf Bultmann, simply pushed aside the doctrine of the pre-existence as a piece of mythology that had been introduced into the early church. Bultmann was prepared to confess Jesus of Nazareth as the eternal Son insofar as in him the eternal God and Father revealed himself.[84] He is eternal only insofar as in him something eternal manifests itself. Here again, there is at best a difference of degree with every other human being: for instance, it is true of each human being that God put eternity (Heb. *olam*) in their heart (Eccl. 3:11). In my view, such liberal claims do not comport with the clear statements by the apostles, at least if the latter are viewed from a standpoint that rejects any interpretation that is foreign to the Scripture itself.[85]

---

84. Regarding this and related views, see Bultmann's pupil Kuschel (1990).
85. Cf. Althaus (*RGG* 5:492–93).

6.8.2 Was Jesus As a Man Pre-Existent?

Does the doctrine of the pre-existence of the Logos mean that Jesus was pre-existent? Some believe that this was indeed the case, not only according to Christ's divine nature but also according to his human nature. They view him in the sense of an archetype, in the way rabbinic Judaism viewed great men like Adam, Enoch, and Moses, and also the tabernacle, the temple, and the two tables of the Torah as pre-existent.[86] This involves a heavenly "look alike" (Ger. *doppelganger*) of the earthly person or object, more or less the way Hebrews 8:5 speaks of the "pattern" (model, example; Gk. *typos*) of the tabernacle that was shown to Moses on the mountain, and 9:23 about "the heavenly things." This is something basically different from a heavenly person, who existed before, and descends from heaven to the earth. In this way, the Logos, the eternal Son of God, came down to earth. Can we say that, similarly, the *Man* Jesus Christ descended to earth, as though his human nature also existed before the incarnation?

1 Corinthians 15:47 seems to point in this direction: ". . . the second man is from heaven." But this is only apparent. Here, "from" indicates not origin, but character: the first man has an earthly, material body, the second man since his resurrection has a heavenly, spiritual body (cf. vv. 44–49). Here, "from heaven" means "of a heavenly nature." The context makes clear that the verse is not speaking about Jesus at his incarnation but about Jesus at his resurrection.[87] In contrast to "the man of dust (earthly material)," that is, the first Adam, whose image we bear before our own resurrection, we find "the man of heavenly material," so to speak, whose image we will bear after our own resurrection (vv. 48–49).

Nevertheless, the pre-existence of the *Man* Jesus has been defended several times.[88] Origen asserted that the incarnation had occurred in two stages: before the foundation of

---

86. Mackintosh (1914, 449).
87. Cf. Fee (1987, 791–93).
88. See the survey by Bloesch (1997, 135–43).

the world, the Logos possessed a human soul, and then in the fullness of time, he possessed a human body. The idea of the pre-existence of the *Man* Jesus returned in the pietist movement within early Protestantism with theologians like Sebastian Franck, Caspar Schwenckfeld, who claimed that Jesus was from eternity the God-Man, with a body of "spiritual flesh," and Valentin Weigel, who claimed that from eternity past the Son possessed a human nature.

Isaac Watts, who wrote the hymn *O God, Our Help in Ages Past*, agreed with Origen, and taught a pre-existent human soul, which had been created in personal union with the Logos. In the same period, Emanuel Swedenborg claimed that Jesus from eternity had been both God and Man. Ignoring the doctrine of the Trinity, he taught that the Father and the Son were one person, so that from eternity God had possessed human within himself. This is the ultimate consequence of having been created in the image and after the likeness of God: what we call "human" had been present from eternity within God himself. Paul Tillich replaced the notion of the "divine nature" of Christ with the notion of the "God-Man unity" in Jesus Christ, and saw this unity rooted in the "eternal God-Man unity," which had become historical reality in Jesus as the Christ.

According to Donald Bloesch, K. Runia taught that there is strong evidence for the idea of the "pre-existence of the Man Jesus of Nazareth as the Eternal Son of God."[89] However, it seems to me that Bloesch has read too much into this phrase. He also quoted Harry Rimmer, who stated that YHWH of the Old Testament and Jesus of the New Testament are the same person.[90] I would rather say that YHWH of the Old Testament is the Triune God, whom we learn to know more fully in the New Testament, namely, in the person of Jesus Christ, who himself is the second person of the Trinity. Therefore, John can say that, when Isaiah saw the glory of YHWH (Isa. 6), he

---

89. Runia (1974, 7).
90. Rimmer (1943, 31–67).

saw the glory of *Jesus*, and spoke of *him* (John 12:39-41). But this does not imply that the humanity of Jesus was present already in YHWH in the Old Testament.

The most influential theologian whose thought moved toward the notion of a pre-existent humanity of the Logos was Karl Barth. He assumed a kind of middle position: Jesus' flesh had been foreknown and chosen from all eternity. In eternity he possessed a form of flesh, and therefore he was able to enter into a body of flesh; the flesh had been latently or implicitly present in the Logos.[91] Basically, this view was related to Barth's concern about the humanity of God: what we call humanity had been present in God's being from eternity.

6.8.3 Evaluation

The greatest objection against the views mentioned above is that in both cases we encounter a reduction of the incarnation (the *becoming* flesh). In this view, there is no eternal "fleshless Logos" (Gk. *logos asarkos*) who, in the fullness of time, received a share in blood and flesh (Heb. 2:14), no Logos who *became* flesh (John 1:14). In the liberal view there *is* no question of an eternal, personal Logos, identical with the ontically eternal Son of God. In the second view, there is only a Logos who appeared to be flesh.[92]

With regard to the latter view, it is mistaken to identify the teaching that Jesus was the Old Testament Angel of YHWH with teaching the pre-incarnate humanity of the Logos.[93] Earlier, I defended the same identification—the Angel of YHWH is the pre-incarnate Christ—without at all believing that, before his incarnation, the Logos was already in some way human. In my view, we may legitimately speak of a pre-incarnate Jesus as long as we recognize the anachronistic element in this way of speaking: stated clearly, the pre-incarnate person is

---

[91]. See, e.g., Barth (*CD* III/2=16, §47.1:48–49), where he speaks of "the pre-existence of the man Jesus."
[92]. See the extensive criticism by Thielicke (1966).
[93]. Bloesch (1997, 140).

the Son, or the Logos, but this is the same person as the One whom we know, since the incarnation, as Jesus Christ.

I conclude this discussion with a clarifying survey by Wolfhart Pannenberg:

> [I]f the Father is from all eternity the One he is shown historically to be in relation to Jesus his Son, and through him, then we cannot think of the Father apart from the Son. This means on the one hand that the risen Lord is exalted to eternal fellowship with the Father. His relationship to the eternal Father as the Son, however, means on the other hand that the Son was linked to the Father before the beginning of the earthly existence of Jesus. The relation reaches back also to the time before his earthly birth.
>
> If the relation to the historical person of Jesus of Nazareth in eternity characterizes the identity of God as Father, then we must speak of a preexistence of the Son, who was to be historically manifested in Jesus of Nazareth even before his earthly birth.[94]

All these considerations may help us to understand that we cannot view the title "Son of God' in the New Testament simply as an honorific title for the Messiah. First, for Jewish tradition, the title "Son of God" was not at all a familiar alternative term for the Messiah (cf. §4.7). Second, in the New Testament the name "Son of God" is repeatedly associated with pre-existence and perfect deity; this will be discussed in chapter 7 below.[95]

6.9 Typological Christology
6.9.1 The Significance of Typology

Within this context of discussing the pre-existence of Christ, I would like to emphasize the significance of biblical typology.[96] Exodus 25:9 and 40 recounts that Moses received the

---

94. Pannenberg (1994, 2:367–68).
95. Cf. Sevenster (*RGG* 1:1753).
96. Two general standard works on typology are those by Habershon (1957) and Fairbairn (1975); see also Ouweneel (2000a, 34–36); C. A. Evans (*DJG* 862–66).

The Pre-Incarnate Christ

command to make the tabernacle according to the "pattern" that God would show him on Mount Sinai. Hebrews 8:5 says of the Aaronic priests: "They serve a copy and shadow of the heavenly things. For when Moses was about to erect the tent, he was instructed by God, saying, 'See that you make everything according to the pattern that was shown you on the mountain'" (cf. Exod. 25:40). Here, the writer says that the tabernacle was an earthly "copy" of heavenly things. These heavenly things were the reality—though the sacrifice of Christ had yet to occur—so that the earthly tabernacle would correspond to the heavenly reality that existed when God was telling Moses about the tabernacle.

In a certain sense, I see in this episode something significant for all typology. The types of Christ in the Old Testament correspond with a person who at the same moment was a reality in heaven: the pre-incarnate Christ. To be sure, the Word had yet to become flesh, the work of atonement had yet to be accomplished. But Revelation 13:8 (NKJV) literally speaks about ". . . the Lamb slain from the foundation of the world." In God's eternal, anticipatory counsel the atonement was a fact from eternity; in the "scroll" it was written about him (Ps. 40:7; Heb. 10:7). In the very quality of being a *Lamb*, Christ "was foreknown before the foundation of the world" (1 Pet. 1:19–20). "If the serpent bites before it is charmed, there is no advantage to the charmer" (Eccl. 10:11). When the serpent "bit" in paradise, the "charming" had already occurred in God's eternal counsel, and thus was as real as if it had taken place on earth. This is what I mean when I say that a biblical type is the earthly counter-image of a heavenly reality.

The search for biblical types is legitimized by the New Testament, where the Greek word *typos* occurs with the meaning intended here in Romans 5:14 (Adam) and 1 Corinthians 10:6 (the wilderness journey); consider as well the Greek word *antitypos* in Hebrews 9:24 and 1 Peter 3:21.[97] In Galatians 4:21–22

---

97. See *EDR* 1:§14.2.

Paul says, "Tell me, you who desire to be under the law, do you not listen to the law [i.e., Torah/Pentateuch]? For it is written that Abraham had two sons, one by a slave woman and one by a free woman," and so on (see vv. 22–31). Here, the apostle implicitly challenges the readers themselves to search for types in the Old Testament. In 1 Corinthians 10:11, he writes about Israel's Old Testament vicissitudes: "Now these things happened to them as an example [Gk. *typikōs*, "type-wise"), but they were written down for *our* instruction, on whom the end of the ages has come" (cf. 9:9–10; italics added), and in Romans 15:4, "[W]hatever was written in former days was written for *our* instruction, that through endurance and through the encouragement of the Scriptures we might have hope" (italics added).

Typology must not be confused with allegorical interpretation, as has happened so often. Since Philo and Origen, the use of allegory was often designed to eliminate the literal meaning of the Old Testament.[98] In typology, the literal meaning is always maintained and always has priority. Moreover, in an allegory like *The Pilgrim's Progress* by John Bunyan, every detail has a symbolic meaning, whereas in typology only the main lines have symbolic meaning. Therefore, when Berkouwer in his Christology criticizes the allegorical interpretation, he seems to distinguish the latter insufficiently from typology.[99] Good typology never undermines grammatical-historical exegesis, but at the same time, *following the lead of the New Testament*, this kind of exegesis wishes to tap into a deeper layer of meaning. In this way, this kind of exegete continually hears from and about Christ in the Old Testament message, in cases where one who throws out the typological baby with the allegorical bath water hears much less.

---

98. The terminology is confusing, though: if Paul says, "[T]his may be interpreted *allegorically*" (Gal. 4:24), he in fact means what *we* are now calling "typologically."
99. Berkouwer (1954, 120–30).

6.9.2 Personal Types[100]

Following the historical order of the Old Testament, I will present here some types that in the New Testament are unequivocally adduced as such, and we will notice immediately that most of them have a clearly soteriological significance.

Adam. In Romans 5:12–21 and 1 Corinthians 15:45–49, Paul identifies the first Adam as a type, or, if one wishes, as an antitype (for there is more contrast than similarity), in contrast to the second man, the last Adam. Through the former, death and condemnation have entered into the world, whereas through the latter, life and justification have come. The first man, Adam, was created as a living soul (cf. Gen. 2:7); the last Adam became a life-giving spirit through his death and resurrection. The first man was an earthly being made from dust, the second man is in his resurrection a heavenly, spiritual being. The first Adam was the head of the old human race, the second Adam is the head of the renewed human race.

Abel. Here again there is especially contrast (Heb. 12:24): we have come "to Jesus, the mediator of a new covenant, and to the sprinkled blood that speaks a better word than the blood of Abel." However, there is also similarity: Abel is the first of the "woman's offspring" (Gen. 3:15; Cain represents the serpent's "offspring"), just as Jesus is chief among the "woman's offspring" (see §4.3.1). Of both, the heel was figuratively bruised (cf. Gen. 49:17, "Dan shall be a serpent in the way, a viper by the path, that bites the horse's heels so that his rider falls backward," where Dan, whose name in Revelation 7 is strikingly absent, has often been associated with the Antichrist; just after this, Jacob exclaims, "I wait for your salvation, O LORD," v. 18).

Melchizedek. The letter to the Hebrews links Jesus with Melchizedek in one of the most explicitly typological passages of the New Testament:

---
100. See Habershon (1957, 122–42, 165–74; also see §4.2 and references there concerning Old Testament types).

> For this Melchizedek, king of Salem, priest of the Most High God, met Abraham returning from the slaughter of the kings and blessed him, and to him Abraham apportioned a tenth part of everything. He is first, by translation of his name, king of righteousness, and then he is also king of Salem, that is, king of peace. He is without father or mother or genealogy, having neither beginning of days nor end of life, but resembling [Gk. *aphōmoiōmenos*] the Son of God he continues a priest forever. See how great this man was! (Heb. 7:1-4a).[101]

Isaac. In Hebrews 11:17-19, Isaac is the "son of the father" *par excellence*, as well as the firstborn, as well as the "risen" one (figuratively speaking), and as such he is a clear type of Christ. In Galatians 4:22-31, Paul contrasts two "orders" or administrations: the former is characterized by Ishmael, standing for Mount Sinai, the mount of slavery; the latter by Isaac, standing for Mount Zion, the mount of freedom in Christ.[102] English Bible teacher Ada Habershon pointed especially to Isaac the shepherd as a type of Christ, as well as to other shepherds like Abel, Jacob, Joseph, Moses, and David.[103]

Jacob. Jesus said to Nathanael, "[Y]ou will see heaven opened, and the angels of God ascending and descending on the Son of Man" (John 1:51). In this way he presented himself as the true Jacob. In other words, the dream of Jacob about the ascending and descending angels has become reality with Jesus. And at Jacob's well, Jacob is the great patriarch, who through the well granted living water to his offspring, just as Christ grants living water to his people (John 4:5, 10).[104]

Moses. In 1 Corinthians 10:1-4, Moses is a type of Christ: just as the Israelites were "baptized" into Moses, believers today are baptized into Christ Jesus (Rom. 6:3). Of course, there are more parallels between Moses and Christ;[105] in contrast to

---

101. For the exegesis, see Ouweneel (1982, 1:86–89).
102. See more extensively, Ouweneel (1997a, 284–306).
103. Habershon (1957, chapter 15).
104. Ratzinger (2007, 240–41).
105. See Ouweneel (2001a, 178–80; 2003, Excursus 8).

the Torah of Moses we have the Torah of Christ. Moses was the first lawgiver, Christ is the new Lawgiver. Moses was the leader of God's people from their exodus from Egypt until their entrance into the promised land, Christ is the leader of God's people from their exodus from the slavery of sin and Satan until the end of the ages. And so on.

Aaron. To be sure, the letter of Hebrews places great emphasis on Jesus being priest after the order of Melchizedek (5:6, 10; 6:20; 7:11, 17). However, typologically speaking, it is preeminently Aaron who is the model for the priesthood that Jesus performed on the cross (Heb. 2:17-18; 9:11-15, 24-28; 10:11-14), and performs in heaven at the present time (Heb. 3:1; 4:14-16; 7:25-28; 8:1-2).

David. In chapter 4 I quoted many psalms that, in the literal sense, deal with David, but in the New Testament they come to have a Messianic thrust. This is the same as saying that, in such cases, David is a type of Christ. This is no surprise: as the first true king of Israel (Saul having been the opposite of a true king) he was the model for the great son of David, the Messianic King of Israel. These similarities extend to the Messiah occasionally being called "David" (§4.5.1).

Solomon. When Jesus says in Matthew 12:42, "[B]ehold, something greater than Solomon is here," this is not meant as a contrast but as a superlative. Solomon was the idealized king of Israel, according to his name the prince of *peace*, in whose days the kingdom Israel enjoyed peace and extended from the Euphrates to the border of Egypt (1 Kings 4:21; see especially Ps. 72). As such he was an excellent type of Christ as the Messianic prince of peace. Solomon was *the* son of David *par excellence*, the beloved of God (2 Sam. 12:24-25), *the* foreshadowing of *the* son of David (cf. 2 Sam. 7:14 with Heb. 1:5b).

Jonah. In Matthew 12:39-40 Jesus says: "An evil and adulterous generation seeks for a sign, but no sign will be given to it except the sign of the prophet Jonah. For just as Jonah was three days and three nights in the belly of the great fish, so will the Son of Man be three days and three nights in the heart of the earth." Here, in his figurative death and resurrection Jonah is a type of Christ.

6.9.3 Types in Genesis and the Feminine Bible Books

Types in Genesis especially have received much attention.[106] The most important (anti)types of Christ are Adam, Abel, and Isaac, in a limited sense also Jacob (especially in relation to his two brides, for whom he served in order to acquire them; see below), and particularly Joseph, both in his humiliation (the rejection by his brothers) and in his exaltation (as viceroy over the world of his day). William Lincoln called Adam the type of the Coming One, Isaac the typological Son, Jacob the typological Servant, and Joseph the typological Ruler. If we also add David, then Joseph and David are the most perfect types of Christ, first in Joseph's rejection (his father's darling was reject by his jealous brothers; see for David 1 Sam. 17:28), then in his exaltation to the throne, ruling over Egypt and Israel, respectively. In Moses' case as well, there was first a period of being rejected by his brothers (cf. Acts 7:23–29), after which God exalted him to be the leader of his people.

In contrast to these types of Christ, we find types of the bride of Christ: to Adam belongs Eve, to Isaac belongs Rebekah, to Jacob belong Leah and Rachel, to Joseph belongs Asenath, and to Boaz belongs Ruth. The two brides of Jacob have been identified as Israel and the church from the nations, but in various ways: bishop Ambrose interpreted Leah as the period of the law (i.e., Israel) and Rachel as the period of grace (i.e., the church of the Gentiles).[107] Evangelical expositors turned this exegesis around: Christ came for Israel (Rachel), but received the Gentile church (Leah)—but ultimately he re-

---

106. See Jukes (1875); Coates (n.d.); Grant (n.d.); Lincoln (n.d.); Macintosh (n.d.); as well as Habershon (1957).

107. *De Jacob et vita beata* l.ii.5, § 25; so also Gregory the Great, *Moralia in Job* l.xxx.25, § 72, and Irenaeus, *Adversus Haereses* l.iv.21, § 3; see Jukes (1875, 346); Lincoln (n.d., 116–17).

ceives Israel (Rachel) as well.[108] In this context, it is remarkable that the Egyptian Asenath, the Midianite Zipporah, and the Moabite Ruth were brides from among the Gentiles, corresponding to the church, which is virtually entirely from the Gentiles.

Moses' bride was Zipporah, David's bride was Abigail; both became prominent when Moses and David had not yet been exalted, so to speak. In this typology, Christ is the bridegroom, as he says himself in Matthew 9:15; recall as well the wedding of the Lamb (Rev. 19:7-9). Asenath is a type of the bride of Christ during the time of his exaltation. In these types, the bride represents the church, whereas the brothers of Joseph obviously represent Israel. In the cases of Moses and David, Israel represents itself as it were, over which both of these men exercised leadership.[109]

We also notice here the three "feminine" Bible books, in which the feminine protagonists are a type of the bride of Christ, or of God: Ruth in the book of Ruth (Boaz being a type of Christ),[110] the bride in the Song of Solomon (the bridegroom being a type of Christ),[111] and Esther in the book of Esther (Ahasuerus being a type of God).[112] In the book of Ruth, Boaz functions as the redeemer (Heb. *Go'el*)—a fascinating figure in the Old Testament (Lev. 25:25-26; Num. 5:8; 35:12-27 ["avenger of blood" is literally "redeemer of blood"]; Job 19:25; Isa. 54:5, 8), who in this quality clearly is a type of the New Testament Redeemer, but also of the righteous Avenger of his people.

6.9.4 Non-Personal Old Testament Types

In addition to a number of personal types, the New Testa-

---

108. Scott (1880, 17); Darby (n.d.-c, 61, 68); Coates (n.d., 214); Smith (n.d., 39–59); Ouweneel (1991, 90–91).
109. Abraham Ibn Ezra believed that Moses was the "king in Yeshurun [i.e., Israel]" (Deut. 33:5), but this exegesis has not been widely accepted.
110. Habershon (1957, 134).
111. See Ouweneel (1973).
112. See Ouweneel (n.d.-b).

ment refers to a number of non-personal matters in the Old Testament in which Christological types are perceived.

Noah's ark. In 1 Peter 3:20-21, Peter writes about "the days of Noah, while the ark was being prepared, in which a few, that is, eight persons, were brought safely through water. Baptism, which corresponds to [lit., is an *antitype* of] this, now saves you, not as a removal of dirt from the body but as an appeal to God for a good conscience." Here we find a typological parallel, and at the same time a contrast (Gk. *Antitypos*), between the ark, which carried Noah and his own people safely through the waters of death, and Christ, who through baptism carries his own people as it were safely through the waters of death.[113]

The Lamb of God. In John 1:29 and 36, John the Baptist refers to Jesus as the "Lamb of God" (cf. 1 Pet. 1:19; Rev. 5:6, 8, 12-13 and many other places). This ties in, first, with the Passover lamb of Exodus 12 (cf. 1 Cor. 5:7), and second, with the lambs that were offered as daily sacrifices (Exod. 29:38-42), and third, with the important place of the lamb, or rather, the young ram, in the Israelite sacrificial service in general. This is the same as saying that the lamb in the tabernacle and temple service was a type of Jesus as the Lamb of God. This ties in with the sacrificial terminology in general in the New Testament (Eph. 5:2; Heb. 9:14, 23-28; 10:5-14; 1 John 2:2; 4:10).

The Lion of Judah. In Revelation 5:5, Jesus is described as "the Lion of the tribe of Judah, the Root of David." This is a clear reference to Genesis 49:9, "Judah is a lion's cub; from the prey, my son, you have gone up. He stooped down; he crouched as a lion and as a lioness; who dares rouse him?" This is followed by the Messianic verse 10: "The scepter shall not depart from Judah, nor the ruler's staff from between his feet, until tribute comes to him [or, Shiloh comes; see §4.3.5]; and to him shall be the obedience of the peoples."

The manna. In John 6:32-58, Jesus compares himself to the

---

113. See more extensively, Ouweneel (2005b, 72-73).

The Pre-Incarnate Christ

manna, the "bread" that "descended" from heaven every day to feed the Israelites in the wilderness and to grant them life. Moreover, the fine flour in Leviticus 2 points to Jesus' perfect life, the grain of wheat (John 12:24) to Jesus' death, and the sheaf of the firstfruits (Lev. 23:10-14) to Jesus' resurrection.[114]

The rock. In 1 Corinthians 10:4, Paul says of Israel, "[T]hey drank from the spiritual Rock that followed them, and the Rock was Christ" — that is, the rock that quenched Israel's thirst in the wilderness was a type of Christ who does the same for his people.

The law. In 2 Corinthians 3:3, Paul draws a parallel with the Ten Commandments that were written on tablets of stone: similarly, Christ is now written on the tablets of flesh, viz., on believers' hearts. The Torah, which exhibits parallels with the Chokhmah in Proverbs 8 and with the Logos in John 1, points to Christ (cf. Ps. 40:8 ISV, "Your Law is part of my inner being").[115]

The bronze serpent. In John 3:14-15, Jesus compares himself to the bronze serpent in the wilderness: both were "lifted up," so that the person who looked at the serpent and looks at Jesus, respectively, would be saved.

The tabernacle/temple. In John 2:19-21, Jesus compares himself to the temple. This is the same as saying that the Old Testament tabernacle and later the temple were a type of Christ: just as the Shekhinah formerly dwelt in the tabernacle and the temple, it dwelt in Christ as God's habitation on earth. At other times, Jesus is compared to the foundation of the temple (1 Cor. 3:11; Eph. 2:20a), or with the cornerstone of the temple (Matt. 21:42 par.; Eph. 2:20b; 1 Pet. 2:6-7; cf. Ps. 118:22), in which cases it is the church that is being typologically represented in the temple (1 Cor. 3:16-17; 2 Cor. 6:16; Eph. 2:21-22).

Ada Habershon mentioned a number of other important types that are not explicitly referred to as such in the New

---

114. Habershon (1957, 30–32); cf. Ouweneel (2001b, §4.1).
115. See more extensively, Ouweneel (1998, 59–60; 2001a, 130).

Testament, like the various Old Testament sacrifices as pointing to Jesus' atoning sufferings and death (Lev. 1–7; cf. Heb. 10:1–10),[116] the budding staff of Aaron as a sign of life out of death (Num. 17), the living bird in the cleansing of the leper (Lev. 14:6), the passage through Jordan (Josh. 3–4), the "third day" and the "three days and three nights" in the Bible (Gen. 1:9–13; 22:4; 40:20; 42:18; Exod. 3:18; 19:11, 16; Josh. 1:11; 3:2–3; Num. 10:33; 2 Kings 20:5; Hos. 6:2; Jonah 1:17), all pointing to Christ's resurrection, and further the ark of the covenant pointing to the person of Christ.[117] In addition, we may think of other utensils in the tabernacle and temple, like the frankincense, the two altars, the candlestick, the four colors in the tissues, and so on, far too many to deal with here.

---

116. See extensively *EDR* 5, and the forthcoming *RT* III/3.
117. Habershon (1957, chapters 5, 6, and 8).

Chapter 7
The Deity of Christ

[We are] waiting for our blessed hope,
the appearing of the glory of our great God and Savior Jesus Christ,
who gave himself for us to redeem us from all lawlessness
and to purify for himself a people for his own possession
who are zealous for good works.

Titus 2:13-14

7.1 Jesus Is God
7.1.1 John's Writings

JESUS CHRIST IS a blessed miracle worker. He is a great teacher and prophet. According to Christians, he is the Messiah of Israel. According to many, after his death, resurrection, and ascension, he now resides at the right hand of God in heaven. However, all of this does not adequately express *who* he is. We will never really know him if we fail to discern, in addition to his perfect humanity (see chapter 8), his perfect deity as well. He is the *Man* Christ Jesus, the mediator between God and humanity (1 Tim. 2:12) — but he could become this only because at the same time he was and is our great *God* and Savior (Titus 2:13; cf. 2 Pet. 1:1). This vital subject, which has so often been contradicted, not only by Jews and Gentiles but also by confessing Christians,[1] deserves our full attention.

In addition to the evidence we have already found in the Old Testament (chapter 4), we find in the New Testament some direct references to the deity of Jesus.[2] We considered John 1:1-2 above. Some have tried to weaken the reference to the deity of Christ by emphasizing that in the expression "the Word was God" (Gk. *theos ēn ho logos*) there is no article before *theos*; thus, the New World Translation of the Jehovah Witnesses renders the Greek as "the Word was a god." This rendering finds no support in the text, since in verses 6, 13, and 18 the article is lacking as well, without anyone doubting that the text speaks of God in the ordinary sense. See further in §6.6.2 and 7.6.1, where I point to verse 18 (NIV): "No one has ever seen God, but the one and only Son, *who is himself God* and is in closest relationship with the Father, has made him known."

In John 20:28, Thomas confesses Jesus as "my Lord and my God" — where the nouns are anarthrous (Gk. *ho kyrios mou kai ho theos mou*).[3] In light of John's comprehensive testimony it is far-fetched to assume that in his enthusiasm Thomas' reach is exceeding his grasp, or that he worships God "in Jesus" as distinct from the Man Jesus. As surely as he calls him his "Lord" (cf. John 4:1; 6:23; 11:2; 13:14; 20:2, 13, 18, 20, 25; 21:7, 12), he calls Jesus his "God." Equally clearly, Clement, bishop of Rome, wrote the following near the end of the first century (or is it an anonymous writing of the mid-second century?): "Brethren, we ought so to think of our Lord Jesus Christ as of God, as of the judge of quick and dead,"[4] that is, not *as if* he is

---

1. See, e.g., the discussion in Borg and Wright (1999, 145–68).
2. See extensively, Harris (1992).
3. Brown (1994a, 188–89; cf. 194).
4. 2 Clement 1:1 (http://www.earlychristianwritings.com/text/2clement-hoole.

God, but: we must think about Jesus the same way we think about God; or, we must think about him in his quality of God. This interpretation is supported by the addition "the judge of quick and dead" because this is a reference to God (1 Pet. 4:5) as well as to Jesus (Acts 10:42; 2 Tim. 4:1).

There is not a single explicit New Testament reference to Jesus' deity that has not been heavily debated. Consider this powerful Johannine statement: "[W]e know that the Son of God has come and has given us understanding, so that we may know him who is true; and we are in him who is true, in his Son Jesus Christ. He is the true God and eternal life" (1 John 5:20).[5] It seems self-evident that "he" (Gk. *houtos*, "this one") refers back to the One mentioned last: Jesus Christ, and this is what many expositors conclude. However, others have argued that *houtos* summarizes everything that 1 John has said about God: this being—he who is true, who was revealed in and through his Son, the One with whom we have been united by his Son—is the true God and eternal life. However, on this interpretation, the sentence becomes tautological: ". . . we are in him who is true. . . . He is the true God." We must also consider that it is the Son who is the source of eternal life (1:2; cf. John 11:25; 14:6). Therefore, John is arguing that, because Jesus is the true God, the One who is in him is also in the Father. Thus, at the end of his letter, as a kind of climax, John proclaims the full deity of Jesus.

Please also notice the expression "God the Almighty" (Heb. *El Shaddai*, Gk. *ho theos ho pantokratōr*). This is YHWH, which is evident, for instance, from 2 Corinthians 6:18, where *kyrios pantokratōr* is the Greek rendering of the Hebrew YHWH *Shaddai*. In Revelation, we find the Greek word *pantokratōr* many times (1:8; 4:8; 11:17; 15:3; 16:7, 14; 19:6, 15; 21:22), sometimes clearly distinct from Christ, or the Lamb. In most passages, the title is linked with the title *kyrios ho theos*, which is the rendering of Old Testament YHWH *Elohim*. However, in the

---
html).
5. See the discussion by Marshall (1978a, 254–55n47); Barker (1981, ad loc.).

first two passages, the title is also linked with the description "[the One] who is and who was and who is to come" (1:8; see the same expression in 1:4), or, "[the One] who was and who is and who is to come" (4:8). This is peculiar because the One "who is to come" in Revelation is, of course, none other than Christ (1:7; 2:5, 16, 25; 3:11; 16:15; 22:7, 12, 20; cf. 14:14; 17:14; 19:11–16). YHWH *Elohim*, who eternally was and eternally is, is the God who is to come in the person of Christ; he (singular!) who will reign is both "our Lord" (YHWH) and "his Messiah" (11:15, 17; 19:6). It is YHWH *Elohim* who says, "I am the Alpha and the Omega," that is, "the first and the last" (1:8; 21:6; cf. Isa. 44:6b; 48:12b) — but it is Christ who is able and allowed to say the very same things (1:17; 2:8; 22:13).

7.1.2 Paul's Writings

Romans 9:5 is another passage on which there has been much debate: ". . . from their [i.e., Israel's] race, according to the flesh, is the Christ, who is God over all, blessed forever."[6] The RSV (cf. NABRE) translates: ". . . of their race, according to the flesh, is the Christ. God who is over all be blessed for ever." In fact, the matter is a question of punctuation. The text literally says, "from whom the Christ according to [the] flesh the being over all God blessed forever." The RSV places a period after "flesh" and reads the rest as a doxology, not to Christ but to God. The traditional translations view "Christ" as the antecedent of "the being," and thus apply the rest of the sentence to Christ.

Without entering any further into the linguistic aspects, I would claim only that the text can be used as an argument for Christ's deity with some prudence. I disagree with the argument that Paul never uses *theos* as a predicate for Christ.[7] It

---

6. See extensively, Murray (1968, 2:245–48).
7. Dodd (1932, 152); see also Messianic Jewish theologian Shulam (1998, 340), who claimed that Paul nowhere referred to Yeshua as God, with the possible exceptions of Phil. 2:6 ("he was in the form of God") and Rom. 10:9–10; the latter reference is strange, because in this passage Jesus is not called God.

is possible to render 2 Thessalonians 1:12 as "... our God and Lord Jesus Christ," although this is less likely because of the location of the Greek word *hēmōn* ("our") after *theou* ("God") (see §6.6.2 on 2 Pet. 1:1).[8] This is different in Titus 2:13: "... of our great God and Savior Jesus Christ," where *hēmōn* comes after *sōtēros* ("Savior"), and thus connects *theou* and *sōtēros*. Therefore, the traditional translation is very strong, even though the GNV and others render it as "of that mighty God, and of our Savior Jesus Christ."

In other statements, Paul comes very close to using *theos* for Christ. Earlier I mentioned Philippians 2:6 ("he was in the form of God") and referred to Colossians 1:19 ("in him all the fullness of God was pleased to dwell") and 2:9 ("in him the whole fullness of deity dwells bodily"). No statements come closer to implicitly saying that Christ himself shares in the deity. At the same time, we notice with John Murray that the reason that Paul so seldom uses the title *theos* for Christ is that, with him, *ho theos* is often the personal name of the Father, and *ho kyrios* ("the Lord") that of Christ (Rom. 1:7; 5:1, 11; 6:23; 7:25; 8:39; 10:9; 14:6; 15:6, 30; 16:20).[9] Christ's being (placed) "over all" (i.e., all creation) in Romans 9:5 agrees with Christ being *ho kyrios*—but then this verse also indicates that he is *theos*.[10]

At this point, I remind the reader of the many Old Testament passages that refer to YHWH but which in the New Testament are directly applied to Jesus (see the extensive survey in §6.2.3). The Septuagint renders YHWH as *kyrios*, a term that in the New Testament is applied almost everywhere to Christ. In Luke 1:16, the term can refer to both God and Christ. In Acts 10:36 and Romans 10:12, Christ is called "Lord of all." In 1 Corinthians 2:8 and James 1:21, Christ is the "Lord of glory."

---

8. Brown (1994a, 180).
9. Murray (1968, 2:248).
10. See Brown (1994a, 181–84) on Titus 2:13; Rom. 9:5; 1 John 5:20; 2 Pet. 1:1; he points out (193) that in all these cases we are dealing with doxologies, which are possibly much older than the letters concerned.

Not only "God is *kyrios*," but also "Jesus is *kyrios*" (Rom. 10:9; 1 Cor. 12:3) — a title that Jesus implicitly claims for himself (Mark 12:35-37 par.). In agreement with this, he sometimes calls his followers "slaves" (less correctly, "servants," Gk. *douloi*, Matt. 10:24-25; 18:23; 24:45-46; 25:14-23; Mark 13:34; Luke 12:37-38, 43; 17:10; 19:13-17; John 13:16; 15:20), thus implying that he is their Lord and Master.

In 1 Timothy 6:15, God, as distinct from Christ, is "the King of kings and Lord of lords" (Gk. *ho basileus tōn basileuontōn kai kyrios tōn kyrieuontōn*, lit., "the King of the reigning ones and Lord of the ruling ones"; cf. Deut. 10:17; Ps. 136:2-3). But in Revelation 19:16 (cf. 17:14) it is the Lamb who is called "King of kings and Lord of lords" (Gk. *basileus basileōn kai kyrios kyriōn*).

In Acts 20:28 we read that Paul tells the elders of Ephesus that God has obtained the church "through his own blood" (Gk. *dia tou haimatos tou idiou*; [N]KJV, ESV, NIV) or "through the blood of his own [Son]" (CJB, GNT, RSV). We may honestly wonder on what basis other than theological bias one would translate the Greek phrase differently than the former way. This former (preferred) rendering means nothing other than that the Triune God has obtained his church through the blood of the *Man* Jesus Christ, but this Man *is* God, namely, God the Son. Such a formulation is not strange for the apostle who also penned Titus 2:13.

7.2 Jesus' Claims to Deity
7.2.1 Equality with God

Jesus is God — to me this claim is just as certain as the fact that he never said, "I am God." In his situation, such a statement would have been totally incomprehensible to his listeners, including his followers.[11] Jesus rarely publicly acknowledged that he was the Messiah, in order not to create any misunderstandings. All the greater would the misconception have been had he spoken openly of his deity. Yet he definitely claimed

---
11. Rahner (1971, 31).

to be divine, but then implicitly, in a covert way, such that his followers could acknowledge his full deity only later, through the power of the Holy Spirit.

In this section, we begin from the conviction that the Gospels are fundamentally—theologically as well as historically—trustworthy (see chapter 5). When therefore Harry Kuitert asserted that nowhere in the Synoptic Gospels did Jesus call himself Son of God,[12] he could only have been referring to the Synoptic Gospels from which he himself had first removed all of Jesus' references to his divine Sonship. The passages involved include Matthew 11:27 par.; 28:19; Mark 13:32; consider also Matthew 21:37-39 par.; 22:41-45 par.; in addition we have those passages where Jesus does not contradict the fact that he is called Son of God by others. Kuitert, and so many liberal theologians like him, could dismiss such passages only by asserting that Jesus did not say it that way, or did not mean anything special with it, or that the references were inserted later as components of the church's theology. This involves passages in which Jesus speaks of himself as the unique Son alongside his Father.

Another sophism by Kuitert is this:

> The strongest argument against God-on-earth, which can be verified by historical investigation, is that Jesus himself could not have believed it. Jesus was a Jew, his religion was the Jewish religion and a Jew cannot call himself Son of God (in the trinitarian sense). That is in fundamental conflict with his faith.[13]

This argument can be easily refuted. First, the seeds of the doctrine of the eternal Son of God are contained in the Old Testament (see chapter 4); and second, Kuitert is the victim of circular reasoning: if Jesus was *only* a Jew, he could not believe in himself as the Son of God; however, if he was the Son of God, he was much, much more than only a Jew. Therefore, he remained the Jew who was faithful to the Torah, but at the

---

12. Kuitert (1999, 62–63, 106–107); cf. D. R. Bauer (*DJG* 769–75).
13. Kuitert (1999, 129).

same time he broke through the boundaries of the Judaism of his day. He did not oppose it, but went beyond and surpassed it (cf. Matt. 5:17-20), in a way that, *in retrospect*, turned out to have been revealed in the Old Testament.

Our first example of Jesus' implicit claims of divinity was that *he made himself equal with God*. We see this in the Synoptic Gospels, and especially in John's Gospel. In John 5:18, the Jews understood very well that the way Christ spoke about God as his own Father implied that he made "himself equal with God." Jesus confirmed this with many implicit references to his deity in verses 18-26: the Son does what the Father does, the Son gives life as the Father gives life, all must honor the Son as they honor the Father, the Son has life in himself as the Father has life in himself.

When the Jews ask him, "Who do you make yourself out to be?" (John 8:53), Jesus answers among other things: "[B]efore Abraham was, I am" (v. 58; cf. vv. 24, 28; see §6.7.2 above). He says, "Whoever has seen me has seen the Father" (14:9), and, "All that the Father has is mine" (16:15), and to his Father: "All mine are yours, and yours are mine" (17:10).

In John 10:30 Jesus says, "I and the Father are one," and again the Jews draw the right conclusion: "[Y]ou, being a man, make yourself God" (v. 33). Without hesitation Jesus speaks of "we" and "us" when speaking of the Father and himself: "[M]y Father will love him, and we will come to him and make our home with him" (John 14:23); "Holy Father, keep them in your name, which you have given me, that they may be one, even as we are one" (17:11; v. 21 [KJV], "one in us"; v. 22: "one even as we are one").[14] He also says that the Father is in him, and he in the Father (v. 21; 14:10), that the Father knows him as he knows the Father (10:15), and: "[N]o one knows the Son except the Father, and no one knows the Father except the Son and anyone to whom the Son chooses to reveal him" (Matt. 11:27 par.). Moreover, we have seen in

---

14. In anyone else's mouth this would have been blasphemy, said Ethelbert Stauffer, quoted in Berkouwer (1954, 170).

The Deity of Christ

other passages that Christ declared his eternal pre-existence, thereby implying his deity (§6.7).

It is remarkable that Jesus never equated God's Fatherhood of himself with God's Fatherhood of the disciples, or of people in general. He taught his disciples to pray "our Father" (Matt. 6:9), as had long been the custom of the Jews (Isa. 63:16; 64:8); but he himself never spoke of "our Father," nor did he ever pray to God as "our Father," but exclusively as "Father" (e.g., John 12:27-28) or "my Father" (e.g., Matt. 26:39). More than that: he prayed in the presence of his disciples, but *he never prayed together with them*. When he refers to God as the Father of the disciples, he says, "your (heavenly) Father" (many times, including fifteen times in the Sermon on the Mount). Even where a clear connection exists between him and his disciples, he does not say "our Father," but "my Father and your Father' (John 20:17).

7.2.2 Four Other Claims to Deity

Second, *Jesus accepted worship*. In Isaiah 42:8 and 48:11, YHWH says that he gives his glory to no other, and in 45:23 that to him every knee will bow. Nevertheless, Philippians 2:9-10 tells us that God has "highly exalted" Jesus, and "bestowed on him the name that is above every name, so that at the name of Jesus every knee should bow, in heaven and on earth and under the earth." The Isaiah passages underscore the fact that ordinary creatures are never allowed to receive worship, and at times sharply refuse it; we see this in the case of Peter (Acts 10:25-26), of Paul and Barnabas (14:11-15), and of the angel in Revelation 19:10 and 22:8-9. Nevertheless, Jesus receives such divine worship without any problem, expressed by the Greek verb *proskuneō*, "to bring homage" or "adoration," "to worship" (Matt. 2:2, 8, 11; 8:2; 9:18; 14:33; 15:25; 20:20; 28:9, 17; Mark 5:6; Luke 24:52; John 9:38). The verb was also used in connection with the deification of rulers (cf. Matt. 18:26), such as the Roman emperors.[15] This point alone weakens David

---

15. Schönweiss and Brown (1992, 875–76).

Flusser's assertion that the Synoptic Gospels do not clearly indicate that Jesus demanded that others accept the high aspirations that resulted from his high self-consciousness.[16]

This same honor is expressed with other verbs: people "fall down" before Jesus (Mark 5:33; Luke 8:47; cf. John 18:6), they "kneel" before Jesus (Mark 1:40; 10:17), or "fall on one's face" before Jesus (Luke 5:12), "fall at Jesus' feet" (Mark 5:22; 7:25; Luke 8:41), and of the healed leper we read that "he fell on his face at Jesus' feet, giving him thanks" (Luke 17:16). In Luke's Gospel we read five times about people at Jesus' feet (7:38; 8:35, 41; 10:39; 17:16). By accepting this homage, or worship, as something to which he was entitled (John 5:23), Jesus implicitly demonstrated his deity. Some have spoken of the *communicatio adorationis* because the *Man* Christ is the object of worship *because he is God*.[17] We must not separate the divine and human natures of Christ; the entire *person* is worshiped.[18]

Third, *Jesus presented himself as the Judge of the world*. God is called "the Judge of all the earth" (Gen. 18:25; cf. Eccl. 12:14). Yet, Jesus says, "[T]he Father judges no one, but has given all judgment to the Son" (John 5:22; cf. v. 27; Matt. 25:31–46; Acts 17:31; 1 Cor. 4:4–5; 2 Cor. 5:10; 2 Thess. 1:7–9; Rev. 19:15). He presents himself as the Son of Man, who will execute judgment on all the nations (Matt. 25:31–46; he is the One "who is to judge the living and the dead," 2 Tim. 4:1). This is the remarkable prophetic language of Psalm 96:13, for example, where we read that YHWH "comes to judge the earth. He will judge the world in righteousness, and the peoples in his faithfulness" (cf. 98:9); the One who is coming for this is the Messiah. The judgment seat of God (Rom. 14:10) is identical with the judgment seat of Christ (2 Cor. 5:10).

Fourth, *Jesus granted divine forgiveness*. After Jesus had forgiven the sins of the paralytic (Mark 2:5 par.), the scribes un-

---

16. Flusser (2007, 126).
17. See Heyns (1988, 249–50) on the four *communicationes* that Christology traditionally distinguishes; Berkhof (1981, 324) mentions three of them.
18. Berkouwer (1954, 289–90).

derstandably asked: "Why does this man speak like that? He is blaspheming! Who can forgive sins but God alone?" (v. 7). People can forgive only those sins that have been committed against *them* (Matt. 6:12, 14; Luke 17:3-4), but other sins no one can forgive except God (cf. Isa. 43:25; 44:22).[19] Therefore, Jesus either committed blasphemy, as the scribes suggested, or he is God. He himself answered (not describing himself as God but as Man): "'But that you may know that the Son of Man has authority on earth to forgive sins' — he said to the paralytic — 'I say to you, rise, pick up your bed, and go home'" (vv. 10-11).

It is remarkable to see here the astonishment of the people that God had given such *authority* to humans (Matt. 9:8). There would have been no ground for such amazement if people had realized that Jesus is God; compare Acts 5:31, "God exalted him at his right hand as Leader and Savior, to give repentance to Israel and forgiveness of sins." Recall Colossians 3:13 (NKJV), ". . . even as Christ forgave you," and the parallel in Ephesians 4:32, ". . . as God in Christ forgave you." To say that Christ forgives is the same as saying that God in Christ forgives.

Fifth, *Jesus granted life*. In 2 Kings 5:7 the king (Jehoram?) rightly claimed that only God can make alive (cf. 1 Sam. 2:6; Ps. 119:25, 37), and can cure a person of his leprosy. In Matthew 8:1-4 (par.) the leper did not doubt for a moment that Jesus was able to cure him, but he was unsure of Jesus' willingness to do so. The Lord not only had the power but also the will to do this. His word, "I will, be clean" (v. 3), is the sovereign will of divine power to cure the man of his leprosy. In an even more powerful way, his life-giving power is manifested in raising the son of the widow of Nain (Luke 7:11-17), the daughter of Jairus (8:40-56 par.), and Lazarus (John 11:1-44). Generally speaking, it is "God who raises the dead" (2 Cor. 1:9), but Jesus claimed: "[A]s the Father raises the dead

---

19. The local church *can* have a mediating function in this (John 20:23; cf. 2 Cor. 2:7, 10).

and gives them life, so also the Son gives life to whom he will" (John 5:21; cf. vv. 28-29). Astonishingly, he called himself "the resurrection and the life" (11:25).

To be sure, Jesus' followers also raised the dead. He had commanded them: "Heal the sick, raise the dead, cleanse lepers, cast out demons" (Matt. 10:8). However, to this end he gave them his own *authority* (v. 1). When his followers raised the dead (Acts 9:40; 20:9-10), it was through Jesus' authority, not through anything they inherently possessed within themselves, an authority that Jesus possessed inherently. They were only instruments, not agents: "[T]hey went out and preached everywhere, while *the Lord* worked with them and confirmed the message by accompanying signs" (Mark 16:20). "By the name of Jesus Christ of Nazareth, ... this man is standing before you well" (Acts 4:10; cf. v. 30). "God also bore witness by signs and wonders and various miracles and by gifts of the Holy Spirit distributed according to his will" (Heb. 2:4).

Above all, Jesus demonstrated his divine sovereignty by rising from the dead: he was "declared to be the Son of God in power according to the Spirit of holiness by his resurrection from the dead" (Rom. 1:4; cf. John 2:19; 10:18). He said, "For this reason the Father loves me, because I lay down my life that I may take it up again. No one takes it from me, but I lay it down of my own accord. I have authority to lay it down, and I have authority to take it up again" (John 10:17-18). Viewed from the standpoint of human responsibility, Jesus had been (passively) put to death by people (Acts 2:23; 3:15; 7:52; 10:39); viewed from the standpoint of Jesus' own divine capacities, he (actively) "laid down" his life at God's time, and "took it up again" at God's time. He was (passively) "*raised* from the dead by the glory of the Father" (Rom. 6:4), but he (actively) "*rose* from the dead" by his own divine power (Acts 10:41). Similarly, he was (passively) "taken up" in glory by God's power (1 Tim. 3:16), but he (actively) "ascended on high" by his own divine power (Eph. 4:8-10).

7.2.3 Three Other Claims to Deity

Sixth, *Jesus speaks of "his" angels*. This is a small detail that is easily overlooked. In the Gospels, Jesus often speaks about himself as the "Son of Man" (see §§4.8 and 4.9). Thus, it is about himself that he says, "The Son of Man will send *his* angels" (Matt. 13:41), and, "[T]he Son of Man is going to come with *his* angels in the glory of his Father" (16:27), whereas these are ordinarily called "angels of God" (Matt. 22:30 [cf. 4:6]; Luke 12:8-9; 15:10; John 1:51; Heb. 1:6-7; Rev. 3:5).[20] In the same context, Jesus also speaks about "his" kingdom (Matt. 13:41; 16:28), whereas this is usually called the kingdom of God (but see Rev. 11:15, "the kingdom of our Lord and of his Christ," and 12:10, "the kingdom of our God and the authority of his Christ").

Seventh, *Jesus is Lord of the Sabbath*. The Sabbath is an institution of God, as is emphasized time and again in the Torah; it is *the* sign of the Sinaitic covenant (Exod. 31:13, 17; Ezek. 20:12, 20). No one may violate this institution; trespasses of the Sabbath commandment are severely punished by God. Jesus honored and obeyed this commandment, but in his own free (non-pharisaic) way. The moment he was confronted on this point he boldly replied: "[T]he Son of Man is lord of the Sabbath" (Matt. 12:8 par.); that is, as a Jew he was under the Sabbath commandment, but at the same time, as a divine person, he was above any of the commandments because he himself was the Giver of these commandments.

Eighth and finally, *Jesus is the Son*. The fact that Jesus is "the Son" must be distinguished from the fact that he is "Son of God."[21] Jesus' divinity comes much more clearly to the fore in the title "the Son" than in the title "Son of God," even in a passage such as Mark 13:32 ("no one knows . . . , nor the Son"). In the letter to the Hebrews the title occurs five times

---

20. Actually, we also read about the archangel Michael and "his angels" (Rev. 12:7), and about Satan and "his" angels (Matt. 25:41)—but no angels belong to *men* like the Son of Man.
21. Ratzinger (2007, 321, 335).

(1:2, 8; 3:6; 5:8; 7:28), in Paul's letters once (1 Cor. 15:28), six times in 1 John (2:22-24; 4:14; 5:12), and once in 2 John (1:9). Most often Jesus describes himself this way, eighteen times in John's Gospel alone. It is only "the Son" who knows the Father; that is, because of the equality of being, he perceives the being of the Father (Matt. 11:27; Luke 10:22; cf. John 1:18). The fact that human beings, too, come to "know" the Father (John 17:3) is only because the Son has become their life (1 John 5:11-12).

Ethelbert Stauffer offers this summary:

> As the Son of God He has *exousia* [authority].... He has the power to remit sins, which according to Jewish tradition God alone enjoyed. He will sit on the throne of God and judge the world. He appropriates the offices and to some degree the names (e.g., Logos) of [ancient] intermediary beings, and in their place He is the Mediator of creation [John 1:3; 1 Cor. 8:6; Col. 1:16-17; Heb. 1:2b] and of salvation history (1 C. 10:4; Hb. 1:1). He stands high and predominant above the angels....
>
> Jesus wages God's battle against the prince of this world, who constantly attacks Him from the first to the last of His activity, and indeed of His life (Luke 22:28).... He enters the house of the strong man and hurls him from his throne [Mark 3:27; Luke 10:18; John 12:31; 16:11]. He drives out demons with the finger of God, and rules them with the power of God [Luke 11:20; cf. Mark 5:7].[22]

Jesus' *exousia* cannot be compared with that of any human being. As A. van de Beek put it:

> In the Sermon on the Mount, Jesus does not just present an alternative way of life but places himself above Moses. Only God can do such a thing. That is why Jesus does not say, as the Old Testament prophets do, "Thus says the Lord," but "And I say unto you" [Matt. 5:22, 28, 32, 34, 39, 44]. His speaking with authority [Gk. *exousia*] is not the preponderance of an authentic

---

22. Stauffer (*TDNT* 3:102–103).

personality but the authority possessed by Godself.[23]

7.3 Jesus' Divine Attributes
7.3.1 The God-Christ Connection

Jesus possessed all the attributes of the Deity: in, through, and for him, all things were created; all things exist by the power of his person (Col. 1:16-17; cf. John 1:3; Heb. 1:2-3); he sends the Holy Spirit (John 15:26); he gives life to whom he wishes (John 5:21); his Spirit inspired the Holy Scriptures (1 Pet. 1:10-11); he places people in the ministry (1 Tim. 1:12; cf. 1 Cor. 12:5); he dwells in the believer (John 14:23; Eph. 3:17; Col. 1:27); he sanctifies them (Eph. 5:26; Heb. 2:11); and he protects them (John 10:28). People believe in him just as they believe in God (14:1), and they pray to him just as they pray to God (Rom. 10:12-13; 1 Cor. 1:2; 16:22 [*Maranatha!* "Lord, come!"]; 2 Cor. 12:8; cf. Acts 7:59; 8:22; 9:13-14).

Otto Weber showed how the New Testament refers to the name of Christ the same way the Old Testament refers to the name of God.[24] Important examples are:

(a) *Meeting in the name:* Matthew 18:20 (cf. Exod. 20:24; Lev. 22:32).

(b) *Believing in the name:* John 1:12; 2:23; 3:18; Acts 3:16; 1 John 3:23; 5:13 (cf. Gen. 15:6; Exod. 14:31; Ps. 33:21).

(c) *Praying in (or, to) the name:* John 14:13-14; 15:16; 16:23-26 (cf. 1 Kings 8:29, 33, 35, 43).

(d) *Being saved through the name:* Acts 4:12; 10:43 (cf. Ps. 54:1; Joel 2:32).

(e) *Miracles through the name:* Acts 4:30 (cf. Ps. 75:1; 105:1-2; Isa. 25:1).

We have a similar situation when it comes to the "face" ("presence") of God or of Christ: the "face of the Lord" (Gk. *prosōpon tou kyriou*) refers to God in Acts 3:19, and to Christ in 2 Thessalonians 1:9 (cf. also 2 Cor. 4:6). In an analogous way,

---

23. Van de Beek (2002a, 142–43).
24. Weber (1981, 1:415–19).

we hear about the "glory" of the Father (Rom. 6:4), of God (Acts 7:55), of the Lord (= God: Luke 2:9; = Christ: 1 Cor. 2:8), and of Christ (Mark 13:26; John 1:14; Titus 2:13; 1 Pet. 4:13; 5:1).

In the baptismal formula of Matthew 28:19, Jesus himself indicates that there is only one single name in (or, unto) which people are baptized, and this single name is that of the Father, the Son, and the Holy Spirit. Several times, they are mentioned in one breath, for instance: "the kingdom of Christ and God" (Eph. 5:5), "the grace of our God and the Lord Jesus Christ" (2 Thess. 1:12), often at the beginning or the end of New Testament letters. Take these sentences: "[M]ay our God and Father himself, and our Lord Jesus, direct our way to you" (1 Thess. 3:11), and: "[M]ay our Lord Jesus Christ himself, and God our Father, . . . comfort your hearts" (2 Thess. 2:16-17), in which the Greek verb has the singular form, as if only one person were involved.

In 1 John, "he" is used for the Father and Son without distinction. Thus, 2:24 speaks about abiding in the Son and in the Father, but verse 25 continues: "And this is the promise that he [singular!] made to us—eternal life." In 2:28, "he" must refer to Christ because the text speaks of his coming; but in verse 29 "he" refers to God because the righteous is born of him. In 3:1b "him" must refer to the Father of verse 1a, but the text continues in verse 2: "[W]e know that when he appears we shall be like him," which clearly refers to the Son. Although the Father and the Son are distinct persons, John speaks of them as being one (cf. John 10:30).

7.3.2 List of Attributes

All of the divine attributes that are applicable to the Father—or more generally, to God—are applicable to the Son as well.[25]

---

25. As the Athanasian Creed puts it: "7. Such as the Father is: such is the Son; and such is the Holy Ghost. 8. The Father uncreate[d]: the Son uncreate[d]: and the Holy Ghost uncreate[d]. 9. The Father incomprehensible [unlimited]: the Son incomprehensible [unlimited]: and the Holy Ghost incomprehensible [unlimited, or infinite]" etc. (Lat. 7. *Qualis Pater, talis Filius, talis*

Here is a concise list of twelve attributes in alphabetical order.[26]

(1) *Glory.* Jesus speaks of the glory that he had with the Father before the world existed (John 17:5); he is the "Lord of glory" (1 Cor. 2:7; James 2:1). The glory of God is, as it were, reflected in the face of Jesus Christ (2 Cor. 4:6). Thus, his face can be "like the sun shining in full strength" (Rev. 1:16; cf. Matt. 17:2), yes, his glory may even be "brighter than the sun" (Acts 26:13).

(2) *Grace.* God is a "God merciful and gracious" (Exod. 34:6; 2 Chron. 30:9; Neh. 9:17, 31; Ps. 86:15; 103:8; 111:4; 112:4; 116:5; 145:8; Joel 2:13; Jonah 4:2), and this grace is reflected in the Son: "grace and truth" came through him (John 1:17). "For you know the grace of our Lord Jesus Christ, that though he was rich, yet for your sake he became poor, so that you by his poverty might become rich" (2 Cor. 8:9). People "wondered at the words of grace which proceeded out of his mouth" (Luke 4:22 ASV).

(3) *Holiness.* In the Old Testament, especially in Isaiah, God is frequently called the "Holy One," but Christ is also called with this name (Mark 1:24 par.; John 6:69; Acts 2:27; 13:35; 1 John 2:20; Rev. 3:7; cf. Luke 1:35).

(4) *Immutability.* In Hebrews 1:10–12, the author applies Psalm 102:25–27, which was originally addressed to YHWH, now to Christ: ". . . you will remain . . . you are the same." Hebrews 13:8 says, "Jesus Christ is the same yesterday and today and forever." What is true of the Father is true of the Son: he is "the Father of lights, with whom there is no variation or shadow due to change" (James 1:17).

(5) *Love.* God is love (1 John 4:8, 16), but we also hear of "the love of Christ that surpasses knowledge" (Eph. 3:19; cf.

[et] *Spiritus Sanctus.* 8. *Increatus Pater: increatus Filius: increatus [et] Spiritus Sanctus.* 9. *Immensus Pater: immensus Filius: immensus [et]Spiritus Sanctus*) (Schaff [1919, 96]).

26. Cf. Chafer (1983, 304–305, 340–42, 401–402); see also *RT* II/1, especially chapters 7 and 8.

John 15:13; Rom. 8:35; 2 Cor. 5:14).

(6) *Omnipotence*. The risen Christ said, "All authority in heaven and on earth has been given to me" (Matt. 28:18); Paul speaks of "the power that enables him [i.e., Christ] even to subject all things to himself" (Phil. 3:21), and: ". . . in him all things hold together." Hebrews 1:3 says that "he upholds the universe by the word of his power" (this must have been true even of the "helpless" babe in the manger!).[27] We have seen that, through the addition "he who is to come," the name "Almighty" (Gk. *pantokratōr*) is applied to Christ in Revelation (1:8; 4:8) (§7.1.1). In John 17:24, the Son ventures to say to the Father: "Father, I *will* [Gk. *thelō*[28]] that they also, whom thou hast given me, be with me where I am" (KJV), whereby he declares himself to be equal to (not identical with!) the Father.

(7) *Omnipresence*. Wherever believers are present in the name of Christ, he is in their midst (Matt. 18:20); he is always with believers (28:20); he fills all in all (Eph. 1:23); together with the Father, he makes his home with every believer (John 14:23; Eph. 3:17).

(8) *Omniscience*. Jesus says, "[N]o one knows the Father except the Son" (Matt. 11:27); ". . . just as the Father knows me and I know the Father" (John 10:15). "I am he who searches mind and heart" (Rev. 2:23; cf. Jer. 11:20; 17:10; 20:12, where this is said of YHWH). He knows what is in humans (John 2:25). Peter says, "Lord, you know everything."[29]

(9) *Peace*. The New Testament speaks equally of the "peace of God" (Phil. 4:17) and of the "peace of Christ" (Col. 3:15). Jesus said to his disciples: "Peace I leave with you; my peace I give to you" (John 14:27).

(10) *Vitality*. Many times, God is called "the living God"

---

27. Calvin mentioned the example of the Jesus asleep in the ship (Mark 4:38–40), who, while asleep, was acting as God to reveal to his disciples the majesty of God's saving love; quoted in Graafland (1982, 63).
28. "I want" is stronger than "I desire" (ESV).
29. On Mark 13:32 ("concerning that day or that hour, no one knows, . . . nor the Son") see §§2.2.1 and 3.7.2; see further §8.2.3.

(from Deut. 5:26 to Rev. 7:2). God is the one who has life in himself in its original sense, the Father giving this life from eternity to the Son, so that the latter has it "in himself" (John 5:26). Hence, from eternity God is the Life-Giver (Father) as well as the Life-Receiver (Son). Jesus is the "Author [or, Prince; Gk. *archēgos*, also: Origin] of life" (Acts 3:15), and the "life-giving spirit" (1 Cor. 15:45).

(11) *Wisdom.* In Romans 16:27, God is described as the "only wise God." Jesus Christ is in his person the "wisdom of God" (1 Cor. 1:24; cf. v. 30; Col. 2:3). He is not only wise, but he *is* divine wisdom in his own person, just as God *is* spirit (John 4:24), light (1 John 1:5) and love (4:8, 16).

(12) *Faithfulness.* God is "faithful" (1 Cor. 1:9; 10:13; 2 Cor. 1:18; 1 Thess. 5:24; Heb. 10:23; 11:11; 1 Pet. 4:19; 1 John 1:9). The same is said of Jesus Christ (2 Thess. 3:3; 2 Tim. 2:13; Heb. 2:17; 3:2); he is the "faithful and true witness" (Rev. 3:14; cf. 1:5; 19:11).

7.3.3 Implications

What are the implications of all these things? The conclusion has been drawn by many theologians that, at a certain time, Jesus was deified by his followers but that God the Son became Man in the fulness of time, and revealed himself as such to his followers. The point is not that there was a Man who resembled God, but that God the Son since the fullness of time has begun to resemble Man. The point is not that Jesus resembles God but that God resembles Jesus. In the words of Michael Ramsey, the archbishop of Canterbury: the significance of the confession that "Jesus is Lord" is not only that Jesus is divine but that God is "Christlike."[30] With a variation on 1 John 1:5, God is Christlike, and in him is no unChristlikeness at all. Stated concisely, as a Man, Christ *has been made kyrios* (Acts 2:36) — but it is equally true that the *kyrios*, as we know him from the Old Testament, *has been made Man.*

William Ramsay added that the Christlikeness of God im-

---
30. Quoted in Ford and Higton (2002, 505–506).

plies that Christ's sufferings and resurrection are the key to the deepest meaning of God's deity. When God became Man, his significance as God came to light in a way never before expressed. The self-surrender, the incarnation, the suffering love, were not additions to the divine experience, or mere incidents in divine history. According to Ramsay, by becoming Man, God revealed the meaning of what it is to be God. God became Man, not because he would have been incomplete without humanity or because he would have depended on creatures for his own existence, but because in himself he is the perfection of love.

7.4 The Eternal Father and the Eternal Son[31]
7.4.1 Fatherhood and Sonship

If, in the Old Testament, God is called "Father," that is, the Father (Begetter and Caretaker) of the people of Israel (Deut. 32:6; Isa. 63:16; 64:8; Mal. 1:6; 2:10; cf. Exod. 4:22; Deut. 1:31; 8:5; 14:1; Ps. 103:13; Isa. 45:11; Jer. 31:20; Mal. 3:17; John 8:41), this description does not necessarily express who God is in himself. A title expresses *what* someone is, for instance, by referring to a certain office, but a name expresses *who* someone is. If within time God *became* the Father of Israel by "begetting" the nation, or when Israel as a nation was "born" (cf. Exod. 4:22; Deut. 14:1), the term "Father" refers to God within time, not to God in his eternal being. Undoubtedly, God's Fatherhood with respect to Israel reflects some of his eternal attributes, such as his love, but fatherhood itself in this meaning is not an eternal attribute because Israel is not from eternity.

It is only in the New Testament that we learn that God the "Father" (in the sense of Creator) is identical to the *eternal* Father as well as the *eternal* Son (as well as the *eternal* Spirit, Heb. 9:14), and that therefore *this* fatherhood and *this* sonship do

---

31. In addition to consulting commentaries and dogmatics handbooks, I have received help for this section from Hocking (1934), Harlow (1974), Smith (1986), Bellett (n.d.), and Pollock (n.d.). See more extensively, Ouweneel (1978a).

indeed express who God was and is in himself from eternity: Father, Son, and Spirit. In the New Testament sense, Christ is the Son, distinct from the Father; but in the Old Testament meaning of the notion of "Father" (i.e., Creator, Redeemer, Caretaker of his people), it is the Messiah who is the "Eternal Father" (Isa. 9:6).

The *concept* of fatherhood in our world concerns the relationship of a male person toward a child. A father is the father of that child because he has begotten that child. Usually this also implies that he takes care of the child, raises the child, and maintains a relationship of intimacy with the child; therefore, a foster father is also called a father. Thus, fatherhood is not an absolute quality but a relative quality: there exists no father who never had a son or a daughter.

When we apply this to Christ, we must notice immediately that God's fatherhood with regard to him has a double aspect because Jesus is both God and Man. Jesus is both Son of God and Son of Man. His sonship is twofold because his person is twofold. However, the matter is even more complicated than this. The name "Son of Man" is linked exclusively with his humanity, but the name "Son of God" is linked with both his deity and his humanity. Thus, Jesus' divine sonship is twofold as well: he is the eternal Son of God as a divine person, but he is also the Son of God because as a human being he was begotten by God from Mary (Luke 1:35; cf. Ps. 2:7). Because Mary was the mother of the Man Jesus Christ, and God was his Father, this Man, begotten by God, could be rightly called "Son of God." Davidic kings were also called "son of God" (cf. 2 Sam. 7:14; Ps. 2:7), but this was based upon adoption, though Psalm 2:7 uses the verb "to beget" (meant here in a figurative way if we take the text here in its primary sense). Jesus was *really* begotten by God from Mary. Of course, here "begetting" is still a metaphor but in the case of Jesus its meaning is greater than with the Davidic kings because he had no human father. In this sense, he is unique: no other human being has ever been begotten in this way from

THE ETERNAL CHRIST: GOD WITH US

a woman. In this sense, too, Jesus is the unique Son of God.

7.4.2 Eternal Sonship

We just saw that Jesus is Son of God because he was begotten by God from Mary. But this is only one reason why he bears the name "Son of God," and not the most important reason. The designation "Son of God" is not only one of his names as Man, but first and foremost his name as a divine person. He was not only a Son born to the Most High God (Luke 1:32, 35), for, although Jesus' human birth was unique, *all* Israelites were "sons of the LORD, your God" (Deut. 4:1, Heb. *banim l'YH-WH Elohēchem*). But Jesus was and is also the Son of the *Father* (2 John 1:3), the eternal Son of the eternal Father (cf. John 17:1, 5, 24; 1 John 1:3). He is the *only* (Gk. *monogenēs*) Son of God, an expression that refers to his absolute uniqueness (see §7.6.2). God spoke "in [the] Son" (Gk. *en huiōi*, Heb. 1:1), that is, God himself spoke as a divine person, and this person is the Son. And Jesus *proved* to be Son of God in this sense: "[B]y being raised from the dead he was proved to be the mighty Son of God, with the holy nature of God himself" (Rom. 1:4 TLB). All these passages and many others show that Jesus' sonship is connected not only with his humanity but also with his deity.

This brings us to an important point. If the designation "Son of God" is the name of an eternal, divine person, it must be clear that this person was Son from eternity, and therefore that the Father was Father from eternity. Genuine names of a divine person are necessarily just as eternal as that person himself. Jesus is the Son in person, and this person is eternal. If Christ on earth was Son as a perfectly divine person, he was eternally the Son; and if the Father is the Father of a perfectly divine person, he was eternally the Father, just as the Holy Spirit is the "eternal Spirit" (Heb. 9:14).[32] Jesus' sonship is just as immutable and permanent as his eternal, divine person, and similarly the fatherhood of the Father is just as immutable and permanent as his eternal, divine person. The

---

32. See *EDR* 1:76–77, 145–46, 155).

relationship between divine persons, namely, the Father and the Son, could not have had a beginning in time any more than these divine persons themselves had a beginning in time.

It is important to notice here that the early church's increasing understanding of the eternal sonship of Christ did not imply a form of mythologizing, but rather a defense against mythology. What is mythological is the idea of a historical, human son of a God who "as such" cannot really have a son, or at best have an adopted son. The understanding of the eternal sonship of Christ is a demythologizing of the idea of God in the sense that the confession "God in Christ" necessitates a new view of God himself. God does not simply beget or adopt a son,[33] God *is* Father and Son (and Spirit). It is not only that "Jesus is God" according to a speculative list of divine features to which Jesus corresponds, but especially that "God is *Jesus*": the being of God is genuinely manifested in the coming and the sacrifice of Jesus Christ.

This is also important as a reply to Jews and Muslims in particular who argue that "God cannot have a Son." In one respect they are perfectly right. The God of Christian believers does not simply *have* a Son. No, this very God *is* Father, Son, and Holy Spirit.

7.5 God Manifested
7.5.1 Son and Sons of God

To understand the sonship of Christ, it may be helpful to highlight its difference with the sonship of believers. It is quite possible for God to become, within time, the Father of a certain human being, precisely because this person *is* a human being and not a divine person. However, could we say that, within the Deity, one divine person could *become* the Father of another divine person? I can imagine that the second person in the Trinity could become Son through the incarnation, and that the first person in the Trinity became the Father of this human being by begetting him. But can we imagine that

---
33. See *RT* II/1, chapters 9 and 10.

one person in the Deity *became* the Father of another *divine* person? It is pointless to designate the persons in the Deity as Father, Son, and Holy Spirit if the Father and the Son are only Father and Son with respect to each other from the time of the Son's incarnation.

I realize that we must be careful here because we are dealing not with *logical concepts* but with the *theological metaphors*[34] "father" and "son." This means that the predicates that belong to the concepts of "father" and "son" cannot automatically be applied to the theological metaphors "Father" and "Son." We can do this only with predicates that are supplied by Scripture itself. This is indeed the case with the *eternal* fatherhood of the Father and the *eternal* sonship of the Son, as we will see.

Thus, there is a basic difference between Christ's sonship and that of the believers. Christ *was* Son of God and *became* a human being, while remaining the Son of God. Believers *were* human beings and *became* sons of God, while remaining human beings. However, in spite of this difference, the believers' sonship also teaches us something about the true significance of sonship, and therefore also about the sonship of Christ. Although it has often been asserted that, on earth, the Son *as such* was subordinate to the Father,[35] we must realize that, in the Bible, sonship is *contrasted* several times with submission and subordination: "The slave does not remain in the house forever; the son remains forever. So if the Son sets you free, you will be free indeed" (John 8:35–36). "For you did not receive the spirit of slavery to fall back into fear, but you have received the Spirit of adoption as sons, by whom we cry, 'Abba! Father!'" (Rom. 8:15).

> [W]hen we were children, [we] were enslaved to the elementary principles of the world. But when the fullness of time had come, God sent forth his Son, born of woman, born under the

---

34. Elsewhere (Ouweneel (1995, §4.2) I have followed Herman Dooyeweerd in preferring the logical term "idea" to the linguistic term "metaphor," but here I am employing common theological parlance.
35. See *RT* II/1, chapters 9 and 10, on subordinationism.

law, to redeem those who were under the law, so that we might receive adoption as sons. And because you are sons, God has sent the Spirit of his Son into our hearts, crying, "Abba! Father!" So you are no longer a slave, but a son, and if a son, then an heir through God (Gal. 4:3-7).

Even in the case of believers, sonship is linked with maturation and freedom. This is even clearer in a passage that refers to Jesus himself (Heb. 5:8): "Although [Gk. *kaiper*] he was a son, he learned obedience through what he suffered." This Greek conjunction *kaiper* indicates a contrast between sonship and obedience (submission, subordination). It was not *because* he was ("only") a Son that he had to learn obedience, but *in spite of* his sonship. This clearly shows that sonship—not to be confused with childhood[36]—is linked with equality, not with submission.

7.5.2 Co-Equality

Even the non-Jesus-believing Jews felt very keenly that Jesus' claim of sonship did not make him subordinate to the Father but rather co-equal with him: "This was why the Jews were seeking all the more to kill him, because ... he was even calling God his own Father, making himself equal with God" (John 5:18; cf.10:33; 19:7). Of course, this does not deny that *as a human being*, because of his human condition, Christ stood *under* God. On earth, he was dependent on and submitted to the Father as far as his human *position* was concerned; but this is something very different from being subordinate to the Father as far as his divine *nature* was concerned. John carefully maintains this distinction: on the one hand, he emphasizes the equality of these two divine persons (3:31; 5:17-18, 22-23;

---

36. Jesus is never called "child of God," except where Gk. *pais* apparently has the sense of "servant" (Acts 3:13, 26; 4:27, 30; cf. v. 25!). Believers' childhood refers to (spiritual) birth from God (John 1:12), through which they come to bear the features of God (Eph. 5:1; Phil. 2:14-15; 1 John 3:9-10). This "sonship" refers more to position (Gk. *huiothesia* = being *placed* as sons); it is something that one "receives" (Gal. 4:5), and to which one is "destined" (Eph. 1:5); see *RT* III/4.

8:58; 10:30; 16:15), while on the other hand he shows us Christ as a human being in a position of submission (3:35; 5:19; 8:29; 10:18; 12:49; 14:28; 15:10).

If the names "Father" and "Son" are applicable only *after* the incarnation and do not represent an essential, eternal relationship within the Godhead, then there is no manifestation of God in the flesh. In other words, if the names "Father" and "Son" are only names under which we know these divine persons after the incarnation of the second person of the Godhead, then these names do not express who and what these persons were from eternity. In that case, we do not really know God. We would have some knowledge of his attributes, and perhaps of the fact that God is three persons in one. But we would have no revelation of *who* these persons are, and their relationship to each other. We would have a revelation only of what it pleased God to *become* through the incarnation, namely, Father, Son, and Spirit.

However, this is not at all the message of the New Testament.[37] Believers have been introduced into the *eternal* fellowship of the Father and the Son (cf. John 17:21; 1 John 1:3), not into a fellowship that had been called into existence for the occasion. We are allowed to know how God eternally lived in love, for the relationship between the Father and the Son is an eternal relationship of glory and love (John 17:5, 24, 26). The object of the Father's love, the Son resting in his bosom (John 1:18), was made known to humanity,[38] and by grace believ-

---

[37]. Regarding this extensively, see the Appendix at the end of this book, about the (un)knowability of God. If, according to the traditional doctrine of the divine attributes, God is unknowable in his essence, then so is the Trinity, for nothing can be more proper to his being than his trinity. But in this case, the Father has not revealed the *eternal Son* (Matt. 16:17), nor has the Son revealed the *eternal Father* (Matt. 11:27), but only their post-incarnational relationship.

[38]. Cf. the parallel with John himself: "Just as Jesus, the Son, knows about the mystery of the Father from resting in his heart [John 1:18], so too the Evangelist has gained his intimate knowledge from his inward repose in Jesus' heart [John 13:25]" (Ratzinger [2007, 222–23]).

ers have been introduced into the same love. The Bible does not allow us to rob the Father of the eternal, unspeakable joy of his divine love and fellowship. The names "Father" and "Son" are the very expression of this eternal love relationship between these divine persons: from eternity, the Son was "the Son of his love" (Col. 1:13 NKJV).

7.5.3 God's Self-Revelation

Through the names "Father," "Son," and "Holy Spirit," believers know the three divine persons as they were from eternity in their mutual relationships. Thus, 1 John 1:2 can say that, first, "eternal life"—that is, the Son (5:20)—was "with the Father," and then, secondly, that it was "made manifest to us." This implies that, before it was made manifest, it was with the Father, and thus the Father was already Father before the incarnation of the Son. The fellowship of the Father and the Son (cf. v. 3) was not brought about by the incarnation but was *revealed* through it as something that had existed already."[T]he Son of God appeared" (3:8). He did not *become* Son through the incarnation but was *revealed* through it as the One who had been Son, and still was the Son. Similarly, where Christ revealed the name of the Father (John 17:6) he did not reveal what the first person in the Godhead was pleased to *become* through the incarnation, or what names it pleased him to *adopt*, but Christ revealed *who* this person *was*, and from eternity had *been*: the Father.

This is the ongoing testimony of the New Testament. The subject of eternal election was the God and *Father* of our Lord Jesus Christ (Eph. 1:3-5), and he predestined believers to be conformed to the image of his *Son* (Rom. 8:29). Thus, eternal life consists in believers knowing God as Jesus Christ had known him from eternity: as *Father*, and knowing Jesus Christ as the Father had known him from eternity—as *Son*: "Father, ... this is eternal life, that they know you, the only true God, and Jesus Christ whom you have sent" (John 17:1, 3). Christ was sent into the world by the *Father* (John 5:36-38; 6:44, 57;

8:16, 18; 10:36; 11:42; 12:49; 14:24; 17:3, 8, 18, 21, 23, 25; 20:21; 1 John 4:14);[39] he came (lit., went out) from the *Father* (John 16:28); God sent his *Son* into the world (John 3:17; 1 John 4:9-10; cf. Rom. 8:3; Gal. 4:4; Matt. 23:37 par.).

The name "Son" is primarily a divine name, which had been assigned to him before his incarnation, namely, from eternity. It was the *Son* whom God had "appointed the heir of all things" (Heb. 1:2). Similarly, the *Father* created all things in, through, and for his beloved *Son* (Col. 1:12-16). And if Melchizedek is "resembling the Son of God," this is because of the way he — who was himself an ordinary human — is presented in Genesis 14: ". . . without father or mother or genealogy, having neither beginning of days nor end of life" (Heb. 7:3). As a Man, Jesus definitely had a mother, a genealogy, a beginning of days (when he was born) and an end of life (when he died). But as the eternal Son of God, he did *not* have "beginning of days" or "end of life." From eternity he is the Son, just as the Father from eternity is the Father, both "having neither beginning of days nor end of life."

7.6   The Eternal Father-Son Relationship
7.6.1   John 1:14-18

John 1:14 tells us: "And the Word became flesh and dwelt among us, and we have seen his glory, glory as of the only Son from the Father, full of grace and truth." Notice the beautiful contrast with verse 1: "the Word *was*" stands over against "the Word *became*"; "the Word *with God*" stands over against "the Word *among us*"; "the Word was *God*" stands

---

39. It is true that the disciples were also sent "into the world" (John 17:18), and of course this cannot mean that they came from outside the world; but it is hard to say the same of the Son if he explicitly tells us: "I came *from* the Father [Gk. *para tou patros*, from his presence]," and *thus* I "have come into the world" (16:28). Nor can it be said of the disciples that they came "from above" (cf. 3:31; 8:23), "from heaven" (cf. 3:31; 6:51, 58), or "from the Father" (cf. 1:14; 16:28). The Son being sent does not necessarily point to a subordinate position, essential to his humanity, which is evident from the fact that the Holy Spirit was sent as well, without an incarnation (14:26; 15:26; 16:7; Luke 24:49; Gal. 4:6; 1 Pet. 1:12).

over against "the Word became *flesh*."⁴⁰

The apostles observed the incarnate Word, and perceived his glory through the veil of his flesh (cf. §8.7); and this glory was that of an only Son who had come "from" his Father. In the Man Jesus, they saw the glory of One who eternally had been in the presence of his Father, with the same dignity that the Father possessed, even though, in his humble state, the Son gave all honor to the Father in everything that was revealed in this glory. After this, verse 18 explains how the apostles knew the Word: he was personally known to them as the Son who always⁴¹ was and is in the bosom of the Father, but also had come from him, and through the Spirit had revealed the Father. They knew him as the only Son who had come down from the place that, in a sense, he had never left, the place of perfect nearness to God and of perfect love to God as his Father: in the bosom (at the heart) of the Father.

Today, there is a certain preference for the reading *monogenēs theos* in John 1:18,⁴² so that the translation becomes: "the only God [or the only One, God⁴³] who is in the bosom of the Father" (see §6.6).⁴⁴ If the reading is authentic, it constitutes a remarkable testimony for the eternal deity of the Son alongside the Father. The Man Jesus, the incarnate Word of God, is at the same time the only God who is in the bosom of the Father. *God* (Gk. *theos* without the article) has made known *God* (Gk. *theos* without the article), that is, one divine person has made known another divine person as he knew him from eternity; the Son made known the Father (cf. Matt. 11:27). He made him known, not as he knew him when he was on earth as a Man, but as the *Son* who had come from the presence of

---

40. Brown (1966, 23–24).
41. See the remarkable words in John 3:13, which have been preserved in many, though not in all important manuscripts: the Son of Man "who is in heaven" (Gk. *ho ōn en tōi ouranōi*): the *Man* who spoke with Nicodemus was at the same time *God* the Son in heaven, in the Father's bosom.
42. See Metzger (1975, 198).
43. Berkouwer (1954, 175) drops the commas: ". . . the only begotten Son."
44. Cf. Brown (1994a, 178–79).

the *Father*.

The Greek participle *ho ōn* in John 1:18 indicates the eternal place where the only begotten Son belonged by nature, and which he, as the omnipresent God, had never left. The Greek preposition *eis* does not mean, as has been asserted, that, at a certain moment, the Son *took* his place in the Father's bosom. The Greek preposition *eis* can very well indicate "the place where" or "the condition in which" (cf. Mark 1:9; Acts 8:23). Perhaps it can be best understood as a reference to the position of two persons who are turned toward each other while sitting or reclining at table (cf. Luke 16:22-23; John 13:23).[45] Thus, the picture is that of the Son eternally lying in the bosom of the Father, turned toward him in the perfect enjoyment of their mutual bliss, love, fellowship, and pleasure. Reclining at table and dining together is a common biblical picture of fellowship (Matt. 8:11; Luke 12:37; 13:29). Christ made God known as the One who was in this position: he revealed the Father's heart as the One who had experienced from eternity how this heart beat for *him*.

7.6.2 Only Begotten and Firstborn

The expression "only" or "only begotten" (Gk. *monogenēs*) in John 1:18 deserves our special attention. The root *genos* can have many meanings, including the meaning of "kind" (Matt. 13:47; 17:21; Mark 9:29; 1 Cor. 14:10). The Greek word *monogenēs* has this meaning: "one of its kind," that is, "unique" (NIV: "one and only"). In the New Testament, it is used for an only child, which is unique because this child is the only one bearing the family features (see Luke 7:12; 8:42; 9:38; Heb. 11:17). Five times the expression is applied to Christ (John 1:14, 18; 3:16, 18; 1 John 4:9). It points to him as the unique Son of the Father, the sole representative and expression of God's being and nature. The term indicates that, by nature, he is the Son because of a familial relationship, and that he is unique in this. This renders John 3:16 peculiarly beautiful, for this verse

---

45. Morris (1971, 114 note).

explains that the value and greatness of God's gift lies in the unique sonship of the One given. The same is true for John 3:18 because the expression "the name of the only (begotten) Son" underscores the perfect revelation of God's being and nature. These find expression in the name of him who, precisely because from eternity he stood in a unique relationship to the Father, was given by him as the object of faith.

The more modern translations prefer the rendering "only" (or "unique") to "only begotten," and understandably so. In ordinary Greek, composite words with *-genēs* point to derivation rather than to birth; even without a reference to derivation, *monogenēs* can be used more generally in the sense of "the only one of its kind," "unique," "unmatched," "incomparable."[46] In the Septuagint, the Hebrew word *yachid* is sometimes rendered as *monogenēs* (e.g., Judg. 11:34), but sometimes as *agapētos* ("beloved"; Gen. 22:2, 12, 16; Jer. 6:26; Amos 8:10; Zech. 12:10). Of course, an only child is particularly loved by their parents. Therefore, it has been presumed that the Greek phrase *ho huios mou ho agapētos* ("my beloved Son") in Mark 1:11 and 9:7 (par.)[47] and *ho monogenēs huios* ("the only Son") in John overlap in meaning to some extent. It would go too far, though, to assert that *monogenēs* is only a predicate of value or love. It implies that the eternal relationship of the pre-incarnate second person to the first person in the Godhead is that of an only, unique, beloved Son to his Father.

A comparable but very different term is *prōtotokos*, "firstborn" (from *prōtos*, "first," and *tokos*, "birth, descent, progeny," from *tiktō*, "to give birth"). Jesus was literally the "firstborn" of Mary (Luke 2:7; cf. the literal "firstborn" of Egypt, Heb. 11:28). In a figurative sense, Christ is "the firstborn of all creation" (Col. 1:15), "the firstborn from the dead" (v. 18; cf.

---

46. Büchsel (*TDNT* 4:737–39); he quoted Parmenides, who called Being *monogenēs*, which cannot mean "only *begotten*," because Being is not begotten.
47. Cf. "my chosen Son" in Luke 9:35 (NABRE), which underscores the Father's special affection for his Son (the Received Text has here "my beloved Son" [cf. KJV]).

Rev. 1:5), or in short, "the firstborn" (Heb. 1:6). Once the term is applied to believers in the expression "the assembly [or, church] of the firstborn who are enrolled in heaven" (Heb. 12:23). In this sense of the term, the idea of a figurative birth or begetting is no longer obviously present.[48] This can be illustrated by Psalm 88:28 (LXX; English Bibles: 89:27): "I will make [Gk. *thēsomai*] him the firstborn," in which "making" excludes birth and suggests adoption instead (cf. 2:7). Here, the term implies both that the person concerned is the first in ranking and that he is loved by God (cf. Exod. 4:22, "Israel is my firstborn son"). The latter element, "loved by God," is shared with the term *monogenēs*, but in the element "first in ranking" it differs essentially from it: *monogenēs* is the unique one—there is no other of his kind—but *prōtotokos*, the "first in ranking," suggests that there *are* others, in whose company he takes the prime position.

Because the idea of birth or begetting is wholly absent in *prōtotokos*, the term does not necessarily refer to some earlier moment in time. In Romans 8:29, Christ as the Son is simply the first in ranking within the fellowship of believers. In Colossians 1:18 and Revelation 1:5, though it is true that, within time, Christ was the first to be raised to true resurrection life (other than Lazarus and others), it is at least as important that Christ is the first in ranking and dignity among those who rise from the dead. Similarly, also in the age to come, Christ will be seen as the first in ranking and dignity (Heb. 1:6).

7.6.3 Colossians 1 and Proverbs 8

In this context, Colossians 1:15 ("He is the image of the invisible God, the firstborn of all creation") is no doubt the most difficult Bible passage, and at the same time one of the most important ones for our subject.[49] In the light of the entire New Testament, the verse cannot mean that Christ was born as the first of the entire creation, that is, that he was the first of all

---

48. Cf. Michaelis (*TDNT* 6:874, 877–78).
49. Bruce (1984, 59); cf. extensively, Hockel (1965).

creatures. The verse provides no support for Arianism, for the next verse qualifies the statement by saying: "*For* in him *all things* [without any exception] were created, in heaven and on earth, . . . *all things* were created through him and for him." He can hardly have created himself. He is the firstborn of all creation *because* he is the Creator; that is, if the Creator shares in the creation by becoming Man, he is necessarily the first in ranking among all the creatures. Here again, the term *prōtotokos* primarily indicates the ranking and dignity of Christ: "firstborn *over* all creation" (NIV); "supreme over all creation" (CJB); "superior to all created things" (GNT). He is such because he created all things.

If we include the factor of time, Christ is also the firstborn *before* all creation; as verse 17a says, "He is before all things." He is the One who *was* there when the work of creation began. The line of thought ends in verse 18b: ". . . so that in everything he might have the supremacy." An interesting rabbinic parallel is the description *qadmono shel ʿolam*, "first of the world," used by Rabbi Eleazar ben Rabbi Simeon for God himself.[50]

An interesting question, little discussed in the commentaries, is whether the expression "firstborn of all creation" is applicable to Christ also in his humanity. Some have argued that Adam was the first man, but he was not the firstborn, and could not be such. How could it be said of Christ, whose birth on earth occurred after so many years, that *he* was the firstborn? The truth is that as Son and Heir, he *could* be nothing else when he entered his own creation. It is a matter of ranking, not of time. When he through whom the world had been created shared in creation, he was necessarily the firstborn among all creatures.[51]

At this point we must add a few words on Proverbs 8:22, "The LORD possessed me [i.e., Wisdom] at the beginning of his work, the first of his acts of old." The word "possessed" is the Hebrew word *qanani*, also rendered as "acquired" (CSB). The

---
50. Gen. Rabbah 38.7 [on 11:2]; see Bruce (ibid.).
51. Kelly (1964, 96–97).

Septuagint rendered it as *ektisen me* ("created me," cf. AMP, RSV). The Targum also has a word for "create." This translation is supported by Sirach 1:4, 9 and 24:8, which say that wisdom was "created" by God. The Greek verse led to confusion among the church fathers, who were convinced that the Wisdom in Proverbs 8 is Christ; it also played a great role in the debate with the Arians. No wonder: the passage seemed to say that Christ, who is the true Wisdom of God (1 Cor. 1:24), had been created by God at a certain moment before the foundation of the world. However, some church fathers rightly pointed out that the LXX rendering *ektisen me* was simply incorrect, and suggested its replacement by *ektēsato* ("acquired, possessed"; cf. *possedit* in the Vulgate) in accordance with the Hebrew verb used, *q-n-h*.[52]

There is no reason to render the opening verb in Proverbs 8:22 with any other meaning than "to acquire" or "to possess." However, the rendering "brought forth" is acceptable (cf. NIV; cf. a similar term in v. 25) because it may suggest eternal generation[53] (see next section), whereas "created" would exclude this. The main reason why the Greek phrase *ektisen me* is unacceptable is that it would lead to an objectionable contradiction. In Proverbs 8 Wisdom is primarily a divine attribute, no matter how much it is personified here. The question is how God could have "created" one of his own attributes. Does this mean that during a certain "period" before the foundation of the world, he was not wise, and then created his own wisdom? We may wonder through what wisdom God could have done this. If Proverbs 8 speaks of "bringing forth," this must be eternal generation because God was necessarily wise from eternity. If therefore this wisdom is personified, and this personification is (rightly) applied to Christ,[54] then Christ, too,

---

52. Koehler-Baumgartner (ad loc.) did postulate another verb *q-n-h*, which would mean "to create"; but there is no single verse (except perhaps Ps. 139:13) where *q-n-h* could not possibly mean "to acquire" or "to possess."
53. Here "generation" means "begetting" or "begottenness."
54. For a discussion of this interpretation of Prov. 8, as well as the Sophiological (i.e., Mariological) interpretation, see Ouweneel (1998, 59–66). In brief:

The Deity of Christ

was generated from eternity. This is why Origen was the first to use the passage as an argument for the eternal generation of the Son.[55] We must now deal with this subject a bit more extensively.

7.7 Eternal Generation
7.7.1 Main Arguments

The teaching that the Son was eternally born from, or begotten by, the Father was developed rather early in church history. It was also included in the Nicene Creed: "And in one Lord, Jesus Christ, the only begotten Son of God, born of the Father before all ages. God from God, Light from Light, true God from true God, begotten, not made, one in being with the Father; through whom all things were made" (Lat. *Et in unum Dominum nostrum Jesum Christum, Filium Dei unigenitum, ex Patre natum ante omnia saecula. Deum de Deo, Lumen de Lumine, Deum verum de Deo vero, genitum non factum, consubstantialem Patri; per quem omnia facta sunt*). What are the biblical and theological arguments for this being "born from the Father before all ages" (Origen: *aiōnios gennēsis*, "eternal birth/begottenness")? In addition to the argument given in §7.6.2 based on Proverbs 8, consider the following additional arguments.

First, a generation from eternity necessarily seems to be contained in the notions "Father" and "Son" as such. Why are two eternal, divine persons called Father and Son? These theological metaphors differ from the logical *concepts* of "father" and "son"; that is, they have no masculine gender, there is no sexual intercourse, no involvement of a mother, no rearing of the son, no emancipation of the son with respect to the father, and so on.[56] Nevertheless such metaphors must have

---

Wisdom is either (a) the eternal Torah, or (b) the Sophia who was incarnate in the Virgin Mary, or (c) Jesus Christ.

55. *First Principles* I.2.1–4; also cf. Brown (1994a, 207–10) and Hengel (1995, 212–14) on the identification between *Chokhmah* (Wisdom) and *Logos* (Word) in John 1.
56. Bavinck (*RD* 2:308).

some correspondence with the concepts concerned. The *only* real quality of a father as such, in its original meaning, is that he has begotten a child, and the *only* real quality of a son as such, in its original meaning, is that he is a male descendent. Even if the masculinity and the implied mother are omitted, this essential feature remains: being a descendant. Thus, it seems unavoidable to introduce the idea of a (necessarily eternal) generating, in which the Son has been (or, is being) eternally generated by the Father, not in the logical-conceptual but in the theological-metaphorical sense, yet as an ontic reality. The Father-Son relationship can hardly be only an eternal, intimate love relationship, for in that case it would be totally unclear why the One is called Father, and the other One Son. As far as we can see, the designations could just as well have been reversed, or replaced by a Husband-Wife or a Two-Companions metaphor.

At the same time, we must add that eternal generation is not necessarily the only possible explanation of the Father-Son relationship; in principle, eternal adoption is another option, regardless of how we should construe this.[57] From eternity, the second person of the Godhead would then be described as the Son of the first person of the Godhead, who therefore from eternity bore the name of Father. One argument for this could be that the spiritual sonship of believers in the New Testament, which is modelled after the sonship of Christ, is not connected with begetting and birth but with adoption and position. This is why the Greek word *huiothesia* ("sonship") is often translated "adoption as sons" (Rom. 8:15, 23; Gal. 4:5; Eph. 1:5).[58]

7.7.2 More Arguments

Second, if there were no eternal generation, nor any eternal

---

57. Cf. the parallel with adoption within time in 2 Sam. 7:14 [cf. Heb. 1:5]; Ps. 2:7; 89:26–27.
58. Better "adoption as sons" than "as children"; in volume III/4 of this series, I will deal more extensively with the distinction between (spiritual) "child" and "son."

procession of the Spirit,[59] we could hardly avoid the danger of tritheism.[60] We would still be able to say that the three divine persons share in the same Deity, but how can this Deity be anything more than merely a generic unity of the three persons, such as, for instance, the members of a family? In this case, the three persons are not only distinct but also separated, like the persons in any group within our created world who may belong closely together, yet are separated individuals. We might still confess the "one God," but in what sense would such terminology differ from the statement that husband and wife are "one human being" in the sense of Genesis 1:27 and 2:24? However, if there *is* an eternal generation and an eternal procession, we understand that, within the one Deity, the Father has generated, and generates, the Son from eternity, and the Holy Spirit had proceeded, and proceeds, from eternity from the Father (and the Son?). From eternity to eternity, the Father is the cause (Gk. *aitia*; Lat. *causa*) of the Son, and the Father (and the Son?) is (are?) forever the cause (Gk. *aitia*; Lat. *causa*) of the Holy Spirit.

Nonetheless, this argument of the threat of tritheism is not entirely convincing. The history of theology shows how easily those who emphasize the distinction between the three persons are accused of tritheism, and how easily those who emphasize the unity of the three persons are accused of modalism (see the previous volume). It is not evident *a priori* why the accusation of tritheism in the case of not accepting the idea of an eternal generation and procession is more valid than the accusation of modalism when the idea of an eternal generation and procession *is* accepted. Just as someone teaching the eternal generation and procession can still maintain the distinction between the three hypostases—and thus is not a modalist—similarly someone doubting the eternal generation and procession can still maintain the ontic and numerical unity of the three hypostases—and thus is not a tritheist.

---

59. See *EDR* 1:§1.3) and *RT* II/3.
60. See *RT* II/1:chapters 9 and 10.

A person is not necessarily a modalist if they cannot explain how the Deity can be three distinct persons, just as a person is not necessarily a tritheist if they cannot explain how the three persons can be ontically and numerically one God.

Third, the term *monogenēs*, which literally means "only begotten" or "only-born" (DLNT), has been adduced as an argument for the Son's eternal generation. However, we have seen (§7.6.2) that the term does not necessarily include the idea of birth or begetting; it can refer to what was unbegotten and unborn from eternity (see Parmenides on Being). Only if other arguments point in that direction can the term serve to support the notion of eternal generation. Similarly, in the term *prōtotokos* the element of birth or begetting is never necessarily implied. On the contrary, it is excluded in Psalm 89:27, as we have seen. Christ is the first in ranking and dignity in each domain and in every group, without *prōtotokos* necessarily telling us that he reached this position through eternal generation.

7.7.3 Collateral Arguments

To the main arguments just considered I will add five secondary arguments. Abraham Kuyper pointed to Micah 5:1, where the Hebrew plural *motzaot* ("goings out, origins") is thought to refer to Christ's eternal generation and his eternal appointment as Messiah in the counsel of God.[61] Of course, this is begging the question. An eternal "going out" of the Messiah — whatever this may mean — is not necessarily the Son's eternal "going out" from the Father (see further §6.2.1). C. F. Keil provided a persuasive argument why Micah 5:1, even though it speaks of the Messiah's eternal origin, cannot refer to the Son's eternal generation by the Father.[62] The plural itself, "goings out," seems to imply that, before his birth in Bethlehem, the Messiah had "gone out," in the sense of "appeared," many times. Keil included in these "goings out" an

---

61. Kuyper (*DD* 1:3, 217).
62. Ibid.

eternal "going out" of the Messiah "before all worlds," followed by many "goings out" within time, especially as the Angel of YHWH. But he excluded the Son's eternal generation by the Father, or that of the Logos by God, apparently because eternal generation was seen as an eternally continuous activity, which would conflict with the plural "goings out." Another argument is that a generation of the Son by the Father is far beyond the scope of Micah, or of the Old Testament in general.

Perhaps the most impressive New Testament argument is derived from John 5:26, "[A]s the Father has life in himself, so he has granted the Son also to have life in himself," and John 17:24, ". . . to see my glory that you have given me because you loved me before the foundation of the world." The context makes clear that Jesus is speaking of a life and a glory that have been granted or given to him from eternity. As Augustine remarked, the Father has life in himself, which no one gave him, whereas the Son has life in himself that the Father gave him,[63] and did so from eternity. This glory, and this life that has been granted to the Son from eternity, comes closest to the idea of an eternal generation. A father generates ("gives life to") his son; thus, the Father gives life to his Son from eternity.

According to Kuyper, by far the most important argument for the eternal generation of the Son is based upon Psalm 2:7, "You are my Son; today I have begotten you."[64] In agreement with this, Herman Bavinck suggests that Hebrews 1:5 (cf. vv. 2–3) refers to the eternity when Christ was begotten by the Father as Son.[65] This argument is not very strong, though. There are no special reasons to link Hebrews 1:5 more with verses 2–3 than with Christ's humanity and present position beyond the angels in verses 3b–4. Moreover, Psalm 2 refers primarily to the adoption of David, or of the Davidic king, as son

---

63. Quoted in Morris (1971, 319.
64. Kuyper (*DD* 1:3, 210–20).
65. Bavinck (*RD* 2:274–75).

of God (cf. 2 Sam. 7:14; Ps. 89:26–27). Only secondarily, this can be applied to the Messiah's begetting (cf. Acts 13:33; Heb. 1:5; 5:5; Rev. 2:27; 19:13), which apparently refers to his virgin birth as a human being (cf. Luke 1:35; see §9.1), not necessarily to his eternal generation, which lies far beyond the scope of the Psalm.

Many expositors believe that the phrase in 1 John 5:18b, "he was born of God" (Gk. *ho gennētheis ek tou theou*), refers to Christ.[66] Some versions (e.g., the CJB) translate the phrase as "the Son of God." However, even if this interpretation were correct (such a description for Christ is highly unusual), nothing persuades us to think here of the Son's eternal generation instead of the virgin birth, especially in view of the parallel with believers.[67] If the text is interpreted this way, it is referring to the *Man* Christ Jesus, associated with other people, believers, and not to the eternal Son.

Finally, some believe that in John 1:13 we should read, "he who was born of God" (viz., Christ; Gk. *hos egennēthē*), and not "those who were born of God" (Gk. *hoi egennēthēsan*), although the former textual reading enjoys very little support.[68] Even if this reading were correct, which is highly unlikely, this would point instead to the virgin birth rather than to eternal generation.[69] In my view, "born of *God*" would always refer to the virgin birth; we would need the phrase "born of the *Father*" to accept it as a possible reference to eternal generation.

7.7.4 Evaluation

The results of our investigation are rather meagre. All the more remarkable, then, that the early church spoke about this with such vigor and persuasion. In addition, consider what Herman Bavinck wrote more recently about the Son's eternal generation.

---

66. See Marshall (1978a, 252, and references).
67. Cf. Medema (1993, 220) and Lalleman (2005, 214–15).
68. Büchsel (*TDNT* 4:741).
69. Cf. Morris (1971, 100).

The Deity of Christ

Accordingly, he was not brought forth by the will of the Father out of nothing and in time. Rather, he is generated out of the being of the Father in eternity. Hence, instead of viewing "generation" as an actual work, a performance (Gk. *energeia*), of the Father, we should ascribe to the Father "a generative nature" (Gk. *physis gennētikē*). . . . It is not an act of an antecedent decreeing will, like creation, but one that is so divinely nature to the Father that his concomitant will takes perfect delight in it. . . . We must, accordingly, conceive that generation as being eternal in the true sense of the word. It is not something that was completed and finished at some point in eternity, but an eternal unchanging act of God [the Father; see the next section], at once always complete and eternally ongoing. Just as it is natural for the sun to shine and for a spring to pour out water, so it is natural for the Father to generate the Son. The Father is not and never was ungenerative; he begets everlastingly.[70]

This is all very attractive, but how much of this is biblically-exegetically *warranted*? I prefer openly to confess my doctrinal ignorance than glibly to follow the early creeds and church fathers. The only thing that must and can be absolutely clear is that the divine Son is as eternal as the divine Father. The rest is theological hypothesis—in certain respects, a very satisfactory hypothesis, offering an explanation for certain biblical data, but no more than that. It is certainly not the *only possible* explanation of the biblical data. Therefore, in my view, our hypothetical conclusion in this matter should never be elevated to the status of a faith dogma that is binding upon all Christians, as is in fact the case with the Nicene Creed.

The view of Paul Althaus is quite acceptable, viz., that the idea of eternal generation has no theological warrant, implies an inadmissible application of the father and son metaphors, and inevitably leads to subordinationism (subordination of the Son to the Father). Althaus claimed that theology knows nothing about the generation of the Son, and thus can say

---

70. Bavinck (*RD* 2:309–10).

nothing about it.[71] In my view, no one can refute such statements other than on the basis of ecclesiastical tradition. Moreover, Reformed Christians are undeniably more sensitive about this tradition than Evangelical Christians (who actually often fall into the opposite danger: an ahistorical biblicism).

Interestingly, Justin Martyr compared the generation of the Son with a light that is kindled, and with a word that goes forth from someone's mouth.[72] He used the picture of a fire that kindles another fire, yet remains the same. Tertullian argued that Father and Son cannot be separated, like a trunk and a branch, a well and a stream, the sun and a sunbeam.[73] God generates the Logos like the root generates the fruit, the well brings forth the river, and the sun produces the beam. Athanasius argued that, just as the sun is inconceivable without light, and the well without water, so the Father is inconceivable without the Son. The Father always speaks, that is, the Word always was and is with him.[74] Just as it is the property of the sun to radiate the light, and of the well to produce the stream, so too generation is characteristic of the Father. He never was, and never will be, without generation; his generation is speaking, that is, producing the Word, and as his speaking is eternal, so too his generating is eternal.[75] We could think here of the Son as the "radiation" (Gk. *apaugasma*) of God's glory (Heb. 1:3).

If there is truth in the hypothesis of the Son's eternal generation, these are all useful and beautiful pictures—but no more than that.

---

71. Althaus (1952, 698).
72. *Apology* II.6; *Dialogue with Trypho* 61.100.128.
73. *Adversus Praxean* 2v.
74. *Against Arius* II.2; *To Serapion* II.2.
75. Bavinck pointed here to Origen, Athanasius, John of Damascus, Augustine, Thomas Aquinas, Amandus Polanus, Gisbertus Voetius, the *Synopsis* (Polyander, et al. [1625]), and J. H. Scholten (*RD* 2:310); see Velde (2015).

7.8 The Father and the Son
7.8.1 Subordinationism

As we now investigate the biblical revelation concerning God the Father and God the Son more closely, we remember that the Father can be known as Father only in relation to the Son. Therefore, much that would need saying in this respect has been said in previous sections. However, several remaining points deserve our attention now.

The name "Father" is associated with the person within the Deity who is traditionally called the "first" person. In a certain sense, "God" can be viewed as the name of a "person" as well, but not as the exclusive name of one of the three persons. The three are one God, that is, they share in one divine being. Bavinck noted that the designation "God" is not a proper name;[76] this is correct insofar as the Hebrew term *elohim* and Greek term *theos* are generic designations. Therefore, the Bible also speaks of "gods"; God is the "God of gods" (Deut. 10:17; Josh. 22:22; Ps. 136:2; Dan. 2:47; 11:36). YHWH *is* a proper name; it is the name of the person whom we call God, that is, the Triune God. The name YHWH may never be attributed exclusively to the Father; it belongs to the Son and the Spirit as well. With regard to the Son, we saw this in §§6.2–6.5 above; as for the Spirit: the YHWH of Isaiah 6 is called the Holy Spirit in Acts 28:26-27.[77]

What basis exists for the traditional reference to the Father as the "first" person of the Deity? The Bible does not contain any numerical designations for the three divine persons. There is no objection against such designations as such; sometimes they are a help if we must avoid the terms "Father" or "Son" in a certain formulation. However, when the word "first" refers to some *primacy* of the Father, some measure of subordinationism is inevitable.[78] We may wonder whether this is not inherent to traditional trinitarianism. If the Father has

---

76. Bavinck (*RD* 2:307).
77. *EDR* 1:§3.2; see also *RT* II/3.
78. Cf. Trillhaas (1972, 113).

the active properties (Lat. *notiones*) of generation and procession, but the Son has only one active property of procession and one passive property of generation, and the Spirit only one passive property of procession, does this not tend toward ontic subordinationism within the Deity? Though we might reject Schleiermacher's view of the Trinity, in this respect he had a point.[79] Moreover, in the thinking of many believers, it seems self-evident that, where the Bible speaks of God Almighty or of YHWH, the Father is meant.[80] This is not always wrong, but neither is it always correct (see §7.1.1 on linking the title "Almighty" to Jesus Christ).

Despite the frequent warnings against subordinationism by traditional trinitarianism, the latter did not always remain free of the former. Bavinck's claim that "both in the Old and in the New Testament, God is the Father who occupies the first place"[81] is linked to a number of Bible passages that do not mention the Father, but do mention God. In some passages this clearly refers to the Father, namely, where his relationship to the Son is involved; we should not forget that, in the Bible, the Son is usually called the Son of *God*, and only once the Son of the *Father* (2 John 3). However, in many cases we must think instead of the Triune God. John 12:41 is a key verse. Tending toward subordinationism is also Bavinck's claim that "[t]he name 'God,' ascribed to the Father in particular, means that in the divine economy he is first. It is an official title, as it were, a designation of his rank and position, just as among humans, all of whom participate in the same nature, there are nevertheless distinctions of social standing and honor."[82]

Similarly, Walter Kaiser continually referred to "God the Father" in a number of cases where one should speak instead

---

79. Schleiermacher (1928, 743–44).
80. Cf. the Apostles' Creed: "I believe in God, the Father Almighty"; the Nicene Creed: "We believe in one God, the Father Almighty."
81. Bavinck (*RD* 2:272).
82. Ibid., 273.

of the Triune God.[83] The danger of subordinationism exists also in the statement by A. van de Beek that "the texts about the subjection and obedience of Christ should not be placed over against his divinity, but his perfect representation of God should be seen precisely *in* his subjection and obedience."[84] But how can one view Jesus' deity in his submission other than in the sense of the Son's subordination to the Father?

The principal basis for the logical primacy of the Father — *not* primacy in ranking — lies in the doctrine of the eternal generation of the Son. If the Son is eternally generated by the Father, the Father is logically (not chronologically!) the first, and the Son is the second. And if the Holy Spirit proceeds eternally from the first and the second persons, he is logically the third. Moreover, there is a logical order in the *works* of the Deity. If all things are *from* (Gk. *ek*) the Father, as their origin, he is logically the first. If all things are *through* (Gk. *dia*) the Son, as the Mediator through whom the things that are from the Father are brought about, he is logically the second (cf. 1 Cor. 8:6). And if all things that are from the Father and are brought about through the Son are brought about *in* the power of (Gk. *en*, i.e., *en instrumentalis*) the Holy Spirit, he is logically the third (cf. Luke 4:1; Eph. 2:18).

However, here again we must not exaggerate these distinctions. Colossians 1:16 says that all things were created "through" (Gk. *dia*), but also "in" (Gk. *en*), and even "(un)to" or "for" (Gk. *eis*) Christ. This seems sufficient reason to understand Romans 11:36 to be referring to the Triune God and not only to the Father: "[F]rom [Gk. *ex*] him and through [Gk. *dia*] him and to [Gk. *eis*] him are all things."

7.8.2 Synergy

All three persons of the Deity are inseparably involved in all the divine works; as tradition states it: "the works of the Trinity are outwardly undivided" (Lat. *opera trinitatis ad extra sunt*

---

83. Kasper (1983, Part II, chapter 1).
84. Van de Beek (2002a, 129).

indivisa). But this does not deny the clear distinction in the contribution to these works made by each of the divine persons. I have discussed this elsewhere with regard to the Holy Spirit,[85] and now do so more specifically with regard to the Father and the Son.[86]

(a) *Creation*. All things are from the Father and through the Son (cf. 1 Cor. 8:6); all things were made through the Logos (John 1:3; cf. Col. 1:16; Heb. 1:2). However, this does not mean that the Son created everything. When we use the active voice to say, "God created all things" (Eph. 3:9), we can state this with the passive voice: "[A]ll things were created by God." In the latter phrase, the Greek would not use the preposition *dia* (which means "through"), but *hypo*. But when the reference is to Christ, invariably the Greek preposition *dia* or *en* is used, never *hypo*. We can say that the world was created "by (*hypo*) God," but not that it was created "by (*hypo*) the Son/the Word," only "through (*dia*)" or "in (*en*) the Son/the Word." It is therefore incorrect to translate "*by* him were all things created" (Col. 1:16) instead of "*in* him," in the power of his person.[87] Equally incorrect is the KJV and others that render "all things were made *through* him" as "*by* him" (John 1:3). Not the Son, or the Word, created all things but *God* created all things *through* the Son, or the Word.

(b) *Reconciliation*. God gives his Son (John 3:16; Rom. 8:32), the Father commands him to lay down his life (John 10:17–18). Noteworthy is Colossians 1:19–20, "[I]n him all the fullness of God was pleased to dwell, and through him to reconcile to himself all things." In fact, the text says "the Fullness." This is the fullness not of the Father,[88] but of the Deity, as in chapter 2:9; strictly speaking, this is the Triune God. This means that it

---

85. *EDR* 1:§3.2.30.
86. Cf. Chafer (1983, 305–308).
87. Surprisingly the AMP, BRG, Darby, ESV, GNV, (N)KJV, and NASB are all mistaken here.
88. This is the erroneous rendering of the NKJV (and many others): "For it pleased [the Father that] in Him all the fullness should dwell."

The Deity of Christ

pleased all the fullness of the Triune God to dwell in the *Man Christ Jesus* (viz., in his body, 2:9), while this Man *is* at the same time the Son of God, that is, one of the persons within the Trinity.[89] Indeed, it can be said of Christ that he came to "reconcile us both [i.e., Jew and Gentile] to God in one body through the cross" (Eph. 2:16). But, as with creation, it is said that, "while we were enemies we were reconciled to God by [through, Gk. *dia*] the death of his Son. . . . [W]e also rejoice in God through [Gk. *dia*] our Lord Jesus Christ, through [Gk. *dia*] whom we have now received reconciliation" (Rom. 5:10–11). ". . . God, who through [Gk. *dia*] Christ reconciled us to himself and gave us the ministry of reconciliation; that is, in Christ God was reconciling the world to himself" (2 Cor. 5:18–19).

(c) *Resurrection and ascension.* It is noteworthy that, in all redemptive actions, Christ is presented as both passive and active.[90] In my view, the former is more related to his human, the latter more to his divine nature. He was given up, or delivered (Gk. *[para]didōmi*), by God (John 3:16; Rom. 8:32; cf. 1 John 4:9–10), but he also *gave himself* (Matt. 20:28; Mark 10:45; Gal. 1:4; 2:20; Eph. 5:2, 25; 1 Tim. 2:6; Titus 2:14). He was killed by people (Acts 2:23; 3:15; 5:30; 7:52; 10:39), and in a sense killed by God (Ps. 22:15), but he also *laid down his own life* (John 10:11, 15, 17a; 15:13; 1 John 3:16). He was raised by God from the dead (Matt. 16:21; 17:23; 20:19 par.; Acts 2:24, 32; 3:15; 4:10; 5:30; 10:40; 13:30; 17:31; Rom. 6:4; Eph. 1:20; Col. 2:12), but he also *raised himself* (Luke 24:7, 46; Rom. 1:4).[91] He

---

89. Kelly (1964, 99–100).
90. Cf. Berkouwer (1965, 211).
91. This distinction is based on the difference between Gk. *egeirō* and *anhistēmi*, but I admit that this difference is not large; the translations often render them both with "to rise" and "to raise." Ordinary people also "rise" from the dead (Mark 12:23, 25). Unequivocal are two passages: John 2:19, 21 ("Jesus answered them, 'Destroy this temple, and in three days I will raise it up.' . . . But he was speaking about the temple of his body") and 10:17–18 ("For this reason the Father loves me, because I lay down my life that I may take it up again. No one takes it from me, but I lay it down of my own accord. I have authority to lay it down, and I have authority to take it up again").

was taken up by God into heaven (Mark 16:19; Luke 24:51; Acts 1:1, 9, 11, 22; 1 Tim. 3:16), but he also *went up himself* to heaven (John 6:62; Eph. 4:8–10; 1 Pet. 3:22). He was seated by God at his right hand (Eph. 1:20), but he also *sat down himself* at God's right hand (Mark 16:19; Heb. 1:3; 8:1; 10:12; 12:2).

(d) *Other actions.* The Holy Spirit is given and sent by the Father (John 14:16, 26), but also sent by the Son from the Father (15:26). As the Father raises the dead and gives them life, so also the Son gives life to whom he will (5:21). Both the Father and the Son make their home with the believer (14:23). That is, the one God and Father of all believers is over all and through all and in all (i.e., all believers[92]) (Eph. 4:6), but the Son also dwells in the believers (3:17). It is said of God in general (2 Cor. 3:6), and of Christ in particular (1 Tim. 1:12), that he appoints people to ministry. Paul calls himself an apostle through (Gk. *dia*) Jesus Christ and God the Father (Gal. 1:1). In the diversity of ministries and services we recognize the one Lord and also the one God (1 Cor. 12:5–6). The church is God's people (Acts 15:14; 1 Pet. 2:10), but also Christ's people (Titus 2:14). It is the church of God (Acts 20:28), but also of Christ (Rom. 16:16). The church is the house or temple of God (1 Cor. 3:16; 2 Cor. 6:16; Eph. 2:22; 1 Tim. 3:15), but also the body of Christ (Rom. 12:5; 1 Cor. 12:27; Eph. 1:22–23; 4:12; 5:30; Col. 1:18, 24). Believers are sanctified by God the Father (Jude 1), but also by Christ (Eph. 5:26; Heb. 2:11). They are safely kept in the Father's hand (John 10:29), but also in the Son's hand (v. 28).

7.8.3 The Three Together

In addition to the examples just mentioned, the three persons are often mentioned together,[93] at least if we accept that in

---

92. Variant reading: "above all, and through all, and in you [or, us] all," which is sometimes taken to mean that God is above and through all *people*, but only *in* the believers (cf. John Gill, https://biblehub.com/commentaries/ephesians/4-6.htm).
93. It is therefore rather strange that, according to Trillhaas (1972, 107), only four clear passages can be adduced as a basis for the doctrine of the Trinity:

such enumerations "God" usually refers to the Father. Let me begin with the baptismal formula of Matthew 28:19, ". . . baptizing them in [or, into] the name of [a] the Father and of [b] the Son and of [c] the Holy Spirit."

In Romans 1:1–4 we hear about the gospel of [a] God, concerning [b] his Son Jesus Christ, who was declared to be the Son of God in power according to [c] the Spirit of holiness by his resurrection from the dead. In 8:3–4 we find [a] God, [b] his own Son, and [c] the Spirit. In 8:11 and 15:16, 30, [b] Jesus Christ, [a] God, and [c] the Spirit are mentioned together.

In 1 Corinthians 12:3–6 we hear about [c] the Spirit, [b] the Lord, and [a] God. In 2 Corinthians 1:19–22, we find [a] God, [b] the Son of God, and [c] the Spirit, and in 13:14, [b] the Lord Jesus Christ, [a] God, and [c] the Holy Spirit. In Galatians 4:6–7, we find [a] God the Father, [b] Christ, and [c] the Spirit of God's Son (cf. Rom. 8:15–17).

Ephesians 1:3–14 begins with [a] the God and Father of [b] our Lord Jesus Christ, and leads to the sealing with [c] the Holy Spirit. In verse 17 we find [a] the God of [b] our Lord Jesus Christ, the Father of glory, who gives [c] the Spirit[94] of wisdom and of revelation. In 4:4–6, we hear about [c] the one Spirit, [b] the one Lord, and [a] the one God and Father of all.

In 2 Thessalonians 2:13, Paul refers to [a] God, [b] the Lord, and [c] the Spirit. In Titus 3:4–6, we find the love of [a] God, who has renewed us by [c] the Holy Spirit, whom he poured out on us richly through [b] Jesus Christ our Savior.

Hebrews 10:29–31 speaks of [b] the Son of God, [c] the Spirit of grace, and [a] the living God. In 1 Peter 1:2 we hear of the elect according to the foreknowledge of [a] God the Father, in the sanctification of [c] the Spirit, for obedience to [b] Jesus Christ. In 4:14 we find that upon those who are insulted

---

Matt. 28:19; 1 Cor. 12:3–6; 2 Cor. 13:13, and Eph. 4:4–6. This biblical basis is not at all restricted to one or a few passages but is found throughout all of Scripture. But when it comes to passages, I supply in the text many more in which we find the three divine persons together.

94. See for the uppercase "S," *EDR* 1:80, 129, 203, and *RT* II/3.

for the name of [b] Christ rests [c] the Spirit of glory and of [a] God. The ancient insertion in 1 John 5:7 says, "[T]here are three that bear witness in heaven: the Father, the Word, and the Holy Spirit; and these three are one."[95] In Revelation 1:4–6, we hear of [c] the seven spirits[96] before the throne, and of [b] Jesus Christ, and of [a] his God and Father.

In all these passages, not only is the unity of the three divine persons being implicitly emphasized, but light is shed also on the distinction between the three persons and their works.[97] It is the Father sending the Son into the world, not the Spirit; and it is the Father and the Son sending the Spirit into the world, not the reverse. It is the Son who became flesh and sacrificed himself, not the Father or the Spirit. It was the Holy Spirit who was poured out, not the Father or the Son. We call upon the Father in the name of the Son, not the reverse, and not in the name of the Spirit either (John 16:23, 26). In the consummation, it is the Son who is subordinated to the Father, not the reverse (1 Cor. 15:28). However, with these distinctions we must not move to the other extreme. We must always keep the balance between both the unity in the trinity, and the trinity in the unity. In none of the works of each of the three divine persons does the person involved ever stand alone. As a Man, Christ says on the cross: "My God, my God, why have you forsaken me?" (Matt. 27:46; Mark 15:34; cf. Ps. 22:1). But as the Son, he says a little earlier: "Behold, the hour is coming, indeed it has come, when you will be scattered, each to his own home, and will leave me alone. Yet I am not alone, *for the Father is with me*" (John 16:32). This is why we should not say that the Son was forsaken on the cross by "the Father"; we have no warrant for such a statement.

---

95. Even though it is highly unlikely that this phrase is authentic, it nonetheless forms a very ancient testimony to the doctrine of the Trinity in the early church; cf. Metzger (1975, 715–17); see also the note in the NKJV.
96. Translations alternate between "spirits" and "Spirits"; not all expositors agree that the Holy Spirit is meant here.
97. Cf. Schlink (*RGG* 6:1035–36).

Chapter 8
The Humanity of Christ

He was manifested in the flesh,
   vindicated by the Spirit,
   seen by angels,
proclaimed among the nations,
   believed on in the world,
   taken up in glory.

1 Timothy 3:16

8.1 Human Properties
8.1.1 Youth and Relatives

IN THIS AND the following chapters, we will be discussing the *Man* Jesus Christ. First, we will discuss his *person* (chapters 8–10), then his *life* (chapter 11), and then his *death* and *resurrection* (chapter 12).

In the New Testament, that Jesus is truly Man is just as important as that he is truly God.[1] This is because only as a Man he could be the mediator between God and humanity (1 Tim. 2:5). The apostle John says that one who denies this true

---

1. Pope Leo the Great, *Sermon 7 on the Birth* (*Patrologia Latina* 54.216), "It is an equally dangerous evil to deny the truth of the human nature in Christ as to refuse to believe that his glory is equal to that of the Father."

humanity of Jesus is in the grip of the spirit of the Antichrist (1 John 4:2-3; 2 John 1:7). God became *flesh* (John 1:14), which involves his entering into and sharing total human existence. The entire fullness of God dwells in Jesus *bodily* (Col. 2:9), that is, in the *Man* Jesus, even now, after his ascension. It is also as a *Man* — more concretely, as the Son of Man — that he will come again, as he himself testified several times (Matt. 10:23; 13:40-41; 16:27-28; 19:28; 24:27, 30, 37, 39, 44; 25:31; 26:64 par.). In the Gospels, the title "Son of Man" is linked with (a) Jesus' authority on earth (e.g., Mark 2:10, 28 par.), (b) his sufferings, death, and resurrection (e.g., Mark 8:31; 9:9; 10:33 par.; also Matt. 8:20; see how in 25:34-40 the Son of Man identifies himself with those who are hungry, thirsty, strangers, poor, sick, and prisoners), and (c) his second coming (e.g., Mark 8:38; 13:26 par.).[2]

Many times, Jesus calls himself the Son of Man, and sometimes simply "man" (Matt. 4:4; John 8:40), and others call him "man" (Matt. 26:72, 74 par.; Mark 15:39; Luke 23:4, 6, 14, 47; John 4:29; 5:12; 7:46; 9:11, 16, 24; 10:33; 11:47; 18:17, 29; Acts 5:28; Rom. 5:15; 1 Cor. 15:21; 1 Tim. 2:5), with as a highlight the almost prophetic statement of Pilate, "Behold the man" (John 19:5; Latin: *Ecce Homo*, a well-known theme in the visual arts).

In the Gospels, there is a constant tension between Jesus being an ordinary man while at the same time being so much more than that. Like every other human being, he was born of a mother (Matt. 1:25; Luke 2:6-7), and in this respect he is more man than Adam was.[3] As a child, he increased in wisdom and in stature, and was submissive to his earthly parents, like any other ordinary child (Luke 2:40, 51-52; cf. 1 Sam. 2:26). He knew the games that children played on the streets

---

2. See Hengel (1995, 58–63); Kärkkäinen (2003, 26); Ratzinger (2007, 328); Sjöberg (1955); Goppelt (1981, 178–90).
3. Actually, Adam was from the earth (*matter*), which is also a "mother" (Lat. *mater*); see the remarkable parallel between the earth and the womb in Job 1:21 and Ps. 139:13–15.

(Matt. 11:16–17). He was the (legal) son of a carpenter (13:55), was himself a carpenter (Mark 6:3), and during eighteen years (from his twelfth to his thirtieth) was active in a nondescript, but local town in Galilee (Matt. 2:23; John 1:45–46; cf. 7:41, 52). He belonged to an ordinary family with parents, brothers, and sisters; four of his brothers are known to us: James, Joseph (or Joses), Judas, and Simon (Matt. 13:55–56; Mark 6:3). Apparently, he shared positive experiences with this family: "If a son asks for bread from any father among you, will he give him a stone? Or if [he asks] for a fish, will he give him a serpent instead of a fish? Or if he asks for an egg, will he offer him a scorpion?" (Luke 11:11–12 NKJV).

As for the familial status of his biological brothers and sisters, according to Eastern Orthodox tradition, these were children of Joseph from an earlier marriage, and thus were Jesus' stepbrothers and stepsisters. According to Roman Catholic tradition, these were sons of Mary's sister, and thus cousins of Jesus. An argument for the latter could be that the Mary who was the sister of the Virgin Mary (Jesus' mother) and Clopas' wife was probably the same as Mary, the mother of James and Joseph/Joses, who could have been identical with Jesus' biological brothers (cf. John 19:25 with Matt. 27:56, 61; 28:1 and Mark 15:40, 47; 16:1). Note as well that Jesus' brothers seem to be older than he because they try to control him (Matt. 12:46–47 par.; John 7:3–4), and Mary does not seem to have other children of her own because on the cross Jesus entrusts her to the apostle John (John 19:25–27).[4] It is remarkable that all names of Jesus and his relatives are found in the Hexateuch (Gen. – Josh.): Jesus = Joshua; James = Jacob; Mary = Miriam. Joses (= Joseph), Sim(e)on, and Judas (= Judah) were originally sons of the patriarch Jacob. The custom of naming children after the patriarchs arose during the Maccabean period (among the sons of the priest Mattathias were Simon and Judas).

---

4. See the discussion by Meier (1991, 318–32); Stein (1996, 82–84); Bloesch (1997, 87–88); Van Bruggen (1998, chapter 5).

8.1.2 Humanness

Jesus' ordinary humanness is so impressive. The God whom the world cannot contain, more precisely God the Son, chose to dwell for nine months in the womb of a virgin. He chose to be cared for by human parents, and to obey them. He who *is* the eternal Torah submitted himself as a Man to his own Torah. God not only *became* human, he voluntarily *submitted* to humans: to his parents (Luke 2:51), and to the authorities (Matt. 17:24-27; John 19:11). In the midst of a world in which so many people strive to become as great as possible, God became a *child*. He said, "Assuredly, I say to you, unless you are converted and become as little children, you will by no means enter the kingdom of heaven. Therefore, whoever humbles himself as this little child is the greatest in the kingdom of heaven" (Matt. 18:3-4) — but no one ever *became* a child as literally, as radically as he did. We may try to become like children in the spiritual sense, but not in the physical sense, for our existence *began* with childhood. God *became* a child in the most absolute sense of the word. Thus, he became what the child is: unpretentious, capable of wonder, capable of a childlike trust in people.

There was a time when humans strove to become "God" (Gen. 3:5), and they still do. This means trying to become what people associate with deity: complete power, perfect knowledge, emancipation, self-realization. But the miracle happened: God instead became a human being, and this entailed obedience and submission. Hence it was easy for him who was once a child himself to welcome and bless other children: "And he took a child and put him in the midst of them, and taking him in his arms, he said to them, 'Whoever receives one such child in my name receives me, and whoever receives me, receives not me but him who sent me'" (Mark 9:36-37). "Let the children come to me; do not hinder them, for to such belongs the kingdom of God. Truly, I say to you, whoever does not receive the kingdom of God like a child shall not enter it" (10:14-15).

Jesus became like human beings in every respect (Phil. 2:7; Heb. 2:17), and in all things he was tempted like other people, but was without sin (Heb. 4:15; see chapter 10). He experienced hunger (Matt. 4:2; Mark 11:12; Luke 4:2; cf. Mark 3:20; 6:31) and thirst (John 19:28; cf. 4:7), and he ate and drank (Mark 2:15-16; 14:18, 22; Luke 7:34, 36; 24:42-43). He experienced weariness after walking (John 4:6), and after becoming tired he knew the refreshment of sleep (Mark 4:38 par.). In his weak moments, he was strengthened by an angel from heaven (Luke 22:43). He broke down under the heavy cross (cf. Matt. 27:32). We do read, though, that he "bore" our diseases (Matt. 8:16-17), but not that he himself ever became sick. Is this self-evident? In other words, are hunger, thirst, and fatigue "sinless" weaknesses that are simply proper to our humanity, whereas illnesses—think of the common childhood diseases—are a consequence of the Fall?

I do not find this distinction adequate.[5] Could not hunger, thirst, and fatigue be viewed as consequences of the Fall as well, especially in the light of Genesis 3:19a ("By the sweat of your face you shall eat bread")? And if Jesus knew these things from experience, why did he not also experience ordinary ailments and aging symptoms? In John 8:57, the Jews estimated Jesus to be almost fifty years old, whereas perhaps he was only thirty-three; his life afflictions had possibly given him an older appearance. We can offer nothing more than this kind of (speculative) consideration when it comes to whether Jesus was ever ill. At any rate, not all disease is a consequence of personal sin.[6]

8.1.3 The "Ordinary" Jesus

Especially conservative Christians have a bit of trouble with any talk of the "ordinary" Jesus. Some believers project the image of the glorified Christ back upon his public ministry, and imagine that he walked through Galilee with an aura around

---

5. *Contra* Jennings (1966, 619).
6. Ouweneel (2004, chapter 7).

him, almost wearing a halo. They cannot imagine Jesus as someone who in many respects was just like other humans, and they are embarrassed by Gospel references to Jesus as someone who got tired, became morose, was inconspicuous in a crowd, and was treated as a fanatic and a demagogue.[7]

How human Jesus was is apparent in particular from the fact that he suffered physically, and underwent physical death ("yielded up his spirit," Matt. 27:50; GNT: "breathed his last"), just like every human being. The thoroughly human element in this is expressed in the statement that Jesus "was crucified in weakness" (2 Cor. 13:4) — a weakness that is placed on the same level with *our* human weakness (cf. also 12:9).[8] After his resurrection he remained entirely human: he could be touched and held (Matt. 28:9; John 20:17, 27), he reclined at table with his followers (Acts 1:4 NIV), and he ate and drank with them (Luke 24:42-43; Acts 10:41). He breathed on his disciples, and laid his hands upon them (John 20:23; Luke 24:50).[9] Both before his death and after his resurrection, John's statement was true: "That which was from the beginning, which we have heard, which we have seen with our eyes, which we looked upon and have touched with our hands, concerning the word of life..." (1 John 1:1). Over against the thought that Jesus was a phantasm (ghost), we hear the Savior's reassuring word: "It is I" (Mark 6:49-50).

Jesus' true humanity implies that he is a human being who can be identified in space and time. The Apostles' Creed, which is so full of mysteries, suddenly gives him an identification in time by telling us that he "suffered under Pontius Pilate." Why does this disturbing and dishonorable name appear in this short creed? Precisely because it identifies Jesus'

---

7. Brown (1994a, 27). Cf. the debates as to whether modern Bible translations in which Jesus is speaking ordinary, everyday language are irreverent.
8. Modern forms of Docetism still cannot accept that Jesus could suffer, like Christian Science (Mary Baker Eddy) and Transcendental Meditation (Maharishi Mahesh Yogi); cf. Bloesch (1997, 58–59).
9. Regarding the *differences* between Jesus' body before his death and after his resurrection, see §13.7 below.

place in history. As the apostolic father Ignatius wrote in his letter to the Trallians: Jesus "was descended from David, and was also of Mary; he was truly born, and ate and drank. He was truly persecuted under Pontius Pilate; he was truly crucified, and [truly] died, in the sight of beings in heaven, and on earth, and under the earth. He was also truly raised from the dead."[10]

The facts of his life concretely took place at the beginning of the present era, in an identifiable country: Israel, and in identifiable towns: Bethlehem, Nazareth, Cana, Capernaum, Jericho, Jerusalem, and others. We learn his name: friend and enemy, and even the evil spirits, call him Jesus of Nazareth or Jesus the Nazarene (Mark 1:9, 24; 10:47; 14:67; 16:6 par.). Although it is possible that our very reverence for Jesus arouses some Docetism in every orthodox heart, the visitor to Israel today can suddenly realize with a shock: he walked *here*, he spoke *here*, he suffered *here*.[11] Christian painter Rien Poortvliet beautifully expressed it in the title of one of his books: *He Was One of Us*.[12]

The modesty in every orthodox heart prevents us from speaking, for instance, about Jesus' sexuality. On the one hand, could he be truly human if he did not have a normally developed sexuality? On the other hand, it is difficult for us, sinners, to imagine that *this Jesus* was truly a Man who could look at a woman without any lustful intent (cf. Matt. 5:28).

8.1.4 Human Soul/Spirit

It is part of Christ's true humanity that he possesses not only a human body but also a human soul and a human spirit. Behind this manner of speaking lies a passage like 1 Thessalonians 5:23, "[M]ay your whole spirit and soul and body be kept blameless at the coming of our Lord Jesus Christ." It is impossible to derive from such a statement an anthropolog-

---

10. http://www.newadvent.org/fathers/0106.htm.
11. Jager (n.d.).
12. Poortvliet (2004).

ical trichotomy (or, a dichotomy), just as we can derive no tetrachotomy from Luke 10:27, "You shall love the Lord your God with all your heart and with all your soul and with all your strength and with all your mind." This is not the place to deal with this matter,[13] nor can we enter here into the multitude of meanings that the terms "soul" and "spirit" can have.[14] Here we can merely state the fact that the New Testament distinguishes in Jesus a soul and a spirit in a clearly human sense, which underscores[15] his true humanity.

The expression "my soul" often means nothing more than "I" or "me" (cf., e.g., Ps. 6:3; 16:10; 34:2; 143:6),[16] and "my spirit" often means the same (Ps. 77:3, 6; 142:3; 143:4). In other passages this may be the case too, such as, "My soul magnifies the Lord, and my spirit rejoices in God my Savior" (Mary in Luke 1:46-47). I think of Jesus' soul: "My soul is very sorrowful, even to death" (Matt. 26:38 par.). "Now is my soul troubled. And what shall I say?" John 12:27). At another place, the term "soul" or "spirit" clearly refers to Jesus' human life: "[Y]ou will not abandon my soul to Hades" (Acts 2:27). "Jesus . . . yielded up his spirit" (Matt. 27:50). "Father, into your hands I commit my spirit!" (Luke 23:46); "he bowed his head and gave up his spirit" (John 19:30).

In other passages, Jesus' inner being (his deliberations, emotions, decisions) as Man are involved: "[T]he child grew and became strong in spirit" (Luke 1:80). "Jesus, perceiving in his spirit . . ." (Mark 2:8); "he sighed deeply in his spir-

---

13. See extensively Ouweneel (1986a, chapters 5 and 6; 2007, chapters 5–8; 2018, chapter 6).
14. See Ouweneel (1984, §2.3.3).
15. The word "proves" would be too strong because, remarkably enough, the Bible sometimes also speaks of *God's* soul (Isa. 1:14; Matt. 12:18) and spirit (Gen. 6:3). Human body parts are ascribed to God, like hair (Dan. 7:9), a mouth (Deut. 8:3), a nose (33:10), nostrils (Exod. 15:8), arms (Deut. 33:27), hands (2:15), fingers (Exod. 8:19), feet (Ps. 18:9), eyes (2 Chron. 16:9), and ears (Num. 11:1).
16. Sometimes, the text says "my glory (or, honor)" (Heb. *Kevodi*; Ps. 4:2; 16:9; 57:8; 108:1), which some translations sometimes render as "my soul."

it" (8:12). "Jesus ... was deeply moved [or, indignant] in his spirit" (John 11:33). "Jesus was troubled in his spirit" (13:21). Of course, this human "spirit" of Christ must be carefully distinguished from him as the "life-giving spirit" (1 Cor. 15:45) as well as from the divine "Spirit of Jesus/Christ" (Acts 16:7; Rom. 8:9; Phil. 1:19; 1 Pet. 1:11), that is in fact none other than the Holy Spirit.[17]

In Apollinarianism, named after Apollinaris of Laodicea, the human soul/spirit of Jesus is denied. The Logos, or the Son, is thought to have been the spirit of Jesus' human body. The ultimate consequence of this is that Jesus was not truly a human being because he possessed only a human body, not a human soul/spirit. Scripture teaches us otherwise: at the very place where Jesus' own soul comes into the foreground, and is sharply distinguished from God, the humanity of his soul comes to light in the clearest way. When he exclaimed, with all his soul, in the deepest anguish: "My God, my God, why have you forsaken me?," it was not Jesus viewed according to his deity who is calling; it was his human soul crying out. Never was his soul more human than at this moment, so to speak. Denying that Jesus possesses a human soul/spirit is the same as denying that he knows genuine human feelings and inner experiences, and that is the same as denying his humanity.

8.2   Human Knowledge
8.2.1   Perfect Knowledge

It is remarkable to see how much Jesus knew about things from the past, or about things happening simultaneously somewhere else, or about things in the future. Some examples:

(a) *Past things.* Jesus had never met the Samaritan woman before, but he knew about her past (John 4:18). Jesus knew about Nathanael sitting under the fig tree before Philip called him (John 1:47-50).

---
17. See *EDR* 1.

(b) *Simultaneous things.* "Jesus, perceiving in his spirit that they thus questioned within themselves . . ." (Mark 2:8). Jesus knew what his disciples had been arguing about among themselves (9:33-35). He told his disciples, "Go into the village in front of you, and immediately as you enter it you will find a colt tied, on which no one has ever sat" (11:2). Jesus knew what was in the hearts of his admirers (John 2:24-25). "Then Jesus told them plainly, 'Lazarus has died'" (11:14).

(c) *Future things.* "From that time Jesus began to show his disciples that he must go to Jerusalem and suffer many things from the elders and chief priests and scribes, and be killed, and on the third day be raised" (Matt. 16:21 par.). "You see all these [things of the temple], do you not? Truly, I say to you, there will not be left here one stone upon another that will not be thrown down" (24:2; see also all the precise predictions in vv. 5-42). Jesus predicts that Judas will betray, and Peter deny him (26:25, 34). "Go into the city, and a man carrying a jar of water will meet you. Follow him" (Mark 14:13-14).[18]

In some cases, we might be reading about a "word of knowledge" that Jesus received through the Holy Spirit (cf. 1 Cor. 12:8 NKJV), but this does not explain every case. Thus, his disciples even testified: "Now we know that you know all things" (John 16:30), and: "Lord, you know everything" (21:17). Especially John's Gospel often refers to Jesus' perfect knowledge: "[H]e himself knew what was in man" (2:25). "Perceiving then that they were about to come and take him by force to make him king . . ." (6:15). "Jesus, knowing in himself that his disciples were grumbling about this, . . ." (6:61). "Jesus knew from the beginning who those were who did not believe, and who it was who would betray him" (v. 64; cf. vv. 70-71). "Jesus knew that his hour had come to depart out of this world to the Father" (13:1). "Jesus, knowing that the Father had given all things into his hands, and that he had come

---

18. Cf. Brown (1994a, 44–58). Jesus' knowledge of the future is a fascinating matter in the light of the urgent questions that Open Theism has raised with regard to God's knowledge of the future; see *RT* III/1.

from God and was going back to God, ..." (13:3); "he knew who was to betray him" (13:11). "Jesus knew that they wanted to ask him" (16:19).

8.2.2 Limited Knowledge?

As for Jesus' knowledge of future things, we also read, "Then Jesus, knowing all that would happen to him, ..." (John 18:4). This statement is remarkable because it seems to be at odds with Jesus' supplication in Gethsemane: "Father, if you are willing [Matt. 26:39, if it be possible], remove this cup from me" (Luke 22:42). The two textual versions suggest that Jesus did not yet know definitively what the Father wanted, or whether avoiding the cup was possible. On the one hand, Raymond Brown argued that the verse shows that, for Jesus, the future was a mystery, a fear, and a hope just as it is for us, and that he thus is an example for us, who go through similar trials.[19] Some have argued that Jesus knew what the Scriptures said about his coming sufferings, and that he could not possibly have believed that these prophecies could be changed. Scripture had to be fulfilled, and thus these sufferings had to occur. Therefore, we must understand Jesus' prayer not so much as a literal supplication but as a grievous utterance of pain.[20]

There seem to be other things that Jesus really did not know. He often asked people questions for information. Sometimes these were obvious test questions, but in other cases we get the impression that Jesus did not know the answer to the question. Thus, he asks the father of the boy with the unclean spirit, "How long has this been happening to him?" (Mark 9:21), and he asks Martha concerning the body of Lazarus, "Where have you laid him?" (John 11:34). In Mark 5, he perceives that power had gone out from him, and asks, "Who touched my garments?" (Mark 5:30). We also read about matters into which Jesus can enter only after having heard about

---

19. Brown (1967, 105).
20. Stein (1996, 217).

them, apparently not having known them before (Matt. 8:10; 9:12; 14:13; Mark 2:17; Luke 7:9; 8:50; John 9:35; 11:4, 6). The fact that, as a twelve-year-old boy, he asked the teachers questions, and that he increased in wisdom (Luke 2:46, 52), also suggests that he did not know everything. The most noteworthy is of course Mark 13:32, "But concerning that day or that hour [of the future glorious things], no one knows, not even the angels in heaven, nor the Son, but only the Father" (on this see §§2.2.1 and 5.9.1 above).

There are other indications that Jesus did not know the future in all its details. Notice the "perhaps" in Matthew 15:32, "I do not want to send them away hungry, so that they may not perhaps become-exhausted on the way" (DLNT); apparently, he was unsure about this. Even more remarkable is Mark 11:13, "And seeing from afar a fig tree having leaves, He went to see if perhaps He would find something on it" (NKJV); apparently, he did not yet know that the tree contained no fruit. The same is true for the "if" in certain statements: "[I]f you do not repent, you will all perish as they did" (Luke 13:3, 5 NABRE); *whether* the people being addressed would repent was apparently still unknown.

8.2.3 Complication

How much Jesus knew as Man on earth relates to how, if Jesus knew *everything*, he could wonder or marvel at anything. As human beings, we wonder about things we have not experienced before, or have not expected, or which we thought would be different from what they were. The Bible tells us, "He marveled because of their unbelief" (Mark 6:6), and, "When Jesus heard this, he marveled" (Matt. 8:10; cf. Luke 7:9). Especially the latter statement is noteworthy: Jesus hears something that makes him marvel, or wonder. This must mean that he sometimes encountered new, as yet unknown things. In support of this, recall that on the cross Jesus first tasted the wine that was offered him, and then refused to drink it (Matt. 27:34).

This is a complicated matter, for two reasons. On the one hand, Simon the Pharisee expected that even an ordinary prophet possessed supernatural knowledge: "If this man were a prophet, he would have known who and what sort of woman this is who is touching him, for she is a sinner" (Luke 7:39; cf., e.g., 1 Sam. 10:1-8[21]). We read that in a situation where the teachers and the Pharisees opposed Jesus: "Jesus perceived [Gk. *epignous*] their thoughts" (Luke 5:22); "he knew [Gk. *ēdei*] their thoughts" (6:8); and in another situation, "Jesus, knowing [Gk. *eidōs*[22]] their thoughts, said, 'Why do you think evil in your hearts?'" (Matt. 9:4; cf. Ps. 94:11; 139:1-6; Heb. 4:13; Rev. 2:23).

On the other hand, in the Old Testament we sometimes get the impression that God himself did not know certain things beforehand, or did not know them for sure ("*now* I know that you fear God," Gen. 22:12). In other cases, God undertook certain actions to find out how a situation was (Gen. 2:19; 11:5; 18:21; 22:1, 12; Exod. 16:4; Deut. 8:2; 13:3; Judg. 2:22; 3:4; 2 Chron. 32:31).[23] In other words, the matter of *God's* omniscience is already so complicated that it is hardly fair or possible to compare this with the knowledge Jesus had as a Man while on earth.[24]

Matters are further complicated by the fact that Jesus was, and is, both God and Man. From God the Son we expect omniscience, but from the Man Jesus we expect ignorance as to certain matters. Indeed, the reality that Jesus did not (yet) know certain things at certain moments can be explained in terms of

---

21. Cf. also Ezekiel, who received several visions about things happening in Jerusalem (e.g., Ezek. 4:8–10:24).
22. Some important manuscripts have Gk. *idōn*, "seeing."
23. For many other examples, see extensively, Boyd (2001, 100–109): God often says "perhaps," "if," or "how long?" with regard to the future, is disappointed about certain things that happen, repents about things he did, relents about things he intended to do, and so on.
24. Roman Catholic exegesis of Mark 13:32 maintains the omniscience of the Man Jesus, e.g., with an appeal to Gen. 22:12 just mentioned; so too Augustine, Gregory the Great, and Thomas Aquinas; see Berkouwer (1954, 212).

his humanity, and in particular from the fact that he emptied himself (§8.7): "Jesus purposely laid aside temporarily the exercise of his omniscience as part of what was involved in his becoming man."[25] Some argue that the phrase "nor the Son" in Mark 13:32 "refers only to the relationship that Christ has to God by virtue of His office . . . , a relationship that does not make Him omniscient."[26] On this point, the most careful view is the claim: ". . . yet, [Jesus] also does not know the day. It is not possible to completely explain this; we stand here before the great miracle of him who is God and Man."[27]

8.3 Jewish Characteristics
8.3.1 The Importance of the Matter

Today, a discussion of Jesus as a genuine Jew (both ethnically and religiously) cannot be omitted in any Christology. For centuries, Christology has paid little or no attention to this matter. This was the case surely since the rise of replacement and spiritualizing theology, that is, those theologies in which prophecies pertaining to Israel were spiritualized and the church was regarded as having replaced Israel as God's people, often with the claim that the church is the true (spiritual) Israel. During this development, Jesus' Jewishness was viewed as less relevant. In the twentieth century, this situation underwent a drastic change.

By way of introduction, I quote A. van de Beek, who wrote with regard to Romans 9:5 ("To them [i.e., Israel] belong the patriarchs, and from their race, according to the flesh, is the Christ, who is God over all, blessed forever"):

> In Romans 9 it is argued in terms of the two-natures doctrine that the human nature [of Jesus] may not be understood in an

---

25. Wessell (1984, 753); cf. Van Leeuwen (1928, 171) about Jesus' limited knowledge; Cyril of Alexandria, quoted in Brown (1994a, 28), also argued that Jesus descended to such a humble position that he shared all that belongs to our nature, including ignorance. Brown himself wondered concerning Jesus' perfection whether omniscience is a perfection *for human beings*.
26. Ridderbos (1987, 452).
27. Grosheide (1954, 370).

individual sense. It comprises the nation in which he lived. Before Christ is the second Adam, he is Son of Israel. Denial of Israel in his unique relationship thus entails a docetic Christology.[28]

Robbing Jesus of his Jewishness is robbing him of his true identity as a human being.

In 1982, the Orthodox Jewish New Testament scholar Pinchas Lapide asked the Roman Catholic dogmatician Karl Rahner:

> Assuming that I could provide you with convincing proof that the Lord's Prayer amount to a shortened version of the synagogue liturgy, that the entire Sermon on the Mount along with the admonition to love one's enemies developed from rabbinical constructions, that virtually all the parables of Jesus achieve their full measure of meaning only from their Jewish background . . . would you then be prepared to concede that Jesus' spiritual Jewishness must count as an indispensable component of Christology?[29]

Rahner immediately and correctly conceded that the Jewish spiritual world at the time of Jesus is of indispensable significance, although he added that some historical elements in Jesus need not be normative for a Christian.

Jesus was born of a Jewish mother (cf. Gal. 3:16, offspring of Abraham), and thus born under the Torah (Gal. 4:4). He came from the tribe of Judah (Heb. 7:14), more precisely, from the house of David (Rom. 1:3). The apostolic father Ignatius wrote: he "was descended from David, and was also of Mary."[30] Does this connection between Mary and the house of David mean that she too personally descended from the house of David? I believe that Luke 1:32 strongly points in this direction: "He will be great and will be called the Son of the Most High. And the Lord God will give to him the throne

---

28. Van de Beek (2002b, 199).
29. Rahner and Lapide (1987, 52).
30. See note 10 (http://www.newadvent.org/fathers/0106.htm).

of his father David." How could Mary, who would become pregnant as a virgin, understand that Jesus would be an offspring of David if she herself did not descend from David? Or did she have to understand that Jesus would only be a legitimate son of David because he would be the lawful son of her future husband Joseph (v. 27)?

There is a difficulty here, though, because Elizabeth, her "relative" (Gk. *syngenis*, v. 36), was "from the daughters of Aaron" (v. 5), that is, from the priestly line in the tribe of Levi. This seems to indicate that Mary, too, was from the tribe of Levi—unless she, for instance through her (traditionally identified) father Joachim, did indeed descend from David, but through her (traditionally identified) mother Anna belonged to the tribe of Levi. We can only speculate here; but the possibility that Mary, too, was a descendant from David, must be kept open.[31] Actually, even if Mary descended from the priestly line in the tribe of Levi, we must remember that the first priest, Aaron, married Elisheba (the name is the Hebrew form of Elizabeth), the daughter of Amminadab and the sister of Nahshon (Exod. 6:23), and thus from the tribe of Judah (Num. 1:7). Thus, *every* descendent of Aaron was not only a Levite but also a Judahite.

For the formal descent of Jesus this is of little consequence; the only thing that counted was the lineage of the father, whether of his biological or of his legal father through the latter's marriage with Mary. Matthew has no problem proving that Jesus is the son of David (1:1; cf. 9:27; 12:23; 15:22; 20:30-31; 21:9, 15), and supplying us with the line of descent from David to Joseph (1:6-16, 20), and at the same time arguing that Joseph was not the biological but the legal father of Jesus (1:18-25).

---

31. We will discuss in the next chapter the speculations about whether Jesus' Davidic genealogy in Luke 3:23-38 was in fact that of his mother Mary (cf. §11.1.1).

8.3.2 More Jewish Characteristics

Additional features of Jesus' Jewishness include that he was circumcised on the eighth day, just like every other Jewish boy (Luke 2:21; cf. Gen. 17:10-12). He must have been young when he learned to recite the Shema: "[Y]ou shall love the LORD your God with all your heart and with all your soul and with all your mind and with all your strength." He learned to pray the Aramaic Qaddish: "Your name may be magnified and hallowed. . . . And he may establish his kingdom during your life"; the Lord's Prayer that he taught his disciples (Matt. 6:9-13; Luke 11:2-4) is similar to this.[32]

At twelve years of age, Jesus' parents took him to Jerusalem at the occasion of Pesach (Luke 2:41-50); given his age, it is possible that he underwent a kind of initiation ritual that later became known as bar mitzvah (cf. §11.3.2). From an early age, he had the habit of attending the services in the synagogue: "[A]s was his custom, he went to the synagogue on the Sabbath day" (Luke 4:16). At times, he read the Scriptures publicly there, as the same verse shows. This means that he was able to read, in contrast to the assertion of the Jesus Seminar[33] (cf. John 8:6; Mark 2:25; Matt. 12:5, 10, 26; 19:4). Jesus had "never studied" (Gk. *mē memathēkōs*, John 7:15) in the sense of having a formal rabbinic training (cf. "uneducated," Gk. *agrammatoi*, in Acts 4:13), but this did not mean that he was illiterate. On the contrary, he quoted all the books of the Torah, most of the Prophets, and some books of the Writings.[34] He also seems to have worn the *tsitsit*, the tassels on the corners of the garments, as prescribed in Numbers 15:38-40. Matthew 9:20 and 14:36 (par.) speak of the "fringe" of Jesus' garment; "fringe" (Gk. *kraspedon*) is the same as "phylacteries" in 23:5. Geza Vermes was convinced that in all these cases the Greek

---

32. In fact, there is *nothing* in the Lord's Prayer that an orthodox Jew could not pray as well—it is therefore all the more amazing that this is the very prayer that has become the standard prayer of Christianity.
33. Funk (1998, 274).
34. See C. A. Evans in Bockmuehl (2001, 15–21).

word *kraspedon* is referring to the *tsitsit*.[35] Only in this way can we understand why the woman with the discharge of blood touched this very part of Jesus' garment.[36]

Jesus' native language was probably Aramaic; some of his Aramaic sayings have been preserved in the New Testament:[37] Cephas (*Kefa*, "stone," John 1:42 CJB), *raca* ("empty-headed idiot," Matt. 5:22 AMP), *mammon* (Luke 16:9-13 NKJV), *Boanerges* (actually *b'nē r'am?*, "sons of thunder," Mark 3:17), *Talitha cumi* ("little girl, arise," 5:41), *corban* ("offering," 7:11), *Ephphatha* (actually *Etptah*, "be opened," 7:34), *Abba* ("Father," 14:36; cf. Rom. 8:15; Gal. 4:6), *Eloi, Eloi, lema sabachthani?* ("My God, my God, why have you forsaken me?" 15:34).[38] In addition to this, Jesus could read and understand Hebrew (Luke 4:16-20; cf. John 7:15 NKJV, Gk. *grammata oiden*, "knows letters"). Jesus possibly spoke Greek in Tyre, Sidon, and Decapolis (Matt. 15:21; Mark 7:31), with Greek visitors (John 12:20-36), and with Pilate.[39]

According to the Talmud, a father must support his son, teach him a craft (in Jesus' case, this was likely carpentry), find a wife for him, and teach him the Torah.[40] I will discuss this craft and this wife in §11.3.1 below. As for instruction in the Torah, Joseph taught Jesus the religion of the fathers, and familiarized him with the synagogue (cf. Luke 4:16). "And the child grew and became strong, filled with wisdom. And the favor of God was upon him. . . . And Jesus increased in wisdom and in stature and in favor with God and man" (Luke

---

35. Vermes (1993, 16).
36. Ouweneel (2001a, 120n76). Perhaps this is also the meaning in Zech. 8:23, "In those days ten men from the nations of every tongue shall take hold of the robe of a Jew" (cf. Jamieson–Fausset–Brown, https://biblehub.com/commentaries/zechariah/8-23.htm).
37. Stein (1996, 86–87).
38. Matt. 27:46 has *Ēli* (with an eta), not *Eloi* (with an epsilon); a minor textual variant for *sabachtani* is *asabthani*, the reading followed by Luther (and known worldwide through Bach's *St. Matthew's Passion*).
39. Regarding the languages Jesus spoke, and his reading and writing capacities, see extensively, Meier (1991, 255–78).
40. Qiddushin 30a.

2:40, 52). For him, it was more true than for Paul, that he "was advancing in Judaism beyond many of my own age among my people, so extremely zealous was I for the traditions of my fathers" (Gal. 1:14). If, at an advanced point in his career, the apostle Paul could say, "I had done nothing against our people or the customs of our fathers" (Acts 28:17), then this was just as true of Jesus, though unlike Paul he possibly never had any formal education from rabbis (John 7:15; Acts 22:3). It has been argued that Joseph was a good Pharisee, and taught Jesus in this tradition, so that Jesus could call himself a Pharisee (cf. Acts 23:6; Phil. 3:5).[41]

8.3.3 Jesus the Faithful Jew

In every respect, Jesus lived, spoke, and acted in faithful submission to the Mosaic Torah. As E. P. Sanders put it, the Synoptic (!) Jesus lived as a law-abiding Jew. He accepted Deuteronomy 6:5 ("love God") and Leviticus 19:18 ("love your neighbor") as the two "greatest commandments" (Matt. 22:36-40), and his saying, "Do to others" (Matt. 7:12) was based upon Leviticus 19:18 and 34. By choosing these, Jesus concentrated on the passages that others in his time viewed as central, too. He attended synagogue services, he ate no pork or shellfish, he did not work on the Sabbath. He accepted the sacrificial system as atoning (Matt. 5:23-24) and cleansing (Mark 1:40-44). Just like other Jewish teachers he warned his followers not to sacrifice until injustice had been put right, and grievances had been resolved (Matt. 5:23-26). He also paid the temple tax — in a very remarkable way (17:24-27). As for the Sabbath, there were two alleged violations: his disciples plucked grain (Mark 2:23-28), and he laid hands on a sick woman to heal her (Luke 13:10-17).[42] In both cases, there was

---

41. Bruners (2006); he also pointed to the role of Mary, who was influenced by Jewish apocalyptic writings as is evident, Bruners claimed, from her song (the *Magnificat*).
42. Only two "violations"!? See also Matt. 12:10–13 (the man with the withered hand); Luke 13:10–17 (the disabled woman); 14:1–6 (the man who had dropsy); and in addition to the Synoptics, John 5:16 (the crippled man in

a legitimate defense: hunger goes beyond the law, and the Sabbath is made for people, not people for the Sabbath; owners untie their animals and lead them to water on the Sabbath. All of this is mentioned by Sanders.[43]

Thus, despite assertions to the contrary by some,[44] Jesus never attacked, criticized, or cast doubt upon the Torah. He did sharply criticize the way the scribes and the Pharisees had distorted, restricted, and weakened elements of the Torah.[45] In fact, Jesus generally did not attack even the so-called *oral* Torah, that is, the commandments ostensibly given by the Lord on Mount Sinai that were not set forth in the written Torah but were supposedly preserved in Jewish tradition, and later set forth in the Talmud. Jesus' basic acceptance of this tradition is evident from Matthew 23:2-4, "The scribes and the Pharisees sit on Moses' seat, *so do and observe whatever they tell you*, but not the works they do. For they preach, but do not practice. They tie up heavy burdens, hard to bear, and lay them on people's shoulders, but they themselves are not willing to move them with their finger." Thus, Jesus clearly and pointedly advised the people to faithfully follow the teachings of the Torah scholars, which also entailed the application of the oral Torah.

During his earthly life, Jesus always kept the Torah strictly, according to the interpretations of the Torah that were generally accepted in those days. This was not simply because this was all "before Calvary," or "before Pentecost" (Acts 2), as if since then things would have drastically changed. Jesus himself had said, "Do not think that I have come to abolish the Law or the Prophets; *I have not come to abolish them* but to fulfill them" (Matt. 5:17). Paul and the other apostles, too, lived after Pentecost in exactly the same way as Jesus had done

---

Bethesda); 9:1–14 (the man born blind).
43. Sanders (1990, 90).
44. E.g., Schweizer (1971b, 32).
45. Ouweneel (2001a, 103–06); so also, e.g., Vermes (1973, 35; 1993, 21).

The Humanity of Christ

before Easter: as law-abiding Jews.[46] Peter and John went to the temple to attend to the evening sacrifice (Acts 3:1). And about twenty years after his conversion, Paul counted himself among the strictest Torah-abiding Israelites. After he had been taken captive, he told the governor Felix, "After an absence of several years, I came to Jerusalem to bring gifts for the poor of my nation and *to offer sacrifices*" (24:17 CEB; which indeed he had done: see 21:26).[47] Afterward, he said to Governor Festus, "Neither against the law of the Jews, nor against the temple, nor against Caesar have I committed any offense" (Acts 25:8). All of this means that after Paul's conversion he faithfully kept the Torah. And to King Agrippa he said, "My manner of life from my youth, . . . is known by all the Jews. They have known for a long time, . . . that according to the strictest party of our religion I have lived as a Pharisee," that is, also after his conversion (26:4–5). To the Jewish leaders in Rome he said, "I had done nothing against . . . the customs of our fathers" (28:17), that is, against both the written and the oral Torah.

If such faithful Torah-keeping was true for this follower, even long after Pentecost, how much more was it true for the Master.[48]

8.4 Confidence in God
8.4.1 The Praying Jesus

It belongs to Jesus' genuine humanity that he customarily prayed to his God and Father: "[H]e came out and went, as was his custom, to the Mount of Olives" (Luke 22:39), in order to pray (Matt. 26:36). Luke in particular emphasizes that Jesus prayed on many occasions—times when other Gospels do not always mention his praying—and thus expressed his

---

46. Ouweneel (2001a, 106–17).
47. In both Acts 21:26 and 24:17, many translations employ the rendering "offering(s)" for the Gk. *prosphora(s)*, in order, it seems, to hide the fact that genuine *animal* sacrifices were involved; according to Num. 6:16–17 these sacrifices included a burnt offering, a sin offering, and a peace offering.
48. Regarding Jesus and the Torah extensively, see volume I/2 in this series.

dependence upon God: at his baptism (3:21), before choosing the twelve apostles (6:12), on the Mount of Transfiguration (9:28-29), in intercession for Peter (22:32), in Gethsemane (vv. 41, 44); or we find a general statement (5:16; 9:18; 11:1).[49] Eight prayers of Jesus have been reported to us, containing two thanksgivings (Matt. 11:25-26 par.; John 11:41-42) and three supplications (John 12:27-28; 17:1-26; Matt. 26:38 par.; cf. Heb. 5:7-9), in addition to the three prayers on the cross (Matt. 27:46; Luke 23:34, 46).[50]

Some interpreters see in Mark 13:32 ("nor the Son") evidence that even Jesus had to live by faith (confidence in God).[51] In this faith relationship, he was so familiar with the Father that he even addressed him with the confidential *Abba*, which means "Father," perhaps the colloquial "Papa" or "Daddy" (Mark 14:36; cf. Rom. 8:15; Gal. 4:6). As far as we know, if Jews offered free prayers, no ordinary Jew would ever have ventured to address God this way.[52]

Sometimes Jesus was so busy "that they could not even eat" (Mark 3:20). But he also took the time to be at a quiet place with his disciples: "And he said to them, 'Come away by yourselves to a desolate place and rest a while.' For many were coming and going, and they had no leisure even to eat" (6:31). Or he sought solitude: "But now even more the report about him went abroad, and great crowds gathered to hear him and to be healed of their infirmities. But he would withdraw to desolate places and pray" (Luke 5:15-16). "In these days he went out to the mountain to pray, and all night he

---

49. Cf. Ratzinger (2007, 132): "Jesus' entire ministry arises [in Luke's Gospel] from his prayer, and is sustained by it. Essential events in the course of his journey, in which his mystery is gradually unveiled, appear in this light as prayer events. Peter's confession that Jesus is the Holy One of God [John 6:69] is connected with encountering Jesus at prayer (cf. Lk 9:18[–20]); the Transfiguration of Jesus is a prayer event (cf. Lk 9:28[–29])."
50. Bockmuehl (1994, 129–40); I am not including the prayer that Jesus taught his disciples (Matt. 6:9–13).
51. Lane (1974, 482).
52. Grün (2002, 19).

continued in prayer to God" (6:12). Jesus could work hard as well as relax; this was evidence of his need of inner rest and confidence. I use the word "relax" on purpose because his desire was not just prayer, which in fact entails new spiritual effort. On the contrary, relaxation suggests that he took time for enjoying "the lilies of the field, how they grow," and for the beauty even of "the grass of the field" (Matt. 6:28, 30).

8.4.2 The Trusting Messiah

It is quite remarkable that Hebrews 2:13a, in supplying us a proof of Jesus' perfect humanity, gives a quotation from Isaiah 8:17 (LXX; cf. 2 Sam. 22:3 LXX; Isa. 12:2): "I will put my trust in him." The argument in Isaiah 8 is as follows: because of Israel's unfaithfulness, God would bring Assyria as a scourge over the people. Instead of putting their trust in false alliances, Israel should have put its trust in YHWH, and honored him (Isa. 8:5-13). It was the same when the Messiah was on earth. In *him* YHWH manifested himself, *he* wanted to be a "sanctuary" for his people. Instead, he became to them a stone of offense and a rock of stumbling (Isa. 8:14; cf. Rom. 9:33).[53]

But now the tone of the prophecy changes. The Messiah, first seen as Immanuel, "God with us," is now typologically viewed as a humble Man on earth. Isaiah himself is now a type of the Messiah, surrounded by his disciples (Isa. 8:16). After Israel has rejected God and his Messiah and has been dispersed, the Messiah—and with him the true remnant of Israel—says, "I will wait for the LORD, who is hiding his face from the house of Jacob, and I will hope in him [LXX: I will put my trust in him]. Behold, I and the children whom the LORD has given me are signs and portents in Israel from the LORD of hosts, who dwells on Mount Zion" (Isa. 8:17-18).

The Messiah puts his trust in God, with whom things will never get out of hand: one day, all of Israel *will* be saved, and Christ will be placed over the "world to come" (Heb. 2:5). Jesus is not just God in a human garment. He is so truly Man

---
53. See extensively, Ouweneel (1982, 43).

that, just like any other believer, he has learned to live in confidence toward, and dependence upon, God. He did not just assume a human form (cf. Heb. 2:14), but he really was "made like his brothers in every respect" (Heb. 2:17), be it "without sin" (Heb. 4:15).

The apostle Peter gave a Messianic interpretation of Psalm 16:8-11 in Acts 2:25-31, and thus, apparently, viewed Psalm 16 as a Messianic Psalm (see §4.1.1). In this context, Psalm 16:1 is noteworthy: "Preserve me, O God, for in you I take refuge." Actually, this is not just the Messiah's voice; the faithful remnant is closely connected with him here. When he walked on this earth, he was perfectly dependent upon God—so how could the "many sons" (Heb. 2:10) be anything else? They are on the way to the Promised Land, travelling through many perils and troubles. Christ is involved in this in three ways.

(1) Christ is the glorified *goal* at the end of the believers' road; this is the writer's subject in Hebrews 12:1-2.

(2) Christ is the *high priest*, who carries them all the way to the end through his work of intercession; this is the subject of 2:17-18; 4:14-16, and 7:25.

(3) Christ is—and this is our topic right now—the shining *example* of true confidence in God for those who are on the road. All opposition by Israel could not shake this trust. Compare Isaiah 49:4 and 50:4-11, passages that first speak of Christ's confidence in God, which is subsequently applied to the faithful remnant.

8.4.3 Nine Mountains of Prayer and Worship

In my view, the emphasis of Calvinism on Jesus' faith and confidence in God is closer to Scripture than certain views of Roman Catholicism. According to the traditional Catholic doctrine, terms like "temptation," "faith," and "hope" cannot be reconciled with the divine nature of Jesus. In opposition to this, a Reformed theologian like Abraham Kuyper has strongly emphasized that Jesus really and truly lived here on earth by *faith* in God.[54] Some have pointed here to passages that, in some translations, speak of the "faith *of* Jesus" (Rom. 3:22, 26; Gal. 2:16; 3:22; Rev. 14:12 KJV), but I wonder whether these are good evidence for "Jesus the believer." Expositors generally believe that these passages speak of "faith *in* Jesus," the faith of which Jesus is the object, not the subject (objective genitive).

Jesus' trust in God is closely related to "the mountain," that "locus of God's particular closeness"[55] (cf. Ps. 48:1; 99:9; 121:1; 148:7-9). I found nine references to such a mountain, which are all connected with Jesus' life of prayer and worship, or his being worshiped by others.

(1) The mountain of temptation ("a very high mountain," Matt. 4:8); Jesus explains to Satan the significance of worshiping God. This was possibly Mount Tabor or Mount Hermon.

(2) The mountain of the Sermon on the Mount (Matt. 5:1; here, Jesus has much to say about prayer: 5:44; 6:5-13; 7:7-8, 11). Tradition says this was what later was called the Mount of Beatitudes, near the Sea of Galilee.

(3) The mountain where Jesus chose the twelve apostles (Mark 3:13-19; in Luke 6:12-16, Jesus spends the night before this in prayer). One tradition says this was on the Horns of Hattin.

(4) The mountain of the prayer during the storm on the Sea of Galilee (Matt. 14:23-33; Mark 6:46-51; John 6:15-21); probably one of the mountains (north)east of the Sea (the Golan).

(5) The mountain where Jesus fed the crowd (Matt. 15:29, 36; John 6:3, 11; Jesus gives thanks to God for the food that he

---

54. Quoted in Bloesch (1997, 63).
55. Ratzinger (2007, 308); "The 'mountain' is the place where Jesus prays—where he is face-to-face with the Father. And that is exactly why it is also the place of his teaching [Matt. 5:1], since his teaching comes forth from this most intimate exchange with the Father" (66). "The mountain is the place of ascent—not only outward, but also inward ascent; it is a liberation from the burden of everyday life, a breathing in of the pure air of creation; ... it gives one an inner peak to stand on and an intuitive sense of the Creator" (309).

is going to give); probably again one of the mountains (north) east of the Sea (the Golan).

(6) The Mount of Transfiguration ("a high mountain," Matt. 17:1; Mark 9:2; here again, Jesus is praying, Luke 9:28). Again, this was possibly Mount Tabor or Mount Hermon.

(7) The mountain of Jesus' supplication: the Mount of Olives (Matt. 26:30, 36 par.), where Jesus prays three times, vv. 39, 42, 44). This was also the mountain of Jesus' End Time Sermon (Matt. 24:3; Mark 13:3), of Jesus' entrance into Jerusalem (Matt. 21:1-9; Luke 19:37: here it is the people praying to God in praise and thanksgiving), and of Jesus' ascension (Luke 24:50, here the ascension leads to worship by the disciples; Acts 1:9, 12)

(8) The mountain of the cross[56] (Matt. 27:33 par.; the first, the middle, and the last of Jesus' seven sayings on the cross are prayers: v. 46; Luke 23:34 and 46).

(9) The mountain of the risen Lord: "[T]he eleven disciples went to Galilee, to the mountain to which Jesus had directed them" (Matt. 28:16); here the disciples are worshiping Jesus (v. 17). Was this again Mount Tabor? Or the Mount of Beatitudes?

8.4.4 Humiliation, Yet Greatness

In §7.5.1 we concluded from Hebrews 5:8 that submission and obedience do not go along with Christ's eternal Sonship, but they do with his position as Man on earth, just like notions such as trust and confidence in God. These elements are part of his humiliation. This position of a humble, obedient human was correlative with his incarnation. Therefore, John's Gospel tells us many times that God, or the Father, "sent" the Son (3:34; 5:25, 36-37; 6:29, 44, 57; 8:16, 18, 42; 10:36; 12:49; 14:24; 17:21, 25; 20:21), namely, "into the world," that is, from outside (3:17; 17:3, 18). This movement "from outside" points to

---

56. The Bible does not speak of a mountain or a hill, but tradition identifies Golgotha as "Calvary Hill" or "Sacred Mount(ain)." Golgotha comes from Heb. *gulgolet*, "skull," which presumably refers to the form of the hill.

his divine nature: the Son coming into the world. The "sentness" points to his human nature: this is a dependent, obedient Man who is "sent."

In this position of obedience, the Father can also give him commandments: "I have power to lay it [i.e., my life] down, and I have power to take it again. This commandment have I received of my Father" (10:18). "I have not spoken on my own authority, but the Father who sent me has himself given me a commandment—what to say and what to speak" (12:49). "I do as the Father has commanded me, so that the world may know that I love the Father" (14:31). "If you keep my commandments, you will abide in my love, just as I have kept my Father's commandments and abide in his love" (15:10).

It is interesting to ponder whether Jesus as the Son of Man is less than Jesus as the Son of God. Surely in those cases where the designation "Son of God" does not necessarily go any further than Israel's Messiah begotten by the Holy Spirit (Ps. 2:7; Luke 1:35), we *cannot* claim this. On the contrary, it sometimes seems as if Jesus esteems the designation "Son of Man" more highly than that of "Son of God" (in the sense just mentioned).[57] After Nathanael's exclamation, "Rabbi, you are the Son of God! You are the King of Israel!" (John 1:49), Jesus replies, "Because I said to you, 'I saw you under the fig tree,' do you believe? You will see *greater things* [!] than these. . . . Truly, truly, I say to you, you will see heaven opened, and the angels of God ascending and descending on the Son of Man" (vv. 50-51). The question arises whether Jesus intended to say that the glorified "Son of Man," who rules over all creation (Heb. 2:5, 8) belongs to the "things greater" than the Son of God who is King over Zion (Ps. 2:6-7; cf. Luke 1:32-33).[58]

---

57. The link that Jesus often makes between his self-designation "Son of Man" and Dan. 7:13 shows how mistaken is the suggestion of the Jesus Seminar that "Son of Man" means no more than "this mother's son," i.e., simply "human being"; see Funk (1999, 47, 97); cf. Theissen and Merz (1998, 541–53); Knight (2004, 111–23); Van Bruggen (1999, §4.2).
58. So, e.g., Kelly (1966, 36).

8.5 Jesus' Personality
8.5.1 Grief and Joy

Every person has a personality, that is, an aggregate of stronger and weaker inner features and properties through which one person distinguishes himself from another. Did Jesus have a personality? Or should we say instead that he distinguished himself from *all* people by not having any less strong properties? Without romanticizing, we can state that he was characterized by great equilibrium and inner balance. In addition to patience (2 Pet. 3:15), meekness (Matt. 11:28; 21:5; 2 Cor. 10:1), humility (Matt. 11:28), determination (Luke 9:51), goodness (2 Cor. 10:1), and faithfulness (2 Thess. 3:3; 2 Tim. 2:13; Heb. 2:17; 3:2), here are other examples highlighted in the in-depth studies by the Benedictine monk, A. Grün.[59]

Jesus wept several times, for instance, on the way to Jerusalem: "And when he drew near and saw the city [i.e., Jerusalem], he wept over it" (Luke 19:41). Or in the story of Lazarus: "[H]e said, 'Where have you laid him?' They said to him, 'Lord, come and see.' Jesus wept. So the Jews said, 'See how he loved him!'" (John 11:34–36). The letter to the Hebrews says, "In the days of his flesh, Jesus offered up prayers and supplications, with loud cries and tears, to him who was able to save him from death" (Heb. 5:7). Several times, Jesus or others spoke of his being moved or troubled: "When Jesus saw her [i.e., Martha] weeping, and the Jews who had come with her also weeping, he was deeply moved [or, was indignant] in his spirit and greatly troubled" (John 11:33). "Now is my soul troubled. And what shall I say? 'Father, save me from this hour'? But for this purpose I have come to this hour" (12:27). "After saying these things, Jesus was troubled in his spirit, and testified, 'Truly, truly, I say to you, one of you will betray me'" (13:21).

In addition, Jesus definitely experienced moments of joy: "In that same hour he rejoiced in the Holy Spirit and said, 'I

---

59. Grün (2002).

thank you, Father, Lord of heaven and earth'" (Luke 10:21).[60] "Rejoiced" (Gk. *hēgalliásato*) is a rather weak rendering; "overflowed with joy" (CEB), or "rejoiced, exuberant in the Holy Spirit" (MSG) is better; there is an element of "shouting" or "exulting" in the basic meaning of the verb (e.g., Acts 2:26). Jesus spoke a few times of "my joy" (John 15:11; 17:13). And Hebrews 12:2 says, "Jesus, . . . who for the joy that was set before him endured the cross, despising the shame" (Heb. 12:2). The harmony that existed within him between his sadness because of circumstances and his joy in God comes to expression in the peace that he possessed and with which he could comfort others: "Peace I leave with you; my peace I give to you. Not as the world gives do I give to you. Let not your hearts be troubled, neither let them be afraid" (John 14:27).[61]

Jesus' joy was part of his reputation: just as John the Baptist had the fame of an ascetic, Jesus had, as he himself put it, the reputation of a "glutton and a drunkard, a friend of tax collectors and sinners" (Matt. 11:19); in short, he had the reputation of being a party person. The Old Testament tells us that wine "cheers God and men" (Judg. 9:13), and is given "to gladden the heart of man" (Ps. 104:15). "A feast is made for laughter, wine makes life merry" (Eccl. 10:19 NIV). To all Christian teetotalers it must be said, "Jesus is inconceivable apart from the biblical culture of wine."[62] His first miracle through which he manifested his glory was changing water into wine (John

---

60. Through Umberto Eco's novel *The Name of the Rose*, one may wonder whether Jesus ever laughed when he lived on earth. Grün (2002, 119): "Today, this is no longer a question in our fun society. Instead, we have trouble with the fact that Jesus wept." And this: "For Buddha the contact with the world is the source of all suffering. Therefore, he breaks off this contact, in order to smilingly experience his inner freedom. Jesus [however] allows himself to be touched. He passes through the suffering. He feels the sorrow. He weeps about it because it moves him very deeply. Jesus, the man who wept, is closer to me than Buddha, the unmovable and untouchable" (120; cf. also 164).
61. We find the same balance in Phil. 2:27 ("sorrow upon sorrow") versus 1:18; 2:17–18; 3:1; 4:4, 10 ("rejoice").
62. Berger (2004, 173).

2:1-11). Realizing how large the six jars were—each two or three "measures," one "measure" being about ten gallons (39 liters)—and how many guests were present at such a village wedding (about two hundred to six hundred?), we can calculate that Jesus supplied enough wine for each guest to have possibly enjoyed more than one gallon of wine.[63] Of course, we may apply this spiritually; Jesus provides an inexhaustible source of blessing and joy, and this shows his glory. But this does not change the fact that each guest received more than one gallon of wine!

In this context, some commentators point to a story about Jesus that is preserved only in Arabic.[64] In this story, Jesus had two very different disciples: the one, Peter, was often sad, and cried out of deep despondence. The other, John, was as happy and jubilant as if he had the world by the tail. When Jesus was asked about both, he said: "I prefer John. . . ."

To be sure, laughing for joy is something other than laughing about funny stories. Though we would not describe Jesus as being "humoristic," he could be very witty. A beautiful example is this statement to the religious hypocrites: "You blind guides, straining out a gnat and swallowing a camel!" (Matt. 23:24). The scribes and Pharisees were so legalistically meticulous that, if the smallest gnat was floating in their cup of wine, this had to be filtered out. But if a camel was floating around in their cup, they thoughtlessly gulped it down. We may count on it that people laughed when Jesus said such things. Or take this lovely Eastern exaggeration: "I'd say it's easier to thread a camel through a needle's eye than get a rich person into God's kingdom" (Luke 18:25 MSG). In this respect, Jesus stood in a tradition familiar with wit, as seen, for instance, in Proverbs: "A person who is lazy and wants to stay home says, 'What if there is a lion out there? Really, there

---

63. How Berger (2004, 174) can arrive at eighteen and one-half gallons (seventy liters) is a riddle to me; did he count only the wedding couple and their parents?
64. Ibid., 189.

might be a lion in the street!'" (26:13 ERV). Proverbs is full of this type of humor.

8.5.2 Rage and Tenderness

Jesus could be genuinely indignant: people "were bringing children to him that he might touch them, and the disciples rebuked them. But when Jesus saw it, he was indignant [Gk. *ēganaktēsen*] and said to them, 'Let the children come to me; do not hinder them, for to such belongs the kingdom of God'" (Mark 10:13-14). "When Jesus saw her [i.e., Martha] weeping, and the Jews who had come with her also weeping, he was deeply moved [was indignant, Gk. *enebrimēsato*] in his spirit and greatly troubled. . . . Then Jesus, deeply moved [or, indignant] again, came to the tomb" (John 11:33, 38). His indignation was directed toward the power of death and Satan, as in John 11, or the sins and weaknesses of people, as in Mark 10; the people themselves he loved. This wondrous balance of indignation toward people's acts and the grief on behalf of the people *themselves* comes beautifully to light nowhere more clearly than in Mark 3:5, "[H]e looked around at them with *anger, grieved* at their hardness of heart."

During Jesus' first cleansing of the temple (John 2:14-17), we hear nothing about anger or indignation, although he acted decisively: "[M]aking a whip of cords, he drove them all out of the temple, with the sheep and oxen. And he poured out the coins of the money-changers and overturned their tables" (v. 15). Yet, we perceive a tone of severe admonition in these words, which is hardly conceivable without some anger: "Take these things away; do not make my Father's house a house of trade." At the second cleansing of the temple (Matt. 21:12-13; Mark 11:15-17; Luke 19:45-46), we find the same; here again, there is a strong accusation: "He said to them, 'It is written, "My house shall be called a house of prayer," but you make it a den of robbers'" (Matt. 21:13). Yet, it is possible that Jesus carried out these cleansings with great determination, accompanied by great calmness.

Jesus' decisiveness was never in conflict with his own claim: "I am gentle and lowly in heart" (Matt. 11:29). He was so humble that he washed his disciples' feet (John 13:1-15; cf. Luke 22:25-27), and called them his friends (Luke 12:4; John 15:15). But in Gethsemane (John 18:4-8), and before Caiaphas (Matt. 26:64) and Pilate (John 19:11), he could also demonstrate his majesty. And if needed he did not shrink away from making enemies (Mark 11:15-19).[65] He was the great peacemaker (Mark 5:34; 9:50; Luke 2:14; 7:50; 8:48; 19:38, 42; 24:36; John 14:27; 16:33; 20:19, 21, 26), but if it could not be avoided, he accepted the division that he caused (Luke 12:51-53).[66]

Sometimes Jesus seemed to be unnecessarily harsh. In Luke 11 he was invited to the home of a Pharisee for dinner. The host is amazed that Jesus did not wash his hands before eating, to which Jesus replies, "Now you Pharisees cleanse the outside of the cup and of the dish, but inside you are full of greed and wickedness. You fools! Did not he who made the outside make the inside also? But give as alms those things that are within, and behold, everything is clean for you" (vv. 39-41). Then Jesus went on to pronounce general woes upon the Pharisees and the scribes. One might think that this reply was too sharp toward someone who had invited him into his house. However, Jesus saw through the hypocritical motives of his host (cf. 7:44-46).

Toward someone who came to him with sincere motives he could be very lovely and tender. A beautiful example is the man (the "rich young man," Matt. 19:20-21) mentioned in Mark 10:21, "Jesus, looking at him, *loved him*, and said to him, 'You lack one thing: go, sell all that you have and give to the poor, and you will have treasure in heaven; and come, follow me.'"[67] As harshly as he responded to the hypocrite, with equal amiability he responded to the sincere person. Moreover, there are many examples of the intense compassion and

---

65. Cf. Grün (2002, 40–46).
66. Ibid., 47–49.
67. See ibid., 130–33, for other examples.

sympathy he showed toward contagious lepers, the dangerously possessed, and public sinners, people whom others would have avoided (Matt. 9:36; 14:14; 15:32; 20:34; Mark 1:41; Luke 7:13). He did so without ignoring the sins committed; here again, his responses were always balanced. We see this in the case of the adulterous woman (John 8:2-11), to whom Jesus says, "'Woman, where are they? Has no one condemned you?' She said, 'No one, Lord.' And Jesus said, 'Neither do I condemn you; go, and from now on sin no more'" (John 8:10-11).[68]

This is important: when Jesus freely ate and drank with tax collectors, prostitutes, and other outcasts (Matt. 9:10-11; 11:19; 21:31-32; Luke 7:34; 15:1), he never allowed himself to be affected by their defilement; rather, he brought *them* into the cleansing presence of God. When addressed by others on this point, he replied to his self-righteous opponents with an ironic word play: I came to help not people who (believe they) do not need help, but people who do need help.

8.5.3 Other Features

In Gethsemane, Jesus experienced great anguish (Gk. *adēmoneō*, "to be in great distress or anguish") with regard to what awaited him in his hours of suffering: the Father's cup (Matt. 26:37-38; Mark 14:33-34; cf. Luke 22:44 [agony, Gk. *agōnia*], and much earlier: Luke 12:50 [Gk. *synechō*, here: "to be in distress"]). Over against this was his tremendous courage. He exhorted his disciples: "Why are you afraid [Gk. *deiloi*], O you of little faith?" (Matt. 8:26; cf. 14:31). In Gethsemane he openly confronted those who had come to capture him: "Then Jesus, knowing all that would happen to him, came forward and said to them, 'Whom do you seek?' They answered him, 'Jesus of Nazareth.' Jesus said to them, 'I am he.' . . . [Then] they drew back and fell to the ground" (John 18:4-6). In Luke 22:52-53 we read: "Then Jesus said to the chief priests and officers of the temple and elders, who had come out against

---

68. I am aware that some doubt the authenticity of this passage.

him, 'Have you come out as against a robber, with swords and clubs? When I was with you day after day in the temple, you did not lay hands on me. But this is your hour, and the power of darkness.'" Several other examples could be given of the courage with which he met his opponents.

Jesus loved to be alone (Matt. 2:22; 4:12; 14:13, 23; Luke 9:18), but he was not a loner. Friendship gave him joy. "Like all of us, he needed friendship, and enjoyed it in the house of Lazarus, Mary, and Martha."[69] Jesus was a friend of tax collectors and sinners (Matt. 11:19 par.). He called Judas "friend," and Lazarus, and all his disciples he called "friends" (Matt. 26:50; John 11:11; Luke 12:4). He once said,

> Greater love has no one than this, that someone lay down his life for his friends. You are my friends if you do what I command you. No longer do I call you servants [or, slaves], for the servant [slave] does not know what his master is doing; but I have called you friends, for all that I have heard from my Father I have made known to you (John 15:13-15).

This necessarily involved a certain distance ("You are my friends if you do what I command you"), but it also involved the intimacy that belongs to friendship ("all that I have heard from my Father I have made known to you").

Jesus' love extended to the children as well (Matt. 19:13-15 par.). "The disciples [who wanted to hinder the children] remain bound to Pharisaic thinking. By their total lack of humor, the Pharisees have no feeling for children. They think that playing with children is a waste of time for orthodox people, and hinders them in reaching the world to come."[70] I agree with Grün, and I think it is even more interesting when we turn this around: by his sense of humor, Jesus understood the importance of children and their play; he even quoted their games in Matthew 11:16-17. Children must become adults in order to share in the kingdom of heaven, as the Pharisees be-

---

69. Verkuyl (1992, 197).
70. Grün (2002, 112).

lieved, but adults must become like children in order to enter the kingdom of heaven, as Jesus explained (18:3-4). This does not mean that they should become childish (infantile); rather, they should be childlike (plain and humble, not arrogant).

His love extends to men and women alike, in a perfectly pure way. Concerning the latter point, Charles Moule expressed his amazement that all the Gospels, without exception, paint for us the remarkably detailed portrait of an attractive young man, moving freely among women of every kind, including the most infamous, without a trace of embarrassment, unnaturalness, or prudishness, yet in each encounter preserving integrity of character.[71]

8.5.4 Divine Suffering?

After everything I have written about Jesus' emotional life, let me add a few remarks about whether Christ on earth suffered only according to his human nature, or also according to his divine nature. This question is especially problematic against the background of the doctrine that God is incapable of suffering.[72] Some early church fathers (Ignatius,[73] Origen) taught that God has no emotions, and therefore according to his divine nature Jesus has none, either. They assert this in spite of, for instance, Isaiah 63:9 (CSB), "In all their suffering, he suffered."[74] We cannot simply discard the numerous passages about God's wrath, anger, rage, joy, grief, love, and hatred, and even his fear (Deut. 32:27) and disappointment (Isa. 5:2).

The so-called *pathos* of God received special attention through the work of Jewish thinker Abraham Joshua Hes-

---

71. Moule (1967, 63).
72. Cf. Küng (1987, 518–25); König (1975, 111–24).
73. *Letter to Polycarp* 3, God is impassible (http://www.newadvent.org/fathers/0110.htm).
74. Actually, Bernhard of Clairvaux, in his commentary on the Song of Solomon, argued against this: "God cannot suffer, but he can 'suffer *with*'" (Lat. *impassibilis est Deo, sed non incompassibilis*)—quoted in Ratzinger (2007, 87)—but is not *compassion* a form of *passion*, "suffering"?

chel,[75] who called the preaching of the prophets "pathetic theology," and placed this over against the early Christian view of God's *apatheia*, adopted from Plato and the Stoics: God cannot suffer. If by this we understand that God is free and independent of humans and of human influences, there is no problem. However, the Greek view of the "apathetic" God also entailed that God is insensitive to, and uninterested in, human matters, and would not need any partners. Israel's prophets, however, did not proclaim an unmoved, unconcerned, neutral God, but One who was intimately involved emotionally with his people. Only in a conceptual use of such terms as God's independence and freedom, on the one hand, and his sympathetic involvement with his people, on the other hand, could we construe contradictions between them. God is the God who can decide freely and autonomously to be intensely moved by, and involved with, his people. God's grief, and even his "relenting" (Gen. 6:6-7; Exod. 32:12, 14; 1 Sam. 15:11, 35; 2 Sam. 24:16; 1 Chron. 21:15; Jer. 15:6; 18:8, 10; 26:3, 13, 19; 42:10; Joel 2:13-14; Amos 7:3, 6; Jonah 3:9-10; 4:2)[76] with regard to his people, are never in conflict with his power and freedom.

From this idea that according to his being, God is incapable of suffering, arose in the sixthcentury *theopaschitic* conflict: if God cannot suffer, and Jesus is truly God, how then could Jesus suffer while living on earth? In reference to the biblical language about the wrath of God, for example, some like to speak of unwarranted primitive anthropopathisms. To this claim, Emil Brunner rightly responded that people arguing like this do not know the *holy* God and the *Lord* God of the Bible.[77]

When the idea that God cannot suffer is rejected, the problem whether Jesus according to his divine nature knew emotions disappears as well. This seems to be a better approach

---

75. Heschel (1936).
76. Cf. the apparent contradiction between Num. 23:19 and 1 Sam. 15:29.
77. Brunner (1950, 162) *contra* Julius A. L. Wegscheider.

than blurring the distinction between the two natures, as does A. König,[78] and to some extent also K. Barth.[79] The latter fully identified the history of Jesus Christ with the history of God: Christ's sufferings are God's sufferings, Christ's self-sacrifice is God's self-sacrifice. G. C. Berkouwer criticized Barth for not clearly distinguishing the relationship between Jesus and God: Jesus surrendered himself to God, suffered under the striking hand of God, and stepped in as Mediator between God and humanity.[80] This criticism did not lead Berkouwer to deny that Christ suffered also according to his divine nature.[81]

8.6 The Exceptional Incarnation
8.6.1 A Truly Human Body

As we saw in chapter 7, there is a continuing struggle in the New Testament to avoid emphasizing Jesus' deity at the expense of his humanity, and to avoid emphasizing Jesus' humanity at the expense of his deity. Thus, John reported that Jesus said, "I thirst" (John 19:28) not so much because of human weakness but in order "to fulfill the Scripture." This does not entail denying anything of Jesus' true humanity; but Jesus' humanity should not compromise anything of his deity.

This fits the entire picture of John 18 and 19, where Jesus was hardly being led by guards and soldiers, but always "went out" or "came forward" or "came out" (Gk. *exēlthen*, 18:1, 4; 19:5, 17) autonomously, sovereignly. He always takes the initiative, even when he appears to be entirely in the control of his enemies. Jesus is not (passively) killed (cf. Acts 2:23; 3:15; 5:30; 7:52) but he (actively) "lays down" his own life (10:17–18). Also note that he did not (passively) "breathe his last" (Matt. 27:50 GNT, Gk. *aphēken to pneuma*), but (actively) "handed over the spirit" (John 19:30 NABRE, Gk. *paredōken to pneuma*) — a distinction that gets blurred in many Bible trans-

---

78. König (1975, 117–18).
79. Barth (*CD* IV/1=21, §59).
80. See the comments by Berkouwer (1956, 297–310).
81. Berkouwer (1977, 246–47).

lations.

At the same time, beginning with John 1:14 ("the Word *became* flesh"), this Gospel writer John fights against the early forms of Docetism that arose in his day. Docetism is the doctrine that Jesus did not truly become a human being but temporarily adopted a human pseudo-body. The term Docetism comes from Greek *dokeō*, "to seem." In a wider sense, Docetism involves any doctrine that calls into question Jesus' true humanity. Thus, the Gnostic Valentinus[82] speculated that Jesus merely fed himself with divinity; he ate and drank in a special way without excreting his solid substances. He had such a capacity of continence that the food within him was not digested, for he experienced no corruption. The idea was that Jesus' body would have been merely a kind of wrapper, which could just as easily be dispensed with, just as the three celestial beings in Genesis 18 had apparently adopted a kind of body for the occasion without really becoming human.

Basically, Docetism was rooted in the ancient Greek conviction that matter is inferior to spirit, and that it is inconceivable that the divine could ever be associated with matter. For the same reason, it is claimed that the Deity could not have created the world in a direct way but only through an intermediate being, the so-called demiurge (lit., "worker [on behalf of God] for the people").[83] Docetism also taught that death involves the liberation of the soul from matter, so that the idea of a resurrection of the dead is ridiculous, or at least highly undesirable (cf. the Greek response in Acts 17:32). Ignatius combated Docetism.[84] However, this opposition did

---

82. Quoted in Ford and Higton (2002, 79).
83. This idea also played a role in Arianism, which taught that Jesus himself was this demiurge.
84. "Now, He suffered all these things for our sakes, that we might be saved. And He suffered truly, even as also He truly raised up Himself, not, as certain unbelievers maintain, that He only seemed to suffer, as they themselves only seem to be [Christians]. And as they believe, so shall it happen unto them, when they shall be divested of their bodies, and be mere evil spirits"; Letter to the Smyrnaeans 2; cf. 5; also cf. his letter to the Trallians 10.

not prevent millions of Christians from focusing far more on their own physical death (and their "going to heaven") than on the second coming of Christ and their own resurrection.

8.6.2 Jesus Still Human Today

Many orthodox Christians find it strange that Jesus Christ should still be truly Man, even after his resurrection and ascension, and during his glorification at the right hand of God. They think that Jesus would no longer need his humanity and his human body. In opposition to this, we find the clear testimony of the New Testament. First, to be sure, Jesus' resurrection body in many respects must have been different than before. There was continuity (it was the buried body that was raised; cf. Rom. 8:11), but there was also discontinuity: with his resurrection body he could enter a closed room, and his encounters with his followers now had the character of appearances (Mark 16:9, 12, 14; Luke 24:34; Acts 1:3; 9:17; 10:40; 13:31; 26:16; 1 Cor. 15:5-8[85]). However, this body was just as real and physical as the body he had before his resurrection. It could be touched, it could ingest food, and it bore the scars of his sufferings (Matt. 28:9; Luke 24:37-43; John 20:17, 20, 25, 27; Acts 10:41).[86]

Second, at his ascension Jesus did not lay aside his resurrection body — presuming this would have been possible — for Colossians 2:9 says, "[I]n him the whole fullness of deity dwells [present tense!] *bodily*," that is, right now, Jesus dwells in heaven in his glorified body.

Third, when Jesus returns, he will still be a Man, for he will bear the title "Son of Man" (Matt. 10:23; 13:40-41; 16:27-28; 19:28; 24:27, 30, 37, 39, 44; 25:31; 26:64; so also Mark-John) (cf. §§4.8-4.9 above).

---

85. Cf. especially 1 Cor. 15:35–49, where Paul deals generally with the differences between the present physical body and the resurrection body; see further in §13.7.
86. Berkouwer (1954, 205) believed that 1 John 5:6 (Jesus came "by water and blood") must "probably" be understood as an anti-docetic polemic as well.

However, fourth, what will life be like in eternity for the Son, after he has given back ("delivered") the kingdom to the Father (1 Cor. 15:24)? A. A. van Ruler took an extreme position by speaking of a "Messianic intermezzo": when one day the creation is consummated in the kingdom of God, there will be neither a place nor a need for the Mediator.[87] At that time, the incarnation will be annulled; there will be no more "(Man) Jesus." The Son will recede within the inner being of the Trinity. From eternity, it was God's desire to live with *human beings*, but not to need a Mediator; a mediator was needed only as a temporary emergency measure to solve the problem of sin.[88] If this were correct, then indeed the Son *would* have assumed a human body only temporarily. Then Docetism would ultimately triumph, for the Word would never have truly *become* flesh (John 1:4).

But Jesus did not assume a human body for a period of time. He "partook" (Gk. *meteschen*) of blood and flesh (Heb. 2:14). His "assumption of flesh" (Lat. *assumptio carnis*) cannot be undone; from the incarnation into all eternity, his humanity belongs to his being just as inseparably as his deity.[89] In opposition to the heretics of his time—according to Irenaeus[90] these were identified as Cerinthus and his followers—John confesses Jesus as one who has "come [Gk. *elēlythota*] in the flesh" (1 John 4:2), or one who is "coming [Gk. *erchomenon*[91]] in the flesh" (2 John 1:7), that is, as a true human, with a body of flesh that belongs to him forever.

This does not necessarily mean that Jesus will be Medi-

---

87. Van Ruler (1947, especially 90–94; 1969, 164–78; 1978).
88. See the summary by Van de Beek (2006, 139–40); see also the objections by Van Genderen and Velema (2008, 510–11), and especially those by Berkouwer (1972, 430–32).
89. Therefore, there can be no gradual incarnation, as Pannenberg posited (1991, 427).
90. *Adversus Haereses* I.26.1; regarding the errors that John combated, see extensively, Marshall (1978a, 14–22).
91. A timeless present tense, through which the emphasis is put all the more strongly on the person who is denied; Jesus is the One coming in flesh.

ator forever in the sense that he would mediate our fellowship with, and contemplation of, the Father. This statement is prompted by John 14:6-9, where Jesus says, "I am the way, and the truth, and the life. No one comes to the Father except through me. . . . From now on you do know him and have seen him. . . . Whoever has seen me has seen the Father." Does this mean that believers will forever see the Father only in and through the Man Jesus Christ? I see three options here, the first of which can be rejected immediately, but the choice between (b) and (c) is more difficult: in eternity (a) Jesus will be neither Man nor Mediator. (b) Jesus will remain both Man and Mediator. (c) Jesus will remain Man but not Mediator.

Herman Bavinck preferred (b) such that, in Christ's Mediatorship, it is no longer a matter of seeing God but of Christ's relationship to the church:

> Christ is and remains [forever] the head of the church, from whom flows all life and blessedness to it throughout all eternity. Those who would deny this must also arrive at the doctrine that the Son will at some point in the future shed and destroy his human nature; and for this there is no scriptural ground whatever.[92]

Abraham Kuyper also testified clearly to Jesus' eternal humanity: "Christ became Man, and will eternally remain Man. He will not ever lay down his humanity but lives in our flesh, and will forever live in our flesh."[93] F. W. A. Korff suggested that according to Calvin Jesus' humanity would not continue forever.[94] However, according to G. C. Berkouwer, Calvin taught in his commentary on 1 Corinthians that there will be an end to Jesus' mediation as far as the contemplation of God is concerned, but not necessarily to his humanity.[95] Personally, I find option (b) most compelling: Christ will remain both

---

92. Bavinck (*RD* 3:482).
93. Kuyper (1887, 31, 195).
94. Korff (1940, 251).
95. Berkouwer (1972, 431–32); cf. Bavinck (*RD* 3:482).

Man and Mediator, not only in relation to his church but also for the contemplation of God. This is because he will forever remain the Logos (the expression of who God is), and the image of God (the imprint of his being). Our access to God will forever be through him who is God's Logos, God's image, God's imprint.

Even though there may be doubt concerning this eternal Mediatorship, at least we must maintain in opposition to Van Ruler and others that Christ remains a human being forever. Believers also remain human beings forever, but their humanity is essentially different from that of Christ. His humanity is unique because of his pre-existence. No ordinary human being "comes in the flesh" because he or she *is* "flesh" — human matter — from the beginning of his or her existence. Christ, however, as the eternal Son, in the fullness of time (Gal. 4:4), *partook* of human flesh. Therefore, he *was* (and *is*) the eternal Word, but he *became* flesh (John 1:14) in order to remain flesh forever just as he will remain the eternal Word forever. What descends from heaven is the Word that has become human. This descending from heaven coincides with his incarnation. He who descends is the eternal Son, who from this same moment will also be flesh forever (cf. John 6:51–55).

8.6.3 Mythological Aspects?

Today, many view the notion of incarnation as mythological. But this conclusion is less obvious than anti-supernaturalism wishes us to believe. It is hardly conceivable that Hellenist myths concerning incarnated gods — which actually never involve gods that were supposed to have really become flesh — would have penetrated that early into the Gospels, which had been written relatively early, and by uneducated followers of Jesus.[96] For this hypothesis, liberal theologians needed to invent pre-Pauline Hellenistic churches, for whose existence no evidence has ever been found. The earliest New Testament

---

96. Neill (1977, 61); see more generally, Erickson (1991) and Davies et al. (2004); more critical is Küng (1987).

writings refer to Jesus' divinity. Equally misplaced is the idea that God would have become incarnate many times, such as in the Buddha. In fact, the understanding of incarnation behind such views has nothing to do with the biblical incarnation. The one Logos became flesh once and for all; thus, only one person can be the incarnation of the one God, and he could become incarnate only once.[97]

Behind every mythological view of the incarnation we find a mistaken starting point.[98] The solution is not to explain ("from below") how it could be possible that Jesus is God, but rather to explain ("from above") how it is possible that the Son of God became flesh. The proper question is not: Can a human being be God? but rather: Can God become Man? The idea that any human being could ever be called God seems inconceivable *a priori*; even the most orthodox Christian would never assume such a thing concerning any human being. That these same Christians nevertheless call Jesus "God" is rooted not in some deification of a human being but in a totally different belief, namely, the incarnation of God. It is impossible to make any human being to be God, even the most remarkable wisdom teacher or redeemer who ever lived. However, it is *not* impossible or inconceivable *a priori* that God would become Man. The Christian faith teaches not that Jesus became God, but that God became Jesus, and did so before the Christian faith came into existence.

8.7 Self-Emptying
8.7.1 Becoming Man, Even Slave

Because of the pre-existence of the eternal Son of God, his incarnation involved a self-emptying (Gk. *kenōsis*; Phil. 2:7). For those who were always human, this could not be the case; but it was for him through whom God had created all human beings, and who now himself became part of that creation. Because it was in, through, and for him that all things were

---

97. See various contributions in Goulder (1979).
98. Erickson (1985, 677–81).

created, he was, from the moment he became part of that creation, necessarily the "firstborn of all creation" (Col. 1:15; see §7.6.3 above). This is an *honorary* title; but it does not change the fact that the incarnation as such constituted *humiliation* for him.

Many expositors have assumed that the words of Philippians 2:6–11 formed a pre-Pauline hymn; verses 6–8a literally say: Christ Jesus, who

> Though he was in the form [Gk. *morphē*] of God,
>> did not count equality [Gk. *to einai isa*] with God a thing to be grasped,
>
> but emptied [Gk. *ekenōsen*] himself,
>> by taking the form [Gk. *morphēn*] of a servant [or, slave; Gk. *doulou*],
>
>> being born in the likeness [Gk. *homoiōmati*] of men.
>
> And being found in human form [Gk. *schēmati*], he humbled himself. . . .

First, in contrast to the *morphē* of God, we find the *morphē* of not just a man ("being born in the likeness of men") but of a *slave*. This was added humiliation. It entails that, in addition to sharing in the *being* of God, it now also belongs to his *being* that he is and remains forever a *slave* (or, in a milder rendering, a *servant*), and not simply a human being. He was a slave on earth in order to accomplish the work of God ("[W]hoever would be first among you must be slave of all. For even the Son of Man came not to be served but to serve," Mark 10:44-45). But today as well, he still consecrates himself to his church in order to serve her (cf. Eph. 5:25-26 NIV, ". . . to make her holy, cleansing her by the washing with water through the word"). And in his kingdom, forever, he will dress himself for service, invite his followers to recline at table, and come and serve them (Luke 12:37): "For who is the greater, one who reclines at table or one who serves? Is it not the one who reclines at table? But I am among you as the one who serves" (22:27).

Second, he not only assumed the *morphē*, the essence, of a

human being but also the *schēma*, the outward form of a human. That is, he is a human being in his essence—his humanity belongs so essentially to his being that he will remain Man forever—*and* he is a human being in his outward appearance, his behavior, his walk and talk.[99]

Third, taking the form of a slave and the figure of a human being is called "emptying." It was a voluntary act of Jesus—he emptied *himself*—out of his gracious love: "[Y]ou know the grace of our Lord Jesus Christ, that though he was rich, yet for your sake he became poor, so that you by his poverty might become rich" (2 Cor. 8:9). What this "emptying" exactly means is examined in the next sections.

8.7.2 What Is *Kenōsis*?

The phrase "emptying himself" (Gk. *heauton ekenōsen*) in verse 7 must be distinguished from the phrase "humbled himself" (Gk. *etapeinōsen heauton*) in verse 8. As Wolfhart Pannenberg wrote,

> The self-humbling obviously refers to the earthly path of obedience that led Jesus to the cross, but the self-emptying seems to start with the divine equality of the Son that he renounced so as to take to himself the slave-existence of human conditions of life.[100]

However, this quotation immediately leads us to ask whether the self-emptying really entailed refraining from being equal to God? In other words, what does the phrase "emptied himself" Gk. *heauton ekenōsen*) mean, and what exactly did Jesus' "emptying" (the English theological term is *kenosis*) involve?

This notion must be described very carefully, because, on the one hand, the full import of the "emptying" (Gk. *kenos* = "empty") must be maintained, whereas, on the other hand,

---

99. For the distinction between *morphē* and *schēma*, see Romans 12:2, "Do not be conformed [Gk. *syschēmatizesthe*, assume the outward appearance] to this world, but be transformed [Gk. *metamorphousthe*, i.e., in your inner being] by the renewal of your mind"; see also J. Behm (*TDNT* 4:742–59).
100. Pannenberg (1994, 2:375).

against the backdrop of all New Testament teaching, it must not be suggested that Jesus would have *laid aside* the "form of God," or part of his divine attributes. What *kenosis* does entail is closely related to the meaning of "did not count equality with God a thing to be grasped," because *kenosis* forms a contrast with this. To begin with, consider the variety in the translations: ". . . did not count equality with God a thing to be grasped (marginal note: a thing to be held on to for advantage)" (ESV); ". . . to be exploited" (CSB); ". . . did not regard equality with God a thing to be grasped *or* asserted [as if He did not already possess it, or was afraid of losing it]" (AMP); "he did not think that his being equal with God was something to use for his own benefit" (ERV); "He had equal status with God but didn't think so much of himself that he had to cling to the advantages of that status no matter what" (MSG).

The fundamental issue here is the meaning of the Greek word *harpagmos* ("robbery, rapine"). Is it the "thing robbed" (in the sense of a possession to which one clings at all costs), *or* is it something worth robbing? That is, is the text saying that the pre-incarnate Christ already possessed equality with God, and decided not to cling to it, *or* that he did not have to reach out for equality with God because he already possessed it? The subsequent phrase "but emptied himself" leads various expositors to prefer the former view,[101] along with various Bible translations. However, this does *not* mean that Christ relinquished his equality with God.[102] John's Gospel is full of evidence that Jesus continually claimed his equality with God (see §7.2.1 above). The point instead is that Jesus did not insist on manifesting, while on earth, all the glory and majesty of his

---

101. E.g., Matter (1965, 48–49); Wuest (1970, 64–65); Kent (1978, 123, 127); Müller (1984, 79–81 including notes 5–7); Kramer (1996, 71, 74); *contra*, e.g., Greijdanus (1925, 47); Kennedy (1979, 436–37).

102. *Contra* H. Bavinck, who wrote that ". . . at his incarnation he exchanged 'the form of God' (*morphē theou*, Phil. 2:6) for the 'form of a servant' (*morphē doulou*, Phil. 2:7), . . . [H]e had put aside 'the form of God' (*morphē theou*) that was his . . ." (*RD* 3:435).

deity.¹⁰³ He could have done so; however, he did not cling to that manifestation of glory and splendor, but he emptied himself of it. This is the "becoming poor" (Gk. *eptōcheusen*) in 2 Corinthians 8:9. In his inner being, he was and remained God, but he chose to become a Man, and in his outer appearance, to present himself to humanity not as God, but as a Man, yes, as a slave. But at the same time, he did it in such a way that, to those who were able to see, "the glory as of the only begotten of the Father" still shone through the veil of his humiliation and self-emptying (John 1:14).¹⁰⁴

Christ remained in the form of God, he continued sharing in the being of God, but he laid aside "the fully glorious, so to speak, fully divine majestic revelation"¹⁰⁵ belonging to the Godhead; or rather, he veiled it; he "refrained from the manifestation of his divine glory."¹⁰⁶ This, then, is how we un-

---

103. K. Schilder (1939, 23) wrote:
    ". . . Rather, he removed the divine glory from the sphere of human *observation*. Where the torrent of a judgment that unleashed God's energy could have been expected, there comes instead of this a tiny baby who lays himself in a manger, and surrenders himself under that judgment; that baby is empty, and that manger is empty, and his later sitting and standing are empty, along with his hanging on the cross. Empty of the radiance of the immeasurable light that blinds eyes, empty of the omnipotent power that smashes spears and makes mountains smoke."
104. A. Kuyper wrote that, in contrast to the Lutherans, the Reformed taught ". . . that the Son of God had *not* laid aside his glory, but had merely *covered* it with the veil of his human nature" (1887, 199). Bavinck taught that Christ had "concealed his divine nature behind the garment of a weak human nature; no one saw in him or could see in him the Only Begotten of the Father, except with the eye of faith (John 1:14)" (*RD* 3:435). K. Schilder observed that ". . . over the form of God, so to speak, he put on the form of a servant; he who was in the form of the Sovereign, the Subduer, the tax gatherer, put on over that form the garment of the subject, the one subdued, the taxpayer" (1939, 24).
105. Greijdanus (1925, 48).
106. Kramer (1996, 72); early Protestant theologians spoke of the "concealment" (Lat. *occultatio*) or "suppression" (Lat. *suppressio*) of the divine attributes of Christ during his earthly life, and combated the idea of a "loss" (Lat. *amissio*), "deposition" (Lat. *depositio*), or a "refraining from" (Lat. *abditio*) of divine attributes.

derstand the "emptying": not as a laying aside of his divine nature and being, for then he would have ceased to be God, but as a veiling of all his splendor. We understand the Greek participle *labōn* here in a causative or instrumental way: he emptied himself *by* taking on the form of a slave, with all humility, unimportance, unattractiveness, and unsightliness that belongs to the status of being a slave (cf. Isa. 53:2–3). Humanity itself still displays, after the Fall, a certain luster and glory (cf. Ps. 8), but Jesus refrained from even *this* by becoming not merely human but the lowest of humans: a slave. His divine glory was concealed behind the insignificance of the slave that he became. "Foxes have holes, and birds of the air have nests, but the Son of Man has nowhere to lay his head" (Matt. 8:20; Luke 9:58).[107]

8.7.3 The Kenotic Theory

Up to this point, we have examined what Jesus' self-emptying (Gk. *kenosis*) involved. We concluded that Jesus did not give up the "form of God," or even part of his divine attributes. When assuming the form of a slave he did not lay aside the form of God.[108] This claim is denied, however, in the so-called kenotic theory, or kenoticism.[109] This view claims that Jesus was first God, then became Man, and then became God again. This erroneous view reminds us of modalism or Sabellianism:

---

107. In John 19:30, "laying his head" (Gk. *tēn kephalēn klinēi*) is the same as "bowed his head" (*klinas tēn kephalēn*): the cross was the only place on earth where Jesus could "lay" his head, namely, in death.
108. Cyril of Alexandria, quoted in Ford and Higton (2002, 96–97), said that what Christ was before the incarnation (he was God, the true, only begotten Son, light, life, and power) he maintains without any loss; what he was not, he, as he became visible, assumed because of the divine plan. Thus, the Word became Man without ceasing to be what he was; he remained God as he became manifest in our form. He did not change his nature, nor did he merely seem to become Man. He did not change the nature of his divinity into the substance of his flesh, nor the substance of his flesh into the nature of his divinity.
109. In addition to some nineteenth-century theologians (J. C. K. von Hofmann, F. H. R. Frank, and others), see Mackintosh (1914, 463–90); Kennedy (1979, 437); see the comments by Berkouwer (1954, 37–42).

God manifests himself at certain times as the Father, at other times as the Son or the Holy Spirit.[110]

The kenotic theory claims that the expression "in the form of God" means "after the image of God," or that Jesus at his incarnation had laid aside some of his divine attributes, such as his omnipotence, omniscience, and omnipresence (Gottfried Thomasius[111]), or even his deity as such, or his divine way of existing (Wolfgang Geß: his deity is "transformed" into his humanity).[112] These views do not at all necessarily follow from the biblical text; on the contrary, Christ was omnipotent, omniscient, and omnipresent also in his human existence (see §7.3 above). Moreover, these views threaten outright the doctrines of God's immutability, of the deity of Christ, and of the divine Trinity. In kenoticism, we lose the New Testament truth that *God* enters into this world in Jesus: Immanuel, "God with us."

This is not to say that the kenotics had nothing right. Thus, this doctrine of God's immutability is quite challenging. This doctrine is affected by the claim that the *kenōsis* implies a certain un-deification of God. But conversely, one wonders how, if God is really immutable, the Logos, who is God, could ever *become* flesh. Does the notion that God can become something that he was not really comport with God's immutability?

Further, the kenotics drew our attention to the problem involving exactly who is the One who emptied himself: Christ *after* his incarnation, during his life on earth, or *during* his incarnation; in my view, they rightly argued the latter. The kenotics also asked whether Jesus was exalted only according to his human nature (Phil. 2:9), or whether *he himself* was ex-

---

110. Was it a slip of the pen when Van Genderen and Velema (2008, 469) wrote: "The Reformed tradition interpreted the incarnation of the Word as a *laying aside* or veiling of the divine glory" (italics added)?
111. See the quotation of him in Ford and Higton (2002, 353–55); see also Weber (1983, 2:141–42); Beker and Hasselaar (1981, 151–54); Bloesch (1997, 61).
112. See the refutation by Berkhof (1981, 327–29); Ward (1962); Fuller (1965, 232); Bonhoeffer (1966, 98–102); Müller (1984, 83–85n9).

alted, that is, according to his entire being. One can take these questions seriously without agreeing with all the kenotics' answers.

Paul Althaus accused the kenotics of affecting the "Christological mystery":

> Making statements about Christ's self-awareness as human and divine surpasses the authority and possibilities of theological thought.
>
> The paradox of the incarnation must not be belittled by such theories. The full tension of the confession concerning Jesus Christ must be maintained. It is precisely in the true, unabridged, unchanged humanity of Jesus that God's *entire* glory and power are present for us . . . . One must not wish to rationalize this divine miracle [of God's entering into his Son's sufferings on the cross] by a theory that allows God to be present and active in Jesus Christ only insofar as this does not break through the boundaries of the human according to our concepts. But we should not try to directly point out the deity ontologically in the humanity of Christ [as classical Christology tried]. The deity is present under [Jesus'] humanity in a hidden way, only revealed to faith, but cannot be viewed, and thus surpasses each possibility of a theory. The fact that it is this way, that God enters into the hiddenness of his deity under [the form of] humanity, that is the Kenosis.[113]

---

113. Althaus (*RGG* 3:1245–46).

Chapter 9
The Virgin Birth of Christ

"Joseph, son of David, do not fear to take Mary as your wife, for that which is conceived in her is from the Holy Spirit.
She will bear a son, and you shall call his name Jesus, for he will save his people from their sins."
All this took place to fulfill what the Lord had spoken by the prophet:
"Behold, the virgin shall conceive and bear a son, and they shall call his name Immanuel (which means, God with us)."

Matthew 1:20-23

[B]ehold, you will conceive in your womb and bear a son, and you shall call his name Jesus.
He will be great and will be called the Son of the Most High.
And the Lord God will give to him the throne of his father David, and he will reign over the house of Jacob forever,
and of his kingdom there will be no end. . . .
The Holy Spirit will come upon you, and the power of the Most High will overshadow you;
therefore the child to be born will be called holy —
the Son of God.

Luke 1:31-33, 35

9.1 Jesus Begotten of a Virgin
9.1.1 The Miracle of the Virgin Birth

THE SO-CALLED "virgin birth" of Jesus is linked inseparably to other important Christological subjects: Jesus' eternal pre-existence and deity, the miracle of the incarnation, his sinlessness (see next chapter), and thus his fitness for accomplishing the work of redemption. The virgin birth refers to Jesus' birth from a virgin, without the intervention of any man. As Gregory of Nazianzus wrote (freely rendered), Jesus was begotten as a Man as well as born as a Man; born of a woman, who was a virgin.[1] The fact that he was born points to his human nature; the fact that he was born of a virgin points to his divine nature. In his human nature, he had no father; in his divine nature, he had no mother. I add to this that God was his divine, heavenly Father, and Joseph of Nazareth was his legal earthly father.

Throughout biblical history, several times God had miraculously given the joy of motherhood to a sterile woman (Rebekah, Rachel, Manoah's wife, Hannah), sometimes even an aged woman (Sarah, Elizabeth, and according to tradition, Joachim's wife Anna[2]). However, in all these cases the begetting was performed by a man, even if he was of advanced age (Abraham, Zechariah, Joachim). Abraham was even "dead," that is, impotent, in terms of the power of begetting (cf. Rom. 4:19). Depending on one's choice of manuscript readings, Hebrews 11:11 can be rendered as follows (and I think this is the proper intention of the text): "By trusting, he [i.e., Abraham] received potency to father a child, even when he was past the age for it, as was Sarah herself; because he regarded the One who had made the promise as trustworthy" (CJB). Thus, a double miracle was involved: aged Abraham received the potency to father a child, and aged Sarah received the capacity to conceive in her womb. However, this does not change the fact that Abraham physically fathered his son Isaac, just as

---

1. Quoted in Ford and Higton (2002, 93).
2. First mentioned in the apocryphal Protoevangelium of James.

Zechariah received the power to father John the Baptist, and Joachim to father Mary.

How different it was with the virgin birth of Jesus, which completely excluded any male role. This is comparable to John 1:13, "... born, not of blood nor of the will of the flesh nor of the will of man, but of God," which some have understood to refer to the virgin birth of Jesus. The text refers to the regeneration of those who come to faith, but the parallel is obvious: it occurs "not of the will of [any] man." Mary is perfectly right in asking: "How will this be, since I do not know a man?" (Luke 1:34 ESV note). This is one of those places where the verb "to know" has the connotation of sexual intimacy (cf. Adam in Gen. 4:1; Joseph in Matt. 1:25). Mary's question is: How can I conceive without having sexual intercourse with any man? The angel's reply is, in one interpretation, that the Holy Spirit will, as it were, take over the role of the man in this miraculous virgin birth: "The Holy Spirit will come upon you, and the power of the Most High will overshadow you" (Luke 1:35; see further below).

9.1.2 The Holy Spirit: Begetting or Giving Birth?

In this chapter, I will follow the metaphor of God himself assuming the role of the human father. Yet, we must express ourselves carefully here. As Mary listened to the words of Gabriel, who must have spoken Aramaic or Hebrew, she heard the (usually) *feminine* word *ruach*.[3] Thus, the person who understands Hebrew always "hears" a "she" who is at work in the work of the Spirit. The feminine gender of *ruach* makes it clearer how the Holy Spirit in Genesis 1:2 is presented as a mother bird "hovering" over the waters just as a bird hovers over its young. In Hebrew, the verb "to hover" is *r-ch-ph*, "to hover, soar, move gently, quaver" (cf. Deut. 22:6, "the mother [bird] sitting on the young or on the eggs") (the form "hovering," *merachephet* is again feminine). In the next volume in this series, we will discuss far more extensively the maternal

---

3. Note that in Luke's Gk. version we read the neuter noun *pneuma*.

aspects of the Holy Spirit, or of God generally.

Believers are "born of [the] Spirit" (Gk. *gennēthē ex pneumatos*, John 3:5); this expression is entirely analogous with this one about Christ: "born of woman" (Gk. *genomenon ek gynaikos*, Gal. 4:4; cf. John 16:21). It sounds as if the Holy Spirit himself is a "woman" from whom believers are born, in contrast with their earthly mother (John 3:4). John 1:13 says that believers are "born of God" (Gk. *ek theou egennēthēsan*), which is the same expression. The Greek verb that is used, *ginomai*, can mean both "to beget (to father)" by a man and "to bear (to give birth to)" by a woman.

In the Gnostic-Christian (second century?) *Odes of Solomon* 24, the Spirit is the feminine dove,[4] who descended upon Jesus at his baptism. The text says (Ode 19): "The Holy Spirit opened Her bosom, and mixed the milk of the two breasts of the Father."[5] In a similar sense, the Armenian writer Nerses Snorhali compared drinking the living water of the Spirit with a child drinking from their mother's breast.[6] In the so-called Gospel of Hebrews, Jesus speaks of "my Mother, the Holy Spirit." In the Gospel of Thomas, Jesus places his earthly mother (Mary) and father (Joseph) over against his heavenly Mother and Father. The Syrian Aphrahat said, "As long as a man has not taken a wife, he loves and reveres God his father and the Holy Spirit his mother, and he has no other love."[7]

Because Mary is Jesus' mother, we may assume that, in the begetting and birth of Jesus, the Holy Spirit assumed the role of the heavenly, spiritual Father. But this not at all self-evident. When the angel says, "The Holy Spirit will come upon you, and the power of the Most High will overshadow you" (Luke 1:35), the Greek verb is *episkiazō*, "to overshadow." We

---

4. The Gk. noun *peristera* ("dove") in Luke 3:22 is a feminine noun.
5. http://gnosis.org/library/odes.htm.
6. Burgess (1989, 6–7, 172–73); a similar image is found with Catherine of Siena; see Burgess (1997, 114).
7. http://www.academia.edu/24856498/The_Mother-Spirit_in_the_Syrian_Tradition_Aphrahat_and_Ephrem.

find this word in Exodus 40:29 (LXX; cf. MT and English versions: v. 35): "Moses was not able to enter the tent of meeting because the cloud settled on [Gk. *epeskiazen*, overshadowed] it, and the glory of the LORD filled the tabernacle." This is a reference to what the rabbis called the *Shekhinah*, the glorious Presence of God. Jewish literature viewed her as a parallel with the divine *Chokhmah* ("Wisdom"). The *Shekhinah* led Israel to the wilderness, and the deuterocanonical book of Wisdom 10:15-21, tells us the same of the Wisdom (*Chokhmah*). Both *Shekhinah* and *Chokhmah* are feminine words. In Hebrew ears it was perfectly normal to think of this overshadowing power as a heavenly feminine being.

Thus, it is quite possible that when Mary heard the words spoken by Gabriel, she did not think at all of the Spirit as a heavenly (fatherly) Begetter but as this heavenly feminine power that was to overshadow her. The Holy Spirit was to hover over her as "She" had once hovered at the beginning of creation (Gen. 1:2). We may still say that Jesus was divinely begotten in the womb of Mary, but then by the *Father*, through the power of the motherly Spirit. In other words, Jesus had, so to speak, two divine Parents: the Father and the Spirit, and two earthly parents: his legal father Joseph, and his biological mother Mary, as some of the church fathers had already expressed it (see above).

9.1.3 Virginal Begetting or Virgin Birth?

Actually, it would be more accurate to speak of "virgin begetting" than of "virgin birth," as several authors have proposed.[8] This shifts attention from the birth to the begetting. As we saw, and as we will see, this begetting of Jesus in Mary's womb was not the effect of sexual intercourse but of an exceptional, supernatural intervention of God the Father through

---

8. Brown (1973, 27–28); Moody (1981, 417); Bloesch (1997, 88, 90); Van de Beek (2002a, 148–57); Borg and Wright (1999, 171–86); B. Witherington (*DJG* 70).

the Holy Spirit.[9] However, there is no reason to assume that Jesus' birth was supernatural as well. From the fourth century, we encounter speculation about the virginity of Mary, not only at the conception (Lat. *ante partum*) of Jesus, but also during and after parturition (Lat. *in partu, post partum*). In effect, this would mean that Mary's hymen would have remained intact during parturition, and that subsequently she never had sexual intercourse with her husband.

Let us begin with the latter point: the consequence of this speculation would be that the "brothers" of Jesus (Matt. 13:55; Mark 6:3) were in fact stepbrothers, that is, sons of Joseph by an earlier marriage (see more extensively in §8.1.1 above). Or they might have been cousins, which is the traditional Roman Catholic view, but the view of Luther and Calvin as well. However, in the second and third century, some believed that Jesus' brothers and sisters were simply children of Mary herself, born after Jesus. This is the most natural interpretation of Mark 6:3, "Is not this the carpenter, the son of Mary and brother of James and Joses and Judas and Simon? And are not his sisters here with us?"

If the latter view is correct, there is no reason to maintain the notion of a permanently intact hymen of Mary. Yet, the Protoevangelium of James (19:19–20:3) tells us that, after the birth of Jesus, the midwife conducted a digital exam to confirm that Mary's hymen was still unaffected, and thereby concluded that a virgin really had given birth to a child. This kind of docetic-gnostic speculation finds no basis in the Bible, and does not pertain at all to Christology, but rather to Mariology.[10] Such Mariological speculations have often been abused to eliminate the doctrine of the virgin birth,[11] whereas Christology and Mariology have very little to do with each other.

Interestingly, the notion of the perpetual virginity (Lat. *semper virgo*) of Mary lived on in Protestantism, for instance,

---

9. For the role of the Holy Spirit, see *EDR* 1:§6.1.1 and *RT* II/1.
10. Van de Beek (2002a, 148); cf. Bloesch (1997, 87).
11. Berkouwer (1965, 125–27, 141–42).

with Martin Luther, John Calvin, Ulrich Zwingli, and John Wesley.[12] No doubt this was due to the age-old exaltation within the Christian church of virginity in general, and that of Mary in particular. As with so many other female saints, it was easier for women to maintain their sanctity if they remained virgins all their lives.

Apart from these speculations about the perpetual virginity of Mary, the term "virgin birth" is certainly not wrong, for at the birth of Jesus Mary was still a virgin in the sense that she had never had sexual intercourse with any man (Matt. 1:25). Therefore, the Apostles' Creed and the Nicene Creed rightly confess, "born of the virgin Mary," (Lat. *natus ex virgine Maria* and *ex Maria virgine*, respectively).[13]

9.1.4 The Virgin Birth in the Quran

Noteworthy is also the testimony of the Quran, considering the fact that, apparently, Muhammad obtained most of his knowledge of divine things from contemporaneous Jews and Christians (no matter how he distorted it):

> And mention in the Scripture Mary, when she withdrew from her people to an eastern location. She screened herself away from them, and We sent to her Our spirit [here: angel], and He appeared to her as an immaculate human. She said, "I take refuge from you in the Most Merciful, should you be righteous." He said, "I am only the messenger of your Lord, to give you the gift of a pure son." She said, "How can I have a son, when no man has touched me, and I was never unchaste?" He said, "Thus said your Lord, 'It is easy for Me, and We will make him a sign for humanity, and a mercy from Us. It is a matter already decided'" (Surah 19:16–21).[14]

Another important statement is found in Surah 21:91, "And

---

12. O'Meara (1966, 111–45).
13. Berkouwer (1965, 108); see extensively 107–50, where he combats Emil Brunner in particular, and evaluates the more positive view of Karl Barth.
14. https://m.clearquran.com/downloads/quran-english-translation-clearquran-edition-allah.pdf.

she who guarded her virginity, We breathed into her of Our spirit, and made her and her son a sign to the world." Please note that such a virgin birth is never claimed for Muhammad.

I use this opportunity to point to more significant differences between Jesus and Muhammed, not according to Christians but according to the Quran itself. The list gives a number of characteristics of Jesus that, as far as I know, were never claimed for Muhammad. The references are to various Surahs (chapters) in the Quran (I leave aside the testimony of the Hadith and of early Muslim scholars).

(1) Jesus is compared to the first man, Adam (3:59).

(2) Jesus was virgin-born of the most exalted woman[15] (19:20-22; cf. 2:87).

(3) Jesus was faultless (2:87, 253; 3:45-46; 6:85; 19:19) (see our next chapter).

(4) Jesus was the Messiah (Anointed One) (3:45; 4:157, 171-172; 5:72, 75; 9:30-31).

(5) Jesus was the Word of God (4:171; 19:34).

(6) Jesus was the Spirit from God (4:171; cf. 58:22).

(7) Jesus received God's assistance from the Holy Spirit (2:253; 5:110).

(8) Jesus is the Mighty and Wise (5:118; cf. 43:63).

(9) Jesus was a great healer of the sick (3:49-51; 5:109-110).

(10) Jesus was a performer of many other miracles (2:87, 253; 3:49; 5:110; 19:29-30; 61:6).

(11) Jesus was taken to heaven by God (3:55; 4:158).

(12) Jesus will be prominent in the world to come (3:45; 5:109-110).

9.2   Biblical Testimony
9.2.1   The Testimony of Matthew and Luke

This is what Matthew tells us:

---

15. Mary is the only woman mentioned by name in the entire Quran; one of the Surahs (19) is entirely devoted to her.

The Virgin Birth of Christ

> Now the birth of Jesus Christ took place in this way. When his mother Mary had been betrothed to Joseph, before they came together she was found to be with child from the Holy Spirit. And her husband Joseph, being a just man and unwilling to put her to shame, resolved to divorce her quietly. But as he considered these things, behold, an angel of the Lord appeared to him in a dream, saying, "Joseph, son of David, do not fear to take Mary as your wife, for that which is conceived in her is from the Holy Spirit. She will bear a son, and you shall call his name Jesus, for he will save his people from their sins." All this took place to fulfill what the Lord had spoken by the prophet: "Behold, the virgin shall conceive and bear a son, and they shall call his name Immanuel" (which means, God with us) [Isa. 7:14]. When Joseph woke from sleep, he did as the angel of the Lord commanded him: he took his wife, but knew her not until she had given birth to a son. And he called his name Jesus (1:18–25).

And this is the testimony of Luke:

> In the sixth month the angel Gabriel was sent from God to a city of Galilee named Nazareth, to a virgin betrothed to a man whose name was Joseph, of the house of David. And the virgin's name was Mary. And he came to her and said, "Greetings, O favored one, the Lord is with you!" But she was greatly troubled at the saying, and tried to discern what sort of greeting this might be. And the angel said to her, "Do not be afraid, Mary, for you have found favor with God. And behold, you will conceive in your womb and bear a son, and you shall call his name Jesus. He will be great and will be called the Son of the Most High. And the Lord God will give to him the throne of his father David, and he will reign over the house of Jacob forever, and of his kingdom there will be no end." And Mary said to the angel, "How will this be, since I am a virgin?" And the angel answered her, "The Holy Spirit will come upon you, and the power of the Most High will overshadow you; therefore the child to be born will be called holy—the Son of God" (1:26–35).

There are several differences between the two stories, which some have used to cast doubt on the fact of the virgin birth as such. It has been shown, however, that the two stories can be fully harmonized.[16] At least the central message is clear: Jesus was begotten by the Holy Spirit, and not by any human male. It is quite far-fetched to suggest that in Luke 1:32-35 the begetting by the Holy Spirit does not necessarily exclude a normal begetting by a man.[17] Mary's point is precisely that she does *not* have a husband, or any man with whom she might have had sexual intercourse. And the point of the angel's reply is that she does not need such a man because the begetting would be performed through the power of the Holy Spirit. Mary was a virgin, legally pledged to be married to Joseph, who both before and after the wedding had no intercourse with her, at least not until her child was born (Matt. 1:25).

Elsewhere I discussed various details in this story.[18] Thus, the first two phrases in Luke 1:35, separated by "and" ("The Holy Spirit will come upon you, and the power of the Most High will overshadow you"), form a parallel similar to a Hebrew poetic parallelism, or even a song. That is to say, the Holy Spirit and the power of the Most High amount to basically the same thing. It is similar to Acts 10:38 and 1 Corinthians 2:4, where the "Spirit and power" basically means "the power of the Holy Spirit" (cf. Acts 1:8; 1 Thess. 1:5), or in 2 Peter 1:16, where "the power and coming of our Lord Jesus Christ" means his "powerful coming" or his "coming in power." The power of the Holy Spirit would come upon the virgin Mary, and rest upon her (cf. Gen. 1:2; Micah 3:8; Zech. 4:6 [human "power" versus the Spirit]; Luke 1:17; 4:14; Rom. 15:13, 19; Eph. 3:16), as a consequence of which she would become pregnant.

---

16. See, e.g., Machen (1930); Brown (1973, 34–35); more pessimistic about possible harmonization is Meier (1991, 211–14).
17. Fitzmyer (1973, 567); Knight (2004, 75); cf. Macquarrie (1998, 32–36).
18. *EDR* 1:§6.1.1 (see the references there); see also *RT* I/2.

Another noteworthy detail is that we are dealing here more with the power than with the person of the Holy Spirit. This is illustrated by the lack of the Greek article before *pneuma hagion* ("Holy Spirit") as well as before *dynamis* ("power"). It is similar in Matthew 1:18 and 20, where the article is lacking as well: Jesus' begetting was "from Holy Spirit" (Gk. *ek pneumatos hagiou*). This corroborates the idea that it is not the person of the Spirit who is viewed as the Begetter here; rather, it is God, or the Father, who is the Begetter, through the power of the Spirit.

A third remarkable detail is that the result of this begetting by God in the power of the *Holy Spirit* was a human being who himself is (literally) called "that holy thing" (or perhaps "that holy [child]"[19]): the text literally says, "that holy [thing? child?] to be born will be called Son of God" (cf. KJV [not NKJV!], ASV, BRG, GNV). That is, the child is just as holy as the Spirit through whose power he was begotten. Notice here that Joseph understandably thought of a very *un*holy explanation for Mary's pregnancy (Matt. 1:19), namely fornication.[20] But the Bible gives us the *most holy* explanation for it: a holy child was to be begotten through the power of the Holy Spirit without any masculine intervention (vv. 18, 20).

9.2.2 Other Biblical Testimony

It is not very accurate to claim, as has been done in the past, that the other Gospels contain no hint at all of Jesus' virgin birth, though we do acknowledge that the evidence is indirect. Thus, the fact that the people in Nazareth called Jesus the "Son of Mary" (Mark 6:3) is very unusual. A boy was named after his father, even if the father had already passed away (unless the father's name was unknown); thus, we do read about "the son of Joseph" (Luke 3:23; 4:22; John 1:45; 6:42) or

---

19. The form, *to hagion*, is neuter, but Greek *teknon*, "child," is also neuter.
20. Because Joseph and Mary were betrothed, one might even speak of adultery here, since the law viewed the two as a married couple, even if they did not yet live together in marriage.

"the carpenter's son" (Matt. 13:55), even though Joseph apparently had already died. Naming a person after their mother was possibly an expression of disdain, but it seems instead related to the Jewish rumors concerning Jesus involving the story that his birth had been illegitimate.[21] In remarkable contrast to this, the classical Muslim scholar Abdulla al-Baiwadi wrote that in Islam, Jesus is viewed as the Son of the virgin Mary and is believed to have been begotten by the creational Word of God.[22]

Rumors like those mentioned must have originated somewhere; either they are correct (at least at their core), or they are rooted in some misunderstanding. At a minimum, they suggest that Jesus' birth was remarkable in certain respects. We can easily imagine that Joseph's fiancée getting pregnant generated the rumor of fornication. Perhaps this explains the question of Jesus' opponents in John 8:19, "Where is your f/ Father?" Even more explicit was their insinuation in verse 41, "*We* were *not* born of sexual immorality," with the presumed implication: 'You were." That John appeared to be aware of such rumors strongly suggests that he was familiar with the virgin birth of Jesus.[23] The fact that John does not express this explicitly does not mean that he did not know about it. Take, for instance, three events with Jesus at which John was present—in the house of Jairus (Mark 5:37), on the Mount of Transfiguration (9:2), and in Gethsemane (14:33)—yet he tells us nothing about these events. In other words, John did not tell us in his Gospel everything that he knew about Jesus (John 21:25).

A. van de Beek wrote:

---

21. Stauffer (1960, 16); Cranfield (1963, 195); Lane (1974, 202–203); Wessell (1984, 665); Meier (1991, 225–27) is careful. Regarding these rumors in Jewish literature, see SBK 1:39–43; Origen, *Contra Celsum* I.18.
22. Stauffer (1960, 17–18).
23. Morris (1971, 461–62); Tenney (1981, 96); Van de Beek (2002a, 150). Meier (1991, 227–29) again expresses reluctance on this point. If John 8:1–11 is authentic, these insinuations relate remarkably to Jesus' attitude toward this woman who was caught in adultery.

> The next perspective on the list—that Jesus, to his credit, was born of a woman of questionable standing—seems an attractive view to many modern people. For God clearly seeks those who are lost. However, the problem is that the biblical texts do not give any credence to this view.

And a bit later:

> We have seen what the alternative leads to: infidelity or virginity. As to the first, I have never observed that biblical authors cover up the unfaithfulness of people. Quite the opposite: it is brought out in the open. For only the truth sets free. It would be God-awful if at the very moment of God's definitive liberation the truth is obfuscated. That is why I do not believe the story of unfaithfulness at all, and will have to come to terms with the much more diffiult story of the virgin birth.[24]

9.3 Objections
9.3.1 Mythology

From the earliest days of church history, the doctrine of the virgin birth has belonged to the core confession of Christians, as is clear from Ignatius, a direct pupil of the apostle John. Around the year 110 he wrote to the church in Ephesus (chapter 18): "For our God, Jesus Christ, was, according to the appointment of God, conceived in the womb by Mary, of the seed of David, but by the Holy Ghost."[25] Similar statements can be found with Aristides, Justin Martyr, Irenaeus, and Tertullian. Earlier I referred to the Nicene-Constantinopolitan Creed: "... who for us, humans, and for our salvation, came down from heaven, and was incarnate by the Holy Spirit, [born] of the Virgin Mary, and was made man..." (Lat. *qui propter nos homines et propter salutem nostram descendit de coelis et incarnatus est de Spiritu Sancto ex Maria virgine, et homo factus est*).

In more recent times, people have often tried to purge the doctrine of the virgin birth from Christian teaching as though

---
24. Van de Beek (2002a, 154–55).
25. http://www.newadvent.org/fathers/0104.htm.

it were a piece of ancient mythology. However, there are sharp contrasts between the begetting of Jesus and the mythological stories involving the begetting and birth of divine sons, in which certain gods, temporarily assuming a human form, associate with earthly women. A well-known example is the Greek supreme god Zeus, who fathered children with earthly women such as Leda (children: Pollux and Helena) and Europa (child, e.g., Minos).[26] In these cases, sexual intercourse was certainly involved, comparable with what Genesis 6:1-4 tells us about the "sons of God," or "sons of the gods," "divine beings" (CEB, ISV) or "angels" (cf. Job 1:6; 2:1). These celestial beings assumed male bodies and had sexual intercourse with the "daughters of man" (human women), and had children with them. On the basis of this passage, Tertullian argued that women, especially "unblemished virgins," must cover themselves in order not to arouse the sexual desire of angels;[27] according to some, 1 Corinthians 11:10 also refers to this: "That is why a wife [or, woman] ought to have a symbol of authority [i.e., a covering] on her head, because of the angels" — but several other interpretations of this difficult verse have been proposed.

The — often vulgar — stories about begettings by gods disguised as people cannot compete with the very different and lofty story of the purely spiritual begetting of Jesus in Mary's womb. Moreover, as authors, Matthew and Luke seem to draw from a much older oral tradition, in which the virgin birth was already stably enshrined. This tradition came from the very beginning Jewish period of the early church, when Greek mythologies would hardly have been able to influence them. Whatever one may think of so-called form criticism, according to its own criteria (the emphasis on the "setting in life" [Ger. *Sitz im Leben*] of a Bible story) there is support for the view that the stories about Jesus' virgin birth originate

---

26. Berger (2004, 53–54).
27. *De virginibus velandis* 7.

from an early time of New Testament history.[28]

Viewed in this light, it is regrettable and not very understandable that Wolfhart Pannenberg—actually in the wake of many[29]—could speak so easily of the "apparently legendary nature of the narrative."[30] John P. Meier was more careful. He argued that decisions regarding the virgin birth tradition are made largely on the basis of a person's philosophical views about the miraculous, and the weight that one assigns to the later church doctrine.[31] Klaus Berger was right in blaming the anti-supernaturalist rejection of the virgin birth for excluding *a priori* "the miraculous because it commands God to operate exclusively within the framework of the Kantian criticism of reason."[32]

9.3.2 An Ovum of Mary?

It is part of the non-mythical but soberly factual character of the history in Matthew 1 and Luke 1 that the Gospel writers do not speculate about what exactly occurred in Mary's womb. With the begetting of the Messiah, the *way in which* the divine was associated with the human (Mary) is merely hinted at by the Greek verbal forms *epeleusetai* (from *eperchomai*, "to come on/over") and *episkiasei* (from *episkiazō*, "to overshadow") in Luke 1:35. Those who wish to know more easily find themselves engaged in idle discussions, such as asking whether, at the begetting of Jesus, an ovum of Mary was involved.

We must realize that for only three centuries now, human semen (sperm cells) and ova have been known to exist, since the discoveries of Antoni van Leeuwenhoek. It is no coincidence that, in the biblical languages, the words for "seed" refer to both human semen and plant seeds: *zera^c* in Hebrew (e.g., Gen. 1:29 and 38:9), *sperma* in Greek (e.g., Matt. 13:4–8 and 1 John 3:9) (which is still the case in modern languages). The

---
28. Erickson (1985, 744, including n15).
29. Barth cites B. Bartmann (*CD* I/2=3, §15.3:183).
30. Pannenberg (1994, 2:318).
31. Meier (1991, 230).
32. Berger (2004, 56).

ancient understanding was that the male semen was "sown" in the womb just as a seed of wheat is sown in the field. The fact that the father and the mother contribute equally to the genetic constitution of the child was still totally unknown.

The metaphorical connection between the soil of the earth and the womb of the mother extended to the view that coming from the womb was like coming from the earth: "My [unborn] frame was not hidden from you, when I was being made in secret, intricately woven in the *depths of the earth*" (Ps. 139:15). And conversely, when, after death, the body is laid in the earth, it is like returning to the womb of one's mother: "Naked I came from my mother's womb, and naked shall I return *there*" (Job 1:21 NKJV) (see chapter 8, note 3 above).

Against this backdrop, it is quite understandable that theologians before about 1700 did not see it as a problem that Jesus, through the operation of the Holy Spirit, came forth from the womb of Mary, much as the earth produced plants without sowing, but through the Spirit (in Genesis 1:11–12, esp. v. 2). These theologians would definitely have had a problem with any involvement of male semen in the begetting of Jesus. Today we have an additional problem: was a female ovum involved in Jesus' begetting? And what theological difference could it make whether a person is conceived from only a female ovum, or from an ovum fertilized by a sperm cell?

It is noteworthy that this kind of problem is hardly ever raised in theology. First, there is an understandable reluctance to speak of such a sacred matter. Second, perhaps there is a lack of biological awareness of the underlying problems. Third, traditional theology is strongly oriented toward pre-1700 theology; its scholarly problems are often dictated by ancient tradition. Fourth, perhaps theologians experience such a discussion as idle since an unequivocal conclusion seems out of reach.

To be sure, though the discussion is certainly interesting, it leads quickly to a stalemate. On the one hand, there are those who *deny* the involvement of an ovum of Mary. I remember how, long ago, a believing British physician insisted to me that "the womb of Mary did not contribute anything to the development of the fetus." Later, a believing French physician also insisted the same. Perhaps the thought of the involvement of an ovum of Mary was repulsive to them, with which I can sympathize. However, because they were physicians, the theological problems may have been less obvious to them. In my view, their denials bordered on Docetism and Gnosticism. This is because, if no ovum of Mary was involved, the question arises: What then was the origin of Jesus' humanity? If his human nature was created entirely anew, how could he be called a son of Mary, or even a son of Adam (Luke 3:23-38)? How could he be called their true *descendant*? How could he even be a genuine human being at all? Was Mary only a surrogate mother — carrying someone else's child in her womb — or was she the real, physical mother of Jesus? Not the possible involvement of male semen, but definitely the involvement of an ovum of Mary made her his real mother, I would think.

On the other hand, the *affirmation* of the question mentioned (was Jesus conceived from an ovum of Mary?) generates its own, new questions, such as: How could Jesus, if born of Mary's ovum, be free of Mary's sinfulness? Roman Catholic theologians have tried to solve this problem through the dogma of Mary's immaculate conception (proclaimed in 1854), which entails the idea that Mary was conceived in the womb of her mother Anna without being infected with original sin. This does *not* mean, as some have suggested, that Mary would not have needed a Redeemer; the idea is rather that God applied to her in the womb the redemption that was to be accomplished by her son Jesus. In spite of this restriction, however, this entire "solution" merely shifts the problem from a sinless son to a sinless mother. Moreover, if God could ensure that a woman, in this case Mary, who had been begotten by a sinful man from a sinful mother, was herself without sin, then he would certainly be able to this with a man, in this case Jesus, who was not begotten by a sinful man. Therefore, I do not consider these points to be an insurmountable objection against the thought that Jesus would have been conceived from an ovum of Mary.

Moreover, other biological questions might be still more difficult to answer: If Jesus was born of an ovum of Mary, without the involvement of a sperm cell, how could he have been anything other than a genetic clone of Mary? An ovum that has not been fertilized by a male sperm cell but matures to development will necessarily produce a girl because of the absent Y chromosome. Or did God, for this occasion, create a sperm cell, which fertilized Mary's ovum, as Millard Erickson suggested?[33] But if this were necessary, why could this not just as well have been a sperm cell of Joseph? In my view, it would have been sufficient if God had created a Y chromosome (cf. §§9.4.1–9.4.2).[34] But let me leave this area of biological speculation for what it is. The questions are obvious and acceptable, but their answers leave us in the dark. If our answers lack solid footing, we must leave the questions unanswered, even though any serious scientist or scholar hates to admit ignorance in a certain part of their field of study.

9.3.3 Other Objections

One objection against the doctrine of the virgin birth is that, at important moments, Mary does not at all seem to believe that Jesus was begotten in a supernatural way. In Luke 2:48, she says to the twelve years old Jesus, "your father and I," as if Joseph and not the Holy Spirit were the true father of Jesus. However, this can be easily refuted. Mary's statement is entirely in accordance with the fact that legally Joseph was indeed Jesus' father. Jesus was born within Joseph's marriage

---

33. Erickson (1985, 752).
34. Speaking about "creating," what would orthodox theologian Johan Verkuyl have meant when he spoke about "a *creation* within the virgin Mary and a birth from her" (1992, 196)?

with Mary (the opposite of "out of wedlock"), and this made Joseph his legal father. Compare these statements: ". . . Jacob the father of Joseph the husband of Mary, of whom Jesus was born" (Matt. 1:16). "Is not this the carpenter's son?" (13:55). "Is not this Joseph's son?" (Luke 4:22). "Jesus of Nazareth, the son of Joseph" (John 1:46). "Is not this Jesus, the son of Joseph, whose father and mother we know?" (6:42). Actually, Luke clearly says, "Jesus . . . , being the son *(as was supposed)* of Joseph" (Luke 3:23).

A rabbi once told me (near the Wailing Wall in Jerusalem), "Jesus was either the Son of God, or he was (through Joseph) the son of David—you cannot have both." My answer was that we *can* have both: because Joseph was his legal father, he was a descendant of Joseph's forefather David; and Jesus was Son of God, both because he was the eternal Son of the Father (e.g., John 17:24) and because he was begotten of Mary through the Holy Spirit (Luke 1:35).

Was the latter fact publicly known, especially to Jesus' relatives and his family's friends? In Mark 3:21, we read: "[W]hen his family [other renderings: his friends] heard it, they went out to seize him, for they were saying, 'He is out of his mind.'" Some have argued that these people would not possibly have said this had they known through Joseph or Mary that he had been begotten in a supernatural way. However, first, it is not certain that the Greek expression *hoi par' autou* (lit., "those who were with him," or "who belonged to him") really means "relatives"; they seem to be distinct from "his mother and his brothers" in verse 31. Second, even if his relatives or companions knew of his supernatural birth, this does not mean that they understood his words and acts, or that they would have accepted them. And as far as his unbelieving brothers were concerned (cf. John 7:5), it is not at all certain what they knew or understood about his supernatural begetting, or whether they would have believed it.

Some authors rejecting the doctrine of the virgin birth adduce the argument that this notion occurs only in Matthew and Luke. This is correct—but how much biblical evidence do people need before they will accept a biblical truth? For various reasons, Mark and John supply us with no birth story, nor do they mention his virgin birth. It would be much harder to explain if they had indeed described Jesus' birth but not his supernatural begetting.

In addition, what does it tell us that neither in Acts nor in the epistles do the apostles refer to this doctrine? Does this mean that they did not know about it? In the book of Acts, all the emphasis lies on the atoning death of Christ, and on his resurrection in particular. And as for the apostle Paul, I acknowledge that Galatians 4:4 ("born of a woman") is hardly evidence for, or even a hint of, Jesus' virgin birth, as has been suggested.[35] But neither is this verse an argument *against* this doctrine. In summary: we cannot conclude from this verse that this doctrine was unknown to Paul.

The greatest problems with respect to the virgin birth of Christ reside not in theological considerations as such, but rather in the anti-supernaturalistic prejudice, which dismisses Matthew 1 and Luke 1 as mythical or, if one wishes, midrashic.[36] However, there is no mythological or midrashic tone at all in Matthew 1 and Luke 1; rather we find the sober tone of the narrator, which provides such a sharp contrast, with not only the mythologies of those days, but also the apocryphal gospels, especially the Protoevangelium of James. No doubt the story of Matthew 1 and Luke 1 has theological significance, but so does every story in the New Testament Gospels. Any emphasis on its theological significance may not be

---

35. See, e.g., Geldenhuys (1983, 108); the same is true for Gen. 3:15; see, e.g., Leupold (1942, 169); Morris (1976, 122).
36. See the summary of the objections in Carson (1984, 71–74); see also Orr (1908); Machen (1930); Edwards (1943); Bruce (1962); Gromacki (1974); Miguens (1975); Murray (1991, 134–36); Stein (1996, 63–68, 78–80); Bloesch (1997, 80–107); MacLeod (1998), and conservative commentaries on Matthew and Luke; more critical: Boslooper (1962); Brown (1973, 1977).

abused to belittle the factuality of the event.

9.4 Theological Significance
9.4.1 Link with the Incarnation

The theological significance of the virgin birth is evident enough. Jesus is the Son of God because his birth was miraculous. Actually, the opposite is true as well: his birth is miraculous because he is the Son of God. He existed as the *eternal* Son of God before his human birth, and a miraculous birth was appropriate for such a person. But Luke 1:35 emphasizes instead that he is Son of God in his *humanity*, namely, because of his miraculous birth. He is not only the incarnate Son of God (cf. John 1:14 with v. 18), but also a Man begotten by the Holy Spirit, and as such Son of God as well. And there is this third aspect: by virtue of his resurrection he "was declared [NIV: appointed; RSV: designated] to be the Son of God in power according to the Spirit of holiness by his resurrection from the dead, Jesus Christ our Lord" (Rom. 1:4). In summary, he *was* the Son of God from eternity; in a second sense he *became* Son of God by being begotten by the Spirit; and thirdly, he was *designated* to be the Son of God in and by his resurrection.

The church father Tertullian argued that the virgin birth of Jesus constituted an essential part of the doctrine of the incarnation.[37] Without the event of the virgin begetting of Christ there could and would not have been any incarnation of the Logos. This is because, if Jesus had had not only a human mother but also a human father, it is hard to understand how he could be anything more than just a human.

This argument is not entirely convincing. If the human nature that Jesus inherited from his mother did not prevent him from being perfectly and entirely God, why would this have been prevented if he had also had a human father? If the Logos became flesh through the womb of Mary, why could he not have become flesh through the male sperm of an earth-

---

37. Tertullianus, *Adversus Marcionem* 4.10.

ly father?[38] The reverse questions seem to be equally valid: If the incarnation of the Logos excludes a human father, why does this incarnation not equally exclude a human mother? Indeed, God could have created the second Man (1 Cor. 15:47) in a direct way, just as he created the first man, Adam, in a direct way, without the intervention of a father and a mother. In such an act of creation, the womb of Mary would not have been necessary. However, the objection against such an argument is that in this case Jesus would not have been a son of Adam (Luke 3:23-38).

Here, the matter of Mary's ovum is relevant again: if Jesus' deity entailed that his birth was not due to a male sperm, it might be equally true that his birth was not due to a female ovum either. In this case, Mary's womb was only the "channel" through which the Son of God supernaturally entered the world.

Millard Erickson rightly argued that the doctrine of Tertullian reeks of Apollinarianism, which teaches that the divine Logos assumed the place of one of the normal "components" of human nature, namely, the soul.[39] Just as Jesus possessed not only a human body but also a human soul/spirit, he also possessed all that the father and the mother normally contribute to the child (including the Y chromosome). Just as God could have produced a normal person through a virgin begetting this child, that is, without this child being the incarnate Word, so too the incarnation is conceivable without the virgin begetting Jesus. We believingly accept[40] the doctrine of the virgin birth because the Bible clearly teaches it—not because it is a theological necessity. God in his sovereignty decided that the Logos would enter the world of human beings by means of a virgin birth.

---

38. Cf. Bloesch (1997, 99–100).
39. Erickson (1985, 755).
40. We do not "believe *in* the virgin birth," but we believe *in* the *Lord* who was born of a virgin; cf. Van de Beek (2002a, 156).

9.4.2 Link to Jesus' Sinlessness

The virgin birth is linked to the sinlessness of Jesus (see the next chapter); here again, people have claimed that this sinlessness would be inconceivable without the virgin birth.[41] However, if having an earthly sinful mother, or at least a mother who was of sinful ancestry, was no hindrance for Jesus' perfect sinlessness, why would having an earthly father be a hindrance for Jesus' sinlessness?[42] Or does the problem lie on a different level, namely, that of sexual desire? Indeed, Augustine said about Jesus: "Begotten and conceived without any lust of carnal desire, and thus without primordial sin." In this representation of the matter, humans are sinful because they were born from their parents' sexual desire—a thought without any basis in the Bible whatsoever.[43]

Augustine's view of human sexuality was quite unbiblical.[44] He read 1 Corinthians 7:6 as follows: "Now I say this as forgiveness, not as a command." (Lat. *Hoc autem dico secundum veniam, non secundum imperium*), and understood this as follows: If *venia* would indeed mean "forgiveness" here (although far more likely it means "concession"), then sexuality (see v. 5) must involve sin. If God allows sexual intercourse, then in fact this is a sin, but one for which forgiveness is promised *a priori*. Please note, intercourse as such is not sin, for God commanded it indirectly by telling Adam and Eve to multiply (Gen. 1:27; see also 2:24). No, what Augustine deemed to be sinful was *sexual desire*. To him, Jesus could not possibly have been a product of the sexual desire between two human beings! Such a view goes far beyond the biblical data. Jesus' virgin birth has to do with his deity—not with the avoidance

---

41. Augustine, *Enchiridion* 13.4; see also, e.g., Orr (1908, 190–201); Bavinck (*RD* 3:290, 294); Von Campenhausen (1964, 79–86); for a more extensive discussion, see Berkouwer (1965, 132–46).
42. Cf. what was said earlier about the doctrine of Mary's immaculate conception, and thus her supposed sinlessness, which simply shifts the problem: how could Mary, born of sinful parents, be sinless (see §9.3.2)?
43. Cf. Ouweneel (1998, §§3.2–3.4).
44. Ibid., 87–88.

of human sexual desire.

In order to explain the relationship between Jesus' virgin birth and his sinlessness, other scholars looked more in a biological direction, and speculated about the way in which original sin might be genetically transferred through male semen, but not through the female ovum. According to the American physician Albert S. Anderson, the virgin begetting demanded three divine steps: first, the removal of Mary's "sin mutation" from her ovum; second, the addition of a newly created Y chromosome; and third, the duplication of the entirely sin-free somatic chromosomes in order to arrive at a complete set of chromosomes for Jesus.[45] Of course, the greatest weaknesses, if not outright erroneous factors, in this argument include the assumption of such a thing as a "sin mutation" in any biological sense, and more generally the view that inheriting primordial sin would be a purely genetic (biological) matter. Our sinful nature is far more than a matter of DNA molecules, far *beyond* anything that is physical.

In addition to this we encounter other biological speculations; for instance, there have been those who sought a connection with the natural phenomenon of animal parthenogenesis, that is, the development of eggs of unfertilized females into full-grown organisms. Origen came up with this idea.[46] We noted earlier the difficulty that parthenogenesis can produce only females, and that such females are genetic and phenotypical clones of their mother (§9.3.2).[47]

No biblical basis exists for the assumption that ordinary people could be sinless if only they had no earthly father, which amounts to the idea that sinful human nature is genetically transferred through the father, or — even worse — through the sexual act, which is viewed as inherently sinful. The latter has been asserted, not only by Augustine, but also

---

45. Anderson (1976, 104).
46. See Smith (1940, 92); Kessel (1988, 25).
47. This ties in with the view of Kessel (see previous note) insofar as the latter views Jesus not as masculine, but as androgynous.

by Gregory the Great, Ambrose, Thomas Aquinas, and Martin Luther, and in the nineteenth century by conservative Protestants such as H. Olshausen and J. P. Lange.[48] Throughout the centuries, the doctrine of the virgin birth has been distorted by such mistaken views of human sexuality. One wonders how, in the view of such scholars, God could ever have allowed the Song of Solomon to have entered the biblical canon. Even if this book is entirely spiritualized, its basic text is thoroughly erotic. If sexual desire were inherently sinful, how could God have used it as a metaphor for the love between God and his people?

9.4.3 Significance of the Biblical Testimony

Jesus was sinless, but not because he had no earthly father, for mothers are sinful as well (cf. Job 15:14; Ps. 51:5). Nor was he sinless because he was not born of sexual desire, for people are not sinful because of their parents' sexual desire. No, Jesus was sinless because God begot him through the *Holy* Spirit in such a mighty way that he was *holy* from the very moment of his conception (Luke 1:35). But if this is so, then the same Holy Spirit could have ensured, in the process of begetting by an ordinary earthly father, that nothing sinful would be attached to the begotten child. As Calvin put it, we declare Christ free of all stain not just because he had been begotten from his mother without intercourse with a man, but because he was sanctified by the Spirit, so that the begetting was pure and unstained.[49] In other words, what explains the sinlessness of Jesus is not the virgin birth as such, but rather the mighty, overwhelming work of the Holy Spirit. No biological theories in any form can explain both the deity and the sinlessness of Jesus — only what God did in Mary through the Holy Spirit can offer such an explanation.

In summary, we are compelled to believingly accept the

---

48. Heyns (1988, 256); Bloesch (1997, 100–01); cf. Ouweneel (1998, §§3.3 and 3.4).
49. Calvin, (1960, 2.12.4).

virgin begetting of Jesus not by an *a priori* theological reason, whether his deity or his sinlessness. Therefore, A. van de Beek is correct when he writes: "Theologically, the virgin birth is not necessary."[50] No, the most compelling reason to believingly accept the virgin begetting of Jesus is that the Bible teaches it unequivocally. The virgin birth underscores the significance of the incarnation of the Logos. As Karl Barth put it:

> The dogma of the Virgin birth is thus the confession of the boundless hiddenness of the *vere Deus vere homo* and of the boundless amazement of awe and thankfulness called forth in us by this *vere Deus vere homo*. It eliminates the last surviving possibility of understanding the *vere Deus vere homo* intellectually, as an idea or an arbitrary interpretation in the sense of docetic or ebionite Christology. It leaves only the spiritual understanding of the *vere Deus vere homo*, i.e., the understanding in which God's own work is seen in God's own light.[51]

The uniqueness of this incarnation is matched by the uniqueness of how the Man Jesus Christ was begotten in Mary's womb. No speculations about sperm cells and ova, or about Y chromosomes, about "sin genes," and other DNA, will ever bring this magnificent miracle any closer to us. And let us not forget: the miraculous begetting of Jesus' through the power of the Holy Spirit is equaled by the miraculous "begetting" of the believer's new self through the power of the Holy Spirit (see John 3:5; Titus 3:5). The expression "not by the will of man" in John 1:13 could almost point to a kind of virgin birth: just like Jesus, believers are born of their "mother," the Holy Spirit, without the intervention of any man.[52]

---

50. Van de Beek (1998, 144).
51. Barth (*CD* I/2=3, §15.3:187).
52. *EDR* 1:82, 141. Remarkably enough, Irenaeus and Tertullian—quoted in Bloesch (1997, 92–93)—followed by many second- and third-century authors, read John 1:12–13 as follows: ". . . those who believe in the name of him who was born, not of blood nor of the will of the flesh nor of the will of man, but of God."

Chapter 10
The Sinlessness of Christ

For our sake he made him to be sin who knew no sin, so that in him we might become the righteousness of God.

2 Corinthians 5:21

. . . one who in every respect has been tempted as we are, yet without sin.

Hebrews 4:15

He committed no sin, neither was deceit found in his mouth.

1 Peter 2:22

You know that he appeared in order to take away sins, and in him there is no sin.

1 John 3:5

10.1 Jesus' Guiltlessness
10.1.1 Is It Human to Sin?

AS WE TURN now to consider the biblical teaching concerning Jesus' sinlessness, we must remember that this is possible only within the framework of a much broader examination of the precise nature of sin. I have carried such an examination elsewhere;[1] important questions must be raised concerning, first, the relationship between the pre-Fall Adam and the post-Fall Adam and his descendants, and second, the relationship between the first Adam and the last Adam, Christ. Raising these questions is necessary because we seek to know both the extent of Jesus' sinlessness and its relationship to that of the pre-Fall Adam. If Jesus was sinless, was it possible in principle for him, just like the first Adam, to fall into sin? And what does this mean for believers who belong to Christ? Could they, in principle, fall into sin again in their future eternity? Many of these questions are dealt with in other volumes in this series.

What does it mean that Jesus never sinned? If this were true, some people assert, he would be nothing more than a legendary hero. People say: "To err is human" (Lat. *Errare humanum est*); if Jesus was truly human, he must have erred once in a while, not only, for instance, in arithmetic or linguistics, but also in more serious matters. Such erring is sin. Real human beings are not perfect; they do not always keep the commandments of God; they sometimes go astray. It is impossible to imagine a real human being who is not occasionally off the mark.

People who argue like this forget, or do not wish to see, two important points. First, Jesus was not just any human. He was the second Man, the last Adam, prototype of an entirely new kind of humanity. This alone is sufficient to argue that originally sinning was not an essential part of being human, and that therefore Jesus could definitely have been a Man without ever sinning. He was a Man of a different kind. He exhibited not only many similarities to people descending from the first Adam, as we will see shortly, but also remarkable differences, such as his sinlessness. Bible passages that are true for "normal" (sinful) people (1 Kings 8:46; Job 15:14; Ps. 14:2-3; 53:2-3;

---

1. See *EDR* 2:chapters 10–14; see also Ouweneel (2018, chapters 8–10).

146:34; Prov. 20:9; Eccl. 7:20; Jer. 17:5, 7; Rom. 3:10-20; 1 John 1:10) were not applicable to the very different type of humanity that Jesus represented.[2]

Second, even with the first Adam sin was not an essential part of his being human. Genesis 1 and 2 show us that sin does not belong to humanity as it originally came forth from God's hand. This point is of the greatest importance in opposition to any form of theistic evolution, which accepts a gradual development of nature, including of *Homo sapiens*.[3] In the beginning, the creation was "very good" (Gen. 1:31). The wolf dwelt with the lamb, so to speak, the leopard lay down with the young goat, the calf with the lion, the cow with the bear (cf. Isa. 11:6-7; 65:25). Once, long ago, humanity was not stained by sin. Sin became attached to humanity from the Fall onward, but this does not mean that sin originally, *creationally*, belonged to what is human. Here we see the enormous importance of the historicity of the Fall, because it made a separation between humanity not yet stained and humanity stained with sin.

10.1.2 Jesus' Moral Excellence

Our certainty that there was a time when sinful humanity did not exist is matched by our certainty that Jesus is the prototype of the new humanity in which sin will no longer dwell. Therefore, we should not be asking: Is Jesus just as human as we are? — because this would imply his sinfulness — but: Are we already, or are we on the way of becoming, just as human as Jesus is?[4] The answer is that, through the redemption that is found in Jesus, we can become so.[5]

It is noteworthy that Jesus is called "a/the Righteous One" (Heb. *tzaddiq*, Gk. *dikaios*) on various occasions: by Pilate's wife (Matt. 27:19), and perhaps by Pilate himself (v. 24), by

---

2. Berkouwer (1954, 196).
3. See extensively Ouweneel (2018).
4. Erickson (1985, 721).
5. Regarding this subject, see the future volumes in this series that deal with soteriology.

Peter (Acts 3:14; 1 Pet. 3:18), by Stephen (Acts 7:52), by Ananias (Acts 22:14), by John (1 John 2:1), and perhaps by James (5:6, depending on the interpretation). The same thought appears in Paul's writings; for example, Jesus was "vindicated (justified, declared to be righteous) by the Spirit" (1 Tim. 3:16). Some of these and others called him "the Holy One" (Heb. *qadosh*, Gk. *hagios*) on various occasions: demons (Mark 1:24; Luke 4:34), Peter (John 6:69), John (1 John 2:20), Jesus himself (Rev. 3:7); the angel Gabriel (Luke 1:35: lit., "that Holy Thing"); note as well the use of Greek *hosios* (Heb. *chesed* and *chasid*) in Rev. 15:4 (the redeemed speaking) and 16:5 (an angel speaking).

All these passages constitute a powerful testimony to the moral excellence of Christ. However, they are not proof of his sinlessness because believers are called righteous and holy as well, whereas sin remains in them as long as they remain in this life (Rom. 7:20; 1 John 1:8). We therefore need more thorough evidence concerning Jesus.

What is also noteworthy are the multiple testimonies to Jesus' innocence by his non-religious judges, both Pilate (Matt. 27:23-24; Mark 15:14; Luke 23:4, 22; cf. Acts 3:13) and Herod (Luke 23:14). In John 18:38 and John 19:4 and 6, we hear Pilate emphatically say three times: "I find no guilt in him," or "in this man" (cf. Luke 23:4). Judas said, "I have sinned by betraying innocent blood" (Matt. 27:4). "[T]he chief priests and the whole council were seeking testimony against Jesus to put him to death, but they found none. For many bore false witness against him, but their testimony did not agree" (Mark 14:55-56). Pilate's wife warned her husband, "Have nothing to do with that righteous man" (Matt. 27:19). One of the criminals on the cross said to the other criminal, "This man has done nothing wrong" (Luke 23:41). And the centurion at the cross said, "Certainly this man was innocent!" (v. 47). This is all very important in any examination of Jesus' trial—but again, judicial innocence or guiltlessness is not the same as sinlessness.

10.1.3 Deeper Testimony

Jesus was not only guiltless but also sinless; that is, not only could he not be accused of grave trespasses worthy of judicial trial, but he had actually committed no sins at all, which of course goes much further. To find out what the Bible has to say about this, let us first listen to Jesus' own testimony. In the midst of his opponents he asked the question: "Which one of you convicts me of sin?" (John 8:46). That is, who can bring any evidence that I have committed sin—a question that received no answer. Apparently, nobody *could* bring in any complaint against him. Imagine what asking such a question involves. Who among us would venture to do so, especially in the midst of enemies? What person in their right mind would dare challenge others to point out one single sin within them?

Earlier in John 8, Jesus had said to the accusers of the adulterous woman: "Let him who is without sin among you be the first to throw a stone at her." The text continues: "But when they heard it, they went away one by one, beginning with the older ones" (vv. 7, 9). Each of those accusers realized that he did not fulfill Jesus' condition. The *only* one who did not go away was Jesus himself; he was the only one standing there who was without sin—but he did not stone the woman. Not because *she* was innocent, but because *he* was merciful. A little later his opponents asked him, "Who are you?" Jesus said to them, "Just what I have been telling you from the beginning" (v. 25). Here was a Man who was what he said, and who said what he was. He was totally transparent to those around him. He could speak this way because, as he himself said, he always did things that were pleasing to his Father (v. 29b). And no one around him could prove the opposite.

Elsewhere in the Gospel we hear Jesus saying, "My food is to do the will of him who sent me and to accomplish his work" (John 4:34). "I have not spoken on my own authority, but the Father who sent me has himself given me a commandment—what to say and what to speak. And I know that his commandment is eternal life. What I say, therefore, I say as the Father has told me" (12:49-50). "I have kept my Father's commandments and abide in his love" (15:10). Even when he speaks of such sovereign acts as laying down his life and taking it up again, he refers to his obedience: "For this reason the Father loves me, because I lay down my life that I may take it up again. No one takes it from me, but I lay it down of my own accord. I have authority to lay it down, and I have authority to take it up again. This charge I have received from my Father" (10:17-18).

It is true that Jesus' opponents sometimes accused him of specific transgressions of the law, in particular violations of the First and Fourth Commandments: "This was why the Jews were seeking all the more to kill him, because not only was he breaking the Sabbath [cf. Luke 6:2, 9-10; 13:14; 14:3-4], but he was even calling God his own Father, making himself equal with God" (John 5:18; cf. v. 33). "We have a law, and according to that law he ought to die because he has made himself the Son of God" (19:7). However, Jesus could legitimately be accused of transgressing the First Commandment only if his claim of coequality with God the Father were untrue. Jesus never transgressed the Fourth Commandment as such, but only the legalistic additions to this commandment that the Pharisees had invented.[6]

10.1.4 A Sinless Nature

The full question we need to ask is not simply whether Jesus ever sinned, that is, committed sinful acts, but whether he had a sinful nature, that is, whether he was *able* to sin. We read about this in Hebrews 4:15, which tells us that Jesus is "one who in every respect has been tempted as we are, yet without sin." Some translations render the latter expression (Gk. *chōris hamartias*) as "without sinning" (AMPC, RSVCE), but in my view this is not a proper rendering. If Jesus never sinned, this does not necessarily mean that he *could* not or *might* not have

---

6. Berkouwer (1954, 241).

sinned; it does not clarify whether he had a sinful nature as such (the "flesh" in its ethical-religious sense). The same is true for 1 Peter 2:22, "He committed no sin, neither was deceit found in his mouth." "Sin apart" (Darby) or "apart from sin" (YLT) would be a better rendering in Hebrews 4: in all of his actions, words, and thoughts, Jesus was "apart from sin," severed from sin as such (the sinful nature, the power of sin).

Clearer still is Paul's statement, "For our sake he made him to be sin who knew no sin, so that in him we might become the righteousness of God" (2 Cor. 5:21), and especially John's statement, "You know that he appeared in order to take away sins, and in him there is no sin" (1 John 3:5). Jesus was "a lamb without blemish or spot" (1 Pet. 1:19; cf. Heb. 9:14). Therefore, from the moment of his conception he could be called "holy" (Luke 1:35). Interestingly, even the Quran (2:87, 253; 3:45–46; 6:85; 19:19) testifies that Jesus was sinless[7] — although it claims that he shared this quality with other great figures in Islam.[8]

Perhaps we should say that a term like "holy" is preferable to several other terms we have used so far: "sinless," "guiltless," "unstained, "without blemish," and even "innocent" (lit., not harming). These terms are all negative; all of them indicate what Jesus was *not*. J. Verkuyl preferred the Dutch expression *volkomen gaaf*, which is something like "perfectly whole."[9] Nevertheless, we cannot avoid using negative terms — the Bible itself uses them (e.g., Matt. 27:4; Heb. 7:26; 9:14; 1 Pet. 1:19) — in order to explain that Jesus was sinless.

10.2 The Temptation of Jesus[10]
10.2.1 To Sin and to Be Able (Not) to Sin

Jesus could not be attracted, allured, seduced, or enticed by sin. Sin found no point of attachment in him, unlike with or-

---

7. Surah 2:87, 253; 19:19.
8. Surah 3:45–46; 6:85. Interestingly, the Quran (47:19; 48:2) does point to sins (*dhanbika*) of Muhammad himself, for which he had to ask forgiveness (*wastaghfir*).
9. Verkuyl (1992, 210–11).
10. See G. H. Twelftree (*DJG* 821–27).

dinary people because they have a sinful nature (the "flesh"). He was and is "holy, innocent, unstained, separated from sinners" (Heb. 7:26). Here the Greek word for "separated" is *kechōrismenos*, which is derived from the word *chōris*, "without" (see "without" in Heb. 4:15). Because Jesus is God, the statement of James 1:13 is true of him: "God cannot be tempted with evil."

We must make a careful distinction here between the objective and subjective qualities of temptation. The former involves putting snares or stumbling-blocks in a person's way, hoping that this person will fall into sin. The subjective quality involves the inclination to fall into sin, inwardly feeling tempted by sin, tending to give way to it. It is obvious that Jesus was tempted in the objective sense. This happened not only during his forty days in the wilderness (Matt. 4:1 par.) for, at the end of these temptations, we read that the devil "departed from him until an opportune time" (Luke 4:13). This implies that, at a later time, he tempted Jesus again (cf. 22:46, 53). Jesus told his disciples at one point: "[Y]ou are they who have continued with me in my temptations" (v. 28 DRA). In order to tempt Jesus, the devil used his opponents, such as the Pharisees, the Sadducees, the Herodians, the lawyers (Matt. 16:1, 3; 22:18, 35; Luke 10:25; 11:16), and even some of Jesus' disciples (Matt. 16:22-23).

In Hebrews 2:18 we read, "[B]ecause he himself has suffered when tempted, he is able to help those who are being tempted." Jesus is a high priest "who in every respect has been tempted as we are, yet without sin" (4:15).

Now the question arises: How *real* were these temptations if Jesus was not *able* to sin? In other words, could he have been *subjectively* tempted by sin? The temptations were real and objective in the sense that if Satan tried, for example, to entice the hungry Jesus to change stones into bread, Jesus would have been able to do so. He *was able* to do something that, if he *had* done it, would have been sin. He was physically able to do things that would have been sinful. However, he was not tempted in any subjective sense; that is, the temptation did not cause any weakness within him, any inclination to give in to the temptation.[11] In summary, this is how theologians have stated the matter for centuries:

(a) Before the Fall, Adam did not yet possess a sinful nature, but two things were true of him:
* *posse peccare* (he was able to sin)
* *posse non peccare* (he was able not to sin).
(b) For fallen humanity, two things are true:
* *posse peccare* (being able to sin)
* *non posse non peccare* (not being able not to sin).
(c) For Jesus, two things were true:
* *non posse peccare* (he was not able to sin)
* *posse non peccare* (he was able not to sin).
(d) For believers at present, two things are true:
* *posse peccare* (they are able to sin)
* *posse non peccare* (they are able not to sin).
(e) For believers in eternal bliss, two things are true:
* *posse non peccare* (they are able not to sin)
* *non posse peccare* (they are not able to sin).

10.2.2 Temptation and Weakness

Jesus became fully acquainted with all the ways that the devil could tempt God's people in order to make them stumble, thus preventing them from reaching their final goal. However, because he had no sinful nature, Jesus did not experience these temptations as weaknesses. Therefore, he himself did not need a high priest. But he is now the high priest for God's children because for *them* these temptations do entail weaknesses, crisis situations in which they experience the inclination to fall into sin.[12]

Thus, Jesus did experience temptation—in the objective sense—and in his omniscience he experienced the weakness-

---
11. *Contra* Robinson (1973, 96); cf. Van de Beek (2002a, 41–48).
12. See Ouweneel (1982, 63).

es that accompany temptation for sinful people; Jesus "needed no one to bear witness about man, for he himself knew what was in man" (John 2:25; cf. Rev. 2:23). However, he did not experience temptation in the subjective sense, that is, arising from his personal nature, nor did he experience sin itself as something that played an active role in his own life (2 Cor. 5:21). He is able to sympathize with the weaknesses of others (Heb. 4:15), but he himself did not experience them.

To Jesus was applicable the opposite of what was applicable to the high priest Aaron. The latter could deal gently with the ignorant and wayward *because* he himself was beset with weakness. But Jesus can deal gently with the ignorant and wayward, *although* he himself is *not* beset with weakness. Therefore, he was *not* obligated to offer sacrifice for his own sins just as he did for those of the people (Heb. 5:2-3; cf. Lev. 16:6, 11-14). "[T]he law appoints men in their weakness as high priests, but the word of the oath, which came later than the law, appoints a Son who has been made perfect forever" (7:28). In brief, Jesus did know the temptations but not the weaknesses that accompany them in sinners.

Of course, we are referring here to a specific kind of weakness, namely, the inner inclination to yield to a sinful temptation. Jesus did not experience this weakness; but he certainly experienced other weaknesses. He was even "crucified in weakness" (2 Cor. 13:4). He experienced the weaknesses that are part of a life of persecution, opposition, suppression, and rejection (cf. 11:29-30; 12:5, 9 and especially v. 10: "For the sake of Christ, then, I am content with weaknesses, insults, hardships, persecutions, and calamities. For when I am weak, then I am strong"). But Jesus was not weak when Satan tried to entice him to sin.

It goes without saying that this standpoint has led to much discussion.[13] Many have argued that though Jesus may never

---

13. See Erickson (1985, 719–21). Van de Beek (2002a, 45) says, "The question of sinlessness demands close scrutiny. . . . If we place Jesus too much in the realm of sin, he becomes a sinner just like us and has to carry his own guilt.

have sinned, he certainly was *able* to sin. For, if he could not be tempted in the subjective sense, did he then really *experience* temptation? It is pointed out by these people, for instance, that in Gethsemane Jesus definitely experienced agony (Luke 22:44).[14] However, the text does not speak of a temptation by the devil; it was the agony of Jesus' own inner conflict when he was confronted with the cup that he was going to drink: the cup of the atoning sufferings and being forsaken by God. The very fact that he was without sin made it horrible for him that he was going to be *made* sin (2 Cor. 5:21).[15] This is not to say that Satan was not involved in this inner conflict; what I am saying is that experiencing agony because of the horrors to come is not the same as experiencing the weakness that yields to temptation.

This is an important distinction: agony differs from an inner inclination to fall into sin. The fact that Jesus was in agony but was not inclined to shrink from his suffering is shown, first, by the fact Jesus' own will remains continually subject to the Father's will: "[N]ot my will, but yours, be done" (Luke 22:42). He says to Peter, "Put your sword into its sheath; shall I not drink the cup that the Father has given me?" (John 18:11). Jesus knew all along that he would have to die on the cross: ". . . the Son of Man must be lifted up" (3:14). "And what shall I say? 'Father, save me from this hour'? But for this purpose I have come to this hour. . . . I, when I am lifted up from the earth, will draw all people to myself" (12:27, 32). "Then Jesus, knowing all that would happen to him, . . ." (18:4). However, all this removed nothing from the agony of his experience.

Second, it is precisely to *others* that Jesus says to his disciples at the same occasion: "Why are you sleeping? Rise and pray that you may not enter into temptation" (Luke 22:46). Could he, who himself prayed so earnestly, then have entered into "(subjective) temptation" (in the sense of being inclined

---

If we keep him too far away from sin, he cannot bear any of it."
14. Berkouwer (1954, 248).
15. Ibid., 250.

to yield to sin)?

Third, Jesus does point to a different path: "Do you think that I cannot appeal to my Father, and he will at once send me more than twelve legions of angels?" (Matt. 26:53). However, there is no hint that Jesus seriously considered using this possibility.

10.2.3 Physical and Moral

Sin had no inner attractiveness for Jesus. Therefore, he could say, "[T]he ruler of the world (Satan) is coming. And he has no claim on Me [no power over Me nor anything that he can use against Me]" (John 14:30 AMP). Because of Jesus' sinlessness, the devil found no vulnerable point where he could attack him.[16] Does this mean that a sinless person is unable to really experience temptation? This is not self-evident. On the contrary, one might argue the very opposite, namely, that the person who *falls* into the temptation has not really experienced it, since the temptation ceases at the moment of falling. Rather the one who endures the temptation until the very end has genuinely experienced it. The fact that Jesus was immune to sin does not mean that he did not experience temptation; on the contrary, he had to keep resisting them until the bitter end.

If we ask whether Jesus was able to sin, we must realize that, in this entire discussion, the phrase "be able to" can mean two quite different things. Satan wished to entice Jesus to change stones into bread, then jump from the pinnacle of the temple, and then bow down before him. *Physically* speaking, Jesus was able to do all three things—and *if* he had done them, he would have sinned. However, this is not the same as being *morally* able to do these things. Only in the physical sense, not in the moral sense, can we speak of the possibility of Jesus sinning. Thus, Abraham Kuyper spoke of the possibility of Jesus sinning, but through the connection of his human with his divine nature it was "absolutely impossible that

---

16. Morris (1971, 659–60).

that possibility would become reality."[17]

Similarly Herman Bavinck wrote that

> [Jesus] is one with the Father and always carries out his Father's will and work. For those who confess this of Christ, the possibility of him sinning and falling is unthinkable.... For in that case either God himself would have to be able to sin—which is blasphemy—or the union between the divine and the human nature[s] is considered breakable and in fact denied.[18]

We cannot say that Jesus was able to sin according to his human nature, but not according to his divine nature. For that is to sever the two natures—something against which the Chalcedon Formula emphatically (and rightly) warns.

Jesus was innocent like the pre-Fall Adam—but he did not possess a sinful nature like the post-Fall Adam. Both the innocent Adam and the fallen Adam could be tempted by the devil, and fall into sin. Jesus was different from both of them. He was that wholly other One, the *last* Adam; therefore, morally speaking, he *was* unable to be enticed by sin. He was not only able to avoid sinning (Lat. *potuit non peccare*, "he was able to not sin")—and indeed did not sin—but he was also unable to sin (Lat. *non potuit peccare*, "he was not able to sin") because of the union of his human and his divine natures. All the more horrible for him, then, to be "*made* sin" on the cross (2 Cor. 5:21), as we will see in the soteriological volumes to follow.

10.3 The "Likeness of Sinful Flesh"
10.3.1 The Meaning of Romans 8:3

In the present context, it is worthwhile to look at Romans 8:3, because in this verse we seem to hear a different tone: "For God has done what the law, weakened by the flesh [Gk. *dia tēs*

---

17. Kuyper (*DD* 3:3:§6, 11); cf. Kuyper (1946, 1:114): Jesus' human nature would have been "overwhelmed by" eternal death "if the divinity of the Son had not supported that human nature, which is to say, if the infinite capacity of the divine nature had not mitigated the human nature in connection with its being overwhelmed" (our translation).
18. Bavinck (*RD* 3:314).

sarkos], could not do. By sending his own Son in the likeness of the flesh of sin [Gk. *sarkos hamartias*] and for sin [or, as a sin offering] he condemned sin in the flesh [Gk. *en tēi sarki*]."

What does it mean that God sent his own Son "in the likeness of the flesh of sin [a freer rendering: the sinful flesh]"? Compare this with the free rendering of the ERV: "God ... sent his own Son to earth with the same human life that everyone else uses for sin." This helps us to understand what the text means, but what is lost here is the pun that the apostle Paul seems to be making; the first time he uses the Greek word *sarx* ("flesh"), he means the "sinful nature": the law was made powerless with respect to humans because, as a consequence of their sinful nature, they were unable to do what the law commanded. The second and third times he uses the Greek word *sarx*, it means "body": Christ came in a body, which in our case, as ordinary humans, is a body affected by sin.

Our attention now is on the expression "in the likeness of the sinful flesh." The Greek word for "likeness" (*homoiōma*) does not suggest that in Jesus' human soul or body there would be something illusory or unreal, as if there were only some (vague) similarity between Jesus' humanity and ours. Paul does not deny the true humanity of Jesus. However, he wishes to avoid the suggestion that Jesus would have appeared in "sinful flesh."[19] Paul wanted to show that the Father sent his Son into this world of sin, misery, and death in a manner that brought him into the closest possible relationship to sinful humanity without becoming sinful himself.[20] I would put it this way: God sent his Son in a body that was exactly like our sinful body, with this difference that, in his case, his body was not affected by sin.

The goal of this sending was "for sin" (Gk. *Peri hamartias*),

---

19. Cf. this formulation of Tertullian, *De carne Christi* 16: we are liberated "not from the flesh of sin ... but from the sin of the flesh" (Lat. *non carnem peccati ... sed peccatum carnis*).
20. Murray (1968, 280); cf. Harrison (1976, 87); Wuest (1977, 128–29); Denney (1979, 645–46).

in view of the solution of the problem of sin, as is clear from the last phrase: God "condemned sin in the flesh"; he condemned humanity's sin in and through the atoning surrender of his Son's "flesh" on the cross.

Some translations and commentaries render the Greek phrase *peri hamartias* as "sin offering." This is because the Hebrew *chata'ah* or *chattat* can mean both "sin" and "means to remove sin," that is, "sin offering." Thus, *l'chattat* means either "for sin" or "as a sin offering" (Lev. 4:3; Num. 8:8; 15:27). Sometimes, it can obviously only mean the latter (Num. 6:11; 7:16 etc.; 8:12; 15:24; 28:15; cf. Lev. 15:30, *chattat* = "as a sin offering"). The Septuagint sometimes renders *chata'ah*/*chattat* when it means "sin offering" as *hamartias*, "[something] of/for sin" (Exod. 29:14), but it also uses the Greek expression *peri hamartias*, "for sin" (Num. 6:11; 7:16 etc.; 8:8, 12; 15:24, 27, 30; 28:15; cf. Lev. 4:3 *peri tēs hamartias*). In Hebrews 10:6 and 8, *peri hamartias* clearly means "sin offering." Therefore, in Romans 8:3, the apostle Paul possibly had this meaning in mind, so that we could render his words as follows: "God . . . sent his own Son in the likeness of sinful flesh and *as a sin offering*."

Precisely because Jesus' own flesh was *not* sinful flesh, he was able to become the true and only sin offering, the atoning sacrifice that removed sin. In Jesus' pure flesh, God could execute his judgment upon the sins that stain *our* sinful flesh. Therefore, Romans 8:3 definitely cannot be interpreted to suggest imperfection in Jesus' humanity; rather, the very opposite: because of his perfect humanity, the sins of fallen human beings could be judged in him, and in him alone (cf. again 2 Cor. 5:21; 1 Pet. 2:22, 24; 1 John 3:5).

10.3.2 Objections

Despite the testimony of the church fathers and the Reformers, several significant theologians have denied that Jesus could not sin, such as E. Irving,[21] one of the main pioneers of

---

21. See the quotation from Irving in Ford and Higton (2002, 364–66); he was vigorously opposed on this point by John N. Darby (*CW* 15:1–15) and Wil-

the Catholic Apostolic Church, H. F. Kohlbrugge,[22] and Karl Barth.[23] These authors did maintain that Jesus was personally sinless, but

> inwardly and outwardly his situation was that of a sinful man. ... [T]he nature which God assumed in Christ is identical with our nature as we see it in the light of the Fall. If it were otherwise, how could Christ be really like us? What concern would we have with Him? We stand before God characterised by the Fall. God's Son not only assumed our nature but He entered the concrete form of our nature, under which we stand before God as men damned and lost.[24]

If Christ really partook of *our* flesh, then this was our *sinful* flesh, argued Karl Barth, for there is no other human flesh. Barth's fallacy here is, in my view, evident from his appeal to 2 Corinthians 5:21 ("he made him to be sin") and Galatians 3:13 (Christ became "a curse for us"), in not seeing that these words do not refer to the incarnation but to Christ's work of atonement on the cross.

Not only in the New Testament, but also in the last centuries the enemies of Christ had to testify about his sinlessness. Even D. F. Strauss, the bitterest enemy of everything supernatural in the Gospels and whose work has done more to destroy faith in Christ than that of any other liberal author, testified at the end of his life of the moral perfection of Christ: "This Christ . . . is historical, not mythical; is an individual, not mere symbol. . . . He remains the highest model of religion within the reach of our thinking; and no perfect piety is possible without his presence in the heart."[25]

Theological objections to the notion of Christ's sinlessness might be due in part to Jesus' humanity being viewed as

---

liam Kelly (1890).
22. See Van Genderen and Velema (2008, 458–59), who also denied Jesus' peccability.
23. Barth (*CD* IV/2=24, §64.2:86 and passim).
24. Barth (*CD* I/2=3, §15.2:156–57).
25. Quoted by Smith (1970, 11).

standing entirely on its own. This danger in Christology may also be encountered in the doctrine of God and in that of the Trinity. Such an independent treatment occurs nowhere in the New Testament. For instance, in Romans 8 Jesus' humanity is viewed strictly from a soteriological viewpoint. Basically, every consideration concerning God and Christ receives its significance from soteriology: Jesus truly became Man (a) in order to redeem us from sin, and to turn us into new people, (b) to intercede for us as long as we are still in this body, and (c) to show us the true essence of humanity as intended by God, and in this to be an example for us.

10.4 Could Jesus Err?
10.4.1 Smaller Examples

In addition to the objections already mentioned, several other problems have been suggested regarding the notion of Jesus' sinlessness. One of these is that on certain occasions Jesus supposedly erred. Even if one were not to identify such errors as directly sinful, they do belong to the brokenness of human existence since the Fall: to err is human. If Jesus is a true Man, we may also expect that the limitations of his humanity involved his occasional erring. He may have been sinless in the absolute sense of the word, but was he perhaps "human enough" to be able to err?[26]

One such supposed error was that Jesus ascribed the five books of the Torah to Moses (Mark 12:26; Luke 20:37). However, even if not everything (or nothing at all) in these five books had been written down by Moses, Jesus is describing the Pentateuch as Jews had done throughout the centuries (see Josh. 8:31–32). Jesus does not contradict Scripture here (see the frequent designation in Acts and the epistles), but rather the assertions of Old Testament critics—and these assertions are rejected or criticized by other Old Testament scholars, (see *RT* I/1, chapter 11).

---

26. Cf. Erickson (1985, 710).

Some have asserted[27] that Jesus was mistaken when he said that David entered the house of God "in the time of Abiathar the high priest" (Mark 2:26), which should be the time of Ahimelech (1 Sam. 21:2-7). However, this could simply mean "in the time of the high priest Abiathar (who was so much better known than his father Ahimelech)." Jesus allegedly erred when he said that the martyr Zechariah was the son of Barachiah (Matt. 23:35, a confusion with the *prophet* Zechariah, Zech. 1:1) instead of the son of Jehoiada (2 Chron. 24:20-22) — unless Jesus really meant the *prophet*.[28]

To be sure, Jesus' followers sometimes erred, even if such erring cannot always be called sin. Take the apostle Paul who said to the high priest Ananias, "God is going to strike you, you whitewashed wall! Are you sitting to judge me according to the law, and yet contrary to the law you order me to be struck?" Those who stood by said to Paul, "Would you revile God's high priest?" Paul replied, "I did not know, brothers, that he was the high priest, for it is written, 'You shall not speak evil of a ruler of your people'" (Acts 23:3-5). With everything we know about Jesus, could we imagine Jesus ever having to apologize for such an error: "Sorry, I did not know that..."?

10.4.2 More Substantial Examples

A far more important example of an alleged mistake of Jesus was that he supposedly predicted that he would return before all his contemporaries had died (Mark 9:1; 13:30 par.). Since this prediction was not fulfilled, he apparently had been mistaken. This interpretation has been strongly defended by Albert Schweitzer.[29] However, in neither case can it be proven that Jesus was speaking about his second coming.

Consider the first incident. Mark 9:1 says, "Truly, I say to you, there are some standing here who will not taste death un-

---

27. Brown (1994a, 37–38).
28. Cf. Archer (1982, 362, 337–38).
29. Schweitzer (1956).

til they see the kingdom of God after it has come with power." In my view, these words were fulfilled in the transfiguration of Jesus on the mountain, an event that took place immediately after these words (vv. 2–8). The key to this interpretation is the insight that Jesus' transfiguration was a presentation of the coming kingdom in power. This is corroborated by 2 Peter 1:16–18,

> [W]e did not follow cleverly devised myths when we made known to you the power and coming of our Lord Jesus Christ, but we were eyewitnesses of his majesty. For when he received honor and glory from God the Father, and the voice was borne to him by the Majestic Glory, "This is my beloved Son, with whom I am well pleased," we ourselves heard this very voice borne from heaven, for we were with him on the holy mountain.

Thus, the event of the transfiguration of Jesus was a *tableau vivant* of the coming Messianic kingdom.

In the other proof text, Mark 13:30, we read, "[T]his generation will not pass away until all these things take place." Three interpretations of this verse have been given that seem worth mentioning. First, Jesus speaks of the generation that would live—during the next forty years—to see the destruction of the temple in AD 70. Second, he speaks of the future generation during the last days before Jesus' return (but would Jesus have called this "*this* generation"?). Third, the Greek *genea* must be understood here not as a quantitative notion at all (a period of, say, forty years) but as a qualitative notion: this "kind" of people will remain until the arrival of the kingdom in glory. See *genea* in Mark 8:12, "this generation," *or* as many have it, "you people." Also compare the related Greek term *genos* in 9:29, "This kind" (ESV). In this case, Jesus is saying that this kind of (carnal, worldly) people will not pass away before the Messianic kingdom will arrive.

In Matthew 24 and Luke 21, there is no suggestion at all—as some have argued—that Jesus' return would occur soon.

THE ETERNAL CHRIST: GOD WITH US

On the contrary, Jesus is suggesting that he might stay away much longer than the disciples might think or wish; compare the statement, "My master is delayed" by the wicked slave (Matt. 24:48; cf. 25:5), and the expression "after a long time" in the parable of the talents (25:19). This interpretation is not contradicted by a passage like Matthew 10:23 ("you will not have gone through all the towns of Israel before the Son of Man comes").

10.5 Was Jesus' Baptism Needed?
10.5.1 The Anticipation of the Cross

Some people have argued that by allowing himself to be baptized by John the Baptist, Jesus showed that he was not sinless. John proclaimed "a baptism of repentance for the forgiveness of sins" (Mark 1:4), and Luke tells us in one breath that "all the people were baptized," and "Jesus also had been baptized" (3:21). Is it therefore not obvious, these people argue, that Jesus, too, apparently belonged to those who needed to repent and to receive the forgiveness of sins?

Some contemporary expositors assert things like this.[30] Klaus Berger heavily criticized them, arguing:

> No one can sufficiently praise God's holiness, therefore do not eschew any repetition of the expression of humility.... Therefore, according to Luke 3:21 [Jesus] prays before his baptism. He would not "need" it, but the fact that he speaks with his Father is the sign that he loves him, and is associated with him. Jesus does not "need" to be baptized, rather he has no reason to eschew an encounter with his heavenly Father. Other than us, he does not think from the urgent need, as if God's acting toward us is ultimately determined and caused by our need. From a biblical viewpoint, the opposite is true: the baptism by John is, in its origin, an encounter with the living God, hence the living water as image of God's vitality and purity (cf. also John 7:38–39 and the image of the source in the Gospel of Thomas

---

30. See the critical analysis by Meier (1994, 106–16).

13³¹). A limitation [of baptism's meaning] to forgiveness of sins is not at all urgently necessary.³²

Berger argued that Jesus' prayer must not be understood as a prayer for forgiveness but as a prayer for the Holy Spirit (cf. Luke 11:13):

> Time and again, the early Christians pray for the Holy Spirit [cf. Acts 1:14]. And therefore it says—actually only in Luke— that the heavens were opened "when Jesus was praying." In the Middle Ages, people see in Jesus' baptism, which he did not need to take away any guilt of his, an analogy with the redemption on the cross: because Jesus, the Righteous One without stain or blemish, had himself baptized, he, already here in his baptism, vicariously took upon himself the sins of others.³³

We might say that already here Jesus was demonstrating his *readiness* to vicariously take upon himself the sins of others. At least it is perfectly clear that Jesus allowed himself to be baptized in anticipation of his sufferings on the cross.

10.5.2 Sin and Righteousness

Let me add here two important points concerning Jesus' baptism. The first one is the amazement of John the Baptist: "I need to be baptized by you, and do you come to me?" (Matt. 3:14). This cannot mean anything other than this: if one of us two needs to be baptized, it is I,³⁴ with this apparent implication: by nature, I too am a sinful human being, just like the others whom I baptize, but you are not. D. A. Carson wrote, "John the Baptist was a humble man; conscious of his own sin, he could detect no sin Jesus needed to repent of and con-

---

31. "[Y]ou have drunk, you have become intoxicated at the bubbling spring that I have measured out" (https://www.biblicalarchaeology.org/daily/biblical-topics/bible-versions-and-translations/the-gospel-of-thomas-114-sayings-of-jesus/).
32. Berger (2004, 57–58).
33. Ibid., 58.
34. Bruce (1979, 85).

fess. So John thought that Jesus should baptize him."[35] This does not necessarily mean that John was entirely conscious of the fact that Jesus, in addition to being the Messiah, the Son of God, was the perfectly Sinless One. But he did realize that, whereas he himself was definitely a morally outstanding man, he was only an inconspicuous man compared to Jesus.[36]

Second, Jesus' reply to John is important: "Let it be so now, for thus it is fitting for us to fulfill all righteousness" (v.15). Jesus did not need John's baptism for his own supposed unrighteousnesses, but in view of "all righteousness." Much has been written about the precise meaning of this, but at least we can say that Jesus' baptism was part of the will of God concerning his path of life on earth. With this baptism, he took upon himself the office of servant of God in order to walk the path of obedience and service. This baptism was one of the conditions to his introducing the wonderful righteousness of God into this world; as he told his disciples: "[S]eek first the kingdom of God and his [i.e., God's] righteousness" (Matt. 6:33; cf. 5:20). Most basically, we may say that Jesus willingly underwent baptism not because he was unrighteous but precisely because he was righteous *and* had come to take upon himself the unrighteousnesses of others.[37]

This is also the way Joseph Ratzinger read the text.[38] "Righteousness" is the human answer to the Torah, the acceptance of God's will. Jesus' baptism means that he says yes to

---

35. Carson (1984, 107).
36. Tasker (1961, 49).
37. Cf. Berkouwer (1954, 244–45). Remarkably, the second-century Gospel of the Nazarenes tells us that Mary asked Jesus to undergo baptism by John. Jesus replied, "In what respect did I sin that I should go and be baptized by him? Unless what I have said is [a sin of] ignorance."
38. Ratzinger (2007, 17–20). He also referred to Paul Evdokimov, who pointed to 2 Kings 2:8 and 14: "The Jordan was turned back by Elijah's [not Elisha's] coat, and the waters were divided leaving a dry path. This is a true image of Baptism by which we pass through life" (1990, 296). Actually, I do not see an image of baptism in this event—rather I see such an image in Israel's passage through the Red Sea (Exod. 13–14), as did Paul (1 Cor. 10:1–2).

the entire will of God, and also that he exhibits his solidarity with sinful people, who are guilty but who reach out for righteousness. In a certain sense this means, said Ratzinger, that Jesus is already shouldering the burden of the sins of people, and carries it into the Jordan, the threatening flood of death. Together with Jonah, Jesus says as it were, "Pick me up and hurl me into the sea; then the sea will quiet down for you," in order thus to save the mariners (Jonah 1:12). Therefore, Jesus' baptism anticipates the cross: his baptism is the acceptance of death for the sins of people, while the heavenly voice—"This is my beloved Son"—is an anticipation of the resurrection (cf. Rom. 1:4). In this way, we also understand that Jesus himself calls his coming death a "baptism"; he said to some disciples, "Are you able to drink the cup that I drink, or to be baptized with the baptism with which I am baptized?" (Mark 10:38), and: "I have a baptism to be baptized with, and how great is my distress until it is accomplished!" (Luke 12:50).

From the beginning, Jesus traveled the road of righteousness. In his case, "increasing in wisdom" (Luke 2:52) never implied some unlearning of foolishness, unlike with every other ordinary child. Similarly, the phrase "learning obedience" in Hebrews 5:7 does not necessarily imply that he would ever have been *dis*obedient. Rather, this saying must be linked with Hebrews 2:10, "[I]t was fitting that he, for whom and by whom all things exist, in bringing many sons to glory, should make the founder of their salvation *perfect* through suffering"; and 5:9, "being made perfect, he became the source of eternal salvation to all who obey him."

Here again, this does not mean that Jesus had to unlearn certain *im*perfections; this would be entirely foreign to the tenor of Hebrews. Rather, here "perfecting" means "bringing to the perfect end of a career," or "bringing into a perfect position" that would make the person involved fit for a certain office.[39] The expression refers to Jesus' experiences as a Man

---

39. Ouweneel (1982, 38, 41); Berkouwer (1954, 248–49).

on earth that made him perfectly fit to become our compassionate high priest. Jesus was made perfectly familiar with all the sufferings that the "many sons," who are on their way to glory (Heb. 2:10), will have to undergo. When he had reached the end of his earthly walk, he had become perfectly capable of taking upon himself his high priestly service for the benefit of all who were yet to accomplish *their* earthly walk.

10.5.3 Did Jesus Reject the Qualification "Good"?

One day, a rich ruler came to Jesus, and asked him, "Good Teacher, what must I do to inherit eternal life?" (Mark 10:17; Luke 18:18). According to Mark 10:18, Jesus responded to this with these remarkable words (cf. Luke 18:19): "Why do you call me good? No one is good except God alone." In Matthew 19:16-17, the situation is a little different. Here, the rich young man does not call Jesus "Good Teacher," but asks "what good deed must I do?," to which Jesus replies, "Why do you ask me about what is good? There is only one who is good" (cf. §5.6.2).

As a truly humble and obedient Man, Jesus always gives God the honor that he deserves.[40] But the question here is this: Does this also mean that Jesus rejects the designation "good" because he would not find himself to be entirely good? This would be in total conflict with the testimony that Jesus gives about himself in other passages. I already referred to various passages in John's Gospel (4:34; 8:29, 46; 15:10). One would drive a wedge between John and the Synoptic Gospels if one were to claim that Mark and Luke cast doubt on the goodness of Jesus. Moreover, these very Gospels reveal Jesus teaches his disciples to confess their sins, and to pray for forgiveness (Matt. 6:12; Luke 11:4), without ever telling us that Jesus had to confess sins himself, or had to ask for forgiveness.

What Jesus is really doing here is challenging the rich ruler, who apparently had a rather shallow view concerning "the

---

40. Grundmann (*TDNT* 1:16): the point of Jesus' question is not his own sinlessness but rather the honor of God.

good."⁴¹ This is evident from the fact that he claimed he had kept all the commandments Jesus had mentioned—in itself an impossible task—but turned out to be unable, or unwilling, to follow Jesus. The young man came to Jesus like one good man comes to another good one, to learn from him some new lessons. Perhaps he even considered Jesus to be better than himself; perhaps, as he may have thought, Jesus knew something he himself did not yet know, namely, how one can inherit eternal life. In any case, he found himself to some extent "good," too. But Jesus showed him that one who speaks of "the good" must identify this by means of the highest possible criterion, and this is God himself.

Thus, the question "Why do you call me good?" does not mean: "Your designation 'good' does not apply to me but only to God," but rather: "Do not use the word 'good' all too superficially, purely out of politeness."[42] The criterion for anything that is truly good lies not in humans, not in shallow conventions, nor for instance, in the legalistic requirements of the scribes and the Pharisees, but in God alone. Nothing must be called "good" that does not flow from God's own goodness. What is really good resides not in the outward maintenance of the commandments but in a heart entirely attuned to God.

That Jesus cannot possibly have meant that he himself was not good is evident from an important clue in the passage. Jesus does not want anyone to call him "good" as long as this person does not understand what they are saying.[43] To put it even more strongly, Jesus refers to *himself* as the criterion of what is truly good: if the rich young man really wished to know what is good he had to learn to follow Jesus: "If you would be perfect, go, sell what you possess and give to the poor, and you will have treasure in heaven; and *come, follow me*" (Matt. 19:21 par.). The good can be found in *God* alone;

---

41. Lane (1974, 365).
42. Bruce (1979, 248).
43. This might also be one of the reasons why Jesus did not want people to address him all too superficially as the Messiah ("the Christ") (cf. 8:29–30).

one who wishes to find it must come to *Jesus*. Thus, this is the reverse of what the critics are claiming. Insofar as one wishes to find in this passage a statement about whether Jesus is sinless, *this* is the key: not a denial of Jesus' sinlessness but rather a confirmation of it: those who follow him will find the good of God in their lives. This is because Jesus is so close to the Father that he could say, just a short time before this event: "[W]hoever receives me, receives not me but him who sent me" (Mark 9:37).

10.6   The Holy and Righteous One
10.6.1 Jesus Is "Risky"

In summary, we must conclude that the doctrine of Jesus' sinlessness is of the greatest theological significance. Without this sinlessness, Jesus could never have become the sacrifice for the sins of any humans. For an ordinary person, this Bible statement is true: "Truly no man can ransom another, or give to God the price of his life, for the ransom of their life is costly and can never suffice, that he should live on forever and never see the pit" (Ps. 49:7–9). However, of Jesus it is said, "For our sake he made him to be sin who knew no sin, so that in him we might become the righteousness of God" (2 Cor. 5:21). "[T]here is one God, and there is one mediator between God and men, the man Christ Jesus, who gave himself as a ransom for all" (1 Tim. 2:5–6). "You know that he appeared in order to take away sins, and in him there is no sin" (1 John 3:5).

A sinless human is as much a miracle in the moral world as a virgin birth is a miracle in the physical world.[44] Jesus' sinlessness is a supernatural miracle, granted by God. It was also a necessary miracle, without which the redemption of humans would not have been possible—not even for an omnipotent God. God's flawless plan of redemption demanded a flawless Redeemer. As wicked as humanity's sinfulness was, so perfect did the Redeemer have to be. God can never cease being God (cf. 2 Tim. 2:13); he cannot remove and forgive un-

---

44. Bruce (1892, 410).

righteousness and unholiness without his own righteousness and holiness having found full and perfect satisfaction, which is possible only through someone who himself is the Righteous and Holy One.

"Sinlessness" is a negative term; it tells what Jesus is *not*. Therefore, it is good to emphasize the positive side as well, as we have just mentioned: in the New Testament, Jesus is the Righteous and the Holy One. And "holy" means: "shocking, strange, dangerous, forcing on the knees, large and unfathomable."[45] Jesus is "dangerous":[46] his sinlessness is risky for us because it brings to light our own sinfulness all the more poignantly. No matter what excuses we may have for our sins (God's laws are too hard; so many excuses and mitigating circumstances may be adduced; etc.), they evaporate when we consider *this* sinless Man, who perfectly kept all God's commandments, and thus brings to the full light our own moral paltriness.

As long as we do not really know him, we can look around among our fellow humans, and wonder which one of us is "the greatest" (Luke 9:46), or even have a "dispute" about it (22:24). It happens all the time, even today, among Christians and non-Christians. However, when we begin to recognize the greatness of Jesus, we discover that we all are the "smallest." Only he is great: "[C]onsider how great this man is" (Heb. 7:4 DRA). If Jesus asks, "Who is the greatest in the kingdom of heaven?" (Matt. 18:1), the answer must ultimately be that the King himself is necessarily the greatest.

10.6.2 A Place of Rest

The significance of Jesus' baptism by John was especially that he received the Holy Spirit. The dove, which in Genesis 8:9 "found no place to set her foot," represents the Holy Spirit, who, throughout the ages, "restlessly" wandered through the

---

45. Berger (2004, 100).
46. He is "not safe," as Mr. Beaver tells Susan in *The Lion, the Witch and the Wardrobe* by C. S. Lewis (2002): "'Course he isn't safe. But he's good."

world to look "down from heaven on the children of man, to see if there are any who understand, who seek after God" (Ps. 14:2; 53:2), one on whom she could find a place to set her foot. "They have all fallen away; together they have become corrupt; there is none who does good, not even one" (Ps. 14:3; 53:3) — until Jesus reached out in prayer to his heavenly Father, and received the Spirit. Among all the millions of people who had ever lived on this earth, there was literally only one on whom the Spirit "found a place to set her foot" — a place of rest — without that person first needing regeneration and redemption.

In a hymn written by poet Julius Anton von Poseck, "On the Lamb Our Souls Are Resting," we find these words: "God is satisfied with Jesus, / We are satisfied as well"; or more literally: "The One on whom God rests with pleasure, is the One on whom we have been put to rest as well"). God *rests* on him. After having observed his Son for thirty years in the concealment of his youth and of the carpenter shop, heaven opened up, and these passionate words were uttered (Matt. 3:17): "This is my beloved Son, with whom I am well pleased" — "not only because he was from eternity my beloved Son in my bosom but also because of what and who he was for *me* and before *me* as a Man on earth." God found eternal rest in the very same person in whom every true believer has found his or her eternal rest: his Son, our Savior.

Klaus Berger wrote,

> When God through Jesus Christ enters the world, this world experiences God's presence in his Son as the mother of all sabbaths [i.e., as the great everlasting time of rest]. And every time Jesus will perform a healing on the sabbath, the proverb is true: "A greater than the sabbath is here" [cf. Matt. 12:42], here God himself has come to rest.[47]

That is, God rested on the sabbath (Gen. 2:3), but now God rests in his own Son, who is greater than the sabbath. And

---

47. Berger (2004, 67).

also, the sabbath is not the worst time to heal the sick—as Jesus' opponents asserted (Matt. 12:10; Mark 2:24; 3:2; Luke 13:14; 14:3; John 5:18; 9:16)—but the very best time. Every such healing is a foreshadowing of the eternal wholeness and rest that will characterize God's coming eternal sabbath.

10.6.3 The Mount of Transfiguration

Again, we must pay attention to the words of the heavenly Father concerning Jesus on the Mount of Transfiguration (Matt. 17:1-13 par.). In opposition to liberal theologians, who prefer to push aside the transfiguration of Jesus as such an "unbelievable" story, Berger called this event "the secret axis of the gospel," "the theological center of Mark's Gospel," "the central place of God's self-revelation."[48] Nowhere else does what God thinks of his Son become more gloriously evident, as does the purpose of sending this Son into the world.

To the many people baptized by John and listening to his preaching, God testifies of the unique position of his Son, so that no one will view Jesus as a penitent sinner like the others who were being baptized. However, on the Mount of Transfiguration, God has a much higher purpose with his heavenly declaration. At the *low* elevation of the Jordan River—more than eight hundred feet *below* sea level—God testified that Jesus is higher than all sinners. But at the *high* elevation of the Mount—perhaps more than eighteen hundred feet *above* sea level—God testified that Jesus is higher than God's greatest servants on earth, Moses and Elijah. The latter two were only servants (cf. Heb. 3:5-6)—Jesus is the Son. At the river, we learn that Jesus is the best of men; on the mount, we learn that Jesus is the best of God's servants.

In his treatise on this event, Klaus Berger casually wrote in a parenthesis about Jesus praying (cf. Luke 9:18, 28): "Jesus always prays alone."[49] This is correct: Jesus does not organize

---

48. Ibid., 68–69, 71; according to Gooding (2007, ad loc.), the same event is the axis in Luke.
49. Berger (2004, 71; see more extensively, 137).

any prayer meetings with his disciples. At some occasions we *hear* him pray, especially in John 17, but this is a different matter. Actually, even on this occasion he prayed alone. He did so because of his unique relationship with the Father. He did teach his disciples to pray: "Our Father in heaven . . . ," but he never prayed this *together with* them. One reason was that he could never pray: ". . . and forgive us our debts, as we also have forgiven our debtors. And lead us not into temptation . . . ," for such words could never pass his lips.

When an ordinary human being approaches God, they must always first humble themselves, make themselves "small." "He must become greater; I must become less," said as great a man as John the Baptist (John 3:30 NIV; cf. Matt. 11:11). Sin makes us "large" (arrogant, proud, rebellious), and therefore, when we repent, we must always become "small" before God. But Jesus *is* already small before his Father, precisely because he is so great. He is perfect in his humility—"I am gentle and lowly in heart" (Matt. 11:29)—but he never had to *humble* himself because he always was humble already. An immature believer, who lives by trial and error and is conscious of their weaknesses, may sometimes doubt whether God always hears them. But Jesus could say, "Father, I thank you that you have heard me. I knew that you always hear me" (John 11:41-42). Today, the mature believer can say the same (with confidence, Heb. 4:16; 10:19), not because of their greatness—they still come humbly—but because of Jesus' greatness.

10.7 Stumbling Over Jesus
10.7.1 "Sweet" Jesus
Much in the fascinating and encompassing study by Klaus Berger sheds variegated light on the moral perfection of Jesus, even from the viewpoint of what is "offensive" in Jesus.[50] Jesus is perfect, even in instances where his opponents call him "offensive."

---

50. Ibid., 88–95.

The Sinlessness of Christ

Children's Bibles, Romantic-era painters, Hollywood movies, and sentimental authors have saddled humanity with the picture of a sweet, gentle, soft, understanding, effeminate Jesus. This is one reason why Christmas is so popular: it exalts the picture of the sweet innocent little Jesus. As God's holiness and judgment fades into the background of Christian thinking, we are left with the pastel shaded picture of "sweet Jesus," as portrayed in this hymn:

> *I want to be like Jesus,*
> *So lowly and so meek;*
> *For no one marked an angry word*
> *That ever heard him speak.*

This picture is very different from that of the Jesus who provokes, who is offensive, who says politically incorrect things, who unsettles people, who even mocks them. Jesus never spoke an angry word? Read Matthew 11:20-24 par.; 23:1-36 par.; Mark 3:5; Luke 6:24-26. Jesus was always meek? Read John 2:13-22; Mark 11:15-19. In fact, it is strange that this is the picture of Jesus that so many Christians prefer, which then is put forth as an example for his followers: I want to be like Jesus, always meek, never angry. Indeed, many revolutionary Christian leaders, from some church fathers to the Reformers, have been depicted as great sinners because of their alleged lovelessness, that is, their anger, their lack of meekness. In reality, they often (not always, of course) were doing nothing but following the Master.

In the New Testament epistles, we are called upon to not offend each other (make another stumble); for instance, in 1 Corinthians 8:13, "[I]f meat make my brother to offend, I will eat no flesh while the world standeth, lest I make my brother to offend" (KJV; cf. v. 9; 10:32; 2 Cor. 6:3; Rom. 14:13). However, Jesus hardly seems to do anything but offend other people. Some of us may like to distinguish here between irritating people (the subjective sense of offending), and causing them to stumble and fall (the objective sense of offending). However, it is questionable whether the New Testament draws a sharp line between these two meanings.[51] Jesus irritated a lot of people—and would some of us not call this a sin, too? If we remove our rose-colored glasses for a moment, through which we usually consider Jesus, we will have to learn to deal with this irritating Jesus, and to determine for ourselves how this irritating Jesus fits into our picture of the sinless Jesus.

10.7.2 Dubious Actions

Let me mention some examples of what appear to be plainly sinful actions that Jesus seems to strangely recommend in his parables, ones that indeed irritated the spiritual leaders very intensely.[52]

(1) Jesus seems to recommend violence as a means to enter the kingdom of God (Matt. 11:12; Luke 16:16; cf. 13:24).[53] Would we not reply that violence must be rejected under all circumstances?

(2) It is immoral to buy a field from someone at a fair price, and later to hide from the seller that that field contains a treasure. Moreover, it is foolish to sell *everything* one possesses before buying something (Matt. 13:44). This is just as foolish as selling *all* of one's possessions in order to buy a single precious pearl (vv. 45–46).

(3) It is foolish and irresponsible—if not outright sinful—to leave behind ninety-nine sheep in the mountains or in the wilderness, unprotected, in order to find one lost sheep; and, to put it mildly, it is quite strange to rejoice in finding that one sheep more than in having kept the ninety-nine others (Matt.

---

51. Cf. in the Gospels [KJV] Matt. 5:29–30; 11:6; 13:21, 41, 57; 15:12; 18:6–9; 24:10; 26:31, 33 (par.).
52. Berger (2004, 350, 354–55, 389); in the text, I am supplementing his examples. Our inability nowadays to understand Jesus' "recommending" these kinds of "sins" is, according to Berger (2004, 350–54), because we confuse morality and religion. He deals extensively with several of these "irritations" listed here (354–73).
53. This seems true unless Jesus means that *enemies* try to eliminate the kingdom of God.

15:12-13; Luke 15:1-6).

(4) You ought not to throw a debtor into prison until he has paid the last penny (Matt. 18:32-34); first, this does not work (if he is in prison, how will he get the money to pay you back?); second, lifelong imprisonment is a disproportionate punishment for debtors.

(5) It is unjust to kill a wedding guest simply because he does not wear the proper clothes, or to kill a servant only because he was lazy (Matt. 22:11-13; 25:30).

(6) Jesus strangely compares the coming of the Son of Man with that of an undesirable and unpredictable thief in the night (Matt. 24:43-44 par.; cf. 1 Thess. 5:2, 4; 2 Pet. 3:10; Rev. 3:3; 16:15).

(7) You cannot leave young girls outside in the middle of the night, as the bridegroom does, with all possible risks — and this only because they did not have enough oil with them (Matt. 25:10-12).

(8) "[T]o everyone who has will more be given, and he will have an abundance. But from the one who has not, even what he has will be taken away" (Matt. 25:29; Luke 19:26). Isn't this simply unfair?

(9) And is it not unfair to organize a banquet for a son who has wasted his inheritance, while never to have granted a modest party for the son who always behaved well (Luke 15:20-32)? Who would recommend or accept such behavior on the part of any father?

(10) It is strictly forbidden to falsify promissory notes, and it is even a sin to praise people who do such things (Luke 16:4-8).

10.7.3 The Irritating Jesus

Of course, in the examples just given what is decisive is not some bourgeois ethic, but rather the religious point that Jesus wishes to make in each case mentioned. It was this very point — the point of one's attitude toward God and his kingdom—that repeatedly irritated the "morally impeccable" Pharisees and scribes, elders, and priests. Was such irritation of opponents necessary, or inevitable, or desirable? we ask ("morally impeccable" as we ourselves are). Yes, it was highly necessary shock therapy. Jesus is this very type of perfect person who, having come into this world, can do nothing but irritate the imperfect-but-all-too-"pious" people: "[T]his is the judgment: the light has come into the world, and people loved the darkness rather than the light because their works were evil" (John 3:19).

In each of the examples given, Jesus' opponents strained out the ethical gnat, but swallowed the religious camel (cf. §8.5.1). In the shadows, these people could present themselves as very pious; but when the bright light shone upon them, their stains and filthiness came to light. Consider these explanations of a few of the examples given earlier.

(1) It requires religious "violence" to overcome the powers that wish to prevent you from entering the kingdom of God. (2) It requires the highest "price" for someone to become a disciple of Jesus. (3) Jesus cared more about the one lost "sheep" than about the ninety-nine sheep that were lost, too, but did not know it, or did not wish to admit it. And so on.

No wonder such people get offended. Jesus himself said about this, "[B]lessed is the one who is not offended by me" (Matt. 11:6). Therefore, he also says, "Do you think that I have come to give peace on earth? No, I tell you, but rather division" (Luke 12:51), namely, between those who are irritated and those who swallow their irritation and follow him. Conversely, those who become followers of Jesus will also themselves cause "offenses." As Jesus himself said, "Woe to you, when all people speak well of you, for so their fathers did to the false prophets" (Luke 6:26). And: "If they persecuted me, they will also persecute you" (John 15:20).

Those who felt offended by Jesus or his followers are the self-appointed "wise" men, who tell the weaker people: "We know that this man is a sinner" (John 9:24). No wonder! Imagine, Jesus healed a man—and thus performed work—during the sabbath rest ordained by God himself! Jesus ate with tax collectors and sinners, something "good" people never do, of course. Jesus was involved with bad women: he allowed himself to be anointed by an immoral woman, and let an adulterous woman, caught in the act, go free after having embarrassed her accusers. Jesus spoke sharply against certain revered Jewish traditions. Jesus constantly hurt the feelings of the spiritual leaders of God's people. He openly ridiculed them with his clever replies. Jesus even uttered the most terrible accusations about them.

This is one of the most remarkable aspects of Jesus' sinlessness: he repeatedly does things that, also in our orthodox churches, would be greeted with frowns. If we were to do one of the irritating things that he did—maintaining relationships with dubious characters, "unnecessarily" shocking people by attacking their sacred traditions, embarrassing spiritual leaders—in quite a few churches or congregations we might be put under church discipline. As Christians, we must not offend each other—but Jesus seemed to do this all the time. We are supposed to follow Jesus—but apparently only the sweet, meek, and mild Jesus, who never spoke an angry word, and never provoked or offended people.

Yet, it cannot be too difficult to discern spiritually between the kind of "offenses" by which *sinners* are unmasked and *sinful* offenses. Jesus himself said, "[I]t must needs be that offences come; but woe to that man by whom the offence cometh!" (Matt. 18:7 KJV). But this concerns "temptations" (ESV), "stumbling blocks" (NASB). This is not what Jesus brought. He unmasked the seducers, but he never seduced anyone; he never caused the vulnerable to stumble or fall (cf. Paul's treatment of this subject in 1 Cor. 8–10).[54] Rather, Jesus is the One who raised the fallen ones (cf. Matt. 14:31).

---

54. For a dissertation-length treatment of this very subject, involving detailed exegesis of Rom. 14 and 1 Cor. 8–10, see Kloosterman (1991).

Among other things, true, Spirit-worked repentance is also this: no longer to be offended by Jesus, no longer to stumble over him, no longer to be irritated by him, but to let oneself be raised by him, and to acknowledge that he is right in everything that he states concerning our lives. Those who take offense say, "We know that this man is a sinner." But Jesus replies, "[B]lessed is the one who is not offended by me" (Matt. 11:6 par.). Such a person discovers not only that Jesus is *not* a sinner but rather the best of all humans, and even the very person who saves sinners: "[T]he Son of man is not come to destroy men's lives, but to save them" (Luke 9:56 KJV).

10.8 Jesus and Women
10.8.1 Lust: the Gravest Sin

It is remarkable that, in traditional Christianity, the notion of sin is linked so strongly with sexuality. The word "immoral" refers to what conflicts with morality, and this is something that pertains to all of human life. But in current parlance, the term "immoral" very often refers to sexual immorality. We all know what the "morality police" do. And if someone is put under church discipline because he or she "is living in sin," we almost know for sure that this person must be committing sexual immorality. Indeed, few interpreters doubt that the sinful woman in Luke 7:37 was an adulteress or a prostitute. And since Mary Magdalene was a woman from whom seven demons had gone out (Luke 8:2), tradition is certain that she must have been a prostitute.

This linking of sin to sexuality goes very far back in church history. In antiquity, the significance of the Fall was sought especially in the loss of sexual innocence. Some church fathers, especially Augustine, were convinced that, before the Fall, Adam and Eve did not experience any sexual *desire*; these church fathers believed that sexual desire is a consequence of the Fall.[55]

Indeed, no sin was viewed as so horrible—and so typi-

---
55. See extensively, Ouweneel (1998, 80–81, 86–95).

cal of what sin in its essence is—as engaging in one's "carnal pleasures," including sexual desire as such. In the New Testament catalogs of evil acts, sexual sins often head the lists (see, e.g., Rom. 1:26-32; 13:13; 1 Cor. 5:9-11; 6:9-10; 1 Tim. 1:9-10; Titus 3:3; Rev. 21:8). There are few sins against which believers are warned more often than against sexual sins (fornication, adultery, homosexuality). This concerns not only illicit sex but also sexual abuse, male abuse of power against women, disregard for women. At the same time, the Bible never condemns sexual desire as such—only the abuse of it, that is, outside the marriage bond. The apostle Paul even acknowledged the legitimacy of sexual desire:

> The husband should give to his wife her conjugal rights, and likewise the wife to her husband. . . . Do not deprive one another [of these rights], except perhaps by agreement for a limited time, that you may devote yourselves to prayer; but then come together again, so that Satan may not tempt you because of your lack of self-control (1 Cor. 7:3-5).

Interpreters have sometimes abused this statement from Genesis 3: "Your desire shall be for your husband, and he will rule over you" (v. 16b NIV). However, the "rule" identified here is not an aspect of the creation order, but an evil and inevitable consequence of the Fall. Behind this, sexual urges play a role: women are "dangerous" (they induce male sexual desire), and therefore they must be either "taken," or moved to the sideline. Some church fathers, and later many medieval church leaders, viewed women either as whores or as holy (i.e., if they remained virgins, abstaining from all forms of sexuality).[56]

10.8.2 Sinlessness and Women

How does the matter of sexual desire relate to the question of Jesus' sinlessness? In §8.5.3 we read a description of Jesus as an attractive young man, moving confidently among women

---

56. See ibid.

of all types, including most infamous ones, without a trace of sentimentality, unnaturalness, or prudishness, yet preserving at each point integrity of character.[57] The sinless Jesus demonstrated what a sinless attitude toward women entails: he *honored* women, he *exalted* them.

Traditional theologians often emphasize what Jesus did *not* do with or to women: he did not include them in the circle of disciples and apostles, and they were not elders and deacons. Actually, these assertions are questionable; there were definitely also female disciples (Luke 8:2-3; Acts 9:36;[58] cf. Luke 24:9, 33 with John 20:19, and Acts 1:2-3 with v. 14). We read of brother Andronicus and sister Junia, "outstanding among the apostles" (Rom. 16:7 NIV).[59] Phoebe was a "deacon" (not a "deaconess"; Gk. *diakonos*) in the church of Cenchreae (Rom. 16:1); 1 Timothy 3:11 has been taken to speak of female "deacons"; and in 1 Timothy 5:2 one might read female presbyters.[60] Despite the wide divergence of interpretations, let us emphasize all the more how Jesus brought believing women into greater prominence.

Klaus Berger provided the following remarkable enumeration. In the Gospels, three times Jesus raised dead people, once it involved a woman (the daughter of Jairus; Mark 5:21-43), and twice he did it on behalf of women: the widow at Nain (Luke 7:11-17) and the sisters Martha and Mary (John 11:1-44).[61] When it came to following Jesus' example of true servitude, women were his best followers (Luke 4:39; 8:1-3; 10:40; John 12:2; cf. 1 Tim. 5:10). This pertained also to their

---

57. Moule (1967, 63).
58. In this verse Luke used the feminine Gk. noun *mathētria*, "female disciple."
59. Often, the accusative Gk. noun *Iounian* is derived from the male form *Iounias* (Junias). However, the name Junias is not known in Hellenistic Greek, whereas the name Junia is. Origen and Chrysostom understood this to refer to a woman; see the discussion of Den Boer (1985, 81–82).
60. Ibid.; the interpretation of all these passages depends on people's biases about the role of women in the church.
61. "For creational life granted on earth always comes from the women, and is 'addressed' to them always first" (Berger [2004, 435]).

loyalty: *women* were present at Jesus' death and at his burial (Matt. 27:55-56, 61), and *women* were the first witnesses of his resurrection (28:1-10). Their tears were precious to Jesus, whether borne of the grief of the mother of the young man in Nain (Luke 7:13), or of the sinful woman (v. 38), or of Mary of Bethany (John 11:33), or of the grief of the women who accompanied him on his way to the cross (Luke 23:27-28), or the grief of Mary Magdalene (John 20:13).

Jesus' care extended to women who were pregnant, or were nursing infants (Matt. 24:19 par.), to widows who had to live on very little money (Luke 21:2-4 par.), to women who had to bear the burden of menstruation, especially if it did not cease (Matt. 9:20 par.). Women anointed him (Luke 7:37-38; Matt. 26:7).[62] Berger also observed that the three elements of anointing—perfume, blood, and tears—are the liquids that very intensively characterize the life of women.[63]

10.8.3 Touch Without Lust

Jesus was sinless, also—and many would say: even—in his relationships with women. One might argue that men can deal with women in a safe way as long as there is no touching. However, the remarkable thing is that, wherever we read that Jesus was touched physically, this was done by women. Thomas might seem to be an exception (John 20:27); but although Jesus invited Thomas to touch him, we do not read that Thomas actually did so. But women did! Of course, Jesus was touched by John the Baptist during his baptism (Matt. 3:15-16 par.), and by Nicodemus and Joseph of Arimathea at his burial (John 19:38-42); and men will certainly have touched him on other occasions. But women touched him in special ways. In such cases we might issue a warning: think of the danger of erotic feelings and thoughts, and even the danger of actual erotic touches. Rightly so. But Jesus permitted himself to be touched by the woman who suffered from a

---
62. Ibid., 230-31.
63. Ibid., 232.

discharge of blood (Matt. 9:20 par.), by a sinful woman (Luke 7:38), by Mary of Bethany (John 12:3 par.), and by women after his resurrection (Matt. 28:9).

Indeed, Jesus could afford, so to speak, being touched by women. This was not necessarily because he did not experience erotic feelings, a matter about which we have no biblical evidence. The discussion about this matter is always uncomfortable, and was traditionally always related to the ancient theological question whether Adam and Eve before the Fall experienced erotic feelings.[64] Regardless of the conclusions we draw from this discussion, it is certain that possible erotic feelings never led to sinful thoughts, desires, fantasies, or actions in the case of Jesus. Because he was sinless, he did not need to avoid women because they were allegedly dangerous. Instead, he could accept them in sinless love, and honor the place that God had intended for them from the beginning.

Together, man and woman had been called to subdue the earth and to reign over God's creation (Gen. 1:28). It is only in Christ that full justice is done to God's intention: "There is neither Jew nor Greek, there is neither slave nor free, there is no male and female, for you are all one in Christ Jesus" (Gal. 3:28). In Christ, the natural differences between men and women, given with the creation order, have not been removed. Therefore, they still marry and procreate. But what *is* removed are all the differences that were caused by the Fall. In Christ, women do not have to be avoided or shunned as a consequence of the twofold sin of the man: his hunger for power (dominance, imperiousness) as well as his fear of the "dangerous" woman. Elevation of women is possible only when men are freed from this twofold sin. The sinless Jesus paved the way for this elevation.

---

64. Cf. Ouweneel (1998, §§3.3 and 3.4), where I reject the negative answer to this question.

Chapter 11
The Life of Jesus[1]

God anointed Jesus of Nazareth with the Holy Spirit and with power.
He went about doing good and healing all who were oppressed by the devil, for God was with him.

Acts 10:38

11.1 Circumstances of Jesus' Birth[2]
11.1.1 Nazareth

IN ISRAEL, HARDLY any place could be more inconspicuous than Nazareth, a town (Gk. *polis*, Matt. 2:23; Luke 1:26; 2:4, 39) in Galilee. It is mentioned nowhere in ancient writings, including the Old Testament. The question by the godly Nathanael,

---

1. The text of this chapter is a revised and expanded version of Ouweneel (1986b, chapters 2 and 3). Without ignoring the many problems involved in this issue, it has presupposed the fundamental historical reliability and unity of the Gospels; see extensively C. L. Blomberg (*DJG* 291–97); Stein (1996, 46–49); Van Bruggen (1998, especially chapters 4–13). I realize that each of the four Gospels has its own specific character, and they exhibit significant differences among themselves; see chapter 5 above, and *RT* I/1.
2. See B. Witherington (*DJG* 60–74, s.v. "Birth of Jesus"); Knight (2004, 57–79).

"Can anything good come out of Nazareth?" (John 1:46) arose from wondering about, and perhaps also contempt for, this unsightly, worthless little village in "Galilee of the Gentiles" (Matt. 4:15; WYC: "of heathen men"). In this village lived a young woman, actually still a girl: Mary. Tradition[3] mentions her parents Joachim and Anne. This does not fit into the idea that Luke 3:23-38 offers us the genealogy of Mary, which mentions a certain Heli as father (v. 23). However, today this idea of a Marian genealogy finds little support.[4] It is quite possible that Mary's parents were indeed Joachim and Anne, which does not then require us to accept all the legends about their marriage and about Mary's birth (cf. §8.3.1 above).

Mary was pledged to be married to Joseph, a descendent from the royal house of David (Matt. 1:6-16). Joseph was not a king but a carpenter (Gk. *tektōn*, craftsman, woodworker; Matt. 13:55; Mark 6:3),[5] in a corner of a land occupied by the Romans and ruled by the Idumean Herod the Great. To this Mary, the angel Gabriel (cf. Dan. 8:16; 9:21) appeared, in her own home (Luke 1:28, *pros autēn*), to announce to her that she would become the mother of the Messiah, the royal son from the house of David, who would receive the eternal kingship from God's hand, according to God's promise (see chapter 4). Gabriel also told her explicitly that her husband-to-be would not be the child's father, but that she would become pregnant by the power of the Holy Spirit (see chapter 9). The answer of

---

3. See especially the Gospel of the Nativity of Mary, the Gospel of Pseudo-Matthew, the Protevangelium of James, and the *Legenda Aurea*, a collection of stories about Mary, Jesus, and other saints (c. 1260).
4. See Brown (1977, 57-94); Liefeld (1984, 861-62); Meier (1991, 28 note 47); B. Witherington (*DJG* 65); D. S. Huffman (*DJG* 256-58); Stein (1996, 69-71); Van Bruggen (1998, 116-20); cf. Carson (1984, 62-65). Morris (1974, 100-101) leaves room for it, and Geldenhuys (1983, 150-52) defends it. If both genealogies are those of Joseph, it is strange that, in Matt. 1:16, Joseph is called a son of Jacob, and in Luke 3:23, a son of Heli. People have tried to explain this difference in various ways, e.g., by positing a levirate marriage.
5. Justin Martyr (*Dialogue with Trypho* 88) says that Jesus made ploughs and yokes.

this godly girl was: "Behold, I am the servant of the Lord; let it be to me according to your word" (Luke 1:38).

When Joseph, who, as was appropriate, had not had any intercourse with her, found out that his bride-to-be was pregnant, he did not wish to press charges against her, which might have resulted in the death penalty for her (Deut. 22:20-24). Instead, he wished to break the engagement quietly. This is one of the reasons why Matthew 1:19 calls him a "righteous" man, a *tzaddiq*: a true *tzaddiq* not only keeps the law but is also a meek and a merciful person. To him, too, an angel appeared, who explained the exceptional situation to him, and encouraged him to take Mary as his wife. In this way, Joseph would become the child's legal father, so that through him Jesus would be a legal son of David, with full title to the latter's throne. If we consider the legal power of the levirate marriage (Deut. 25:5-10; cf. Gen. 38:1-11, 26: Ruth 3-4), we understand that, for one's title to the throne, legal descent counted just as strongly as biological descent.

It was Joseph who had to give to the newborn child the name "Jesus" (Gk. *Iēsous*; Matt. 1:21), that is, either the Hebrew *Yehoshuah* ("YHWH is salvation," "Joshua" in Exod. 24:13), or the shorter form, for instance *Yēshuah* ("YHWH saves, is Savior," cf. "Jeshua" in Neh. 7:7).⁶ Joseph did what he was told to do, and married Mary, but had no intercourse with her as long as her child was not yet born (Matt. 1:25).⁷

Did this child have to be born in Nazareth? "How can the Christ [i.e., the Messiah] come from Galilee? . . . Look into it, and you will find that a prophet does not come out of Galilee"

---

6. The latter name is used for Jesus by Messianic Jews; cf. Stern (1992, 4–5). See more extensively, Meier (1991, 205–208). The name occurred rather frequently in the first century; in the New Testament we know "Jesus Barabbas" (Matt. 27:16–17 NIV), Jesus called Justus (Col. 4:11), and Bar-Jesus ("son of Jesus," Acts 13:6).
7. The verse has been taken to suggest that, after Jesus' birth, Joseph did have intercourse with Mary, which contradicts Roman Catholic teaching on this point (see §8.1.1 above).

(John 7:41, 52 NIV). This was correct.[8] However, "[t]he king's heart is a stream of water in the hand of the LORD; he turns it wherever he will" (Prov. 21:1). Thus, he led the heart of the mighty emperor, Augustus, who was considered to be the divine redeemer and peacemaker of the world. He was the very person who unwittingly arranged the circumstances for the *true* Redeemer and Prince of Peace, the son of David, to be born in Bethlehem, according to the saying of Micah (5:2).[9]

11.1.2 Time of Birth

Caesar Augustus gave the order that "all the world [Gk. *oikoumenē*]," that is, the Roman Empire,[10]

> should be registered. This was the first registration when Quirinius was governor of Syria. . . . And Joseph also went up from Galilee, from the town of Nazareth, to Judea, to the city of David, which is called Bethlehem, because he was of the house and lineage of David, to be registered with Mary, his betrothed, who was with child (Luke 2:1-5).

Jesus' birth was not a mythical fantasy, but occurred in identifiable space and time.[11] In the sixth century, the Roman abbot Dionysius Exiguum tried, with the help of deficient data, to calculate the beginning of our era, and made a mis-

---

8. According to Ridderbos (1930, 27), Tenney (1981, 88), and others, it was *in*correct because Jonah, for example, did come from Galilee (cf. Talmud: Sukkah 27b: "There was not a tribe in Israel from which there did not come prophets"); two Gk. manuscripts of John (P^{66} and P^{75}) contain the alternative reading we are following (rendered in the NIV, NASB, NRSV), in which the Pharisees used the present tense of the Gk. verb *egeirō*, perhaps to say: "Notice that a prophet never comes forth from people such as these Galileans"; see Morris (1971, 434n108).
9. "Augustus may be compared with Cyrus in the Old Testament [Isa. 44:28; 45:1], who must serve God's people as an instrument in God's hand" (Berkouwer [1965, 92]).
10. Cf. *oikoumenē* in Acts 17:6, again in the sense of the Roman Empire; cf. Ouweneel (2003, 46, 91).
11. Our knowledge of this environment of Jesus continually increases through studies about the Roman empire and Palestine in the first century; see Barnett (1998, chapter 4).

take of at least five years. Today, it is generally accepted that King Herod the Great died in the year 4 BC, and at that time Jesus had been born, and the wise men from the east had come and gone. In connection with their visit, Herod had used a margin of two years for eliminating any potential threat to his throne (Matt. 2:16). Joseph and Mary had already fled to Egypt, where they stayed until the death of Herod (vv. 14-15, 19-20). All of this points to a birth year of no later than 5 BC, and perhaps as early as 8 or 7 BC.[12]

Regarding the time of year when Jesus was born, elsewhere I have argued that it was not around December 25,[13] and that the time of Sukkoth (the Feast of Booths, September/October) is a reasonable alternative; such a pilgrims' festival was an excellent time for a census.[14] Zechariah the priest was serving in the temple according to his division (the eighth: that of Abijah; Luke 1:5; 1 Chron. 24:10), near the fourth month of the religious year. The conception of John the Baptist took place a few weeks later (Luke 1:23-24), and the conception of Jesus in the sixth month after this (v. 26). This brings us to the seventh month of the religious year for the birth of Jesus; this is the month of Sukkoth. It is interesting that John literally says (John 1:14), "[T]he Word became flesh and dwelt-in-a-tent among us"; the Greek verb is *eskēnōsen* (related to the Greek noun *skēnē*; Heb. *sukkah*, "booth" or "tent"). It is quite possible that, during the Feast of Booths, Jesus came to live among us in the "booth" of his human body.

---

12. B. Witherington (*DJG* 66-70); H. W. Hoehner (*DJG* 118-122); Stein (1996, 52-56).
13. It is highly unlikely that Jesus was born on December 25, first, because at that time of year there are no sheep in the fields; second, the winter is an impossible time for a census. The only true reason that Christmas is celebrated on December 25 is that on, or around, this day pagan midwinter festivals were celebrated, as in ancient Rome the *Natalis Invicti (solis)* ("[re] birth of the invincible [sun]": the days begin to lengthen again. The date has also been associated with the birth of the Egyptian goddess Isis, with pagan moon festivals, and with the Indo-Iranian godhead Mithra(s); see Ouweneel (2003, 72).
14. Ouweneel (2001b, §2.3.2).

11.1.3 The Census

Regarding the registration of the entire Roman Empire that Luke mentions, we have only vague indications,[15] but that is not surprising. Little of the historiography of that time has survived. There is some evidence that, under Augustus, the Romans had a registration (a census for the purpose of taxation) every fourteen years. Such a census occurred in AD 6, as we will see shortly, and therefore apparently also in 9 or 8 BC. Evidently such a census near the end of Herod's rule is quite possible. Augustus gradually came to view Herod as a subject, and Judea as Roman territory. The Jews had to swear an oath of fidelity to both Herod and Augustus. A census may also very well have been part of a census of the entire empire. There is some evidence of such registrations in various parts of the empire between 11 and 8 BC, such as in Egypt (10–9 BC). As for Egypt, a papyrus from AD 104 describes a census just like the one mentioned in Luke 2.[16]

The Roman governor proclaimed that, in view of the census, all those who were not residing in their town of birth had to return there. In this way, it could be determined how much farmland every landowner possessed, in order to assess these to determine the tax liability. Married women had to travel with their husbands in order to determine the number of members in each family. And thus, Mary traveled with Joseph to Bethlehem because this was the hometown of the house of David (Ruth 4:11, 21–22; 1 Sam. 16:1, 18; 17:15; 20:6).

The time of this census is identified more precisely with the mention of Quirinius as governor of Syria. This Publius Sulpicius Quirinius, former consul at Tome (12 BC), was an imperial legate (deputy commander) in Syria-Silicia from 6 to 9 BC. At the beginning of this regime, he organized the cen-

---

15. See Grosheide (1954, 1–2); Greijdanus (1955, 57–60); Morris (1974, 81–83); Bruce (1979, 470–71); Archer (1982, 365–66); Geldenhuys (1983, 99–100, 104–106); Liefeld (1984, 843–44); see also Gollwitzer and Lapide (1984).
16. See Ramsay (1915, 255–74): "The Augustan Census-System."

sus in Judea mentioned in Acts 5:37, after Archelaus had been deposed, and this territory had become a Roman province.[17] Although we have no direct historical evidence for this, it is quite possible that Quirinius had been a ruler earlier in Syria. The date of this rule is conjectured to have been sometime between 12 and 7 BC. This range includes the years 9 or 8 BC just mentioned, which may be yet another hint about the year of Jesus' birth.

11.2 The Birth of Jesus
11.2.1 Stable or Cave

Joseph and Mary had to travel for four days southward from Nazareth to Bethlehem, a very difficult journey for a woman with an advanced pregnancy.[18] Bethlehem lay on the main road from Jerusalem to Hebron; its former name was Efrath. There, Rachel, wife of the patriarch Jacob, had been buried (Gen. 35:16, 19; 48:7). There, Ruth had gleaned ears of grain in the field of Boaz (Ruth 2). There, David had been born (1 Sam. 16:1, 13, 18; 17:12, 58). And there, after the fall of Jerusalem through King Nebuchadnezzar, the company of Johanan, to which the prophet Jeremiah belonged, had made a stop on their way to Egypt (Jer. 41:17). Thus, it was highly likely that Bethlehem had a caravansary, a large inn for travelers, along this important north–south road.

However, for Joseph and Mary no place was available, possibly because they had come from a region (Galilee) known for revolutionary activity, so that their direct descent

---

17. Acts 5:37 reminds us of Judas the Galilean, who claimed that people were to pay taxes to God alone, and not to the Romans. He initiated a revolt that failed miserably. His followers formed the party of the Zealots, that is, the "zealous ones." One of Jesus' disciples probably came from that party; see Luke 6:15; Acts 1:13.
18. Regarding Bethlehem as the place of Jesus' birth, see Bockmuehl (1994, 25–29). Liberal theologians often call the Bethlehem birth episode a myth, based upon the supposed Davidic descent of Jesus, and assume that he was born at Nazareth; see, e.g., Theissen and Merz (1998, 164–65). For a much more balanced view, see Meier (1991, 214–16), who believed that, purely on the basis of historical arguments, the question must remain open.

from David was a sensitive matter. Therefore, they had to be satisfied to lodge in a stable, or in one of the caves in the neighborhood, which provided shelter for shepherds and animals.[19] Such shepherds were outside in the fields near Bethlehem, and became the first to hear the angelic message about the newborn Savior, the Messiah, the Lord. According to the Protevangelium of James, Mary began her first labor pains when they had arrived in Bethlehem, so that Joseph carried her in his arms into the cave.[20] There, according to that same source, Mary gave birth to her child with the help of a local midwife. According to the custom of those days, she wrapped the baby boy in swaddling clothes, and for lack of anything better, she laid him in a manger for animals. This weird cradle became the sign that would enable the shepherds to find the child. Angels gave voice to the first testimony concerning the newborn King, and shepherds became the first worshipers (Luke 2:6–20).

As the law prescribed, the boy was circumcised after eight days (cf. Gen. 17:12); this must have happened in Bethlehem as well, administered presumably by a local "circumciser" (Heb. *mohel*). On this occasion, the boy received the name "Jesus" (Heb. *Yeshuah*). After the obligatory forty-day ritual cleansing, his parents brought the offering of the poor in nearby Jerusalem, on the basis of which his mother was declared clean by the priest (Lev. 12). Because Jesus was a firstborn son, they also consecrated him to YHWH, as happened with all firstborn boys (Exod. 13:2, 12, 15).[21] In the temple, they met Simeon,

---

19. Instead of "manger" (Gk. *phatnē*), Epiphanius reads "cave" (Gk. *spēlaion*); so does the Protevangelium of James 18–22; Justin Martyr, *Dialogue with Trypho* 78, 5; Origen, *Against Celsus* I, 51.
20. At the foot of the hill Ramat Rachel, halfway between Jerusalem and Bethlehem, are the rarely visited remains of a Byzantine church, built over the rock where Mary supposedly rested, and where her water broke.
21. In my view, Meier (1991, 210–11) strongly exaggerated the alleged inaccuracies in Luke 2:22–24 (Luke has the cleansing ritual for Mary coincide with the dedication ritual for Jesus), thus discrediting Mary as a possible eyewitness in Luke's account (cf. 1:1–4).

who had received the promise from God that he would not die before he had seen the Messiah,[22] as well as the elderly widow Anna, who had served God daily in the temple, and had looked forward to the Messiah (Luke 2:21-38).

11.2.2 The "Kings" (?)

In those days, Joseph and Mary must have found residence in a stone or clay dwelling ("house," Matt. 2:11). That was where they were visited by the Magi, the wise men from the east (Matt. 2:1-12). Apparently, these were pagan astrologers, who had deduced the birth of an important Jewish king from observing a new star.[23] Perhaps through the Jews in the Diaspora they were familiar with the prophecy of Balaam: "[A] star shall come out of Jacob, and a scepter shall rise out of Israel" (Num. 24:17). The term Magi originally referred to a priestly class in the nation of the Medes; Daniel also mentions these "enchanters" in the Babylonian empire (1:20; 2:27; 5:15). Thus, the wise men possibly came from that territory, but perhaps Justin of Nablus (c. AD 150) was right in claiming that they were from Arabia, which at that time referred to the area east of Decapolis and Perea.[24]

Indeed, Arabia is sometimes referred to as the "east country" (Gen. 25:6) or "the East" (Judg. 6:3). Belonging to Arabia were also Seba and Sheba (cf. Gen. 10:7), and this is quite remarkable in the light of the Messianic prophecy in Psalm 72:9-11 (NKJV):

> Those who dwell in the wilderness [i.e., the Arabs living in the deserts] will bow before Him [i.e., the King],
> And His enemies will lick the dust.
> The kings of Tarshish and of the isles

---

22. As a consequence, Simeon is frequently described, or portrayed, as an old man, whereas Luke gives no indication of his age.
23. No other element in Jesus' birth history has been debated more than this one; see Carson (1984, 82) with reference to Schulze (1975).
24. See Grosheide (1954, 25-28); Tasker (1961, 36-37, 40-41); Ridderbos (1987, 37-40); Bruce (1979, 69-71); and Carson (1984, 82-86).

Will bring presents;
The kings of Sheba and Seba
Will offer gifts.
Yes, all kings shall fall down before Him;
All nations shall serve Him.

This is exactly what the wise men from the east did. After arriving in Jerusalem, where Herod's scribes gave them further instruction, they went to Bethlehem, where they honored the child Jesus, and offered gifts to him: gold, frankincense, and myrrh.

Isaiah had said something similar:

Arise, shine, for your light has come,
and the glory of the L ORD has risen upon you. . . .
And nations shall come to your light,
    and kings to the brightness of your rising. . . .
A multitude of camels shall cover you,
    the young camels of Midian and Ephah;
    all those from Sheba shall come.
They shall bring gold and frankincense,
    and shall bring good news, the praises of the L ORD (Isa. 60:1, 3, 6).

Perhaps partly because of such Bible passages, the wise men from the east became known as the "three kings," Caspar, Melchior, and Balthasar[25] — three, because of the number of gifts. Two contrasts are obvious: those who came earlier to visit the manger were not the rich and the mighty, but poor shepherds. The newborn King was honored not by King Herod and the religious leaders from Jerusalem, but by Gen-

---

25. These names did not appear before the eighth century. People suppose that Melchior was a sixty-year-old European, bearded man who gave the gold; that Balthasar was a forty-year-old bearded black man from Saba (Ethiopia) who gave the myrrh; and that Caspar was a twenty-year-old Asiatic young man who gave the frankincense. They represented the three continents known at the time, as well as a man's three phases of life, and thus stood for all humanity.

tile wise men.

11.2.3 The Star and the Shelter

Various explanations of the "star of Bethlehem" have been proposed, a star that was so impressive that it induced the Magi to undertake the long journey to Judea. Some have identified it either as Halley's comet (11 BC), which was visible again in 1986, or as a comet or passing star in 4 BC, known from Chinese stories. Others have pointed to an important conjunction of the planets Jupiter and Saturn in 7 BC. However, all these phenomena did not last long. Perhaps we should think of a supernova, a very rare explosion of a star, which may radiate a hundred million times more light than the sun, dominating the entire night sky, gradually weakening over a number of months. Whatever this star may have been, it aided the wise men in their travel to Bethlehem.[26]

For Herod the Great, the birth of the Messiah came at a very inconvenient time. Perhaps he was already suffering from the horrible disease from which he would die when he heard the rumor in Jerusalem that in Bethlehem a royal child was born, a descendent from the house of David. Herod's world, built in such a cunning way, seemed to be collapsing. This drove him to one of his most heinous actions: murdering the infant boys of Bethlehem (Matt. 2:16-18). The end of his own life drew near without him knowing whether his plan had succeeded. His fear was so great that he tried to take his own life. In the nick of time, he managed to have his own son Antipater executed, and he also gave orders to his sister Salome to hold the chief leaders of the Jews in the arena of Jericho—the city where he lay on his deathbed—in order to have them killed at his death (which execution did not occur).[27]

Warned by an angel, Joseph had fled to Egypt in time. This country was a rather obvious haven: it was relatively

---

26. Books on the star of Bethlehem include Molnar (1999); Kidger (1999); Nieuwenhuis (2000); and Moore (2001).
27. Flavius Josephus, *Jewish War* I.33; *Jewish Antiquities* XVII.6–8.

nearby, it belonged to the Roman Empire as well, but Herod had no jurisdiction there, and after the flight of Jeremiah almost a million Jews had found refuge in that country.[28] After Herod's death, the Holy Family returned to the land of Israel; Matthew 2:15 describes it with a reference to Hosea 11:1, "Out of Egypt I called my son," so that this return exhibits a parallel with the exodus (cf. Exod. 4:22–23). Joseph and Mary did not return to Judea, where Archelaus had become king (§11.4.2), but to their former dwelling place, Nazareth in Galilee.

We do not hear about Joseph again after Jesus had reached maturity, so we must assume that he had passed away. The Gospels tell us only about Mary and about Jesus' brothers and sisters (Matt. 12:46; 13:55 par.). Presumably, Joseph had been much older than Mary, and perhaps these brothers of Jesus were half-brothers, or sons from an earlier marriage of Joseph, or they were sons of a sister of Mary (see §§8.1.1 and 9.1.3 above).

11.3 Jesus' Youth
11.3.1 High or Low Status?

The Bible is virtually silent about the longest period of Jesus' life. He spent his youth in quiet, inconspicuous Nazareth, probably as an apprentice with his (legal) father Joseph, the carpenter. Jesus is called "the son of the carpenter" (Matt. 13:55), and he himself is called "the carpenter" (Mark 6:3). The carpenter's handicraft was certainly not humble: in Jesus' day, the carpenter was a woodcutter, a cabinetmaker, a cartwright, a builder of houses, in short, his labors involved all sorts of woodworking. Jewish scholar David Flusser wrote: "Carpenters were regarded as particularly learned. If a difficult problem was under discussion, they would ask: 'Is there a carpenter among us, or the son of a carpenter, who can solve the problem for us?'"[29]

---

28. Carson (1984, 90–91).
29. Flusser (2007, 33). He hinted at Abodah Zarah 50b, jerJebamot 9b, and jerQiddoesjin 66a, where the Heb. terms *naggara* ("carpenter") and *bar*

The Talmud teaches that a father must provide for his son and do at least three things for him: teach him a craft (in this case, that of the carpenter), find him a wife, and teach him the Torah.[30] We just mentioned the craft, and in §8.3 above we mentioned teaching the Torah. As for finding a wife for the son, in Jesus' case this did not happen. The brothers of Jesus did have wives (1 Cor. 9:5). John Meier needed thirteen pages to reach the conclusion that Jesus probably was not married.[31] Fortunately, the time is past when people tried to explain the reason that Jesus was unmarried to be that sexuality would be something inferior (cf. 1 Tim. 4:1-4). Klaas Schilder gave the following interesting reason for Jesus' unmarried status: Jesus

> is not ashamed to call himself the brother of us all. That is his office. But he would indeed have been ashamed to be called the (physical) father of some of us. *For that is not his office.* His unmarried state is not a pattern for us; nor is it a humiliatingly "high" ideal for one who lacks the charisma of abstinence. His *office* is so very different.[32]

Speculations about Jesus' socio-economic status diverge widely.[33] Robert Funk claimed that it was very low.[34] Because a carpenter is a craftsman, Joseph and Jesus were at the bottom of the economic ladder. Funk also presumed that Jesus belonged to the farming class, since his parables often contain metaphors drawn from agriculture. Other scholars have assumed the opposite, and portrayed Joseph with his son as master builders, frequent travelers who worked in cities like Sepphoris and Jerusalem, who were relatively well-off.[35] In

---

naggara ("son of a carpenter") mean "scholar" (i.e., rabbi) and "son of a scholar" (i.e., a rabbi's pupil).
30. Kiddushin 29a–30b.
31. Meier (1991, 332–45).
32. Schilder (2016, 54); Verkuyl (1992, 197) seeks the reason for Jesus' unmarried state in Matt. 19:12.
33. See the general discussion by Meier (1991, 278–85).
34. Funk (1999, 89–90); cf. Matt. 8:20 and 2 Cor. 8:9 regarding Jesus' "poverty."
35. Albright and Mann (1971, 21–22, 172–73); Riesner (1981, 219); Batey

this case, the idea is that Jesus surrendered his wealthy status at the beginning of his public ministry (cf. Matt. 19:21).

Jesus and his disciples clearly lived consciously as beggars.[36] They depended on gifts and hospitality (as with the family at Bethany, and see also Luke 8:2-3): "Foxes have holes, and birds of the air have nests, but the Son of Man has nowhere to lay his head" (Matt. 8:20 par.). In the same spirit, Jesus sent out his disciples: "Acquire no gold or silver or copper for your belts, no bag for your journey, or two tunics or sandals or a staff, for the laborer deserves his food" (Matt. 10:9-10 par.). Therefore, we must not spiritualize this statement of Jesus: "So therefore, any one of you who does not renounce all that he has cannot be my disciple" (Luke 14:33). The contrast between the poor and rich disciple is this: the former inherits the kingdom of God, but "it is easier for a camel to go through the eye of a needle than for a rich person to enter the kingdom of God" (Matt. 19:24 par.).

11.3.2 Visit to Jerusalem

After describing Jesus' birth and the flight to Egypt, the Bible mentions only one event from Jesus' youth. This was the pilgrimage that he made, as a boy of twelve years old, with his parents to Jerusalem to celebrate Pesach there. He may have done so in previous years, but this one was a special occasion: at the beginning of puberty—for centuries this moment had been fixed at thirteen years of age—a Jewish boy became a "son of the covenant." This custom lives on in the modern ceremony of the *bar mitzvah* ("son of the commandment"); in this way, the boy is declared to be religiously mature (§8.3.2).[37] He is then allowed to read publicly for the first time from the Torah in the synagogue, and ask questions about it, and from this time forward he is obliged to go up to Jerusalem three times a year for the three pilgrimage festi-

---

(1984); Mann (1986, 289).
36. Berger (2004, 483–84).
37. Mishnah: Abot 5:21; Niddah 5:6; Yoma 8:4.

vals: *Pesah* (Passover), *Shavu'ot* (Feast of Weeks) and *Sukkoth* (Feast of Booths) (cf. Deut. 16:16). At this point, then, Jesus is no longer a "child" (Gk. *paidion*, see Luke 2:40) but a "boy," a "young man" (*pais*, v. 43).[38]

In the temple of Herod, the young Jesus had a discussion in Solomon's Portico with the scholars of the Torah (cf. Acts 3:11; 5:12), and surprised them with his intellect and wisdom. When his anxious mother found him in this group, he spoke the words that, more than anything, give us a glimpse of what was in his heart, and what was his calling: "Did you not know that I must be in the things of my Father?" (Luke 2:49 TLV). The expression "in the things of my Father" or "in that which is my Father's" (Gk. *en tois tou patros mou*) has been interpreted in various ways: "in my Father's business" ([N]KJV), or "in the house of my Father" (ESV), that is, the temple. In line with Genesis 41:51 (LXX), the latter is quite possible (cf. Ps. 122:1-2). The importance of these words lies in the fact that young Jesus knew that his actual father was not Mary's husband (see v. 48!) but God. This insight was so profound that, in spite of the angel's explanation (Luke 1:34-35), Luke 2:50 continues with this: Joseph and Mary "did not understand the saying that he [i.e., Jesus] spoke to them."[39]

In addition to these sparse data about Jesus' youth, there are various apocryphal gospels that have tried to fill this gap. Thus, the Arabic Gospel of the Redeemer's Youth tells us about his birth, the vicissitudes during the flight to Egypt (for this, see also the [Greek] Protevangelium of James), the miracles occasioned by the child in Egypt, on the way back to Bethlehem, and afterward in Nazareth. The latter miracles are also found in the (Greek) Infancy Gospel of Thomas. According to this book, the child performed all kinds of prepos-

---

38. Morris (1974, 91); Liefeld (1984, 851). The KJV has "child" in both verses; the ISV has in v. 43 "the young man Jesus."
39. Liefeld (1984, 852); Greijdanus (1955, 82); cf. Bruce (1979, 478), who adds that it was no wonder that they did not understand: even we do not fully understand it.

terous, sometimes malicious miracles. In one of the stories, which appears also in the Quran, Jesus made birds of clay, which he then made to fly away;[40] it must have had an early origin. The Infancy Gospel of Thomas ends with an extensive report of the temple visit in Jerusalem. The work exhibits points of similarity with the (Latin) "History of Mary's Birth and of the Redeemer's Infancy."

These often childish stories in the apocryphal books have very little historical value. A few examples: Jesus "heals" a young man who had been magically turned into a mule; he is venerated by dragons; he carries water in a handkerchief; he gives life to a dried fish; he turns boys into bucks—all these stories are no more than the meaningless products of an inflated imagination. The basic question that we must ask here is whether we may assume that Jesus performed any miracles before his anointing with the Holy Spirit, that is, before his divine ministry actually began.[41]

11.4 Historical Context[42]
11.4.1 Pompei and Antipater

During Jesus' ministry, Judea was an insignificant province in the eastern corner of the Roman Empire. Since their return from the Babylonian exile, the Jews had never really been free (cf. Neh. 9:36–37): successively, they had been part of the Persian empire, of Alexander the Great's Greco-Macedonian empire, and of the eastern empires of his successors (the Diadochi), alternately the Ptolemaic and the Seleucid empires (the "king of the south" and the "king of the north," respectively, in Dan. 11). It was only in 142 BC that Simon, the last of the Maccabees—the famous freedom fighters from the family of the Hasmoneans—acquired national autonomy for the Jews. The

---

40. Surah 5:110; cf. 3:49.
41. *EDR* 1:285.
42. A good survey is offered by, e.g., Witherington (1997, 14–41); Theissen and Merz (1998, 125–84, 225–34). Much contemporaneous historical information comes from Flavius Josephus (which I will not always reference in the footnotes).

grateful people rewarded Simon by proclaiming him and his descendants to be high priests and "ethnarchs" (rulers of the people), "until a true prophet appears" (1 Maccabees 14:41). The latter was a probable reference to the Prophet of the end times, the Messiah himself, who had been announced earlier by Moses (Deut. 18:15; see §4.10 above). The Hasmoneans ruled Israel for more than one hundred years, until Herod the Great became king, the persecutor of the newly born Prophet.

The relative autonomy of the Hasmoneans came to an end when, in 66 BC, the Roman general Pompei conquered Pontus in Asia Minor (cf. Acts 2:9; 18:2; 1 Pet. 1:1) and, moving on to the south, also put an end to the Seleucid (Syrian) empire. In 63 BC, Pompei besieged Jerusalem and conquered the city. Palestine became a vassal territory of Rome; a puppet of the Romans, the Idumean Antipater, got a foothold in Judea. However, when the conflict between Pompei and Julius Caesar broke out later, he shrewdly chose the side of the victor, Caesar. The latter gave Antipater Roman citizenship, exempted him from taxes, and installed him as procurator of Judea. After new conflicts arose both in Rome and in Jerusalem, his son Herod managed to prevail.

11.4.2 Herod and Archelaus

Herod the Great, as history calls him, was a capable ruler and a formidable builder; his greatest achievement was the extension and embellishment of the Second Temple (John 2:20; Luke 21:5). However, Herod longed for honor, and was exceptionally suspicious; a large part of his own family fell prey to his neurotic jealousy. When he died (4 BC), his son Archelaus, with the permission of the emperor Augustus, became Herod's successor in Judea and Samaria (Matt. 2:22). His second son was (Herod) Antipas (i.e., Antipater), who in the New Testament is called "Herod the tetrarch" (Matt. 14:1–11 par.; Luke 3:1–19; 9:7; 23:7–15; Acts 13:1), a tetrarch being a ruler over a fourth part of a territory. He succeeded his father in Galilee and Perea;[43] this is the Herod who had John the Baptist executed (see below). (Herod) Philip the tetrarch succeeded his father in Ituraea and Trachonitis (Luke 3:1; Matt. 14:3).[44]

Because we do not know the exact year Jesus was born, we do not know whether his visit to the temple in Jerusalem, when he was twelve years old, occurred just before or just after the removal of Archelaus. This occurred in AD 6, when emperor Augustus turned Judea into a Roman province and, partly as a consequence of this, the revolt of Judas the Galilean broke out (Acts 5:37). Jesus must have experienced this directly, since the revolt was suppressed in Galilee, and the capital Sepphoris, close to Nazareth, was destroyed. Two thousand of the city's inhabitants were executed on crosses placed on both sides of the main road, stretching far in the northern and the southern directions. Here, Jesus became closely acquainted with the most heinous method of execution applied by the Romans: crucifixion.

From 14 BC, the Roman emperor was Tiberius (cf. Luke 3:1). He appointed in Judea a *procurator* ("governor"). Literally, this was the man who "procured" the taxes, but in practice he was also a ruler, judge, and military commander. Beginning with Coponius, the procurators of Judea succeeded each other quickly. The fourth of them, Valerius Gratus (AD 15–26), lasted a little longer. When he was procurator, the Sadducee Annas (or Ananus; Aramaic: *Chanan*), the son of Seth, was high priest. Valerius Gratus had been appointed by Quirinius (Luke 2:2). He replaced the high priest four times, but as the family head Annas kept playing an important role in the background. The last high priest, whom Gratus appointed presumably in AD 18, was Annas' son in law, Caiaphas (Aramaic: *Yehoseph bar Qaipha*, "Joseph son of Qaipha") (Matt. 26:3,

---

43. The name *Peraia* occurs only in Luke 6:17 (alternate manuscript reading); usually, Perea is described as "[the land] beyond the Jordan" (Gk. *peran tou Iordanou*, Matt. 4:25; Mark 3:8; 10:1).
44. H. W. Hoehner (*DJG* 317–26).

57; Luke 3:2; John 11:49; 18:13–14, 24, 28; Acts 4:6). Caiaphas served in his office until AD 36, but Annas retained a leading position, as is evident from the Bible passages mentioned.[45]

In AD 26, Gratus was succeeded by Pontius Pilate, who served in the office of procurator until AD 36. He was constantly quarreling with the Jews by provoking them in various ways. Thus, he took money from the temple treasury (cf. Mark 12:41; John 8:20) in order to build an aqueduct for the water supply of Jerusalem. When (during a festival?) tens of thousands of people protested against this theft, Pilate sent disguised troops against them, and many were massacred. Perhaps Luke 13:1 is referring to this, speaking of "Galileans whose blood Pilate had mingled with their sacrifices." The famous Jewish intellect in Alexandria, Philo, described Pilate as a cruel, stiff-necked, quick-tempered, corrupt, callous, and beastly person.[46] Pilate feared only one man: his emperor (cf. John 19:12).

11.4.3 The Forerunner

One of the most remarkable figures of the New Testament is John the Baptist (Heb.: *Yochanan hamatbil*).[47] Jesus testified about him: "[A]mong those born of women there has arisen no one greater than John the Baptist"; but he added, "Yet the one who is least in the kingdom of heaven is greater than he" (Matt. 11:11), apparently because John, who died prematurely, was not allowed to enter into this kingdom.[48]

John had the stature of an Isaac because, like Sarah, his mother was barren, and only at an advanced age bore a child through God's miraculous intervention (Luke 1:5–25). In both

---

45. For an extensive discussion of these matters, see Flusser (2007, 151–55).
46. H. W. Hoehner (*DJG* 615–17). See extensively, Flusser (2007, 155–62).
47. B. Witherington (*DJG* 383–91); Meier (1994, 19–99); Stein (1996, 90–101); in addition to data from the New Testament, we know a few things about John the Baptist through Flavius Josephus, *Jewish Antiquities* XVIII.116–19; on this, see Barnett (1998, 58–59).
48. For other explanations, see Bruce (1979, 172–73) and Carson (1984, 264–65).

cases, the miracle was announced in a supernatural way (Gen. 17:15–16).

John also had the stature of a Samson and a Samuel because all three of them were born of barren women, and exhibited features of a Nazirite (Num. 6:1–21; Judg. 13:2–14; 16:17; 1 Sam. 1:11).

John had the stature of an Elijah as well; both wore garments of hair with a leather belt around their waist (2 Kings 1:8; Matt. 3:4), and John acted "in the spirit and power of Elijah, to turn the hearts of the fathers to the children" (Luke 1:17; cf. Mal. 4:5–6). If Israel had believingly accepted John, he would have been the "Elijah who is to come" (Matt. 11:14; 17:12–13; Mark 9:12–13). Now, apparently, Elijah's coming must await the last days (Mal. 4:5–6).

John the Baptist was the last and greatest prophet before the Messiah's coming, and was the latter's immediate forerunner (cf. Matt. 3:3 with Isa. 40:3).[49] For years, he had been prepared by God for this great moment (Luke 1:80), and received his calling when the time for it had arrived (3:2). Thus, he began to appeal to the people to repent and convert:

> You brood of vipers! Who warned you to flee from the wrath to come? Bear fruits in keeping with repentance.... I baptize you with water, but he who is mightier than I is coming, the strap of whose sandals I am not worthy to untie. He will baptize you with the Holy Spirit and fire (Luke 3:7–8, 16).[50]

John baptized his converts in the river Jordan with "a baptism of repentance for the forgiveness of sins" (Mark 1:4) as the outward sign of their spiritual cleansing and preparation for the coming of the Messiah. There is a clear connection with the Jewish *mikveh* (the Jewish ritual bath).[51] Yet, this baptism

---

49. Something very different from being Jesus' "mentor," as Meier (1994, see subtitle) called him (see especially 116–30). Jesus never belonged to John's "disciples" (see §11.2.3 at the end).
50. See *EDR* 1:70–73.
51. See Ouweneel (2001a, §7.2.1).

was new in the sense that, until now, only pagan converts to Judaism had undergone this *mikveh*, that is, proselyte baptism.[52] This new baptism of Jews by John indicated that Jews, too, needed repentance and spiritual cleansing.

When the Messiah appeared on the scene, he amazed John by desiring that he would baptize him, Jesus, along with the others: ". . . Let it be so now, for thus it is fitting for us to fulfill all righteousness" (Matt. 3:15; see §10.5.2). The humble prophet, who viewed himself only as a "voice" and a servant (John 1:23, 27), also had to baptize the Messiah, through which event the latter lovingly united himself with the repentant and faithful ones in Israel. For John, this was proof that Jesus was indeed the Messiah (vv. 33-34);[53] hence his joyful exclamation when he observed Jesus in the crowd: "Behold, the Lamb of God, who takes away the sin of the world!" (v. 29), and a day later briefly, "Behold, the Lamb of God!" (v. 36).

Not long after the beginning of his ministry, John was imprisoned by Herod the tetrarch (Matt. 4:13; 11:2-6; Luke 3:19-20), and later, at the instigation of his wife Herodias and her daughter, Salome, he was beheaded (Matt. 14:1-12 par.).[54] Thus he became the first martyr for the name of Jesus. In the meantime, he had founded his own "school"; several times we hear about the "disciples of John" (Matt. 9:14; 14:12; Mark 2:18; 6:29; Luke 5:33; 7:18; John 3:25), perhaps as late as during

---

52. SBK 1:102–12; regarding proselytes (Gk. *prosēlytoi*), see Matt. 23:15; Acts 2:10; 6:5; 13:43.
53. It is pure speculation on the part of Flusser to assert that the voice from heaven ("This is my beloved Son, with whom I am well pleased," Matt. 3:17) in reality spoke the words of Isa. 42:1, "Behold my servant, whom I uphold, my chosen, in whom my soul delights; I have put my Spirit upon him; he will bring forth justice to the nations" (2007, 140–41 and references). The voice's words can be understood as a combination of Isa. 42:1 and Ps. 2:7; Brown (1994a, 117).
54. See Flavius Josephus (*Jewish Antiquities* XVIII.117–119). It is remarkable that a "lifelong friend" (or "foster brother") of Herod, Manahen (Heb. Menachem), later became one of the prophets and teachers in Antioch (Acts 13:1).

Paul's missionary journey.[55]

11.5 Jesus' Ministry
11.5.1 Dating

When he was baptized by John, the Messiah manifested himself to the people for the first time, and began his public ministry among Israel. This ministry must have lasted more than three years, since John's Gospel mentions four annual festivals occurring during this public preaching.[56] Near the beginning of Jesus' ministry, the Passover was mentioned in John 2:13 and 23. In 4:35 it is apparently winter ("There are yet four months, then comes the harvest"; thus, the time of sowing had taken place two months before). In 5:1 we hear of "a feast of the Jews," which presumably was either Passover (Heb. *Pesach*), or Pentecost (Heb. *Shavu'ot*), or the Feast of Booths (Heb. *Sukkot*). In John 6:4, Passover was near, and in 12:1 we hear of the Passover during which Jesus was crucified. The time from the first to the last Passover was exactly three years. The first Passover was preceded by a few months of ministry, during which Jesus was baptized, spent forty days in the wilderness, and performed his opening activities in Galilee. The entire earthly ministry of Jesus thus lasted less than three and a half years.

According to the Gospels, the Passover celebrated in the year of Jesus' crucifixion fell on a Friday — it was the evening with which the Sabbath began (Luke 23:54; John 19:31)[57] —

---

55. Acts 19:1, 3; see *EDR* 1:185–87.
56. Some modern theologians, who do not take John's chronology very seriously, assume that Jesus' ministry may not have lasted much more than a year.
57. This ties in with the fact that Jesus rose "on the third day" (Matt. 16:21 par.), which was on a Sunday (Mark 16:2). Apparently, the expressions "after three days" (Mark 8:31 par.) and "three days and three nights" (Matt. 12:40) must be read in this light, that is, Friday, Saturday, and Sunday, such that a part of a day is counted as a full day; see Archer (1982, 327–29). The term "Preparation" (Gk. *Paraskeuē*) in John 19:31 is a common reference to the Friday of the festival; see Morris (1971, 776–77, 816); Archer (1982, 375–76).

which helps us date Jesus' ministry.[58] Astronomers have determined that, within the relevant period, AD 30 and 33 were the only years in which the Passover, that is, Nisan the 14th, fell on Friday.[59] The opinions on which of the two years is correct vary enormously. Some point out that, according to Luke 3:23, Jesus was about thirty years of age at the beginning of his ministry, which ties in better with AD 30 as the year of his crucifixion. But according to others, John 8:57 ("you are not yet fifty years old") suggests that, against the end of his earthly life, Jesus was already in his forties. This ties in better with AD 33.[60]

Some conclude from John 2:13 and 20 that the first Passover was forty-six years after 20 BC, that is, in AD 27. This would again point to AD 30 as the year of the crucifixion. However, others believe that the number forty-six can refer to a closed period of building, and also that the actual beginning of Herod's building activities can be put a little later. Some conclude from Luke 3:1 that the ministry of John the Baptist began in AD 28 or 29, since this was the fifteenth year of the emperor Tiberius. The year of the crucifixion would then be 33. But others believe that the fifteenth year of the "rule" (not the "emperorship") of Tiberius can also go back to the beginning of his co-rulership together with emperor Augustus, and this could be AD 11 or 12. In this case, the year of the crucifixion would be AD 30. We will leave this discussion for what it is, and accept the most current chronology, according to which Jesus' ministry began at the end of AD 26, and ended in AD 30.

---

58. Cf. P. L. Maier's article in Vardaman and Yamauchi (1989).
59. Others believe that this Friday was Nisan the *15th*; see note 129.
60. H. W. Hoehner (*DJG* 119–22) and Van Bruggen (1998, 92–109) chose the latter; Meier (1991, 401–02) and Theissen and Merz (1998, 157–60) chose AD 30; J. B. Green (*DJG* 149) and Stein (1996, 56–60) left it undecided.
It may hardly be taken as an argument for dating the crucifixion, but it *is* remarkable that between the years 30 and 70 we have exactly forty years— an important period in Scripture (the wilderness journey, ruling periods of Saul, David and Solomon).

11.5.2 Spiritual Background

Herod, the tetrarch of Galilee and Perea, Pontius Pilate, the procurator in Judea, and the high priests, Annas and Caiaphas, were the protagonists who would play such an important role during Jesus' ministry, and in particular at the end of his earthly life.[61]

During Jesus' life on earth, the temple ministry was still in full operation. Every evening and every morning, a burnt offering was presented in the priestly court, with a concomitant offering of frankincense in the sanctuary, with a choir singing with musical accompaniment, and collective prayers were offered (Luke 1:9, 10, 21-22; Acts 3:1). The priests performed their services according to their twenty-four divisions (Luke 1:5, 8; 1 Chron. 24). In addition to the prescribed sacrifices the people brought voluntary sacrifices (Acts 21:23-26). Three times a year, the Israelites went up to Jerusalem for the main festivals: the Passover (Heb. *Pesach*, Luke 2:41-50; John 2:13, 23; 6:4; 11:55; 12:1), Pentecost or the Feast of Weeks (Heb. *Shavu'ot*, Acts 2:1; 20:16; 1 Cor. 16:8), and the Feast of Booths (Heb. *Sukkot*, John 7:2, 3, 8, 10).[62] For the maintenance of the temple, all Jews annually had to pay a tax of half a shekel or two drachmas (Matt. 17:24-27). In addition to this, there were voluntary gifts (Mark 12:41-44).

---

61. The mention of Pilate in the Apostles' Creed concretizes Jesus' story within the totality of world history, according to Rufinus (c. AD 400); cf. Berkouwer (1965, 153–59); Van de Beek (2002a, 158). Van Genderen and Velema (2008, 482) saw the significance of this mention also in the fact that as the representative of the then world power, Pilate condemned Jesus innocently (cf. Heidelberg Catechism Q&A 38). Ratzinger viewed the emperor and Jesus as the embodiments of "two different orderings of reality," which do not *have to* exclude each other but do so if the emperor presents himself as a god. Jesus *must* contradict this, with the consequence of death: "Luke's mention of Pontius Pilate casts the shadow of the Cross over the beginning of Jesus' public activity" (2007, 11–12). With the mention of the name of Pontius Pilate [Luke 3:1], the shadow of the cross lies already over the beginning of Jesus' activity.
62. In addition to this, John 10:22 mentions the Feast of (Re-)Dedication (or, Renewal, viz., of the temple, 165 BC), which is the Feast of Hanukkah.

For the many Jews in the Diaspora, who could not easily travel to Jerusalem, it was very important that in addition to the temple there were synagogues (meeting places). These buildings, erected since the Babylonian exile, were places where people prayed, sang, and read from the Scriptures, for instance in Damascus (Acts 9:2, 20), on Cyprus (13:5), in Pisidian Antioch (vv. 14–15), Iconium (14:1), Thessalonica (17:1), Berea (v. 10), Athens (v. 17), Corinth (18:4, 7–8, 17), and Ephesus (vv. 19, 26; 19:8). They existed in the land of Israel as well; we hear about the synagogues of Galilee (Matt. 4:23; 9:35 par.) and Judea (Luke 4:44), and specifically about the ones in Nazareth (Matt. 13:54; Luke 4:16), Capernaum (Mark 1:21; Luke 7:1, 5; John 6:59), and Jerusalem (John 9:7, 22, 34; Acts 6:9). During the services in the synagogues, first a part of the Torah was read, and then the associated passage (the Haphtharah) from the prophets. Then there was the opportunity to explain what had been read (Luke 4:16–30; Acts 13:14–41; 15:21). Where there was no synagogue, the Jews often looked for a place of prayer somewhere in the open air, as, for instance, in Philippi (Acts 16:13).

Presumably, the founders of the religious services in the synagogues were the "scribes" or "lawyers," that is, the Torah scholars. Originally, they were political or judicial officials (Heb. *soferim*, "secretaries," 2 Sam. 8:27; 20:25; KJV "scribes"). After the Babylonian exile, they were particularly those who copied, preserved, and interpreted the law: "Ezra . . . was a scribe skilled in the Law of Moses that the LORD, the God of Israel, had given, . . . Ezra the priest, the scribe, a man learned in matters of the commandments of the LORD and his statutes for Israel" (Ezra 7:6, 11). Usually they were priests, who probably lived together in clans (guilds?) (cf. 1 Chron. 2:55). In the New Testament period, when many of the scribes were not priests, their task was threefold: they preserved and copied the Old Testament; they gathered pupils around them to teach them the law in the temple or synagogue (Luke 2:46; John 18:20); and in Jerusalem, as Torah scholars or teachers, they were charged with the application of the Torah, namely, as judges in the Jewish Council, the Sanhedrin (from the Greek word *synedrion*, "gathering"), the highest judicial institution in Israel (Matt. 22:35; Mark 14:53; Acts 4:5).

11.5.3 Pharisees and Sadducees

The Torah scholars were not unified; in the days of the Maccabees the religious parties arose that are so familiar to us through the New Testament: the Pharisees and the Sadducees.[63] The word "Pharisees" (Heb. *p'rushim*) means "separated ones," a designation that probably implies that they kept themselves at a distance from the "crowd that does not know the law" (John 7:49). Because of their (supposed) greater holiness and devotion to God, they felt elevated above the masses (Luke 18:11-12). They constituted "the strictest party" within Jewish religion (Acts 26:5), strongly represented in the Jewish Council (23:6), "zealous for the law" (21:20; cf. Phil. 3:5), and for the "tradition of the elders" (Matt. 15:1-9; 23:1-36; Mark 7:1-13; Luke 11:37-44). They were doctrinally orthodox (Acts 23:8), although they judged divorce rather lightly (Luke 16:14-18).

The reason why Jesus often attacked them so sharply was that hypocrisy was often concealed behind their zeal for the law (Matt. 6:2; 23:13-29; Luke 12:1), with some exceptions, like Nicodemus (John 13:1), Gamaliel (Acts 5:34), and Saul of Tarsus (23:6; Phil. 3:6). The core of their doctrine was observing the law as well as newly elaborated commandments applied to new circumstances, a practice existing since the exile (the "tradition of the elders," or "ancients," that is, the traditions handed down by earlier generations of Torah teachers). Famous Pharisees were Hillel and Shammai (1st century BC), who founded rather different schools.

The Hebrew name of the Sadducees is *tz'duqim*, "Zadokites," that is perhaps, followers of Zadok the priest (2 Sam. 8:17; 15:27,

---

63. B. D. Chilton (*DJG* 401–104); S. Westerholm (*DJG* 609–14); Meier (2001); Van Bruggen (1999, chapter 1 and Appendix 1, "The Pharisees").

35). The little that we know about them comes mainly from Flavius Josephus.[64] The social class from which they came was higher than that from which the Pharisees came, and included particularly the priests (Acts 4:1–2; 5:17). They were amply represented in the Jewish Council (23:6). Their doctrine was quite conservative; they rejected the "tradition of the elders," and wished to observe only the law of Moses. They recognized only the Torah (Pentateuch), and therefore rejected doctrines that they considered to be later inventions, doctrines about the resurrection of the dead, about angels, and about spirits (Matt. 22:23; Acts 23:8). They emphasized that humans choose freely between good and evil, and therefore they were harsh judges.

During the rule of John Hyrcanus I (134–104 BC), the Pharisees and the Sadducees entered into a civil war against one another. During the reign of King Alexander Janneus (103–76 BC), the Sadducees enjoyed supremacy, but under his widow, Salome Alexandra (76–67 BC), the Pharisees enjoyed supreme power; for the first time, they acquired a place in the Jewish Council, alongside the Sadducees (cf. Acts 23:6).

The Pharisees were the opponents of the Herodians, the political followers of the family of Herod (Matt. 22:16; Mark 3:6; 12:13). The Herodians tried to seduce the people to follow pagan practices (the "leaven of Herod"? Mark 8:15), and insisted upon full submission to the Romans and paying taxes to the Romans. Since this was opposed by the Pharisees, both parties were interested in Jesus' answer about the imperial tax (§11.11.2). Actually, the Sadducees were no friends of Herod either. The latter had executed forty-five of them because they had resisted his entry into Jerusalem.

11.5.4 Other Movements

The sect of the Essenes was theologically akin to the Pharisees, but their ascetic way of life made them very different from the Pharisees. In the modern era, we have learned more about the Essenes through the discovery of the Dead Sea Scrolls, which presumably had been produced by them,

---

64. *Jewish Antiqities* II.8.14.

THE ETERNAL CHRIST: GOD WITH US

and through the excavations of their presumed Qumran settlement near the Dead Sea. The Essenes are not mentioned in the Bible, but the apostle Paul may have referred to them (and others?) in the epistle to the Colossians.[65] They formed a Jewish mystical, radically ascetic brotherhood (cf. Col. 2:23), very strict in observing the Mosaic Law (Col. 2:20-22), especially the sabbath (Col. 2:16-17). However, they rejected marriage (Col. 3:18-19), and also abstained from wine and meat (Col. 2:16). They did not believe in the resurrection of the body (Col. 1:18). They venerated angels (Col. 2:18b). Therefore, in their view, true wisdom was only known to some (Col. 1:23b, 28; 2:2-3). Because of supposed doctrinal similarities, it has sometimes been assumed that John the Baptist was a member of this movement for a while,[66] but this is pure speculation.

One aspect of Judaism around the beginning of the present era must be mentioned, namely, the so-called "apocalyptic" literature. Between about 200 BC and AD 100, many apocalyptic Jewish works appeared. These books supply us with predictions about the latter days in the form of often bizarre symbols, visions, and celestial journeys. They have therefore been compared with the New Testament book of Revelation (Greek: *Apokalypsis*, hence the term "apocalyptic"), with this difference, that the latter belongs to the apostolic Scriptures, whereas the Jewish apocalyptic writings are apocryphal (non-canonical, though related). The main works among them are the first (or, Ethiopian) and the second (or, Slavic) book of Enoch,[67] the book of Jubilees, the Assumption of Moses,[68] the Ascension of Isaiah,[69] 2 Esdras (Vulgate: 4 Esdras or Ezra), and the (Syrian) Apocalypse of Baruch (or, 2 Baruch).

---

65. Long before the discovery of the Dead Sea Scrolls, Lightfoot (1879, 349–419) defended this view; see, more recently, Bruce (1984, 17–26).
66. Rather recently, Ratzinger (2007, 14) claimed this.
67. Jude 14 is presumably a quotation from 1 Enoch 60:8.
68. According to Clement of Alexandria, Origen, and others, Jude 9 is a citation from this book.
69. The phrase "sawn in two" in Heb. 11:37 probably refers to this book (5:11–14).

The books are apocryphal, yet the doctrine concerning the last things and the coming of God's kingdom presented in them is very important because it tells us something of the eschatological expectations of many Jews around the time of Jesus' birth. In his own teaching, Jesus employed terminology used in the apocalyptic writings, as when he spoke, for instance, about the "present (or, this) age" and the "age to come" (Matt. 12:32; Mark 10:30; Luke 18:30; 20:34–35). The apostles did the same (Eph. 1:21; Gal. 1:14; 1 Tim. 6:17; Titus 2:12; Heb. 6:5; 9:9). In 2 Esdras (7:30–33, 113), the "age to come" follows the day of resurrection and divine judgment. Pharisaic rabbis (the schools of Hillel and Shammai), too, spoke of the two "ages," separated by the resurrection. They connected the "age to come" with "the things of the Messiah," which in its Old Testament sense refers to the rule of the Messiah on the throne of David in Zion. The faithful in Israel lived in the expectation of this "age" (cf. Luke 2:25, 38).

11.6 The Beginning of Jesus' Ministry
11.6.1 The First Disciples

After Jesus had been baptized by John, he withdrew to the south. In the desert of Judea, stretching along the Dead Sea, he fasted for forty days, and was tested by Satan, God's adversary (Matt. 4:1–11; Luke 4:1–13).[70] In contrast to Adam,[71] Jesus splendidly withstood the three temptations, and showed who he was: a perfect Man, unconditionally faithful to God, his Father. He returned to the Jordan, where he turned two of John's disciples into his own disciples: Andrew (John 1:40, Gk. *Andreas*) and John (Heb. *Yochanan*, possibly a cousin of

---

70. Stein (1996, 102–11); Berger (2004, 256–60); Ratzinger (2007, 25–45).
71. A possible connection exists between Jesus' temptations and Eve's temptations: "[T]he woman saw [a] that the tree was good for food, and [b] that it was a delight to the eyes, and [c] that the tree was to be desired to make one wise" (Gen. 3:6; also cf. 1 John 2:16: "[a] the desires of the flesh and [b] the desires of the eyes and [c] pride of life") and the three temptations of Jesus (in the order of Luke 4:1–12).

Jesus,[72] not to be confused with John the Baptist[73]).

Andrew found his brother Simon (Heb. *Shimᶜon*), to whom Jesus gave the Aramaic name *Kepha* ("rock," Greek: *Kephas*, Latin: *Cephas*; translated into Greek: *Petros*, English: Peter, from *petra*, "rock"). This Simon, or Peter, became the chief spokesman among the disciples. John presumably warned his brother James (*Yaᶜaqov*, Jacob). These four men were all Galilean fishermen. In addition to them, Jesus found two more Galilean disciples (John 1:43–51), Philip (Gk. *Phil[h]ippos*) and Nathanael (Heb. *Nathan'el*), presumably the same as Bartholomew (Gk. *Bartholomaios*, from Aramaic *Bar Tolmai*, "Son of Tolmai," the latter name coming from Gk. *Ptolemaios*, "Ptolemy"[74]).

With them Jesus went to Galilee where all of them had grown up, to spend some more quiet time among relatives and friends. There, he also performed his first sign, which underscored his peculiar personality and calling. A week after his return from the Jordan, he attended a wedding in the town of Cana (not far from Nazareth), from where Nathanael/Bartholomew had come (John 21:2). When the wedding wine ran out, Jesus changed some six hundred liters (159 U.S. gallons) of water into wine. In this way, he demonstrated that he was not only a preacher of penitence, such as John the Baptist, or a strict ascetic, such as the contemporaneous Essenes, but that he was the One who came to bring life and joy (cf. §8.5.1).[75] After the wedding, he went with his relatives and his first

---

72. This claim is based on the conclusion from Matt. 27:56, Mark 15:40, and John 19:25 that John's mother, Salome, was the Virgin Mary's sister; see Morris (1971, 811); Dods (1979, 858); but cf. §8.1.1 above.
73. This is the problem of churches named after St. John: many are dedicated to John the Baptist (e.g., Plattsburgh, NY; Gouda, Netherlands), some to John the Evangelist (e.g., Pawling, NY; 's-Hertogenbosch, Netherlands), and some to both (St. John Lateran, Rome, Italy).
74. A Syrian tradition says that his name was "Jesus" (Heb. *Yehoshua*), and that because of his Master he adopted a different name.
75. Regarding the historical as well as symbolic significance of John 2:1–11, see Hengel (1995, chapter 5); Ratzinger (2007, 249–54) discerned a reference to Jesus' own eschatological wedding.

disciples to the commercial and fishing center Capernaum (Kfar-Nahum), near the Sea of Galilee.[76] There, he rested for a short period of time.

11.6.2 The First Passover

Soon, the first test occurred during Passover in Jerusalem (AD 27). Jesus probably took the road to Jericho running along the western bank of Jordan, and from there the steeply rising road — about twenty-five kilometers (sixteen miles) — to Jerusalem. During Passover, the temple tax was collected, and for that reason the temple court was full of money changers. Cattle dealers were selling sacrificial animals, so that Israelites did not have to bring them from home. In order to purify the temple cult, Jesus chased the animals from the court with a whip of cords (John 2:13-16).[77] Only someone like the Messiah was entitled to do this, and therefore the temple police asked about his authorization. Jesus gave this enigmatic reply: "Destroy this temple, and in three days I will raise it up." Of course, the Jews thought he was speaking about the temple of Herod, but Jesus was referring to his own body and to his resurrection. *This* would be the Messianic sign *par excellence* (cf. Matt. 12:39-40; see further §12.2.1).

During that Passover week, Jesus' first public ministry occurred. Many Jews were quite impressed with it, and came to "faith," but this "faith" did not yet have much depth (John 2:23-25). However, Jesus did have quite an important conversation with a prominent rabbi, a Pharisee and member of the Jewish Council, named Nicodemus (John 3:1-21; cf. 7:50; 19:39). Jesus pointed out to him that his entrance into the kingdom of God would come not through his knowledge and observation of the law, but only through the inner renewal

---

76. This body of water was also called the Sea (or Lake) of Tiberias, or the Sea/Lake of Gennesaret (Luke 5:1), a name derived from Heb. *Chinnereth* (Num. 34:11), which means "harp," because of the lake's shape.
77. There is a prophetic element in this action: "At that time [i.e., in the age to come] there will not be any merchants buying and selling things in the Temple of the Lord All-Powerful" (Zech. 14:21b ERV); see Hengel (1995, 56).

of regeneration, which can be brought about by God's Spirit alone.[78] For this to occur, Nicodemus and every other human would have to believe in *him*, the Son of Man, for he was the only Son of God, who was going to die in order that whoever believed in him would have eternal life (John 3:15-16).[79]

After this visit to Jerusalem, Jesus probably spent the rest of the year (AD 27) in the countryside of Judea, but we know nothing about this stay. Perhaps he counted on receiving a better hearing among the population of the plains of Judea than among the Jews of Jerusalem, on whom the influence of the religious leaders was much stronger. In the countryside, quite a few people were baptized by Jesus' disciples—not by Jesus himself (John 4:2)—creating intense irritation among the Pharisees. Perhaps in order to avoid a confrontation, Jesus travelled back to Galilee by the end of AD 27. This time, he chose the road along Sychar, near Shechem, through the region of Samaria. Jews usually avoided this road because from ancient times they detested the Samaritans (see 2 Kings 17; Neh. 4 and 6). The Samaritan woman—who was living in sexual immorality—was all the more surprised when Jesus the Jewish man spoke to her at Jacob's well. It was to her that Jesus declared for the first time that he was the Messiah (John 4:25-26).

11.7 First Journey through Galilee
11.7.1 Healings and Deliverances

In describing Jesus' ministry, we start from the rather generally accepted thesis that Mark provides the most accurate chronological ordering of events. This can be harmonized with the orders found in Matthew and Luke which deviate somewhat from Mark's chronology.

If we carefully consider the data, we conclude that Jesus made three journeys through Galilee (see §§11.7-11.9). The first of these journeys began in Cana, where he healed the son

---

78. Cf. *EDR* 1:197–99, and *RT* II/3.
79. See *RT* III/4.

of a Jewish official of King Herod Antipas. The man had asked for his help presumably because he knew Jesus from the Passover celebration in Jerusalem (John 4:46-54). Jesus then chose his domicile at Capernaum (Matt. 4:13; perhaps in the house of Peter, who was married; 8:14; 1 Cor. 9:5). From there, he made his first journey through the towns and villages of Galilee. In the synagogues and in the open air, he appealed to people to repent and convert because, with his coming, the kingdom of God was at hand.

The region along the lake was quite prosperous. The brothers Andrew and Peter, John and James, who still practiced their craft as fishermen, abandoned flourishing enterprises when Jesus called them to be his disciples (Matt. 4:18-22). Perhaps it was in thriving Capernaum, where they lived, that Jesus performed most of his miracles. There he healed a possessed man during the synagogue service (Mark 1:21-28; Luke 4:31-37), and on the same day Peter's mother-in-law, who lay sick in his home, and many other town inhabitants (Matt. 8:14-17; Mark 1:29-34; Luke 4:38-41). He even healed a leper there (Matt. 8:1-4; Mark 1:40-45; Luke 5:12-16). In Capernaum he also healed a paralytic who, because of the enormous crowd, was let down through the roof of a house where Jesus was teaching (Matt. 9:1-8; Mark 2:1-12; Luke 5:17-26).

Because of all these miracles, Jesus came into increasing conflict with the Pharisaic scribes (Torah scholars), especially when he forgave the paralytic man his sins ("Who is this who speaks blasphemies? Who can forgive sins but God alone?" Luke 5:21), when he called as disciple Matthew (alias Levi), a Jew who was a tax collector employed by the hated Romans (Matt. 9:9-13; Mark 2:13-17; Luke 5:27-32), and especially when he did not abide by the traditions of the Pharisees (Matt. 15:1-20; Mark 7:1-23). He did not observe their commandments about fasting and about the Sabbath insofar as these went beyond Scripture, and he allowed his disciples to pluck heads of grain on the Sabbath (which *was* permitted on other days) (Matt. 9:14-17; 12:1-8; Mark 2:18-28; Luke 5:33-39; 6:1-5).

On the Sabbath day Jesus healed a man with a withered hand in the synagogue (Matt. 12:9-14; Mark 3:1-6; Luke 6:6-11). This aroused the rage of the Pharisees so strongly that, at this early stage they consulted together with the Herodians, whom they detested, as to how they might eliminate Jesus. However, they were unable to prevent ever increasing crowds, also from other regions, from coming to Jesus to listen to him on the shore of the lake.

11.7.2 The Twelve Disciples

During this same period, from his many disciples (from Latin *discipulus*, "pupil, follower"; Gk. *mathētēs*) Jesus chose twelve special ones, who were also called "apostles" (Gk. *apostolos*, "envoy, messenger") (Matt. 10:1-4; Mark 3:13-19; Luke 6:12-16).[80] These were the following men (to whose information I add the traditional description of how their lives ended):

(1) *Simon* (Heb. *Shimʿon*), nicknamed *Cephas* (more correctly: *Kefa*) or *Peter* (both meaning "rock," John 1:42), son of Jonah (Matt. 16:17) or John (John 21:15-17), the spokesman among the later twelve apostles (Acts 1-12). He was crucified (upside down) in Rome.

(2) His brother *Andrew* (Gk. *Andreas*), from Bethsaida (John 1:44), originally a disciple of John the Baptist, and perhaps Jesus' first disciple (John 1:35-40). He was crucified on a so-called Andreas cross (in the form of an X) at Patros (Greece).

(3) *John* (Heb. *Yochanan*) and (4) *James* (Heb. *Yaʿaqov*, "Jacob"), nicknamed "the Great" or "the Elder" (Lat. *Jacobus Maior*), sons of Zebedee and Salome. John and James were called Boanerges ("Sons of Thunder," Mark 3:17). They were from one of the towns on the shore of the Lake of Galilee. Peter, James, and John formed the inner circle of disciples (cf. Mark 5:37; 9:2; 14:33). Among the apostles, James was the first

---

80. M. J. Wilkins (*DJG* 178-81); Stein (1996, 112-22).

martyr (Acts 12:1-2, killed with the sword at Jerusalem),[81] whereas John was the last apostle to die (and possibly the only one to die a natural death[82]), namely, at Ephesus. If we follow the common identification—John = the disciple whom Jesus loved (John 13:23; 19:26; 20:2; 21:7, 20), = the "other disciple" (18:15-16), = the author of John's Gospel[83]—it is remarkable that a Galilean fisherman could have been "known to the high priest" (John 18:15). Either Zebedee was a prosperous fisherman with commercial contacts in Jerusalem, including in the high priestly family, or John's mother Salome, presumably a (half) sister to Mary (see note 72), and thus related to Elizabeth (Luke 1:36), was of the high priestly family (v. 5); John himself was perhaps a priest.[84]

(5) *Matthew* (Heb. *Mattai* = *Levi* the tax collector, son of Alphaeus, and the author of Matthew's Gospel), from Capernaum (Matt. 9:1, 9). As a former collaborator with the Romans, his position contrasted with that of former resistance fighters Simon the Zealot and perhaps Judas Iscariot (see below). He was killed with a halberd in Egypt or in Parthia.

(6) *Philip* (Gk. *Phil[h]ippos*), from Bethsaida (John 1:44; 12:21) (Andrew and Philip are the only Greek names in the group; see §11.6.1). He died as a martyr in the Phrygian city of Hierapolis (mentioned in Col. 4:13).

(7) *Bartholomew* (Heb. *Bar Tolmai* = *Nathanael*, Heb. *Nathan'el*; see §11.6.1), from Cana (John 21:2). He was beaten to death in Albanapolis (Armenia).

(8) *Thomas* (Heb. *T'oma*), or (Gk.) *Didymus* (both meaning "Twin"; John 11:16; 20:24; 21:2). He was killed with a spear in Mylapore near Madras (India).

(9) *James* (Heb. *Ya'aqov*, "Jacob"), son of Alphaeus (not nec-

---

81. An ancient and widespread tradition has it that this James is buried in Spain, in Santiago [i.e., Saint James] de Compostela.
82. Reportedly after several unsuccessful attempts to kill him.
83. Irenaeus held to this identification; cf. John 19:20, 35; 21:20, 24–25.
84. So Eusebius, *Historia Ecclesiae* III.31.3; see Morris (1971, 752n32); cf. Ratzinger (2007, 222–27).

essarily a brother of Matthew), nicknamed "the Less(er)" or "the Younger" (Lat. *Jacobus Minor*), and sometimes viewed as identical with James, "the Lord's brother" (Acts 12:17; 15:13; 21:18; Gal. 1:19), who was nicknamed "the righteous one," and was the author of the epistle of James; this James along with Peter and John were viewed as "pillars" (Gk. *styloi*) in the early church (Gal. 2:9). He was stoned and clubbed to death in Jerusalem.

(10) *Jude* (Heb. *Yehudah*), son (or brother?[85]) of James; he was also called Thaddaeus (from Aram. *tadda*, "brave"), and in some manuscripts Lebbaeus (from Heb. *lev*, "heart") (Matt. 10:3). He was crucified at Edessa.

(11) *Simon* (Heb. *Shim`on*) the Zealot ("zealous one," possibly a former member of the Zealots; see note 17). Also called "Simon Kananaios" (Matt. 10:4; Mark 3:18), which means the same thing as Zealot (Luke 6:15), Heb. *qanna* and Gk. *zēlos* both mean "zeal, envy." The Zealots viewed themselves as zealous for the sake of God, like Phinehas (Num. 25:6-13), Elijah (1 Kings 18:40; 2 Kings 1:10, 12), and Mattathias (1 Macc. 2:17-28).[86] Simon was crucified either in Britain or in Persia.

(12) *Judas* (Heb. *Yehudah*) Iscariot (a word derived from Sicarian?[87]), who later betrayed Jesus, and possibly was the only non-Galilean. He committed suicide, and was replaced by Matthias (from Heb. *Mattai*, like Matthew; Acts 1:15-26), who was stoned, and then beheaded, at Jerusalem.

Reviewing the group, it is quite surprising to find among these twelve two people named James (i.e., Jacob), two named Simon, and two named Jude or Judas; they remind us of the patriarch Jacob and two of his sons, Simeon and Judah.

---

85. If he was a brother, this Jude, like James, was a brother (half-brother? step-brother?) of Jesus (cf. Matt. 13:55; Mark 6:3).
86. Ratzinger (2007, 177–78).
87. The Sicarians (or Sicarii) were Jewish stealth political assassins (Acts 21:38), a radical wing of the Zealots; thus, among Jesus' disciples there may have been two former freedom fighters. Others explain Iscariot as Heb. *Ish Keryot*, "man from [the town of] Keryot," or link the name to Issachar.

The apostles were mostly "uneducated, common men" (Acts 4:13), whom Jesus chose—apart from Judas—to proclaim his person and doctrine throughout the entire world (cf., e.g. Acts 10:36), and to obtain disciples for the kingdom of God (cf. Matt. 28:19). Apparently, at least seven of them were fishermen (John 21:2-3).[88]

11.7.3 The Sermon on the Mount

During those days Jesus gave his famous Mountain Sermon ("Sermon on the Mount," Matt. 5-7). Tradition tells us that he did so on the slope of Karnē Hattin ("Horns of Hattin, or Hittim"), which lay west of the lake. In fact, Jesus probably gave this sermon in different segments on different occasions; compare the differences and similarities with the "Valley Sermon" in Luke 6:20-49 (see v. 17, "on a level place").[89]

In this sermon, or these sermons, Jesus explained the basic principles that would apply in the "kingdom of heaven," that is, the "heavenly" (divine) kingdom to be established on earth under his leadership. In doing so, he did not add human commandments to the Mosaic Law, as the Pharisees did, but he interpreted that very same law in its moral and spiritual depth.[90] He also warned how the disciples who wished to live according to his commandments would be treated: "Blessed are you when others revile you and persecute you and utter all kinds of evil against you falsely *on my account*. Rejoice and be glad, for your reward is great in heaven" (Matt. 5:11-12). On the mountain, and afterward on the "level place," he taught his disciples true fellowship, true benevolence, true prayer, true fasting, true faith confidence, true judgment of oneself and of others, and true *living* out of a renewed heart.

Not only through preaching but also through his actions, Jesus kept showing how concerned he was about the poor and

---

88. New Age thinking attaches great significance to the fact that Jesus chose fishermen, and not, as God did in the Old Testament, shepherds; see Ouweneel (1998, 157–58).
89. See Van Bruggen (1998, 148–49, 172–74).
90. See extensively, Ouweneel (2001a, 123–29), and vol. I/2 in this series.

distressed, both within Israel and outside of Israel. In Capernaum, he healed the mortally ill slave of a Roman centurion (a commander of one hundred soldiers) (Matt. 8:5-13; Luke 7:1-10). At the city gate of Nain, two hours southeast of Nazareth, he raised from the dead the only son of a widow (her breadwinner) (Luke 7:11-17). Everywhere he healed those possessed, paralytics, blind, deaf, and lepers. As the apostle Peter put it later, "He went about doing good and healing all who were oppressed by the devil, for God was with him" (Acts 10:38).

During those days John the Baptist, who had been imprisoned by Herod Antipas, sent messengers to ask Jesus whether he truly was the Messiah. John, too, was a weak and sinful person, depending on God's grace and mercy. Jesus was the perfect One, the unique One. He simply pointed to his Messianic actions of preaching and healing. But he also magnificently defended John by calling him the greatest prophet of all times. He blamed the religious leaders for not having accepted John's message, just as they were refusing to accept his own ministry.

In a tangible way, these matters were illustrated during a visit to the house of a Pharisee, who clearly showed his contempt for Jesus, whereas, by way of contrast, a woman with a reputation for being immoral, came with obvious repentance to find grace and forgiveness with him (Luke 7:36-50).[91]

11.8 Second Journey through Galilee
11.8.1 Preaching and Expounding

It was still during the spring of AD 28 that Jesus made a new journey through the towns and villages, and everywhere preached the gospel of the kingdom of God. The term "gospel" (Gk. *euangelion*; or *evangelion*, "evangel") was well-known in the Roman world, where it referred to the "good news" of the emperor, who was viewed as an incarnate deity, the miracle-working giver of blessing and salvation to hu-

---

91. Regarding this woman, see Berger (2004, 233–35).

manity. The latter's birth, maturation, and enthronement are *evangelia*, but by definition all his ordinances are "good news" as well. Christ adopted all these features and proclaimed *his* "evangel" as the incarnate, miracle-working, salvation-bringing King.[92] The tension between these two "gospels" was often clearly felt in the apostles' ministry. Some were accused of "acting against the decrees of Caesar, saying that there is another [i.e., a different, Gk. *heteros*] king, Jesus" (Acts 17:7). Jesus was the alternative king (Gk. *basileus*), the better option, so to speak.

In Jesus' permanent company were not only the twelve disciples but also several well-to-do women, who "provided for them out of their means" (Luke 8:1–3). Among them were Mary Magdalene, that is, Mary from Magdala (Heb. *migdal*, "tower"), a village near the lake; she had been healed by Jesus from severe demonic possession. Another one was Joanna, the wife of Herod's household manager (Gk. *epitropos*, a kind of finance minister; perhaps he was the official whose son Jesus had healed; John 4:46–54).

During this period, Jesus healed a possessed man who was blind and mute (Matt. 12:22–32; Mark 3:20–30; Luke 11:14–23). The Pharisees were outraged about this. Their hatred was so great that they ventured to assert that Jesus cast out the demons with the help of "Beelzebul, the prince of demons" (i.e., Satan). As Jesus showed, this accusation was not only absurd but also a horrible blasphemy of the Holy Spirit, through whom Jesus spoke and acted.[93] The Pharisees and the Torah scholars did not understand him at all. Even people in his company (Gk. *hoi par' autou*, Mark 3:21) sometimes thought that he was out of his mind, and tried to correct him.

Jesus was not disturbed by these things; according to him, his true family ("brothers and sisters") were those who accepted his word (Matt. 12:46–50; Mark 3:31–35; Luke 8:19–21). He sat and taught on the lakeshore (Matt. 13:1; Mark 4:1). In the

---

92. Cf. G. Friedrich (*TDNT* 2:724–25); Ratzinger (2007, 46–47).
93. See *EDR* 1:150–52; *RT* II/3.

form of parables, he began to explain that the word of God's kingdom would go out into all the world. Eventually, most of his disciples would be recruited from the Gentiles, and thus the message of the kingdom of God would go to the ends of the earth. In this way, he explained future developments — positive as well as negative — in the kingdom of God.[94] The crowd did not understand any of this. Once they returned to the house, it was only to his disciples that he explained the parables, but it is questionable whether they understood his explanation, since they did not yet possess the Holy Spirit.

11.8.2 New Tokens of Power

When the evening had come, Jesus went with his disciples into a boat, and asked them to sail to the other side of the lake in order to escape the crowd (Matt. 8:23-27; Mark 4:35-41; Luke 8:22-25). Jesus quietly slept in the stern as a heavy storm arose — as occurred occasionally due to air currents suddenly sweeping across the lake — and the boat nearly capsized. When the disciples in deadly fear roused him from sleep, he put their unbelief to shame by calming the storm and the lake by a single word of power.

On the other side of the lake was the country of the Gerasenes (or Gergesenes, or Gadarenes[95]) (Matt. 8:28-34; Mark 5:1-20; Luke 8:26-39). There, Jesus liberated two demon-possessed men who had confronted him, and drove the demons into the pigs that were being kept there (for the Jews, these were unclean animals that they were not supposed to keep![96]). The herd ran into the lake and drowned, which aroused the inhabitants to such intense anger that they chased Jesus away.

Jesus again crossed the lake, and soon an enormous crowd assembled on the other side. An important man came for-

---

94. See extensively, *RT* IV/3.
95. Gerasa and Gadara were Greek-speaking towns on the east side of the lake, belonging to Decapolis (i.e., "ten cities"), a large territory, to which even Damascus and Philadelphia (now Amman) belonged.
96. Cf. Lev. 11:7; all the greater, then, was the shame of the prodigal son for having to herd pigs (Luke 15:15).

ward from the crowd, Jairus, the "ruler of the synagogue," that is, the leader of the public service in the synagogue, who as such must have known Jesus quite well. His daughter was dying, and Jairus begged Jesus to come with him (Matt. 9:18–26; Mark 5:21–43; Luke 8:40–56). The sensation-hungry crowd surrounded them as they set out to Jairus' house. On the road, a woman was healed of her chronic discharge of blood, simply by touching the fringe of Jesus' garment (§8.3.2). During this delay, the news came that the child had already died. Yet, Jesus continued to Jairus' house, chased the curious away, and, once in the house, raised the girl from death—a magnificent message for the entire region.

Presumably it was in this period that Jesus journeyed to Jerusalem with his disciples to celebrate "a feast of the Jews" (John 5:1), that is, either Passover or Pentecost (in the spring of AD 28), or Booths (during the fall, at the end of the entire harvest).[97] There, Jesus visited the pool of Bethesda,[98] where a crowd of sick people was present because of the occasional healing power of the water.[99] On the Sabbath, Jesus healed a man there who had been paralyzed for thirty-eight years, an event that again brought Jesus into conflict with the religious leaders. This time, he gave a very clear testimony about himself as the divine Son of the Father (see §7.2.1).

11.9 Third Journey through Galilee
11.9.1 New Preaching

Once again, Jesus conducts ministry in his beloved Galilee.

---

97. John 5 speaks of the last judgment, but this does not help identify the feast of v. 1, since this judgment is traditionally associated with four festivals: Passover, Pentecost, New Year, and Booths (Mishnah: Rosh Hashanah 1:2). Some manuscripts have the article: "*the* feast"; this suggests the Feast of Booths (cf. 7:2; Lev. 23:39; 1 Kings 8:2, 65; 12:32); see Morris (1971, 299n6).
98. Or "Bethzatha" (GNT and many others).
99. At least, this is told by the less strong manuscript testimony in vv. 3b and 4 (by the ESV and others rightly mentioned in a footnote only), in which it is an open question whether the water miracle involved a divine healing, an occult healing, or just a popular belief.

This time he attended the synagogue service on the Sabbath in Nazareth, the town where he had grown up, and where the people had known him as a child.[100] During the service, he read the Messianic prophecy from Isaiah 61, and applied this directly to himself, but without performing a miraculous sign (Matt. 13:53-58; Mark 6:1-6; Luke 4:16-30). The Nazarenes mocked him, and when he reproached them for their unbelief, they became so enraged that they dragged him to one of the high hills in the neighborhood in order to throw him off the precipice. However, at that moment Jesus simply walked away from among them without them being able to do anything.

Jesus now left the town of his youth for good, and again travelled throughout all Galilee. His compassionate heart was full of concern for the many people who were afflicted by diseases, sins, and fears. This time, he also used his disciples, sending them two by two through the region to heal the sick and to preach the gospel, without fearing enemies of the gospel (Matt. 10:5-15; Mark 6:7-13; Luke 9:1-6). Thus, he indirectly prepared many generations of servants for the task of preaching and serving, which they were to perform until his second coming, in the face of every conceivable persecution and oppression.

11.9.2 Feeding the Crowd

This forecast of persecution was underscored in a painful way, right then and there, when Jesus received the news that John the Baptist had been beheaded. His own disciples had returned after their missionary trip with enthusiastic stories about their experiences, but the grieving and tired Master took them by boat to a quiet place on the other side of the lake (Matt. 14:12-13; Mark 6:30-32). There, for a short time, they would be free of the crowd, and regain their strength. However, that pause did not last long. The enthusiastic crowd was

---

100. This is a good example of how confusing the chronology of the Synoptics can be, for Luke places this almost at the beginning of Jesus' ministry.

tracking their boat, and walked around the lake to be waiting for Jesus when he arrived.

When Jesus saw their spiritual poverty, his heart was softened by it, and again he began to teach them, until evening. It was a tiring matter, teaching a crowd of probably more than ten thousand people! The disciples did not like the view, and at the end of the day insisted that Jesus send the people away, so that they could find some food—which, in that neighborhood, seemed an impossible task. Jesus simply replied: *"You should give them food!"* One of them, Andrew, found a boy who had with him five loaves and two fish. For Jesus, this was enough; in his hands, the food multiplied until there was enough for everyone present. At the end, twelve baskets full of broken pieces of bread were left over (Matt. 14:13-21; Mark 6:30-44; Luke 9:10-17; John 6:1-14).

People were so impressed by the miracle—imagine a Messiah who can end all of our economic problems! (cf. Ps. 132:15)—that they wished to make him king on the spot. But of course, Jesus could not accept this; the people did not have a proper idea of his Messianic kingship, which was less about food for the stomach, and more about food for the heart.

11.9.3 Walking on the Lake

Jesus sent the people away, asked his disciples to sail to the other side, while he went to a mountain to pray in solitude. Another storm arose on the lake, and this time the Master was not with the disciples. But during the night, he came to them, walking on the water,[101] so that the disciples thought he was a ghost. After they had recognized him, Peter, always first in everything, climbed overboard in order to walk toward the Lord. What faith! And what a disaster when he got scared, and for this reason began to sink. Jesus saved him, quieted the

---

101. On the significance of this fact, see Ouweneel (2003, 327–31). Macquarrie (1998, 36–39) also emphasized the deeper, spiritual meaning of this walking on the water, but he did so at the expense of the literal meaning. Cf. also Job 9:8b (CSB), "he . . . treads on the waves of the sea."

storm, and thus safely reached the other side of the lake with his disciples (Matt. 14:22-33; Mark 6:45-52; John 6:15-21).

They arrived again in the territory where Jesus earlier had destroyed the herd of pigs. We now see the results of the preaching by the demon-possessed man who had been liberated (Matt. 14:34-36; Mark 6:53-56). People came to Jesus from every direction, he preached to them, and he healed their sick.

After his return to Capernaum, he went to the synagogue there, and taught the people. The crowd that he had sent away the evening before, and that had sought him everywhere, found him in that same synagogue. At this time Jesus explained to them the precise significance of the earlier miraculous multiplication of bread and fish (John 6:22-65). What he had offered was not a solution to some economic problem but a symbolic presentation of himself, the true "bread of life," who had come into the world as a Man in order to give his life for all those who would believe in him. Thus, he would become for them the spiritual food through which they would have eternal life. Most people found this an incomprehensible and disappointing explanation, and abandoned him. Solemnly, Jesus asked his disciples whether they would not rather go away as well. Peter expressed the feelings of them all in saying, "Lord, to whom shall we go? You have the words of eternal life" (vv. 66-71).

11.10 Jesus' Final Activities
11.10.1 Various Places

The events just described took place not long before Passover in AD 29, which Jesus probably celebrated in Jerusalem again. However, he did not stay long in Judea because the religious leaders were continually after him. His "hour" — the time set by the Father — had not yet come, so Jesus returned to Galilee. He stayed there the entire summer of 29, until the Feast of Booths. After a debate with the Pharisees about the "tradition of the elders" — which Jesus rejected (Matt. 15:1-20; Mark

7:1-23)—he withdrew with his disciples in the opposite direction, to the north, to the region of the harbor city of Tyre in Phoenicia. Although that region was quite hostile toward the Jews, Jesus found Eastern hospitality there with a Gentile no less (Mark 7:24). He did not remain hidden; a woman from the region requested his help for her daughter. Jesus tested her by claiming that she was not entitled to his help, for he had come for the Jews first (Matt. 15:21-28; Mark 7:24-30). But the woman did not claim any rights but asked only for grace—and this Jesus could not refuse.

Back in Galilee, Jesus healed many sick, moved on to Decapolis, and healed a deaf man (Mark 7:31-37). In the surroundings of the lake, he performed a second miraculous feeding of a large crowd (Matt. 15:32-39; Mark 8:1-10).[102] Then he crossed the lake again, and arrived at the western shore near Dalmanutha (in the neighborhood of Magdala? cf. Matt. 15:39). After a brief debate with the Pharisees (Matt. 16:1-12; Mark 8:11-21; Luke 12:54-56), he went by boat to Bethsaida, from where Andrew, Peter, and Philip had come, on the northeast side of the lake. There, Jesus healed a blind man (Mark 8:22-26), then moved on to the far north, to the neighborhood of Caesarea Philippi, a city built by Philip the tetrarch in honor of Caesar (i.e., emperor) Tiberius.

Here, Jesus asked his disciples this famous question, "Who do you say that I am?" (Matt. 16:15). As happened so often, Peter took the initiative: "You are the Christ [i.e., the Messiah, the Anointed (King)], the Son of the living God" (vv. 13-20;

---

102. The two miraculous bread multiplications form a counterweight against many critics. If the one feeding had been described in Matthew and the other in Luke, they would have viewed this as a typical form of a vague tradition, which were contained in the Gospels as two contradictory versions. In reality, however, the two stories appear in the same Gospels, both in Matthew and in Mark (although some critics still speak of a duplication!); cf. Lane (1974, 271–72); Carson (1984, 357–58); Wessell (1984, 686). Grosheide (1954, 248) emphasizes the significance of the repetition of this miracle. This corroborates the suggestion, that there could very well have been two cleansings of the temple (see note 124).

Mark 8:27–30; Luke 9:18–21). Jesus explained to him that only the Father in heaven could have revealed this to him. Jesus was going to build *his* church on himself, Jesus, as the foundation of this church, this Jesus as Peter had confessed him, or on this apostolic confession, or possibly on people like Peter.[103]

Moreover, Jesus gave to Peter the "keys" of the kingdom of heaven, that is, the authority with which he would be qualified to allow people into the discipleship of Christ (cf. Peter's admissions in Acts 2:14–36; 8:14–17; 10:1–11:18). At the same time, Jesus also announced for the first time his sufferings, death, and resurrection (Matt. 16:21; Mark 8:31; Luke 9:21–22). The response by Peter ("This shall never happen to you") and the reprimand by Jesus ("Get behind me, Satan") depict Peter as the half-healed blind man, who saw the people walking like trees (Mark 8:22–25).[104] Peter's response was "Satanic" because it was of the same character as the third temptation in Matthew 4:8–9: a world empire without the cross.[105]

11.10.2 The Transfiguration

Before Jesus set foot upon the path of his final sufferings and death, he showed to his three main disciples his divine and royal glory on the "mount of transfiguration" (a "high mountain"; tradition identifies it as Mount Tabor, not far from Nazareth, but many consider Mount Hermon, more to the north, to be more likely) (Matt. 17:1–8; Mark 9:2–8; Luke 9:28–36).[106] Undoubtedly there is a deep connection here with Exodus 24:16, "The glory of the LORD dwelt on Mount Sinai, and the cloud covered it six days. And on the seventh day he called to Moses out of the midst of the cloud."[107] There are many

---

103. The text is explained in many different ways; see a survey in Carson (1984, 367–70).
104. Brown (1994a, 117).
105. Ratzinger (2007, 42).
106. W. L. Liefeld (*DJG* 834–41; Stein (1996, 167–76); on the central significance of this story in the Gospel, see Berger (2004, 68–74).
107. Cf. Gese (1977), quoted in Ratzinger (2007, 355).

parallels, such as the involvement of Moses in both cases, the mention of the cloud (Luke 9:34), and that both Moses and Jesus shone radiantly because of their encounters with God on the mountain (Exod. 34:29-30; Luke 9:29).

There, during the night, Jesus was transfigured (Gk. *metemorphōtē*); that is, his appearance was changed. The disciples saw him, his face shining like the sun, and heard him speaking with Moses and Elijah, the greatest men of God in the Old Testament, representing the Torah and the prophets, respectively.[108] God himself called from heaven: "This is my beloved Son, with whom I am well pleased; listen to him" (cf. Deut. 18:15, where Moses says, "The LORD your God will raise up for you a prophet like me from among you, from your brothers — it is to him you shall listen"). Greater glory was hardly conceivable — and yet, the subject of the conversation between the three was the impending sufferings and death of Jesus in Jerusalem: they "spoke of his departure [Gk. *exodos*], which he was about to accomplish at Jerusalem." In 2 Peter 1:15, the Greek word *exodos* refers to Peter's death, but in Luke 9:31 it is something that Jesus would actively "accomplish" (Gk. *plēroun*): "a departure from this life, a passage through the 'Red Sea' of the Passion, and a transition into glory...."[109] It is striking that after the exodus from Egypt that Moses had led, he is occupied here with a new and definitive exodus.[110]

In this significant event, and in God's magnificent words about his Son, Jesus was given to see the "joy that was set before him," in order to thus give him the strength to endure the cross, and to withstand the hostility of sinners toward him (Heb. 12:2-3).

After having descended the mountain, Jesus and his three

---

108. Cf. their being linked in Mal. 4:4–5 and (without mention of their names) in Rev. 11:6, as well as the fact that both Elijah and, according to Jewish tradition (Flavius Josephus, *Jewish Antiquities* IV.8.48) also Moses ascended to heaven; moreover, both men had beheld a theophany on Horeb (Exod. 24; 1 Kings 19); so Stein (1996, 172).
109. Ratzinger (2007, 311).
110. Berkouwer (1965, 204) links Jesus' *exodos* with his ascension.

disciples were immediately confronted with harsh reality. At the foot of the mountain, a large crowd had gathered around a father with a "lunatic" son (KJV; Matt. 17:14-18; Mark 9:14-27; Luke 9:37-43). Jesus blamed the other disciples that they had not been able to heal the boy and free him from his demon. He returned with his disciples to Galilee, where the tax collectors bothered him about the temple tax (Matt. 17:24-27). Jesus provided this through the miracle of the shekel in a fish's mouth. For the rest, this stay in Capernaum was significant because of Jesus' teaching to his disciples: on subjects such as who was the greatest in God's kingdom, on the little and the weak, on forgiving one's brother (Matt. 18). For the second time, he spoke of "the church" (v. 17), and in this way again anticipated the future, when his followers would no longer be dealing with the leaders of Israel, but with the Christian church.

11.10.3 The Feast of Booths

In the fall of AD 29, Jesus' brothers—who did not yet believe in him—had already urged him to be in Jerusalem during the Feast of Booths in order to show his miracles to the Judeans (John 7:1-9). He departed at the last minute, and again traveled through Samaria, possibly because the road on the west bank of the Jordan had already become impassable due to the early rains. The Samaritans did not give the festival pilgrims a warm welcome. In contrast to his disciples, he responded gently to this lack of hospitality (Luke 9:51-56).[111] He sent out seventy of his followers to go ahead of him in order to preach the gospel of God's kingdom in all the places that he would pass through (Luke 10:1-12).

There has been much speculation as to which contemporaneous followers of Jesus, apart from the Twelve, might have belonged to the seventy (i.e., 7 x 10; other manuscripts:

---

111. My interpretation suggests that Jesus is on his way to the Feast of Booths. Others interpret Luke 9:51 to indicate that he is on his way to the last Passover; still others presume that, beginning with these events, Luke has collated events from various journeys to Jerusalem; see Morris (1974, 177–78); Bruce (1979, 535–36); Geldenhuys (1983, 293); Liefeld (1984, 931–32).

72, i.e., 6 x 12; 78 and 12 both being sacred numbers). Tradition has suggested that this included virtually all well-known disciples, such as Mark, Luke, Cleopas (Luke 24:18), Ananias (Acts 9:10), the seven of Acts 6:5, the first four mentioned in 13:1, Epaphras (Col. 1:7; 4:12), Agabus (Acts 11:28; 21:10), and so on. This group of "the seventy" reminds us of the seventy sons of Jacob (Exod. 1:5), but also of the seventy or seventy-two nations of the world (Gen. 10);[112] perhaps, sending out "the seventy" was a portent of the coming world mission (of Matt. 28:19).[113] Please note that the limitation of Matthew 10:5-6 ("Go nowhere among the Gentiles and enter no town of the Samaritans, but go rather to the lost sheep of the house of Israel") is lacking in Luke 10.

Along the way, Jesus told his famous parable of the good Samaritan, who had mercy upon a mistreated Jew who had been attacked by robbers and abandoned by his own religious leaders (vv. 25-37). Throughout the entire journey, Jesus gave very important teaching: about genuine praying, about the hypocrites among the Pharisees, about the dangers of material wealth, about the "signs of times," and so on (Luke 11).

During the Feast of Booths, Jesus moved among the celebrating crowd, which became heavily divided over the question of whether he was the Messiah (John 7). Indirectly, Jesus himself gave the answer by shouting loudly that the people had to believe in *him* (v. 38). Shortly thereafter, the Pharisees tested him by bringing an adulterous woman to him. Instead of condemning *her*, he exposed *their* hypocrisy (8:2-11).[114] Moreover, he demonstrated his own divinity and heavenly mission so clearly that they almost stoned him (8:12-59).

A new conflict arose when Jesus healed on a Sabbath, a man born blind. On this occasion, he explained to the Phari-

---

112. See Ouweneel (2003, 108).
113. Ratzinger (2007, 179).
114. The passage is possibly a later addition to John's Gospel—see Morris (1971, 882-84)—but even so, it can certainly be referring to an actual event.

sees that, as a good Shepherd, he cared for his sheep, whereas they were only blind (note the contrast!) and heartless "hirelings" (9:1–10:21).[115]

11.10.4 To Perea and Back

Two months later, Jesus was again in Jerusalem, namely, during the Feast of Hanukkah or Renewal (celebrating the re-dedication of the temple by the Maccabees in 164 BC). Here again, some Jews tried to stone him for his claim of divinity (10:22–42). Thereupon, Jesus left for Perea (the territory east of the Jordan River). The most likely chronology of Jesus' ministry justifies the presumption that in Perea, Jesus spoke such famous parables as that of the laborers in the vineyard (Matt. 21:33–46; Mark 12:1–12; Luke 20:9–19), of the excuses by invited wedding guests (Matt. 22:1–14; Luke 14:15–24), of the lost sheep, the lost coin, and the prodigal son (Luke 15), of the dishonest manager, of the rich man and the poor Lazarus (unless this was an actual event[116]) (Luke 16), of the unrighteous judge, and of the Pharisee and the tax collector (18:1–14). Jesus also gave teaching on divorce, he blessed little children, and met the young, rich synagogue ruler, for whom his attachment to his wealth was too strong (Matt. 19; Mark 10:1–31; Luke 18:15–30).

In the same period, at the beginning of AD 30, Jesus received news that his friend Lazarus had become ill (John 11).[117] Jesus finally arrived in Bethany on the fourth day after Lazarus had died and had been buried. In the company of a large crowd, Jesus went with the sisters to the tomb, had

---

115. Without any basis, but with impressive self-assurance, the Jesus Seminar asserted that the kind of blindness that Jesus could heal was psychosomatic in nature. This is because, ostensibly, blindness that had an organic basis would have required magic for its healing, "and Jesus was probably not a magician," according to Funk (1999, 101). So, then, would magicians have more power than Jesus? This would mean that the devil has more power than God.

116. See the arguments by Summers (1974, 195), including that a real historical figure is introduced (Abraham), and the protagonist has a name (Lazarus).

117. Regarding the trustworthiness of this story, see Berger (2004, 92–95).

the stone removed, and shouted with a loud voice, "Lazarus, come out!" (v. 43). Lazarus' raising provoked a strong reaction of hatred: the leaders now made their definitive plan to kill Jesus, and even Lazarus. However, Jesus' hour had not yet come. He withdrew to the town of Ephraim, a half-day's travel north of Jerusalem (v. 54). There, he waited until the end of March, that is, almost until Passover, before beginning his last journey to Jerusalem.

After being in hiding for weeks, Jesus told his disciples that he would go up to Jerusalem.[118] There, the religious leaders would sentence him to death and deliver him to the Romans, who would crucify him. However, after three days he would rise from the dead. The disciples hardly seemed to have heard this last phrase; they were terribly frightened, and followed him in anxious tension.

About a week before Passover, Jesus approached Jericho. The entire town came out to see the rabbi who had been sought by the leaders for quite some time. The chief tax collector, Zacchaeus, who was a man of small stature, climbed a sycamore tree in order not to miss Jesus (Luke 19:1-10). Jesus called him to come down from the tree, and openly announced that he wished to stay with this collaborator with the Romans. The penitent Zacchaeus became a saved man.

Outside Jericho, Jesus met a blind beggar, named Bartimaeus. Surrounded by an enormous crowd, Jesus healed him (Matt. 20:29-34; Mark 10:46-52; Luke 18:35-43). Jesus continued his journey to Jerusalem, along the lonely, rocky road that led from the deep Jordan valley (about 850 feet below sea level) up to the elevated city of Jerusalem (2,460 feet above sea level). The Master did not yet travel straight to Jerusalem itself. He stopped in the village of Bethany, which lay on the slopes of the Mount of Olives, to stay there with his beloved friends, Martha, Mary, and Lazarus (John 12:1). There, he spent the Sabbath and part of the Sunday before Passover.

---

118. Why Jesus did so has been explained in very different ways; see the discussion by Knight (2004, 162–66).

THE ETERNAL CHRIST: GOD WITH US

The Passion Week or Holy Week, as it is called, had now begun.

Chapter 12
The Passion Story

> ... *Christ Jesus, who, though he was in the form of God, did not count equality with God a thing to be grasped, but emptied himself, by taking the form of a servant, being born in the likeness of men.*
> *And being found in human form, he humbled himself by becoming obedient to the point of death, even death on a cross.*
>
> Philippians 2:5–8

12.1 The Passion Week
12.1.1 Palm Sunday and Monday

ON SATURDAY NIGHT, after the Sabbath, when according to the Jewish view, the Sunday had already begun,[1] Jesus dined in Bethany in the house of Simon, a leper who had been healed by him; he was possibly the husband of Martha (Matt. 26:6-13; Mark 14:3-9; John 12:1-8). During dinner, Martha's sister, Mary, stood up and anointed the head and the feet of Jesus

---

1. The fact that for Israel the new day begins with sunset not only goes back to Gen. 1 but also has an eschatological significance (Rom. 13:12; 1 Thess. 5:4–10). This was six days before Passover (John 12:1).

with a pound of nard perfume, which had the value of a full year's salary.[2] The disciples were outraged at such a waste of money, but Jesus implicitly said that Mary had understood better than any other person what was going to happen with him. He would die, and she had anointed him, as it were, in view of his burial.

The next day — this must have been on Sunday morning — Jesus headed for Jerusalem. He walked over the ridge of the Mount of Olives along the Roman road, surrounded by a crowd of pilgrims who were also on their way to the feast.[3] Another crowd, full of political expectations, came out of the city to meet him and to prepare a Messianic entrance for the rabbi who had been sought everywhere (Matt. 21:1-11; Mark 11:1-11; Luke 19:28-40; John 12:12-19). Apparently with the prophecy of Zechariah 9:9 in mind, Jesus asked two disciples to fetch the colt of a donkey from a befriended owner in the village of Bethphage. The people spread their clothes on the animal and on the road, while Jesus sat down on the young donkey, and rode down the slope of the Mount of Olives. The excited crowd wove branches of palm trees, and shouted the Messianic blessing (Ps. 118:26), "Hosanna to the Son of David! Blessed is the King who comes in the name of the Lord! Blessed is the coming kingdom of our father David! Peace in heaven and glory in the highest!" (cf. §4.13.5).

The crowd shouted, the Pharisees were outraged, but Jesus himself wept as he saw the radiant city, because its inhabitants did not really believe in him, and because it would be totally destroyed within four decades. He entered through the gate of the city, which thronged with the tumult. In great excitement, the people told each other: "This is the Prophet!"

---

2. The ointment had a value of three hundred denarii (Mark 14:5; John 12:5); a denarius was a day's wage for a laborer (Matt. 20:2), and since there were about three hundred working days in a year, this amounted to a year's worth of wages.
3. L. A. Losie (*DJG* 854–59); Stein (1996, 177–84); Knight (2004, 166–69: "Triumphal entry").

(cf. §4.10). He visited the temple square;[4] there, he calmly observed the melee. In the evening, he left the city to spend the night again with his friends in Bethany.

On Monday, he returned to Jerusalem. During the walk, he became hungry and turned to a fig tree to see whether already some early fruits could be found beneath the leaves. When he found nothing, he cursed the fig tree; this turned out to be a symbolic cursing of the hypocrites among the people, who gave the false impression of appearing to bear fruit for God (Matt. 21:18–19; Mark 11:12–14).[5]

Having arrived in the temple, Jesus repeated the temple cleansing that he had carried out at the beginning of his ministry (Matt. 21:12–17; Mark 11:15–19; Luke 19:45–48).[6] God's temple had to be a house of prayer (cf. Isa. 56:7), not a "den of robbers," that is, a place for the dishonest pursuit of profit. At the same time, Jesus could not fail to show mercy, and he healed the lame and the blind in the temple square, to the chagrin of the chief priests and the scribes. These also had to listen to the shouts of the children, cheering the Messiah. In the evening, Jesus again withdrew to Bethany, to spend the night there.

12.1.2 Tuesday and Wednesday

The next day, upon Jesus' return to Jerusalem, the disciples discovered that the cursed fig tree had withered to its very

---

4. According to a Christian tradition, he entered through the Golden Gate, also called the Gate of Mercy (Bab el Rahmeh). According to a Jewish tradition, upon his arrival the Messiah would enter Jerusalem through this gate (cf. Ps. 24:7–10). Therefore, sultan Süleyman (around 1540) had the gate bricked up. The present-day gate dates from about 640.
5. Cole (1961, 176–77); Carson (1984, 445); Wessell (1984, 725–26); cf. the expositions by Grosheide (1954, 320) and Lane (1974, 402). Berger (2004, 384–86) rejects this view.
6. Many expositors, including a conservative author such as Stein (1996, 186–87), believe there was only one temple cleansing, which John for some reason placed very early in his story. For arguments that there were *two* temple cleansings (or a temple cleansing and a temple sign), see Morris (1971, 188–91), Carson (1984, 441), and Van Bruggen (1998, 135–37).

roots (Matt. 21:20-22; Mark 11:20-26). Jesus explained that this was to be a lesson of faith for them. In a similar way, they too had to learn to form spiritual judgments on matters that they confronted.

Having arrived at the temple square, Jesus demonstrated how wisely he discerned the hearts of his enemies, who did not dare to arrest him in the midst of the pilgrims but did attempt to catch him with their trick questions (Matt. 21:23-22:46; Mark 11:27-12:37; Luke 20:1-44 [10:25-28]). The religious leaders openly asked him about his authority, but Jesus demonstrated to them that they did not possess the spiritual capacity for judging such matters. Moreover, by means of a parable he clearly showed that they would soon kill him, the Son of God. Then God would condemn them, and accept Gentiles as his people. The religious leaders were outraged, but they did not dare to undertake any action against him.

Subsequently, the Pharisees, together with their opponents, the Herodians, tried to catch him with a question about the imperial tax. If he defended it, the former group would accuse him, and if he opposed it, the latter group would accuse him. However, Jesus silenced both groups. He also demonstrated the ignorance of the Sadducees, who tried to ridicule belief in the resurrection with a fanciful hypothetical problem. Overtly Jesus now proclaimed himself not only as David's son but also as David's Lord. In a long, fervent sermon, he exposed all the hypocrisy and popular tripe of both the scribes and the Pharisees (Matt. 23:1-36; Mark 12:38-40; Luke 20:45-47 [cf. 11:37-52]). There was only one scribe (Torah scholar) in the temple square who made a more positive impression (Mark 12:32-34). Jesus' heart went out to him, as it went out to the poor widow who dropped her entire daily allowance into the offering box (Mark 12:41-44; Luke 21:1-4).

When some religious Greeks arrived who wished to talk with him, he explained to them that he was the Son of Man who would die and rise again, and would harvest much fruit among the Gentiles. However, to the unbelieving Jews he announced God's judgment if they refused to repent and convert (John 12:20-25).

After this, Jesus' public ministry definitively ended. With his disciples he left the temple square, and sat down on the slope of the Mount of Olives, with a view of the city. There, he gave his disciples his sermon on the Last Things (Matt. 24-25; Mark 13:1-37; Luke 21:5-36 [12:41-48; 19:11-27]).[7] He explained to them that a hard period was coming, for them as well. The Romans would destroy the city and the temple, as truly happened in AD 70.[8] The Jews would be dispersed throughout the world. There would also be a great tribulation, but all misery would end with his return from heaven, when he would appear in glory on the clouds, and would establish his kingdom on earth. To this his followers would have to look forward, without slackening in faithfulness and vigilance, and with full use of the talents that he would entrust to each of them. This was because at his return he would call all nations to account. This was all still in the distant future; for the present, he overtly announced to his disciples that at Passover he would be crucified.

In the meantime, on Tuesday or Wednesday, the religious leaders debated how they could arrest Jesus (Matt. 26:1-5; Mark 14:1-2; Luke 22:1-2; John 11:45-53). This would be difficult to do during the festival because of the celebrating pilgrims who were favorably inclined toward Jesus. However, they must also have been afraid of Jesus himself, for they allowed all the days and nights before the feast to pass by without seizing him. Nonetheless, it was God's will that the death of the true Passover lamb (1 Cor. 5:7;[9] cf. John 1:29, 36; 1 Pet.

---

7. R.W. Paschal (*DJG* 229-33).
8. Regarding the meaning of Jesus' predictions concerning the temple, see Bockmuehl (1994, 60-76).
9. The Gk. term *pascha* (cf. paschal lamb in RSV; see also Heb. 11:28) is derived from Passover, just as *Pasen* (Dutch), *Pâques* (French), and *Pascua* (Spanish) are derived from *pascha*.

1:19; Rev. 5:12) would occur at the very time of Passover.

That Wednesday was Jesus' last day of rest on earth. Apparently, he spent the day in quietness in Bethany or outside the town, in the neighborhood of the Mount of Olives, alone or with his disciples. The leaders did not close in on him but waited for their chance. For them, it was a happy development that one of Jesus' disciples, Judas Iscariot, offered his services; for a reward, he would advise them regarding a good opportunity for them to arrest Jesus.

12.1.3 Thursday

On Thursday morning, Jesus sent two of his disciples from his inner circle, Peter and John, to Jerusalem, where they had to follow a man with a jar of water on his head—a rare phenomenon in the Near East. This man would take them to the house of a friend, possibly the house of Mary, the mother of John Mark (cf. Acts 1:13; 12:12). There, they would find a well-equipped upper room, where they had to prepare the Passover meal.[10] This was because that evening, at about six o'clock, the night and day of Passover would begin, and Jesus wished to celebrate Passover with his disciples before his final suffering and death.[11]

At the end of the afternoon, Jesus arrived at the upper room with the other disciples. No personnel were available to perform the ritual foot washing, so the disciples hesitantly reclined at table. Each of them felt above doing slaves' work. Then, Jesus himself rose, and washed the disciples' feet (John 13:1-16). This, as he implicitly explained, he would be doing spiritually later in heaven in his high priestly ministry, and similarly, Jesus' followers must spiritually "wash" each oth-

---

10. For many centuries, it has been called the *Seder* meal (*seder* = order), because of its fourteen stages or orders identified in later rabbinic tradition.
11. For a discussion of the complicated question whether Jesus kept the Passover meal on the same day as the rest of Israel, or one day earlier, see Morris (1971, 774-86), Carson (1984, 528-32), Stein (1996, 200-05), and Van Bruggen (1998, 212-19), who maintained that it was a regular Passover meal; Meier (1991, 386-401) chose the other view.

er's "feet."

As they were reclining at table, first Judas was exposed as a traitor by Jesus when as host he gave him the first piece of the bread (Matt. 26:20-25; Mark 14:17-21; Luke 22:21-33; John 13:21-30).[12] This was a traditional gesture, normally done for the one to whom one felt most attached. Only John,[13] who was lying on Jesus' bosom, was allowed to hear the meaning of this moving gesture. Judas left the room immediately, possessed by the devil (Luke 22:3; John 13:2, 27 [cf. 6:70]). In the darkness of night, he went to the religious leaders, who had gathered in Caiaphas' house. There, he probably caused great tension among the leaders. On the one hand, Jesus was soon going to walk to Gethsemane, the orchard on the Mount of Olives; moreover, he spoke of his approaching death—apparently, he was entirely ready for it. What a chance! Apparently, they no longer needed to fear him. On the other hand, tomorrow the feast would be celebrated. Would they manage, within a few hours, to condemn him and have him executed by the Romans, before the day was over?[14] They must have debated this matter for hours, thereby giving Jesus enough time to finish the Passover meal with his disciples.[15]

During this meal, Jesus instituted a new, symbolic meal by taking a piece of the Passover bread (Heb. *matzot*, "unleavened loaves") and saying, "Take, eat, this is my body, which is given for you; do this in remembrance of me." After this, he took one of the Passover cups,[16] and said, "Drink of it, all of you. This cup is the new covenant in my blood, which

---

12. In my view, Judas had left the upper room before Jesus instituted the Lord's Supper.
13. According to tradition, he is both the author of John's Gospel and the "disciple whom Jesus loved" (John 13:23; 19:26; 20:2; 21:7, 20).
14. Actually, the Mishnah (Sanhedrin 11:4) says that the execution of a heretic *must* take place during one of the three main feasts, so that all the people would hear it, and fear (cf. Deut. 17:13; SBK 2:826).
15. For the reconstruction of the last night and day of Jesus' earthly life, I am following Morison (1972) for the most part; see also Medema (1990).
16. Regarding the two cups of Luke 22:17 and 20, see Stern (1992, 144).

is poured out for many for the forgiveness of sins" (Matt. 26:26-30; Mark 14:22-26; Luke 22:15-20; cf. 1 Cor. 11:23-25). Since that time, millions of Christians have celebrated[17] this "supper,"[18] or remembrance meal, or Eucharist,[19] not only as a commemoration of Jesus' sufferings and death but also as a foretaste of the eternal festival meal with the Lord, the banquet prepared in the kingdom of God (Mark 14:25).[20]

Jesus still had many other things to say to his disciples, especially about the future, when he would be going away from them to the Father's "house," where he would prepare a place for them. In the meantime, he would send to earth the Holy Spirit, the Helper (Advocate, Counselor), who would always be with them to encourage, lead, and instruct them (John 14). After having sung the final hymns (Ps. 114-118) — Psalm 118 having a particular Messianic-eschatological significance — he went out with his disciples into the night on their way to the Mount of Olives.

12.2 The Last Night
12.2.1 Gethsemane

It was already late at night when Jesus and the disciples walked through the softly illuminated city (it was full moon). Was it still within the house, or was it on the road ("Rise, let us go from here," John 14:31b), that Jesus spoke with his disciples about himself as the true vine (John 15:1-6)? In and through him they would be able to bear fruit for the honor of the Father, they would live together in love, and they would be able to endure oppressions and persecutions. To encour-

---

17. Actually, we find the institution of the Lord's Supper not in Matt. and Mark but only in Luke 22 and 1 Cor. 11, where we read the words "do this in remembrance of me." Because of this institution, Theissen and Merz (1998, 405) called Jesus a "founder of a cult."
18. Gk. *deipnon*, "meal" (1 Cor. 11:20), or more specifically "evening meal, supper," in Luke 14:12 distinct from *ariston*, "midday meal, lunch."
19. Derived from the Gk. verb *eucharisteō*, "to thank" (Luke 22:17, 19; 1 Cor. 11:24).
20. Cf. Hengel (1995, 69–70); Brown (1994b, 66).

The Passion Story

age them, Jesus spoke again of the coming of the Holy Spirit, but at the same time he made it even clearer that first he would die and rise and leave them and return to the Father (John 16). Then there was the solemn moment when he stood still, and looked up to the starry sky, and prayed earnestly to his Father for his disciples, and for those who would believe in him through them (John 17): "Holy Father, keep them in your name, . . . that the love with which you have loved me may be in them, and I in them" (vv.11, 26).[21]

The little company descended to the valley of the Kidron, crossed the brook, and climbed the slope of the Mount of Olives to the estate of Gethsemane, possibly the property of a friend (Matt. 26:31–46; Mark 14:27–42; Luke 22:31–46; John 13:36–38). On the road, the overconfident Peter received the warning that, during that same night, he would deny his Lord three times. At the entrance to the garden, Jesus left eight disciples behind, and took with him that same Peter, as well as the brothers John and James, into the garden in order to keep awake with him, as he prayed. Here, the approaching divine judgment that he was to endure on the cross overwhelmed him so strongly that he, sorrowful and troubled, prayed to be saved from this.[22] But, he added, "not my will, but yours, be done" (§10.2.2). Three times he sent up his ardent supplication, and three times he returned to his three disciples to find them asleep. The third time he let them continue sleeping. He knew that the traitor was near, and full of inner surrender and confidence he now faced the coming heavy hours.

---

21. In my view, the term "high priestly prayer" is not accurate because there is a distinction between the *Son* speaking to or with his *Father* (John 17; 1 John 2:2) and the high priest speaking (as a *man*) to God (Heb. 4:14–16; 7:25). Barrett (1955, ad loc.) had his own objections to the term, which, in his view, does insufficient justice to all the matters that are dealt with in John 17.
22. On the nature of Jesus' sorrow (or anguish, agony), see Stein (1996, 215–17).

12.2.2 Deliberations

In the meantime, the spiritual leaders must have extensively deliberated after receiving Judas' news. This was because the time was remarkably suitable, especially because the victim himself seemed so willing. However, there were immense problems: according to Jewish law, in cases of a complaint that demanded the death penalty, it was not the judges who were allowed to imprison the accused, but only the witnesses could do so. Such a trial could not be held during the night, either. Moreover, would Pilate be willing to impose the death sentence just before the seven-day feast of Passover and Unleavened Bread?[23]

It is quite conceivable that Caiaphas, or another prominent envoy, presented himself to the procurator, Pontius Pilate, that same night. Pilate happened to be in the city in view of the feast, together with his wife, Claudia Procula.[24] The cruel, insensitive Pilate presumably promised a quick conviction and sentence, otherwise the Jewish leaders probably would not have ventured to arrest Jesus that very night. Pilate presumably told his wife about it, thus inadvertently causing her to have a bad night. She must have had some sympathy for this Jewish rabbi. The fact that, next morning, *her* husband would have to condemn this man without anything resembling a serious trial literally caused her to have nightmares (Matt. 27:19). This was one of those events that would give the trial of the next day a somewhat different turn.

The way was free for the Jewish leaders. The next morning, the Jewish Council would have to swallow the two illegal actions that now were going to be committed. First, now heading out to arrest Jesus were not the accusing witnesses, but Caiaphas' temple guard. And second, contrary to the law

---

23. Regarding the Passover and the Feast of Unleavened Bread, see Mark 14:1, 12 par.; cf. Acts 12:3; 20:6; and 1 Cor. 5:7–8.
24. She reportedly was a granddaughter of emperor Augustus, and the illegal daughter of Claudia, the third wife of emperor Tiberius. One tradition tells us that she became a Christian; Eastern churches venerate her as a saint.

the court hearing would have to be held that very night, before Jesus would be brought before Pilate the next morning. Judas went with the soldiers, and through a traitor's kiss identified whom they had to arrest (Matt. 26:47-56; Mark 14:43-50; Luke 22:47-53; John 18:3-12).[25] Jesus uttered a mild reproach, but at the same time he showed his power: when the soldiers told him that they were seeking Jesus of Nazareth, and Jesus said only, "I AM" (§6.7.2), the entire band fell to the ground, including apparently Judas. Yet, Jesus willingly surrendered, and intervened on behalf of his disciples. Peter drew a sword and cut off an ear from one of Caiaphas' servants. Jesus healed the ear, and explained to both Peter and the soldiers that his hour had come, that is, the time of his sufferings.[26] He let himself be bound; Peter and the other disciples ran off.

12.3 The Jewish Trial[27]
12.3.1 The Accusing Witnesses

Very early that Friday morning, while it was still dark, the leaders came together in the house of Annas, Caiaphas' father-in-law and head of the high priestly family. Jesus was taken to this place first (John 18:13). At a later stage, the judicial hearing was continued in the — possibly adjacent — palace of Caiaphas (Matt. 26:57-68; Mark 14:53-65; Luke 22:54-55, 63-65; John 18:19-24). The actual trial by the Jewish Council

---

25. Regarding the "why" of Judas' treason, see Stein (1996, 218–19), as well as the reconstructed Gospel of Judas, according to which Judas was a pious man who helped Jesus to accomplish his ministry according to God's plan; see Van der Vliet (2006).
26. This is sufficient to explain why those expositors are wrong who think that Jesus was content with the two swords that were offered him (Luke 22:38); his word, "It is enough," instead implies a rejection of the entire offer; cf. Greijdanus (1941, 2:230–31); Geldenhuys (1983, 571–72); Liefeld (1984, 1029–30).
27. Much has been written on this subject; I refer to the contributions of the lawyer Douglas Linder on various websites. See also (from very different viewpoints) Blinzler (1970); Strobel (1980); Medema (1990); B. Corley (*DJG* 841–54); Brown (1994b); Crossan (1995); Watson (1995); Stein (1996, 224–39); Theissen and Merz (1998, 440–66); Wampler (2000); Knight (2004, 182–92); and Van Bruggen (1998, 251–63).

was to be held only in the (early) morning; this nightly session was an illegal hearing, during which Caiaphas, who was in a great hurry, sought to create the right mood for the trial. First, he interrogated Jesus about his teaching in general, but Jesus boldly referred him to his thousands of listeners.

According to Jewish law, there was no prosecutor, but only accusing witnesses. These witnesses themselves were to be killed if they testified falsely about anything that would warrant the death penalty (Num. 35:30; Deut. 17:6-7; 19:15-19). Therefore, the hearing became serious only when the accusing witnesses were heard. What Caiaphas needed for his summary judgment was testimony that, in line with Jewish law, was given by at least two agreeing witnesses, *and* was serious enough to entice the—partly critical—Council[28] to render a death sentence. At first, there were only many false, and thus contradictory witnesses, which were useless for Caiaphas. But eventually there were two witnesses who declared, "This man said, 'I am able to destroy the temple of God, and to rebuild it in three days.'" *This* was an accusation of magic and sacrilege, which two points, if the charge was strong enough, were sufficient for a death sentence.[29] However, Caiaphas realized that this was insufficient for moving the Council to pronounce a death sentence for *this* man.

A highly significant fact! For these reasons: both that the testimony was not contradicted, and that Caiaphas nevertheless rejected it, showed that this had not been staged in advance—and that the accusation therefore was true (even if the witnesses had completely misunderstood Jesus). It thus cannot be denied that Jesus had once said that he would not only be killed, but would raise in three days the temple of his body (cf. John 2:19-22).

Of course, in the search for the historical Jesus it is of the

---

28. Cf. John 12:42; think further of people like Nicodemus (John 7:50–51) and Joseph of Arimathea (Luke 23:50–51); cf. also Acts 23:1–9.
29. Regarding magic, see Exod. 22:18; cf. Deut. 18:10–12; regarding sacrilege, cf. Jer. 26:1–19; see also Rosh Hashanah 17a; Tosefta Sanhedrin 13:5.

greatest interest that his statement that he would rise from death on the third day must be viewed as authentic. Please note: (a) this testimony was accepted by Caiaphas; (b) it was totally misunderstood; (c) Matthew and Mark, who report this testimony, do not explain it further; and (d) a very different Gospel writer, John, tells us that Jesus had made this statement in referring to his resurrection. This is all a beautiful example of something that historians would call powerful evidence for authenticity: Jesus must really have announced his own resurrection; this was not an invention of the early church (cf. §13.4.2).[30]

The negative role of Peter in Matthew 16:21-23 also makes it impossible to view this passage as a piece of theology invented by the church because Peter was one of the greatest heroes of the early church. That is to say, if Jesus accused him of playing the devil's role, something momentous must have happened that had stirred Peter's indignation. This weighty event was Jesus' announcement of his death and resurrection (although the latter was apparently overheard by Peter), which was straightforwardly rejected by Peter. Therefore, Jesus' announcement that he would rise on the third day (v. 21) cannot be anything other than authentic.[31]

12.3.2 Another Illegal Act

At this point, Caiaphas committed another illegal act. If the testimonies were either contradictory, or insufficiently strong, he was obliged to dismiss the case. Instead, entirely contrary to Jewish law, he himself began to interrogate the accused, under oath, in order that Jesus might incriminate himself. In the common Jewish manner (whereby not the defendant but the judge himself took the oath), he adjured Jesus by the living God to say whether he was the Messiah, the Son of God. Because of this oath, in terms of Jewish law, Jesus was obliged to answer and to openly confess that he was the Messiah.

---

30. Morris (1971, 198–99), with reference to C. F. D. Moule.
31. Stein (1996, 161–62).

Jesus confessed an additional truth: he referred to his second coming as the "Son of Man," implying that he would return on the clouds of heaven (cf. Dan. 7:13), and that, before this, he would be seated at the right hand of God in heaven (alluding to Ps. 110:1). This confession was exactly what Caiaphas wanted to hear because, to him, this was blasphemy. He tore his robes, ostensibly out of sorrow (cf. already Gen. 37:29, 34; 44:13), and the great majority of the council declared that Jesus deserved the death penalty. That their judicial impartiality was a mere pretense is evident from the mocking and hatred that they then poured out on the accused.

In the meantime, not all of the disciples remained aloof. The disciple John was an acquaintance of the high priest, perhaps through familial bonds or through commercial contacts, since his father Zebedee was a fisherman with possible business contacts in the capital. Peter, together with John, had also entered the house of Caiaphas, and was warming himself at a fire in the courtyard, together with the servants of the high priest. Three times he was asked whether, or accused that, he was a disciple of Jesus, and three times he denied it, as Jesus had foretold (Matt. 26:69-75; Mark 14:66-72; Luke 22:56-62; John 18:15-18, 25-27). Then a rooster crowed. And during the judicial hearing, Jesus turned around to Peter, standing in the courtyard, and looked him in the eyes. With a shock, Peter remembered what Jesus had foretold. He went outside and wept bitter tears of remorse. Subsequently, Peter was restored to the circle of the disciples, but Judas, the traitor, killed himself (Matt. 27:3-10; Acts 1:18-19).

Jesus likely had to spend a few remaining hours in a cell in the high priest's palace. The next morning, at an early hour, the members of the Jewish Council were rustled together (Matt. 27:1; Mark 15:1; Luke 22:66-71), probably in Solomon's Portico.[32] When they learned that Jesus had called himself the

---

32. The colonnade of Solomon (Gk. *stoa tou Solomōnos*; cf. John 10:23; Acts 3:11; 5:12) was a pre–Herodian (but not necessarily Solomonic) portico, where the Torah teachers normally gave their lessons.

Messiah, and even the Son of God, as well as the Son of Man in the sense of Daniel 7, they could do nothing but sentence him to death because of this alleged greatest possible blasphemy. Now, the sentence needed only to be ratified by the procurator, so that Jesus could be crucified that very same morning. Thus, two things were unequivocally established through this mock trial: Jesus had predicted that he would rise from death on the third day, and the Jewish leaders condemned him because he called himself God's Son (cf. John 19:7).

Indeed, what had irritated the Jewish leaders was not Jesus' political Messianic pretensions, as in the case of Barabbas, and later, Bar-Kochba. The Jewish leaders were accustomed to such imposters. Rather, the irritant was that he had made himself equal to God. As Joseph Ratzinger observed,

> The fact that Jesus' trial was then presented to the Romans as the trial of a political Messiah reflects the pragmatism of the Sadducees. But even Pilate senses that something completely different was really at stake here—that anyone who really seemed to be a politically promising "king" would never have been handed over to him to be condemned.[33]

12.4 The Roman Trial
12.4.1 No Immediate Ratification

Given the deliberation of the previous evening, the leaders undoubtedly felt certain that the unconscionable Pilate would ratify their sentence without any further ado. This is evident from various details of what was now happening. Such a quick ratification agrees with everything we know of Pilate from non-biblical historical sources. However, God arranged the circumstances in such a way that, *if* Jesus were to be crucified, the Gentiles would be equally culpable in the execution of Jesus Christ.

Look at what happened. While the streets of Jerusalem were still quiet, in the very early morning, the Jewish leaders

---
33. Ratzinger (2007, 304).

took Jesus to the palace of Herod, where Pilate resided during the feast, and where he sat in judgment. In order not to defile themselves in view of Passover, the leaders remained outside the fence, whereas the prisoner was led by a Roman escort into the courtroom (Matt. 27:2, 11-31; Mark 15:1-20; Luke 23:1-25; John 18:28-19:16). The Jewish leaders waited impatiently outside for the formal ratification of their sentence by the procurator. A signature would have sufficed.

However, lo and behold, the procurator himself came out, and began asking the Jewish leaders: "What accusation do you bring against this man?" This implied that he wanted a formal trial, a trial whose outcome was not *a priori* certain at all! Therefore, the Jewish leaders reacted furiously, and at first glance, rather strangely: "If this man were not doing evil, we would not have delivered him over to you." In other words, why do you not simply ratify *our* sentence, after *we* already determined that he deserves death?

Yes, why not? What moved this Roman to suddenly show so much consideration for a Jewish prisoner? This is one of the most important and interesting questions in all these legal procedures. I see three possible motives. First, perhaps Pilate had personal motives to thwart the Jewish leaders at that moment.

Second, his wife Claudia Procula had sent him a troubling note: "Have nothing to do with that righteous man, for I have suffered much because of him today in a dream" (Matt. 27:19). For Pilate, this would have sufficed to try to avoid a sentence. His wife was more important to him than judicial arguments by the hated Jews.

However, as the trial advanced, a third motive was expressed: outside the courtroom, Pilate began a conversation with Jesus, this remarkable, amazing, impressive man, who was obviously harmless and innocent. *This* is why the trial took such a weird turn: Pilate really tried everything to save Jesus from a death sentence. This also made him all the more guilty when he finally did acquiesce to the Jewish leaders.

12.4.2 Trying to Save Jesus

First, Pilate tried to shift responsibility to the Jewish leaders, but these reminded him of the fact that they needed his consent to perform an execution. (This in itself was remarkable because, in the case of Stephen, they did not hesitate to stone him to death; Acts 7.)

Second, Pilate discovered that Jesus was a Galilean, and therefore tried to transfer his case to his enemy, Herod Antipas, the tetrarch of Galilee. The latter happened to be in the city as well, probably in a Maccabee palace near the Wailing Wall. In doing this, Pilate was paying honor to Antipas with the hope of decreasing his hostility. He succeeded in this, but Herod did send Jesus back to him (Luke 23:6–12). The weird result of these actions was that Herod and Pilate, who had been enemies, became friends that very day.

Third, Pilate remembered the custom of granting amnesty at every Passover to a prisoner. He gave the Jewish leaders the choice between Jesus and a dangerous guerrilla. The group of Jews, having by now grown into a considerable crowd, did not hesitate to choose the latter. It was a remarkable contrast, however: the rebel Jesus Barabbas (i.e., "son of the father") (Matt. 27:16–17 CEV) and the "rebel" Jesus, the Son of the Father. In a certain sense, the resistance fighter Barabbas was also a "Messianic figure," so the people had to choose, as it were, between two allegedly pretending "Messiahs."[34] David Flusser emphasized that Barabbas was a hero of the people, so that Pilate committed a stupid error by presenting this very man to the people.[35]

Fourth and last, Pilate had Jesus beaten and mocked by his soldiers and rudely dressed in a scarlet robe and a crown of thorns. In this way, he hoped to elicit the pity of the gathered Jews ("Behold the man," John 19:5; Lat. *Ecce Homo*). Howev-

---
34. Ratzinger (2007, 40–41).
35. Flusser (2007, 164–66).

er, they were not impressed. On the contrary, they invoked Jesus' blood upon themselves, and unanimously demanded his crucifixion.

Pilate remained stubborn, until the Jewish leaders struck him in his weakest spot: his relationship to the emperor. If he were to release Jesus, he would—they argued—be setting free a resistance fighter, a revolutionary, an enemy of the emperor (John 19:12). Such a person could unleash a revolt among all the people and make himself king. Could Pilate take *that* risk? In this way, the man was induced not only to ratify the sentence of an unknown defendant—as he had done so often without batting an eye—but also to pronounce the sentence of death on a man he knew to be innocent, a man respected by his own wife Claudia, a righteous witness of God and the Son of God himself (v. 7). Pilate literally washed his hands of the matter (Matt. 27:24)—but in reality, as the representative of the Gentile world empire, he made himself equally culpable of the justice-perverting condemnation of Jesus, just as the Jewish leaders had done earlier.

Please note that in the past, the guilt of the Jewish leaders for Jesus' death has been one-sidedly emphasized, with horrible consequences. Today the opposite often occurs by people underscoring that not the Jews but the Romans sentenced Jesus to death, and nailed him to the cross. However, this view clearly conflicts with the testimony of the book of Acts: Jesus was crucified just as much by the people in Jerusalem and their Jewish leaders as he was by Pilate (2:23, 36; 3:14-15; 4:10; 5:30; 7:52; 10:39). But it is equally true that it was the Gentiles (Gk. *ta ethnē*, i.e., the Romans) who mocked, flogged, and killed Jesus (Matt. 20:19; Mark 10:34; Luke 18:32-33).

12.5 The Crucifixion of Jesus
12.5.1 The Act of Crucifying

The Jewish leaders did not waste any time; in fact, their actions were driven by a shortage of time. The convicted Jesus received his own clothes again, and, according to custom, was led through the busiest streets as a warning to the people. This is the route that people subsequently called the *Via dolorosa*, "The Way of Grief." Jesus also carried the crossbeam himself. The procession left the city to go to Golgotha (Matt. 27:32; Mark 15:21; Luke 23:26-32; John 19:17). At the time, Golgotha lay outside the city wall (cf. Heb. 13:12); today it lies within the Turkish city wall (if we accept the—highly likely—tradition that Golgotha lies within the Church of the Holy Sepulchre built later).

On the road, the soldiers met a man who was just coming in from the field, Simon of Cyrene, far away from his homeland—Cyrene was a Greek city in modern Libya—perhaps either to celebrate Passover in Jerusalem or having retired in Jerusalem. The soldiers pressed him to take the crossbeam from Jesus so that the procession would not lose too much time. An enormous crowd was going on foot, pilgrims from all parts of the world, as well as people from Jerusalem. More and more people were coming from the city to watch the procession. The rabbi who had been teaching all week in the temple square and had performed miracles was going to be crucified! The hearts of many women were overwhelmed, and they cried, but Jesus told them that they could better weep for themselves, for unspeakable horrors would soon descend upon *them*. This was fulfilled in the Jewish-Roman war of AD 66-73.

Having arrived at the place of execution—it was about nine o'clock in the morning—Jesus was offered aromatic wine, prepared by women to alleviate his pain.[36] However, he refused; apparently, he wished to endure the sufferings as fully as possible. He was then unclothed and crucified; he was laid on the ground, his hands (actually his wrists) were nailed to the crossbeam with large nails, and then the beam was drawn up, probably with ropes, and attached to the erect beam that had been set in the ground (Matt. 27:33-44; Mark

---

36. Cf. Sanhedrin 43a, which appeals to Prov. 31:6.

15:22-32; Luke 23:33-43; John 19:17-27).[37] Jesus prayed, "Father, forgive them, for they know not what they do." His feet had been nailed to a footrest. Above his head,[38] a sign had been attached with the words: "This is Jesus the Nazarene, the King of the Jews" (cf. §5.6.1), written in Hebrew, Greek, and Latin. This superscription irritated the Jewish leaders, and they complained to Pilate, but this time he stood his ground — no doubt divinely led, although he was not conscious of this.

On both sides of Jesus, two guerrillas were crucified. These were rebels, guerrillas, or insurrectionists (Gk. *lēistai*) not ordinary thieves, as one might conclude from many Bible translations; ordinary thieves would not have been crucified. Perhaps the middle cross had originally been intended for Barabbas.[39] The clothes of the crucified ones were divided among the soldiers, but they cast lots for Jesus' beautiful tunic, which may have been a gift from friends.

The Greeks and Romans had adopted the method of execution through crucifixion from the Phoenicians and/or the Persians. It was one of the most heinous forms of execution. Originally intended only for slaves, the punishment was found too horrible even by some Romans, such as the Roman philosopher Cicero. In 314 the Christian emperor Constantine abolished crucifixion. The dying process usually lasted at least thirty-six hours, sometimes many days. Therefore, it was necessary that a centurion with several soldiers would guard the cross, so that nobody could liberate the condemned. The pain was unbearable. The entire body was stretched out, and after a time the arteries of the head and the stomach were overloaded with blood, which caused a hideous headache. Because of the nail-fixed arms, the thorax was distorted to such an extent that the victim almost suffocated, and occasionally had to raise himself up on nailed feet to get some air. The thirst was

---

37. See J. B. Green (*DJG* 146–63: "Death of Jesus").
38. This explanation assumes that this cross was in the traditional form of †, and not the form of an X or a T; cf. Hislop (1959, 197–205).
39. So Carson (1984, 569).

indescribable. Finally, fever and heavy convulsions set in.[40]

12.5.2 The Bystanders

Jesus was severely mocked by the chief priests and scribes and the elders of the nation, and more generally, by "those who passed by" (Matt. 27:39-40; Mark 15:29-30). However, Luke 23 gives a little more positive picture of (some of) the ordinary people. When Jesus was on his way to Golgotha, "there followed him a great multitude of the people and of women who were mourning and lamenting for him" (v. 27); "the people stood by, watching, but the rulers scoffed at him" (v. 35). We read that after Jesus' death, "And all the crowds that had assembled for this spectacle, when they saw what had taken place, returned home beating their breasts" (v. 48).[41] This underscores the cleft between the Jewish leaders, who had made themselves co-responsible for Jesus' death, and the majority of the people, who were grief-stricken because of his crucifixion.

The leaders shouted (Matt. 27:43), "He trusts in God; let God deliver him now, if he desires him. For he said, 'I am the Son of God.'" Their words allude to Psalm 22:7-8, "All who see me mock me; they make mouths at me; they wag their heads; 'He trusts in the LORD; let him deliver him; let him rescue him, for he delights in him!'" There is also a remarkable similarity to Wisdom 2:16-20, where the *wicked* say about the righteous:

> They boast of having God for their Father, and believe that when all is said and done, only the righteous will be happy. But we'll see if that's true! Let's see what will happen when it's time for them to die! If the righteous really are God's children, God will save them from their enemies. So let's put them to the test. We'll be cruel to them, and torment them; then we'll find

---

40. See extensively B. Smalhout, www.catechese.net/rorate/scripts/nws_art.php?id=25061, and www.rorate.com/rorate/scripts/nws_art.php?id=25077; cf. Stein (1996, 244–48); Van de Kamp (2005, 133–37).
41. This contrast is emphasized by Flusser (2007, 224–36).

out how calm and reasonable they are! We'll find out just how much they can stand! We'll condemn them to a shameful death. After all, they say that God will protect them.

The two crucified guerrillas also mocked Jesus until a remarkable change occurred in one of them. This man repented and begged Jesus for mercy in view of the coming kingdom after the resurrection. Jesus promised that immediately he would forever be with Jesus (cf. Phil. 1:23; 1 Thess. 4:17), and where Jesus is there is paradise (Luke 23:39-45).[42] Paradise, not hell. The statement of Van de Beek ("after his death Jesus went to hell")[43] may be supported by the Apostles' Creed—if the Latin term *infernus* means "hell" and not "hades" (the realm of the dead, lit., "netherworld")—but it is not supported by the New Testament, not even 1 Peter 3:18-19.[44]

The four women who had followed Jesus from Galilee were standing near the cross: Mary Magdalene, Mary the wife of Clopas,[45] Mary the mother of Jesus, and her sister Salome, the wife of Zebedee and mother of the disciples John and James (Matt. 27:55-56; Mark 15:40-41; Luke 23:49; John 19:25-27). John was standing there as well, the only one of the twelve remaining near Jesus. Peter had hidden himself out of remorse, and the other disciples had probably fled to Bethany and other nearby places. Perhaps they and their friends there were still ignorant of all that had happened.

Jesus looked at his mother and his cousin, John, and despite his own grief, showed his deep love for Mary by entrusting her to John's care: "Woman, behold, your son!," and to John, "Behold, your mother!" At that moment, it became too much for the already cruelly tortured Mary. John lovingly took her with him, and also Salome apparently pitied her sis-

---

42. Cf. Ouweneel (2020, chapter 7).
43. Van de Beek (2002a, 172-76).
44. See *EDR* 1:146-48, 200.
45. According to one tradition, this Clopas was a brother of Joseph, Mary's husband; according to another, he was one of the husbands of Anne, Mary's mother, so "Mary of Clopas" was not his wife but his daughter.

The Passion Story

ter; we know that she was present at the burial of Jesus. Two other women remained behind, watching the sorrowful scene until the end. They were Jesus' only friends at his death.

12.6 The Death of Jesus
12.6.1 Last Sayings

At noon, when Jesus had been hanging on the cross for three hours, the sun became covered as it were by the hand of God, so that darkness spread across the land for three hours, between twelve and three in the afternoon (Matt. 27:45-54; Mark 15:33-39; Luke 23:44-48; John 19:28-37). This cannot have been an ordinary eclipse of the sun, for this type of phenomenon can occur only at new moon, whereas at Passover, on the fourteenth day after the new moon, it was the time of full moon. Moreover, such an eclipse does not last for three hours. Whether this darkness had a natural explanation, at a minimum it was a sign of disaster and judgment (cf. Amos 8:9-10).

The Bible is silent about this most horrible stage in Jesus' suffering, in which God's full judgment descended upon him.[46] It was horrible but also magnificent—horrible because the holy Jesus had been made sin, and a holy and righteous God had to forsake him. Magnificent because it was the finest revelation of God's love toward sinners ever to occur.[47]

The only thing the Bible tells us about these three hours is that, near the end, a grievous cry came from Jesus' lips: "My God, my God, why have you forsaken me?" (Heb. *Ēli, Ēli, lema sabachtáni?*;[48] cf. Ps. 2:1). The bystanders said—ignorantly or (more likely) mockingly?—that he was calling for the prophet Elijah (cf. Mal. 4:5). Jesus now knew that the end was

---

46. Regarding the soteriological significance of this suffering, see vol. III/3 in this series.
47. Cf. R. Earle in Henry (1962, 138).
48. The manuscript readings of this statement differ in Matt. 27:46 and Mark 15:34: *Ēli* or *Elōi*, *lema* or *lama* or *lima*, *sabachthani* or *sabaktani* or *azaphthani*. Ps. 22:1 has *Ēli, Ēli, lama ᶜazavthani?* The version *Elōi, Elōi, lama sabachthani?* is the Aramaic rendering of the Hebrew text.

THE ETERNAL CHRIST: GOD WITH US

near, and he said, in order to fulfill the Scripture, "I thirst." Someone drenched a sponge in a vessel of sour wine, put it on a hyssop branch, and let the suffering Man drink, under the protests of the bystanders. John tells us emphatically (John 19:28) that Jesus said this in order to fulfil the Scriptures; compare Psalm 69:21, "They put gall in my food and gave me vinegar for my thirst."

Then Jesus cried, "It is finished!" (in Greek this is one word: *tetelestai*, derived from *telos*: "goal": "The goal has been reached!"). The great work that he had come to accomplish on earth had been brought to an end; as he had said before, "I glorified you on earth, having accomplished[49] the work that you gave me to do" (John 17:4). It was at the ninth hour that he said this, that is, about three o'clock in the afternoon. This was the very moment when, in the temple, the Passover lambs were being slaughtered, and evening prayer was being said by the pilgrims. It was the very moment when, centuries earlier, Elijah had said his prayer to let fire come down from heaven (1 Kings 18:36-38). It was the very moment when Ezra had said his solemn prayer on behalf of the sinful people (Ezra 9:5-15). It was the very moment when the angel Gabriel had come to visit the praying prophet Daniel with an important message concerning Israel's future (Dan. 9:20-27). It was the time when Peter and John later visited the temple to pray there (Acts 3:1), and the time when an angel later appeared to the praying Cornelius (10:3).

Jesus connected, as it were, with all these prayers, and according to Jewish custom, said with a loud voice, "Father, into your hands I commit my spirit!" (or, "my human life"; Luke 23:46) — though he was the only one to add the name "Father" (cf. Ps. 31:5). The great work had been finished and now Jesus could surrender his earthly life. This was not just "breathing his last" (Gk. *aphēken to pneuma*, Matt. 27:50), but also with divine authority actively surrendering his human

---

49. Gk. *teleilōsas*, from the same verb *teleioō*, "to complete," as *tetelestai*.

life unto death (Gk. *paredoken to pneuma*, John 19:30; cf. 10:18, "I lay it [i.e., my life] down of my own accord. I have authority to lay it down, and I have authority to take it up again," viz., in resurrection).

12.6.2 The Events Surrounding Jesus' Death

It was a dramatic moment. While the chief priests believed they had triumphed over Jesus, in the temple the curtain of the Most Holy place was torn in two, from top to bottom, demonstrating that any human intervention was excluded. About that moment, a priest was offering the evening frankincense on the golden altar. He must have looked with dismay into the sanctuary, only to see what was *lacking* there: the ark of the covenant (cf. Jer. 3:16) and the *Shechinah* (at the dedication of the Second Temple [Ezra 6:16-18; Hag. 2:1-10] we do not hear of a new descent of the pillar of the cloud). At the same time, a severe earthquake occurred, so that the rocks were split and the tombs were opened. After Jesus' resurrection, many bodies of deceased saints were raised, who came forth from the graves, entered the holy city, and appeared to many (Matt. 27:52-53).[50]

The Roman centurion, seeing all this, was deeply shocked and exclaimed, "Truly, this Man was righteous—he was a Son of God!"[51] The crowd was stunned; full of self-reproach and fear, the people beat their breast. Had Jesus died in this both horrible and impressive way? What could they now expect for themselves?

The leaders remained cold-blooded. The corpse of the one crucified was not permitted to remain hanging on the cross after sunset (cf. Deut. 21:22-23), all the more because the next day would be a double or triple Sabbath (cf. John 19:31): it

---

50. This is the way Wenham (1981) interprets the text; because of the term "appearing" (cf. Mark 16:9; Luke 24:34; Acts 9:17; 13:31; 26:16; 1 Cor. 15:5-8), these Old Testament believers must have received resurrection bodies, as a first harvest of Jesus' resurrection; see Carson (1984, 581-82).
51. Regarding this remarkable Roman confession (reminiscent of the Roman son of the supreme deity, Apollo), see Ouweneel (2003, 349).

was the seventh day of the week, *and* the first day of the Feast of Unleavened Bread, *and* the Sabbath before the day of the sheaf of the firstfruits (Lev. 23:5-11). Therefore, they requested Pilate to put an end to the lives of the crucified, so they might remove their bodies from the crosses. Pilate granted permission, and the soldiers put an end to the agony of the two guerrillas by breaking the shins with a club or a hammer (John 19:31-33; Lat. *crurifragium*). As a consequence, the weight of the crucified would have come to rest all the more heavily on the nails or ropes holding the arms, and they would have died more quickly but also more painfully. The soldiers did as they had been told.

Coming to Jesus' cross, they found to their amazement that he had already died. A soldier wanted to make sure, and likely acting on his orders, pierced Jesus' side with a spear, just below the ribs, up into the heart region. Immediately, both blood and a watery liquid came out. Various physiological explanations have been given for this.[52] Later, John gave the spiritual meaning of blood and water (1 John 5:6-8).[53] Here again, Jesus was the perfect Passover lamb: he died at the very moment when the Passover lambs were dying in the temple, he gave his blood for atonement, and not one of his bones was broken (cf. Exod. 12:6-7, 46).

12.7 Jesus' Burial[54]
12.7.1 The Rich Man's Tomb

Usually, the body of a crucified person remained on the cross until it had been devoured by animals or had rotted away. Sometimes, as a favor, family and friends were allowed to bury the body. A man named Joseph of Arimathea[55] received permission from Pilate to bury the body of Jesus (Matt. 27:57-

---

52. Cf. Morris (1971, 819–20 including notes 88–91).
53. Cf. *EDR* 1:159–60.
54. J. B. Green (*DJG* 88–92); Stein (1996, 254–57).
55. Arimathea is possibly Ramataim-Sophim, or Rama (1 Sam. 1:1, 19), either where Samuel was born and lived (7:17), and was visited by David (19:18); or Rama near Bethlehem (Josh. 18:25; Judg. 4:5; Jer. 31:15; Matt. 2:18).

61; Mark 15:42–47; Luke 23:50–56; John 19:38–42). Joseph was a rich, prominent man, a member of the Jewish Council, good and righteous, a man who had not approved of Jesus' execution but rather had surreptitiously become a disciple of his. He received help from another member of the Council, Nicodemus (see John 3:1, 4, 9; 7:50), who brought about seventy-five pounds (John 19:39; Gk. *litras hekaton*, "one hundred *litras*") of myrrh and aloes with which to anoint the body.

Joseph had bought a shroud, in which they wrapped the body with the spices. Some believe that this is the same as the famous shroud of Turin, on which one can vaguely discern the image of a crucified man, but others hold this to be a medieval fake.[56] The two friends laid Jesus' body in a new tomb, which Joseph had hewn out of the rock in a neighboring garden. Time apparently did not allow opportunity to look around for another burying place; thus, Isaiah 53:9 was fulfilled: "He was assigned a grave with the wicked, but he was with a rich man at his death" (CSB).

Two Galilean women, who were probably unknown to these prominent inhabitants of Jerusalem, watched the scene from a distance, and remembered the location of the tomb. They were Mary Magdalene and Mary the wife of Clopas. It was getting dark in the garden; Sabbath was near. The women returned to the house where Peter and John, Mary the mother of Jesus, and Salome were present, to spend the Sabbath there in the greatest sadness and despondency. On that Sabbath, the Jewish leaders, with Pilate's permission, placed a large round stone in front of the tomb, sealed it with the imperial seal, and placed a guard in front of it to prevent theft of the body.

12.7.2 Descending into the Netherworld?

What should we think of the phrase in the Apostles' Creed that, after his burial, Jesus "descended into the netherworld" (Gk. *katelthonta eis ta katōtata*, Lat. *descendit ad inferna*)? The

---

56. See Cassanelli (2002); Zugibe (2005); and Whiting (2006).

Greek word *katōtata* is "depths, low places"; in Ephesians 4:9, we read that Jesus "descended into the lower regions [Gk. *katōtera*] of the earth" (which is often explained as Hades) and in Psalm 139:15 (LXX), "in the depths [Gk. *katōtatō*] of the earth." Thus, although the words *enfer* (French) and *infierno* (Spanish) mean "hell," the Latin word *inferna* means "netherworld, hades, realm of the dead." It comes from *inferus*, "being under [often: in the netherworld]" (cf. "inferior"). The confusion is continued in older English translations of the Apostles' Creed, where *hades* is rendered "hell."

The phrase in question forms a later addition to the Creed, so that some have proposed that it be removed.[57] Or does it confess something biblically meaningful? Peter's quotation from Psalm 16:10, "[Y]ou will not abandon my soul to Sheol" (Acts 2:27), suggests that, between his death and resurrection, Jesus was in Sheol or Hades (the realm of the dead, the netherworld). But what does this mean? There are various explanations, including that Jesus descended into Hades, either to liberate from it the believers who had died before him, or to preach the gospel to the Gentiles and unbelievers. All of this is rather speculative, and is definitely not in view in Ephesians 4:9, 1 Peter 4:4-6, and probably not 1 Peter 3:19-20 either.[58]

It seems to me closer to the truth to say that Jesus descended into Hades, not for the human beings thought to sojourn there, but rather to break the power of the devil. Jesus became Man "that through death he might destroy the one who has the power of death, that is, the devil" (Heb. 2:14). "The reason the Son of God appeared was to destroy the works of the devil" (1 John 3:8). After this dethroning of Satan, from now on Jesus possesses "the keys of Death and Hades" (Rev. 1:18).[59]

John Calvin looked in a different direction. He sought to apply the words "descended into Hades" to the hellish agony that Jesus endured in Gethsemane and on the cross. This is

---

57. Vleugels and Verhoeff (2006, 180n16).
58. Regarding this, see *EDR* 1:146–48.
59. Cf. Ratzinger (2007, 19–20).

The Passion Story

a sympathetic approach,[60] but I see two objections: first, the Creed mentions this descent explicitly *after* Jesus' burial; and second, there is no basis for understanding the Latin word *inferna* to mean "hell." Therefore, it is better to follow the lead of the Westminster Confession, which understands the Latin phrase *descendit ad inferna* simply to be stating that, between his death and resurrection, Jesus was in the realm of death.[61] In this sense, we can understand the age-old parallel with Jesus' baptism, namely, as a descent into death (cf. Rom. 6:4): "Descended into the waters he bound the strong man" (cf. Luke 11:21–22), said Cyril of Jerusalem; and, "Going down into the water and emerging again are the image of the descent into hell and the Resurrection," said John Chrysostom.[62]

---

60. As is the similar approach of the Heidelberg Catechism, Q&A 44.
61. Berkhof (1981, 340–43); Berkouwer (1965, 174–79); Van Genderen and Velema (2008, 484–86); cf. Heyns (1988, 263).
62. Quoted in Ratzinger (2007, 19).

Chapter 13
Jesus' Resurrection and Ascension

> *Therefore God has highly exalted him and bestowed on him the name that is above every name, so that at the name of Jesus every knee should bow, in heaven and on earth and under the earth, and every tongue confess that Jesus Christ is Lord, to the glory of God the Father.*
>
> Philippians 2:9–11

13.1 The Resurrection of Jesus
13.1.1 Introduction

IN THE NEXT sections, as in the previous ones, a harmony of the Gospels forms the basis of my discussion.[1] Precisely in the resurrection stories, this is not easy at all; I therefore give the following "reconstruction" of the events with great reservation.

The seriousness with which one assesses the difficulties of the harmonization depends on one's theological paradigm.

---

1. As we saw, for a historical survey of Jesus' life this is unavoidable, but a harmony of the Gospels *cannot* be the starting point for an exegetical and dogmatic approach (see §5.2.1).

Some seek to smooth out all the discrepancies between the four Gospels,[2] as much as others seek to magnify these differences.[3] Perhaps we should neither fret about nor exaggerate these discrepancies.[4] Frank Morison argued that they are evidence for the authenticity of the resurrection stories. The declarations of witnesses in a court case may deviate at certain points — it would be strange if they did *not* — whereas their presentation of the core of the matter is unanimous.

It is the same with the Gospels. If the Gospel writers had offered four accounts that in a sophisticated way would neatly fit together, the suspicion would have been much higher that they had literally copied each other (leaving us with only one Gospel), or that, at a later stage, a redactor would have tidied up the stories.[5]

13.1.2 The Discovery of the Empty Tomb

In addition to Nicodemus, the women had bought spices, too. After the Sabbath, they wished to visit the tomb in order to anoint the body of Jesus with more care than had been possible in the haste of the late Friday afternoon. They were unaware that a guard had been posted there. Early on Sunday morning, while it was still dark, at least four women set off to the tomb: Mary Magdalene, Mary the wife of Clopas and mother of James and Joses, Salome, and Joanna (who was the wife of Herod's household manager, and therefore on Friday morning had been preoccupied with her duties) (Matt. 28:1-8; Mark 16:1-8; Luke 24:1-12; John 20:1-10).[6] While or perhaps before they were on their way, and without them knowing it,

---

2. E.g., Archer (1982, 347–56).
3. See, e.g., Schweizer (1971a, 46–47); Lapide (1983, 32–40).
4. Van de Beek (2002a, 180) claimed straightforwardly that the Gospel writers' versions of the resurrection cannot be harmonized, which in my view is a bit too strong.
5. See especially Morison (1972, chapter 14). The truth of the resurrection cannot depend on precisely how many women were at the tomb, and who saw the living Lord first; cf. Theron (1996, 406).
6. Perhaps there was a fifth woman: Susanna (cf. Luke 8:3 with 24:10).

a severe earthquake had occurred near the tomb, and an angel had appeared in a blinding light. He had rolled away the stone from before the opening of the tomb and was sitting on it.[7] The guards had fled, scared to death.

Meanwhile, the women were anxiously wondering who would roll away the heavy stone in front of the tomb. In the light of early morning, they were able to see the tomb—and saw, to their utter amazement, that the large stone *had* already been rolled away. Moreover, one glance into the tomb showed them that it was empty. In their initial panic, they must have quickly conferred with each other, for something serious had occurred. Peter and John must be warned! One of the women, Mary Magdalene, perhaps the youngest of them, agreed to return home immediately to warn the two disciples. The other women carefully entered the burial chamber. An angel was there, who looked like a young man, and was accompanied by a second angel. The first one told the frightened women:

> Do not be alarmed. You seek Jesus of Nazareth, who was crucified. He has risen; he is not here. See the place where they laid him. But go, tell his disciples and Peter that he is going before you to Galilee. There you will see him, just as he told you (Mark 16:6–7).

The women ran to the disciples, fearful, but at the same time full of new wonder and joy. Apparently, they had chosen a different road, for Peter and John did not encounter them on their way to the tomb. Mary Magdalene had come to them and had told them that the Lord had been taken from the tomb, and she did not know what people had done with him. Peter immediately ran ahead, but John overtook him, and arrived at the tomb first. He glanced inside, and then followed Peter, who by then had arrived, too, and without hesitation had entered the burial chamber. They did not see any

---

7. From John 20:19 it is clear that the angel rolling away the stone was not needed for Jesus to get *out* of the tomb, but for his followers to get *into* the tomb.

angels, but they did see the linen cloths in which Jesus had been wrapped. The face cloth lay folded up in a place by itself. It was an orderly scene, not the kind of disorder one would expect in the case of a theft.

At that moment, it dawned on John. The possibility of the resurrection had not occurred to the disciples for a moment, but now John suddenly remembered Jesus' own words: "The Son of Man must suffer many things, . . . and be killed, and on the third day be raised." Slowly the men returned home, marveling about what might have happened.

13.2 The First Appearances
13.2.1 The Women and Peter

Apparently, Mary Magdalene had followed the two men to the tomb at a slower speed, and now it was her turn to enter the burial chamber (John 20:11-18; Mark 16:9-11). She too saw the angels, who asked her why she was weeping. She answered: "Because they have taken away my Lord, and I do not know where they have laid him."[8] She did not wait for a reply and left the burial chamber. Through her tears, she saw in the garden a strange man, who asked her, "Woman, why are you weeping? Whom are you seeking?" She thought that it was the gardener, and asked him whether *he* had laid "him" in another place. The stranger uttered just one word: "Mary!" Then her eyes were opened,[9] and she exclaimed, "Rabboni!" (i.e., Teacher). She had recognized Jesus, and fell at his feet. However, she had to learn that she could not cling to him because the risen Jesus would return to his Father. That message she had to pass on to the disciples. It was with respect to them that Jesus now spoke for the first time of "my brothers," and about "*your* Father . . . *your* God."

Mary hurried back to the disciples, who were sitting to-

---

8. Her words remind us of those of the bride in Song 3:1–3 (Grün 2002, 38). Regarding her encounter with Jesus, see Berger (2004, 244–46).
9. And her ears as well: the good shepherd "calls his own sheep by name and leads them out" (John 10:3; cf. vv. 3–5 and 27).

gether in sadness. "I have seen the *Lord!*" she exclaimed, and told them what he had said to her. The grieving company simply could not believe it.[10] Somewhat later, the other women arrived, reporting how they, too, had seen Jesus (Matt. 28:9-10). He had met them halfway, and had greeted them in the usual way. They had fallen at his feet, and he had told them that they had to go to Galilee, to meet him there. The disciples were possibly on the edge of irritation, for they simply *could* not believe such girl talk.

During the course of that Sunday, one of them changed his mind: Simon Peter. This was because Jesus also appeared to *him* (Luke 24:34; 1 Cor. 15:5). The Bible does not tell us what they discussed, but we may assume that they spoke of Peter's denial of the Master, of his deep remorse, and of Jesus' forgiveness. When Peter, too, told the others that he had seen Jesus, and had spoken with him, the disciples had no choice but to believe him. A profound ecstasy came over them. In the meantime, most of the other disciples had joined Peter and John. They sat together on this wondrous day in the house where they were staying, the doors closed for fear of the Jewish leaders.

By then, these leaders had understood, too, that strange things had happened in the garden of the tomb (Matt. 28:11-15). The fleeing guards had come to them to report what they had seen, after which the serious matter was discussed in the Jewish Council. They feared that the empty tomb would cause a stir, and that belief in Jesus among the people could be inflamed again. Faith in a risen Jesus would be stronger and more invincible than faith in a Jesus who had not died! They decided to give the soldiers much money along with orders that the latter spread the story that the disciples had

---

10. According to the Jewish law, a woman could not serve as a witness, except when she had to declare in court that a man had died, so that the widow could remarry (Rosh Hashanah 22a). According to Lapide (1983, 96), it is ironic that in the Gospels, women testified concerning a man who had come back to life.

come during the night, as they (the guards) were asleep, and that they had stolen the body of Jesus. This highly implausible lie was spread vigorously among the Jews, and kept many of them away from the truth.

13.2.2 The Emmaus Disciples

At dusk on that same Sunday, two of Jesus' followers who were not apostles were walking from Jerusalem to the village of Emmaus, where they lived, some two hours away (Luke 24:13-35).[11] While they were speaking about all that had happened, Jesus joined them, but due to some divine intervention[12] they did not recognize him. Jesus asked them what they were talking about. They stood still, looking sad; did this stranger not know what had occurred in Jerusalem with Jesus of Nazareth? They had presumed this Jesus was the Messiah, but now it was the third day since he had been crucified. That very morning the tomb had been found empty, and some women claimed that they had seen angels. But that was all they could tell. Remarkably, the stranger did know about the matter, for he rebuked their unbelief, and began to explain in detail from the Old Testament that the Messiah had to endure all these sufferings in order to enter into his glory.

Having arrived in Emmaus, Cleopas[13] and his companion (wife?) insisted that the stranger stay with them because night had fallen. He accepted their invitation, and during the meal he functioned as their host. He said the blessing, broke the bread, and gave it to them. Then suddenly their eyes were opened; was it the wounds in his hands that awakened

---

11. The precise location of this village is unknown; at least five locations have been proposed, within a range of 60 stadia (60 times c. 185 m = c. 11.1 km = c. 7 miles), or perhaps (according to a less reliable reading) 160 stadia (c. 29.6 km = 18.4 miles).
12. Cf. Gen. 19:11; 2 Kings 6:18; 2 Cor. 3:14–16, which actually speaks of a (temporary) blinding as a divine judgment.
13. Some claim that this name is Aramaic *Chalphai*, in Greek: Cl(e)opas (cf. John 19:25) or Halphaios (Alpheus; cf. Matt. 10:3 par.; Acts 1:13); these names have often been thought to be identical (e.g., by Jerome). Others argue that Cleopas is an abbreviation of Cleopatros.

them? However, at the very moment they recognized Jesus, he disappeared (cf. Acts 8:39). The two looked at each other, and acknowledged what his wonderful exposition of the Scriptures had meant to them—and now it became evident who had been the expositor! Delightfully, they walked those two hours—now in the dark—back to Jerusalem. There they found ten of the twelve disciples (minus Judas and Thomas; see below), at least four women, and perhaps other followers, who in the meantime had become convinced that the Lord had risen. The Emmaus disciples could now confirm this with their wonderful experience.[14]

There may have been *many* more followers of Jesus present at this time, considering that, after the Lord's ascension, one hundred twenty followers were waiting for the Holy Spirit (Acts 1:15), such as Joseph Barsabbas and Matthias and other anonymous disciples (v. 23) and "many" women (Luke 8:3); think also of the seventy (or seventy-two) disciples of Luke 10:1, 17. In 1 Corinthians 15:6 we read of "more than five hundred brothers" who saw the risen Lord. Nicodemus and Joseph of Arimathea no doubt belonged to the secret followers (John 19:38–39), just like Cleopas (Luke 24:18), the owner of the colt (19:33–34), the owner of the upper room (Matt. 26:18), along with Mary, the mother of (John) Mark (Acts 12:12), and Mark himself (people have often thought he is the young man mentioned in Mark 14:51–52).

---

14. The liberal New Testament scholar John Dominic Crossan, a prominent member of the Jesus Seminar, was quoted in Ford and Higton (2002, 427), to say that the Emmaus story is a metaphorical condensation of the first years of Christian doctrine and practice into one parable-like afternoon. Emmaus never happened. Emmaus always happens. Dietrich Bonhoeffer (1967, 489) said something similar, but he at least believed in the reality of the risen Lord. He argued that even today the Unknown One meets people in such a way that they can only ask the question, "Who are you?," no matter how often they try to avoid it. The encounter with Jesus is not the same as the encounter with Socrates and Goethe. It is impossible to avoid the person of Jesus because he lives. It *is* possible to avoid Goethe, for he is dead.

13.2.3 The Twelve and Many Others

It was a joyful company there in that house. But the most joyous was yet to happen. As they reclined at table, Jesus suddenly appeared in their midst (Luke 24:36-49; John 20:19-23). His resurrection body was not stopped by closed doors and windows. Their first response was shock. Was this a phantom? Jesus reassured them: "Peace be with you!" He reproached them for their unbelief and showed them his pierced hands and side, so that they could see that it was really him. They were even allowed to touch him,[15] to determine that he was not a ghost but a human being of flesh and bones. The last doubt of the rejoicing disciples was eliminated when, before their eyes, Jesus ate a piece of broiled fish.

It has been argued, and perhaps rightly so, that Jesus' resurrection body was indeed "flesh and bones" (Luke 24:39), *not* "flesh and blood," as his body had been before his death (cf. Heb. 2:14). This is because he had given his blood as a sacrifice (Matt. 26:28; Heb. 9:7, 14), and "flesh and blood" cannot inherit the kingdom of God (1 Cor. 15:50). This question is related to the more profound question concerning the differences between Jesus' mortal body and his resurrection body (see §13.7).

After having eaten, Jesus began to explain that his sufferings, death, and resurrection had been the necessary fulfilment of the words of the prophets. Only in this way could repentance for the forgiveness of sins be proclaimed from now on in his name to all nations. And as the first witnesses of his resurrection, *they* were being called to do this. As the Father had sent him, so now the risen Lord was sending them. However, he ordered them to begin their preaching only after they had received the Holy Spirit in Jerusalem. With a view toward this, he breathed on them (cf. God's breathing in Gen. 2:7, and

---

15. We may assume a distinction between the "touching" (*krateō*) by the women, which Jesus allowed (Matt. 28:9), and the "touching" (*haptō*, here in the sense of "holding") by Mary Magdalene, which was not allowed (John 20:17).

cf. 1 Cor. 15:45, Jesus as the life-giving spirit), and said, "Receive Holy Spirit." Notice the lack of the article here, which seems to underscore the preliminary character of this granting of the Spirit; the *person* of the Spirit would not descend before the next upcoming day of Pentecost (Acts 2:1-13).[16]

That evening, Thomas had not been present among the disciples. His enthusiastic friends visited him and said: "We have seen the Lord!" (John 20:24-29). Thomas refused to believe it; he would believe only if, with his own fingers, he were to touch the wounds in Jesus' hands and side. The next Sunday evening, Thomas was persuaded to be present. Jesus appeared again with his greeting of peace, and immediately addressed Thomas by inviting him to do as he had wished. But Thomas no longer needed to touch Jesus' wounds; he was already convinced. Ashamed as well as joyful, he bowed down and stammered, "My Lord and my God!" He received one more reproach: he had believed only after he had seen. Blessed would be the millions who, throughout the ages, would come to faith without having seen what Thomas was now seeing.

13.3 Later Appearances
13.3.1 In Galilee

The risen Christ appeared several times more to both individuals and groups, on one occasion to more than five hundred followers at a time, many of whom could subsequently testify of this appearance (1 Cor. 15:6). Jesus also appeared to his (half- or step-)brother James (v. 7), who during Jesus' ministry had not believed in him (John 7:5). Perhaps it was this event that led to his conversion;[17] at any rate, in Acts 1:14, we find Jesus' brothers among the early believers. Later, James became a prominent leader of the congregation in Jerusalem, and the author of the epistle of James (Gal. 1:19; 2:9; Acts 12:17;

---
16. See vol. II/3 in this series, chapter 6.
17. This had possibly occurred much earlier, since tradition identifies him as one of the "seventy" mentioned in Luke 10:1.

15:13-21; 21:18). Around AD 62, James suffered martyrdom in Jerusalem.[18]

As we saw, both before and after his death and resurrection, Jesus had told his disciples that they would meet their risen Master in Galilee. Therefore, when the week of the Feast of Unleavened Bread ended, the disciples traveled to the land of their birth, and waited. The fishermen among them resumed their former craft. Seven of them took a boat out on the Sea of Galilee, but did not catch anything that entire night (John 21:1-14). Disappointed, they returned to the shore in the early morning, where they saw an unknown man standing on the beach, who asked them whether they had caught anything edible. After their negative response, the man advised them to cast their net on the other side of the boat. This time, they caught a net full of fish. The *sensitive* John was the first to recognize Jesus, and the *energetic* Peter immediately jumped overboard to wade to Jesus. The others dragged the net ashore. Jesus had prepared a charcoal fire along with a meal of fish (strictly speaking, he did not need *their* fish) and bread. They ate breakfast together.

During this meal, Peter was reinstated among the disciples (John 21:15-23). At the very time when Peter was profoundly humbled, Jesus entrusted to him the highest ministry: tending and feeding the Shepherd's sheep, in particular, the lambs. Jesus also foretold that Peter would suffer martyrdom, and alluded to the fact that John would survive all of the apostles. According to tradition, both predictions were fulfilled literally: Peter was crucified in Rome (c. AD 64), and John died at a very advanced age in Ephesus (c. 90-100).

13.3.2 Once More in Jerusalem

Jesus must have appeared to his disciples many other times, for Luke writes that to the apostles Jesus "presented himself alive ... by many proofs, appearing to them during forty days

---

18. Flavius Josephus, *Jewish Antiquities* 20.9.1; Eusebius, *Historia Ecclesiae* 2.23.1–18.

Jesus' Resurrection and Ascension

and speaking about the kingdom of God" (Acts 1:2-3). On one of these occasions—it was near a mountain in Galilee, where the Master had made an appointment with them—he gave them the famous Great Commission:

> All authority in heaven and on earth has been given to me. Go therefore and make disciples of all nations, baptizing them in the name of the Father and of the Son and of the Holy Spirit, teaching them to observe all that I have commanded you. And behold, I am with you always, to the end of the age (Matt. 28:18-20; cf. Mark 16:15).

To this Mark adds these words of Jesus:

> Whoever believes and is baptized will be saved, but whoever does not believe will be condemned. And these signs will accompany those who believe: in my name they will cast out demons; they will speak in new tongues; they will pick up serpents with their hands; and if they drink any deadly poison, it will not hurt them; they will lay their hands on the sick, and they will recover (vv. 16-18).[19]

The last encounter with the disciples occurred again in Jerusalem. It was a Thursday, the fortieth day after Jesus' resurrection (Acts 1:3). The disciples were still curious whether Jesus would now establish the Messianic kingdom for Israel (vv. 6-8). Jesus did not contradict this, or condemn the question as such—as many have suggested—but explained to them that the time had not yet arrived for this to happen. The Father had determined when it *would* happen; in the meantime, the disciples had to wait in Jerusalem until the moment they would receive the Holy Spirit. After this, beginning at Jerusalem, then in Judea and Samaria, and then to the far corners of the world, they would testify this about the living Lord: "Thus it is written, that the Christ should suffer and on the third day rise from the dead, and that repentance for the forgiveness of sins should be proclaimed in his name to all

---

19. See *EDR* 1:102, 265, 287-88, 315.

nations, beginning from Jerusalem" (cf. Luke 24:46–47).

After having said this, he took his disciples outside the city, to the Mount of Olives, to the place where the road goes to Bethany (v. 50). There, he lifted his hands, and as he was blessing them, he was carried up from them (v. 51). The disciples watched until a cloud took him out of their sight. As they were still gazing into the sky, they saw two angels, who told them that one day this Jesus would return from heaven in the same *way* as they saw him go into heaven (Acts 1:6–11) — and, we may add, at the same *place* (Zech. 14:4). The Lord who had been taken up went to sit down at the right hand of God in heaven (Mark 16:19; cf. Ps. 110:1). The disciples returned to Jerusalem with great joy. They could be found in the temple, where they were continually blessing God, waiting for the pouring out of the Holy Spirit (Luke 24:52–53; Acts 1:12–14).

13.4 The Significance of Jesus' Resurrection
13.4.1 A Historical Turning Point

Biblical theology finds its clearest starting point and interpretative key in the resurrection of Jesus Christ.[20] Even if liberalism has often contradicted this, all theology stands or falls with the historical, bodily resurrection of Christ; it forms the heart of Christian faith. It is therefore no wonder that so many attacks have been directed toward this very resurrection.

When it comes to the resurrection of Jesus Christ, only three options are available: either it is an illusion, a delusion, a form of self-conceit to which a number of *good* people have fallen prey. Or it is the most refined and noxious lie in world history, spread by *evil* people, who have perfidiously misled billions of people. Or it is the most important, most impressive, and most influential fact of world history.[21] One thing is

---

20. Filson (1956, 25).
21. From the rich apologetic literature concerning the resurrection, I have consulted the following: Berkhof (1981, 346–49); Berkouwer (1965, chapter 7); Green (1967); Stott (1971); McDowell (1972); Tenney (1972); Ladd (1975); Riss (1977); Wilson (1977); Thierry (1978); Craig (1988; 1989); Vos (1990); Pannenberg (1994, 2:343–72); G. R. Osborne (*DJG* 678–87);

certain: belief in the resurrection of Jesus constitutes the heart of Christianity. It was not a moral preaching of love, peace, and righteousness that formed the kernel of the message of Jesus' first witnesses, but the proclamation of the *historical fact* of the resurrection (Acts 2:32; 3:15; 4:10; 5:30). This is because the resurrection is the necessary demonstration of the power and divinity of Jesus of Nazareth (Rom. 1:4), of the finished work of atonement (4:24). It is also the triumph over Satan and his powers (Heb. 2:14-15; 1 John 3:8), and the absolute condition for the forgiveness and redemption of believers (1 Cor. 15:14-19), and for a new way of life (Rom. 6:4; Col. 2:12; 3:1). Among those who have heard and understood the gospel, from the time of Jesus' resurrection only those who believe with their hearts that God has indeed raised him from the dead will be saved (Rom. 10:9).

Therefore, in my view it is entirely contrary to the spirit of the New Testament to assert: "The resurrection stories in the four Gospels are not meant to inform the reader about historical facts. They have first and foremost a *theological* significance. Therefore, they cannot be used as prooftexts for the *fact* that Jesus was raised from the dead."[22] As happens so often, theology and history are here being played off against each other. For the apostles who preached (Acts 2-5), and also for the apostle Paul, the *historical fact* of Jesus' resurrection has tremendous theological significance; but according to them, this significance evaporates if the *historical fact* did not exist. As long as one abandons the anti-supernaturalistic

---

Verkuyl (1992, chapter 15); Bockmuehl (1994, 147–55; 2001, 102–18); Brown (1994a, 162–70); LaHaye (1997); Van de Beek (2002a, 176–80); Stein (1996, 259–76); McGrath (2008); Strobel (1998; 2004); Wright in Borg and Wright (1999, 111–27, and the contradiction by Borg, 129–42); Walker (2000); Wright (2003); Zacharias (2004); Berger (2004, chapter 18); Van Bruggen (1998, 167–87); G. Fracke in Chung (2005, 67–89); partly critical: Van Gennep et al. (1989; with contributions by F. O. van Gennep, R. Zuurmond, H. J. de Jonge, H. Berkhof, M. R. Spindler, and M. de Jonge); Theissen and Merz (1998, 474–511); Knight (2004, 193–223).

22. Den Heyer (2003, 89).

bias that "corpses cannot become alive,"[23] it is not difficult to acknowledge that the empty tomb, the empty shroud, and the appearances described by Jesus' followers are best explained by assuming that Jesus rose from the dead.

Someone has observed that

> [a]n irony of history lies in the fact that in a day when people wish to shed the worldview of the New Testament through "demythologizing" [*ala* Bultmann], people are busy at the same time attempting to rise above the dualistic [soul/body] dichotomy and regain appreciation for the significance of the "body."[24]

This means that, in our time, a view involving a kind of "spiritual" resurrection of Jesus, in which the body is and remains dead while the spirit comes alive, is no longer possible. For without a bodily resurrection, no spiritual resurrection is possible, since body and spirit are one. A resurrection from death is a resurrection of the *body* (cf. Matt. 27:52; Rom. 8:11; Rev. 20:13, and the implication of Matt. 10:28). The fact that the apostle sometimes spoke of a being raised in a spiritual sense (Eph. 2:6; Col. 2:12) and called the resurrection body a "spiritual" body (1 Cor. 15:44) — which is something completely different from an "immaterial" body — does not contradict this at all.

Jesus' resurrection is the axis of world history. It cannot be compared to the earlier resurrections of people like Lazarus, who returned to natural life and must have died again later.[25]

---

23. Brown (1994a, 25 note) claims that historicity is not determined by what we think to be possible or likely, but by the age and reliability of the evidence (cf. 62).
24. Cf. Berkouwer (1965, 187–88; our translation).
25. This was not seen by the orthodox Jewish New Testament scholar Pinchas Lapide, who wrote somewhere that Paul was mistaken when he called Jesus the "firstfruits" of deceased believers (1 Cor. 15:20; cf. Col. 1:18), since six persons had been raised before him (1 Kings 17:22; 2 Kings 4:34–35; 13:21; Luke 7:14–15; 8:54–55; John 11:43–44). See, however, his lovely booklet on the resurrection (Lapide [1983]), in which he testifies of his faith in Jesus' resurrection, also in opposition to Christian modernists. The orthodox Jew David Flusser (2007, 154–55) was convinced that reliable reports

In contrast to this, the resurrected Jesus is the "firstfruits of those who have fallen asleep" (1 Cor. 15:20), the first one belonging to a totally new order of existence, in which sin, death, and Satan no longer have any power, an order in which incorruptible life is reigning (2 Tim. 1:10 JUB; 1 Cor. 15:42-44, 52-54). Jesus was not a phantom but a living, tangible person of flesh and bones — yet, in his resurrection body, Jesus entered the locked room of the disciples. He was now a human being of a different order, a new world, the resurrection world. Those of this higher world who make themselves visible, audible, as well as tangible within the empirical world are said to "appear"[26] to people (in addition to Jesus, see Matt. 27:53).

In the resurrection of Jesus Christ, *the* resurrection that will be experienced by all people becomes manifest — although after their physical resurrection, unbelievers will still be as "dead" as before (Rev. 20:12). Jesus' resurrection entails the breakthrough of the new life that one day will become fully manifest in the new creation (cf. Rom. 8:18-25). In Jesus' resurrection, the resurrection of the creation has begun. In his own person he embodies resurrection and life (John 11:25).

13.4.2 Scientific Argumentation

Throughout the centuries, the historical evidence for Jesus' resurrection has been investigated not only by theologians but also by historians[27] and lawyers[28] — people who are used to

---

existed that the crucified One appeared to Peter and others (1 Cor. 15:3–8).
26. This meaning is present is several Greek verbs: in addition to *horaō*, there is *phainō, phaneroō, emphanizō,* and *optanomai*.
27. Historian Thomas Arnold (1859, 324) wrote that for many years he had studied the histories of other times, and investigated and weighed the evidence of those who wrote those histories, and yet he knew of no fact in the history of humanity that, to the understanding of a fair investigator, had been demonstrated by better and fuller evidence than the great God-given sign that Christ died and rose from death.
28. Greenleaf (1965); Morison (1972); Anderson (1968) described the conversion of the criminal justice lawyer Frank Morison, who planned to write a book *against* the resurrection but was overwhelmed by the arguments for it; Josh McDowell (1997, 87–95) had a similar experience. Smith (1965,

evaluating declarations of witnesses and the claimed historicity of events. After extensive examination, many of them have testified that the historical and judicial evidence for the resurrection is extensive and irrefutable, and that no fact in history has been documented and demonstrated better and more convincingly than the resurrection of Jesus. Only prejudiced opinions that any resurrection is inherently unacceptable have discredited the evidence for Jesus' resurrection. Thus, people who have no clear idea of the nature, scope, and authority of the natural sciences have believed that a resurrection from death is scientifically unacceptable. They fail to realize that the natural sciences may describe the normal course of things in nature but cannot say anything for or against anything that is unique, miraculous, or supernatural, or what they *think* to be unique, miraculous, or supernatural.[29]

There have always been people for whom the resurrection of Jesus was unacceptable, not so much because of intellectual objections, but because of their conscience.[30] Naturally, for humans the resurrection is unacceptable because they are sinners—sinners who are fully aware of the very great consequences for their own responsibilities, for their present lives, and for their eternal future *if* Jesus Christ were really alive. *If* he is living right now at the right hand of God, in a glorified state, he will also be returning to judge the living and the dead (Acts 10:42). Accepting or not accepting Jesus' resurrection is not primarily a scientific but an existential matter. Of course, this is not to deny that the resurrection is a historical fact suf-

---

423–25) quoted the lawyer Lord Lyndhurst (John Singleton Copley, d. 1863), Green (1967, 53–54) the British justice Lord Darling, Stott (1971, 47) the lawyer Sir Edward Clarke. All these lawyers testified that, in a legal trial, the evidence for Jesus' resurrection would be accepted as legal, valid, and convincing (or similar terms).

29. We often encounter the same phenomenon with respect to the ministry of healing, where miraculous healings are simply dismissed either as scientifically impossible or as scientifically explainable, whereas before the event these critics had declared any healing to be inconceivable.

30. See more extensively, Ouweneel (2005a, chapter 16).

ficiently convincing to the intellect (cf. the way Paul adduces rational arguments for the resurrection in 1 Cor. 15:1-9), because the heart and the intellect are not opposed to each other; reason is nothing else than a function of the human heart.[31]

Of course, the reliability of the resurrection as a historical fact depends primarily on the trustworthiness of the statements by the witnesses, and thus of the Gospels in the New Testament. These were written by direct eyewitnesses, or by men who were closely associated with the eyewitnesses (cf. Luke 1:2). Luke tells us that he wrote his Gospel on the basis of careful historical investigation (vv. 3-4), and "many infallible proofs' (Acts 1:3 NKJV). The Gospels were written within a few decades after the resurrection, that is, at a time that numerous eyewitnesses of Jesus' ministry (including hostile ones!) were still alive. If the Gospels contained false stories about the resurrection, these would have been contradicted by many opponents, and it would have been impossible for Christianity to expand so quickly and widely. Indeed, the early Christians were confronted with many adversaries, among them people who had been in Jerusalem at the time of the crucifixion. These opponents fiercely combated the Christians — but they could not catch them telling lies. Rather these opponents themselves spread lies (Matt. 28:11-15).

What is more, we find that the Gospel writers tell us very honestly that even Jesus' closest followers had difficulty with the resurrection: "[T]he eleven disciples went to Galilee, to the mountain to which Jesus had directed them. And when they saw him they worshiped him, but some doubted" (Matt. 28:16-17). "But they were startled and frightened and thought they saw a spirit. . . . And while they still disbelieved for joy and were marveling, he said to them, 'Have you anything here to eat?'" (Luke 24:37, 41). These doubts, fears, and amazement make the story all the more credible: one does not find such reactions in piously invented legends, but they *are* found in

---

31. See extensively, Ouweneel (2014).

authentic testimonies.[32]

One of the most remarkable facts in the Gospels relating to the resurrection is that the disciples were not the only ones to speak about the resurrection: Jesus himself had predicted many times that, after his crucifixion, he would rise from death. He even foretold that this would occur on the third day (Matt. 16:21; 17:22-23; 20:17-28; 26:32 par.; see also John 10:17-18; 11:25).[33] Here is a man who not only predicted his own martyrdom—which to some extent could be foreseen—but also announced that a few days later he would return from death! Of course, the critics can claim that the Gospel writers simply put such words into Jesus' mouth. However, there is strong evidence that Jesus must have said something like this, for we saw in §12.3.1 that during the pre-trial before Caiaphas, one statement by Jesus was ascertained beyond any doubt, namely, that in three days he could rebuild the broken-down "temple," that is, his own body. Jesus undeniably announced his own resurrection on the third day. In itself, this is not a proof for the resurrection; but it does constitute powerful support for other evidence of the resurrection.

13.4.3 Alternative Hypotheses

People have tried many times to discredit the historical evidence for Jesus' resurrection. Let us briefly look at the most important hypotheses.

(1) *Jesus did not die at all.* According to this view of the German rationalist Karl H. G. Venturini, Jesus lost consciousness on the cross, recovered in the coolness of the tomb, and then appeared to his disciples. But this view totally overlooks the horrible injury to Jesus' limbs, his utter weakness through a great loss of blood, the lethal nature of the five open and unattended wounds, the stiffly wrapped cloths, and the heavy

---
32. Van de Beek (2002a, 176–77).
33. In Jewish counting, the Sunday is the third day after Friday. The New Testament also uses the expressions "after three days" (Mark 8:31; 9:31; 10:34), and "three days and three nights" (Matt. 12:40), in which parts of a day/night are counted as a full day/night.

stone in front of the tomb. Moreover, the critical modernist David F. Strauss argued that it is inconceivable that a half dead person crawls out of a tomb, needs care and treatment, in the end succumbs to his wounds, and yet gave his disciples the impression that he was the victor over death, the Prince of life—as they proclaimed afterward.[34]

(2) *The body was stolen by the disciples.* This was the slander spread by the Jewish leaders (Matt. 28:11-15), but it is easily refuted. First, the disciples have had neither the courage nor the ability to do this. A well-trained guard stood in front of the tomb, and the heavy stone (weighing perhaps more than 4,000 pounds, according to the custom of the time) had been sealed with the imperial seal, which no sensible person would dare to break. Second, the disciples would not have considered committing theft. They were far too desperate (think of the Emmaus disciples and the disciples' unbelief toward the women) and far too scared (they sat anxiously together, having the doors locked for fear of the Jews). Third, the alleged theft of the body and subsequent worldwide spread of the lie of the resurrection conflicted entirely with the high moral standard of their teaching and of their own lives, and with the steadfastness of their faith in the midst of all persecution, and their preparedness to die for their alleged lie. From all this, it is evident that the disciples themselves firmly believed that Jesus had risen.

(3) *The body was carried to another place* (either by Joseph of Arimathea, or by the Jews or the Romans). At first glance, this seems a rather realistic explanation. However, we cannot think of any sensible reason why Joseph would have removed the body. If he did, he must have done so during the night from Saturday to Sunday. As a disciple of Jesus, would he have allowed Christianity to be based on the misunderstanding of the empty tomb? Would he not have honestly pointed out the real tomb? And what is more, would the Jews

---

34. Strauss (1972).

not have known about this new tomb, and have hastily called attention to it as soon as the early church began to grow after the Day of Pentecost? This would also have happened if the Jews or the Romans had removed the body. Nothing was easier for the Jews, who would have known the new tomb, than to triumphantly produce the dead body of Jesus. This would have suppressed the apostles' preaching once and for all. Instead of this, the Jews spread the rumor that the body had been stolen. This proves that they could not deny that the tomb was empty — they never denied the guards' report — and that they did not know (or did not want to know) what had caused its being empty. Moreover, no hypothesis about a stolen or removed body can explain the neatly arranged cloths of the dead body still in the tomb, or the guards fleeing from the tomb.

(4) *The women were mistaken about the correct tomb.* This view, defended by Kirsopp Lake and others, theorized that it was so dark on that Sunday morning that the women mistook another, empty tomb for the tomb of Jesus. Such an absurd theory is possible only by denying a number of biblical facts. First, Mark 16:2 tells that the women arrived at the tomb just *after* sunrise. Second, John 20:15 shows that we may fairly assume that a gardener was already at work. Third, if the resurrection story were based on a mistake concerning the tomb, the Jews would have hastened to identify the correct tomb and to produce the body. In order to make his view more likely, Lake suggested that, only after some weeks had passed, the women would have told their story — in the meantime embellished — to the disciples, who on that Sunday were still fleeing to Galilee. However, it is unrealistic to suppose that the disciples would have been far away from Jerusalem, whereas the female followers of Jesus would have stayed behind for several weeks in the dangerous city. Moreover, one of them was probably the mother of two disciples (Salome), and another woman was possibly also the mother of two disciples (Mary, Clopas' wife).

13.5 Three Facts
13.5.1 The Empty Tomb
No matter what one thinks of the resurrection stories, four facts are beyond any reasonable doubt. First, the tomb was empty. On the next Sunday morning, the tomb where Jesus had been laid on Friday night was undeniably empty (apart from the cloths). It can hardly be disputed that the people saw the correct tomb.

Second, the emptiness of the tomb cannot be explained by claiming that a man who was only apparently dead regained his consciousness and crawled out of the tomb.

Third, it is inconceivable that the body had been stolen.

Fourth, it is equally inconceivable that others had legally removed the body and buried it elsewhere.

Look again at the broad picture. The guards have fled filled with fear. The very heavy stone had been rolled away, definitely not by the guards, nor by any thieves. The cloths in which the body had been wrapped lay there, neatly arranged. Not only was the tomb empty, but so was the shroud.

13.5.2 The Changed Disciples
Then there was the problem that the disciples underwent a profound change in their behavior within a short period of time. Imagine a clinical psychologist coming forward to explain this amazing change. I have mentioned this point before, but I wish to stress it a little more strongly.

On Sunday morning, the followers of Jesus formed a desperate, pathetic group of cowards. They had lost all self-confidence, sat anxiously together behind closed doors (John 20:19), and did not believe the women's reports of the resurrection. However, that very same evening, and surely fifty days later, these cowards had been transformed into bold witnesses of Jesus, who fervently and fearlessly preached the message about the risen Lord. Each one of them was prepared to give his life for him — and in fact, each one of them, except the apostle John, subsequently suffered martyrdom.

How can we explain this bizarre transformation? Is it at all conceivable that these men simply invented the story of the resurrection, and spread it throughout the world either as a form of self-delusion or as deliberate deceit? People who do such things expect a certain positive result. But what advantage did these men derive from their delusion or deceit? Did their total commitment to the risen Jesus bring them honor, wealth, higher social status, or material benefits? Their sole reward was that they were beaten, stoned, thrown before the lions, tortured, and crucified. However, no one could stop them from speaking and witnessing about the risen Jesus. What could explain such behavior other than the resurrection itself?

13.5.3 The Appearances

There are numerous confirmations of the empty tomb and of the radical transformation of the disciples, which the disciples themselves provide: they saw the risen Jesus, they touched him, they spoke with him, and this went on for no fewer than forty days (Acts 1:3). No one has begun to resolve successfully the problems mentioned in the two previous sections, problems associated with explanations less plausible than the one offered by the disciples: Jesus had risen from the dead.

However, plausibility is not proof. The disciples testified that Jesus had appeared to them. But how reliable and acceptable are their testimonies? They communicate the very strong impression that they were not imposters. However, could these simple, well-intentioned people not have become victims of hallucinations, or other illusions, and thus have deceived themselves and others?

Three considerations clarify why this is hardly conceivable. First, one person could obviously mistake a hallucination for a genuine appearance. But how could a large group of people hallucinate simultaneously without an objectively perceivable phenomenon having occurred? Jesus did appear

Jesus' Resurrection and Ascension

several times to large groups of people. On the first Sunday evening, at least sixteen or seventeen[35] (probably many more) people were present. At the ascension of Jesus, probably many more were present, if we take into account the hundred and twenty disciples who were together in the temple (Acts 1:15) in the days immediately thereafter. Most importantly, we recall the five hundred brothers to whom Jesus appeared at the same time (1 Cor. 15:6). The majority of them were still alive in Paul's day, so that he could direct his readers to them for testimony about what they had seen. It is inconceivable that five hundred disciples had seen the same hallucination at the same time.

Second, one of the remarkable aspects of Jesus' appearances was his tangibility. The disciples did not see the ghost of a dead person, as Hamlet supposedly did in the beginning of Shakespeare's tragedy *Hamlet*. On the contrary, the risen Jesus could be touched and held. He shared many meals with his followers, beginning the first Sunday night, with the Emmaus disciples and all the gathered disciples, then later at the Sea of Galilee, and apparently on several other occasions.

Third, perhaps one might imagine that the loyally devoted Mary Magdalene, or the soft, sensitive John would be given to hallucination (although, normally, devoted and sensitive people do not get hallucinations, either). But this is inconceivable with certain other people. The melancholic, critical Thomas was certainly not easily impressionable concerning the resurrection. The impulsive but rational Peter can hardly be imagined as a victim of phantom appearances. And what about James, Jesus' brother, a close relative who was highly skeptical about the person of Jesus, but who after Jesus' death became an ardent follower, the leader of the church in Jerusalem, and ultimately a martyr for Jesus? Everything we know about hallucinations contradicts the notion that, generally

---

35. Eleven apostles minus Thomas (John 20:24), plus the two Emmaus disciples, plus Mary the mother of Jesus, Mary Magdalene, Mary the mother of James, plus Johanna, and Susanna(?) (Luke 8:3; 23:49; 24:9, 33).

speaking, such people would be susceptible to hallucinations, let alone would be so radically transformed by them.

Most importantly, such an explanation can hardly be true for the man who underwent the greatest transformation. He was a brilliant rabbi, steeped in Judaism, entirely congenial to the spiritual leaders, fully convinced of the lie that Jesus' disciples had stolen his body. No opponent of the Jesus sect was more fervent than he was. However, from one day to the other, this man changed into an equally fervent Christian, the most gifted and devoted witness of the *living* Jesus. On several occasions, he testified that on the road to Damascus, he had seen Jesus in glory (Acts 9:1-19; 22:6-18; 26:12-18; cf. Acts 23:6; 1 Cor. 9:1; 15:8; Gal. 1:13-14; Phil. 3:4-6). Is it conceivable that a man like Saul of Tarsus became a Christian through a hallucination—something that he certainly was not subconsciously desiring? After years of solitude, during which he could critically evaluate his alleged hallucination, he never once doubted his experience. On the contrary, he became an astute defender of the historicity of the resurrection. Nothing can satisfactorily explain such a transformation—unless Saul of Tarsus really saw, and spoke with, the living Lord. Such conversions to Christ still occur, among Jews, Muslims and areligious people, conversions that have the same effect on the people involved. God transforms people with power; not just a little, or just halfway, but radically.

As we review all the arguments for the bodily resurrection of Jesus, the words of the great Jewish scholar Joseph Klausner seem appropriate. He argued that, had the four Gospel writers invented such credible and highly similar reports about the Nazarene, this would have been a miracle greater than all the miraculous acts of Jesus put together.[36]

13.6 Why No Public Appearance?
13.6.1 Three Reasons
One of the first Enlightenment theologians, Hermann Samuel

---
36. Quoted in Lapide (1983, 126).

Reimarus, raised a question that, at first sight, seems unanswerable. He wrote,

> Even if we had no other scruples concerning the resurrection of Jesus, the one that he did not appear publicly would be sufficient in itself to overthrow any plausibility; for it can never be reconciled with the purpose for which Jesus is supposed to have come into the world.[37]

The question seems logical: If Jesus appeared so many times to his followers, why did he never appear in public, to the entire world, or at least to the Jewish leaders, to Pilate and Herod, or to the emperor in Rome? The answer is not all that difficult. There are five possible answers.

First, the claim cannot be right that the non-public appearance of the risen Jesus is "sufficient in itself to overthrow any plausibility" of the resurrection story. If there are—as many believe—sufficient independent reasons to accept the *historical* fact of the resurrection of Jesus, these can never be discarded by a purely *theological* question. The fact that Jesus did not appear in public is a negative fact, an argument from silence, and does not change the historical arguments supporting the resurrection.

Second, the New Testament makes very clear why the risen Jesus did not appear to all people, or to the Jewish leaders. The apostle Peter said,

> God raised [Jesus] on the third day and made him to appear, not to all the people but to us who had been chosen by God as witnesses, who ate and drank with him after he rose from the dead. And he commanded us to preach to the people and to testify that he is the one appointed by God to be judge of the living and the dead (Acts 10:40-42).

To be considered as worthy of personally beholding the risen Lord, and thus to become a witness of him, one had to have been a friend of Jesus during his ministry on earth (cf. 13:30–

---

37. Reimarus (1778), quoted in Lapide (1983, 42).

31). Perhaps Jesus' brother or cousin James was the only exception (apart from Saul of Tarsus, but this was only after the ascension). At first, James did not believe in Jesus (John 7:5), but after the resurrection he received a prominent position in the early church (Acts 12:17; 15:13; 21:18; cf. also the other brothers: 1:14). The risen Jesus appeared separately to him (1 Cor. 15:7).

Third, people who refuse to accept God's Word would not recognize the risen Lord if he were to appear to them. This was the case already at that time, with Jesus' own followers: "And when they saw him they worshiped him, but some doubted" (Matt. 28:17). Jesus said, "If they do not hear Moses and the Prophets, neither will they be convinced if someone should rise from the dead" (Luke 16:31). This is very important: people will not accept anything as evidence unless they are *prepared* to view it as evidence.[38] As Blaise Pascal put it, "There is enough light for those who only desire to see, and enough obscurity for those who have a contrary disposition."[39] As Eduard Schweizer observed, "[P]roof cannot be given of Jesus' resurrection. Here, too, very much as in the crucifixion of Jesus, God exposes himself to scepticism [sic], doubt, and disbelief, renouncing anything that would compel men to believe."[40] Or, as I would argue, proofs can be objectively provided, but subjective certainty depends on the willingness of the hearers.

13.6.2 Two More Reasons

Fourth, why would the resurrection of Jesus be more credible if the Jewish leaders had seen him (assuming their willingness to admit that they had seen the risen Jesus)? Why is the testimony of trustworthy witnesses like the apostles insufficient, when it is just as credible as that of any outsider who would have seen him? Jesus said to Thomas, who had doubt-

---

38. Cf. Ouweneel (2005a, chapter 4) on the nature and meaning of evidence.
39. http://www.ccel.org/ccel/pascal/pensees.viii.html.
40. Schweizer (1971a, 49).

ed the testimony of the other disciples, "Have you believed because you have seen me? Blessed are those who have not seen and yet have believed" (John 20:29). This is the point at issue—faith. The disciples had not only personally seen the risen Jesus, but he needed also to become the object of their faith, as he had said shortly before his death: "You believe in God; believe also in me" (14:1 NIV). It is precisely because Jesus had appeared to them but would not be staying with them (cf. 20:17) that the risen Jesus had to become an object of faith.

In this respect, the disciples were no different from believers who had never beheld the risen Lord in person but who, through the Holy Spirit, know him as the object of faith, too. As Peter said, "Though you have not seen him, you love him. Though you do not now see him, you believe in him and rejoice with joy that is inexpressible and filled with glory, obtaining the outcome of your faith, the salvation of your souls" (1 Pet. 1:8–9).

Fifth, there is an eschatological reason. If the risen Lord would have appeared to all people, by definition the last day would have arrived: "Behold, he is coming with the clouds, and every eye will see him, even those who pierced him, and all tribes of the earth will wail on account of him" (Rev. 1:7). In other words, that Jesus did not appear to all people is related to the Messianic kingdom arriving at the second coming of Christ, not at his resurrection. In the meantime, his servants go out into the world in order to recruit followers for Jesus (cf. Matt. 28:19; Mark 16:15; Luke 24:46–47), "until the fullness of the Gentiles has come in" (Rom. 11:25). Between his ascension and his second coming, Jesus appears to people only by way of exception. In the New Testament, we know of Stephen (Acts 7:55–56), Saul of Tarsus (Acts 18:9; 22:14,18; 23:11; 26:16; 1 Cor. 9:1; 15:1), and the apostle John (Rev. 1:17; 5:6).[41]

---

41. In recent years some have reported that Jesus appeared to orthodox Jews and Muslims, especially in dreams, who as a consequence came to faith (see www.jesusvisions.org/chapt01.shtml and www.youtube.com/watch?v=7tL-

In the meantime, Christians "walk by faith, not by sight" (2 Cor. 5:7). The testimony of the apostles, having seen Jesus (cf. 1 Cor. 9:1), suffices for all other believers. This is all the more true because their testimony has been set forth in the New Testament. To paraphrase Luke 16:31, if they do not listen to the apostolic testimony in the New Testament, neither will they be convinced if someone should rise from the dead.

13.7 The Theological Significance of Jesus' Resurrection
13.7.1 Natural and Spiritual

The apostle Paul emphasized in his epistles that we can and must be fully convinced that our faith is based upon the well-determined historical fact of the bodily resurrection of Jesus, and not on a myth or a legend. I say "bodily" resurrection—apart from explaining the quality of Jesus' resurrection body (cf. 1 Cor. 15:35-49)—because some believe in a spiritual resurrection of Jesus, but not in a physical resurrection. Paul speaks differently: it was the *mortal* body of Jesus that had become alive again (cf. Rom. 8:11). In other words, Jesus rose from death with the body that he had before his death.[42] The belief that Jesus rose spiritually, while his corpse remained a corpse, is held by some out of pure bias, not because it can be reconciled with the statements of the apostles, either in Acts (1:22; 2:24, 31-32; 3:15; 4:10, 33; 5:30; 10:40-41; 13:30, 34, 37; 17:31; 26:23) or in the epistles (Rom. 4:24-25; 6:4-5, 9; 7:4; 8:11, 34; 10:9; 1 Cor. 6:14; 15:4, 12-17, 20; 2 Cor. 4:14; 5:15; Gal. 1:1; Eph. 1:20; 2:1; Phil. 3:10; Col. 2:12; 3:1; 1 Thess. 1:10; 4:14; 2 Tim. 2:8; 1 Pet. 1:3; 3:21).

People may say, of course, that they disagree with Paul on this matter; but they cannot assert that Paul leaves any room for an ethereal resurrection, not even in 1 Corinthians 15:44, "It is sown a natural body; it is raised a spiritual body. If there is a natural body, there is also a spiritual body." The "natural body" (Gk. *sōma psychikon*, the body as dominated by the

---

HQB–sxkY&NR).
42. Van de Beek (2002a, 180).

soul, i.e., the biotic-psychical body) is here being contrasted to the "spiritual body" Gk. *sōma pneumatikon*, the body as dominated by the spirit) — yet definitely a *body*. The Gospel writers tell us that this body could be touched and held (Matt. 28:9; John 20:17, 27), that the unsuspecting Emmaus disciples did not distinguish it from an ordinary body (Luke 24:13-31), and that Jesus could eat with this resurrection body (Luke 24:42-43; Acts 10:41).[43] Again, the Bible contradicts any suggestion that Jesus' corpse remained a corpse, which then supposedly appeared as a ghost.[44]

At the same time, Jesus' resurrected body was different.

(1) He no longer made ordinary visits to his disciples but simply and suddenly appeared, like angels appeared, and then suddenly disappeared from their sight (Mark 16:9; Luke 24:31, 34; Acts 9:17; 13:31; 26:16; 1 Cor. 15:5-8; cf. Matt. 27:53; Luke 9:8, 31; cf. Matt. 1:20; 2:13, 19; Luke 1:11; 22:43; 24:23; Acts 7:35).[45]

(2) He entered the room where they were staying while the doors were locked (John 20:19, 26), something we never read about before his death; this phenomenon explains why the angel rolled the stone away from the tomb not to let Jesus out, but to let the eyewitnesses in.

(3) When people recognize the risen Jesus, strange misunderstandings occur (Luke 24:16, 31; John 20:14; 21:7; cf. Matt. 28:17), partly because he could appear in various forms (Mark 16:12).

The apostle Paul tried to explain in what sense Jesus' resurrected body was different with this comparison: the former body relates to the resurrection body as a grain of wheat to

---

43. W. Kelly argued that Jesus, having a body, could eat, and having a spiritual body, did not need to eat (*BT* 9:181).
44. Before Jesus' death and resurrection, his disciples saw him at night on the lake thinking he was a phantom, a ghost (Matt. 14:26 par.); after the resurrection, this never happened to them.
45. He was "no longer bound to time and place," according to Verkuyl (1992, 250).

the full plant with blade and ear (1 Cor. 15:35-44); one could also say: as a flower bulb to the flower, or as a caterpillar to the butterfly.

13.7.2 Seven Truths

In the spiritual testament left to us by the aging apostle Paul (cf. Philem. 9) we read, "Keep your attention on Jesus Christ as risen from the dead" (2 Tim. 2:8 HCSB). All who do so in faith, all who confess with their mouth that Jesus is Lord, and believe in their heart that God raised Jesus from the dead (Rom. 10:9-10), may be convinced of the following seven truths.[46]

(1) Believers' sins are forgiven, they are justified by faith, and nothing can ever condemn them: ". . . us who believe in him who raised from the dead Jesus our Lord, who was delivered up for our trespasses and raised for our justification" (Rom. 4:25-5:2; see also Acts 13:30-39; 1 Cor. 15:17; 1 Thess. 1:10). The resurrection proves that God has accepted the work of Christ (cf. John 17:4-5).

(2) Believers are delivered from a senseless and empty, sinful life, and changed into new creatures in Jesus Christ, with a magnificent new meaning and destination (Rom. 7:4; 10:10-11; 2 Cor. 5:15-19).

(3) Through baptism, believers are united with Christ "in order that, just as Christ was raised from the dead by the glory of the Father, we too might walk in newness of life" (Rom. 6:4; cf. 2 Cor. 5:15; Col. 2:12; 1 Pet. 3:21).

(4) Believers receive the life of the risen Christ, so that God views them as (spiritually) raised – already now – together with Christ, and sitting with him in the heavenly places (Eph. 1:20-2:6; cf. Col. 2:12); the resurrection of believers is entailed in Jesus' resurrection.

(5) During their life of faith, believers are privileged to know that the risen Jesus at the right hand of God intercedes for them (Rom. 8:34; cf. Heb. 4:14-16; 7:25).

---

46. Cf. Van Genderen and Velema (2008, 493–96).

(6) Believers' actual, spiritual life exists where the risen Lord is: "If then you have been raised with Christ, seek the things that are above, where Christ is, seated at the right hand of God. Set your minds on things that are above, not on things that are on earth. For you have died, and your life is hidden with Christ in God" (Col. 3:1–3).

(7) If believers pass away before the second coming of Jesus, at this second coming they will be raised from the tomb, just like Jesus (Rom. 8:11; 1 Cor. 6:14; 15:12–23; 2 Cor. 4:14; Phil. 3:10–11; 1 Thess. 4:14; 1 Pet. 1:3).

The resurrection does not conflict with reason (*contra* the Enlightenment), it is not a myth (*contra* liberalism), it is not a phenomenon in the apostles' experience that can be dismissed on psychological grounds (*contra* kerygmatic theology), nor is it an event that surpasses all historical analysis (*contra* neo-orthodoxy). But neither is the resurrection simply an event that can be explained in historical categories, apart from its theological and especially its existential meaning. A person is saved not by believing in the *fact* of the resurrection as such, but by appropriating in one's personal life of faith the *everlasting value* of the historical, bodily resurrection of Jesus. Stated more clearly: a person is saved only by an existential encounter with the living Lord himself.

13.8 Jesus' Ascension
13.8.1 The Reports

In §6.1.1, I described three states and seven positions occupied by Christ. Thus far, we have dealt with (a) the *pre-incarnate* Christ (chapter 6), (2) the *incarnate* Christ (chapters 7–11), (3) the *dead* Christ (chapter 12), and (4) the *risen* Christ (§§13.1–6). We will now deal with (5) the *exalted* Christ (§§13.8–9). Eschatology deals with (6) the *returning* Christ, and (7) the *eternally ruling* Christ.[47]

Of the four Gospel writers, we can be certain that the apostles Matthew and John were present at the ascension of Jesus;

---
47. See *EDR* 10.

yet these are the two authors who did not write about it (cf. §5.3.1). It is as though Matthew continues the line of Jesus' earthly ministry until his return to earth, and the glorious establishment of the kingdom of heaven on earth. From a somewhat different viewpoint, we find something similar with John, as in this mysterious statement to Peter: "If it is my will that he [i.e., John] remain until I come, what is that to you?"[48] The apostolic collaborator, Mark, who *perhaps* was present at the ascension (cf. Mark 14:51-52 [was Mark this "young man"?]; Acts 12:12), writes, "So then the Lord Jesus, after he had spoken to them, was taken up into heaven and sat down at the right hand of God" (Mark 16:19).

By the way, the latter passage is important over against those who claim that Jesus' resurrection and ascension were one event, and that Jesus sat at the right hand of God from the day of his resurrection.[49] The risen Lord said to Mary that he had "*not* yet ascended to the Father" (John 20:17); this occurred forty days *after* Passover. In the New Testament, Jesus does not sit at God's right hand without being "taken up in glory" (1 Tim. 3:16). As a consequence, Jesus' appearances before his ascension, as A. van de Beek observes, are much "more earthy, 'human'" than his glorious appearance to Paul, that is, *after* his ascension (Acts 26:13-14).[50]

The report on the ascension by Luke[51] in his Gospel and in Acts is the most extensive: "And he led them out as far as Bethany, and lifting up his hands he blessed them. While he blessed them, he parted from them and was carried up into heaven" (Luke 24:50-51).

---

48. Jesus suggests that in principle John's ministry might last until his return. Indeed, through his inspired writings his ministry lasts until Jesus' second coming, according to Darby (n.d.-d, 378–79).
49. See Zwiep (2003, 53, also note 5 and references): "From the day of the resurrection, Christ is the exalted Lord, sitting at the right hand of the Father."
50. Van de Beek (2002a, 184).
51. Tradition includes Luke among the seventy mentioned in Luke 10:1, about whom he alone reports; if this is correct, the proselyte Luke was an early disciple.

And when [Jesus] had said these things, as they were looking on, he was lifted up, and a cloud took him out of their sight. And while they were gazing into heaven as he went, behold, two men stood by them in white robes, and said, "Men of Galilee, why do you stand looking into heaven? This Jesus, who was taken up from you into heaven, will come in the same way as you saw him go into heaven" (Acts 1:9-11; cf. vv. 2 and 22).

The frequency with which Jesus predicted his resurrection[52] was inversely proportional to his speaking about his ascension. Usually he referred to it indirectly, first, by speaking of his sitting at God's right hand (Matt. 26:64 par.), and second, by speaking of his second coming. That is, there can be no return from heaven, and no descending on the clouds of heaven, without first having ascended to heaven (Matt. 24:30; 26:64; cf. 10:23; 13:40-41; 16:27-28; 19:28; 24:27, 37, 39, 44; 25:31). Several times in John's Gospel, Jesus uses the verb "to ascend" (Gk. *anabainō*) in reference to his imminent return to heaven: "No one has ascended [Gk. *anabebēken*[53]) into heaven except he who descended from heaven, the Son of Man" (3:13). "Then what if you were to see the Son of Man ascending to where he was before?" (6:62). "Jesus said to [Mary Magdalene], 'Do not cling to me, for I have not yet ascended to the Father; but go to my brothers and say to them, "I am ascending to my Father and your Father, to my God and your God"'" (20:17).

13.8.2 The Testimonies

In the book of Acts, the apostles speak several times of Jesus' ascension. Peter says, "Being therefore exalted at the right hand of God, ... For David did not ascend into the heavens, but he himself says, 'The Lord said to my Lord, "Sit at my right

---

52. H. F. Bayer (*DJG* 630–33).
53. Notice here the remarkable perfect tense, which has been explained in various ways; perhaps the most obvious explanation is that Jesus views himself in a sense as never having left heaven, as is suggested by several manuscripts reading in v. 13b, "... the Son of Man *who is in heaven*" (NKJV).

hand, until I make your enemies your footstool"'" (2:33-35). Subsequently he talked about ". . . Jesus, whom heaven must receive until the time for restoring all the things" (3:20-21). Later he acknowledged that "God exalted [Jesus] at his right hand as Leader and Savior, to give repentance to Israel and forgiveness of sins" (5:31). Stephen confessed in the last moment of his life, while beholding the glory of God: "Behold, I see the heavens opened, and the Son of Man standing[54] at the right hand of God" (7:56).

The apostle Paul speaks of Jesus having "ascended on high" (Eph. 4:8-10), being "highly exalted" (Phil. 2:9), "taken up in glory" (1 Tim. 3:16; cf. Mark 16:9; Luke 9:51; Acts 1:2, 11), who is now "at the right hand of God" (Rom. 8:34), and tells us about God who seated Jesus "at his right hand in the heavenly places" (Eph. 1:20; cf. Col. 3:1). The apostle Peter writes about "Jesus Christ, who has gone into heaven and is at the right hand of God, with angels, authorities, and powers having been subjected to him" (1 Pet. 3:21-22). Hebrews speaks five times about Jesus at the right hand of God (1:3, 13; 8:1; 10:12; 12:2). In all these cases, the allusion is to Psalm 110:1, "The LORD says to my Lord: 'Sit at my right hand, until I make your enemies your footstool'."

Of course, terms like "ascending," "taking up," "exalting" (literally, "lifting up") are all metaphorical, as is being "caught up together with them in the clouds to meet the Lord in the air" (1 Thess. 4:17). They fit into the ancient worldview, in which the sky extends like a vault over the earth (cf. Job 22:14; Amos 9:6; also Gen. 1:6-8, 14-17, 20 NIV); the heavens are "above" (Deut. 11:21; Josh. 2:11; 1 Kings 8:23; Ps. 50:4; 103:11; Jer. 4:28; 31:37; Acts 2:19). Ascending to heaven is "going up" (cf. 2 Kings 2:1, 11; John 1:52; Acts 10:11, 16). Even if we no longer hold this worldview, we are not entitled to dis-

---

54. "Standing," not "sitting," perhaps to come to Stephen's help; it has been suggested that if Israel at that moment had accepted his testimony, and had believed, Jesus would have returned (cf. Peter's suggestion in Acts 3:19-20).

miss the ascension as ahistorical. The spiritual reality behind the metaphorical language of "ascending" ("going up") must not be denied. Jesus has been taken up into heaven, which is true reality, even though we cannot localize it in our three-dimensional world. His sitting in the throne of God, at his right hand, illustrates that as the heavenly Lord, he has all power in heaven and on earth, that is, in the entire universe (Matt. 28:18).

We may add here that in the verb "to lift up" (Gk. *hypsoō*) we encounter a fascinating ambiguity in the New Testament: with regard to Jesus, it can refer to his ascension (see above), but also to his having been lifted up on the cross: "[A]s Moses lifted up the serpent in the wilderness, so must the Son of Man be lifted up, that whoever believes in him may have eternal life" (John 3:14-15). "When you have lifted up the Son of Man, then you will know that I am he" (8:28). "'And I, when I am lifted up from the earth, will draw all people to myself.' He said this to show by what kind of death he was going to die" (12:32-33). It is not a coincidence, or a conceptual confusion, that the New Testament uses *hypsoō* both for the crucifixion and for the ascension, because the former is the condition for, and the first step to, the latter. He who was lifted up on the cross was, as a consequence, also lifted up to the right hand of God; the cross was a "way station" in his lifting up. As Joseph Ratzinger observes, John "calls the Lord's Cross an 'exaltation,' an elevation to God's throne on high. John brings Cross and Resurrection, Cross and exaltation together in a single word, because for him the one is in fact inseparable from the other."[55]

In my view, it is too speculative, though, to read such subsequent stages into Isaiah 52:13: "Behold, my servant shall act wisely; he shall be high and lifted up, and shall be exalted." The "high" is thought to refer to the Messiah's resurrection, the "lifted up" to his ascension, and the "shall be exalted" to

---

55. Ratzinger (2007, 73; cf. 315, 332).

his glorification.[56] The text provides insufficient warrant for such an interpretation.

13.8.3 Jesus' Glorification

Of particular significance is the verb "to glorify" (Gk. *doxazō*) with respect to the exaltation of Jesus: "The God of Abraham, the God of Isaac, and the God of Jacob, the God of our fathers, glorified his servant Jesus, whom you delivered over and denied in the presence of Pilate, when he had decided to release him" (Acts 3:13).

We find this term first in John 7:39, ". . . as yet the Spirit had not been given, because Jesus was not yet glorified." This clearly refers to the ascension of Jesus; only after this exaltation could the Holy Spirit descend: "Being therefore exalted at the right hand of God, and having received from the Father the promise of the Holy Spirit, he has poured out this that you yourselves are seeing and hearing" (Acts 2:33). John 8:44 speaks for the second time of Jesus' glorification, now in Jesus's own words and in the present tense: "If I glorify myself, my glory is nothing. It is my Father who glorifies me." The Father glorifies Jesus, for instance, through the miracles that he gives him to do: "This illness does not lead to death. It is for the glory of God, so that the Son of God may be glorified through it" (11:4), and the Holy Spirit will glorify him in his own way (16:14). However, in John 12:16 John speaks concretely of Jesus' ascension: "[W]hen Jesus was glorified, then they remembered that these things had been written about him and had been done to him."

Just as with the verb "to lift up," the verb "to glorify" can refer to the crucifixion, but also to the resurrection and the ascension. In that light, we want to compare the following three Scriptures.

(1) *Crucifixion.* "The hour has come for the Son of Man to be glorified. Truly, truly, I say to you, unless a grain of wheat

---

56. So Jennings (1966, 613); Vine (1971, 166); Bultema (1981, 503); R. E. Stier, quoted by Young (1972, 336), who rejects this view

falls into the earth and dies, it remains alone; but if it dies, it bears much fruit" (John 12:23-24). The time was near when Jesus would be glorified by all humanity; but he could receive this glory only through his sufferings, death, and resurrection.[57] His sufferings on the cross not only entailed a dramatic humiliation (cf. Isa. 52:14; 53:2-4), but also manifested a special glory in him, which even the centurion stationed at the cross observed: "Truly this was the Son of God" (Matt. 27:54).

(2) *From the cross to resurrection and ascension.* "Now is the Son of Man glorified, and God is glorified in him. If God is glorified in him, God will also glorify him in himself, and glorify him at once" (John 13:31-32). This "now" refers back to the departure of Judas and the start of his betrayal, with which Jesus' final suffering begins as well, culminating in his work on the cross. In his suffering and death, he himself would be glorified, and so would God, whose will he fulfilled. In answer to this, God would reward him with his glorification in heaven, and do so "at once," that is, shortly after his death. The phrase "in himself" means not only "with himself" (cf. 17:7 NASB),[58] but also "in God," that is, with divine glory.[59] Some have suggested the need to distinguish between the second to the last phrase and the last phrase: God will glorify Jesus when one day he will come in his royal glory, but he will also glorify him much earlier, that is, "at once," through his resurrection and exaltation at the Father's right hand.[60]

(3) *Resurrection and ascension.* "Father, the hour has come; glorify your Son that the Son may glorify you. . . . I glorified you on earth, having accomplished the work that you gave me to do. And now, Father, glorify me in your own presence with the glory that I had with you before the world existed"

---

57. Grant (1897b, 562); Henry (1918, 246); Dods (1979, 809); Gaebelein (1925, 227–31); Tenney (1981, 128–29); and Stuart (n.d., 263–64).
58. Morris (1971, 631).
59. Dods (1979, 820).
60. Henry (1918, 275–76); Darby (*CW* 25, 272; 33, 246; n.d.-b, 96); Kelly (1966, 278). *Contra* Bouma (1927, 176), who refers the "at once" to the cross.

(John 17:1-5). The Son has glorified the Father by perfectly fulfilling the earthly ministry to which the Father had called him. What follows in the text can be interpreted in two ways: either we take the "now" literally, so that Jesus is asking the Father to glorify him on the cross (see above); or in the submissiveness with which he commits himself to his work on the cross,[61] and now desires to be glorified through the Father raising him from the dead (cf. Rom. 6:4) and exalting him at his right hand. Given the addition "with the glory that I had with you before the world existed," as well as verse 11 ("I am no longer in the world"), where Jesus commits himself to his work on the cross, the second option is clearly preferable.[62] The Son is entitled to ask that he will be glorified by and through the Father as the reward for his accomplished work.

In summary, we conclude that the glorification of Jesus may refer both to his suffering on the cross and to his resurrection and ascension.[63] In other words, John sees these three events as one entity: none of them can be severed from the other two. Jesus' glorification begins with his entering the way of suffering, and is finished when he has been seated at the right hand of God. In this way, we also understand better that the verb "to be lifted up" embodies both the crucifixion and the ascension of Jesus (§13.8.2).

The theological meanings of Jesus' glorification are multiple, and were discussed in part when we dealt with the resurrection (§13.7).

(1) It is the closure and coronation of his finished work of redemption (John 17:4-5; Phil. 2:8-9; 1 Tim. 3:16; Heb. 1:3; 10:12; 12:2).

---

61. Cf. Bouma (1927, 205): "In his awareness of the victory looking beyond Calvary, [Jesus] sees that work as already finished, so that he can say, *I have glorified you on earth*"; cf. also Tenney (1981, 162).
62. Morris (1971, 721) and Tenney (1981, 162) seem to combine the two possibilities on the basis of the idea that suffering, death, resurrection, and ascension form one entity.
63. Tenney (1981, 141) speaks of the "dual dimension" of Jesus' glorification.

(2) It entails his triumph over all the spiritual powers that he defeated (Eph. 1:20-22; Col. 2:10; 1 Pet. 3:22; cf. Acts 2:36).

(3) It marks the present position and status not only of Jesus but also of one who believes in him (Eph. 1:20; 2:1, 6); it is the actual sphere of the believer's life of faith (Col. 3:1-3).

(4) Jesus' ministry in this status is especially high-priestly in nature, and is characterized by intercession and the defense of believers' interests (Rom. 8:34; Heb. 4:14-16; 7:25; 8:1; 1 John 2:1).

13.9 Jesus' "Anakenōsis"
13.9.1 A Man Clothed in Divine Glory

It is worthwhile to pay some more attention to the important phrase in John 17:5, "And now,[64] Father, glorify me in your own presence with the glory that I had with you before the world existed." Jesus' request, "glorify me," does *not* mean that Jesus had lost his divine glory at his incarnation, but it does mean that this glory had been veiled during his earthly life. As we have seen, this is one of the best descriptions of the meaning of his self-emptying (Gk. *kenosis*, Phil. 2:7; see §8.7.2). In a sense, John 17:5 implies the reversal of the *kenōsis*: the veil is removed, which I will describe with the neologism *anakenōsis*.

In such a formulation, we must not lose sight of the fact that the Son became Man in order to remain so forever (cf. §8.7). That is, if the veil that is removed is seen as identical with his human flesh, then our formulation does not work: removing the veil of his flesh in the sense that Jesus set aside the flesh he had adopted is out of the question. We have seen that it is even out of the question that Jesus would set aside his status as servant (or slave). He remains forever in the "form" of God as well as in the "form" of a servant (Phil. 2:6-7).

So what *does* happen in the *anakenōsis*? What is set aside is

---

64. In the light of v. 4 ("having accomplished the work"), this phrase "and now" means that Jesus views the glorification as *deserved* (cf. the "therefore" in Phil. 2:9), according to Berkouwer (1965, 41-44).

not Jesus' humanity, nor his servant form, but the brilliance and splendor of his divine glory is no longer veiled. *This* is the special thing that Jesus asks for in John 17:5. If that veil is removed, he remains human, and thus as the glorified *Man* Jesus Christ he possesses the full splendor of the glory that he had with the Father before the foundation of the world. This is what is new: he remains Man, and servant, but from now on without the *kenōsis*; the veil of his self-emptying has been removed.[65]

We thus discern three stages here.

(1) Before the incarnation, Jesus possesses divine glory as Son of God.

(2) After the incarnation and before the glorification, Jesus is both God and Man, but such that his divine glory is veiled (Gk. *kenōsis*).

(3) At his glorification, Jesus remains both God and Man, but now with a divine glory that is no longer veiled (Gk. *anakenōsis*).

That the Son, who accomplished the work that the Father gave him as a *Man*, now asks as a *Man* to be glorified with the glory that he once had as the *Son* with the Father before the foundation of the world is a truth that has been too little emphasized. An expositor who *was* clearly aware of this was Matthew Henry (beginning of the eighteenth century): Jesus "prays that even his human nature might be advanced to the highest honor it was capable of, his body a glorious body; and that the glory of the Godhead might now be manifested in the person of the Mediator, Emmanuel, God-man."[66]

Jesus did not glorify himself. He had adopted the status of a Man dependent on God in order to *receive* all things — and

---

65. Matthew Henry used the metaphor of a garment in an opposite way to the same effect: "That in his exalted state he resumed this glory, and clad himself again with his former robes of light" (https://www.biblestudytools.com/commentaries/matthew-henry-complete/john/17.html).

66. https://www.biblestudytools.com/commentaries/matthew-henry-complete/john/17.html.

Jesus' Resurrection and Ascension

not to *take* them—even if it is the glory that he had with the Father before the world existed.[67] He received as a *Man* what he had always possessed as a divine person, so that now he possessed this glory as both God and Man.[68] He returned to his former glory, the glory of the Son, but he received it back as a Man, so that now he is the Son—as he had been from eternity—*and* the glorified Man on the throne. This Man now possesses what he, as God the Son, had already possessed from eternity.[69] He asks for this glory, on behalf of not only his personal relationship with the Father but also the work that he, on earth, had accomplished for the Father's glory, with the purpose of being able to share this same glory with believers (v. 22). It was his perfection as Man with which he had accomplished his work that made him ask for this glorification. He did not glorify himself even as the risen One; he had emptied and humbled himself for the glory of the Father. He asks the *Father* to glorify him, even though he expresses his eternal and divine authority by asking to be glorified with the glory that he had with the Father before the world existed.[70]

13.9.2 Shared With, and Beheld By, Believers

The discussion of the soteriological significance of Jesus' death, resurrection, ascension, and glorification must await future volumes in this series; but these events also have Christological significance. Everything that Jesus receives as a *Man*, even the glory that he had with the Father before the world existed, he shares with his own: "The glory that you have given me I have given to them" (v. 22). Jesus is God and is one with the Father—believers are not. However, everything that Jesus received as *Man* believers have received too.[71] At the same time, John 17 makes clear that there is a dimension of his *received* glory that believers cannot share with him but can

---

67. Darby (n.d.-b, 131).
68. Darby (*CW* 25, 291).
69. Darby (*CW* 33, 279).
70. Kelly (1966, 351).
71. Darby (*CW* 26, 328).

only observe: "Father, I desire that they also, whom you have given me, may be with me where I am, to see my glory that you have given me because you loved me before the foundation of the world" (v. 24). There is a similar duality in 1 John 3:2, "[W]e know that when he appears [a] *we shall be like him* [cf. John 17:22], because [b] *we shall see him as he is* [cf. John 17:24]."

Actually, we must identify *three* levels of Jesus' glory: in addition to the glory that he, as the glorified Man, can and does share with believers (v. 22), and in addition to the glory that he cannot share with believers but that *can* be beheld by them (v. 24), there is glory that he cannot share with them, and that cannot be observed by them: the dimension of his divine glory as God the Son.

Since Jesus' glorification, the full splendor of his divine glory is shining again, just like before his incarnation; however, for the first time he is the *Man* Jesus Christ—who at the same time was, and is, and will be the Son of God—in whom this full splendor is manifested. Two individuals in the New Testament observed this. The first is Saul of Tarsus on his way to Damascus: "At midday, O king [Agrippa], I saw on the way a light from heaven, brighter than the sun, that shone around me and those who journeyed with me.... And I said, 'Who are you, Lord?' And the Lord said, 'I am Jesus whom you are persecuting'" (Acts 26:13-15). The name "Jesus" is remarkable here: it is the name with which he was known here on earth in his state of emptying and humbling himself. But it is this *Man*, now glorified in heaven, who shines here with a light brighter than the sun. Compare this statement of Paul: "Therefore God has highly exalted him and bestowed on him the name that is above every name, so that at the name of *Jesus* every knee should bow" (Phil. 2:9-10).

A second example of the splendor of the glorified *Man* Christ Jesus is what John experienced on Patmos: "[I]n the midst of the lampstands [I saw] one like a son of man [or, (the)

Son of Man], ... and his face was like the sun shining in full strength. When I saw him, I fell at his feet as though dead" (Rev. 1:13-17). This "him" is explicitly the Son of *Man*, a Man whose face was shining with the glory of God (v. 13).

Jesus' transfiguration on the mount had been a foretaste of the glory that Saul and John later beheld: "[H]e was transfigured before them, and his face shone like the sun, and his clothes became white as light" (Matt. 17:2; cf. 2 Pet. 1:17, "he received honor and glory from God the Father"). Just as in the two preceding examples, the glory of Christ is compared here to that of the sun — the most beautiful and splendid metaphor within creation of glory that we know.

There is a *Man* in heaven, not on a throne *alongside* the Father, but *on* the throne *of* the Father (cf. Rev. 3:21),[72] at his right hand. A glorified Man. The glory that radiates from him is that of the eternal Son; it is the glory that he possessed before the foundation of the world. And yet it is different: back then, the Son was not yet what he is now: Man. It is also different from what he was on earth: back then he was a Man, but he had set aside the outer glory of his divine Sonship (without ceasing to be the Son). After his ascension, he is glorious in an entirely new way: both as Man and as One unveiled, in the full splendor of his eternal Sonship. And here again his two natures are undivided: as a reward for his finished work, the *one Man* Jesus Christ is now invested with the glory of the eternal Son.

---

72. See extensively Hengel (1995, 148–51).

Bibliography

Aalders, W. J. 1933. *De incarnatie.* Groningen: J.B. Wolters.

Albright, W. F. and C. S. Mann. 1971. *Matthew.* AB 26. Garden City, NY: Doubleday.

Alexander, J. A. (1846–1847) 1980. *Commentary on the Prophecies of Isaiah.* Grand Rapids, MI: Zondervan.

Alexander, R. H. 1986. *Ezekiel.* EBC 6. Grand Rapids, MI: Zondervan.

Alexander, W. L. 1888. *A System of Biblical Theology,* Vol. I. Edinburgh: T. & T. Clark.

Allen, L. C. 1976. *The Books of Joel, Obadiah, Jonah and Micah.* NICOT. Grand Rapids, MI: Eerdmans.

Allen, R. B. 1990. *Numbers.* EBC 2. Grand Rapids, MI: Zondervan.

Althaus, P. 1932. *Grundriss der Dogmatik.* Vol. 2. Gütersloh: Bertelsmann.

_____. 1952. *Die christliche Wahrheit: Lehrbuch der Dogmatik.* 3rd ed. Gütersloh: Bertelsmann.

Anderson, A. S. 1976. "The Seed of the Woman." *Third National Creation Science Conference,* 99–104. St. Paul, MN: Bible-Science Association/Twin-City Creation-Science Association.

Anderson, J. N. D. 1968. "The Resurrection of Jesus Christ." *Christianity Today.* March 29, 4–9.

Anderson, R. 1990. *Daniel in the Critics' Den: A Defense of the Historicity of the Book of Daniel.* Grand Rapids, MI: Kregel.

_____. n.d. *The Coming Prince, or The Seventy Weeks of Daniel.* Edinburgh: Pickering & Inglis.

Archer, G.L. 1982. *Encyclopedia of Bible Difficulties.* Grand Rapids, MI: Zondervan.

Arnold, T. 1859. *Sermons on the Christian Life: Its Hopes, Its Fears, and Its Close.* London: T. Fellowes.

Asch, S. 1939. *The Nazarene.* New York: Routledge & Sons.

Ashley, T. R. 1993. *The Book of Numbers.* NICOT. Grand Rapids, MI: Eerdmans.

Baeck, L. 1938. *Das Evangelium als Urkunde der jüdischen Glaubensgeschichte.* Berlin: Schocken.

Baigent, M., R. Leigh, and H. Lincoln. 1983. *Het Heilige Bloed en de Heilige Graal.* Baarn: Tirion.

_____. 1991. *De messiaanse erfenis.* 2nd ed. Baarn: Tirion.

Baldwin, J. G. 1972. *Haggai, Zechariah, Malachi: An Introduction and Commentary.* Downers Grove, IL: InterVarsity.

Bammel, E. and C. F. D. Moule, eds. 1984. *Jesus and the Politics of His Day.* Cambridge: Cambridge University Press.

Barker, G. W. 1981. *1, 2, 3 John.* EBC 12. Grand Rapids, MI: Zondervan.

Barker, K. L. 1985. *Zechariah.* EBC 7. Grand Rapids, MI: Zondervan.

Barnett, P. W. 1998. *Historische zoektocht naar Jezus.* Zoetermeer: Boekencentrum.

Barrett, C. K. 1955. *The Gospel According to St. John.* London: SPCK.

Barth, K. 2009. *Church Dogmatics. Study Edition.* Translated by G. W. Bromiley et al. Vols. I/1–IV/1. New York, NY: T&T Clark. (Editor's Note: The original fourteen volumes have been published in the *Study Edition* as thirty-one volumes. For citation purposes, the original volume enumeration is followed by the number of the equivalent new volume:

e.g., III/3=18. The sections [§] are identical in both editions. The final number[s] refer[s] to the page[s] in the new *Study Edition*. Sample citation convention: *CD* III/3=18, §51.2:130.)

Batey, R. A. 1984. "Is Not This the Carpenter?" *New Testament Studies* 30:249-58.

Bavinck, H. 2002-2008. *Reformed Dogmatics*. Edited by J. Bolt. Translated by J. Vriend. 4 vols. Grand Rapids, MI: Baker Academic.

Beasley-Murray, G. R. 1954. *Jesus and the Kingdom of God*. London: Macmillan.

Beker, E. J. and J. M. Hasselaar. 1981. *Wegen en kruispunten in de dogmatiek*. Vol. 3: *Christologie*. Kampen: Kok.

Bellett, J. G. n.d. *The Son of God*. London: W.H. Broom.

Ben-Chorin, S. 2001. *Brother Jesus: The Nazarene through Jewish Eyes*. Translated by J. S. Klein and M. Reinhart. Athens, GA: University of Georgia Press.

Bentzen, A. 1952. *Introduction to the Old Testament*. 2nd ed. Copenhagen: G.E.C. Gad Publishers.

Berger, K. 2004. *Jesus*. München: Pattloch.

Berkhof, H. 1964. *The Doctrine of the Holy Spirit*. Atlanta, GA: John Knox Press.

_____. 1966. *Christ the Meaning of History*. Translated by L. Buurman. Richmond, VA: John Knox Press.

_____. 1986. *Christian Faith: An Introduction to the Study of the Faith*. Translated by S. Woudstra. Rev. ed. Grand Rapids, MI: Wm. B. Eerdmans.

Berkhof, L. 1981. *Systematic Theology*. 4th rev. and enlarged ed. Grand Rapids, MI: Eerdmans.

Berkouwer, G. C. 1954. *The Person of Christ*. Translated by J. Vriend. Studies in Dogmatics. Grand Rapids, MI: Eerdmans.

_____. 1956. *The Triumph of Grace in the Theology of Karl Barth*. Translated by H. R. Boer. Grand Rapids, MI: Eerdmans.

———. 1965. *The Work of Christ*. Translated by C. Lambregtse. Studies in Dogmatics. Grand Rapids, MI: Eerdmans.

———. 1972. *The Return of Christ*. Translated by J. Van Oosterom. Studies in Dogmatics. Grand Rapids, MI: Eerdmans.

———. 1977. *A Half Century of Theology: Movements and Motives*. Translated by L. B. Smedes. Grand Rapids, MI: Eerdmans.

Berkowitz, A. and D. (1998) 1999. *Take Hold: Embracing Our Divine Inheritance with Israel*. 2nd ed. Littleton, CO: First Fruits of Zion.

Bernard, J. H. 1979. *The Second Epistle to the Corinthians*. EGT 3. Grand Rapids, MI: Eerdmans.

Bieneck, J. 1951. *Sohn Gottes als Christusbezeichnung der Synoptiker*. Zürich: Zwingli Verlag.

Bivin, D. and R. B. Blizzard. 1984. *Understanding the Difficult Words of Jesus*. Shippensburg, PA: Destiny Image Publishers.

Blackburn, J. S. 1978. *Seek Ye First: A Study of the Kingdom of God*. Wooler: Central Bible Hammond Trust.

Bleeker, L. H. K. 1934. *De kleine profeten*. Vol. 2. Tekst en Uitleg. Groningen: J.B. Wolters.

Blinzler, J. 1970. *The Trial of Jesus: The Jewish and Roman Proceedings Against Jesus Christ Described and Assessed from the Oldest Accounts*. Translated by I. and F. McHugh. Westminster, MD: Newman.

Bloesch, D. G. 1997. *Jesus Christ: Savior and Lord*. Downers Grove, IL: InterVarsity Press.

Bock, D. L. 2002. *Jesus According to Scripture*. Grand Rapids, MI: Baker Academic.

Bockmuehl, M. 1994. *This Jesus: Martyr, Lord, Messiah*. Downers Grove, IL: InterVarsity Press.

Bockmuehl, M., ed. 2001. *The Cambridge Companion to Jesus*. Cambridge: Cambridge University Press.

Boff, L. 1984. *Church: Charism and Power*. London: SCM.

Bonhoeffer, D. 1966. *Christology*. Translated by J. Bowdon. London: Collins. 1982.

———. 1967. *Letters and Papers from Prison*. London: SCM.

Borg, M. J. 1987. *Jesus: A New Vision: Spirit, Culture and the Life of Discipleship*. San Francisco, CA: Harper.

———. 1994a. *Meeting Jesus Again for the First Time*. San Francisco, CA: HarperCollins.

———, et al. 1994b. *The Search for Jesus: Modern Scholarship Looks at the Gospels*. Symposium at the Smithsonian Institute, September 11, 1993. Washington, D.C.: Biblical Archaeology Society.

———. 1998. *Conflict, Holiness and Politics in the Teachings of Jesus*. Rev. ed. Harrisburg, PA: Trinity Press International.

——— and N. T. Wright. 1999. *The Meaning of Jesus: Two Visions*. New York: HarperCollins.

Bornkamm, G. 1960. *Jesus of Nazareth*. Translated by I. and F. McLuskey, with J. M. Robinson. London: Hodder & Stoughton.

Bornkamm, H. 1969. *Luther and the Old Testament*. Translated by E. W. and R. C. Gritsch. Edited by V. I. Gruhn. Philadelphia, PA: Fortress Press.

Boslooper, T. 1962. *The Virgin Birth*. Philadelphia, PA: Westminster.

Bouma, C. 1927. *Het evangelie naar Johannes*. KV. Kampen: Kok.

Bouman, J. 1994. *In gesprek met moslims*. Leiden: Groen & Zoon.

Bousset, W. 1906. *Jesus*. Edited by W. D. Morrison. Translated by J. P. Trevlyan. New York: G. P. Putnam. 1904 (1922). *Jesus*. 4th ed. Halle: Gebauer-Schwetschke.

———. 1970. *Kyrios Christos: A History of the Belief in Christ from the Beginnings of Christianity to Irenaeus*. Translated by J. E. Steely. Nashville, TN: Abingdon Press.

Bowling, A. 1980. "*mal'āk*." *Theological Wordbook of the Old Testament*. Edited by R. L. Harris, G. L. Archer, and B. K. Waltke. 464–65. Chicago, IL: Moody Press.

Boyd, G. A. 1995. *Cynic, Sage, or Son of God: Recovering the Real Jesus in an Age of Revisionist Replies*. Wheaton, IL: Victor Books.

———. 2001. *Satan and the Problem of Evil: Constructing a Trinitarian Warfare Theodicy*. Downers Grove, IL: IVP Academic.

Braaten, C. E. 1966. *History and Hermeneutics*. Philadelphia, PA: Westminster Press.

——— and R. A. Harrisville. 1964. *The Historical Jesus and the Kerygmatic Christ*. New York: Abingdon Press.

Brandon, S. G. F. 1967. *Jesus and the Zealots: A Study of the Political Factor in Primitive Christianity*. Manchester: Manchester University Press.

Braun, C. 1876. *Der Begriff "Person" in seiner Anwendung auf die Lehre von der Trinität und Incarnation*. Mainz: Franz Kirchheim.

Bromiley, G. W. 1978. *Historical Theology: An Introduction*. Grand Rapids, MI: Eerdmans.

Brown, D. 2004. *The Da Vinci Code*. New York: Doubleday. *De Da Vinci Code*. Amsterdam: Luitingh.

Brown, R. E. 1966. *The Gospel According to John*. Vol. 1. Garden City, NY: Doubleday.

———. 1967. *Jesus, God and Man*. Milwaukee: Bruce Publications.

———. 1973. *The Virginal Conception and Bodily Resurrection of Jesus*. New York: Paulist.

———. 1977 (1996). *The Birth of the Messiah: A Commentary on the Infancy Narratives in Matthew and Luke*. 2nd ed. New York: Doubleday.

———. 1994a. *An Introduction to New Testament Christology*. New York: Paulist Press.

———. 1994b. *The Death of the Messiah: From Gethsemane to the Grave*. New York: Doubleday.

———. 1997. *An Introduction to the New Testament*. New York: Doubleday.

Bruce, A. B. 1892. *Apologetics, or, Christianity Defensively Stated.* Edinburgh: T. & T. Clark.

———. 1979. *The Synoptic Gospels.* EGT 1. Grand Rapids, MI: Eerdmans.

Bruce, F. F. 1958. *The Spreading Flame.* Exeter: Paternoster.

———. 1962. "The Person of Christ: Incarnation and Virgin Birth." In *Basic Christian Doctrines.* Edited by C. F. H. Henry. 124–30. New York: Holt, Rinehart & Winston.

———. 1972. *The New Testament Documents: Are They Reliable?* 5th ed. Downers Grove, IL: InterVarsity.

———. 1984. *The Epistles to the Colossians, to Philemon, and to the Ephesians.* NICNT. Grand Rapids, MI: Eerdmans.

———. 1988. *The Book of the Acts.* NICNT. Grand Rapids, MI: Eerdmans.

Brümmer, V. 1988. *Over een persoonlijke God gesproken: Studies in de wijsgerige theologie.* Kampen: Kok Agora.

Bruners, W. 2006. *Wie Jesus glauben lernte.* Freiburg: Herder.

Brunner, C. 1921, repr. 1958. *Unser Christus oder des Wesen des Genies.* Berlin: Oesterheld; repr. Köln/Berlin: Kiepenheuer & Witsch.

Brunner, E. 1950. *Dogmatics.* Translated by O. Wyon. Vol. 1: *The Christian Doctrine of God.* Philadelphia, PA: Westminster Press.

Buber, M. 1961. *Two Types of Faith: A Study of Interpenetration of Judaism and Christianity.* Translated by N. P. Goldhawk. New York: Harper Torchbooks.

Bultema, H. 1981. *Commentary on Isaiah.* Grand Rapids, MI: Kregel.

Bultmann, R. 1952/1955. *Theology of the New Testament.* Translated by K. Grobel. 2 vols. London: SCM.

———. 1958. *Jesus and the Word.* New York: Scribner.

———. 1963. *The History of the Synoptic Tradition.* Translated by J. Marsh. Oxford: Blackwell.

———. 1984. "New Testament and Mythology: The Problem

of Demythologizing the New Testament Proclamation." In *New Testament and Mythology and Other Basic Writings*. Edited and translated by S. M Ogden. 4th ed. 1–43. Philadelphia, PA: Fortress Press.

Buri, F. 1978. *Dogmatik als Selbstverständnis des christlichen Glaubens*. Vol. 3: *Die Transzendenz der Verantwortung in der dreifachen Schöpfung des dreieinigen Gottes*. Bern: Paul Haupt/Tübingen: Katzmann.

Burridge, R. A. and G. Gould. 2004. *Jesus Now and Then*. Grand Rapids, MI: Eerdmans.

Burstein, D., ed. 2004. *Secrets of the Code: The Unauthorized Guide to the Mysteries behind the Da Vinci Code*. New York, NY: CDS Books.

Busch, W. 2004. *Jezus onze bestemming*. Hoornaar: Gideon.

Calvin, J. 1960. *Institutes of the Christian Religion*. Translated by F. L. Battles. The Library of Christian Classics. 2 vols. Louisville, KY: Westminster John Knox Press.

Campenhausen, H. von. 1964. *The Virgin Birth in the Theology of the Ancient Church*. Translated by F. Clarke. London: SCM Press.

Carotta, F. 2005. *Jesus Was Caesar: On the Julian Origin of Christianity. An Investigative Report*. Translated by T. Hendriks et al. Soesterberg, Netherlands: Aspekt.

Carson, D. A. 1984. *Matthew*. EBC 8. Grand Rapids, MI: Zondervan.

Cassanelli, A. 2002. *The Holy Shroud*. Leominster: Gracewing.

Cassels, W. R. 1874. *Supernatural Religion*. London: Longmans, Green & Co.

Chafer, L. S. 1983. *Systematic Theology*. 15th ed. 8 vols. Dallas: Dallas Seminary Press.

Chambers, L. T. n.d. *Tabernacle Studies*. Kilmarnock: John Ritchie.

Charlesworth, J. H., ed. 1991. *Jesus' Jewishness: Exploring the Place of Jesus in Early Judaism*. New York: Crossroad.

Chilton, B. and C. A. Evans, eds. 1994. *Studying the Historical Jesus*. Leiden: Brill.

Chung, S. W., ed. 2005. *Christ the One and Only*. Grand Rapids, MI: Baker.

Cleage, A. B., Jr. 1968. *The Black Messiah*. Trenton, NJ: Africa World Press.

Coates, C. A. n.d. *An Outline of the Book of Genesis*. Kingston-on-Thames: Stow Hill Bible & Tract Depot.

Cohen, A., ed. 1980. *The Twelve Prophets*. SBB. London: Soncino.

_____, ed. 1982–1985. *The Soncino Books of the Bible*. 14 vols. London: Soncino.

_____, ed. 1983. *The Soncino Chumash*. SBB. London: Soncino.

_____, ed. 1985. *The Psalms*. SBB. London: Soncino.

Cole, R. A. 1961. *The Gospel According to St. Mark*. TNTC. Grand Rapids, MI: Eerdmans.

Cornfeld, G., ed. 1982. *The Historical Jesus: A Scholarly View of the Man and His World*. New York: Macmillan.

Craig, W. L. 1988. *Knowing the Truth About the Resurrection*. Ann Arbor, MI: Servant.

_____. 1989. *Assessing the New Testament Evidence for the Historicity of the Resurrection of Jesus*. Lewiston, NY/Queenston, Ont.: Edwin Mellen Press.

Craigie, P. C. 1976. *The Book of Deuteronomy*. NICOT. Grand Rapids, MI: Eerdmans.

Cranfield, C. E. B. 1963. *The Gospel According to St. Mark*. 2nd ed. Cambridge Greek Testament. Cambridge: Cambridge University Press.

Crossan, J. D. 1991. *The Historical Jesus*. San Francisco, CA: HarperSanFrancisco.

_____. 1995a. *Who Killed Jesus?* New York: HarperCollins.

_____. 1995b. *Jesus: A Revolutionary Biography*. San Francisco, CA: HarperSanFrancisco.

Cullmann, O. 1953. *Peter: Disciple–Apostle–Martyr.* London: SCM.

———. 1963. *The Christology of the New Testament.* Translated by S. C. Guthrie and C. A. M. Hall. Philadelphia, PA: Westminster Press.

Dahl. N. A. 1991 *Jesus the Christ: The Historical Origins of Christological Doctrine.* Edited by D. H. Juell. Minneapolis: Fortress.

Darby, J. N. n.d.-a. *The Collected Writings of J. N. Darby.* Available at https://bibletruthpublishers.com/john-nelson-darby-jnd/collected-writings-of-j-n-darby/luc13-14921.

———. n.d.-b. *Synopsis of the Books of the Bible.* Available at https://www.sacred-texts.com/bib/cmt/darby/.

Daube, D. 1956. *The New Testament and Rabbinic Judaism.* London: Athlone Press.

Davies, S. T., D. Kendall, and G. O'Collins, eds. 2004. *The Incarnation.* Oxford: Oxford University Press.

Davis, J. D. 2004. "The Child Whose Name Is Wonderful: An Address on Isaiah IX. 5 and 6 (English Version 6 and 7)." In *Biblical and Theological Studies: Commemorating the 100th Anniversary of Princeton Theological Seminary.* 91–108. Homewood, AL: Solid Ground Christian Books.

Dawes, G. W., ed. 1999. *The Historical Jesus Quest: A Foundational Anthology.* Leiden: Deo.

Deden, D. 1953. *De kleine profeten.* De boeken van het Oude Testament. Roermond/Maaseik: J.J. Romen & Zonen.

De Graaff, F. 1987. *Jezus de Verborgene: Een voorbereiding tot inwijding in de mysteriën van het evangelie.* Kampen: Kok.

De Jonge, M. 1990. *Jezus als Messias: Hoe Hij zijn zending zag.* Boxtel: KBS/Tabor.

———. 1997. *Het verhaal van Jezus volgens de bronnen.* Maarssen: De Ploeg.

Den Heyer, C. J. 1986. *De messiaanse weg.* Vol. 2. Kampen: Kok.

———. 2003. *Van Jezus naar christendom: De ontwikkeling van tekst tot dogma*. Zoetermeer: Meinema.

Dennett, E. 1967. *Daniel the Prophet, and The Times of the Gentiles*. Oak Park, IL: Bible Truth Publishers.

Denney, J. 1979. *St. Paul's Epistle to the Romans*. EGT 2. Grand Rapids, MI: Eerdmans.

Dennison, J. T., Jr., ed. 2008–2014. *Reformed Confessions of the 16th and 17th Centuries in English Translation*. 4 vols. Grand Rapids, MI: Reformation Heritage Books.

De Ru, G. 1974. *De verleiding der revolutie*. Kampen: Kok.

De Wilde, W. J. 1929. *De messiaansche opvattingen der middeleeuwsche exegeten Rasji, Aben Ezra en Kimchi, vooral volgens hun commentaren op Jesaja*. Wageningen: H. Veenman & Zonen.

Den Boer, C., ed. 1985. *Man en vrouw in bijbels perspectief*. Kampen: Kok.

Dibelius, M. 1919. *Die Formgeschichte des Evangeliums*. Tübingen: Mohr (Siebeck).

Dodd, C. H. 1932. *The Epistle to the Romans*. Moffatt New Testament Commentary. New York/London: Harper & Brothers.

_____. 1935. *The Parables of the Kingdom*. London: Nisbet & Co.

_____. 1952. *According to the Scriptures*. London: Nisbet & Co.

_____. 1971. *The Founder of Christianity*. London: Collins.

Dods, M. 1979. *The Gospel of John*. EGT 1. Grand Rapids, MI: Eerdmans.

Doherty, E. 1999. *The Jesus Puzzle: Did Christianity Begin with a Mythical Christ?* Ottawa: Age of Reason Publications.

Douglas, K. B. 1994. *The Black Christ*. Maryknoll, NY: Orbis Books.

Douma, J., ed. 1974. *Oriëntatie in de theologie*. Groningen: De Vuurbaak.

Dunn, J. D. G. 1990a. *Unity and Diversity in the New Testament: An Inquiry into the Character of Earliest Christianity*. 2nd ed. London: SCM.

———. 1990b. *Jesus, Paul, and the Law: Studies in Mark and Galatians*. Louisville, KY: Westminster.

———. 2003. *Christology in the Making*. Vol. 1: *Jesus Remembered*. 2nd ed. London: SCM.

———. 2005. *A New Perspective on Jesus: What the Quest for the Historical Jesus Missed*. Grand Rapids, MI: Baker Academic.

Durand, J. J. F. 1985. *Wegwysers in die dogmatiek*. Vol. 1: *Die lewende God*. 2nd ed. Pretoria: NG Kerkboekhandel Transvaal.

Durrant, M. 1973. *Theology and Intelligibility*. London: Routledge & Kegan Paul.

Duvekot, W. S. 1998. *Wie is toch deze? Jezus' persoon vanuit de Joodse traditie; een poging*. Zoetermeer: Boekencentrum.

Earle, R. 1978. *1, 2 Timothy*. EBC 11. Grand Rapids, MI: Zondervan.

Ebeling, G. 1961. *The Nature of Faith*. Translated by R. G. Smith. London: Collins.

Edelkoort, A. H. 1941. *De Christusverwachting in het Oude Testament*. Wageningen: H. Veenman & Zonen.

———. 1945. *De profeet Zacharia: Een uitlegkundige studie*. Baarn: Bosch & Keuning.

Edersheim, A. 1979 (repr. 1883). *The Life and Times of Jesus the Messiah*. Grand Rapids, MI: Eerdmans.

Edwards, D. 1943. *The Virgin Birth in History and Faith*. London: Faber & Faber.

Ehrman, B. D. 1996. *The Orthodox Corruption of Scripture: The Effect of Early Christological Controversies on the Text of the New Testament*. Oxford: Oxford University Press.

———. 2003a. *Lost Christianities: The Battles for Scripture and the Faiths We Never Knew*. Oxford: Oxford University Press.

———. 2003b. *Lost Scriptures: Books that Did Not Make It into the New Testament*. Oxford: Oxford University Press.

Emmen, E. 1935. *De christologie van Calvijn*. Amsterdam: H.J. Paris.

Erickson, M. J. 1985. *Christian Theology*. 2nd ed. Grand Rapids, MI: Baker Book House.

———. 1991. *The Word Became Flesh*. Grand Rapids, MI: Baker.

Evans, C. A. 1992. *Jesus*. Grand Rapids, MI: Baker.

Evdokimov, P. 1990. *The Art of the Icon: A Theology of Beauty*. Redondo Beach, CA: Oakwood Publications.

Fairbairn, P. 1975. *The Typology of Scripture, Viewed in Connection with the Whole Series of the Divine Dispensations*. Grand Rapids, MI: Baker Book House.

Farmer, W. R. 1964. *The Synoptic Problem*. New York: Macmillan.

———. 1994. *The Gospel of Jesus: The Pastoral Relevance of the Synoptic Problem*. Louisville, KY: Westminster/John Knox.

Fijnvandraat, J. G. 1990. *Babylon, beeld en beest: Bijbelstudies over de profetie van Daniël*. Vol. 2: Chapters 7–12. Vaassen: Medema.

Filson, F. V. 1956. *Jesus Christ the Risen Lord*. Nashville, TN: Abingdon Press.

Fisch, S., ed. 1978. *Ezekiel*. SBB. London: Soncino.

Fitzmyer, J. 1973. "The Virginal Conception of Jesus in the New Testament." *Theological Studies* 34:541–75.

Flesseman-van Leer, E. 1985. *Wie toch is Jezus van Nazareth?* 's-Gravenhage: Boekencentrum.

Flusser, D. 2001. *Jesus*. In collaboration with R. S. Notley. 3rd ed. Jerusalem: The Hebrew University Press.

Ford, D. F. and M. Higton, eds. 2002. *Jesus*. Oxford: Oxford University Press.

Forsyth, P. T. 1909. *The Person and Place of Jesus Christ*. London: Independent Press.

Fortman, E. J. 1972. *The Triune God: A Historical Study of the Doctrine of the Trinity*. Grand Rapids, MI: Baker Book House.

Freke, T. and P. Gandy. 1999. *The Jesus Mysteries*. London: Thorsons.

Fruchtenbaum, A. G. (1989) 1992. *Israelology: The Missing Link in Systematic Theology*. 2nd ed. San Antonio, TX: Ariel Ministry Press.

Fuchs, E. 1964. *Studies of the Historical Jesus*. Translated by A. Scobie. London: SCM Press.

Fuller, R. H. 1965. *The Foundations of New Testament Christology*. New York: Scribner.

Funk, R. W. 1996. *Honest to Jesus: Jesus for a New Millennium*. San Francisco, CA: HarperSanFrancisco.

———. 1998. *The Acts of Jesus: The Search for the Authentic Deeds of Jesus*. San Francisco, CA: HarperCollins.

———. 1999. *The Gospel of Jesus According to the Jesus Seminar*. Santa Rosa, CA: Polebridge Press.

———. 2002. *A Credible Jesus: Fragments of a Vision*. Santa Rosa, CA: Polebridge Press.

——— and R. Hoover. 1993. *The Five Gospels: The Search for the Authentic Words of Jesus*. New York: Macmillan.

Gaebelein, A. C. 1911. *The Prophet Daniel*. London: Marshall Brothers.

———. 1925. *The Gospel of John: A Complete Analytical Exposition of the Gospel of John*. New York: Publication Office "Our Hope."

———. 1965. *The Book of Psalms*. Neptune, NJ: Loizeaux Brothers.

Galling, K. ed. 1986. *Die Religion in Geschichte und Gegenwart*. 6 vols. Tübingen: Mohr (Siebeck).

Garvie, A. E. 1925. *The Christian Doctrine of the Godhead*. London: Hodder & Stoughton.

Geisler, N. L. 1979. "Philosophical Presuppositions of Biblical Errancy." In *Biblical Errancy: An Analysis of its Philosophical Roots*. 305–334. Grand Rapids, MI: Zondervan.

———, ed. 1981. *Biblical Errancy: An Analysis of its Philosophical Roots*. Grand Rapids, MI: Zondervan.

Geldenhuys, N. 1983. *Commentary on the Gospel of Luke*. NIC-

NT. Grand Rapids, MI: Eerdmans.

Gerlitz, P. 1963. *Ausserchristliche Einflüsse auf die Entwicklung des christlichen Trinitätsdogmas.* Leiden: E.J. Brill.

Gese, H. 1977. *Zur biblischen Theologie: Alttestamentliche Vorträge.* München: Chr. Kaiser.

Gispen, W. H. 1954. *De Spreuken van Salomo.* KV. Kampen: Kok.

_____. 1979. *Genesis.* Vol. 2: *Genesis 11:27–25:11.* COT. Kampen: Kok.

Godet, F. 1879. *Commentary on the Gospel of Luke.* Edinburgh: T. & T. Clark.

Goldman, S., ed. 1983. *Samuel.* SBB. London: Soncino.

Gollwitzer, H. 1973. "Inleiding." In *Jezus voor atheïsten.* Edited by M. Machovec. Baarn: Ten Have, p. 5–12.

_____ and P. Lapide. 1984. *Een vluchtelingenkind: Gedachten over Lucas 2.* Baarn: Ten Have.

Gooding, D. 2007. *Volgens Lukas: Een nieuwe verklaring van het derde Evangelie.* Vaassen: Medema.

Goppelt, L. 1981. *Theology of the New Testament.* Translated by J. E. Alsup. Edited by J. Roloff. Vol. 1. Grand Rapids, MI: Eerdmans.

Goslinga, C. J. 1962. *Het tweede boek Samuël.* COT. Kampen: Kok.

Goulder, M. D. 1974. *Midrash and Lection in Matthew.* London: SPCK.

_____, ed. 1979. *Incarnation and Myth: The Debate Continued.* Grand Rapids, MI: Eerdmans.

Graafland, C. 1982. *Wie zeggen de mensen dat Ik ben? Over de Persoon van Jezus Christus.* Kampen: Kok.

Grant, F. W. 1897a. *The Numerical Bible: The Psalms.* New York: Loizeaux Brothers.

_____. 1897b. *The Numerical Bible: The Gospels.* New York: Loizeaux Brothers.

———. n.d. *Genesis in the Light of the New Testament.* New York: Loizeaux Brothers.

——— and J. Bloore. 1931. *The Numerical Bible: Ezekiel.* New York: Loizeaux Brothers.

Grässer, E. 1973. "Motive und Methoden der neueren Jesus-Literatur." *Verkündigung und Forschung* 18:3–45.

Green, J. B., S. McKnight, and I. H. Marshall, eds. 1992. *Dictionary of Jesus and the Gospels.* Downers Grove, IL: InterVarsity.

Green, M. 1967. *Man Alive!* London: InterVarsity.

———. 1992. *Who is This Jesus?* Nashville, TN: Thomas Nelson.

Greene, C. J. D. 2003. *Christology in Cultural Perspective.* Grand Rapids, MI: Eerdmans.

Greenleaf, S. 1965 (repr. 1847). *Testimony of the Evangelists, Examined by the Rules of Evidence Administered in Courts of Justice.* Grand Rapids, MI: Baker Book House.

Greijdanus, S. 1925. *De brief van den apostel Paulus aan de Philippenzen.* KV. Kampen: Kok.

———. 1941. *Het heilig evangelie naar de beschrijving van Lucas.* 2 vols. Kommentaar op het Nieuwe Testament. Amsterdam: H.A. van Bottenburg.

———. 1955. *Het evangelie naar Lucas.* 2 vols. 2nd ed. KV. Kampen: Kok.

Griffith-Thomas, W. H. 1930. *Principles of Theology.* New York: Longmans, Green & Co.

Grillmeier, A. 1975. *Christ in Christian Tradition.* Vol. 1: *From the Apostolic Age to Chalcedon.* 2nd ed. Atlanta, GA: John Knox Press.

Grogan, G. W. 1986. *Isaiah.* EBC 6. Grand Rapids, MI: Zondervan.

Gromacki, R. 1974. *The Virgin Birth: Doctrine of Deity.* Nashville, TN: Nelson.

Grosheide, F. W. 1954. *Het heilig evangelie volgens Mattheüs.*

2nd ed. CNT. Kampen: Kok.

Grün, A. 2002. *Beelden van Jezus*. Tielt: Lannoo/Baarn: Ten Have.

Grunewald, J. 2000. *Chalom Jésus! Lettre d'un rabbin d'aujourd'hui au rabbi de Nazareth*. Paris: Albin Michel.

Guthrie, D. 1970. *New Testament Introduction*. 2nd ed. London: InterVarsity.

Gutiérrez, G. 1988. *A Theology of Liberation: History, Politics and Salvation*. Maryknoll, NY: Orbis Books.

Habershon, A. R. 1957 (1967). *The Study of the Types*. Grand Rapids, MI: Kregel.

Hall, C. A. M. 1968. *With the Spirit's Sword: The Drama of Spiritual Warfare in the Theology of John Calvin*. Richmond, VA: John Knox.

Hamilton, V. P. 1995. *The Book of Genesis Chapters 18–50*. NICOT. Grand Rapids, MI: Eerdmans.

Hanson, R. P. C. 1988. *The Search for the Christian Doctrine of God*. Edinburgh: T. & T. Clark.

Harinck, G., ed. 2001. *De kwestie-Geelkerken: Een terugblik na 75 jaar*. Ad Chartas-reeks 5. Barneveld: De Vuurbaak 2001.

Harlow, R. E., ed. 1974. *God the Son: A Symposium*. Toronto, ON: Everyday Publications.

Harnack, A. von. 1957. *What Is Christianity?* The Library of Religion and Culture. New York: Harper.

Harris, M. J. 1976. *2 Corinthians*. EBC 10. Grand Rapids, MI: Zondervan.

———. 1992. *Jesus As God: The New Testament Use of Theos in Reference to Jesus*. Grand Rapids, MI: Baker Book House.

Harrison, E. F. 1976. *Romans*. EBC. Grand Rapids, MI: Zondervan.

Hasenhüttl, G. 1979. *Kritische Dogmatik*. Graz: Styria.

Head, P. M. 1997. *Christology and the Synoptic Problem: An Argument for Markan Priority*. Cambridge: Cambridge University Press.

Heering, G. J. 1945. *De christelijke godsidee*. Arnhem: Van Loghum Slaterus.

———. 1950. *Geloof en openbaring*. 2 vols. 3rd ed. Arnhem: Van Loghum Slaterus.

Hengel, M. 1995. *Studies in Early Christology*. Edinburgh: T. & T. Clark.

Hepp, V. 1937. *Dreigende deformatie*. Vol. 3: *De vereeniging van de beide naturen van Christus*. Kampen: Kok.

Herford, R. T. 1975 (repr. 1903). *Christianity in Talmud and Midrash*. Jersey City, NJ: Ktav.

Heschel, A. J. 1936. *Die Prophetie*. Krakau: Verlag der Polnischen Akademie der Wissenschaften.

Heschel, S. 1998. *Abraham Geiger and the Jewish Jesus*. Chicago: University of Chicago Press.

Heyns, J. A. 1953. *Die grondstruktuur van die modalistiese Triniteitsbeskouing*. Kampen: Kok.

———. 1977. "Grondlyne van 'n Algemene Wetenskapsleer" and "Teologie as Wetenskap." In *Op weg met die teologie*. 13–228. Edited by J. A. Heyns and W. D. Jonker. Pretoria: NG Kerkboekhandel.

———. 1988. *Dogmatiek*. Pretoria: NG Kerkboekhandel.

Hirsch, E. 1936. *Das Alte Testament und die Predigt des Evangeliums*. Tübingen: Mohr (Siebeck).

Hislop, A. 1959. *The Two Babylons*. Neptune, NJ: Loizeaux Brothers.

Hockel, A. 1965. *Christus der Erstgeborene: Zur Geschichte der Exegese von Kol. 1,15*. Düsseldorf: Patmos.

Hocking, W. J. 1934. *The Son of His Love*. London: C.A. Hammond.

Hodge, C. A. 1872. *Systematic Theology*. Vol. 1. New York: Scribner, Armstrong & Co.

Hoehner, H. W. 1977. *Chronological Aspects of the Life of Christ*. Grand Rapids, MI: Zondervan.

Hoeller, S. A. 1989. *Jung and the Lost Gospels*. Wheaton, IL:

Quest Books.

———. 2002. *Gnosticism: New Light on the Ancient Tradition of Inner Knowing*. Wheaton, IL: Quest Books.

Honig, A. G. 1910. *De persoon van den Middelaar in de nieuwere Duitsche dogmatiek*. Kampen: Kok.

Horsley, R. A. 1989. *Sociology and the Jesus Movement*. New York: Crossroad.

———. 1993. *Jesus and the Spiral of Violence*. Minneapolis: Fortress.

Horton, M. S. 2005. *Lord and Servant: A Covenant Christology*. Louisville, KY: Westminster John Knox.

Hughes, P.E. 1962. *Paul's Second Epistle to the Corinthians*. NICNT. Grand Rapids, MI: Eerdmans.

Hull, M. J. 1974. *Hellenistic Magic and the Synoptic Tradition*. London: SCM Press.

Immink, F. G. 1990. *Jezus Christus profeet, priester, koning*. Kampen: Kok.

Ironside, H. A. 1907. *Notes on the Book of Proverbs*. Neptune, NJ: Loizeaux Brothers.

Jager, O. n.d. *Hier koos de Heer zich vaste voet*. Wageningen: Gebr. Zomer & Keuning.

Jennings, F. C. 1966. *Studies in Isaiah*. 4th ed. Neptune, NJ: Loizeaux Brothers.

Jenson, R. W. 1982. *The Triune Identity: God According to the Gospel*. Philadelphia, PA: Fortress Press.

———. 2001. *Systematic Theology*. Vol. 1: *The Triune God*. New York: Oxford University Press.

Jeremias, J. 1957. *Unknown Sayings of Jesus*. Translated by R. G. Fuller. London: S.P.C.K.

———. 1971. *New Testament Theology*. Vol. 1: *The Proclamation of Jesus*. New York: Scribner.

Johnson, L. T. 1977. *The Literary Function of Possessions in Luke-Acts*. Missoula, MT: Scholars.

———. 1996. *The Real Jesus: The Misguided Quest for the Histor-*

ical Jesus and the Truth of the Traditional Gospels. San Francisco, CA: HarperSanFrancisco.

Jukes, A. 1875. *The Types of Genesis Briefly Considered*. London: Longmans, Green & Co.

Jüngel, E. 1977. *Gott als Geheimnis der Welt*. Tübingen: Mohr (Siebeck).

Juster, D. 1995. *Jewish Roots: A Foundation of Biblical Theology*. Shippensburg, PA: Destiny Image Publishers.

Kabak, A. A. 1972. *Op het smalle pad: De jood uit Nazareth*. 's-Gravenhage: Boekencentrum.

Kähler, M. 1964. *The So-Called Historical Jesus and the Historic, Biblical Christ*. Translated by C. E. Braaten. Philadelphia, PA: Fortress Press.

Kant, I. 2013. *Answer the Question: What Is Enlightenment?* Translated by D. F. Ferrer. Available at https://archive.org/details/AnswerTheQuestionWhatIsEnlightenment/mode/2up.

Kärkkäinen, V.-M. 2003. *Christology: A Global Introduction*. Grand Rapids, MI: Baker Academic.

Käsemann, E. 1954. "Das Problem des historischen Jesus." *Zeitschrift für Theologie und Kirche* 51:125–53.

Kasper, W. 1976. *Jesus the Christ*. Translated by V. Green. New York: Paulist Press.

_____. 1983. *The God of Jesus Christ*. London: SCM Press.

Kaufmann, Y. 1988. *Christianity and Judaism: Two Covenants*. Jerusalem: Magnus Press.

Kaylor, R. D. 1994. *Jesus the Prophet: His Vision of the Kingdom on Earth*. Louisville, KY: Westminster/John Knox.

Keil, C. F. and F. Delitzsch. 1976–1977. *Commentary on the Old Testament*. 10 vols. Grand Rapids, MI: Eerdmans.

Kelly, J. N. D. 1958. *Early Christian Doctrines*. New York: Harper.

Kelly, W., ed. 1856–1920. *Bible Treasury: A Monthly Review of Prophetic and Practical Subjects*. Available at https://bibletruthpublishers.com/bible-treasury/lpvl22465.

———. 1884. "The First Epistle to Timothy." *BT* 15.

———. 1890. "The Catholic Apostolic Body, or Irvingites, Chap. IV. Doctrine. § 4. The Incarnation." *BT* 18:73–77.

———. 1895a. "The Mystery of Godliness." *BT* 20.

———. 1902. *Notes on the Book of Daniel*. New York: Loizeaux Brothers.

———. 1964. *Lectures on Philippians and Colossians*. Oak Park, IL: Bible Truth Publishers.

———. 1966. *An Exposition of the Gospel of John*. London: C.A. Hammond.

Kennedy, H. A. A. 1979. *The Epistle of Paul to the Philippians*. EGT 3. Grand Rapids, MI: Eerdmans.

Kent, H. A., Jr. 1978. *Philippians*. EBC 11. Grand Rapids, MI: Zondervan.

Kessel, E. L. 1988. *The Androgynous Christ: A Christian Feminist View*. Portland: Interprint.

Kidger, M. 1999. *The Star of Bethlehem: An Astronomer's View*. Princeton, NJ: Princeton University Press.

Kidner, D. 1967. *Genesis*. Tyndale Old Testament Commentary. Chicago: InterVarsity.

Kierkegaard, S. 1936. *Philosophical Fragments*. Princeton: Princeton University Press.

King, K. L. 2003. *What Is Gnosticism?* Cambridge, MA: Harvard University Press.

Kittel, G. et al., eds. 1964–1976. *Theological Dictionary of the New Testament*. Translated by G. W. Bromiley. 10 vols. Grand Rapids, MI: Wm. B. Eerdmans.

Klausner, J. 1964. *Jesus of Nazareth: His Life, Times and Teaching*. Boston: Beacon Books.

Klooster, F. 1977. *Quests for the Historical Jesus*. Grand Rapids, MI: Baker.

Kloosterman, N. D. 1991. *Scandalum Infirmorum et Communio*

Sanctorum: The Relation Between Christian Liberty and Neighbor Love in the Church. Neerlandia, AB: Inheritance Publications. Available at http://theoluniv.ub.rug.nl/265/.

Knevel, A. G. and M. J. Paul, eds. 1995. *Verkenningen in de oudtestamentische messiasverwachting.* Kampen: Kok Voorhoeve/Hilversum: Evangelische Omroep.

Knight, J. 2004. *Jesus: An Historical and Theological Investigation.* London/New York: T. & T. Clark.

Knowling, R. J. 1979. *The Acts of the Apostles.* EGT 2. Grand Rapids, MI: Eerdmans.

Knox, J. 1967. *The Humanity and Divinity of Christ.* Cambridge: Cambridge University Press.

Koehler, L. and W. Baumgartner. 1953. *Lexicon in Veteris Testamenti Libros.* Leiden: E.J. Brill.

Koester, H. 1971. "The Structure and Criteria of Early Christian Beliefs." In *Trajectories through Early Christianity.* 205–31. Edited by J. M. Robinson and H. Koester. Philadelphia, PA: Fortress.

Kohler, K. 1894. *Judaism at the World's Parliament of Religions.* Cincinnati, OH: Clarke.

Kohnstamm, P. 1931. *De heilige.* Haarlem: Tjeenk Willink.

König, A. 1975. *Hier is ek! Gelovig nagedink.* Vol. 1: *Oor God.* Pretoria: N.G. Kerkboekhandel.

Koopmans, J. 1938. *Het oudkerkelijk dogma in de reformatie, bepaaldelijk bij Calvijn.* Wageningen: Veenman.

Kopmels, E. 2005. *Christus en cultuur: Beelden van Christus in de moderne theologie.* Budel: Damon.

Korff, F. W. A. 1940. *Christologie: De leer van het komen Gods.* Vol. 1. Nijkerk: Callenbach.

Kramer, G. H. 1996. *Gegrepen door Christus: Bijbelstudies bij de Brief van Paulus aan de Filippiërs.* Vaassen: Medema.

Kretschmar, G. 1956. *Studien zur frühchristlichen Trinitätstheologie.* Tübingen: Mohr (Siebeck).

Kuitert, H. M. 1962. *De mensvormigheid Gods: Een dogma-*

tisch-hermeneutische studie over de anthropomorphismen van de Heilige Schrift. Kampen: Kok.

———. 1999. *Jesus: The Legacy of Christianity.* Translated by John Bowdon. London: SCM Press.

———, A. van de Beek, et al. 1999. *Jezus bij hoog en bij lag: De christologie van Van de Beek en Kuitert.* Kampen: Kok.

Kuitse, R. S. 1992. "Christology in the Qur'an." *Missiology: An International Review* 20:355–69.

Kümmel, [It looks like something is missing here: author's initial, date?] *und Erfüllung.* Basel: Majer.

Küng, H. 1987. *The Incarnation of God: An Introduction to Hegel's Theological Thought as a Prolegomena to a Future Christology.* Translated by J. R. Stephenson. New York: Crossroad.

Kuschel, K.-J. 1990. *Geboren vor aller Zeit? Der Streit um Christi Ursprung.* München: Piper.

Küster, V. 1999. *Die vielen Gesichter Jesu Christi.* Neukirchen-Vluyn: Neukirchener Verlag.

Kuyper, A. 1871. *Het modernisme een fata morgana op Christelijk gebied.* Amsterdam: H. de Hoogh & Co.

———. 1887. *De vleeschwording des Woords.* Amsterdam: J.A. Wormser.

———. 1910. *Dictaten Dogmatiek.* 5 vols. Kampen: J.H. Kok.

———. 1946. *The Work of the Holy Spirit.* Translated by H. De Vries. 3 vols. Grand Rapids, MI: Eerdmans. Available at https://www.ccel.org/ccel/kuyper/holy_spirit.html.

———. 2008. *Encyclopedia of Sacred Theology: Its Principles.* Translated by J. H. De Vries. Edited by B. C. Richards. Vol. 1, 1–53, and Vol. 2 of the original. Available at www.reformingscience.com.

Ladd, G. E. 1952. *Crucial Questions About the Kingdom of God.* Grand Rapids, MI: Eerdmans.

———. 1959. *The Gospel of the Kingdom: Popular Expositions on the Kingdom of God.* Grand Rapids, MI: Eerdmans.

———. 1974. *The Presence of the Future: The Eschatology of Bib-*

lical Realism. Grand Rapids, MI: Eerdmans.

———. 1975. *I Believe in the Bodily Resurrection of Jesus.* Grand Rapids, MI: Eerdmans.

LaHaye, T. 1997. *Jesus: Who Is He?* Sisters, OR: Multnomah Press.

Lake, K. 1907. *The Historical Evidence for the Resurrection of Jesus Christ.* London: Williams & Norgate.

Lalleman, P. J. 2005. *1, 2 en 3 Johannes: Brieven van een kroongetuige.* CNT. Third Series. Kampen: Kok.

Lane, W. L. 1974. *The Gospel of Mark.* NICNT. Grand Rapids, MI: Eerdmans.

Lang, G. H. 1942. *The Histories and Prophecies of Daniel.* London: Oliphants.

Lapide, P. 1983. *The Resurrection of Jesus: A Jewish Perspective.* Translated by W. C. Linss. Minneapolis, MN: Augsburg Publishing House.

Lapide, P. 1984. *Is dat niet de zoon van Jozef? Jezus in het hedendaagse jodendom.* Baarn: Ten Have.

Lapide, P. 1988. *Wie waren er schuldig aan de dood van Jezus?* Kampen: Kok.

Lapide, P. and U. Luz. 1985. *Jesus in Two Perspectives: A Jewish-Christian Dialog.* Translated by L. W. Denef. Minneapolis, MN: Augsburg Publishing House.

Lauterbach, J. Z. 1951. "Jesus in the Talmud." *Rabbinic Essays.* 473-570. Cincinnati: Hebrew Union College.

Leupold, H. C. 1942. *Exposition of Genesis.* London: Evangelical Press.

Lewis, C. S. 2002. *The Lion, the Witch and the Wardrobe.* London: HarperCollins.

———. 2015. *Mere Christianity.* London: HarperOne.

Liefeld, W. L. 1984. *Luke.* EBC 8. Grand Rapids, MI: Zondervan.

Lienhard, M. 1980. *Martin Luthers christologisches Zeugnis.* Göttingen: Vandenhoeck & Ruprecht.

Lightfoot, J. B. 1865. *Saint Paul's Epistle to the Galatians.* London: Macmillan.

———. 1879. *Saint Paul's Epistles to the Colossians and Philemon.* London: Macmillan.

———. 1889. *Essays on "Supernatural Religion".* London: Macmillan.

Lincoln, W. n.d. *Typical Foreshadowings in Genesis.* Glasgow: Pickering & Inglis.

Lonergan, B. 1976. *The Way to Nicea: The Dialectical Development of Trinitarian Theology.* London: Darton, Longman & Todd.

Longenecker, R. N. 1981. *The Acts of the Apostles.* EBC 9. Grand Rapids, MI: Zondervan.

Loofs, F. 1975. *Nestorius and His Place in the History of Christian Doctrine.* New York: Lenox Hill.

Loonstra, B. 1994. *De geloofwaardigheid van de Bijbel.* Zoetermeer: Boekencentrum.

McComiskey, T. E. 1985. *Micah.* EBC 7. Grand Rapids, MI: Zondervan.

McDowell, J. 1972. *Evidence That Demands a Verdict.* San Bernardino, CA: Campus Crusade for Christ.

———. 1979. *Daniel in the Critics' Den: Historical Evidence for the Authenticity of the Book of Daniel.* San Bernardino, CA: Campus Crusade for Christ International.

———. 1997. *Jezus feit of fictie?* Heerenveen: Barnabas.

———. 2006. *The Da Vinci Code: A Quest for Answers.* Holiday, FL: Green Key Books.

McGrath, A. 2002. *Knowing Christ.* New York: Galilee. 2001.

———. 2007. *Christian Theology: An Introduction.* Maiden, MA: Blackwell.

———. 2008. *Resurrection.* Minneapolis, MN: Fortress Press.

Machen, J. G. 1930. *The Virgin Birth of Christ.* New York: Harper & Row.

Mackintosh, C. H. 1914. *The Doctrine of the Person of Jesus Christ.* New York: Scribner.

MacLeod, D. 1998. *The Person Of Christ: Contours of Christian Theology.* Downers Grove, IL: InterVarsity.

Macquarrie, J. 1975. *Thinking about God.* London: SCM.

———. 1981. "Truth in Christology." In *God Incarnate: Story and Belief.* Edited by A. E. Harvey. 24–33. London: SPCK.

———. 1990. *Jesus Christ in Modern Thought.* London: SCM.

———. 1998. *Christology Revisited.* Philadelphia: Trinity Press International.

———. 2003. *Christology Revisited.* London: SCM.

Maier, G. 1982. *Der Prophet Daniel.* Wuppertaler Studienbibel. Wuppertal: Brockhaus.

Maier, J. 1978. *Jesus von Nazareth in der talmudischen Überlieferung.* Darmstadt: Wissenschaftliche Buchgesellschaft.

Mann, C. S. 1986. *Mark.* AB 27. Garden City, NY: Doubleday.

Maoz, B. 2003. *Judaism Is Not Jewish: A Friendly Critique of the Messianic Movement.* Fearn: Mentor.

Markschies, C. 2000. *Gnosis: An Introduction.* Edinburgh: T. & T. Clark.

Marshall, I. H. 1971. *Luke: Historian and Theologian.* Grand Rapids, MI: Zondervan.

———. 1977. *I Believe in the Historical Jesus.* London: Hodder & Stoughton.

———. 1978a. *The Epistles of John.* NICNT. Grand Rapids, MI: Eerdmans.

———. 1978b. *The Gospel of Luke.* NIGTC. Grand Rapids, MI: Eerdmans.

———. 1990a. *The Origins of New Testament Christology.* Leicester: Apollos.

———. 1990b. *Jesus the Savior.* Downers Grove, IL: InterVarsity.

Martin, R. P. 1972. *Mark: Evangelist and Theologian.* Grand Rapids, MI: Zondervan.

Marxsen, W. 1969. *Mark the Evangelist: Studies on the Redaction History of the Gospel.* Translated by J. Boice et al. Nashville, TN: Abingdon.

Massey, G. 1886. *The Historical Jesus and Mythical Christ.* Springfield, MA: Star Publishing Company.

Matter, H. M. 1965. *De brief aan de Philippenzen en de brief aan Philemon.* COT. Kampen: Kok.

Medema, H. P. 1990. *Het proces tegen Jezus.* Vaassen: Medema.

———. 1993. *Het leven is geopenbaard: Bijbelstudies bij de Eerste Brief van Johannes.* Vaassen: Medema.

Meier, J. P. 1991. *A Marginal Jew: Rethinking the Historical Jesus.* Vol. 1: *The Roots of the Problem and the Person.* New York: Doubleday.

———. 1994. *A Marginal Jew: Rethinking the Historical Jesus.* Vol. 2: *Mentor, Message, and Miracles.* New York: Doubleday.

———. 2001. *A Marginal Jew: Rethinking the Historical Jesus.* Vol. 3: *Companions and Competitors.* New York: Doubleday.

Metzger, B. M. 1975. *A Textual Commentary on the Greek New Testament.* 2nd ed. London/New York: United Bible Societies.

Meyer, B. F. 1979. *The Aims of Jesus.* London: SCM.

Michel, O. 1992. "*Ho huios tou anthropou*, the Son of man." *NIDNTT* 3:613–634.

Miguens, M. 1975. *The Virgin Birth: An Evaluation of Scriptural Evidence.* Westminster, MD: Christian Classics.

Miguez Bonino, J. 1974. *Theologie van verdrukten: Een boodschap uit Latijns Amerika.* Kampen: Kok.

Miley, J. 1892. *Systematic Theology.* Vol. 1. New York: Methodist Book Concern.

Miskotte, K. H. 1941. "Halt bij Chalcedon?" *Woord en Wereld* 1941:23–42.

Molnar, M. R. 1999. *The Star of Bethlehem: The Legacy of the*

Magi. Piscataway, NJ: Rutgers University Press.

Moltmann, J. 1993. *The Crucified God: The Cross of Christ as the Foundation and Criticism of Christian Theology*. Minneapolis, MN: Fortress Press.

Montefiore, C. G. 1910. *Some Elements of the Religious Teaching of Jesus According to the Synoptic Gospels*. London: Macmillan.

———. 1930. *Rabbinic Literature and Gospel Teachings*. London: Macmillan.

Moody, D. 1981. *The Word of Truth: A Summary of Christian Doctrine Based on Biblical Revelation*. Grand Rapids, MI: Eerdmans.

Moore, P. 2001. *The Star of Bethlehem*. Bath: Canopus Publishing.

Morison, F. 1972 (repr. 1930). *Who Moved the Stone?* London: Faber & Faber.

Morris, H. M. 1976. *The Genesis Record: A Scientific and Devotional Commentary on the Book of Beginnings*. San Diego, CA: Creation-Life Publishers.

Morris, L. 1971. *The Gospel According to John*. NICNT. Grand Rapids, MI: Eerdmans.

———. 1974. *The Gospel According to St. Luke*. TNTC. Grand Rapids, MI: Eerdmans.

Moule, C. F. D. 1965. *The Gospel According to Mark*. CBC. Cambridge: Cambridge University Press.

———. 1967. *The Phenomenon of the New Testament*. London: SCM.

———. 1977. *The Origin of Christology*. Cambridge: Cambridge University Press.

Müller, J. J. 1984 (repr. 1955). *The Epistle of Paul to the Philippians*. NICNT. Grand Rapids, MI: Eerdmans.

Murray, J. 1968. *The Epistle to the Romans*. NICNT. Grand Rapids, MI: Eerdmans.

———J. 1991. *Collected Writings*. Vol. 2. Edited by I. Murray.

Edinburgh: Banner of Truth.

Nassi, T. 1990. *The Great Mystery: How Can Three Be One?* Cincinnati, OH: Messianic Literature Outreach.

Neander, A. 1847. *The Life of Jesus Christ in its Historical Connexion and Historical Development*. Translated by J. M'Clintock and C. E. Blumenthal. 3rd ed. New York: Harper & Brothers.

Neill, S. 1977. "Jesus and Myth." In *The Truth of God Incarnate*. Edited by M. Green. 58–70. Grand Rapids, MI: Eerdmans.

Neusner, J. 2000. *A Rabbi Talks with Jesus*. 2nd ed. New York: Doubleday.

Nicoll, W. R., ed. 1979. *The Expositor's Greek Testament*. Grand Rapids, MI: Eerdmans.

Niehaus, J. J. 1996. "Theology of Theophany." *NIDOTT* 4:1247–50.

Nieuwenhuis, H. 2000. *De Ster van Bethlehem: Natuurverschijnsel of een wonder?* Franeker: Terlenga's Drukkerij.

Noel, N. 1936. *The History of the Brethren*. Vol 1. Denver, CO: W.F. Knapp.

Noordtzij, A. 1932. *De profeet Ezechiël*. Kampen: Kok.

_____. 1934. *Het boek der psalmen*. Vol. 1: *Psalm 1–70*. Kampen: Kok.

North, C. R. 1956. *The Suffering Servant in Deutero-Isaiah: An Historical and Critical Study*. 2nd ed. London: Oxford University Press.

Oegema, G. S. 1991. *De messiaanse verwachtingen ten tijde van Jezus*. Baarn: Ten Have.

O'Meara, T. 1966. *Mary in Protestant and Catholic Theology*. New York: Sheed & Ward.

_____. 1974. *Loose in the World*. New York: Paulist Press.

O'Neill, J. C. 1995. *Who Did Jesus Think He Was?* Leiden: E.J. Brill.

Orr, J. 1908. *The Virgin Birth of Christ*. London: Hodder & Stoughton.

Oswalt, J. N. 1986. *The Book of Isaiah Chapters 1–39*. NICOT. Grand Rapids, MI: Eerdmans.

Ott, H. 1969. *Wirklichkeit und Glaube*. Vol. 2: *Der persönliche Gott*. Göttingen : Vandenhoeck & Ruprecht.

_____. 1972. *Die Antwort des Glaubens: Systematische Theologie in 50 Artikeln*. Stuttgart: Kreuz Verlag.

_____. 1974. *God*. Edinburgh: St. Andrew Press.

Ouweneel, W. J. 1973. *Het Hooglied van Salomo*. Winschoten: Uit het Woord der Waarheid.

_____. 1978a. *Wat is het Zoonschap van Christus?* Winschoten: Uit het Woord der Waarheid.

_____. 1978b. *Het ontstaan van de bijbel*. Hilversum: Evangelische Omroep.

_____. 1980. *Die Herrlichkeit des Herrn Jesus in den vier Evangelien*. Neustadt: Ernst Paulus Verlag.

_____. 1982. *"Wij zien Jezus": Bijbelstudies over de brief aan de Hebreeën*. 2 vols. Vaassen: Medema.

_____. 1984. *Psychologie: Een christelijke kijk op het mentale leven*. Amsterdam: Buijten & Schipperheijn.

_____. 1986a. *De leer van de mens*. Amsterdam: Buijten & Schipperheijn.

_____. 1986b. *Het ontstaan van het Christendom: De geschiedenis van het Nieuwe Testament*. Hilversum: Evangelische Omroep.

_____. 1988–90. *De Openbaring van Jezus Christus: Bijbelstudies over het boek Openbaring*. 2 vols. Vaassen: Medema.

_____. 1989. *De profeet Jona*. 2nd ed. Alblasserdam: Stg. Boeken bij de Bijbel.

_____. 1991. *Israël en de Kerk, oftewel: Eén of twee volken van God? Confrontatie van de verbondsleer en de bedelingenleer*. Vaassen: Medema.

_____. 1995. *Christian Doctrine: I. The External Prolegomena*, Amsterdam: Buijten & Schipperheijn.

_____. 1997. *De vrijheid van de Geest: Bijbelstudies bij de Brief van Paulus aan de Galaten.* Vaassen: Medema.

———. 1998. *De zevende koningin: Het eeuwig vrouwelijke en de raad van God.* Metahistorische triologie. Vol. 2. Heerenveen: Barnabas.

———. 2000a. *Het Jobslijden van Israël: Israëls lijden oplichtend uit het boek Job,* Vaassen: Medema.

———. 2000b. *De zesde kanteling: Christus en 5000 jaar denkgeschiedenis: Religie en metafysica in het jaar 2000.* Metahistorische trilogie. Vol. 3. Heerenveen: Barnabas.

———. 2001a. *"Hoe lief heb ik uw wet!": De Eeuwige Torah tussen Oude en Nieuwe Verbond.* Vaassen: Medema.

———. 2001b. *Hoogtijden voor Hem: De bijbelse feesten en hun betekenis voor Joden en christenen.* Vaassen: Medema.

———. 2002. "Jezus Christus versus Julius Caesar." *ELLIPS* 240.

———. 2003. *De negende Koning: Het laatste der hemelrijken: De triomf van Christus over de machten.* Metahistorische triologie. Vol. 1. 3rd ed. Soesterberg: Aspekt (Forthcoming in English as *The Ninth King: The Last of the Celestial Empires, The Triumph of Christ over de Powers*).

———. (2003) 2004. *Geneest de zieken! Over de bijbelse leer van ziekte, genezing en bevrijding.* 4th ed. Vaassen: Medema.

———. 2005a. *De God die is: Waarom ik geen atheïst ben.* Vaassen: Medema.

———. 2005b. *Sta op, laat je dopen.* Vaassen: Medema.

———. 2007. *De Geest van God: Ontwerp van een pneumatologie.* EDR 1. Vaassen: Medema.

———. 2008. *De schepping van God: Ontwerp van een scheppings-, mens- en zondeleer.* EDR 2. Vaassen: Medema.

———. 2009. *Het zoenoffer van God: Ontwerp van een verzoeningsleer.* EDR 5. Vaassen: Medema.

———. 2012. *De toekomst van God: Ontwerp van een eschatology.* EDR 10. Heerenveen: Medema.

———. **2014.** *Wisdom for Thinkers: An Introduction to Christian*

Philosophy. Edited by N. D. Kloosterman. Jordan Station, ON: Paideia Press.

———. 2015. *What Then Is Theology?* Edited by N. D. Kloosterman. Jordan Station, ON: Paideia Press.

———. 2016. *The Heidelberg Diary: Daily Devotions on the Heidelberg Catechism*. Edited by N. D. Kloosterman. Jordan Station, ON: Paideia Press.

———. 2018. *Adam, Where Are You? And Why This Matters: A Theological Evaluation of the New Evolutionist Hermeneutics*. Edited by N. D. Kloosterman. Toronto, ON: Ezra Press.

———. Forthcoming. *An Evangelical Introduction to Reformational Theology*. Edited by N. D. Kloosterman. 13 vols. Jordan Station, ON: Paideia Press.

———. n.d.-a. *Leviticus: een serie bijbellezingen*. Hengelo: A. Lievers.

———. n.d.-b. *Het boek Esther*. Alblasserdam: Stg. Boeken bij de Bijbel.

Pagels, E. 1992. *De gnostische evangeliën*. Cothen: Servire.

Pannenberg, W. 1977. *Jesus – God and Man*. Translated by L. L. Wilkins and D. A. Priebe. Philadelphia, PA: Westminster Press.

———. 1994. *Systematic Theology*. Translated by G. W. Bromiley. Vol. 2. Grand Rapids, MI: Eerdmans.

Parrinder, E. G. 1977. *Jesus in the Qur'ân*. New York: Oxford University Press.

Paul, M. J. 1987. "The Order of Melchizedek (Ps 110:4 and Heb 7:3)." *Westminster Theological Journal* 49:195–211.

Payne, J. B. 1962. *The Theology of the Older Testament*. Grand Rapids, MI: Zondervan.

Peabody, D. B., L. Cope, and A. McNicol. 2002. *One Gospel From Two: Mark's Use of Matthew and Luke*. Philadelphia, PA: Trinity Press International.

Pentecost, J. D. 1981. *The Words and Works of Jesus Christ: A Study of the Life of Christ*. Grand Rapids, MI: Zondervan.

Perrin, N. 1963. *The Kingdom of God in the Teaching of Jesus*. Philadelphia, PA: Westminster Press.

_____. 1967. *Rediscovering the Teaching of Jesus*. London: SCM.

_____. 1976. *Jesus and the Language of the Kingdom: Symbol and Metaphor in New Testament Interpretation*. Philadelphia, PA: Fortress Press.

Pesch, R. 1976-1977. *Das Markusevangelium: Erster Teil* resp. *Zweiter Teil*. Herders theol. Komm. NT II/1, 2. Freiburg: Herder.

Picknett, L. and C. Prince. 1998. *Het geheime boek der Grootmeesters: Maria Magdalena, Johannes de Doper en de ware identiteit van de Messias*. Baarn: Tirion.

Pilgrim, W. E. 1981. *Good News to the Poor*. Minneapolis: Augsburg.

Plummer, A. 1922. *Gospel According to St. Luke*. International Critical Commentary. 5th ed. Edinburgh: T. & T. Clark.

Pollock, A. J. n.d.-a. *The Eternal Son*. London: Central Bible Truth Depot.

_____. n.d.-b. *The Tabernacle's Typical Teaching*. London: Central Bible Truth Depot.

Poortvliet, R. 2004. *Hij was een van ons*. Rev. ed. Kampen: Kok.

Price, R. M. 2000. *Deconstructing Jesus*. Amherst, NY: Prometheus Books.

Quispel, G. 1972 (repr. 1951). *Gnosis als Weltreligion*. Zürich: Origo.

Radmacher, E. D. and R. D. Preus, eds. 1984. *Hermeneutics, Inerrancy, and the Bible*. Grand Rapids, MI: Zondervan.

Rahner, K. 1961. *Theological Investigations*. Vol. 1. London: Darton, Longman, & Todd.

_____. 1970. *The Trinity*. New York: Herder & Herder.

_____. 1971. *Ik geloof in Jezus Christus*. Brugge: Desclée De Brouwer.

_____. 1974. "Remarks on the dogmatic treatise 'De Trinitate'." *TI* IV:77-102).

---. 1975. "Der dreifaltige Gott als transzendenter Urgrund der Heilsgeschichte." In *Mysterium Salutis*. 2nd ed. 2:317–401. Edited by J. Feiner and M. Löhrer. Einsiedeln: Benziger.

---. 1979. "The Hiddenness of God." *TI* XVI:227–243.

Rahner K. and P. Lapide. 1987. *Encountering Jesus – Encountering Judaism: A Dialogue*. Translated by D. Perkins. New York: Crossroad.

--- and W. Thüsing. 1980. *A New Christology*. Translated by D. Smith and V. Green. New York: Seabury Press.

Räisänen, H. 1980. "The Portrait of Jesus in the Qur'an: Reflections of a Biblical Scholar." *Muslim World* 70:122-33.

Ramsay, W. M. 1915. *The Bearing of Recent Discovery on the Trustworthiness of the New Testament*. London: Hodder & Stoughton.

Ratzinger, J. 2007. *Jesus of Nazareth: From the Baptism in the Jordan to the Transfiguration*. Translated by A. J. Walker. New York, NY: Doubleday.

Raymond, R. L. 2003. *Jesus Divine Messiah: The New and Old Testament Witness*. Fearn: Mentor.

Reimarus, H. S. 1778. "Von dem Zwecke Jesu und seiner Jünger." *Wolfenbütteler Fragmente IV*. Edited by G. E. Lessing. In *Lessing's Werke*. Berlin: Hempel.

Renan, E. 1863. *The Life of Jesus*. New York: A. L. Burt.

Ridderbos, H. N. 1946. *Zelfopenbaring en zelfverberging: Het historisch karakter van Jezus' Messiaansche zelfopenbaring volgens de synoptische Evangeliën*. Kampen: Kok.

---. 1987. *Matthew*. Translated by R. Togtman. Bible Student's Commentary. Regency Reference Library. Grand Rapids, MI: Zondervan Publishing House.

Ridderbos, J. 1930. *De kleine profeten*. Vol. 2: *Van Obadja tot Zefanja*. KV. Kampen: Kok.

---. 1934. *De profeet Jesaja*. Vol. 2: *Hoofdstuk 40–66*. 2 ed. KV. Kampen: Kok.

_____. 1935. *De kleine profeten*. Vol. 3: *Haggaï, Zacharia, Maleachi*. KV. Kampen: Kok.

_____. 1955. *De psalmen*. Vol. 1: *Psalm 1-41*. COT. Kampen: Kok.

_____. 1958. *De psalmen*. Vol. 2: *Psalm 42-106*. COT. Kampen: Kok.

Riesner, R. 1981. *Jesus als Lehrer*. Tübingen: Mohr (Siebeck).

Rimmer, H. 1943. *The Magnificence of Jesus Christ*. Grand Rapids, MI: Eerdmans.

Riss, R. 1977. *The Evidence for the Resurrection of Jesus Christ*. Minneapolis, MN: Bethany Fellowship.

Rivkin, E. 1984. *What Crucified Jesus?* Nashville, TN: Abingdon Press.

Robinson, J. A. T. 1973. *The Human Face of God*. London: SCM.

Robinson, J. M. 1959. *A New Quest of the Historical Jesus*. London: SCM.

Rohde, J. 1968. *Rediscovering the Teaching of the Evangelists*. Philadelphia, PA: Westminster.

Rosenzweig, F. 1971. *The Star of Redemption*. Translated by W. W. Hallo. New York, NY: Holt, Rinehart & Winston.

Ross, A. P. 1991. *Proverbs*. EBC 5. Grand Rapids, MI: Zondervan.

Rowley, H. H. 1950. "Melchizedek and Zadok (Gen 14 and Ps 110)." In *Festschrift für Alfred Bertholet zum 80. Geburtstag*. 461-472. Edited by W. Baumgartner et al. Tübingen: Mohr (Siebeck).

_____. 1952. *The Servant of the Lord and Other Essays on the Old Testament*. London: Lutterworth Press.

Rumscheidt, H. M. 1972. *Revelation and Theology: An Analysis of the Barth-Harnack Correspondence of 1923*. Cambridge: Cambridge University Press.

Runia, K. 1974. "A 'New' Christology Challenges the Church." *Christianity Today* 18.7:4-8.

_____. 1992. *Het geheim van Jezus Christus*. Kampen: Kok.

Sailhamer, J. H. 1990. *Genesis*. EBC 2. Grand Rapids, MI: Zondervan.

Sanders, E. P. 1985. *Jesus and Judaism*. London: SCM.

———. 1990. *Jewish Law from Jesus to the Mishnah: Five Studies*. London: SCM.

Santala, R. 1992. *The Messiah in the Old Testament in the Light of Rabbinical Writings*. Translated by W. Kinnaird. Jerusalem: Keren Ahvah Meshihit. 1997. *Der Messias im Alten Testament im Licht der rabbinischen Schriften*. Neuhausen-Stuttgart: Hänssler-Verlag.

Saucy, M. 1997. *The Kingdom of God in the Teaching of Jesus in 20th Century Theology*. Dallas: Word.

Schaeffer, F. A. 1982. *The Complete Works: A Christian Worldview*. Vol. 2: *A Christian View of the Bible As Truth*. Westchester, IL: Crossway Books.

Schaff, Philip. 1919. *Creeds of Christendom, With A History and Critical Notes*. Vol. 2. 6th ed. Available at https://www.ccel.org/ccel/schaff/creeds2.html.

Schiffman, M. 1996. *Return of the Remnant: The Rebirth of Messianic Judaism*. Baltimore, MD: Lederer Messianic Publishers.

Schilder, K., ed. 1939. *'t Hoogfeest der Schriften: Studies over de Vleeschwording des Woords*. Goes: Oosterbaan & Le Cointre.

———. 1949/1950. *Heidelbergsche Catechismus*. Vols. 2, 3. Goes: Oosterbaan & Le Cointre.

———. 2016. *Christ and Culture*. Translated by W. Helder and A. H. Oosterhoff. Annotated by J. Douma. Hamilton, ON: Lucerna/CRTS Publications.

Schillebeeckx, E. 1979. *Jesus: An Experiment in Christology*. Translated by H. Hoslins. New York, NY: Seabury Press.

Schirrmacher, C. 1994. *Der Islam 2: Geschichte, Lehre, Unterschiede zum Christentum*. Neuhausen/Stuttgart: Hänssler.

Schirrmacher, T. 2001. *Christus im Alten Testament*. Hamburg: RVB.

Schleiermacher, F. D. E. 1928. *The Christian Faith*. Translated and edited by H. R. Mackintosh and J. S. Stewart. Edingurgh: T. & T. Clark.

Schlink, E. 1983. *Oekumenische Dogmatik: Grundzüge*. Göttingen: Vandenhoeck & Ruprecht.

Schmidt, K. L. 1969 (repr. 1919). *Der Rahmen der Geschichte Jesu*. Darmstadt: Wissenschaftliche Buchgesellschaft.

Schmidt, M. 1949. "Der Ort der Trinitätslehre bei Emil Brunner." *Theologische Zeitschrift* 5:46-66.

Schmiedel, P. W. 1901. "Gospels." *Encyclopaedia Biblica* 2:1761-1898.

Schneider, O. 1953. *Das zweite Buch Samuel*. Paderborn: F. Schöningh.

Schneider, R. 1979 (repr. 1947). *Das Vaterunser*. 6 ed. Freiburg: Herder.

Schoeps, H. J. 1932. *Jüdischer Glaube in dieser Zeit: Prolegomena zur Grundlegung einer systematischen Theologie des Judentums*. Berlin: Vortrupp.

———. 1949. *Theologie und Geschichte des Judenchristentums*. Tübingen: Mohr (Siebeck).

———. 1963. *The Jewish-Christian Argument: A History of Theologies in Conflict*. New York: Holt, Rinehart & Winston.

Schönweiss, H. and C. Brown. 1992. "*Proskyneō*." *NIDNTT* 2:875-79.

Schoon, S. 1991. *De weg van Jezus: Een christologische heroriëntatie vanuit de joods-christelijke ontmoeting*. Kampen: Kok.

Schoonenberg, P. J. A. M. 1969. *Hij is een God van mensen*. 's-Hertogenbosch: Malmberg.

Schuler, B. 1961. *Die Lehre von der Dreipersönlichkeit Gottes*. Paderborn: Ferdinand Schöningh.

Schulze, W. A. 1975. "Zur Geschichte der Auslegung von Matth. 2,1-12." *Theologische Zeitschrift* 31:150-60.

Schumann, O. 1988 (repr. 1975). *Der Christus der Muslime: Christologische Aspekte in der arabisch-islamitischen Literatur*.

2nd ed. Köln: Böhlau Verlag.

Schüssler Fiorenza, E. 1994. *Jesus: Miriam's Child, Sophia's Prophet: Critical Issues in Feminist Theology.* New York, NY: Continuum.

Schwarz, H. 1998. *Christology.* Grand Rapids, MI: Eerdmans.

Schweitzer, A. 1956. *The Quest of the Historical Jesus: A Critical Study of its Progress from Reimarus to Wrede.* Translated by W. Montgomery. New York, NY: Macmillan.

Schweizer, E. 1971a. *Jesus.* Translated by D. E. Green. Richmond, VA: John Knox Press.

_____. 1971b. *The Good News According to Mark.* London: SPCK.

Scott, W. 1880. *Bible Outlines.* Charlotte, NC: Books for Christians.

Sellers, R.V. 1961. *The Council of Chalcedon.* London: SPCK.

Sevenster, G. 1948. *De christologie van het Nieuwe Testament.* 2nd ed. Amsterdam: Holland.

_____. 1986. "Christologie. I. Christologie des Urchristentums." *RGG* 1:1745–62.

Shulam, J. (with H. Le Cornu). 1998. *A Commentary on the Jewish Roots of Romans.* Baltimore, MD: Messianic Jewish Publishers.

Siegel, B. 1976. *The Controversial Sholem Asch: An Introduction to His Fiction.* Bowling Green, OH: Bowling Green University Popular Press.

Sigal, P. 1987. *The Halakhah of Jesus of Nazareth According to the Gospel of Matthew.* Lanham, MD: University Press of America.

Sjöberg, E. 1955. *Der verborgene Menschensohn in den Evangelien.* Lund: Gleerup.

Slavenburg, J. 1992. *De verborgen leringen van Jezus.* Deventer: Ankh-Hermes.

Slotki, I. W. 1983. *Isaiah.* SBB. London: Soncino.

_____. 1985. *Daniel, Ezra, Nehemiah.* SBB. London: Soncino.

Smeets, J. 1991. *Jezus was geen christen*. Kampen: Kok.

Smith, B. T. D. 1937. *The Parables of the Synoptic Gospels*. Cambridge: Cambridge University Press.

Smith, H. 1986. *"Hold That Fast Which Thou Hast."* Belfast: Words of Truth.

──────. 1987. *The Gospel of Mark*. Wooler: Central Bible Hammond Trust.

Smith, J. D. n.d. *The Brides of Scripture*. Glasgow: Pickering & Inglis.

Smith, M. 1978. *Jesus the Magician: Charlatan or Son of God?* London: Gollancz.

Smith, W. M. 1940. *The Supernaturalness of Christ*. Boston: W.A. Wilde.

──────. 1965. *Therefore Stand: Christian Apologetics*. Grand Rapids, MI: Baker Book House.

──────. 1970. *Have You Considered Him?* Downers Grove, IL: Inter-Varsity Press.

Sobrino, J. 1978. *Christology at the Crossroads: A Latin American Approach*. Maryknoll, NY: Orbis Books.

Spurgeon, C. H. 2008. *The Treasury of David: Classic Reflections on the Wisdom of the Psalms*. 3 vols. Peabody, MA: Hendrikson Publishers.

Spykman, G. J. 1992. *Reformational Theology: A New Paradigm for Doing Dogmatics*. Grand Rapids, MI: Eerdmans.

Stanton, G. N. 1989, 2002. *The Gospels and Jesus*. 2nd ed. Oxford: Oxford University Press.

──────. 1995. *The Gospel Truth? New Light on Jesus and the Gospels*. Valley Forge, PA: Trinity.

Stauffer, E. 1960. *Jesus and His Story*. London: SCM.

Stein, R. H. 1996. *Jesus the Messiah: A Survey of the Life of Christ*. Downers Grove, IL: InterVarsity Press.

Stephan, H. 1941. *Glaubenslehre: Der evangelische Glaube und sein Weltverständnis*. Berlin: Töpelmann.

Stern, D. H. 1992. *Jewish New Testament Commentary*. Clarksville, TN: Jewish New Testament Publications.

———. 1997. *Messianic Jewish Manifesto*. 3rd ed. Clarksville, TN: Jewish New Testament Publications.

Stott, J. R. W. 1971. *Basic Christianity*. Downers Grove, IL: InterVarsity.

Strack, H. L. and P. Billerbeck. 1922–1928. *Kommentar zum Neuen Testament aus Talmud und Midrasch*. 4 vols. München: C. H. Beck.

Strauss, D. F. 1972. *The Life of Jesus, Critically Examined*. Translated by G. Eliot. Philadelphia, PA: Fortress Press.

Strobel, A. 1980. *Die Stunde der Wahrheit: Untersuchungen zum Strafverfahren gegen Jesus*. Tübingen: Mohr (Siebeck).

Strobel, L. 1998. *The Case for Christ: A Journalist's Personal Investigation of the Evidence for Jesus*. Grand Rapids, MI: Zondervan.

———. 2004. *The Case for Easter: A Journalist Investigates the Evidence for the Resurrection*. Grand Rapids, MI: Zondervan.

Stuart, C. E. n.d. *Tracings from the Gospel of John, or, Records of the Incarnate Word*. London: E. Marlborough & Co.

Summers, R. 1974. *Commentary on Luke*. Waco, TX: Word Books.

Susman, M. 1987. *Het boek Job en de lijdensweg van het Joodse volk*. Kampen: Kok.

Tasker, R. V. G. 1961. *The Gospel According to St. Matthew*. TNTC. Grand Rapids, MI: Eerdmans.

Taylor, J. B. 1962. "Angel of the Lord." In *The New Bible Dictionary*. 38. Edited by J. D. Douglas et al. Wheaton, IL: Tyndale House Publishers.

Tenney, M. C. 1972. *The Reality of the Resurrection*. Chicago: Moody Press.

———. 1981. *The Gospel of John*. EBC 9. Grand Rapids, MI: Zondervan.

Theissen, G. and A. Merz. 1998. *The Historical Jesus: A Compre-*

hensive Guide. Minneapolis: Fortress.

Theron, P. F. 1996. "Die betroubaarheid van die Skrif en sekerheid." *Ned. Geref. Teol. Tydskrif* 37.3:404–413.

Thielicke, H. 1962. *A Little Exercise for Theologians.* Translated by C. L. Taylor. Grand Rapids, MI: Eerdmans.

———. 1966. *Theological Ethics.* Translated by W. H. Lazareth. Vol. 1. Philadelphia, PA: Fortress Press.

Thierry, J. J. 1978. *Opstandingsgeloof in de vroegchristelijke kerk.* Amsterdam: Buijten & Schipperheijn.

Thomas, J. C., ed. 2010. *Toward a Pentecostal Ecclesiology: The Church and the Fivefold Gospel.* Cleveland, TN: CPT Press.

Thompson, W. M. 1985. *The Jesus Debate: A Survey and Synthesis.* New York: Paulist Press.

———. 1996. *The Struggle for Theology's Soul: Contesting Scripture in Christology.* New York: Crossroad Herder.

Tillich, P. 1968. *Systematic Theology.* Digswell Place, Herts: Nisbett & Co.

Trillhaas, W. 1972. *Dogmatik.* 3rd ed. Berlin: W. de Gruyter.

Troeltsch, E. 1971. *The Absoluteness of Christianity and the History of Religions.* Translated by D. Reid. Richmond, VA: John Knox Press.

———. 1911. *Die Bedeutung der Geschichtlichkeit Jesu für den Glauben.* Tübingen: Mohr (Siebeck).

Troost, A. 1992. "Kritiek op art. 1 van de Nederl. Geloofsbelijdenis." *Opbouw* 36.8:147–49.

Turlington, H. E. 1969. *Mark.* Broadman Bible Commentary 8. London: Marshall, Morgan & Scott.

Tyrrell, G. 1963. *Christianity at the Crossroads.* London: George Allen & Unwin.

Unger, M. F. 1962. *Zechariah.* Grand Rapids, MI: Zondervan.

Van Bruggen, J. 1998. *Christ on Earth: The Gospel Narratives as History.* Translated by N. Forest-Flier. Grand Rapids, MI: Baker.

———. 1999. *Jesus the Son of God: The Gospel Narratives as Message*. Translated by N. Forest-Flier. Grand Rapids, MI: Baker.

———. 2005. *Paul: Pioneer for Israel's Messiah*. Translated by E. M. van der Maas. Phillipsburg, NJ: P&R Publishing.

Van de Beek, A. 1980. *De menselijke persoon van Christus*. Nijkerk: Callenbach.

———. 1987. *De adem van God: De Heilige Geest in kerk en kosmos*. Nijkerk: G.F. Callenbach.

———. 2002a. *Jesus Kyrios: Christology as the Heart of Theology*. Translated by P. O. Postma. Studies in Reformed Theology: Supplement No. 1. Zoetermeer, NL: Meinema.

———. 2002b. *De kring om de Messias: Israël als volk van de lijdende Heer*. Zoetermeer: Meinema.

———. 2006. *Van Kant tot Kuitert: De belangrijkste theologen uit de 19^e en 20^e eeuw*. Kampen: Kok.

Van de Donk, W. B. H. J., A. P. Jonkers, G. J. Kronjee, and R. J. J. M. Plum, eds. 2006. *Geloven in het publieke domein: Verkenningen van een dubbele transformatie*. Amsterdam: Amsterdam University Press.

Van de Kamp, W. 2005. *Het wonder van het kruis: De laatste achttien uur voor Jezus' sterven*. Doetinchem: Crosslight Media.

Van der Kooi, C. 1999. *Hinkelen binnen de lijnen: Enkele krijtstrepen voor een christologie*. Kampen: Kok.

Van der Linden, E. [2001]. *Wie is die man? Joodse visies op Jezus*. Baarn: Ten Have.

Van der Merwe, W. L. 1991. "Metafoor en teologie." *Tydskrif vir Christelike Wetenskap* 27.2:65–108.

Van der Vliet, J. 2006. *Het evangelie van Judas: Verrader of bevrijder?* Utrecht/Antwerpen: Servire.

Van der Woude, A. S. 1973. "De oorsprong van Israëls messiaanse verwachtingen in het Oude Testament en in de vroeg-joodse traditie." *Kerk en Theologie* 24:1–11.

Van Gemeren, W. A. 1991. *Psalms*. EBC 5. Grand Rapids, MI:

Zondervan.

Van Genderen, J. and W. H. Velema. 2008. *Concise Reformed Dogmatics*. Translated by G. Bilkes and E. M. van der Maas. Phillipsburg, NJ: Presbyterian and Reformed Publishing Company.

Van Gennep, F. O. et al. 1989. *Waarlijk opgestaan! Een discussie over de opstanding van Jezus Christus*. Baarn: Ten Have.

Van Leeuwen, J. A. C. 1928. *Het evangelie naar Markus*. KV. Kampen: Kok.

Van Niftrik, G. C. 1961. *Kleine dogmatiek*. Nijkerk: Callenbach.

Van Ruler, A. A. 1947. *De vervulling van de wet*. Nijkerk: Callenbach.

———. 1969. *Theologisch werk*. Vol. 1. Nijkerk: Callenbach.

———. 1978. *Verwachting en voltooiing*. Nijkerk: Callenbach.

Van Uchelen, N. A. 1977. *Psalmen II*. De prediking van het Oude Testament. Nijkerk: Callenbach.

Van Voorst, R. E. 2000. *Jesus Outside the New Testament: An Introduction to the Ancient Evidence*. Grand Rapids, MI: Eerdmans.

Vardaman, J. and E. M. Yamauchi, eds. 1989. *Chronos, Kairos, Christos*. Winona Lake, IN: Eisenbrauns.

Velde, R. T. te et al., eds. 2015. *Synopsis Purioris Theologiae: Synopsis of a Purer Theology. Latin Text and English Translation*. 2 vols. Leiden, Netherlands: Brill. This source is related to Polyander, J., A. Rivetus, A. Walaeus, and A. Thysius. 1625. *Synopsis purioris theologiae*, by J. Polyander, A Rivetus, A. Walaeus, and A. Thysius (1625), and to *Synopsis of Overzicht van de zuiverste theologie*, 2 vols., edited by H. Bavinck (Enschede: Boersma, 1964, 1966).

Venema, H. 1850. *Institutes of Theology*. Edinburgh: T. & T. Clark.

Verhoef, P. A. 1987. *The Books of Haggai and Malachi*. NICOT. Grand Rapids, MI: Eerdmans.

Verkuyl, J. 1992. *De kern van het christelijk geloof*. Kampen: Kok.

Vermes, G. 1973. *Jesus the Jew: A Historian's Reading of the Gospels.* London: Collins.

———. 1983. *Jesus and the World of Judaism.* London: SCM.

———. 1993. *The Religion of Jesus the Jew.* London: SCM.

———. 2002. *Ieder zijn eigen Jezus.* Baarn: Ten Have.

Vine, W. E. 1971. *Isaiah: Prophecies, Promises, Warnings.* Grand Rapids, MI: Zondervan.

Vischer, W. 1935–42. *Das Christuszeugnis des Alten Testaments.* Vol. 1: *Das Gesetz;* vol. 2: *Die früheren Profeten.* Zollikon-Zürich: Evangelischer Verlag.

Vlaardingerbroek, J. 1989. *Jezus Christus tussen joden en christenen.* Kampen: Kok.

Vleugels, G., and M. Verhoeff. 2006. *De leer van de twaalf.* Heerenveen: Protestantse Pers.

Vollenhoven, D. H. Th. 1933. *Het Calvinisme en de reformatie van de wijsbegeerte.* Amsterdam: Paris.

Von Rad, G. 1935. "Das Christuszeugnis des Alten Testaments: Eine Auseinandersetzung mit Wilhelm Vischers gleichnamigen Buch." *Theologische Blätter* 14:249–54.

Vos, A. 1990. *Het is de Heer! De opstanding voorstelbaar.* Kampen: Kok.

Vos, G. 1948. *Biblical Theology: Old and New Testaments.* Grand Rapids, MI: Eerdmans.

Wainwright, A. W. 1969. *The Trinity in the New Testament.* 2nd ed. London: SPCK.

Wakely, R. 1996. "b'r I." *NIDOTT* 4:683–90.

Walker, B. 1990. *Gnosticism: Its History and Influence.* London: HarperCollins.

Walker, P. 2000. *The Weekend that Changed the World: The Mystery of Jerusalem's Empty Tomb.* Louisville, KY: Westminster John Knox Press.

Walvoord, J. F. 1974. *Matthew: Thy Kingdom Come.* Chicago: Moody Press.

Wampler, D. 2000. *The Trial of Jesus: A Twenty-First Century Lawyer Defends Jesus*. Yakima, WA: WinePress.

Ward, W. E. 1962. "The Person of Christ: The Kenotic Theory." In *Basic Christian Doctrines*, edited by C. F. H. Henry. 131–37. Grand Rapids, MI: Baker Book House.

Warfield, B. B. 1929. *Christology and Criticism*. New York: Oxford University Press.

Watson, A. 1995. *The Trial of Jesus*. Athens, GA: University of Georgia Press.

Weber, O. 1981/1983. *Foundations of Dogmatics*. Translated by D. L. Guder. 2 vols. Grand Rapids, MI: Eerdmans.

Wells, G. A. 1996. *The Jesus Legend*. Chicago: Open Court.

———. 1998. *The Jesus Myth*. Chicago: Open Court.

———. 2004. *Can We Trust the New Testament? Thoughts on the Reliability of Early Christian Testimony*. Chicago: Open Court.

Wenham, J. W. 1981. "When Were The Saints Raised?" *Journal of Theological Studies* 32:150–52.

Wentsel, B. 1981. *Dogmatiek*. Vol. 1: *Het Woord, de Zoon en de dienst*. Kampen: Kok.

———. 1987. *Dogmatiek*. Vol. 3a: *God en mens verzoend: Godsleer, mensleer en zondeleer*. Kampen: Kok.

Wessell, W. W. 1984. *Mark*. EBC 8. Grand Rapids, MI: Zondervan.

Whiting, B. 2006. *The Shroud Story*. Madeira Park, BC: Harbour Publishing.

Wiles, M. 1976. "Some Reflections on the Origins of the Doctrine of the Trinity." In *Working Papers in Doctrine*. 1–17. London: SCM Press.

Wilken, R. L. 1984. *The Christians As the Romans Saw Them*. New Haven: Yale University Press.

Wilkins, M. J. and P. Moreland, eds. 1995. *Jesus Under Fire*. Grand Rapids, MI: Zondervan.

Willis, W., ed. 1987. *The Kingdom of God in Twentieth Century*

Interpretation. Peabody, MA: Hendrickson.

Wilson, C. 1977. *The Passover Plot Exposed*. San Diego, CA: Master Books.

Wilson-Kastner, P. 1983. *Faith, Feminism and the Christ*. Philadelphia, PA: Fortress Press.

Witherington, B. 1990. *The Christology of Jesus*. Minneapolis, MN: Fortress.

_____. 1994. *Jesus the Sage: The Pilgrimage of Wisdom*. Edinburgh: T. & T. Clark.

_____. 1997. *The Jesus Quest: The Third Search for the Jew of Nazareth*. 2nd ed. Downers Grove, IL: InterVarsity.

Wolff, H. W. 1990. *Micah: A Commentary*. Translated by G. Stansell. Minneapolis, MN: Augsburg.

_____. 1984. *Jesaja 53 im Urchristentum*. 4th ed. Gießen: Brunnen-Verlag.

Wood, L. J. 1985. *Hosea*. EBC 7. Grand Rapids, MI: Zondervan.

Wrede, W. 1971. *The Messianic Secret*. Translated by J. C. G. Greig. Cambridge: J. Clarke.

Wright, N. T. 1996a. *Jesus and the Victory of God*. Minneapolis, MN: Augsburg Fortress.

_____. 1996b. *The Original Jesus: The Life and Vision of a Revolutionary*. Grand Rapids, MI: Eerdmans.

_____. 2003. *The Resurrection of the Son of God (Christian Origins and the Question of God*, Vol. 3). Minneapolis, MN: Augsburg Fortress.

Wuest, K. S. 1970. *Philippians in the Greek New Testament*. Grand Rapids, MI: Eerdmans.

_____. 1977. *Romans in the Greek New Testament*. Grand Rapids, MI: Eerdmans.

Young, E. J. 1972. *The Book of Isaiah*. Vol. 3: *Chapters 40–66*. Grand Rapids, MI: Eerdmans.

Zacharias, R. 2004. *The Real Face of Atheism*. Grand Rapids, MI: Baker Book House.

Zindler, F. R. 2003. *The Jesus the Jews Never Knew: Sepher Toldoth Yeshu and the Quest of the historical Jesus in Jewish Sources.* New York: AAP.

Zugibe, F. T. 2005. *The Crucifixion of Jesus: A Forensic Study.* 2nd ed. New York: M. Evans & Co.

Zwiep, A. 2003. *Jezus en het heil van Israëls God: Verkenningen in het Nieuwe Testament.* Zoetermeer: Boekencentrum.

Scripture Index

OLD TESTAMENT
Genesis
1	184, 298, 451
1:1	298
1:2	425, 427, 432, 438
1:6–8	604
1:9–13	322
1:11–12	438
1:14–17	604
1:20	604
1:26	30
1:27	359, 445
1:28	488
1:29	437
1:31	451
2	451
2:3	476
2:4	152
2:7	315, 578
2:19	385
2:24	359, 445
3	184, 485
3:5	376
3:6	517
3:15	146, 149, 150, 155, 156, 315, 442
3:16	485
3:19	377
3:20	155
3:22	30
4:1	425
4:25–26	156
6–9	156
6:1–4	436
6:3	380
6:6	81
6:6–7	408
6:9	152
8:9	475
9:27	156
10	537
10:1	152
10:7	497
10:21	156
11:5	385
11:10	152
11:10–27	156
11:27	152, 156
14	191, 350
14:13	156
14:18	191
15:6	37
16:10	288
16:11	288, 291
16:13	288
17:9	157
17:10-12	389
17:12	496
17:15–16	508
18	289, 410
18:1	289
18:2	289
18:13	289
18:17	289
18:17–33	289
18:21	385
18:22	289
18:25	332
19:1	289
19:11	576
19:15	289
19:24	293
21:12	157, 158
21:17	288, 291
21:33	278
22:1	385
22:2	158, 353
22:4	322
22:11–12	288
22:12	353, 385
22:15–18	288
22:16	353
22:18	157
24:7	287
24:16	170

24:40	287	46:29-30	158	19:11	322
24:43	170	47:27	158	19:16	322
25:2	158	47:29	158	20:24	337
25:6	497	47:31	158	21:6	281
25:12	152	48:7	495	22:8-9	281
25:19	152	48:15-16	288	22:18	552
25:23	159	48:16	288	22:28	281
26:3	157	49	162, 166	23:20	286, 288
26:4	157	49:3	159	23:21	288
26:24	157	49:9	320	24	535
28:4	157	49:10	146, 161, 195, 320	24:13	491
28:13	157			24:16	534
28:14	159	49:11-12	162	25:4	229
31:11-13	288	49:17	315	25:9	312
32:28	158	49:18	315	25:40	312, 313
35:10	158	49:22-26	160	28:3	194
35:16	495	49:26	160	28:36	194
35:19	495			28:41	194
35:21-22	158	**Exodus**		29:1	194
36:1	152	1:5	537	29:7	187
36:9	152	3	290	29:14	463
37:3	158	3:2	288	29:21	194
37:13	158	3:4	288, 291	29:33	194
37:29	554	3:5	290	29:38-42	320
37:34	554	3:6	291	29:44	194
38:1-11	491	3:14	11, 49, 303	30:30	187
38:9	437	3:18	322	31:13	335
38:26	491	4:22	210, 212, 296, 342, 354	31:17	335
40:20	322			32:12	408
41:8	159	4:22-23	174, 500	32:14	408
41:51	503	6:23	388	32:32-33	152
42:5	158	8:19	380	32:34	288
42:18	322	12	320	33:2	288
43:6	158	12:6-7	566	33:11	189
43:8	158	12:46	203, 566	33:20-23	189
43:11	158	13-14	470	34:6	339
44:1	159	13:2	496	34:6-7	23
44:13	554	13:12	496	34:29-30	535
44:21	159	13:15	496	35:6	229
45:4	159	13:21	288	39:30	194
45:21	158	14:19	288	40:29	427
45:28	158	14:31	337	40:35	427
46:1-2	158	15:8	380		
46:5	158	16:4	385	**Leviticus**	
46:8	158	16:7	58	1-7	229, 322

Scripture Index

2	321	24:17	497	33:16	288
4:3	463	24:17–19	159	33:27	278, 380
8:12	187, 194	25:6–13	524	34:10–12	189
8:30	194	25:10–13	193		
11:7	528	28:15	463	**Joshua**	
12	496	34:11	519	1:11	322
14:6	322	35:12–27	319	2:11	604
15:30	463	35:30	552	3–4	322
16:6	458			3:2–3	322
16:10	209	**Deuteronomy**		5:13–15	289
16:11–14	458	1:31	342	6:2	290
16:20–22	209	2:15	380	8:31–32	465
19:18	391	4:1	344	18:25	566
19:34	391	5:26	341	22:22	365
22:32	337	6:4	30		
23:5–11	566	6:5	391	**Judges**	
23:10–14	321	8:2	385	2:1–5	288
23:39	529	8:3	380	2:22	385
25:23	171	8:5	342	3:4	385
25:25–26	319	10:17	280, 328, 365	4:5	566
		11:21	604	5:23	288
Numbers		13:3	385	6:3	497
1:7	388	14:1	174, 342	9:13	401
3:3	187	16:16	503	11:34	353
5:8	319	17:6	243	13:2–14	508
6:1–21	508	17:6–7	552	13:12–13	288
6:11	463	17:13	547	13:16	288, 291
6:16–17	393	17:14–20	188	13:18	288
7:16	463	18	188	13:22	288
8:8	463	18:10–12	552	16:17	508
8:12	463	18:15	505, 535		
9:12	203	18:15–18	187, 188	**Ruth**	
10:33	322	19:15	243	2	495
11:1	380	19:15–19	552	3–4	491
12:6–8	189	21:22–23	565	4:11	494
12:8	189	22:6	425	4:17	163
15:24	463	22:20–24	491	4:21–22	494
15:27	463	23:19	268		
15:30	463	25:5–10	491	**1 Samuel**	
15:38–40	389	30:11–14	152	1:1	566
17	322	32:6	342	1:3	161
22:31	288	32:27	407	1:9	161
22:32–35	288	32:39	303	1:11	508
23:19	179, 408	33:5	319	1:19	566
24	160	33:10	380	1:24	161

665

2:6	333	8:2	160	**2 Kings**	
2:26	374	8:13–14	160	1:3	287
3:20	188	8:17	514	1:8	508
4:4	196	8:27	513	1:10	524
7:17	566	12:24–25	158, 317	1:12	524
10:1–8	385	14:17	287	1:15	287
13:14	164	14:20	287	2:1	604
15:11	408	15:27	514	2:8	470
15:29	408	15:35	514–515	2:11	604
15:35	408	19:27	287	2:14	470
16:1	163, 164, 494, 495	20:25	513	4:34–35	584
		22:3	395	5:7	45, 333
16:11	164	23:1–7	191	6:18	576
16:13	187, 495	23:3–5	168	13:21	584
16:18	163, 494, 495	23:4	169	17	520
17:12	163, 495	24:16	408	19:15	196
17:15	494			19:35	287
17:28	318	**1 Kings**		20:5	322
17:58	163, 495	2:25	173	24:6	172
19:18	566	2:27	192	25:27–30	172
20:6	494	2:35	192		
21:2–7	466	4:21	162, 317	**1 Chronicles**	
29:9	287	4:24	162	2:55	513
		5:3	196	3:17–18	173
2 Samuel		8:2	529	5:1	160
2:4	187	8:14	192	9:24	229
5:3	187	8:23	604	13:6	196
5:7	163	8:29	337	21:12–30	287
5:9	163	8:33	337	21:15	408
5:17	175	8:35	337	21:28	192
6:2	196	8:43	337	24	512
6:10	163	8:46	450	24:10	493
6:12	163	8:55	192	28:2	294
6:13–18	192	8:62–64	192	28:5	196
6:14	192	8:65	529	29:23	196
6:16	163	11:15–16	160		
6:18	192	12:32	529	**2 Chronicles**	
7	167	17:22	584	16:9	380
7:12	168	18:36–38	564	24:20–22	466
7:12–16	167	18:40	524	30:9	339
7:14	147, 167, 168, 174, 175, 176, 279, 317, 343, 358, 362	19	535	32:21	287
		19:5	287	32:31	385
		19:9	287		
		19:16	187	**Ezra**	
7:16	168			1:5	162

Scripture Index

1:8	162		361, 399, 509	30:13	199
6:16–18	565	2:8	162	31:5	564
7:6	513	2:8–9	175	33:21	337
7:11	513	2:9	174	34:2	380
7:12–26	211	4:2	380	34:7	289
9:5–15	564	6:3	380	34:9	289
9:9	211	8	153, 183, 184,	34:11	289
			185, 420	34:20	203
Nehemiah		8:2	183	35:5–6	288, 289
4	520	8:4–6	182, 184	37:25	201
6	520	8:5	185, 281	40	153, 201
7:7	491	9:10	201	40:6–8	201, 202
9:17	23, 339	8:6	48, 183	40:7	313
9:31	339	14:2	476	40:8	321
9:36–37	504	14:2–3	450	41:9	203
12:46	278	14:3	476	45	153, 195, 196,
		16	153, 198, 199,		281
Job			200, 396	45:2	55
1	6	16:1	396	45:6	280, 281
1:6	436	16:8–11	147, 200, 396	45:6–7	280, 294
1:21	374, 438	16:9	199, 380	48:1	397
2	6	16:10	198, 200, 380,	49:7–9	11, 474
2:1	436		568	50:4	604
9:6	229	18:9	380	50:21	95
9:8	531	18:17	186	51:5	447
15:14	447, 450	18:50	194	53:2	476
19:25	319	20:6	194	53:2–3	450
22:14	604	22	150, 153, 200	53:3	476
25:6	179	22:1	203, 372, 563	54:1	337
26:11	229	22:2	200, 201	57:8	380
35:7–8	179	22:7–8	561	57:9	199
		22:8	253	68:18	293
Psalms		22:8–9	200	68:33–34	181
2	153, 166, 174,	22:14	200	69	153, 202, 203
	175, 196, 361	22:15	369	69:4	202, 203
2:1	563	22:16	156	69:5	203
2:1–2	174	22:17	200	69:9	202
2:2	194	22:19	201	69:9	202
2:5–7	147	22:23	201	69:19	203
2:6	175	22:25	201	69:21	202, 564
2:6–7	399	22:28	201	69:22–23	202
2:7	44, 92, 147,	23:1	292	69:25	202
	174, 175, 176,	24:7	197	72	153, 162, 176,
	221, 279, 295,	24:7–10	543		195, 196, 317
	343, 354, 358,	28:8	194	72:2	195

667

72:8	154, 215	97:1	285	122:1-2	503
72:8-11	162	97:2	181	130:8	293
72:9-11	497	98:6	285	132	153, 196,
74:1	292	98:9	285, 332	132:10	194
74:12	278	99:1	196	132:15	531
75:1	337	99:1-5	285	132:17	194
75:3	229	99:9	397	136:2	365
77:3	380	100:3	293	136:2-3	328
77:5	278	102	282	139:1-6	385
77:6	380	102:12	282	139:13	356
77:11	278	102:23-24	282	139:13-15	374
77:21	293	102:24	282	139:15	438, 568
78:40	81	102:24-27	282, 293	142:3	380
78:52	293	102:25	282, 339	143:4	380
79:13	293	102:26	282	143:5	278
80	186	102:27	282	143:6	380
80:1	196	103:8	23, 339	144	184
80:2	292	103:11	604	144:3	179
80:8	187, 212	103:13	342	144:3-4	184
80:8-15	212	104:3	181	145:8	23, 339
80:14	186, 187	104:15	401	146:3	179
80:15	186, 212	105:1-2	337	146:34	451
80:17	186, 212	105:15	187	148:7-9	397
80:18	186	106:16	193		
82	281	108:1	380	**Proverbs**	
82:2	281	109:25	203	8	151, 321, 354,
82:6	281	110	191, 192, 200,		356, 357
84:9	194		294	8:22	355, 356
86:15	23, 339	110:1	30, 45, 168,	8:22-31	276
88:28	354		186, 192, 195,	8:23-31	278
89:19-29	168		196, 200, 294,	8:25	356
89:26	175		554, 582, 604	20:9	451
89:26-27	174, 358, 362	110:4	191, 195	21:1	492
89:27	203, 354, 360	111:4	339	26:13	403
89:38	194	112:4	339	30:3	296
89:51	194	114-118	548	30:4	296
90:2	278	116:5	339	31:6	559
90:10	282	118	203, 548		
93:2	278	118:22	204, 321	**Ecclesiastes**	
94:11	385	118:22-23	203	3:11	308
94:14	201	118:25-26	204	7:20	451
95:3	285	118:26	542	7:28	151
95:7	293	119:25	333	9:15	151
96:10	285	119:37	333	10:11	313
96:13	284, 293, 332	121:1	397	10:19	401

Scripture Index

12:14	332		288, 295, 296, 343	40:11	293
				40:28	278
Song of Solomon		9:6-7	30, 145, 165, 168, 172, 176	41:4	303
3:1-3	574			41:8-9	206, 208
		9:7	154, 171, 178, 191, 280	41:8-10	209
Isaiah				42-53	150
1:14	380	10:21	280	42:1	208, 509
2:1-4	166	10:33-34	165	42:1-4	206
2:2-4	174	11	165	42:1-7	204, 207
3:14	303	11:1	82, 165, 173	42:2-4	207
4:2	166	11:1-5	168	42:3	207
5:1-7	212	11:1-10	185	42:6	207, 284
5:2	407	11:2	280	42:6-7	206
6	147, 292, 295, 310, 365	11:4	165	42:8	293, 331
		11:6-7	451	42:19-22	206
6:1	295	11:10	165, 166	42:1	209
6:1-3	293	12:1-6	166	43:2	289
6:3	292	12:2	395	43:10	206, 208, 209, 303
6:5	292, 295	14:12	160		
6:13	166	16:4-5	172	43:13	303
7	170, 171	16:5	165, 169	43:25	303, 333
7-8	280	17:12	180	44:1-2	206, 208
7:1	171	19:1	181	44:1-3	209
7:1-9:7	177	22:13	303	44:6	293, 303, 326
7:6	177	22:20-22	203	44:21	206
7:11-14	171	22:21	296	44:21-22	206, 209
7:13	170, 171,	25:1	337	44:22	333
7:14	76, 164, 168, 170, 171, 172, 176, 178, 279, 280, 431	26:4	278	44:23	209
		28:16	293	44:26	206
		28:29	288	44:28	492
		29:14	9	45:1	492
8	395	30:27	283	45:4	206, 208, 209
8:1-4	176	30:30	283	45:11	342
8:3	171	31:4-5	283	45:21	278
8:5-13	395	32	283	45:23	293, 331
8:8	171, 280	32:1	283	45:23	293
8:10	280	35:6	260	46:3	209
8:14	293, 395	37:16	196	46:4	303
8:16	395	37:36	287	46:10	278
8:17	203, 253, 395	39	177	48:11	331
8:17-18	395	40	201	48:12	293, 303, 326
8:18	176	40-53	206	48:20	206, 208
9:5-6	171	40:3	286, 293, 508	49:1-5	209
9:6	32, 161, 174, 176, 279, 280,	40:3-5	283	49:1-7	204
		40:10	283, 293	49:1-9	204

49:3	207, 208	54:5	319	22:30	172, 173
49:4	396	54:8	319	23	174
49:5–6	159, 162, 207	54:17	206	23:5	168, 172
49:6	154, 166, 206, 284	55:3	200	23:5–6	173, 293
		55:8	34	23:24	78
49:7	207	56:7	543	26:1–19	552
49:8	207	59:15	284	26:3	408
49:8–9	206	59:19–20	283	26:13	408
49:21	164	59:20	284, 293	26:19	408
50:4–11	204, 396	60:1	284, 498	30:9	168
50:6	207	60:1–3	166	31:10	293
50:8–9	203	60:3	498	31:15	147, 566
50:10	207	60:6	498	31:20	342
51:12	179, 303	61	530	31:37	604
51:16	209	61:1–2	203, 206	32:18	280
52–53	205, 208	61:1–3	187, 190	33	174
52:7–10	208	62:11	293	33:11	167
52:11–12	208	63:7–15	289	33:14–16	173
52:12	208	63:9	81, 288, 289, 407	33:15	82, 172
52:13	204, 208, 605			33:16	76
52:13–53:12	204, 208	63:16	331, 342	41:17	495
52:14	607	64:8	296, 331, 342	42:10	408
52:15	208	65:21–25	185	49:36	229
53	147, 149, 153, 205, 206, 209	65:25	155, 451		
		66:1	294	**Lamentations**	
53:1–6	210	66:8	164	3:44	181
53:2	55, 166	66:15–16	293		
53:2–3	420	66:23	166	**Ezekiel**	
53:2–4	207, 607			1:5–10	229
53:3	209	**Jeremiah**		1:26	180
53:3–5	10	2:21	212	2:1	179
53:4	205	3:16	565	2:3	179
53:4–5	201	4:28	604	2:6	179
53:5	156, 205, 209	6:26	353	2:8	179
53:5–12	207	9:24	293	4:8–10:24	385
53:7	56, 205, 209	10:10	278	7:2	229
53:7–8	205	11:20	293, 340	10:14	229
53:8	11, 207, 209	15:6	408	10:21	229
53:8–12	209	17:5	451	15	212
53:9	205, 209, 567	17:7	451	17:23	168
53:10	205, 209	17:10	293, 340	19:10	212
53:11	76	18:8	408	20:12	335
53:12	205, 208, 209, 252	18:10	408	20:20	335
		20:12	293, 340	20:40	167
54:1	164	22:24	172	21:27	162

21:32	162	8:16	490	3:9–10	408
32:7	160	9	210	4:2	23, 339, 408
34:11–23	293	9:20–27	564		
34:23	164	9:21	490	**Micah**	
34:23–24	167, 168	9:24	211, 212,	3:8	432
37:9	229	9:24–27	210	4:4	173
37:24	164	9:26	211	4:9–10	164
37:24–25	167, 168	9:27	211	4:13	164
40–44	174	10:5	283	4:14	164
40:3–5	290	10:5–9	290	5:1	164, 360
40:46	193	10:10–15	290	5:1–2	163
43:4	287	10:13	290	5:2	30, 164, 168,
43:6–7	290	11	504		176, 277, 278,
43:19	193	11:4	229		492
44:15	193	11:36	365	5:3	164, 293
48:11	193	12:6–7	290	5:2–3	163
				5:4	164
Daniel		**Hosea**		5:5–6	164
1:20	497	1:7	294	5:5–9	164
2:27	497	3:4–5	166	5:8	164
2:38	179	6:2	322	7:20	278
2:47	365	9:3	171		
3:25	289	10:1	212	**Habakkuk**	
3:28	289	11	212	1:12	278
5:15	497	11:1	147, 174, 187,	2:14	58
5:21	179		212, 500		
6:23	287			**Haggai**	
7	178, 179, 180,	**Joel**		2:1–10	565
	182, 294, 555	2:13	23, 339	2:7–10	174
7:2	180	2:13–14	408	2:8	287
7:4–6	180	2:32	293, 337		
7:7	180			**Zechariah**	
7:9	181, 293, 380	**Amos**		1:1	466
7:9–10	283	7:3	408	1:11–12	288
7:13	31, 139, 154,	7:6	408	1:12	292
	179, 180, 181,	8:9–10	563	1:12–14	291
	182, 282, 399,	8:10	353	2:6	229
	554	9:6	604	3:1–4	289
7:13–14	162, 181, 195	9:11	278	3:1–5	292
7:14	181, 191, 290	9:11–12	169	3:1–9	193
7:22	31, 283,	9:11–15	169	3:6–10	289
7:23	181			3:7	291
7:23–24	180	**Jonah**		3:8	193
7:27	181	1:12	471	3:8–10	173
8:8	229	1:17	322	4:6	432

671

4:6-10	193	1:6-11	170	4:1-11	517
4:14	193	1:6-12	238	4:2	55, 377
6	174	1:6-16	388, 490	4:3	138
6:5	229	1:12	172	4:4	39, 374
6:11	193	1:16	270, 441, 490	4:6	138, 335
6:12-13	173, 192	1:17	238	4:7	39
6:13	192, 193	1:18	433	4:8	397
8:23	390	1:18-20	76	4:8-9	534
9:9	181, 284, 542	1:18-23	170	4:10	39
9:9-10	168, 196	1:18-25	388, 431	4:12	406
9:10	197	1:19	433, 491	4:13	509, 521
11:4-7	203	1:20	287, 388, 433, 599	4:15	490
11:9-14	203			4:18-22	521
11:13	284, 293	1:20-23	423	4:23	513
12:4-9	284	1:21	78, 293, 491	4:25	506
12:8	288, 289	1:23	78, 82, 171, 280	5-7	237, 525
12:10	156, 197, 284, 293, 353			5:1	397
		1:24	287	5:3-12	242
13:7	203, 284	1:25	374, 425, 429, 432, 491	5:11-12	525
14:4	582			5:17	140, 304, 392
14:5	284	2:1-12	497	5:17-20	330
14:9	284	2:2	276, 331	5:20	470
14:16	284	2:4	276	5:21-22	149
14:21	519	2:4-6	163	5:22	336, 390
		2:8	331	5:23-24	391
Malachi		2:11	331, 497	5:23-26	391
1:2	159	2:13	287, 599	5:27-28	149
1:6	342	2:14-15	493	5:28	336, 379
2:7	287	2:15	147, 187, 212, 500	5:29-30	480
2:10	342			5:31-32	149
3:1	285, 286, 287, 293	2:16	493	5:32	235, 336
		2:16-18	233, 499	5:33-34	149
3:17	342	2:18	147, 566	5:34	336
3:20	169	2:19	287, 599	5:35	294
4:2	150, 169	2:19-20	493	5:38-39	149
4:4-5	535	2:22	406, 505	5:39	336
4:5	286, 563	2:23	165, 375, 489	5:43-44	149
4:5-6	508	3:3	283, 293, 508	5:44	236, 336, 397
		3:4	508	6:2	514
NEW TESTAMENT		3:14	469	6:5-13	397
Matthew		3:15	470, 509	6:9	331
1	437, 442	3:15-16	55, 487	6:9-13	242, 389, 394
1:1	154, 158, 388	3:17	78, 476, 509	6:12	333, 472
1:2-16	233	4:1	456	6:14	333
1:3	160	4:1-10	55, 237	6:28	395

6:30	395	9:27	276, 388	12:18	276, 380
6:33	18, 470	9:35	513	12:18–21	206
7:7–8	397	9:36	405	12:22–32	527
7:11	397	10:1	128, 334	12:23	276, 388
7:12	391	10:1–4	522	12:26	389
7:37	55	10:3	524, 576	12:30	2
8–9	237	10:4	524	12:31–32	249
8:1–4	333, 521	10:5–6	537	12:32	517
8:2	331	10:5–15	530	12:38	276
8:3	333	10:8	128, 334	12:39–40	254, 317, 519
8:5–9	243	10:9–10	502	12:40	152, 276, 510, 588
8:5–13	526	10:10	236		
8:10	384	10:23	374, 411, 468, 603	12:42	168, 317, 476
8:11	352			12:46	500
8:14	521	10:24–25	328	12:46–47	375
8:14–17	521	10:28	584	12:46–50	527
8:16–17	205, 377	10:32	221	13:1	527
8:17	153, 205	10:34–35	304	13:4–8	437
8:19	276	11:2	276	13:21	480
8:20	26, 233, 276, 374, 420, 501, 502	11:2–6	509	13:40–41	374, 411, 603
		11:5	256, 260	13:41	277, 335, 480
		11:6	480, 482, 484	13:44	480
8:23–27	528	11:10	286, 293	13:45–46	480
8:24	55	11:11	478, 507	13:47	352
8:26	405	11:12	480	13:53–58	530
8:28	243	11:14	286, 508	13:54	513
8:28–34	528	11:16–17	375, 406	13:55	375, 428, 434, 441, 490, 500, 524
8:29	138	11:18–19	305		
9:1	523	11:19	401, 405, 406		
9:1–8	521	11:20–24	479	13:55–56	375
9:2	55	11:25	8, 138	13:57	276, 480
9:4	385	11:25–26	394	13:58	255
9:6	58, 133, 276	11:27	9, 46, 138, 329, 330, 336, 340, 348, 351	14:1–11	505
9:8	333			14:1–12	509
9:9	523			14:3	506
9:9–13	521	11:28	55, 223, 400	14:12	509
9:10–11	405	11:29	404, 478	14:12–13	530
9:12	384	12	249	14:13	384, 406
9:13	304	12:1–8	522	14:13–21	531
9:14	509	12:5	389	14:14	405
9:14–17	522	12:8	335	14:19–21	55
9:15	276, 319	12:9–14	522	14:22–33	532
9:18	331	12:10	389, 477	14:23	406
9:18–26	529	12:10–13	391	14:23–33	397
9:20	389, 487, 488	12:15–21	205	14:25	55

14:26	599	17:5	138, 240	20:30-31	276, 388
14:27	304	17:12	305	20:34	405
14:31	405, 483	17:12-13	286, 508	21:1-9	398
14:33	138, 221, 304, 331	17:14-18	536	21:1-11	542
		17:21	352	21:4-5	197
14:34-36	532	17:22-23	276, 588	21:5	276, 400
14:36	389	17:23	369	21:9	204, 277, 388
15:1-9	514	17:24-27	376, 391, 512, 536	21:10	1
15:1-20	521, 532			21:11	276
15:12	480	18	536	21:12-13	403
15:12-13	480-481	18:1	475	21:12-17	543
15:21	390	18:3	9	21:13	403
15:21-28	533	18:3-4	376, 407	21:15	204, 277, 388
15:22	276, 388	18:6-9	480	21:16	183
15:24	234	18:7	483	21:18-19	543
15:25	331	18:12-14	276	21:20-22	544
15:29	397	18:16	243	21:23-22:46	544
15:32	384, 405	18:17	536	21:31-32	405
15:32-39	533	18:20	337, 340	21:33-46	538
15:36	397	18:23	328	21:37	138
15:39	533	18:26	331	21:37-39	329
16	220	18:32-34	481	21:41	244
16:1	456	19	538	21:42	203, 321
16:1-12	533	19:4	389	22:1-14	538
16:3	456	19:12	59, 501	22:11-13	481
16:12	256	19:13-15	406	22:16	276, 51
16:13-20	533	19:16	276	22:18	456
16:15	1, 12, 533	19:16-17	241, 472	22:23	515
16:16	46, 138, 219, 276	19:17	249	22:24	276
		19:20-21	404	22:30	46, 335
16:17	9, 219, 348, 522	19:21	473, 502	22:35	456, 514
		19:22	249	22:36	276
16:17-19	220	19:24	502	22:36-40	391
16:21	369, 382, 510, 534, 553, 588	19:28	277, 374, 411, 603	22:41-45	329
				22:42	1, 6, 12, 233
16:21-23	553	20:2	542	22:42-45	168
16:22-23	456	20:17-28	588	22:43-45	192
16:27	277, 335	20:19	369, 558	22:44	195
16:27-28	374, 411, 603	20:20	331	23:1-36	479, 514, 544
16:28	335	20:20-21	242	23:1-39	237
17:1	398	20:26-28	276	23:2-4	392
17:1-5	234	20:28	10, 56, 205, 235, 304, 369	23:5	389
17:1-8	534			23:13-29	514
17:1-13	477	20:29-34	539	23:15	509
17:2	150, 339, 613	20:30	243	23:24	402

Scripture Index

23:35	155, 466	26:20-29	237	27:23-24	452
23:37	350	26:25	382	27:24	451, 558
23:39	204	26:26-29	241	27:29	276
24	467	26:26-30	548	27:32	377, 559
24-25	545	26:28	56, 235, 578	27:33	398
24:2	382	26:30	398	27:33-44	559
24:3	398	26:31	203, 276, 284, 480	27:34	384
24:5-42	382	26:31-46	549	27:37	239, 276
24:10	480	26:32	588	27:39	153, 200, 203
24:19	487	26:33	480	27:39-40	561
24:27	277, 374, 411, 603	26:34	243, 382	27:42	276
24:30	139, 277, 374, 411, 603	26:36	393, 398	27:43	138, 153, 200, 253, 561
		26:37-38	405	27:45-54	563
24:37	277, 374, 411, 603	26:38	380, 394	27:46	73, 153, 200, 203, 238, 248, 251, 252, 372, 390, 394, 398, 563
		26:39	331, 383, 398		
24:39	277, 374, 411, 603	26:42	398		
		26:44	398		
24:43-44	481	26:47-56	551		
24:44	374, 411, 603	26:50	406	27:50	378, 380, 409, 564
24:45-46	328	26:51-52	18		
24:48	468	26:53	460	27:50-51	237
25:1-12	277	26:57	506-507	27:52	584
25:5	468	26:57-68	551	27:52-53	565
25:10-12	481	26:63	46	27:53	585, 599
25:14-23	328	26:63-64	138, 276	27:54	138, 240, 607
25:19	468	26:63-66	294	27:55-56	487, 562
25:29	481	26:64	139, 196, 277, 374, 404, 411, 603	27:56	375, 518
25:30	481			27:57-61	566-567
25:31	277, 374, 411, 603			27:61	375, 487
		26:69-75	554	28:1	245, 375
25:31-46	332	26:72	374	28:1-8	572
25:34	276	26:74	374	28:1-10	487
25:34-40	374	26:75	143, 243	28:2	245, 287
25:40	276	27:1	554	28:5	245
25:41	335	27:2	556	28:6	78
26:1-5	545	27:3-10	554	28:8	245
26:3	506	27:4	452, 455	28:9	331, 378, 411, 488, 578, 599
26:6-13	541	27:5	77		
26:7	487	27:9-10	203, 284, 293	28:9-10	575
26:11	77, 78, 79	27:11-31	556	28:11-15	575, 587, 589
26:13	3	27:12	276	28:16	398
26:15	56	27:16-17	491, 557	28:16-17	235, 587
26:18	276, 577	27:19	451, 452, 550, 556	28:17	331, 398, 596, 599
26:20-25	547				

28:18	340, 605	2:24	477	6:3	234, 375, 428, 433, 490, 500, 524
28:18-20	581	2:25	389		
28:19	46, 329, 338, 371, 525, 537, 597	2:26	466		
		2:28	47, 374	6:5	256
		3:1-6	136, 522	6:5-6	255
28:20	78, 79, 340	3:2	477	6:6	384
		3:5	403, 479	6:7	256
Mark		3:6	515	6:7-13	530
1	237	3:8	506	6:12-13	256
1:1	44	3:11	44, 138	6:29	509
1:2	286	3:11-12	136	6:30-32	530
1:2-3	283	3:12	134	6:30-44	531
1:3	47	3:13-19	397, 522	6:31	46, 377, 394
1:4	468, 508	3:17	390, 522	6:45-52	532
1:9	352, 379	3:18	268, 524	6:46-51	397
1:11	44, 45, 174, 353	3:20	46, 377, 394	6:48	45
		3:20-30	527	6:49-50	378
1:17	223	3:21	250, 441, 527	6:51	45
1:21	513	3:27	336	6:53-56	532
1:21-28	136, 521	3:28-30	249	7:1-13	514
1:24	45, 194, 304-305, 339, 379, 452	3:31	441	7:1-23	521, 532-533
		3:31-35	527	7:11	390
		4	237	7:24	533
1:29-34	521	4:1	527	7:24-30	533
1:39	136	4:13-20	45	7:25	45, 332
1:40	45, 332	4:35-41	528	7:31	390
1:40-42	45	4:38	46, 377	7:31-37	533
1:40-44	391	4:38-40	340	7:34	390
1:40-45	521	4:39	45	7:36	134
1:41	405	4:41	1, 45	8:1-10	533
1:44	134	5	237, 383	8:11-21	533
2	237	5:1-20	528	8:12	254, 381, 467
2:1-12	136, 521	5:2	243	8:14-21	256
2:5	45, 332	5:6	45, 331	8:15	256, 515
2:7	45, 333	5:7	44, 138, 336	8:16-17	256
2:8	380, 382	5:19	47	8:22-25	534
2:10	45, 374	5:21-43	486, 529	8:22-26	533
2:10-11	333	5:22	45, 332	8:27-30	534
2:13-17	521	5:30	383	8:28-29	219
2:15-16	377	5:33	45, 332	8:29	44, 220
2:17	384	5:34	404	8:29-30	473
2:18	509	5:37	434, 522	8:30	134
2:18-28	522	5:41	390	8:31	374, 510, 534, 588
2:19	44	5:43	134		
2:23-28	391	6:1-6	530	8:38	374

Reference	Pages
9:1	466
9:2	398, 434, 522
9:2-8	467, 534
9:5	276
9:7	44, 45, 240, 353
9:7-9	136
9:9	134, 374
9:12	205
9:12-13	508
9:14-27	536
9:21	383
9:29	352, 467
9:31	588
9:33-35	382
9:36-37	376
9:37	474
9:40	2
9:50	404
10	403
10:1	506
10:1-31	538
10:11-12	235
10:13-14	403
10:14-15	376
10:17	45, 332, 472
10:17-18	241
10:18	249, 472
10:21	404
10:30	517
10:33	374
10:34	558, 588
10:35-37	242
10:38	471
10:44-45	416
10:45	10, 369
10:46	243
10:46-52	539
10:47	379
10:47-48	44
11:1-11	542
11:2	382
11:3	47
11:10	44, 47
11:12	377
11:12-14	543
11:13	384
11:15-17	403
11:15-19	479, 543
11:15-19	404
11:20-26	544
11:21	276
11:27-12:37	544
12:1-12	538
12:2-5	45
12:6	45
12:9	244
12:11	47
12:13	515
12:23	369
12:25	369
12:26	465
12:30	47
12:32-34	544
12:35	136
12:35-37	45, 328
12:36	47
12:38-40	544
12:41	507
12:41-44	512, 544
13:1-37	545
13:3	398
13:20	47
13:26	45, 338, 374
13:27	45
13:30	466, 467
13:32	44, 45, 57, 58, 133, 138, 251, 329, 335, 340, 384, 385, 386, 394
13:34	328
14:1	550
14:1-2	545
14:3-9	541
14:5	542
14:9	3
14:12	550
14:13-14	382
14:17-21	547
14:17-25	237
14:18	377
14:22	377
14:22-25	241
14:22-26	548
14:24	205
14:25	548
14:27-42	549
14:30	243
14:32-42	234
14:33	434, 522
14:33-34	46, 405
14:36	138, 390, 394
14:43-50	551
14:51-52	577, 602
14:53	514
14:53-65	551
14:55-56	452
14:61-62	35, 44, 138
14:61-64	2
14:62	139
14:66-72	554
14:67	379
14:68	243
14:72	243
15:1	554
15:1-20	556
15:14	452
15:19-20	136
15:21	559
15:22-32	559-560
15:26	239
15:29	203
15:29-30	561
15:32	44
15:33-39	563
15:34	200, 203, 238, 251, 372, 390, 563
15:37-38	237
15:39	44, 138, 240, 374
15:40	268, 375, 518
15:40-41	562
15:42-47	567

15:47	375	1:32	49, 163, 344, 387	2:49	49, 138, 163, 503
16:1	245, 375	1:32-33	191, 399	2:50	503
16:1-8	572	1:32-35	432	2:51	376
16:2	510, 590	1:34	425	2:52	384, 390-391, 471
16:5	245	1:34-35	503		
16:6	379	1:35	6, 24, 44, 46, 49, 76, 77, 176, 221, 296, 308, 339, 343, 344, 362, 399, 423, 425, 426, 432, 437, 441, 443, 447, 452, 455	2:51-52	374
16:6-7	573			3:1	261, 506, 511, 512
16:8	245			3:1-19	505
16:9	411, 565, 599, 604			3:2	265, 507, 508
16:9-11	574			3:3	18
16:12	411, 599			3:7-8	508
16:14	235, 411			3:16	508
16:15	581, 597			3:19-20	509
16:16-18	2, 581	1:36	301, 388, 523	3:21	394, 468
16:17-18	128	1:38	491	3:22	6, 138, 174, 308, 426
16:19	370, 582, 602	1:42	82		
16:19-20	47, 48	1:46-47	380	3:23	6, 433, 441, 490, 511
16:20	334	1:76	286		
		1:77	18	3:23-38	49, 154, 155, 172, 388, 439, 444, 490
Luke		1:80	380, 508		
1	437, 442	2	494		
1:1	138, 238	2:1-5	492		
1:1-2	226	2:2	506	3:27	172
1:1-4	43, 229, 496	2:4	163, 489	3:27-31	238
1:2	44, 587	2:6-7	374	3:38	6
1:2-4	238	2:6-20	496	4	237
1:3	43, 138	2:7	55, 353	4:1	367
1:3-4	587	2:9	287, 338	4:1-12	237, 517
1:5	388, 493, 512, 523	2:11	163, 276	4:1-13	517
		2:14	404	4:2	377
1:5-25	507	2:21	389	4:3	138
1:8	512	2:21-38	497	4:9	138
1:9	512	2:22-24	496	4:13	456
1:10	512	2:25	517	4:14	432
1:11	287, 599	2:32	206, 284	4:16	389, 390, 513
1:16	327	2:38	517	4:16-20	390
1:17	286, 432, 508	2:39	489	4:16-30	513, 530
1:21-22	512	2:40	374, 390-391, 503	4:17-21	190
1:23-24	493			4:18	18
1:26	489, 493	2:41-50	389, 512	4:18-19	203
1:26-35	431	2:42-43	287	4:22	339, 433, 441
1:27	388	2:43	503	4:31-37	521
1:28	490	2:46	384, 513	4:34	194, 452
1:31-33	423	2:48	440, 503	4:38-41	521

4:39	486	7:27	286	9:31	535, 599
4:41	138	7:34	377, 405	9:34	535
4:44	513	7:36	377	9:35	240, 353
5	237	7:36–50	526	9:36	12
5:1	519	7:37	484, 487	9:37–43	536
5:12	332	7:38	332, 487, 488	9:38	352
5:12–16	521	7:39	385	9:46	475
5:15–16	394	7:44–46	404	9:50	2
5:16	394	7:47	18	9:51	400, 536, 604
5:17–26	521	7:49	1	9:51–56	536
5:20	18	7:50	404	9:52	287
5:21	1, 521	8	237	9:56	10, 484
5:22	385	8:1–3	486, 527	9:58	420
5:27–32	521	8:2	20, 484	10	537
5:32	10, 18	8:2–3	486, 502	10:1	577, 579, 602
5:33	509	8:3	572, 577, 593	10:1–12	536
5:33–39	522	8:19–21	527	10:7	236
6	237	8:22–25	528	10:9	128
6:1–5	522	8:25	1	10:17	577
6:2	454	8:26–39	528	10:18	336
6:6–11	522	8:27	243	10:21	401
6:8	385	8:28	138	10:22	46, 138, 336
6:9–10	454	8:35	332	10:25	456
6:12	394, 395	8:40–56	333, 529	10:25–28	544
6:12–16	397, 522	8:41	332	10:25–37	537
6:15	495	8:42	352	10:27	380
6:17	506, 525	8:47	332	10:30	55
6:20	18	8:48	404	10:39	332
6:20–23	242	8:50	384	10:40	486
6:20–49	525	8:54–55	584	11	237, 404, 537
6:24–26	479	9	237	11:1	394
6:26	482	9:1–6	530	11:2–4	242, 389
7	20, 237	9:7	505	11:4	472
7:1	513	9:8	599	11:11–12	375
7:1–10	526	9:9	1	11:13	469
7:2–8	243	9:10–17	531	11:14–23	527
7:5	513	9:18	394, 406, 477	11:16	456
7:9	384	9:18–20	394	11:20	336
7:11–17	333, 486, 526	9:18–21	534	11:21–22	569
7:12	352	9:20	219	11:23	2
7:13	405, 487	9:21–22	534	11:37–44	514
7:14–15	584	9:28	398, 477	11:37–52	544
7:16	276	9:28–29	394	11:37–54	237
7:18	509	9:28–36	534	11:39–41	404
7:22	18, 256	9:29	535	11:51	155

12	221, 237	16:9-13	390	20:37	465
12:1	256, 514	16:14-18	514	20:45-47	544
12:4	404, 406	16:16	480	21	467
12:8	221	16:18	235	21:1-4	544
12:8-9	46, 335	16:19-31	18	21:2-4	487
12:10	249	16:22-23	352	21:5	505
12:37	352, 416	16:31	596, 598	21:5-36	545
12:37-38	328	17	221	22	548
12:41-48	545	17:3-4	333	22:1-2	545
12:43	328	17:10	328	22:3	547
12:49	304	17:16	332	22:14-23	237
12:50	405, 471	17:21	286	22:15-20	548
12:51	482	17:24	221	22:17	547, 548
12:51-53	404	17:25	221	22:19	548
12:54-56	533	18:1-14	538	22:19-20	234, 241
13	237	18:4	18	22:20	547
13:1	507	18:11-12	514	22:21-33	547
13:3	384	18:15-30	538	22:24	475
13:5	384	18:18	472	22:25-27	404
13:10-17	391	18:19	73, 249, 472	22:27	416
13:14	454, 477	18:22	18	22:28	336, 456
13:24	480	18:25	402	22:31-38	220
13:29	352	18:30	517	22:31-46	549
13:31-35	237	18:31	205	22:32	394
13:33	276	18:32-33	558	22:37	153, 205
14	237	18:35	243	22:38	551
14:1-6	391	18:35-43	539	22:39	393
14:3	477	19:1-10	539	22:41	394
14:3-4	454	19:8	18	22:42	70, 383, 459
14:12	548	19:10	10, 233	22:43	377, 599
14:13	18	19:11-27	545	22:44	394, 405, 459
14:15-24	538	19:13-17	328	22:46	456, 459
14:21	18	19:26	481	22:47-53	551
14:26-27	223	19:28-40	542	22:52-53	405
14:33	502	19:33-34	577	22:53	456
15	538	19:37	398	22:54-55	551
15:1	405	19:38	404	22:56-62	554
15:1-6	481	19:41	56, 400	22:63-65	551
15:1-7	203	19:42	404	22:66-71	554
15:5	293	19:45-46	403	22:70	138
15:10	46, 335	19:45-48	543	23	561
15:15	528	20:1-44	544	23:1-25	556
15:20-32	481	20:9-19	538	23:4	374, 452
16	237, 538	20:16	244	23:6	374
16:4-8	481	20:34-35	517	23:6-12	557

Scripture Index

23:7-15	505	24:36	235, 404		352, 374, 410, 414, 419, 443, 493
23:14	374, 452	24:36-49	578		
23:22	452	24:37	587		
23:26-32	559	24:37-43	411	1:14-18	350
23:27	561	24:39	77, 578	1:15	301
23:27-28	487	24:39-43	40	1:17	339
23:33-43	560	24:41	587	1:18	190, 271, 276, 295, 299, 324, 336, 348, 351, 352, 443
23:34	238, 243, 394, 398	24:42-43	377, 378, 599		
		24:44	152		
23:35	561	24:44-47	148		
23:38	239	24:46	369	1:21	188, 286
23:39-45	562	24:46-47	582, 597	1:23	283, 509
23:41	452	24:47	18	1:25	188, 190, 286
23:43	83, 238	24:49	350	1:27	509
23:44	263	24:50	378, 398, 582	1:29	13, 50, 205, 276, 320, 509, 545
23:44-48	563	24:50-51	602		
23:45-46	237	24:51	370, 582		
23:46	238, 380, 394, 398, 564	24:52	331	1:30	301
		24:52-53	582	1:33-34	509
23:47	240, 374, 452			1:35	13
23:48	561	**John**		1:35-40	522
23:49	562, 593	1	289, 297, 321, 357	1:36	50, 276, 320, 509, 545
23:50-51	552				
23:50-56	567	1:1	49, 76, 77, 276, 300, 350	1:39	276
23:54	510			1:40	517
23:60	243	1:1-2	271, 292, 294, 295, 305, 324	1:42	146, 276, 390, 522
24:1	245				
24:1-12	572	1:1-3	13, 298	1:43-51	518
24:4	245	1:1-14	275	1:44	522, 523
24:7	369	1:1-18	298	1:45	148, 433
24:9	486, 593	1:3	50, 299, 336, 337, 368	1:45-46	375
24:10	245, 572			1:46	188, 441, 490
24:12	55	1:4	299, 412	1:47-50	381
24:13-31	599	1:6	324	1:49	399
24:13-35	576	1:9	302	1:50	221, 276
24:16	205, 599	1:11	286	1:50-51	399
24:18	537, 577	1:12	337, 347	1:51	316, 335
24:23	599	1:12-13	448	1:52	46, 604
24:25-27	148	1:13	324, 362, 425, 426, 448	2:1-11	401-402, 518
24:26	272			2:13	510, 511, 512
24:27	152	1:14	13, 40, 54, 59, 61, 76, 77, 131, 271, 292, 295, 299, 300, 305, 311, 338, 350,	2:13-16	519
24:31	599			2:13-22	479
24:33	486, 593			2:14-17	403
24:34	235, 411, 565, 575, 599			2:15	403
				2:17	153, 202

2:19	334, 369	4:31	276	6:33-58	301
2:19-21	321	4:34	453, 472	6:35	224, 304
2:19-22	552	4:35	510	6:37	224
2:20	505, 511	4:42	276	6:42	301, 433, 441
2:21	369	4:46-54	521, 527	6:44	349, 398
2:23	337, 510, 512	5	529	6:51	194, 350
2:23-25	519	5:1	510, 529	6:51-55	414
2:24-25	382	5:4	287	6:57	349, 398
2:25	340, 382, 458	5:12	1, 374	6:58	350
3:1	567	5:12-13	12	6:59	513
3:1-21	519	5:16	391	6:61	382
3:2	276	5:17-18	347	6:62	58, 301, 370, 603
3:4	426, 567	5:18	49, 330, 347, 454, 477	6:64	382
3:5	426, 448	5:18-26	330	6:66-71	532
3:9	567	5:19	57, 348	6:69	194, 220, 339, 452
3:13	58, 78, 301, 351, 603	5:21	334, 337, 370	6:70	547
3:14	459	5:22	332	6:70-71	382
3:14-15	321, 605	5:22-23	347	7	537
3:15-16	224, 520	5:23	332	7:1-9	536
3:16	11, 235, 352, 368, 369	5:25	398	7:2	512, 529
		5:26	341, 361	7:3	512
3:17	302, 350, 398	5:27	58, 133, 332	7:5	441, 579, 596
3:18	337, 352, 353	5:28-29	334	7:8	512
3:19	301, 302, 482	5:33	454	7:10	512
3:25	509	5:36-37	398	7:15	390, 391
3:26	276	5:36-38	349	7:29	301
3:29	276	5:39	148, 152	7:3-4	375
3:30	478	5:40	224	7:15	389
3:31	347, 350	5:45	148	7:37	55
3:34	398	5:46	188	7:38	55, 224, 537
3:35	348	6	257	7:38-39	468
4:1	324	6:1-14	531	7:39	606
4:2	520	6:3	397	7:40	276
4:5	316	6:4	510, 512	7:40-41	190
4:6	55, 377	6:11	397	7:41	375, 492
4:7	377	6:14	188, 276, 302	7:42	163
4:10	316	6:15	382	7:46	374
4:18	381	6:15-21	397, 532	7:49	514
4:19	276	6:22-65	532	7:50	519, 567
4:22	210	6:23	324	7:50-51	552
4:24	341	6:25	276	7:52	375, 492
4:25	146, 276	6:29	398	8	453
4:25-26	520	6:32-58	320	8:1-11	434
4:29	374	6:33-51	55		

Scripture Index

8:2-11	405, 537	10:3-5	574	11:35	56
8:6	389	10:7	304	11:38	403
8:7	453	10:11	56, 203, 276, 292, 304, 369	11:41	138
8:9	453			11:41-42	394, 478
8:10-11	405	10:14	56, 203, 276, 292	11:42	350
8:12	304			11:43	539
8:12-59	537	10:15	330, 340, 369	11:43-44	56, 584
8:14	301	10:16	56	11:45-53	545
8:16	350, 398	10:17	369	11:47	374
8:18	350, 398	10:17-18	58, 334, 368, 369, 409, 454, 588	11:49	507
8:19	434			11:52	187
8:20	507			11:54	539
8:23	301, 350	10:18	58, 334, 348, 399, 565	11:55	512
8:24	304, 330			12:1	510, 512, 539, 541
8:25	1, 453	10:22	512		
8:28	304, 330, 605	10:22-42	538	12:1-8	3, 541
8:29	348, 453, 472	10:23	554	12:2	486
8:35-36	346	10:27	574	12:3	488
8:38	301	10:28	337, 370	12:5	542
8:40	374	10:29	370	12:8	79
8:41	342, 434	10:30	49, 73, 77, 248, 330, 338, 348	12:12-19	542
8:42	302, 398			12:14-15	197
8:44	155, 606			12:16	606
8:46	453, 472	10:33	49, 330, 347, 374	12:20-25	545
8:48	55			12:20-36	390
8:53	330	10:35	149, 224	12:21	523
8:57	377, 511	10:36	302, 350, 398	12:23-24	272, 607
8:58	49, 303, 330, 348	11	403, 538	12:24	321
		11:1-44	333, 486	12:27	380, 400, 459
8:59	303	11:2	324	12:27-28	331, 394
9:1-14	392	11:4	384, 606	12:31	336
9:1-10:21	538	11:6	384	12:32	166, 459
9:2	276	11:8	276	12:32-33	605
9:7	513	11:11	406	12:34	1, 191
9:11	374	11:14	382	12:36-41	281
9:16	374, 477	11:15	78	12:37-38	205
9:22	513	11:16	523	12:38	205
9:24	374, 483	11:25-26	224	12:39-41	311
9:34	513	11:25	304, 325, 334, 585, 588	12:41	147, 292, 293, 295, 366
9:35	384				
9:36	1	11:27	302	12:42	552
9:38	331	11:33	381, 400, 403, 487	12:44	224
9:39	302			12:46	224, 302
10:2	276	11:34	56, 383	12:47	10
10:3	574	11:34-36	400	12:49	348, 350, 398,

	399	15:1–6	548	17:8	350
12:49–50	58, 454	15:9	232	17:10	330
13:1	232, 382, 514	15:10	348, 399, 454,	17:11	78, 330, 549,
13:1–15	404		472		608
13:1–16	546	15:11	400	17:13	401
13:2	547	15:13	340, 369	17:18	302, 350, 398
13:3	301, 383	15:13–15	406	17:21	330, 348, 350,
13:11	383	15:15	404		398
13:14	324	15:16	337	17:22	330, 611, 612
13:16	328	15:20	328, 482	17:23	350
13:18	203	15:25	202	17:24	6, 70, 340,
13:19	304	15:26	26, 229, 337,		344, 348, 361,
13:21	381, 400		350, 370		441, 612
13:21–30	547	16	549	17:25	302, 350, 398
13:23	227, 352, 523,	16:4	275	17:26	348, 549
	547	16:7	26, 350	18	409
13:25	348	16:11	336	18:1	409
13:27	547	16:13	78	18:3–12	551
13:31	73	16:13–14	229	18:4	383, 409, 459
13:31–32	607	16:14	606	18:4–6	405
13:36–38	549	16:15	330, 348	18:4–8	404
14	548	16:19	383	18:5–8	304
14:1	224, 337, 597	16:21	302, 426	18:6	332
14:1–3	79	16:23	372	18:11	459
14:3	80	16:23–26	337	18:13	265, 551
14:6	224, 304, 325	16:26	372	18:13–14	507
14:6–9	413	16:28	78, 301, 302,	18:15	523
14:9	295, 330		350	18:15–16	523
14:10	330	16:30	382	18:15–18	554
14:12	128, 224	16:32	81, 372	18:17	374
14:13–14	337	16:33	55, 404	18:19–24	551
14:16	26, 370	17	73, 478, 549,	18:20	513
14:16–17	80		611	18:24	265, 507
14:17–18	78	17:1	138, 344, 349	18:25–27	554
14:18	79, 80	17:1–5	276, 608	18:28	507
14:23	80, 330, 337,	17:1–26	394	18:28–19:16	556
	340, 370	17:3	4, 248, 336,	18:29	374
14:24	350, 398		349, 350, 398	18:31	162
14:26	26, 228, 350,	17:4	564, 609	18:36–37	234
	370	17:4–5	600, 608	18:37	302
14:27	340, 401, 404	17:5	6, 302, 339,	18:38	452
14:28	30, 248, 348		344, 348, 609,	19	409
14:30	460		610	19:4	452
14:31	399, 548	17:6	349	19:5	374, 409, 557
15:1	187, 212, 304	17:7	607	19:6	452

19:7	347, 454, 555, 558	20:18	324	1:9	235, 370, 398
		20:19	235, 404, 486, 573, 591, 599	1:9–11	603
19:11	376, 404			1:11	77, 284, 370, 604
19:12	507, 558	20:19–23	578		
19:17	409, 559	20:20	324, 411	1:12	398
19:17–27	560	20:21	350, 398, 404	1:12–14	582
19:18	200	20:23	333, 378	1:13	227, 495, 546, 576
19:19	239	20:24	523, 593		
19:20	523	20:24–29	579	1:14	234, 469, 486, 579, 596
19:24	153, 201	20:25	77, 201, 324, 411		
19:25	375, 518, 576			1:15	577, 593
19:25–27	375, 562	20:26	404, 599	1:15–26	524
19:26	227, 523, 547	20:27	201, 378, 411, 487, 599	1:18–19	554
19:26–28	238			1:20	202
19:28	55, 202, 377, 409, 564	20:27–28	101	1:22	370, 598, 603
		20:28	3, 300, 324	1:23	577
19:28–37	563	20:29	597	2	198, 392
19:30	238, 380, 409, 420, 565	20:30–31	229	2–5	583
		21:1–14	580	2:1	512
19:31	510, 565	21:2	518, 523	2:1–13	579
19:31–33	566	21:2–3	525	2:9	505
19:34	235, 293	21:7	227, 324, 523, 547, 599	2:10	509
19:35	523			2:14–36	534
19:36	203	21:12	324	2:19	604
19:37	198, 284, 293	21:15–17	522	2:21–22	234
19:38–39	577	21:15–23	580	2:22	234
19:38–42	487, 567	21:17	382	2:22–36	122, 272
19:39	519, 567	21:20	227, 523, 547	2:23	235, 334, 369, 409, 558
19:40	83	21:24–25	523		
19:42	83	21:25	229, 434	2:24	11, 369, 598
20:1–2	245			2:24–32	198
20:1–10	572	**Acts**		2:25–31	147, 396
20:2	227, 324, 523, 547	1–12	522	2:26	234, 401
		1:1	229, 370	2:27	83, 339, 380, 568
20:5–7	55	1:1–2	226, 238		
20:11	143	1:1–8	235	2:30	82, 233
20:11–18	245, 574	1:2	603, 604	2:31	83, 153
20:13	143, 324, 487	1:2–3	486, 581	2:31–32	598
20:14	599	1:3	77, 126, 223, 273, 411, 581, 587, 592	2:32	369, 583
20:15	143, 590			2:33	606
20:15–16	56			2:33–34	235
20:17	20, 201, 252, 331, 378, 411, 578, 597, 599, 602, 603	1:4	378	2:33–35	604
		1:6–8	581	2:34–35	195
		1:6–11	582	2:35–36	235
		1:8	432	2:36	48, 49, 235,

	276, 341, 558, 609	6:5	509, 537	10:35	234
3	188	6:9	513	10:36	327, 525
3:1	393, 512, 564	7	557	10:36-37	48
3:11	503, 554	7:23-29	318	10:37	234
3:13	276, 347, 452, 606	7:30-31	288	10:38	432, 489, 526
3:13-14	234	7:35	288, 599	10:39	334, 369, 558
3:14	452	7:38	288	10:40	235, 369, 411
3:14-15	558	7:49	78	10:40-41	598
3:15	155, 235, 334, 341, 369, 409, 583, 598	7:52	155, 235, 334, 369, 409, 452, 558	10:40-42	595
				10:41	334, 378, 411, 599
		7:53	288	10:42	325, 586
		7:55	338	10:43	233, 337
3:16	337	7:55-56	196, 235, 597	11:26	262
3:19	337	7:56	178, 604	11:28	537
3:19-20	604	7:59	51, 337	12:1-2	523
3:20-21	604	8:12	223	12:3	550
3:21	77	8:14-17	534	12:7	287
3:22-23	188	8:22	51, 337	12:12	227, 546, 577, 602
3:26	276, 347	8:23	352		
4:1-2	515	8:26	287, 292	12:17	524, 579, 596
4:5	514	8:29	292	12:23	287
4:6	265, 507	8:30	39	13	200
4:10	235, 334, 369, 558, 583, 598	8:30-35	205	13:1	505, 509, 537
		8:32	50, 205	13:5	513
4:11	204	8:32-33	153	13:6	491
4:12	337	8:32-35	147	13:14-15	513
4:13	389, 525	8:34-35	149	13:14-41	513
4:25	347	8:39	577	13:20	188
4:25-26	174	9:1-9	235	13:22	164
4:27	276, 347	9:1-19	594	13:22-23	165
4:30	276, 334, 337, 347	9:2	513	13:23	276
		9:10	537	13:23-25	234
4:33	598	9:13-14	51, 337	13:27	149
5:12	503, 554	9:17	411, 565, 599	13:27-28	234
5:17	515	9:20	14, 513	13:29	149, 235
5:19	287	9:22	14	13:30	369, 598
5:28	374	9:36	486	13:30-31	595-596
5:30	155, 235, 369, 409, 558, 583, 598	9:40	334	13:30-39	600
		10:1-11:18	534	13:31	235, 411, 565, 599
		10:3	564		
5:31	235, 276, 333, 604	10:11	604	13:32-33	49, 176
		10:16	604	13:33	174, 176, 295, 362
5:34	514	10:25-26	331		
5:37	495, 506	10:26	45	13:34	176, 598

13:35	153, 339		370	1:26–32	485
13:35–37	198	20:35	235	2:3-10	23
13:37	598	21:10	537	3:10–20	451
13:38–39	233	21:18	524, 580, 596	3:22	397
13:43	509	21:20	514	3:26	397
13:47	206, 284	21:23–26	512	4:19	424
14:1	513	21:26	393	4:24	583
14:11–15	331	21:38	524	4:24–25	598
14:13–15	45	22:3	391	4:25	205
14:22	223	22:6–18	594	4:25–5:2	600
15	169	22:14	452, 597	5:1	327
15:13	524, 596	22:18	597	5:6	194
15:13–21	580	23:1–9	552	5:8	194
15:14	370	23:3–5	466	5:10–11	369
15:16	233	23:6	391, 514, 515,	5:11	327
15:16–17	169		594	5:12–21	315
15:21	513	23:8	514, 515	5:14	313
16:7	80, 381	23:11	597	5:15	10, 374
16:13	513	24:5	118	5:15–19	48
17:1	513	24:17	393	6:3	316
17:3	14	25:8	393	6:4	194, 235, 334,
17:6	492	26:4–5	393		338, 369, 569,
17:7	126, 527	26:5	514		583, 600, 608
17:10	513	26:12–18	594	6:4–5	598
17:17	513	26:13	150, 339	6:6	234
17:22–31	14	26:13–14	602	6:9	194, 598
17:31	332, 369, 598	26:13–15	612	6:23	327
17:32	40, 410	26:16	411, 565, 597,	7:4	598, 600
18:2	262, 505		599	7:20	452
18:4	513	26:22–23	149	7:25	327
18:5	14	26:23	206, 284, 598	8	465
18:7–8	513	28:5	293	8:3	350, 461, 463
18:9	597	28:17	391, 393	8:3–4	371
18:17	513	28:23	223	8:9	80, 349, 381
18:19	513	28:26–27	365	8:11	371, 411, 584,
18:26	513	28:31	223		598, 601
18:28	14			8:15	346, 358, 390,
19:8	223, 513	**Romans**			394
20:6	550	1:1–4	371	8:15–17	371
20:9–10	334	1:3	82, 233, 387	8:18–25	585
20:16	512	1:3–4	6, 76, 122	8:23	358
20:21	126	1:4	6, 77, 176,308,	8:29	160, 210, 354
20:24	126		334, 344, 369,	8:32	235, 368, 369
20:25	126, 223		443, 471, 583	8:33–34	203
20:28	11, 235, 328,	1:7	327	8:34	50, 196, 235,

	292, 598, 600, 604, 609	15:21	205	7:10	236
		15:30	327, 371	7:10–11	235
8:35	340	16:1	486	8–10	483
8:39	327	16:7	486	8:5	47, 91
9	386	16:16	370	8:6	47, 248, 336, 367, 368
9:5	3, 32, 76, 77, 82, 91, 233, 276, 300, 326, 327, 386	16:20	156, 327		
		16:27	341	8:9	479
				8:13	479
		1 Corinthians		9:1	594, 597, 598
9:10–13	159	1:2	47, 51, 337	9:5	234, 265, 501, 521
9:33	293, 395	1:9	341		
10:4	303	1:17–18	234	9:9–10	314
10:6–8	152	1:18–19	9	9:14	236
10:9	47, 276, 327, 328, 583, 598	1:18–25	255	10:1–2	470
		1:23	234	10:1–4	316
10:9–10	326, 600	1:24	6, 151, 276, 341, 356	10:1–12	157
10:10–11	600			10:4	321, 336
10:12	327	1:26–29	9	10:6	313
10:12–13	51, 293, 337	1:30	293, 341	10:11	314
10:16	205	1:30–31	6	10:13	341
11:9–10	202	1:31	293	10:21	47
11:25	597	2	22	10:32	479
11:26	284, 293	2:2	234, 251	11	548
11:29	195	2:4	432	11:10	436
11:36	367	2:7	339	11:20	548
12:2	417	2:8	58, 133, 234, 327, 338	11:23–25	548
12:5	370			11:23–26	234, 241
12:14	236	2:9	47	11:24	548
13:12	541	2:14–15	2	11:26	33, 34
13:13	485	3:11	321	12:3	47, 276, 328
14	483	3:16	370	12:3–6	371
14:6	327	3:16–17	321	12:4–6	248
14:8	47	3:18	9	12:5	337
14:10	23, 332	4:4–5	332	12:5–6	370
14:11	293	4:20	223	12:8	382
14:13	479	5:7	235, 276, 320, 545	12:27	370
14:17	223			14:10	352
15:3	153, 202, 234	5:7–8	550	15	14, 22, 217
15:4	314	5:9–11	485	15:1	597
15:6	327	6–7	22	15:1–7	94
15:8	195, 233, 234	6:9–10	223, 485	15:1–9	587
15:12	165	6:14	598, 601	15:3	51, 205
15:13	432	7:3–5	485	15:3–7	235
15:16	371	7:5	445	15:3–8	585
15:19	432	7:6	445	15:3–19	97

Scripture Index

15:4	235, 598	3:6	370	1:19	234, 265, 524, 579
15:5	234, 575	3:14	154		
15:5–8	411, 565, 599	3:14–16	576	2:9	524, 579
15:6	238, 258, 577, 579, 593	4:4–6	7, 299	2:16	397
		4:5	47	2:20	7, 234, 235, 369
15:6–8	235	4:6	337, 339		
15:7	579, 596, 600	4:14	598, 601	3–6	14
15:8	594	5:7	598	3:1	234
15:12–17	598	5:10	23, 332	3:13	464
15:12–23	601	5:14	340	3:16	152, 157, 387
15:14–19	583	5:15	598, 600	3:19	288
15:17	105	5:15–19	600	3:22	397
15:19	105	5:16	98	3:28	488
15:20	584, 585, 598	5:16–17	4	4:3–7	347
15:21	76, 77, 374	5:18–19	369	4:4	76, 82, 99, 233, 305, 350, 387, 414, 426, 442
15:21–22	76	5:18–21	99		
15:24	223, 412	5:21	60, 76, 205, 449, 455, 458, 459, 461, 463, 464, 474		
15:25	195			4:4–5	222
15:25–26	76			4:5	347, 358
15:27	48, 184			4:6	80, 350, 390, 394
15:28	57, 273, 336, 372	6:3	479		
		6:16	321, 370		
15:35–44	600	6:18	325	4:6–7	371
15:35–49	411, 598	8:9	26, 233, 305, 339, 417, 419, 501	4:14	287
15:42–44	585			4:21	157
15:44	584, 598			4:21–22	313
15:44–49	309	10:1	234, 400	4:21–31	157
15:45	48, 184, 276, 341, 381, 579	10:17	293	4:22–31	314, 316
		11:3	9	4:24	314
15:45–49	315	11:29–30	458	5:11	234
15:47	48, 309, 444	12:5	458	5:21	223
15:48–49	180, 309	12:8	51, 337	6:12	234
15:50	223, 578	12:9	378, 458	6:14	130, 234
15:52–54	585	12:10	458		
16:8	512	13:4	50, 234, 378, 458	**Ephesians**	
16:22	47, 51, 337			1:3–5	349
		13:13	371	1:3–14	371
2 Corinthians		13:14	371	1:5	347, 358
1:9	333			1:16	7
1:11	63	**Galatians**		1:17	165, 248, 371
1:18	341	1:1	370, 598	1:18	2
1:19–22	371	1:4	235, 369	1:20	196, 235, 369, 370, 598, 604, 609
2:7	333	1:13–14	594		
2:10	333	1:14	391, 517		
3:3	321	1:16	222	1:20–22	609

1:20–2:6	600	2:5–11	272	1:15	210, 299, 353, 354, 416
1:21	517	2:6	77, 295, 306, 326, 327, 418	1:15–16	295
1:22	48, 184				
1:22–23	370	2:6–7	305, 609	1:15–17	13, 306
1:23	76, 340	2:6–8	416	1:16	185, 306, 367, 368
2:1	598, 609	2:6–9	94		
2:6	584, 609	2:6–11	51, 120, 416	1:16–17	50, 336, 337
2:16	234, 369	2:7	377, 415, 417, 418, 609	1:16–20	10
2:18	367			1:17	273, 298, 355
2:20	321	2:7–8	233	1:18	13, 353, 354, 355, 370, 516, 584
2:21–22	321	2:8	234, 417		
2:22	370	2:8–9	608		
3:4	9	2:8–11	122	1:19	327
3:8	5, 7	2:9	235, 421, 604, 609	1:19–20	368
3:9	368			1:19–22	13
3:16	432	2:9–10	331, 612	1:20	234
3:17	337, 340, 370	2:9–11	293, 571	1:23	516
3:19	4, 339	2:10–11	293	1:24	370
4:4–6	248, 371	2:11	47	1:27	9, 337
4:6	370	2:12–13	4	1:28	516
4:8	78, 293	2:14–15	347	2–3	14
4:8–10	235, 334, 370, 604	2:17–18	401	2:2	9
		2:27	401	2:2–3	516
4:9	235, 568	3:1	401	2:3	151, 341
4:9–10	272	3:4–6	594	2:9	77, 78, 327, 368, 369, 374, 411
4:10	76	3:5	391, 514		
4:12	370	3:6	514		
4:13	4, 53	3:8–11	4	2:10	609
4:24	180	3:10	598	2:11	233
4:32	333	3:10–11	601	2:12	235, 369, 583, 584, 598, 600
5:1	347	3:18	234		
5:2	235, 320, 369	3:20–21	60	2:14–15	234
5:5	223, 338	3:21	77, 340	2:16	516
5:25	369	4:4	401	2:16–17	516
5:25–26	416	4:10	401	2:18	516
5:26	337, 370	4:17	340	2:20–22	516
5:30	370			2:23	516
		Colossians		3:1	196, 235, 583, 598, 604
Philippians		1	354		
1:18	401	1–2	22	3:1–3	601, 609
1:19	80, 381	1:7	537	3:9–11	180
1:23	83, 562	1:12–16	7, 350	3:13	333
2:5–7	7, 122, 233, 305	1:13	57, 58, 158, 223, 349	3:15	340
				3:18–19	516
2:5–8	541	1:13–14	13	4:3	9

4:10	227		302, 334, 370,	1:1–3	13, 306
4:11	223, 491		373, 452, 602,	1:1–4	272
4:12	537		604, 608	1:2	50, 336, 350, 368
4:13	523	4:1–4	501		
4:14	227	4:1–5	14	1:2–3	306, 337, 361
		5:2	486	1:3	196, 235, 273, 295, 299, 306, 340, 364, 370, 604, 608
1 Thessalonians		5:10	486		
1:5	432	5:18	228, 236		
1:10	598, 600	6:13	234		
2:12	223	6:15	328	1:3–4	361
2:15	235	6:16	59, 64, 83	1:5	50, 147, 167, 174, 295, 317, 358, 361, 362
3:11	222, 338	6:17	517		
4:14	598, 601				
4:17	562, 604	**2 Timothy**		1:6	210, 354
5:2	481	1:9	307	1:6–7	335
5:4	481	1:10	585	1:8	50, 281, 336
5:4–10	541	2:8	233, 598, 600	1:10	50
5:23	379	2:8–10	15	1:10–12	282, 293, 339
5:24	341	2:13	341, 400, 474	1:13	195, 604
		3:16	228	2	183, 185
2 Thessalonians		4:1	223, 325, 332	2:2	288
1:5	223	4:1–4	14	2:3	50
1:7–8	293	4:3	18	2:4	334
1:7–9	332	4:11	227	2:5	395, 399
1:9	337	4:18	223	2:5–9	153
1:12	327, 338			2:6	48, 178
2:8	165	**Titus**		2:6–8	182
2:13	371	2:4	293	2:6–9	147
2:16–17	223, 338	2:12	235, 517	2:7	281
3:3	341, 400	2:13	32, 276, 300, 324, 327, 328, 338	2:8	399
				2:9	77, 183
1 Timothy				2:10	396, 471, 472
1:9–10	485	2:13–14	10, 323	2:11	337, 370
1:12	337, 370	2:14	369, 370	2:12	153, 201
1:15	233	3:3	485	2:13	203, 253, 395
2:5	12, 56, 62, 77, 248, 254, 373, 374	3:4–6	371	2:14	54, 82, 156, 253, 302, 311, 396, 412, 568, 578
		3:5	448		
2:5–6	474	**Philemon**			
2:6	235, 369	9	600	2:14–15	583
2:12	324			2:16–17	82
3:11	486	**Hebrews**		2:17	194, 253, 276, 341, 377, 396, 400
3:15	370	1	282		
3:16	58, 122, 132, 233, 235, 272,	1:1	38, 50, 306, 336, 344		
				2:17–18	317, 396

691

2:18	456		456	12:2-3	535
3:1	276, 317	7:28	336, 458	12:3	234
3:1-6	189	8:1	235, 276, 370,	12:23	354
3:2	341, 400		604, 609	12:24	155, 315
3:5-6	477	8:1-2	317	12:28	223
3:6	50, 336	8:5	309, 313	12:29	23
3:14	50	9:7	578	13:8	293, 304, 339
4	455	9:9	517	13:12	234-235, 559
4:8	193	9:11	276	13:20	277, 292-293
4:13	385	9:11-15	317		
4:14-15	276	9:13-14	202	**James**	
4:14-16	317, 396, 549,	9:14	78, 320, 342,	1:13	456
	600, 609		344, 455, 578	1:17	339
4:15	60, 82, 253,	9:23	309	1:21	327
	377, 396, 449,	9:23-28	320	2:1	339
	454, 456, 458	9:24	313	2:5	223
4:16	478	9:24-28	317	5:6	452
5:2-3	458	9:28	205		
5:5	174, 276, 295,	10	202	**1 Peter**	
	362	10:1-10	322	1:1	505
5:6	191, 317	10:4	202	1:2	371
5:7	201, 400, 471	10:5	306	1:3	598, 601
5:7-8	234	10:5-7	201	1:8-9	597
5:7-9	122, 394	10:5-10	153	1:10-11	337
5:8	57, 336, 347,	10:5-14	320	1:11	80, 148, 205,
	398	10:6	463		381
5:9	471	10:7	306, 313	1:12	350
5:10	191, 276, 317	10:8	463	1:19	50, 205, 276,
6:5	517	10:11	202		320, 455, 545-
6:6	234	10:11-14	317		546
6:20	191, 276, 317	10:12	235, 370, 604,	1:19-20	202, 313
7:1-4	316		608	1:20-21	272
7:1-10	152	10:12-13	195	2:6-7	321
7:3	76, 350	10:19	478	2:6-8	293
7:4	475	10:23	341	2:7	204
7:11	191, 317	10:29-31	371	2:10	370
7:14	82, 160, 233,	10:31	23	2:22	60, 153, 449,
	387	11:11	341, 424		455, 463
7:15-16	76	11:17	352	2:22-25	205
7:17	191, 317	11:17-19	158, 316	2:23	234
7:24-25	77	11:28	353, 545	2:24	153, 252, 463
7:25	292, 396, 549,	11:37	516	2:25	276, 293
	600, 609	12:1-2	396	3:15	276
7:25-28	317	12:2	234, 235, 370,	3:18	205, 452
7:26	76, 276, 455,		401, 604, 608	3:18-19	562

Scripture Index

3:19–20	568	2:1	50, 276, 292,	1:3	344
3:20–21	320		452, 609	1:7	173, 301, 374,
3:21	313, 598, 600	2:1–2	205–206		412
3:21–22	604	2:2	320, 549	1:9	336
3:22	196, 235, 370,	2:16	517	1:9–11	5
	609	2:18	173	3	366
4:4–6	568	2:20	339, 452		
4:5	325	2:22	173	**Jude**	
4:13	338	2:22–24	336	1	14, 370
4:14	371	2:24	338	3	112
4:19	341	2:25	338	9	516
5:1	338	2:28	338	14	516
5:4	277, 292	2:29	338		
5:8	200	3:1	338	**Revelation**	
		3:2	338, 612	1:4	326
2 Peter		3:5	60, 206, 449,	1:4–6	372
1:1	10, 300, 324,		455, 463, 474	1:5	203, 341, 354
	327	3:8	156, 349, 568,	1:5–6	3
1:4	63		583	1:6	223
1:11	223	3:9	437	1:7	198, 293, 326,
1:15	535	3:9–10	347		597
1:16	432	3:16	369	1:8	264, 303, 325,
1:16–18	467	3:23	337		326, 340
1:17	613	4	14	1:9	223
1:17–18	234	4:2	173, 301, 412	1:11	232
3	14	4:2–3	374	1:13	50, 179, 180,
3:10	481	4:8	339, 341		613
3:15	400	4:9	352	1:13–14	283
3:16	59	4:9–10	350, 369	1:13–16	290
3:18	3, 4	4:10	320	1:13–17	613
		4:14	336, 350	1:14	290, 293
1 John		4:16	339, 341	1:15–16	297
1:1	298, 378	5:1	9	1:16	150, 339
1:1–2	299	5:6	235, 411	1:17	293, 303, 326,
1:1–3	58	5:6–8	566		597
1:2	11, 325, 349	5:7	372	1:18	568
1:3	344, 348, 349	5:11–12	336	1:19	232
1:4	23	5:12	336	2:5	326
1:5	341	5:13	337	2:8	293, 303, 326
1:6–7	23	5:18	362	2:16	326
1:8	452	5:20	50, 276, 301,	2:23	293, 340, 385,
1:9	341		325, 327, 349		458
1:10	451			2:25	326
1:15	23	**2 John**		2:27	174, 362
2	14	1	14	3:3	481

693

3:5	335	16:5	452
3:7	203, 339, 452	16:7	325
3:11	326	16:14	325
3:12	252	16:15	326, 481
3:14	341	17:14	326, 328
3:21	613	17:15	180
4–20	23	18:1	297
4:6–8	229	19:6	325, 326
4:8	325, 326, 340	19:7	277
5:5	160, 162, 165, 233, 276, 297, 320	19:7–9	319
		19:10	45, 331
		19:11	165, 293, 341
5:6	276, 320, 597	19:11–16	326
5:8	276, 320	19:13	54, 362
5:9	162	19:14	174
5:10	223	19:15	165, 325, 332
5:12	546	19:16	276, 328
5:12–13	276, 320	19:19–21	175
7	315	19:21	165
7:1	229	20:1	156
7:2	297, 341	20:1–6	273
7:3	297	20:2	150, 155
8:2	50	20:4	277
8:3	297	20:6	277
10:1	297	20:7–9	175
10:1–3	297	20:8	229
10:1–7	290	20:10	156
11:1–2	235	20:12	585
11:6	535	20:13	584
11:8	234, 235	21:2	277
11:15	223, 277, 326, 335	21:6	264, 303, 326
		21:8	485
11:17	325, 326	21:9	277
12:1–5	233	21:14	234
12:5	235	21:22	325
12:7	335	21:23	297
12:9	150, 155	22:4	273
12:10	223, 335	22:7	326
13:8	313	22:8–9	45, 331
14:6–9	297	22:12	283, 293, 326
14:12	397	22:13	264, 293, 303, 326
14:14	179, 326		
14:15–18	297	22:16	160, 165, 233
15:3	325	22:17	277
15:4	201, 452	22:20	47, 51, 326

Subject Index

A

A New Quest of the Historical Jesus 107

Aalders, Willem 69, 71

Aaron 193, 317, 322, 388, 458

Abarbanel, Isaac 178, 204

Abel 155, 315, 316, 318

Abiathar 466

Abigail 319

Abodah Zarah 267, 268, 501

Abraham 26, 49, 154, 157, 158, 191, 289, 303, 314, 316, 330, 387, 424, 538, 606

Abu Huraira 27

Acts of Peter and Paul 260

Acts of Pilate 260

Adam 22, 25, 49, 76, 154, 155, 156, 179, 184, 185, 276, 309, 313, 315, 318, 355, 374, 387, 425, 430, 439, 444, 445, 450, 451, 457, 461, 484, 488, 517

Adler, Hermann 191

Adoptionism 49, 68, 75, 87, 101

Adoptionists 49

Adversus Haereses 173, 229, 318, 412

Adversus Marcionem 443

Adversus Praxean 252, 364

Africa 115

Agabus 537

Against Arius 364

Against Celsus 496

Agapius of Hierapolis 266

Agrippa 393, 612

Ahasuerus 319

Ahaz 170, 171

Ahimelech 466

Akiva, Rabbi 182

Al-Baiwadi, Abdulla 434

Albanapolis 523

Albright 501

Alexander Janneus 515

Alexander, Joseph A. 177, 205

Alexander, R. H. 179

Alexander the Great 504

Alexandria
  48, 54, 62,
  63, 67, 74,
  299, 386,
  420, 507,
  516
Alexandrian school
  62, 63
Allah 24, 25, 26,
  27
Allen L. C.
  164, 278
Allen, R. B.
  160
Alphaeus 268, 523
Alshech, Moses
  205
Althaus, Paul
  71, 86, 308,
  363, 364,
  422
Ambrose 318, 447
America 28
American Revolution
  135
Amman 528
Amminadab
  388
Anabaptists
  72, 82, 84
Anakenōsis
  609, 610
Ananias 452, 466,
  537
Ancient of Days
  31, 181,
  283, 290
Anderson, Albert S.
  446
Anderson, J. N. D.
  585
Anderson, R.
  211
Andrew 146, 517,
  518, 521,

522, 523,
  531, 533
Andronicus
  486
Angel of the covenant
  285, 287
Angel of YHWH
  30, 279, 285,
  287, 288,
  289, 290,
  291, 292,
  294, 295,
  297, 311,
  361
Anglicans 66
Anhypostasis
  70, 71, 72,
  74, 128
Annales 261, 262
Anna 388, 439,
  497
Annas 265, 506,
  507, 512,
  551
Anne 490, 562
Anselm Grün
  232
Anselm of Canterbury
  7, 86, 110
Anti-supernaturalism
  86, 89, 111,
  115, 246,
  414
Anti-supernaturalists
  121, 255
Antichrist 315, 374
Antioch 47, 51, 62,
  67, 509, 513
Antiochian school
  63
Antipater 499, 504,
  505
Antisemitism
  139, 267
Antoninus Pius

259
Aphrahat 426
Apocalypse of Baruch
  516
Apocryphon of John
  19
Apollinarianism
  64, 70, 74,
  87, 102,
  103, 381,
  444
Apollinaris
  61, 62, 65,
  70, 128,
  131, 381
Apollo 565
Apostles 6, 20, 51, 91,
  199, 234,
  235, 258,
  308, 351,
  392, 394,
  397, 442,
  486, 517,
  522, 525,
  527, 576,
  580, 583,
  590, 593,
  596, 598,
  601, 603
Apostles' Creed
  23, 105, 273,
  366, 378,
  429, 512,
  562, 567,
  568
Apostolic Fathers
  258
Aquinas, Thomas
  7, 71, 364,
  385, 447
Arabia 497
Arabic Gospel of the
Redeemer's Youth
  503
Arabic Infancy Gospel

Subject Index

25
Archelaus 495, 500,
   505, 506
Archer, Gleason
   211, 219,
   240, 241,
   243, 244,
   466, 494,
   510, 572
Arianism 64, 66, 87,
   298, 355,
   410
Arians 60, 356
Aristides 435
Ark of the covenant
   195, 322,
   565
Armenia 523
Arnold, Thomas
   585
Artaxerxes I
   211
Ascension 24, 47, 80,
   104, 195,
   227, 235,
   273, 274,
   323, 369,
   374, 398,
   411, 535,
   571, 577,
   593, 596,
   597, 601,
   602, 603,
   605, 606,
   607, 608,
   611, 613
Ascension of Isaiah
   516
Asch, Sholem
   28, 33
Asenath 318, 319
Ashley, T. R.
   160
Asia Minor
   505

Assumption of Moses
   516
Assyria 165, 395
Athanasian Creed
   14, 54, 61,
   133, 248,
   338
Athanasius
   10, 62, 68,
   81, 160,
   364
Athens 513
Athenians 264
Atonement
   47, 275,
   313, 464,
   566, 583
Augustine, Aurelius
   7, 54, 126,
   131, 289,
   291, 361,
   364, 385,
   445, 446,
   484
Augustus 492, 494,
   505, 506,
   511, 550

B

Babylon 207, 208
Babylonian empire
   497
Babylonian exile
   504, 513
Baeck, Leo
   28
Bahrdt, Karl F.
   88
Baigent, M.
   20
Balaam 159, 160,
   497
Baldwin, J. G.
   193
Balthasar 498

Baptism 6, 39, 49,
   102, 134,
   234, 308,
   320, 394,
   426, 468,
   469, 470,
   471, 475,
   487, 508,
   509, 569,
   600
Bar mitzvah,
   389, 502
Bar-Jesus 491
Bar-Kochba
   555
Barabbas 491, 555,
   557, 560
Barachiah 466
Barker, G. W.
   325
Barker, K. L.
   193
Barnabas 206, 331
Barnett, Paul
   17, 91, 94,
   107, 260,
   492, 507
Barth, Karl
   7, 71, 87,
   96, 101,
   102, 103,
   106, 107,
   111, 252,
   311, 409,
   429, 437,
   448, 464
Bartholomew
   518, 523
Bartimaeus
   243, 539
Bartmann, B.
   437
Barton, S. C.
   225
Bastille 84

Batey, R. A. 501
Bauer, D. R. 166, 329
Baumgartner, W. 356
Baur, F. C. 88, 98, 99
Bavinck, Herman 38, 71, 78, 80, 224, 229, 230, 271, 289, 291, 357, 361, 362, 363, 364, 365, 366, 413, 418, 419, 445, 461
Bayer, H. F. 603
Beatitudes 242, 397, 398
Beelzebul 527
Behm, J. 295, 417
Beker, E. J. 78, 123, 421
Belgic Confession 76, 79, 82, 83
Bellett, J. G. 342
Ben-Adam 178, 179, 183, 186
Ben-Chorin, Shalom 28, 34
Ben Dama, Eleazar 268
Ben Gershom, Levi 188
Ben Meir, Shemuel 160
Ben Pandera 269, 270
Ben Rabbi Simeon, Eleazar, 355
Ben Yechiel Michel, Meir Leibush 164
Bentzen, A. 278
Berea 513
Berger, Klaus 16, 92, 114, 116, 143, 239, 257, 401, 402, 436, 437, 468, 469, 475, 476, 477, 478, 480, 486, 487, 502, 517, 526, 534, 538, 543, 574, 583
Berkeley, George 84
Berkhof, Hendrikus 91, 112, 121, 122, 123, 124, 306, 583
Berkhof, Louis 54, 61, 71, 332, 421, 569, 582
Berkouwer, G. C. 8, 9, 11, 12, 41, 54, 57, 60, 69, 70, 71, 76, 78, 86, 103, 105, 106, 123, 125, 132, 133, 147, 149, 150, 151, 154, 170, 191, 246, 248, 249, 253, 254, 271, 272, 294, 298, 304, 314, 330, 332, 351, 369, 385, 409, 411, 412, 413, 420, 428, 429, 445, 451, 454, 459, 470, 471, 492, 512, 535, 569, 582, 584, 609
Berlin Wall 84
Bernard, John H. 98, 99
Bernhard of Clairvaux 407
Bethany 3, 20, 487, 488, 502, 538, 539, 541, 543, 546, 562, 582, 602
Bethesda 12, 392, 529
Bethlehem 163, 164, 277, 278, 279, 360, 379, 492, 494, 495, 496, 498, 499, 503, 566
Bethphage 542,
Bethsaida 522, 523, 533

Subject Index

Biblical Criticism 215, 216
Biblicism 31, 217, 364
Bieneck, Joachim 136
Bithynia 260
Bleeker, L. H. K. 278
Blinzler, J. 551
Bloesch, Donald 1, 3, 73, 74, 75, 79, 86, 87, 90, 112, 114, 171, 309, 310, 311, 375, 378, 397, 421, 427, 428, 442, 444, 447, 448
Blomberg, C. L. 489
Bloore, J. 179
Boaz 151, 318, 319, 495
Bock, Darrell L. 114, 125
Bockmuehl, Markus 91, 114, 117, 225, 265, 389, 394, 495, 545, 583
Boff, Leonardo 17
Bonhoeffer, Dietrich 5, 11, 12, 78, 112, 421, 577
Bonino, M. 17
Book of Jubilees 516
Book of Wisdom 427

Borg, Marcus 17, 107, 108, 109, 113, 114, 324, 427, 583
Bornkamm, Günther 88, 107
Bornkamm, H. 160
Boslooper, T. 442
Bouma, C. 607, 608
Bouman, J. 27
Bousset, Wilhelm 47, 87, 91, 304
Bowling, A. 292
Boyd, G. A. 385
Braaten, Carl 89, 96, 97, 105
Branch 161, 165, 166, 172, 173, 174, 186, 192, 193, 364, 564
Branch of David 161
Brethren Movement 103
Bridegroom 20, 152, 276, 277, 319, 481
Britain 524
Bromiley, G. W. 54
Bronze serpent 321
Brown, Colin 94, 108, 331

Brown, Dan 21
Brown, Raymond 6, 36, 114, 115, 119, 134, 137, 168, 182, 218, 222, 226, 248, 249, 281, 294, 304, 324, 327, 351, 357, 378, 382, 383, 386, 427, 432, 442, 466, 490, 509, 534, 548, 551, 583, 584
Bruce, A. B. 474
Bruce, F. F. 169, 176, 226, 258, 354, 355, 442, 469, 473, 494, 497, 503, 507, 516, 536
Bruners, W. 391
Brunner, Emil 7, 12, 37, 97, 102, 408, 429
Buber, Martin 11, 28, 33
Büchsel 353, 362
Buddha 401, 415
Buitink-Heijblom 177
Bultema, H.

699

178, 284, 606
Bultmann, Rudolf 87, 90, 97, 102, 103, 104, 105, 106, 107, 108, 134, 218, 220, 298, 308, 584
Bunyan, John 314
Burgess 426
Burridge, Richard A. 117, 118, 225
Burstein, D. 21

C

Caesar Augustus 492
Caesarea Philippi 533
Caesaropapism 66
Caiaphas 2, 404, 506, 507, 512, 547, 550, 551, 552, 553, 554, 588
Cain 155, 315
Calvar 392, 398, 608
Calvin, John 3, 63, 71, 74, 80, 83, 85, 133, 175, 187, 190, 200, 218, 230, 289, 291, 340, 413, 428, 429, 447, 568
Calvinism 79, 274, 396
Calvinists 29, 66, 79, 81
Campenhausen, H. von 445
Cana 379, 518, 520, 523
Canterbury 7, 110, 341
Capernaum 379, 513, 519, 521, 523, 526, 532, 536
Carotta, Francesco, 257, 258
Carson, D. A. 220, 249, 255, 256, 442, 469, 470, 490, 497, 500, 507, 533, 534, 543, 546, 560, 565
Cashdan, Eli 193, 197, 286
Caspar 498
Cassanelli, A. 567
Cassels, W. R. 217
Catherine of Siena 426
Catholic Apostolic Church, 464
Celsus 269, 496
Cenchreae 486
Census 493, 494

Centurion 240, 243, 452, 526, 560, 565, 607
Cephas 235, 390, 518, 522
Cerinthus 412
Chafer, L. S. 272, 287, 292, 339, 368
Chalcedon 13, 14, 42, 59, 61, 63, 65, 66, 67, 68, 69, 70, 72, 74, 75, 76, 84, 85, 92, 93, 111, 112, 122, 130, 131, 132, 133, 224, 225, 461
Chalcedonian formula 13, 65, 68, 69, 93, 121, 128, 131
Charismatics 275
Charlesworth, J. H. 28
Chicago Statement on Biblical Hermeneutics 37
Chilton, B. D. 107, 514
China 115
Chokhmah 321, 357, 427
Christ on Earth: The Gospel Narratives as History 124, 125
Christ the Meaning of

Subject Index

History
            124
Christian church
            20, 47, 51,
            66, 429,
            536
Christian Science
            378
Christianity
            1, 8, 15, 16,
            19, 20, 27,
            33, 92, 93,
            103, 108,
            110, 115,
            118, 119,
            139, 140,
            199, 204,
            205, 232,
            264, 269,
            294, 389,
            484, 583,
            587, 589
Christians 4, 24, 25,
            27, 29, 30,
            34, 35, 41,
            51, 61, 66,
            90, 107,
            109, 111,
            125, 129,
            130, 137,
            143, 146,
            153, 154,
            206, 216,
            233, 242,
            246, 257,
            261, 262,
            263, 266,
            267, 268,
            285, 323,
            324, 363,
            364, 377,
            410, 411,
            415, 429,
            430, 435,
            469, 475,
            479, 483,
            548, 587,
            598
Christmas 274, 275,
            479, 493
Christologists
            16
Christology
            1, 4, 6, 9,
            11, 12, 13,
            15, 17, 19,
            21, 24, 25,
            27, 29, 36,
            42, 43, 48,
            49, 50, 51,
            53, 62, 81,
            84, 86, 87,
            91, 92, 93,
            94, 97, 98,
            101, 103,
            106, 109,
            112, 114,
            115, 117,
            119, 120,
            121, 123,
            124, 125,
            126, 127,
            130, 140,
            143, 215,
            216, 218,
            222, 223,
            224, 247,
            274, 275,
            312, 314,
            332, 386,
            387, 422,
            428, 448,
            465
Chrysostom
            486, 569
Chung, Sung Wook
            26, 114,
            583
Church fathers
            32, 55, 66,
            75, 127,
            133, 160,
            200, 291,
            294, 298,
            356, 363,
            407, 427,
            463, 479,
            484, 485
Church history
            10, 66, 357,
            435, 484
Church of the Holy Sepulchre
            559
Cicero   560
Circumcision
            29
Clarke, Edward
            586
Claudia Procula
            550, 556,
            558
Claudius   262
Clement of Alexandria
            48, 54, 299,
            516
Clement of Rome
            324
Cleopas   537, 576,
            577
Clopas   375, 562,
            567, 572,
            590
Coates, C. A.
            318, 319
Cohen, Abraham
            160, 164,
            166, 169,
            175, 183,
            188, 191,
            193, 195,
            197, 198,
            199, 200,
            201, 204,

277, 280,
281, 286,
290
Cole, R. A. 543
Colossae 22
Colwell 299
Communism
  28
Confession of Chalcedon
  61
Coniah 172
Conservatives
  15, 221
Constantine
  31, 66, 560
Constantinople
  13, 31, 63,
  67, 70
Contra Celsum
  434
Copley, John Singleton
  586
Coponius 506
Corinth 22, 513
Corley, B. 551
Cornelius 564
Cornfeld, Gaalya
  28
Council of Chalcedon
  42, 59, 61,
  63, 66, 67,
  84
Council of Constantinople
  31, 70
Council of Ephesus
  63, 253
Council of Nicaea
  31
Covenant 15, 26, 77,
  122, 169,
  195, 207,
  210, 241,
285, 287,
315, 322,
335, 502,
547, 565
Covenant theology
  15
Craig, W. L.
  582
Craigie, P. C.
  188, 189
Cranfield, C. E. B.
  434
Creator 23, 282,
  296, 342,
  343, 355,
  397
Crossan, John Dominic
  17, 113,
  141, 551,
  577
Crucifixion
  34, 232,
  263, 266,
  506, 510,
  511, 558,
  560, 561,
  587, 588,
  596, 605,
  606, 608
Cullmann, Oscar
  93, 220,
  275
Cynicism 17
Cyprus 513
Cyrene 559
Cyril of Alexandria
  62, 63, 74,
  386, 420
Cyril of Jerusalem
  569
Cyrus 204, 492

D
Dahl, Nils Alstrup
114, 115
Dalmanutha
  533
Damascus 57, 75, 364,
  513, 528,
  594, 612
Darby, John N.
  216, 306,
  319, 368,
  455, 463,
  602, 607,
  611
David 6, 55, 58,
  136, 145,
  146, 154,
  158, 161,
  163, 164,
  165, 166,
  167, 168,
  169, 170,
  171, 172,
  173, 175,
  176, 177,
  184, 186,
  191, 192,
  193, 195,
  196, 197,
  198, 199,
  200, 201,
  202, 203,
  233, 259,
  273, 276,
  277, 278,
  316, 317,
  318, 319,
  320, 361,
  379, 387,
  388, 423,
  431, 435,
  441, 466,
  490, 491,
  492, 494,
  495, 496,
  499, 511,
  517, 542,

Subject Index

566, 603
Davidic kings
      164, 170,
      192, 343
Davies, S. T.
      414
Davis, J. D. 178
Day of Pentecost
      579, 590
De Civitate Dei
      289
De Graaff, F.
      302
De Jacob et vita beata
      318
De Jonge, H. J.
      583
De Jonge, M.
      114, 583
De kring rond de Messias
      130
De Ru, G. 17
De Vidas, Eliyahu
      205
De Wilde, W. J.
      197
Dead Sea Scrolls
      32, 116,
      118, 161,
      168, 175,
      193, 515,
      516
Decapolis 136, 390,
      497, 528,
      533
Deden, D. 278
Deity of Christ
      27, 47, 64,
      65, 246,
      292, 308,
      323, 324,
      421
Delitzsch, F.
      175

Demythologizing
      103, 104,
      111, 345,
      584
Den Boer, C.
      486
Den Heyer, C.
      16, 137,
      238, 583
Denney, J. 462
Dennison, J. T., Jr.
      11, 61, 76,
      82
Dialogue of the Savior
      19
Dialogue with Trypho
      364, 490,
      496
Diaspora 497, 513
Dibelius, M.
      134
Dictaten Dogmatiek
      85
Dionysius Exiguum
      492
Dioscurus 66
Disciples 79, 114,
      119, 148,
      234, 245,
      256, 266,
      268, 304,
      331, 340,
      350, 378,
      382, 389,
      391, 394,
      395, 398,
      402, 403,
      404, 405,
      406, 456,
      459, 468,
      470, 471,
      472, 478,
      486, 495,
      502, 508,
      509, 517,

518, 519,
520, 521,
522, 524,
525, 527,
528, 529,
530, 531,
532, 533,
534, 535,
536, 537,
539, 542,
543, 545,
546, 547,
548, 549,
551, 554,
562, 573,
574, 575,
576, 577,
578, 579,
580, 581,
582, 585,
587, 588,
589, 590,
591, 592,
593, 594,
597, 599
Divine attributes
      32, 57, 337,
      338, 348,
      418, 419,
      420, 421
Docetism 5, 46, 70,
      74, 79, 82,
      87, 90, 107,
      110, 301,
      378, 379,
      410, 412,
      439
Docetists 60, 64
Dodd, C. H.
      50, 108, 326
Dods, M. 518, 607
Dogmatics 1, 7, 8, 9,
      37, 38, 52,
      103, 342
Doherty, E.

257,
Dooyeweerd, Herman 346
Douma, Jochem 37, 38, 142
Downing, F. Gerald 17
Dualism   65, 70, 72, 73, 75, 77, 130, 132, 133, 134
Dunn, James D. G. 28, 91, 104, 113, 114, 118, 119, 120, 121, 139, 140, 141, 226
Dutch Council of Churches 124
Duvekot, W. S. 118

E
Earle, R.   236, 563
Earth   7, 8, 9, 26, 33, 58, 76, 78, 79, 80, 81, 93, 109, 118, 124, 125, 138, 141, 154, 157, 159, 168, 181, 183, 195, 196, 198, 215, 229, 231, 234, 252, 255, 257, 272, 273, 275, 282, 283, 284, 293, 297, 306, 309, 313, 318, 321, 329, 331, 332, 333, 340, 344, 346, 347, 351, 355, 374, 379, 384, 385, 395, 396, 398, 401, 407, 408, 416, 418, 420, 421, 438, 459, 462, 470, 472, 476, 477, 482, 486, 488, 512, 525, 528, 545, 546, 548, 564, 568, 571, 581, 595, 597, 601, 602, 604, 605, 607, 608, 611, 612, 613
Easter   94, 97, 105, 111, 119, 120, 140, 274, 275, 393
Eastern Orthodox Churches 13, 69
Eastern Orthodoxy 274, 289
Ebeling, G. 107
Eber   156
Ebionites   101
Eco, Umberto 401
Ecumenical Councils, 13, 66
Eddy, Mary Baker 378
Edelkoort, A. H. 153, 167, 168, 188, 193
Eden   277
Edersheim, Alfred 88
Edessa   524
Edom   159, 160, 169
Edwards, D. 442
Efrath   495
Egypt   174, 187, 189, 212, 317, 318, 353, 493, 494, 495, 499, 500, 502, 503, 523, 535
Ehrman, B. D. 20
Election   159, 349
Eliakim   203, 280
Elijah   151, 188, 286, 477, 508, 524, 535, 563, 564
Elisha   151
Elisheba   388
Elizabeth   388, 424, 523
Emmanuel 610
Emmaus disciples 148, 576, 577, 589, 593, 599
Emmen, E. 78
Empiricism

84
Enchiridion
    445
Enhypostasis
    71, 72, 74
Enlightenment
    15, 36, 42,
    44, 72, 73,
    84, 85, 86,
    87, 88, 90,
    91, 110,
    111, 112,
    115, 215,
    246, 247,
    254, 255,
    257, 308,
    594, 601
Enlightenment theology
    36, 42, 44,
    85, 86, 246,
    257
Enoch   309
Enosh   156
Epaphras   537
Ephah   498
Ephesus   63, 65, 253,
    328, 435,
    513, 523,
    580
Ephraim   161, 196,
    539
Epistles   17, 47, 48,
    223, 233,
    236, 305,
    442, 465,
    479, 598
Erickson, Millard
    60, 82, 97,
    102, 121,
    414, 415,
    437, 440,
    444, 451,
    458, 465
Esau   159

Essenes   515, 516,
    518
Esther   151, 200,
    319
Eternal Father
    296, 297,
    312, 342,
    343, 344,
    348, 350
Eternal generation
    279, 356,
    357, 358,
    359, 360,
    361, 362,
    363, 364,
    367
Eternal Son
    44, 73, 76,
    77, 127,
    131, 231,
    276, 296,
    297, 307,
    308, 309,
    310, 311,
    329, 342,
    343, 344,
    348, 350,
    362, 414,
    415, 441,
    443, 613
Eternity   3, 6, 122,
    165, 273,
    278, 295,
    298, 301,
    303, 305,
    306, 307,
    308, 310,
    311, 312,
    313, 341,
    342, 343,
    344, 348,
    349, 350,
    351, 352,
    353, 356,
    357, 358,

    359, 360,
    361, 363,
    412, 413,
    443, 450,
    476, 611
Ethiopia   498
Ethiopian eunuch
    149, 205
Eucharist   548
Euhemerism
    91, 94
Euphrates   156, 317
Europa   436
Europe   21, 28, 115
Eusebius   227, 266,
    523, 580
Eutyches   65, 67, 131
Eutychianism
    66, 70, 81,
    253
Evangelical tradition
    66
Evangelicalism
    274
Evangelicals
    129
Evans, Craig A.
    107, 117,
    148, 260,
    265, 267,
    312, 389
Evdokimov, Paul
    470
Eve   155, 318,
    445, 484,
    488
Everlasting Father
    145, 176,
    177, 178,
    280, 296
Exclusive Brethren
    103
Existentialists
    92, 129
Extra-biblical sources

Ezekiel 222, 257, 167, 174, 179, 204, 290, 385
Ezra 211, 513, 564

F

Fairbairn, P. 312,
Faith 6, 7, 8, 9, 10, 15, 17, 22, 25, 26, 28, 34, 35, 36, 40, 41, 42, 53, 67, 84, 88, 89, 90, 94, 95, 96, 97, 98, 104, 105, 106, 109, 110, 111, 112, 114, 115, 119, 120, 121, 126, 128, 129, 137, 140, 143, 158, 217, 223, 232, 236, 255, 262, 329, 353, 363, 394, 396, 397, 405, 415, 419, 422, 425, 464, 519, 525, 531, 544, 575, 579, 582, 584, 589, 597, 598, 600, 601, 609
Faithful remnant 207, 396
Faithfulness 23, 169, 172, 285, 293, 332, 341, 400, 545
Fall 60, 184, 377, 420, 450, 451, 457, 461, 464, 465, 484, 485, 488
Farmer, W. R. 114, 226
Fatherhood 280, 331, 342, 343, 344, 346
Feast of Booths 493, 503, 510, 512, 529, 532, 536, 537
Feast of Hanukkah 512, 538
Feast of Unleavened Bread 550, 566, 580
Feast of Weeks 503, 512
Federalism 15
Fee 309
Felix 393
Feminist theologians 15
Festus 393
Fichte, Johann G. 96
Filson, F. V. 582
Fijnvandraat, J. G. 211, 290
First Apology 259
First Commandment 454
First Principles 357
First Quest 87, 88, 93, 106, 107
Fitzmyer, J. 432
Flesseman-van Leer, Ellen 112
Flusser, David 28, 35, 36, 109, 116, 267, 332, 500, 507, 509, 557, 561, 584
Ford, D. F. 3, 27, 55, 70, 78, 341, 410, 420, 421, 424, 463, 577
Forerunner 190, 286, 507, 508
Form criticism 134, 135, 436
Formula of Chalcedon 13, 69, 130, 132, 225
Fourth Commandment 454
Fracke, G. 583
France, R. T. 204
Francis of Assisi 8
Franck, Sebastian 310

Subject Index

Frank, F. H. R. 420
Freke, T. 257
Friedrich, G. 527
Fuchs, Ernst 88, 107
Fuller, R. H. 421
Funk, Robert W. 15, 19, 113, 389, 399, 501, 538

G

Gabriel 162, 289, 425, 427, 431, 452, 490, 564
Gadara 528
Gadarenes 528
Gaebelein, A. C. 202, 211, 290, 607
Galilee 120, 141, 268, 375, 377, 397, 398, 431, 489, 490, 491, 492, 495, 500, 506, 510, 512, 513, 518, 519, 520, 521, 522, 526, 529, 530, 532, 533, 536, 557, 562, 573, 575, 579, 580, 581, 587, 590, 593, 603
Gamaliel 514
Gandy, P. 257
Gate of Mercy 543
Gehenna 277
Geisler, Norman 38
Geldenhuys, N. 442, 490, 494, 536, 551
Gentiles 34, 149, 190, 259, 318, 319, 324, 490, 528, 537, 544, 545, 555, 558, 568, 597
Gerasa 528
Gerasenes 528
Gergesenes 528
Gersonides 188
Gese, H. 534
Geß, Wolfgang 421
Gethsemane 227, 383, 394, 404, 405, 434, 459, 547, 548, 549, 568
Gispen, W. H. 289, 296
Glorification 122, 195, 235, 273, 411, 606, 607, 608, 609, 610, 611, 612
Glory 2, 3, 6, 7, 58, 59, 133, 148, 160, 181, 183, 185, 197, 205, 231, 232, 272, 275, 277, 281, 283, 284, 287, 291, 292, 293, 295, 297, 299, 302, 306, 310, 311, 323, 327, 331, 334, 335, 338, 339, 348, 350, 351, 361, 364, 371, 372, 373, 380, 401, 402, 418, 419, 420, 421, 422, 427, 467, 471, 472, 498, 534, 535, 542, 545, 571, 576, 594, 597, 600, 602, 604, 606, 607, 608, 609, 610, 611, 612, 613
Glossolalia 275
Gnostic theologians 15
Gnosticism 19, 20, 21, 22, 23, 82,

Gnostics 20, 21, 22, 23, 24, 60, 117, 439
God's kingdom 107, 136, 402, 517, 528, 536
Godet, F. 172
Godhead 11, 54, 77, 78, 80, 81, 248, 254, 294, 348, 349, 353, 358, 419, 493, 610
Goethe 577
Gogarten, Friedrich 97, 102
Golan 397, 398
Golden Gate 543
Goldman, Solomon 164, 167, 277
Golgotha 209, 398, 559, 561
Gollwitzer, H. 252, 494
Gomorrah 293
Good Friday 274, 275
Good Samaritan 537
Goppelt, Leonhard 141, 374
Goslinga, C. J., 168, 176
Gospel of Hebrews 426
Gospel of Judas 551
Gospel of Nicodemus 260
Gospel of Pseudo-Matthew 490
Gospel of the Nativity of Mary 490
Gospel of the Nazarenes 470
Gospel of Thomas 25, 426, 468
Gospels 16, 17, 19, 20, 21, 25, 35, 36, 39, 43, 48, 88, 91, 95, 96, 106, 107, 108, 109, 114, 116, 119, 120, 121, 125, 126, 135, 137, 138, 148, 178, 188, 215, 216, 218, 219, 221, 222, 223, 224, 225, 227, 228, 229, 230, 231, 232, 235, 236, 238, 239, 240, 242, 243, 244, 245, 246, 247, 255, 257, 258, 298, 304, 329, 330, 332, 335, 374, 393, 407, 414, 433, 442, 464, 472, 480, 486, 489, 500, 503, 510, 527, 533, 571, 572, 575, 583, 587, 588
Gould, Graham 117, 118, 225
Goulder, M. D. 226, 415
Graafland, C. 14, 15, 71, 78, 81, 340
Grace 4, 66, 77, 78, 126, 183, 197, 231, 307, 318, 338, 339, 348, 350, 371, 417, 526, 533
Grant, F. W. 179, 202, 232, 233, 318, 321, 607
Great Commission 581
Greco-Macedonian empire 504
Greece 522
Greek mythologies 436
Greeks 162, 266, 544, 560
Green, J. B. 511, 560, 566
Green, Michael 21, 264, 265, 582, 586

Subject Index

Greenleaf, S. 585
Gregory of Nazianzus 55, 57, 62, 63, 424
Gregory of Nyssa 62, 63
Gregory the Great 20, 318, 385, 447
Greijdanus, S. 418, 419, 494, 503, 551
Griesbach hypothesis 226
Grillmeier, A. 60, 67
Griffith Thomas, William H. 37
Grogan, G. W. 165, 170
Gromacki, R. 442
Grosheide, F. W. 249, 386, 494, 497, 533, 543
Grün, Anselm 191, 232, 394, 400, 401, 404, 406, 574
Grundmann 472
Grunewald, Jacquot 28
Guardini, Romano 41
Guelich, R. A. 44, 134
Guthrie, Donald 43, 48, 127, 226, 228, 239
Gutiérrez, Gustavo 17

H

Habershon, Ada 312, 315, 316, 318, 319, 321, 322
Hades 2, 18, 83, 380, 562, 568
Hadith 26, 430
Hadrian 262
Hagar 157
Hall, C. A. M. 74
Halley's comet 499
Hamilton, V. P. 161
Hamlet 593
Hannah 424
HaQalir, Eleazar 205
Harinck, G. 237
Harlow, R. E. 342
Harris, Murray J. 98, 99, 324
Harrison, E. F. 462
Harrisville, R. A. 105
Hasmoneans 504, 505
Hasselaar, J. M. 78, 123, 421
He Was One of Us 379
Head, P. M. 226

Heaven 2, 7, 8, 24, 26, 33, 45, 47, 55, 57, 58, 76, 79, 80, 105, 138, 139, 152, 154, 180, 181, 196, 219, 221, 231, 251, 254, 272, 273, 282, 294, 296, 297, 301, 309, 313, 316, 317, 321, 323, 331, 340, 350, 351, 354, 355, 370, 372, 376, 377, 379, 384, 399, 401, 404, 406, 407, 411, 414, 430, 435, 467, 473, 475, 476, 478, 507, 509, 525, 534, 535, 542, 545, 546, 554, 564, 571, 581, 582, 602, 603, 604, 605, 607, 612, 613
Hebrew Christians 29
Hebron 495
Heering, G. J.

304
Hegel, Georg W. F. 73, 96
Heidegger, Martin 104
Heidelberg Catechism 10, 76, 78, 79, 80, 83, 252, 254, 512, 569
Helena 436
Heli 490
Hellenism 92, 94, 104, 141, 142
Hellenistic Christians 30
Hengel, Martin 49, 60, 89, 114, 115, 119, 134, 141, 181, 182, 188, 192, 217, 357, 374, 518, 519, 548, 613
Henry, C. F. H. 563
Henry, Matthew 610
Hepp, Valentijn 71
Heraclitus 91
Herculaneum 264
Herder, Johann Gottfried 41
Heresies 32, 51, 68
Heretics 14, 15, 131, 268, 412
Herford, R. T. 267
Hermetism 22

Herod Antipas 505, 521, 526, 557
Herod the Great 490, 493, 494, 498, 499, 500, 503, 505, 519
Herod the tetrarch 256, 452, 259, 505, 506, 509, 512, 515, 556, 557, 595
Herodians 456, 515, 522, 544
Herodias 509
Heschel, Abraham Joshua 408
Heschel, Susannah 140
Hess, Johann Jakob 88
Heyns, J. A. 149, 271, 332, 447, 569
Hezekiah 171, 177, 178, 204, 283
Hierapolis 266, 523
High priest 2, 191, 192, 193, 194, 265, 268, 276, 297, 396, 456, 457, 458, 466, 472, 506, 523,

549, 554
Higher criticism 216
Higton, M. 3, 27, 55, 70, 78, 341, 410, 420, 421, 424, 463, 577
Hillel 199, 514, 517
Hirsch, E. 147
Hislop, A. 560
Historia Ecclesiae 227, 523, 580
Historia Ecclesiastica 266
History of the World 263
Hobbes, Thomas 94
Hocking, W. J. 342
Hodge, Charles 37
Hoehner, H. W. 211, 493, 506, 507, 511
Hoeller, S. A. 20,
Holiness 6, 185, 334, 339, 371, 443, 468, 475, 479, 514
Holtzmann, H. J. 88
Holy Land 258, 277
Holy One of God 44, 194, 220, 394
Holy Spirit 6, 24, 27, 30, 31, 46, 49, 66, 128,

Subject Index

131, 218, 228, 229, 230, 246, 249, 250, 275, 281, 292, 293, 300, 329, 334, 337, 338, 344, 345, 346, 349, 350, 359, 365, 367, 368, 370, 371, 372, 381, 382, 399, 400, 401, 421, 423, 425, 426, 427, 428, 430, 431, 432, 433, 435, 438, 440, 441, 443, 447, 448, 469, 475, 489, 490, 504, 508, 527, 528, 548, 549, 577, 578, 579, 581, 582, 597, 606

Holocaust 140
Honig, A. G. 132
Hoover, R. 113
Horeb 187, 535
Horns of Hattin 397, 525
Hort, F. J. A. 88
Horton, M. S. 15

House of David 146, 163, 167, 168, 170, 171, 173, 193, 195, 197, 387, 431, 490, 494, 499
Hud 26
Huffman, D. S. 490
Hughes, P.E. 99
Hume, David 84, 94
Humiliation 185, 248, 271, 272, 273, 318, 398, 416, 419, 607
Hymn to Proserpine 17
Hymns 8, 548
Hypostasis 67, 70, 74, 75, 92

I
Ibn Ezra, Abraham 177, 191, 197, 204, 286, 319
Iconium 513
Ignatius 258, 259, 379, 387, 407, 410, 435
Imam al-Bukhari 27
Immanuel 170, 171, 280, 395, 421, 423, 431

Immutability 339, 421
Incarnation 6, 11, 31, 40, 50, 54, 59, 62, 67, 73, 92, 93, 102, 115, 122, 123, 127, 132, 185, 202, 248, 273, 274, 277, 295, 301, 305, 307, 309, 311, 312, 342, 345, 346, 348, 349, 350, 398, 409, 412, 414, 415, 416, 418, 420, 421, 422, 424, 443, 444, 448, 464, 609, 610, 612
India 523
Infancy Gospel of Thomas 503, 504
Inspiration 48, 85, 109, 216, 217, 220, 224, 230, 245
Institutes of the Christian Religion 3
Irenaeus 173, 227, 229, 318, 435, 448, 523,
Ironside 296

Irving, E. 463
Isaac 151, 152, 157, 158, 159, 316, 318, 424, 507, 606
Isai 163
Ishmael 26, 288, 316
Ishmael, Rabbi 268
Isis 493
Islam 25, 26, 27, 434, 455
Islamic Christology 24
Israel 6, 25, 28, 29, 30, 33, 34, 56, 117, 124, 130, 134, 139, 146, 154, 157, 158, 159, 160, 162, 163, 164, 166, 167, 168, 169, 171, 173, 174, 175, 181, 186, 187, 188, 189, 192, 194, 195, 196, 197, 200, 203, 204, 206, 207, 208, 209, 210, 211, 212, 213, 229, 233, 234, 268, 277, 279, 281, 286, 296, 317, 318, 319, 321, 323, 333, 342, 354, 379, 386, 387, 395, 396, 399, 427, 468, 489, 492, 497, 500, 505, 508, 509, 510, 513, 514, 517, 526, 536, 537, 541, 546, 581, 604
Ituraea 506

J

Jacob 146, 158, 159, 160, 167, 192, 270, 284, 288, 315, 316, 318, 375, 395, 423, 431, 441, 490, 495, 497, 524, 537, 606
Jacob of Kefar-Sekaniah 268
Jacob's well 316, 520
Jager, O. 379
Jairus 227, 333, 434, 486, 529
James 19, 169, 235, 242, 265, 375, 424, 428, 442, 452, 490, 496, 503, 518, 521, 522, 524, 549, 562, 572, 579, 580, 593, 596
James ossuary 265
James the son of Alphaeus 268, 523
James the younger 268, 524
Japheth 156
Japhethites 156
Jeconiah 172, 173
Jedidiah 158
Jehoiachin 172, 204
Jehoiada 466
Jehoram 333
Jehovah's Witnesses 299
Jennings, F. C. 283, 377, 606
Jenson, R. W. 74
Jeremiah 25, 172, 204, 495, 500
Jeremias, Joachim 88, 107, 268
Jericho 379, 499, 519, 539
Jerome 576
Jerusalem 28, 51, 55, 140, 148, 162, 163, 164, 196, 197, 210, 227, 234, 237, 265,

Subject Index

        283, 284,
        294, 379,
        382, 385,
        389, 393,
        398, 400,
        441, 495,
        496, 498,
        499, 501,
        502, 504,
        505, 506,
        507, 512,
        513, 515,
        519, 520,
        521, 523,
        524, 529,
        532, 535,
        536, 538,
        539, 542,
        543, 546,
        555, 558,
        559, 567,
        569, 576,
        577, 578,
        579, 580,
        581, 582,
        587, 590,
        593
Jeshua   193, 491
Jesse   163, 165,
        166, 191
Jesuology 27
Jesus Barabbas
        491, 557
Jesus called Justus
        491
Jesus Christ
        1, 3, 4, 5, 6,
        7, 10, 19,
        23, 33, 47,
        48, 50, 67,
        71, 73, 76,
        77, 80, 82,
        83, 96, 105,
        109, 126,
        131, 132,
        151, 166,
        194, 223,
        233, 248,
        258, 259,
        272, 287,
        299, 300,
        301, 304,
        307, 309,
        310, 312,
        323, 324,
        325, 327,
        328, 334,
        338, 339,
        341, 343,
        345, 349,
        357, 366,
        369, 370,
        371, 372,
        373, 379,
        381, 409,
        411, 413,
        417, 422,
        431, 432,
        435, 443,
        448, 467,
        476, 555,
        571, 582,
        585, 586,
        600, 604,
        610, 612,
        613
Jesus Quests
        87, 101
Jesus Seminar
        15, 113,
        114, 117,
        120, 399,
        538, 577
Jesus the Son of God: The Gospel Narratives as Message
        124, 125
Jewish Antiquities
        265, 266,
        499, 507,
        509, 535,
        580
Jewish Council
        514, 515,
        519, 550,
        551, 554,
        567, 575
Jewish expositors
        36, 153,
        155, 160,
        163, 175,
        176, 181,
        197, 267,
        290
Jewish law
        550, 552,
        553, 575
Jewish-Roman war
        559
Jewish War 499
Jews
        13, 14, 16,
        24, 26, 27,
        28, 29, 30,
        31, 32, 34,
        49, 55, 66,
        94, 125,
        130, 139,
        140, 146,
        153, 154,
        158, 162,
        186, 188,
        191, 206,
        210, 239,
        240, 259,
        262, 264,
        266, 269,
        301, 324,
        330, 331,
        345, 347,
        377, 393,
        394, 400,
        403, 429,
        454, 465,
        491, 494,

	497, 499, 500, 504, 507, 509, 510, 512, 513, 517, 519, 520, 528, 529, 533, 538, 545, 556, 557, 558, 560, 576, 589, 590, 594, 597	Jordan River	49 322, 470, 471, 477, 506, 508, 517, 518, 519, 536, 538, 539	Joshua Josiah Judah	151, 188, 193, 289, 290, 375 177, 204 146, 154, 160, 161, 162, 163, 172, 173, 233, 276, 277, 294, 320, 375, 387, 388, 524
Joachim	388, 424, 425, 490	Joseph Joseph, husband of Mary	151, 160, 316, 318, 319, 6, 143, 148, 172, 188,	Judaism	21, 92, 110, 118, 130, 139, 140,
Joahaz	170		197, 265,		141, 142,
Joanna	527, 572		269, 375,		205, 277,
Johanan	495		388, 390,		309, 330,
John Hyrcanus			391, 423,		391, 509,
	515		424, 425,		516, 594
John Mark			426, 427,	Judas Iscariot	
	546, 577		428, 431,		237, 382,
John of Damascus			432, 433,		406, 452,
	57, 75, 364		434, 440,		523, 524,
John the Baptist			441, 490,		525, 546,
	47, 141,		491, 492,		547, 550,
	188, 205,		493, 494,		551, 554,
	283, 286,		495, 496,		577, 607
	287, 301,		497, 499,	Judas the Galilean	
	305, 320,		500, 501,		495, 506
	401, 425,		503, 562	Judas the Maccabee	
	468, 469,	Joseph Barsabbas			197
	478, 487,		577	Jude	524
	493, 506,	Joseph of Arimathea		Judea	162, 492,
	507, 508,		487, 552,		494, 495,
	511, 516,		566, 567,		499, 500,
	518, 522,		577, 589		504, 505,
	526, 530	Josephus, Flavius			506, 512,
Johnson, D. H.			265, 266,		513, 517,
	294		267, 499,		520, 532,
Johnson, L. T.			504, 507,		581
	114		509, 515,		
Jonah	129, 152,		535, 580	Jukes, A.	318
	255, 317,	Joses	375, 428,	Julius Caesar	
	318, 471,		572		258, 505

Subject Index

Junia 486
Juno 264
Jupiter 499
Juster, Dan 30
Justification
  6, 315, 600
Justin Martyr
  160, 259,
  260, 364,
  435, 490,
  496
Justin of Nablus
  497

K
Kabak, Avraham Aharon
  28
Kabbalah 31
Kähler, Martin
  87, 93, 94,
  95, 97, 120,
  215
Kaiser, Walter
  366
Kant, Immanuel
  12, 85, 94
Kärkkäinen, Veli-Matti
  10, 12, 78,
  86, 97, 118,
  274, 374
Käsemann, Ernst
  88, 106,
  107
Kasper, Walter
  112, 367
Kaufmann, Yehezkel
  28, 33, 35
Keil, C. F.
  164, 278,
  279, 360
Kelly, William
  211, 218,
  290, 302,

355, 369,
399, 464,
599, 607,
611
Kennedy, H. A. A.
  418, 420
Kenosis 272, 305,
  415, 417,
  418, 420,
  421, 422,
  609, 610
Kenotic Theory
  420, 421
Kenoticism
  65, 420,
  421
Kent, H. A., Jr.
  418
Kerygma 88, 90, 95,
  96, 97, 105,
  108, 109,
  120
Kerygmatic theology
  97, 601
Kessel, E. L.
  446
Kidger, M. 499
Kidner, D. 287
Kidron 549
Kierkegaard, Søren
  56, 92
Kimchi, David
  178, 197,
  200, 286
King, K. L. 20
Kingdom of God
  18, 113,
  117, 126,
  141, 223,
  231, 241,
  286, 335,
  376, 403,
  412, 467,
  470, 480,
  482, 502,

519, 521,
525, 526,
528, 548,
578, 581
Kingship 58, 161,
  162, 167,
  168, 192,
  194, 282,
  490, 531
Kirkpatrick, Alexander F.
  191
Klausner, Joseph
  28, 33, 267,
  269, 594
Klooster, F. H.
  16, 106
Kloosterman, N. D.
  483
Knevel, A. G.
  163, 167,
  168, 169,
  170, 175,
  177, 188,
  200, 204,
  277, 287
Knight, J. 17, 27, 107,
  182, 399,
  432, 489,
  539, 542,
  551, 583
Knowling, R. J.
  176
Knox, J. 307
Koehler, L.
  356
Kohlbrugge, H. F.
  464
Kohler, Kaufman
  33
König, A.
  407, 409
Kopmels, E.
  88
Koran 24, 25, 26,

715

Korff, F. W. A.
71, 413
Kramer, G. H.
418, 419
Kretschmar, G.
298
Kuitert, Harry
15, 16, 127,
220, 232,
329
Kuitse, R. S.
27
Küng, Hans
112, 407,
414
Kuschel, K.-J.
308
Küster, V.
17
Kuyper, Abraham
133, 229,
237, 360,
361, 396,
413, 419,
460, 461

L
Ladd, G. E.
582
LaHaye, T. 583
Lalleman, P. J.
5, 50, 362
Lake, Kirsopp
590
Lake of Galilee
522
Lake of Gennesaret
519
Lamb 13, 50, 202,
205, 209,
276, 313,
319, 320,
325, 328,
451, 455,
476, 509,
545, 566
Lane, William L.
45, 135,
250, 256,
286, 394,
434, 473,
533, 543
Lang, G. H.
211
Lange, J. P. 447
Lapide, Pinchas
27, 28, 32,
33, 34, 35,
154, 387,
494, 572,
575, 584,
594, 595
Last Things
517, 545
Latin Americans, 15
Lauterbach, J. Z.
267
Lazarus 18, 56, 333,
354, 382,
383, 400,
406, 538,
539, 584
Leah 318
Lebbaeus 524
Leda 436
Lee, Witness
300
Legenda Aurea
490
Lehrman 166, 169
Leo I 65
Leo the Great
373
Leontius of Byzantium
72, 74
Lessing, Gotthold E.
87, 88
Leupold, H. C.
442
Levey, Samson H.
177
Lewis, C. S.
475
Liberal theologians
15, 36, 64,
86, 112,
140, 255,
257, 329,
414, 477,
495
Liberal theology
19, 35, 86,
103, 104,
110, 123,
130, 308
Liberalism 103, 106,
582, 601
Liberals 14, 15, 113,
155, 221
Liberation theology,
17, 18
Libya 559
Liefeld, W. L.
490, 494,
503, 534,
536, 551
Lienhard, M.
81
Life of Claudius
262
Lightfoot, J. B.
88, 217,
516
Lincoln, William
318
Linder, Douglas
551
Lion of Judah
276, 320
Locke, John
84
Logos 13, 49, 54,
60, 61, 62,
63, 65, 67,

Subject Index

70, 71, 72, 74, 86, 87, 91, 98, 101, 102, 103, 122, 127, 131, 202, 275, 289, 291, 292, 294, 295, 297, 298, 299, 300, 305, 307, 309, 310, 311, 312, 321, 324, 336, 357, 361, 364, 368, 381, 414, 415, 421, 443, 444, 448
Longenecker, R. N., 175, 176
Loofs, F. 60, 65
Loonstra, B. 157, 171
Lord Darling 586
Lord Lyndhurst 586
Lord's Prayer 242, 264, 387, 389
Lord's Supper 80, 234, 237, 241, 257, 274, 547, 548
Losie, L. A. 542
Lot 26
Lower criticism 216
Lucian of Samosata 263
Lust 445, 484, 487
Luther, Martin 12, 67, 78, 80, 85, 133, 160, 171, 291, 390, 428, 429, 447
Lutheranism 79, 274
Lutherans 63, 66, 78, 79, 81, 82, 419
Luz, Ulrich 28, 35

M

Maccabees 504, 505, 514, 538
Machen, J. G. 432, 442
Macintosh 318
Mack, Burton Lee 17, 141
Mackintosh, C. H. 75, 309, 420
MacLeod, D. 442
Macquarrie, John 4, 68, 72, 74, 75, 86, 114, 115, 237, 432, 531
Madras 523
Magdala 527, 533
Magi 497, 499
Maharishi Mahesh Yogi 378
Maier, G. 211
Maier, J. 267
Malbim 164

Manahen 509
Mann, C. S. 226, 501, 502
Maoz, Baruch 110
Mara Bar-Serapion 263
Marcion 19, 23
Marduk 91
Mariology 253, 428
Markschies, C. 20
Marshall, I. Howard, 5, 43, 89, 108, 114, 127, 179, 216, 217, 243, 245, 258, 325, 362, 412
Martha 383, 400, 403, 406, 486, 539, 541
Martin, R. P. 46, 255
Martyrdom 580, 588, 592
Marxsen, W. 135
Mary Magdalene 19, 20, 21, 143, 245, 484, 487, 527, 562, 567, 572, 573, 574, 578, 593, 602, 603
Mary of Bethany 3, 20, 487, 488
Mary, mother of Jesus

24, 25, 28,
63, 64, 76,
81, 82, 129,
253, 259,
269, 274,
343, 344,
353, 357,
375, 379,
380, 387,
388, 391,
423, 425,
426, 427,
428, 429,
430, 431,
432, 433,
434, 435,
436, 437,
438, 439,
440, 441,
443, 444,
445, 446,
447, 448,
470, 490,
491, 492,
493, 494,
495, 496,
497, 500,
503, 504,
518, 523,
562, 567,
593
Mary, sister of Martha
406, 486,
539, 541,
542
Mary, wife of Clopas
375, 562,
567, 572,
590
Masoretic text
169, 172,
199
Massey, Gerald
270
Mattathias 375, 524

Matter, H. M.
418
Matthias 524, 577
McComiskey, T. E.
164, 278
McDowell, Josh
21, 155,
211, 250,
582, 585,
McGrath, A.
4, 9, 11,
13, 63, 81,
89, 583
Medema, H. P.
294, 362,
547, 551
Medes 497
Mediator 10, 11, 76,
77, 132,
152, 254,
315, 323,
336, 367,
373, 409,
412, 413,
414, 474,
610
Meier, John P.
15, 16, 18,
19, 28, 90,
95, 106,
109, 119,
139, 226,
228, 231,
242, 243,
260, 265,
375, 390,
432, 434,
437, 468,
490, 491,
495, 496,
501, 507,
508, 511,
514, 546
Melanchthon, Philip
3, 11

Melchior 498
Melchizedek
152, 191,
193, 315,
316, 317,
350
Melito of Sardis
54
Merovingian kings
21
Merz, A. 19, 87, 107,
260, 267,
399, 495,
504, 511,
548, 551,
583
Messiah 6, 14, 25,
27, 28, 29,
30, 31, 32,
33, 34, 35,
45, 91, 98,
101, 117,
130, 134,
135, 136,
137, 138,
143, 146,
148, 149,
150, 151,
153, 154,
155, 156,
157, 158,
159, 160,
161, 162,
163, 164,
165, 166,
167, 168,
169, 170,
171, 172,
173, 174,
175, 176,
177, 178,
179, 181,
182, 184,
185, 186,
187, 188,

Subject Index

190, 192, 193, 194, 195, 197, 198, 199, 202, 203, 204, 205, 206, 207, 208, 209, 210, 211, 212, 213, 215, 219, 256, 267, 276, 277, 278, 279, 280, 281, 282, 283, 284, 285, 286, 292, 293, 294, 295, 296, 307, 308, 312, 317, 323, 326, 328, 332, 343, 360, 361, 395, 399, 430, 437, 470, 473, 490, 491, 496, 497, 499, 505, 508, 509, 510, 517, 519, 520, 526, 531, 533, 537, 543, 553, 555, 576

Messiahship 17, 44, 134, 136

Messianic Jews 27, 28, 29, 32, 491

Messianic King 162, 168, 194, 196, 317

Messianic kingdom 58, 166, 174, 185, 197, 198, 208, 211, 273, 467, 581, 597

Messianic predictions 147, 153

Messianic secret 134, 136

Messiology 27

Metzger, B. M. 351, 372

Meyer, B. F. 91, 111, 220

Michael 280, 289, 290, 335

Michaelis 354

Michel, O. 179, 182

Middle East 263

Midian 498

Midrash Tanchuma 205

Midrashic exegesis 150, 151

Mighty God 145, 176, 177, 178, 280, 296, 327

Miguens, M. 442

Minos 436

Miracles 25, 85, 89, 96, 109, 111, 135, 136, 189, 255, 256, 257, 275, 294, 334, 337, 430, 503, 504, 521, 536, 559, 606

Miriam 375

Mishnah 267, 502, 529, 547

Mithra 493

Moab 159, 160

Modalism 30, 31, 82, 87, 300, 359, 420

Modernism 42, 43, 84

Molnar, M. R. 499

Moltmann, Jürgen 34, 81, 111

Monophysitism 61, 63, 64, 65, 68, 69, 70, 73, 79, 80, 87, 128, 131, 252, 253

Monotheletism 70

Montefiore, Claude G. 28

Moody, D. 427

Moore, P. 499

Moralia in Job 318

Mordecai 151

Moreland, P. 114

Morison, Frank 547, 572, 585

Morris, H. M. 442

Morris, L. 298, 299, 352, 361, 362, 434, 460, 490, 492, 494, 503, 510, 518, 523, 529, 536, 537, 543, 546, 553, 566, 607, 608

Mosaic Law 516, 525

Moses 22, 23, 26, 136, 148, 149, 152, 187, 188, 189, 204, 205, 233, 288, 290, 299, 303, 309, 312, 313, 316, 317, 318, 319, 336, 392, 427, 465, 477, 505, 513, 515, 516, 534, 535, 596, 605

Mother of God 63, 253, 274

Moule, Charles F. D. 45, 60, 114, 118, 407, 486, 553

Mount Hermon 397, 398, 534

Mount of Beatitudes 397, 398

Mount of Olives 284, 393, 398, 539, 542, 545, 546, 547, 548, 549, 582

Mount of Transfiguration 227, 234, 240, 394, 398, 434, 477, 534

Mount Sinai 23, 288, 313, 316, 392, 534

Mount Tabor 397, 398, 534

Mount Zion 283, 316, 395

Mudde 169, 200

Muhammad 24, 26, 27, 429, 430, 455

Mulder 167

Müller, Max 92, 418, 421

Murray, John 326, 327, 442, 462

Muslims 25, 26, 27, 117, 345, 594, 597

Mylapore 523

N

Nachmanides 160, 290

Nag Hammadi 15, 19

Nahshon 388

Nain 333, 486, 487, 526

Nassi, Tzvi 31

Nathan 167

Nathanael 188, 316, 381, 489, 518, 523

Naturalism 42, 111, 216

Nazarenes 118, 470, 530

Nazareth 6, 22, 28, 90, 91, 92, 96, 98, 148, 154, 162, 188, 190, 239, 240, 255, 256, 267, 269, 270, 308, 310, 312, 334, 379, 405, 424, 431, 433, 441, 489, 490, 491, 492, 495, 500, 503, 506, 513, 518, 526, 530, 534, 551, 573, 576, 583

Neander, August 88

Nebuchadnezzar 289, 495

Neill, S. 414

Neo-Gnosticism 19, 117

Neri 172

Nero 261, 262

Nestle-Aland text 299

Subject Index

Nestorianism
 64, 66, 69,
 70, 79, 80,
 82, 87, 128,
 131, 252,
 253
Nestorians 65, 67
Nestorius 63, 64, 67,
 131
Netherworld
 562, 567,
 568
Neusner, Jacob
 28, 33
New Testament scholars
 16, 109,
 113, 114,
 135, 140
New Testament scholarship
 16, 125,
 224, 228
New World Translation
 299, 324
Ng Kam Weng
 26
Nicaea 13, 31, 85,
 224
Nicene Creed
 13, 14, 105,
 357, 363,
 366, 429
Nicene-Constantinopolitan Creed
 435
Nicodemus
 260, 268,
 351, 487,
 514, 519,
 520, 552,
 567, 572,
 577
Niehaus, J. J.
 292
Nietzsche, Friedrich
 92, 94
Nieuwenhuis, H.
 499
Nimrod 91
Noah 22, 26, 156,
 320
Non-Questers
 99, 101,
 106
Noordtzij, A.
 179, 201
North, C. R.
 206
North America
 115

O

Odes of Solomon
 426
Oegema, G. S.
 146
Olshausen, H.
 447
O'Meara, T.
 73, 429
Omnipotence
 58, 59, 340,
 421
Omnipresence
 58, 59, 79,
 340, 421
Omniscience
 59, 340,
 385, 386,
 421, 457
O'Neill, John Cochrane
 114, 115
Open Theism
 382
Origen 75, 269,
 309, 314,
 357, 364,
 407, 434,
 446, 486,
 496, 516
Original sin
 439, 446
Orr, J. 442, 445
Orthodox Christians
 61, 111,
 216, 411
Orthodox Jews
 13, 27, 32,
 34, 154,
 597
Orthodox theologians
 35, 36
Orthodoxy 20, 85, 103,
 106, 130,
 274, 289
Osborne, G. R.
 582
Oswalt, J. N.
 165, 170,
 172, 177,
 280, 296
Ott, H. 8
Ouweneel, W. J.
 19, 22, 29,
 30, 31, 32,
 33, 37, 38,
 39, 40, 52,
 54, 60, 63,
 66, 75, 76,
 83, 84, 85,
 91, 98, 103,
 107, 110,
 131, 147,
 149, 151,
 152, 157,
 163, 183,
 185, 186,
 191, 201,
 204, 211,
 216, 218,
 222, 232,
 258, 273,

277, 281, 282, 297, 306, 312, 316, 319, 320, 321, 342, 346, 356, 377, 380, 390, 392, 393, 395, 445, 447, 450, 451, 457, 471, 484, 488, 489, 492, 493, 508, 525, 531, 537, 562, 565, 586, 587, 596

Oxyrhynchus 19

P

Paganism 21, 30
Pagels, E. 19
Palestine 263, 492, 505
Palm Sunday 541
Pandaros 269
Pannenberg, Wolfhart 13, 40, 54, 57, 60, 63, 71, 72, 73, 96, 97, 111, 141, 297, 312, 412, 417, 437, 582
Pantheras 269
Papias 227
Paraclete 26
Paradise 83, 277, 313, 562
Parmenides 353, 360
Parousia 32, 34
Parrinder, E. G. 27
Parthia 523
Pascal, Blaise 596
Paschal, R.W. 545
Passion Week 540, 541
Passover 235, 263, 268, 320, 503, 510, 511, 512, 519, 521, 529, 532, 536, 539, 541, 545, 546, 547, 550, 556, 557, 559, 563, 564, 566, 602
Patmos 612
Patriarchs 22, 151, 156, 195, 277, 375, 386
Patros 522
Paul 3, 4, 6, 7, 13, 14, 32, 33, 39, 41, 42, 46, 47, 48, 51, 58, 62, 83, 91, 94, 98, 99, 105, 137, 138, 148, 149, 154, 157, 159, 165, 174, 183, 184, 198, 199, 200, 206, 217, 222, 235, 236, 238, 251, 258, 260, 305, 314, 315, 316, 321, 326, 327, 328, 331, 340, 370, 371, 391, 392, 393, 411, 442, 462, 463, 466, 470, 485, 516, 583, 584, 587, 598, 599, 600, 602, 604, 612
Paul, M. J. 163, 167, 168, 169, 170, 175, 177, 188, 192, 200, 204, 277, 287
Paul of Samosata 49, 101
Payne, J. B. 287
Peabody, D. B. 226
Peace 145, 146, 156, 161, 173, 176, 177, 178, 192, 193, 195, 196, 197, 280, 283, 316, 317, 340, 393, 401, 482, 492, 542, 578,

Peels 168
Pentateuch 152, 314, 465, 515
Pentecost 275, 392, 393, 510, 512, 529, 579, 583, 579, 590
Pentecost, Dwight 125, 236
Pentecostal movement 275
Pentecostals 275
Perea 497, 506, 512, 538
Perrin, Norman 139
Persecution 66, 458, 530, 589
Persia 524
Persians 162, 560
Pesach 163, 389, 502, 510, 512
Peter 2, 3, 4, 10, 19, 20, 39, 41, 143, 148, 188, 194, 198, 199, 219, 220, 227, 235, 260, 269, 320, 331, 340, 382, 393, 394, 396, 402, 452, 459, 518, 521, 522, 524, 526, 531, 532, 533, 534, 546, 549, 551, 553, 554, 562, 564, 567, 573, 574, 575, 580, 585, 593, 595, 597, 602, 603, 604
Pharisaism 141
Pharisees 125, 237, 256, 385, 392, 402, 404, 406, 454, 456, 473, 482, 492, 514, 515, 520, 521, 522, 525, 528, 532, 533, 537, 542, 544
Philadelphia 528
Philip 19, 148, 149, 188, 205, 381, 518, 523, 533
Philip the tetrarch 506, 533
Philistines 175
Philo 314, 507
Phinehas 193, 524
Phoebe 486
Phoenicia 533
Phoenicians 560
Picknett, L. 20
Pietist movement 310
Pirie, Alexander 186
Pisidian Antioch 513
Plato 264, 408
Platonism 22
Plummer, A. 172
Pliny the Younger 260, 261
Plymouth Brethren 103
Polanus, Amandus 364
Pollock, A. J. 342
Pollux 436
Polyander, Joannes 85, 364
Polycarp 258, 407
Pompei 504, 505
Pontius Pilate 24, 110, 234, 259, 260, 266, 374, 378, 379, 390, 404, 451, 452, 507, 512, 550, 551, 555, 556, 557, 558, 560, 566, 595, 606
Pontus 260, 505
Poortvliet, Rien 379
Poverty 17, 339, 417, 501, 531
Prayer 7, 8, 112, 142, 195, 205, 242, 261, 264, 383, 387,

389, 394,
395, 396,
397, 403,
469, 476,
478, 485,
513, 525,
543, 549,
564
Prayer of the Virgin in Bartos
264
Prayers 8, 55, 297,
394, 398,
400, 512,
564
Preus, R. D.
37
Price, R. M.
257
Priesthood
50, 174,
191, 192,
193, 194,
317
Priests 3, 151, 313,
382, 405,
452, 458,
482, 505,
512, 513,
515, 543,
561, 565
Prince, C. 20
Prince of Peace
145, 161,
176, 178,
280, 317,
492
Promised Land
157, 208,
317, 396
Prophecies 21, 151,
153, 159,
172, 181,
195, 206,
207, 209,

275, 383,
386
Prophets 22, 25, 26,
27, 38, 45,
109, 136,
148, 149,
182, 188,
190, 266,
267, 290,
306, 307,
336, 389,
392, 408,
482, 492,
509, 513,
535, 578,
596
Protestant expositors
291
Protestantism
17, 254,
274, 310,
428
Protestants 16, 64, 67,
84, 447
Proto Evangelium
155
Protoevangelium of James
424, 428,
442
Psalms of Solomon
168
Ptolemaic empire
504
Pythagoras
263, 264

Q
Q-source 16
Quelle 43, 226
Questers 99, 102,
108, 109,
119, 121,
139, 140
Quirinius 492, 494,

495, 506
Quispel, G.
20
Qumran 516
Quran 429, 430,
455, 504

R
Rachel 318, 319,
424, 495
Radmacher, E. D.
37
Rahner, Karl
28, 33, 34,
35, 112,
154, 328,
387
Rashbam 160
Rashi 160, 164,
165, 175,
177, 178,
188, 191,
195, 197,
204, 286,
296
Räisänen 27
Rama 566
Ramat Rachel
496
Ramsay, William
341, 342,
494
Raphael 289
Rationalism
84, 85, 86,
97, 217
Ratzinger, Joseph
4, 8, 33, 41,
95, 102,
106, 119,
120, 174,
179, 180,
186, 187,
189, 193,
194, 221,

Subject Index

224, 242,
303, 304,
316, 335,
348, 374,
394, 397,
407, 470,
471, 512,
516, 517,
518, 523,
524, 527,
534, 535,
537, 555,
557, 568,
569, 605
Raymond, R. L.
146
Reagan, President
307
Reason 9, 42, 84,
85, 95, 98,
115, 217,
298, 437,
587, 601
Rebekah 159, 170,
318, 424
Received Text
302, 353
Recovery Version
Bible
300
Red Sea 470, 535
Redaction criticism
135
Redeemer 22, 23, 32,
33, 68, 118,
126, 176,
202, 208,
209, 274,
276, 284,
293, 319,
343, 415,
439, 474,
492
Redemption
6, 11, 13,

22, 23, 47,
118, 189,
190, 207,
208, 251,
424, 439,
451, 469,
474, 476,
583, 608
Redemptive history
93
Reformation
72, 75, 84,
112, 126
Reformed expositors
296
Reformers 131, 463,
479
Reimarus, Hermann S.
87, 88, 91,
137, 595
Remnant of Israel
164, 207,
208, 209,
395
Renan, Ernest
87, 88, 140
Rensberger, D.
50
Resurrection
4, 6, 13, 24,
27, 39, 40,
46, 55, 76,
77, 83, 85,
90, 93, 98,
99, 104,
105, 107,
109, 111,
115, 126,
127, 129,
158, 176,
198, 200,
217, 222,
233, 235,
238, 245,
255, 258,

259, 264,
273, 304,
308, 309,
315, 318,
321, 322,
323, 334,
342, 354,
369, 371,
373, 374,
378, 410,
411, 442,
443, 471,
487, 488,
515, 516,
517, 519,
534, 544,
553, 562,
565, 568,
569, 571,
572, 574,
578, 580,
581, 582,
583, 584,
585, 586,
587, 588,
589, 590,
591, 592,
593, 594,
595, 596,
597, 598,
599, 600,
601, 602,
605, 606,
607, 608,
611
Reuben 160
Revelation 2, 31, 37,
41, 85, 102,
107, 138,
167, 220,
224, 291,
296, 348,
349, 353,
365, 371,
419, 477,

725

Ridderbos, Herman 563
  96, 386, 497
Ridderbos, J.
  175, 185, 186, 193, 199, 200, 201, 204, 206, 278, 280, 492
Riesner, R. 501
Rimmer, Harry 310
Riss, R. 582
Ritschl, Albrecht 12, 140, 308
Rivetus, Andreas 85
Rivkin, Ellis 28
Robinson, J. A. T. 457
Robinson, J. M. 107
Rohde, J. 134
Roman Catholic Church 274
Roman Catholic theologians 291, 439
Roman Catholicism 253, 396
Roman Catholics 16, 63, 66, 67, 84, 112
Roman Empire 62, 260, 492, 494, 500, 504
Romanticism 89, 92
Rome 67, 261, 262, 324, 393, 493, 505, 518, 522, 580, 595
Rosenzweig, Franz 28
Rosh Hashanah 529, 552, 575
Rosicrucians 22
Ross, A. P. 296
Rowley, Harold H. 191, 206
Rublev, Andrei 289
Rufinus 512
Rumscheidt, Martin 102
Runia, Klaas 69, 97, 103, 112, 123, 252, 310
Ruth 151, 318, 319, 495

S

Saba 498
Sabbath 47, 148, 335, 389, 391, 392, 454, 476, 477, 483, 510, 516, 521, 522, 529, 530, 537, 539, 541, 565, 566, 567, 572
Sabellian modalism 30
Sabellianism 300, 420
Sadducees 456, 514, 515, 544, 555
Sahih Muslim 27
Sailhamer, J. H. 161
Saints 8, 112, 297, 429, 490, 565
Salih 26
Salome, John's mother 518, 522, 523, 562, 567, 572, 590
Salome, sister of Herod the Great 499
Salome, stepdaughter of Herod Antipas 509
Salome Alexandra 515
Samaria 505, 520, 536, 581
Samaritan woman 146, 381, 520
Samaritans 520, 536, 537
Samians 264
Samson 508
Samuel 188, 508, 566
Sanctification 6, 371
Sanders, E. P. 28, 141, 391, 392
Santala, R. 205
Santiago de Compostela 523

Subject Index

Sarah 157, 424, 507
Satan 150, 155, 156, 186, 231, 250, 317, 335, 397, 403, 456, 458, 459, 460, 485, 517, 527, 534, 568, 583, 585
Saturn 499
Saul 200, 201, 317, 511,
Saul of Tarsus 4, 14, 94, 514, 594, 596, 597, 612, 613
Savior 3, 4, 8, 10, 17, 19, 33, 34, 48, 123, 231, 275, 276, 300, 323, 324, 327, 333, 371, 380, 476, 491, 496, 604
Scapegoat 209, 210
Schaeffer, Francis A. 155
Schaff, Philip 54, 61, 248, 339
Schiffman, Michael 31
Schilder, K. 72, 141, 142, 152, 153, 254, 419, 501
Schillebeeckx, Edward 112, 121, 139
Schirrmacher, C. 27
Schirrmacher, T. 146
Schleiermacher, Friedrich 68, 87, 88, 272, 366
Schlink, E. 8, 372
Schmidt, K. L. 94, 134
Schmiedel, P. W. 247, 249, 254
Schneider, O. 175
Schoeps, H. J. 153
Scholasticism 42, 85
Scholten, J. H. 364
Schönweiss, H. 331
Schoon, Simon 112
Schoonenberg, Piet 71, 112
Schüssler Fiorenza, E. 15
Shroud of Turin 567
Schulze, W. A. 497
Schumann, Olaf 25
Schwarz, Hans 114
Schweitzer, Albert 17, 87, 94, 215, 466
Schweizer, Eduard 3, 96, 392, 572, 596
Schwenckfeld, Caspar 310
Scott, W. 319
Scripture 8, 13, 14, 37, 38, 39, 41, 46, 109, 149, 150, 157, 198, 217, 224, 225, 228, 230, 246, 251, 306, 308, 346, 371, 381, 383, 396, 409, 429, 465, 511, 521, 564
Sea of Galilea 397
Sea of Tiberias 519
Seba 497, 498
Second coming 24, 57, 273, 374, 411, 466, 530, 554, 597, 601, 602, 603
Second Helvetic Confession 61
Second Quest 88, 106, 107, 140
Second Temple 118, 197, 205, 505, 565
Seder meal 546
Sefer Milhamot Adonai 188

Seir 159
Seleucid empire
    504, 505
Sellers, R.V.
    67
Sepphoris 501, 506
Septuagint 47, 161,
    169, 171,
    172, 181,
    185, 193,
    198, 199,
    201, 281,
    303, 327,
    353, 356,
    463
Sermon on the Mount
    237, 331,
    336, 387,
    397, 525
Servant of YHWH
    150, 158,
    204, 206,
    207, 208,
    209
Seth 156, 506
Sevenster, Gerhard
    47, 51, 179,
    305, 312
Sextus Julius Africanus
    263
Sexual desire
    436, 445,
    446, 447,
    484, 485
Shabbat 29
Shakespeare
    593
Shammai 514, 517
Shealtiel 172, 173
Sheba 497, 498
Shechem 520
Shekhinah 30, 287,
    294, 321,
    427

Shem 156
Sheol 198, 199,
    568
Sheth 159
Shiloh 146, 161,
    320
Shulam, Joseph
    32, 326
Sicarians 524
Siegel, B. 33
Simeon 269, 496,
    497, 524
Simon Bar-Jonah
    2, 219
Simon, brother of Jesus
    375, 428
Simon Magus
    22
Simon of Cyrene
    559
Simon Peter
    146, 235,
    518, 522,
    575
Simon the leper
    541
Simon the Maccabee
    191, 504,
    505
Simon the Pharisee
    385
Simon the Zealot
    523, 524
Sinaitic covenant
    335
Sinlessness
    274, 424,
    445, 446,
    447, 448,
    449, 450,
    452, 458,
    460, 464,
    465, 472,
    474, 475,

    483, 485
Sjöberg, E. 374
Slavenburg, J.
    15
Slotki, Israel W.
    165, 177,
    178, 181
Smalhout, B.
    561
Smalley, S. S.
    50
Smith, H. 342
Smith, J. D. 319
Smith, W. M.
    446, 464,
    585
Smyrnaeans
    259
Snorhali, Nerses
    426
Sobrino, J. 15
Socinians 72, 84
Socrates 263, 264,
    577
Sodom 293
Solomon 152, 158,
    162, 167,
    168, 175,
    177, 192,
    195, 196,
    238, 317,
    319, 407,
    426, 447,
    511, 554
Solomon's Portico
    503, 554
Son of Abraham
    154, 158
Son of Adam
    154, 439,
    444
Son of David
    6, 58, 136,
    154, 158,
    166, 167,

Subject Index

168, 169,
175, 186,
192, 199,
276, 277,
317, 388,
423, 431,
441, 491,
492, 542
Son of God 2, 6, 7, 14,
27, 33, 34,
44, 45, 46,
49, 53, 58,
76, 77, 83,
91, 92, 101,
124, 125,
127, 130,
131, 134,
136, 137,
138, 174,
212, 221,
240, 259,
276, 279,
289, 297,
298, 299,
304, 306,
308, 309,
310, 311,
312, 316,
325, 329,
334, 335,
336, 343,
344, 346,
349, 350,
357, 362,
366, 369,
371, 399,
415, 419,
423, 431,
433, 441,
443, 444,
454, 470,
520, 544,
553, 555,
558, 561,
565, 568,
606, 607,
610, 612
Son of Israel
387
Son of Man
10, 12, 33,
44, 45, 48,
58, 133,
134, 137,
138, 139,
141, 178,
179, 180,
181, 182,
183, 184,
185, 186,
212, 221,
248, 249,
250, 255,
276, 277,
282, 283,
290, 316,
318, 332,
333, 335,
343, 351,
374, 399,
411, 416,
420, 459,
468, 481,
484, 502,
520, 544,
554, 555,
574, 603,
604, 605,
606, 607,
612, 613
Soncino Books of the Bible
154
Song of Solomon
152, 319,
407, 447
Sonship 17, 32, 49,
73, 136,
174, 175,
295, 296,
329, 342,
343, 344,
345, 346,
347, 353,
358, 398,
613
Sophia of Jesus Christ
19
Sophiology
21
Soteriology
12, 32, 126,
275, 451,
465
South America
115
Soviet Union
28
Spain 523
Spindler, M. R.
583
Spurgeon, Charles
186, 202
Spykman, G. J.
102
St. Matthew's Passion
390
Stanley, A. P.
98, 99
Stanton, Graham N.
43, 114
Star 159, 160,
497, 499
Stauffer, Ethelbert
330, 336,
434
Stein, R. H.
16, 19, 43,
114, 246,
260, 265,
375, 383,
390, 442,
489, 490,
493, 507,
511, 517,

522, 534, 535, 542, 543, 546, 549, 551, 553, 561, 566, 583
Stephen 178, 288, 452, 557, 597, 604
Stern, David 29, 30, 31, 491, 547
Stier, R. E. 606
Stoics 408
Stott, J. R. W. 50, 582, 586
Strauss, David F. 87, 88, 464, 589
Strecker, G. 50
Strobel, A. 551
Strobel, L. 583
Stuart, C. E. 607
Su'aib 26
Subordinationism 87, 346, 363, 365, 366, 367
Suchnin 268
Suetonius 262
Sukkoth 493, 503
Süleyman 543
Summers, R. 538
Supercessionists 139
Supernaturalism 40, 42, 86, 89, 92, 111, 115, 216, 224, 228, 246, 414

Susanna 572, 593
Susman, Margareta 28
Swedenborg, Emanuel 310
Swinburne, A. G. 17
Sychar 520
Synagogues 205, 262, 513, 521
Synod of Alexandria 62
Synopsis purioris theologiae 85, 364
Synoptic Gospels 39, 43, 48, 116, 219, 225, 227, 228, 232, 242, 304, 329, 330, 332, 472
Synoptics 39, 41, 42, 43, 46, 48, 49, 98, 225, 391, 530
Syria 492, 494, 495
Syro-Ephraimite war 177
Systematic theology 9, 37, 125

T
Tabernacle 152, 229, 309, 313, 320, 321, 322, 427
Tacitus 261, 262
Talmud 154, 165, 172, 176, 181, 182, 195, 267, 268, 269, 270, 277, 390, 392, 492, 501

Tanakh 29, 30, 145, 146, 147, 148, 149, 150, 151, 152, 153, 154, 156, 158, 161, 166, 170, 172, 174, 177, 179, 183, 184, 186, 191, 195, 202, 204, 207, 210, 212

Targum 165, 166, 177, 181, 186, 195, 204, 356
Targum of Jonathan, 173
Tarshish 497
Tasker, R. V. G. 220, 470, 497
Tatian 218, 230
Taylor, J. B. 292
Temple 63, 118, 163, 173, 174, 192, 195, 197, 205, 211, 285, 287, 290, 294, 309, 320, 321, 322, 369, 370, 382, 391, 393, 403, 405, 406,

Subject Index

460, 467, 493, 496, 497, 503, 504, 505, 506, 507, 512, 513, 519, 533, 536, 538, 543, 544, 545, 550, 552, 559, 564, 565, 566, 582, 588, 593

Temple cleansing 543

Tenney, M. C. 434, 492, 582, 607, 608

Terah 156

Tertullian 54, 252, 364, 435, 436, 443, 444, 448, 462

Textual criticism 216

Thaddaeus 268, 269, 524

Thallus 263

The Bible Treasury 219

The Church in the Power of the Spirit 34

The Da Vinci Code 21

The Eternal Kingdom 223

The Jewish Encyclopedia 268

The Lion, the Witch and the Wardrobe 475

The Messianic Secret 134

The Name of the Rose 401

The Pilgrim's Progress 314

The Soncino Talmud 268, 269

Theissen, G. 19, 87, 107, 260, 267, 399, 495, 504, 511, 548, 551, 583

Theodore of Mopsuestia 62, 63

Theologians 13, 15, 17, 33, 35, 36, 38, 39, 53, 57, 64, 79, 86, 88, 93, 94, 98, 102, 105, 107, 111, 112, 113, 114, 121, 137, 140, 141, 146, 154, 177, 204, 218, 220, 221, 223, 225, 246, 247, 255, 257, 258, 291, 308, 310, 329, 341, 414, 419, 420, 438, 439, 457, 463, 477, 486, 495, 510, 585, 594

Theology 1, 3, 7, 9, 13, 15, 17, 18, 19, 21, 25, 27, 35, 36, 37, 38, 40, 41, 42, 44, 46, 47, 49, 50, 65, 69, 75, 85, 86, 89, 97, 98, 102, 103, 104, 105, 110, 111, 119, 120, 123, 124, 125, 128, 129, 130, 131, 134, 135, 141, 143, 187, 218, 220, 221, 222, 224, 230, 239, 246, 257, 274, 275, 308, 329, 359, 363, 386, 408, 438, 553, 582, 583, 601

Theopaschitism 59, 112, 252

Theophilus 238

Theotokos 63, 64, 253

Theron, P. F. 572

Thessalonica 126, 513

Thielicke, Helmut 7, 311

731

Thierry, J. J. 582
Third Quest 88, 108, 110, 113, 117, 118, 131, 141
Thomas 3, 4, 19, 101, 300, 324, 487, 523, 577, 579, 593, 596
Thomas, J. C. 275
Thomasius, Gottfried 421
Thompson, W. M. 150
Throne of David 145, 154, 172, 176, 273, 517
Thurneysen, Eduard 102
Thüsing, W. 112
Thysius, Antonius 85
Tiberius 261, 506, 511, 533, 550
Tillich, Paul 102, 310
To Serapion 364
Tomb 55, 83, 148, 199, 245, 265, 273, 274, 403, 538, 566, 567, 572, 573, 574, 575, 576, 584, 588, 589, 590, 591, 592, 599, 601
Tome 494
Torah 29, 117, 140, 148, 149, 151, 152, 153, 156, 157, 191, 277, 309, 314, 317, 321, 329, 335, 357, 376, 387, 389, 390, 391, 392, 393, 465, 470, 501, 502, 503, 513, 514, 515, 521, 527, 535, 544, 554
Tosefta 267, 268, 552
Traditionalism 110, 132
Trachonitis 506
Trajan 261
Trallians 379, 410
Transfiguration 227, 234, 240, 394, 398, 434, 467, 477, 534, 613
Trillhaas, Wolfgang 8, 365, 370
Trinitarianism 31, 114, 123, 365, 366
Trinity 9, 11, 29, 31, 75, 115, 124, 131, 133, 289, 292, 298, 301, 306, 310, 345, 348, 366, 367, 369, 370, 372, 412, 421, 465
Tritheism 31, 82, 359
Triune God 225, 273, 281, 300, 310, 328, 365, 366, 367, 368, 369
Troeltsch, E. 87, 91
Twelftree, G. H. 455
Twentieth century 27, 28, 38, 87, 99, 101, 102, 116, 121, 135, 138, 146, 386
Typology 150, 312, 313, 314, 319
Tyre 390, 533
Tyrrell, George 95

U
Unger, M. F. 193
Unitarians 72, 84
Uzziah 204

V

Subject Index

Valentinus 410
Valerius Gratus 506
Van Bruggen, Jakob, 19, 114, 124, 125, 126, 219, 233, 243, 260, 265, 375, 399, 489, 490, 511, 514, 525, 543, 546, 551, 583
Van de Beek, Abraham 1, 4, 16, 17, 24, 25, 40, 63, 64, 65, 69, 81, 92, 111, 114, 115, 118, 124, 127, 128, 129, 130, 136, 236, 237, 336, 337, 367, 386, 387, 412, 427, 428, 434, 435, 444, 448, 457, 458, 512, 562, 572, 583, 588, 598, 602
Van de Donk, W. B. H. J. 115
Van de Kamp, W. 561
Van der Kooi, Cornelis 69
Van der Linden, E. 28, 33
Van der Merwe, Willie 38
Van der Vliet, J. 551
Van der Woude, A. S. 167
Van Estrik 175
Van Gemeren, W. A. 175, 185, 192, 195, 199, 200, 201
Van Genderen, J. 72, 180, 271, 412, 421, 464, 512, 569, 600
Van Gennep, F. O. 583
Van Houwelingen, A. A. 127
Van Leeuwen, J. A. C. 386
Van Leeuwenhoek, Antoni 437
Van Ruler, A. A. 412, 414
Van Uchelen, N. A. 281
Van Veen-Vrolijk 287
Van Voorst, R. E. 260
Vardaman, J. 511
Vatican 267
Velde, R. T. 364
Velema, W. H. 72, 180, 271, 412, 421, 464, 512, 569, 600
Venema, H. 288
Venturini, Karl H. G. 588
Verhoef, P. A. 285, 287
Verhoeff, M. 568
Verkuyl, Johan 136, 137, 236, 406, 440, 455, 501, 583, 599
Vermes, Geza 28, 109, 141, 149, 389, 390, 392
Vermigli, Pietro M. 78
Vespasian 262
Via dolorosa 559
Vine, W. E. 606
Virgin birth 31, 85, 89, 93, 104, 109, 123, 127, 155, 362, 423, 424, 425, 427, 428, 429, 430, 432, 433, 434, 435, 436, 437, 440, 441, 442, 443, 444, 445,

733

Vischer, W. E. 446, 447, 448, 474
Vischer, W. E. 147
Vlaardingerbroek, J. 35
Vleugels, G. 568
Voetius, Gisbertus 364
Vollenhoven, Dirk 71
Von Harnack, Adolf 69, 89, 92, 102
Von Hofmann, J. C. K. 420
Von Poseck, Julius Anton 476
Von Rad, G. 150, 287
Vos, A. 582
Vos, G. 287

W
Wailing Wall 441, 557
Wakely, Robin 291, 292
Walaeus, Antonius 85
Walker, B. 20
Walker, P. 583
Wampler, D. 551
Ward, W. E. 421
Warfield, B. B. 247
Watson, A. 551
Watts, Isaac 310
Weber, Otto 12, 13, 86, 337, 421
Wegscheider, Julius A. L. 408
Weigel, Valentin 310
Wells, G. A. 257
Wenham, J. W. 565
Wentsel, B. 124, 174, 179
Wesley, John 429
Wessell, W. W. 45, 386, 434, 533, 543
Westcott, B. F. 88
Westerholm, S. 514
Westminster Confession 569
Westminster Larger Catechism 61, 77, 83
Whiting, B. 567
Wilken, R. L. 260
Wilkins, M. J. 114, 522
Wilson, C. 582
Wisdom 6, 84, 113, 118, 151, 182, 255, 276, 341, 355, 356, 357, 371, 374, 384, 390, 415, 427, 471, 503, 516, 561
Witherington, Ben 15, 17, 28, 91, 107, 113, 114, 141, 427, 489, 490, 493, 504, 507
Wolff, H. W. 205, 206, 279
Wonderful Counselor 145, 176, 280
Wood, L. J. 167
Word of God 54, 96, 257, 351, 430, 434
World Council of Churches 124
Worldview 16, 17, 40, 216, 217, 255, 584, 604
Worship 1, 2, 3, 16, 26, 45, 47, 82, 263, 331, 332, 396, 397, 398
Wright, N. T. 113, 114, 324, 427, 583
Wrede, Wilhelm 94, 134, 135
Wuest, K. S. 418, 462

Subject Index

Y
Yalkut Shimeoni 205
Yamauchi, E. M. 511
Yarmulke 29
Yeshu 267, 268, 269, 270
Yeshua 326
Yeshuah 29, 30, 31, 32, 268, 491, 496
Yeshuology 29
Yeshurun 319
YHWH 11, 23, 30, 47, 58, 150, 157, 158, 173, 185, 196, 204, 206, 207, 208, 209, 279, 281, 282, 283, 284, 285, 286, 287, 288, 289, 290, 291, 292, 293, 294, 295, 297, 303, 310, 311, 325, 326, 327, 331, 332, 339, 340, 361, 365, 366, 395, 491, 496
Yitzchaqi, Shlomo 164
Yom Kippur 205
Young, E. J. 190, 283, 606

Z
Zacchaeus 539
Zadok 193, 514
Zadokian priesthood 191
Zacharias 583
Zealots 495, 524
Zebedee 522, 523, 554, 562
Zechariah, son of Barachiah 466
Zechariah the priest 493
Zedekiah 170, 173
Zephyrinus 81, 127, 128
Zerubbabel 164, 172, 193, 204
Zeus 436
Zindler, F. R. 267
Zion 164, 196, 208, 283, 284, 293, 316, 395, 399, 517
Zipporah 319
Zohar 30, 205
Zoroastrianism 22
Zugibe, F. T. 567
Zuurmond, R. 583
Zwiep, A. 182, 602
Zwingli, Ulrich 57, 80, 429

www.ingramcontent.com/pod-product-compliance
Lightning Source LLC
Chambersburg PA
CBHW060646150426
42811CB00086B/2440/J